IMAGE FUSION

Edited by **Osamu Ukimura**

Image Fusion
Edited by Osamu Ukimura

Published by InTech
Janeza Trdine 9, 51000 Rijeka, Croatia

Publishing Process Manager Iva Lipovic

Technical Editor Teodora Smiljanic

Cover Designer InTech Design Team

Additional hard copies can be obtained from orders@intechopen.com

Image Fusion, Edited by Osamu Ukimura
p. cm.
ISBN 978-953-307-679-9

For EU product safety concerns:
IN TECH d.o.o., Prolaz Marije Krucifikse Kozulić 3, 51000 Rijeka, Croatia,
info@intechopen.com or visit our website at intechopen.com.

Meet the editor

Osamu Ukimura, MD, PhD is an internationally recognized expert in image-guided surgery and diagnosis and minimally invasive therapy for prostate and kidney cancer. He is one of the world's most experienced urologists in transrectal ultrasonography for diagnosis, staging, biopsy and management of prostate cancer. Dr. Ukimura pioneered augmented reality, image-fusion of 3-dimensional ultrasound with CT or MRI and 4-dimensional navigation technologies in the filed of urology. Dr. Ukimura also authored over 100 peer-reviewed publications and book chapters, and was awarded at multiple international medical meetings, and edited book entitled "Contemporary Interventional Ultrasonography in Urology". Current position and title: Professor of Clinical Urology, Institute of Urology, University of Southern California/Norris Cancer Center, Los Angeles, USA and Dedicated Professor of Urology, Kyoto Prefectural University of Medicine, Kyoto Japan.

Contents

Preface

Multiple imaging modalities can complement each other to provide more information to understand the real worlds of objects than the use of a single modality. Image fusion aims to generate a fused single image which contains more precise reliable visualization of the objects than any source image of them. Such a fused image should provide extended information and better perception for human vision or computerized vision tasks. All source images need to be accurately aligned or spatially registered before fusion. Image fusion has been investigated by many researchers in various fields. Several great works in this decade established the basic principles and sub-specialties evolved and grew. Recent efforts have led to the development of a number of algorithms, performance assessment, processing approaches and promising applications. Image fusion technology has successfully contributed to various fields such as medical diagnosis and navigation, surveillance systems, remote sensing, digitalized cameras, military applications, computer vision, etc. However, there are still challenging issues to be resolved over the broad range of its applications, which include the development of further sophisticated algorithms and associated hardware devices to support more reliable, real-time practical applications.

This book presents various recent advances in research and development in the field of image fusion. This monumental work was created through the diligence and creativity of some of the most accomplished experts in different fields. Many authorities have provided their unique concepts and thoughts herein. To enhance readability, the essential processes of image fusion have been graphically represented in each chapter. It is our hope that our efforts have yielded a comprehensive and practical reference source for image fusion for basic scientists and imaging specialists in diverse fields, and that it will be ultimately beneficial for human use and in robotics to achieve more precise and reliable decision making.

Many people have devoted many hours to this project in different ways. First, the editor would like to thank all the authors of the chapters which make this book such a valuable collection of new developments and perspective insights. Furthermore, we would like to thank all the Editorial members of IN-TECH for giving us this opportunity and their support in the timely publication of this book.

Osamu Ukimura
Institute of Urology, University of Southern California, Los Angeles, California, USA
Department of Urology, Kyoto Prefectural University of Medicine, Kyoto, Japan

Part 1

Novel Approaches and Algorithms in Image Fusion

1

F-Transform Based Image Fusion

I. Perfilieva, M. Daňková, P. Hod'áková and M. Vajgl
Institute for Research and Applications of Fuzzy Modeling, University of Ostrava
Czech Republic

1. Introduction

Developments in hardware, sensor quality and imaging technology have attracted a great deal of research interest in image processing and associated fields in the last two decades. Here, we focus particularly on the problem of image fusion due to the fact that it is one of the leading areas of intense research and development activity. Moreover, image fusion is used in many real-world applications such as medical diagnosis with multimodal images (for an overview of medical applications, see Constantinos et al. (2001)), person or weapon detection by automated defense systems and classification of objects (e.g., roads, rivers, mountains and towns) in multi sensor geographical images. (a wide overview of applications can be found in Piella (2003)).

Image fusion aims at the integration of various complementary image data into a single, new image with the best possible quality. The term "quality" depends on the demands of the specific application, which is usually related to its usefulness for human visual perception, computer vision or further processing. As stated in Šroubek & Flusser (2005), if u is an ideal image (considered as a function of two variables) and $c_1,\ldots,c_K$ are acquired images, then the relation between each c_i and u can be expressed by

$$c_i(x,y) = d_i(u(x,y)) + e_i(x,y),\ i = 1,\ldots,K$$

where d_i is an unknown operator describing the image degradation, and e_i is an additive random noise.

Image fusion is a means to obtain an image $\hat{u}$ that yields in some sense a better representation of the ideal image u than is provided by each individual image c_i. There are various fusion methodologies currently in use. The main categories are determined by the level at which the fusion is actually executed Zhang (2010). The methodologies are designed on the basis of the following mathematical fields: statistical methods (e.g., using aggregation operators, such as the MinMax method Blum (2005)), estimation theory Loza et al. (2010), fuzzy methods (see Singh et al. (2004); Ranjan et al. (2005); Ashoori et al. (2008)), optimization methods (e.g., neural networks, genetic algorithms Mumtaz & Majid (2008)) and multiscale decomposition methods, which incorporate various transforms, e.g., discrete wavelet transforms (for a classification of these methods see Piella (2003); a classification of wavelet-based image fusion methods can be found in Amolins et al. (2007), and for applications for blurred and unregistered images, refer to Šroubek & Flusser (2005); Šroubek & Zítová (2006)). The choice of a fusion methodology is basically influenced by parameters relating to the type of degradation operators d_i, the occurrence of noise and the type of outputs of the preprocessing analysis.

The main purpose of this contribution is to show that the F-transform technique is a promising and efficient method for image fusion Daňková & Valášek (2006); Perfilieva & Daňková (2008). The original motivation for the F-transform (an abbreviated name for the fuzzy transform) came from fuzzy modeling Perfilieva (2006; 2007). The purpose was to show that, similarly to traditional transforms (Fourier and wavelet), the F-transform performs a transformation of an original universe of functions into a universe of their "skeleton models" (vectors of F-transform components) in which further computation is easier (e.g., an application to the initial-value problem with a fuzzy initial condition Perfilieva, De Meyer, De Baets & Plšková (2008)). In this respect, the F-transform can be as useful in many applications as traditional transforms (see applications to image compression Perfilieva, Pavliska, Vajgl & De Baets (2008) and time-series procession Perfilieva, Novák, Pavliska, Dvořák & Štěpnička (2008)). Moreover, sometimes the F-transform can be more efficient than its counterparts. Without going into specific details here, we claim that F-transform has a potential advantage over the wavelet transform; while the latter uses a single "mother wavelet" that determines all basic functions, the former can use basic functions with different shapes.

This contribution is organized as follows: Section 2 introduces the F-transform technique and gives an overview of its properties; Section 3 describes the details of image representation for image fusion using the F-transform; Section 4 provides the details of two algorithms (where the first algorithm is a special case of the second one) for image fusion that use image representation based on the F-transform; Section 5 addresses some particular problems in image fusion and highlights the advantages of the optional setting in the introduced algorithm. Finally, conclusions, comments and some future trends in our research are given in the Section 6.

2. F-transform

To find a fused image, we propose two algorithms that are based on the F-transform technique. Before going into the details of image fusion, we give a general characterization and the relevant details of the technique developed herein.

Generally speaking, the F-transform produces an image by a linear mapping from a set of ordinary continuous/discrete functions over a domain P onto a set of functions within a fuzzy partition of P. We assume that the reader is familiar with the notion of the *fuzzy set* and how is it represented.

Below, we explain the F-transform in more detail and adapt our explanation to the purpose of this chapter (we refer to Perfilieva (2006) for a complete description). The explanation will be given for the example of a discrete function that corresponds to the image u.

Let u be represented by the discrete function $u : P \to \mathbb{R}$ of two Variables, where $P = \{(i,j) \mid i = 1,\dots,N, j = 1,\dots,M\}$ is an $N \times M$ array of pixels, and $\mathbb{R}$ is the set of reals. If $(i,j) \in P$ is a pixel, then $u(i,j)$ represents its intensity range.

The F-transform of u corresponds u to the matrix $\mathbf{F}_{nm}[u]$ of F-transform components:

$$\mathbf{F}_{nm}[u] = \begin{pmatrix} F[u]_{11} & \dots & F[u]_{1m} \\ \vdots & \vdots & \vdots \\ F[u]_{n1} & \dots & F[u]_{nm} \end{pmatrix}. \tag{1}$$

Each component $F[u]_{kl}$ is a local mean value of u over a support set of the respective fuzzy set $A_k \times B_l$. The latter is an element of a *fuzzy partition* of the Cartesian product of intervals

$[1,N] \times [1,M]$. Using the fact that a fuzzy partition of a Cartesian product is the Cartesian product of fuzzy partitions, we first introduce this notion for a single interval and then for a Cartesian product of intervals.

Let $[1,N] = \{x \mid 1 \le x \le N\}$ be an interval on the real line $\mathbb{R}$, $n \ge 2$, a number of fuzzy sets in a fuzzy partition of $[1,N]$, and $h = \frac{N-1}{n-1}$ the distance between nodes $x_1,\ldots,x_n \in [1,N]$, where $x_1 = 1, x_k = x_1 + (k-1)h, k = 1,\ldots,n$. Fuzzy sets $A_1,\ldots,A_n : [1,N] \to [0,1]$ establish a *h-uniform fuzzy partition* of $[1,N]$ if the following requirements are fulfilled:

(i) for every $k = 1,\ldots,n$, $A_k(x) = 0$ if $x \in [1,N] \setminus [x_{k-1}, x_{k+1}]$, where $x_0 = x_1$, $x_{N+1} = x_N$;

(ii) for every $k = 1,\ldots,n$, A_k is continuous on $[x_{k-1}, x_{k+1}]$, where $x_0 = x_1$, $x_{N+1} = x_N$;

(iii) for every $i = 1,\ldots,N$, $\sum_{k=1}^{n} A_k(i) = 1$;

(iv) for every $k = 1,\ldots,n$, $\sum_{i=1}^{N} A_k(i) > 0$;

(v) for every $k = 2,\ldots,n-1$, A_k is symmetrical with respect to the line $x = x_k$.

The membership functions of the respective fuzzy sets in a fuzzy partition are called *basic functions*. The example of triangular basic functions $A_1,\ldots,A_n$, $n \ge 2$ on the interval $[1,N]$ is given below.

$$A_1(x) = \begin{cases} 1 - \frac{(x-x_1)}{h}, & x \in [x_1, x_2], \\ 0, & \text{otherwise}, \end{cases}$$

$$A_k(x) = \begin{cases} \frac{|x-x_k|}{h}, & x \in [x_{k-1}, x_{k+1}], \\ 0, & \text{otherwise}, \end{cases}$$

$$A_n(x) = \begin{cases} \frac{(x-x_{n-1})}{h}, & x \in [x_{n-1}, x_n], \\ 0, & \text{otherwise}. \end{cases}$$

Note that the shape (e.g., triangular or sinusoidal) of a basic function in a fuzzy partition is not predetermined and can be chosen according to additional requirements.

We now introduce two *extreme fuzzy partitions* of $[1,N]$ that will be used in the following.

Largest partition. The largest partition contains only one fuzzy set, $A_1 : [1,N] \to [0,1]$, such that for all $x \in [1,N]$, $A_1(x) = 1$.

Finest partition. The finest partition is established by N fuzzy sets, $A_1,\ldots,A_N : [1,N] \to [0,1]$, such that for all $k,l = 1,\ldots,N$, $k \ne l$, $A_k(x_k) = 1$ and $A_k(x_l) = 0$.

If fuzzy sets $A_1,\ldots,A_n$ establish a fuzzy partition of $[1,N]$ and $B_1,\ldots,B_m$ do the same for $[1,M]$, then the Cartesian product $\{A_1,\ldots,A_n\} \times \{B_1,\ldots,B_m\}$ of these fuzzy partitions is the set of all fuzzy sets $A_k \times B_l$, $k = 1,\ldots,n$, $l = 1,\ldots,m$. The membership function $A_k \times B_l : [1,N] \times [1,M] \to [0,1]$ is equal to the product $A_k \cdot B_l$ of the respective membership functions. Fuzzy sets $A_k \times B_l, k = 1,\ldots,n, l = 1,\ldots,m$ establish a fuzzy partition of the Cartesian product $[1,N] \times [1,M]$. In Figure 1, an example of a fuzzy partition of $[1,3] \times [1,4]$ by triangular membership functions is given.

Let $u : P \to \mathbb{R}$ and fuzzy sets $A_k \times B_l$, $k = 1,\ldots,n$, $l = 1,\ldots,m$, establish a fuzzy partition of $[1,N] \times [1,M]$. The (direct) *F-transform* of u (with respect to the chosen partition) is an image of the mapping $F[u] : \{A_1,\ldots,A_n\} \times \{B_1,\ldots,B_m\} \to \mathbb{R}$ defined by

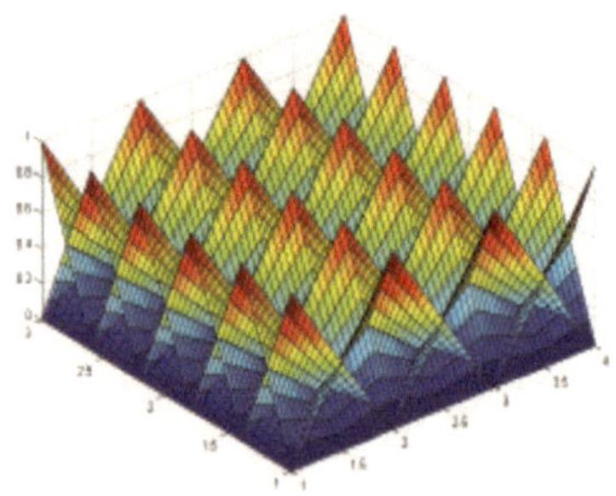

Fig. 1. An example of a fuzzy partition of [1,3] × [1,4] by triangular membership functions.

$$F[u](A_k \times B_l) = \frac{\sum_{i=1}^{N} \sum_{j=1}^{M} u(i,j) A_k(i) B_l(j)}{\sum_{i=1}^{N} \sum_{j=1}^{M} A_k(i) B_l(j)}, \tag{2}$$

where $k = 1,\ldots,n, l = 1,\ldots,m$. The value $F[u](A_k \times B_l)$ is called an *F-transform component* of u and is denoted by $F[u]_{kl}$. The components $F[u]_{kl}$ can be arranged into the matrix representation as in (1) or into the vector representation as follows:

$$(F[u]_{11},\ldots,F[u]_{1m},\ldots,F[u]_{n1},\ldots,F[u]_{nm}). \tag{3}$$

The *inverse F-transform* of u is a function on P, which is represented by the following inversion formula, where $i = 1,\ldots,N, j = 1,\ldots,M$:

$$u_{nm}(i,j) = \sum_{k=1}^{n} \sum_{l=1}^{m} F[u]_{kl} A_k(i) B_l(j). \tag{4}$$

It can be shown that the inverse F-transform u_{nm} approximates the original function u on the domain P. The proof can be found in Perfilieva (2006; 2007).

Example 1 *Let discrete real function $u = u(x,y)$ be defined on the $N \times M$ array of pixels $P = \{(i,j) \mid i = 1,\ldots,N, j = 1,\ldots,M\}$ so that $u : P \to \mathbb{R}$. We now characterize F-transforms of u for two extreme fuzzy partitions introduced above.*

Largest partition. *The largest partition of $[1,N] \times [1,M]$ contains only one fuzzy set, $A_1 \times B_1$, such that for all $(x,y) \in [1,N] \times [1,M]$, $(A_1 \times B_1)(x,y) = 1$. The respective F-transform component $F[u]_{11}$ and the respective inverse F-transform u_{11} are as follows:*

$$F[u]_{11} = \frac{\sum_{i=1}^{N} \sum_{j=1}^{M} u(i,j)}{NM},$$
$$u_{11}(i,j) = F[u]_{11}, \quad i = 1,\ldots,N, j = 1,\ldots,M.$$

It is easy to see that $F[u]_{11}$ is the arithmetic mean *of u.*

Finest partition. *The finest partition of $[1,N] \times [1,M]$ is established by $N \times M$ fuzzy sets $A_k \times B_l$, such that for all $k = 1,\ldots,N$, and $l = 1,\ldots,M$, $(A_k \times B_l)(x_k,y_l) = 1$, and for all $r = 1,\ldots,N$, and $s = 1,\ldots,M$, such that $(k,l) \neq (r,s)$, $(A_k \times B_l)(x_r,y_s) = 0$. The respective F-transform* *components* $F[u]_{kl}$, $k = 1,\dots,N$, $l = 1,\dots,M$, *and the respective inverse F-transform* u_{NM} *are as follows:*

$$F[u]_{kl} = u(k,l),$$
$$u_{NM}(i,j) = u(i,j), \quad i = 1,\dots,N, j = 1,\dots,M.$$

It is easy to see that $u_{NM} = u$.

The following two statements (for the proof see Perfilieva & Valášek (2005)) justify the image-fusion method proposed below. Both are based on the following assumptions: the interval $[a,b]$ is h-uniformly partitioned by $A_1,\dots,A_n$, where $n > 2$ and $h = (b-a)/(n-1)$, f is a continuous function on $[a,b]$, $F[f]_1,\dots andF[f]_n$ are the F-transform components of f with respect to $A_1,\dots,A_n$.

S1. For each $k = 1,\dots,n-1$, and for each $t \in [x_k, x_{k+1}]$ the following estimations hold:

$$|f(t) - F[f]_k| \le 2\omega(h,f), \qquad |f(t) - F[f]_{k+1}| \le 2\omega(h,f)$$

where

$$\omega(h,f) = \max_{|\delta|\le h} \max_{x\in[a,b-\delta]} |f(x+\delta) - f(x)|$$

is the modulus of continuity of f on $[a,b]$.

S2. The k-th component $F[f]_k$ ($k = 1,\dots,n$) minimizes the function

$$\Phi(y) = \int_a^b (f(x) - y)^2 A_k(x) dx.$$

3. Image representation for image fusion: step by step

In the next section, two algorithms for image fusion are presented. Both are based on the F-transform technique, leading to one-level or higher-level decomposition of an image; here we explain the technical details of these decompositions. We assume that the image u is a discrete real function $u = u(x,y)$ defined on the $N \times M$ array of pixels $P = \{(i,j) \mid i = 1,\dots,N, j = 1,\dots,M\}$ so that $u : P \to \mathbb{R}$. Moreover, let fuzzy sets $A_k \times B_l$, $k = 1,\dots,n$, $l = 1,\dots,m$, where $0 < n \le N, 0 < m \le M$ establish a fuzzy partition of $[1,N] \times [1,M]$.
We begin with the following representation of u on P:

$$u(x,y) = u_{nm}(x,y) + e(x,y), \text{ where } 0 < n \le N, 0 < m \le M, \tag{5}$$
$$e(x,y) = u(x,y) - u_{nm}(x,y), \forall (x,y) \in P, \tag{6}$$

where u_{nm} is the inverse F-transform of u and e is the respective residuum. If we replace e in (5) by its inverse F-transform e_{NM} with respect to the finest partition of $[1,N] \times [1,M]$ (see the Example above), the above representation can then be rewritten as follows:

$$u(x,y) = u_{nm}(x,y) + e_{NM}(x,y), \forall (x,y) \in P. \tag{7}$$

We call (7) a *one-level decomposition* of u.
If function u is smooth, then the error function e_{NM} is small, and the one-level decomposition (7) is sufficient for our fusion algorithm. However, images generally contain various types of degradation that disrupt their smoothness. As a result, the error function e_{NM} in (7) is not

negligible, and the one-level decomposition is insufficient for our purpose. In this case, we continue with the decomposition of the error function e in (5). We decompose e into its inverse F-transform $e_{n'm'}$ (with respect to a finer fuzzy partition of $[1,N] \times [1,M]$ with $n' : n < n' \leq N$ and $m' : m < m' \leq M$ basic functions, respectively) and a new error function e'. Thus, we obtain the *second-level decomposition* of u:

$$u(x,y) = u_{nm}(x,y) + e_{n'm'}(x,y) + e'(x,y),$$
$$e'(x,y) = e(x,y) - e_{n'm'}(x,y), \forall (x,y) \in P.$$

In the same manner, we can obtain a *higher-level decomposition*

$$\begin{aligned} u(x,y) &= u_{n_1m_1}(x,y) + e^{(1)}_{n_2m_2}(x,y) + \ldots + e^{(k-2)}_{n_{k-1}m_{k-1}}(x,y) + e^{(k-1)}(x,y), \text{ where} \\ & 0 < n_1 \leq n_2 \leq \ldots \leq n_{k-1} \leq N, \\ & 0 < m_1 \leq m_2 \leq \ldots \leq m_{k-1} \leq M, \\ e^{(1)}(x,y) &= u(x,y) - u_{n_1m_1}(x,y), \\ e^{(i)}(x,y) &= e^{(i-1)}(x,y) - e^{(i-1)}_{n_im_i}(x,y), \text{ for } i = 2,\ldots,k-1 \text{ and } (x,y) \in P, \end{aligned}$$

which can be rewritten as follows:

$$u(x,y) = u_{n_1m_1}(x,y) + e^{(1)}_{n_2m_2}(x,y) + \ldots + e^{(k-2)}_{n_{k-1}m_{k-1}}(x,y) + e^{(k-1)}_{n_km_k}(x,y). \tag{8}$$

Below, we work with the two decompositions of u that are given by (7) and (8).

4. Two algorithms for image fusion

We propose two algorithms:

1. The simple F-transform-based fusion algorithm (SA) and
2. The complete F-transform-based fusion algorithm (CA).

These algorithms are based on the one-level decomposition (7) and the higher-level decomposition (8), respectively. Moreover, the first algorithm is a special case of the second. Both algorithms are derived from the one developed in Daňková & Valášek (2006).
The main role in fusion algorithms is played by the so-called *fusion operator* $\kappa : \mathbb{R}^K \rightarrow \mathbb{R}$, defined as follows:

$$\kappa(x_1,\ldots,x_K) = x_p, \text{ if } |x_p| = \max(|x_1|,\ldots,|x_K|). \tag{9}$$

Note that other definitions of a fusion operator are possible. The choice of a fusion operator is influenced by a type of image degradation encountered. Below, we show that a rather wide class of degradations can be captured by the κ defined above.

4.1 Simple F-transform-based image fusion

Assume that we are given $K \geq 2$ input images $c_1,\ldots,c_K$ with various types of degradation. Our aim is to recognize undistorted parts in the given images and to fuse them into one image. In this section, we describe the algorithm for image fusion based on the one-level decomposition (7).

Each input image $c_i, i = 1,\dots,K$, is assumed to be a discrete real function $c_i = c_i(x,y)$ defined on the $N \times M$ array of pixels $P = \{(x,y) \mid x = 1,\dots,N, y = 1,\dots,M\}$ so that $c_i : P \to \mathbb{R}$. Moreover, the set $[1,N] \times [1,M]$ is assumed to be partitioned by fuzzy sets $A_k \times B_l$, where $k = 1,\dots,n, l = 1,\dots,m$ and $0 < n \leq N, 0 < m \leq M$. Denote $I = \{1,2,\dots,K\}$. The algorithm can be summarized as follows:

(1) Decompose input images $c_1,\dots,c_K$ into inverse F-transforms and error functions using the one-level decomposition (7).

(2) Apply the fusion operator (9) to the respective F-transform components of c_i, $i \in I$, and obtain the fused F-transform components of a new image.

(3) Apply the fusion operator to the to the respective F-transform components of the error functions e_i, $i \in I$, and obtain the fused F-transform components of a new error function.

(4) Reconstruct the fused image from the inverse F-transforms with the fused components of the new image and the fused components of the new error function.

We now proceed with a detailed description of the simple F-transform-based image-fusion algorithm (SA).

Setting:

Step 0. Choose $n, m, 0 < n \leq N, 0 < m \leq M,$ – the numbers of basic functions in the fuzzy partitions of $[1,N]$ and $[1,M]$, respectively.

Initialization:

Step 1. Create the fuzzy partitions $A_1^{(1)},\dots,A_n^{(1)}$ and $B_1^{(1)},\dots,B_m^{(1)}$ of $[1,N]$ and $[1,M]$, respectively.

Denote $A_1^{(2)},\dots,A_N^{(2)}$ and $B_1^{(2)},\dots,B_M^{(2)}$ the finest partitions of $[1,N]$ and $[1,M]$, respectively.

Transformation:

Step 2. For all $i \in I$, compute the direct and the inverse F-transforms of each input image c_i and obtain:

$F[c_i]_{11},\dots,F[c_i]_{nm}$ – the F-transform components of c_i,

$c_{i_{nm}}$ – the inverse F-transform of c_i.

Step 3. For all $i \in I$, compute the error functions: $e_i = c_i - c_{i_{nm}}$. Identify values $e_i(x,y)$, $(x,y) \in P$, with the F-transform components $F[e_i]_{xy}$ of e_i with respect to the finest partitions of $[1,N]$ and $[1,M]$.

Fusion:

Step 4(a). Apply the fusion operator κ to the respective components of the direct F-transforms of the input images c_i, $i \in I$:

$$\kappa(F[c_1]_{11},\dots,F[c_K]_{11}) = \kappa_{11}^{(1)},$$

$$\dots\dots\dots\dots\dots\dots\dots\dots\dots\dots$$

$$\kappa(F[c_1]_{nm},\dots,F[c_K]_{nm}) = \kappa_{nm}^{(1)},$$

and obtain the fused F-transform components of a new image:

$$(\kappa_{11}^{(1)}, \ldots, \kappa_{nm}^{(1)}). \tag{10}$$

Step 4(b). Apply the fusion operator κ to the respective components of the direct F-transforms of the error functions e_i, $i \in I$, with respect to the finest partitions of $[1, N]$ and $[1, M]$:

$$\kappa(F[e_1]_{11}, \ldots, F[e_K]_{11}) = \kappa_{11}^{(2)},$$
$$\cdots\cdots\cdots\cdots\cdots\cdots\cdots\cdots$$
$$\kappa(F[e_1]_{NM}, \ldots, F[e_1]_{NM}) = \kappa_{NM}^{(2)},$$

and obtain the fused F-transform components of a new error function:

$$(\kappa_{11}^{(2)}, \ldots, \kappa_{NM}^{(2)}). \tag{11}$$

Reconstruction:

Step 5. The fused image c is equal to the sum of the two inverse F-transforms with fused components (10) and fused components (11), i.e.:

$$c(x,y) = \sum_{k=1}^{n}\sum_{l=1}^{m} \kappa_{kl}^{(1)} A_k^{(1)}(x) B_l^{(1)}(y) + \sum_{k=1}^{N}\sum_{l=1}^{M} \kappa_{kl}^{(2)} A_k^{(2)}(x) B_l^{(2)}(y),\ (x,y) \in P.$$

4.2 Complete F-transform-based algorithm

In this section, we describe the second algorithm for image fusion, i.e., based on the higher-level decomposition (8). All the assumptions made above remain valid. Moreover, the summarized description of the complete F-transform-based algorithm coincides with the one given above up to the descriptions of their respective decompositions.
We proceed with a detailed description of the complete F-transform-based image fusion algorithm (CA).

Setting:

Step 0. Choose

$k_{\max}$ – maximal number of iterations,
$step$ – coefficient for an increment of the number of basic functions in each fuzzy partitio
n_{start} – starting number of basic functions in the fuzzy partition of $[1, N]$,
m_{start} – starting number of basic functions in the fuzzy partition $[1, M]$,

where $step \le \min(N - n_{start}, M - m_{start})$ and $0 < n(m)_{start} \le N(M)$.
Denote $e_i^{(0)} = c_i$ for $i \in I$.

For $k = 0 \cdot step^k$ **to** $k_{\max}$

Initialization:

Step 1.1. Compute $n = n_{start} \cdot step^k$, $m = m_{start} \cdot step^k$.

Step 1.2. Create fuzzy partitions $A_1^{(0)}, \ldots, A_n^{(0)}$ and $B_1^{(0)}, \ldots, B_m^{(0)}$ of $[1,N]$ and $[1,M]$, respectively.

Transformation:

Step 2. For all $i \in I$, compute the direct and the inverse F-transforms of each function $e_i^{(k)}$ and obtain:

$$F[e_i^{(k)}]_{11}, \ldots, F[e_i^{(k)}]_{nm} \text{ – the F-transform components of } e_i^{(k)},$$
$$e_{i_{nm}}^{(k)} \text{ – the inverse F-transform of } e_i^{(k)}.$$

Step 3. For all $i \in I$, compute error functions: $e_i^{(k+1)} = e_i^{(k)} - e_{i_{nm}}^{(k)}$.

Fusion:

Step 4. Apply fusion operator κ to respective components of the direct F-transforms of functions $e_i^{(k)}$:

$$\kappa(F[e_1^{(k)}]_{11}, \ldots, F[e_K^{(k)}]_{11}) = \kappa_{11}^{(k)},$$
$$\ldots\ldots\ldots\ldots\ldots\ldots\ldots\ldots\ldots\ldots$$
$$\kappa(F[e_1^{(k)}]_{nm}, \ldots, F[e_K^{(k)}]_{nm}) = \kappa_{nm}^{(k)},$$

and obtain the fused F-transform components as follows:

$$(\kappa_{11}^{(k)}, \ldots, \kappa_{nm}^{(k)}). \tag{12}$$

Step 5. $k = k + 1$.

End For

Last step of fusion:

Step 6. For all $i \in I$, identify values $e_i^{(k_{\max}+1)}(x,y)$, $(x,y) \in P$, with the F-transform components $F[e_1^{(k_{\max}+1)}]_{xy}$ of $e_i^{(k_{\max}+1)}$ with respect to the finest partitions of $[1,N]$ and $[1,M]$. Apply the fusion operator κ to the respective F-transform components of $e_i^{(k_{\max}+1)}$:

$$\kappa(F[e_1^{(k_{\max}+1)}]_{11}, \ldots, F[e_K^{(k_{\max}+1)}]_{11}) = \kappa_{11}^{(k_{\max}+1)},$$
$$\ldots\ldots\ldots\ldots\ldots\ldots\ldots\ldots\ldots\ldots$$
$$\kappa(F[e_1^{(k_{\max}+1)}]_{NM}, \ldots, F[e_K^{(k_{\max}+1)}]_{NM}) = \kappa_{NM}^{(k_{\max}+1)},$$

and obtain the fused F-transform components as follows:

$$(\kappa_{11}^{(k_{\max}+1)}, \ldots, \kappa_{NM}^{(k_{\max}+1)}). \tag{13}$$

Reconstruction:

Step 7. The fused image c is equal to the sum of two inverse F-transforms with fused components (12) and fused components (13), i.e.:

$$c(x,y) = \sum_{k=1}^{n_{start}} \sum_{l=1}^{m_{start}} \kappa_{kl}^{(0)} A_k^{(0)}(x) B_l^{(0)}(y) + \dots$$

$$\dots + \sum_{k=1}^{N} \sum_{l=1}^{M} \kappa_{kl}^{(k_{\max}+1)} A_k^{(k_{\max}+1)}(x) B_l^{(k_{\max}+1)}(y) \, (x,y) \in P, \quad (14)$$

where $n_0 = n_{start}$ and $m_0 = m_{start}, \dots, n_{k_{\max}+1} = N, m_{k_{\max}+1} = M$.

4.3 Justification of the algorithms

By **S1**, a smaller modulus of continuity leads to a higher-quality approximation of an input image by its inverse fuzzy transform. If a certain part of the input image is affected by degradation, then by **S2**, the respective F-transform component captures the weighted arithmetic mean and the error function is close to zero at that part. Thus, by the proposed fusion operator κ, we choose components with maximal absolute values that correspond to those parts of the input image which are least degraded.

5. Experimental results

We tested the algorithms described above on examples of input images which are available at "http://irafm.osu.cz/". Two types of degradations were applied to these images so that they appear as either:

1. multi-focus input images, or
2. multi-sensor input images.

Multi-focus input images are affected by degradation in the form of blurring caused by imaging devices (due to their optical properties or display limitations) and/or the complexity of the image subject. Such images are blurred and noisy and generally exhibit further phenomena such as various motions in the field or input images having different resolutions; these effects were neglected in the subsequent experiments, as our aim was only to minimize blurring and noise in the fused image.
In contrast, multi-sensor input images do not contain a priori degraded information. They can be characterized as more likely to be carriers of complementary information coming from different types of sensors. Of course, additional blurring may occur as well as noise and other distortions in the input images. Here, a fused image should contain the most useful information available in the input images.
The following experiments produced a series of fused images. They differed in their initial settings of the values of the algorithms and thus in their resulting quality. Because the latter is not obvious, we focus on a performance of a particular algorithm and demonstrate various fusions that are better than the input originals. Whenever possible, we compare fused images with ideal images. In this case, the Euclidean distance $E(c,d) = \sqrt{\sum_{x \in P}(c(x) - d(x))^2}$ was used as a measure of quality.

5.1 Multi-focus images

In this section, we demonstrate a multi-focus image fusion. In the first two examples, a Gaussian noise was artificially added to an ideal image at complementary or disjoint regions. In the following two examples, real images made by a digital camera were fused.
Ideally, the fused image is produced by combining regions that are in focus. If this is the case, our fusion operator κ defined by (9) works reasonably well. We can explain (and justify) this as follows: if the one-level decomposition is applied, then the error function of a blurred part is smaller than that of the unblurred (sharp) part. Therefore, the maximal absolute values of the F-transform components reflect the level of sharpness, which is important for fusion. In the case of the SA and CA, an important role is played by the initial settings of the values of the algorithm parameters: the number of basic functions, m, n, in the case of SA and CA and the values of the increment, *step*, and the number of iterations, k_{max}, in the case of CA.

5.1.1 Artificial input images

Figs. 2(d) – 2(f) illustrate the use of the SA and the CA in the case of artificially blurred input images Fig. 2(a) and 2(b). The results show that the best choice was the SA with $m, n = 3$. In this case, the fused image was identical to the original one shown in Fig. 2(c), and for this reason, it is not demonstrated. A lower or a higher number of basic functions propagated the blur into the fused images (see Fig. 2(d), 2(e), and 2(f)), with the respective pictures of the pointwise absolute differences shown in Fig. 2(g), 2(h), and 2(i), where the values that are "close to zero" are in "close to black" color. Moreover, the SA, with the optimal choice $m, n = 3$, has a small computational complexity and was thus very fast. Surprisingly, the CA, with $step = 2$ and 8 iterations (see Fig. 2(f)), did not provide a better fusion.
The next example is slightly different: there are two different Gaussian blurs[1] applied to two disjoint regions of the ideal image Fig. 3(c). Unlike the previous case, we were not able to obtain a fused image identical to the ideal one. The results of our fusion algorithms were as follows: the SA required a rather fine partition, with $m, n = 250$ basic functions (see Fig. 3(e), the Euclidean distance is $E = 75.58$), and the CA slightly outperformed the SA (see Fig. 3(f), the Euclidean distance is $E = 72.53$). However, the computational complexity of the first algorithm (SA) was significantly smaller than that of the second (CA). We finally remark that the application of the simplest SA, with $m, n = 1$ (see Fig. 3(d)), produced a very good fusion with the Euclidean distance $E = 187.07$. The quality of fusion was especially good in the background part of the image.

5.1.2 Real input images

5.1.2.1 Grayscale digital input images

Fig. 4 presents the fusion of multi-focus images originating from a digital camera. Due to space limitations, we show here only the SA output Fig. 4(c) and note that it is comparable (measures of quality are almost equal) to the CA. Because we did not have a whole, ideal image at our disposal, we compare "ideal" parts of the input images with their respective parts in the fused image. These "ideal" parts are designated by the two color boxes in Fig. 4(d), referred to as the "left box" and the "right box". In Fig. 4(e) and Fig. 4(f), we see graphs of the pointwise absolute differences between the "ideal" and blurred parts, where again, the values that are "close to zero" are in "close to black" color. It is easily seen that the quality of fusion in the background region (left box) is better than that in the foreground region (right box). This was

[1] A Gaussian blur is a type of an image filter, which combines Gaussian function and the input image by means of convolution.

(a) 1'st blurred image (b) 2'nd blurred image (c) O – Original image

(d) F_1 – fused image by SA with $n, m = 1$ (e) F_2 – fused image by SA with $n, m = 9$ (f) F_3 – fused image by CA with $n_{start}, m_{start} = 1, k_{\max} = 8, step = 2$

(g) $|O - F_1|$ (h) $|O - F_2|$ (i) $|O - F_3|$

Fig. 2. Illustration of various initial setting values of SA and CA applied to a blurred image (Gaussian blur).

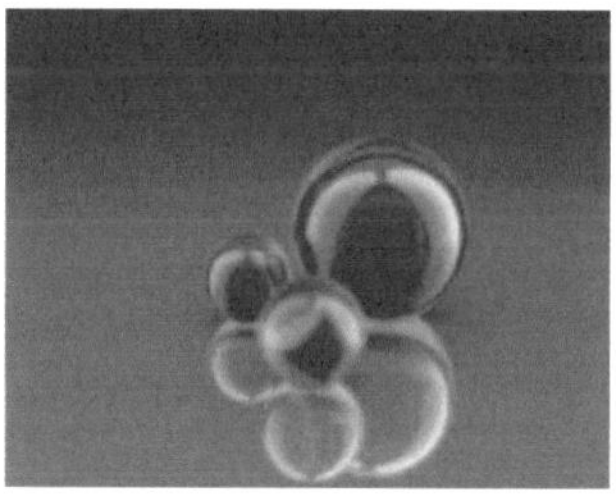

(a) 1'st blurred image

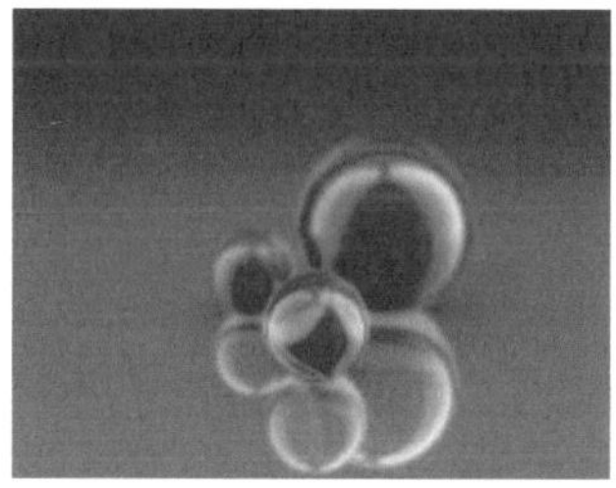

(b) 2'nd blurred image

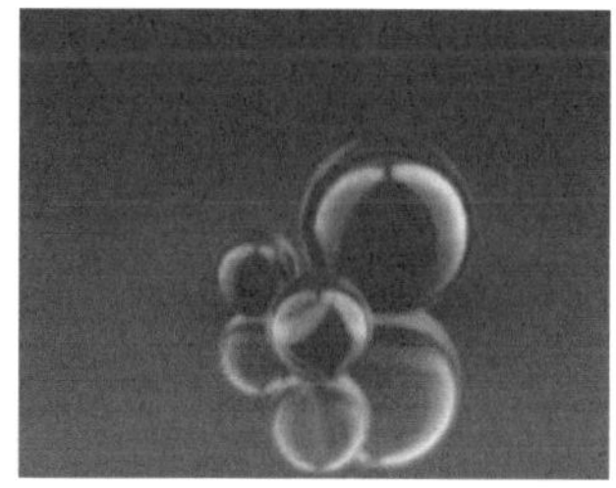

(c) Original image

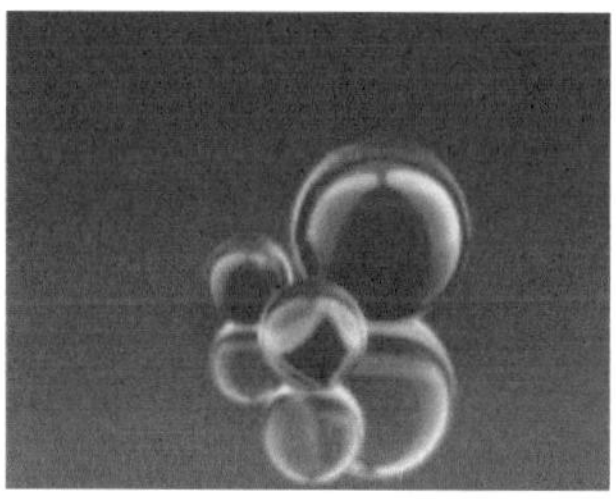

(d) F_1 – fused image by SA with $n, m = 1$

(e) F_2 – fused image by SA with $n, m = 250$

(f) F_3 – fused image by CA with $n_{start}, m_{start} = 1, k_{\max} = 10, step = 2$

(g) $|O - F_1|$

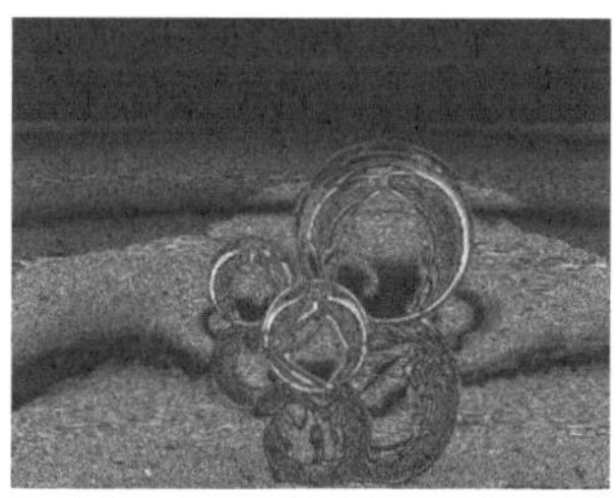

(h) $|O - F_2|$

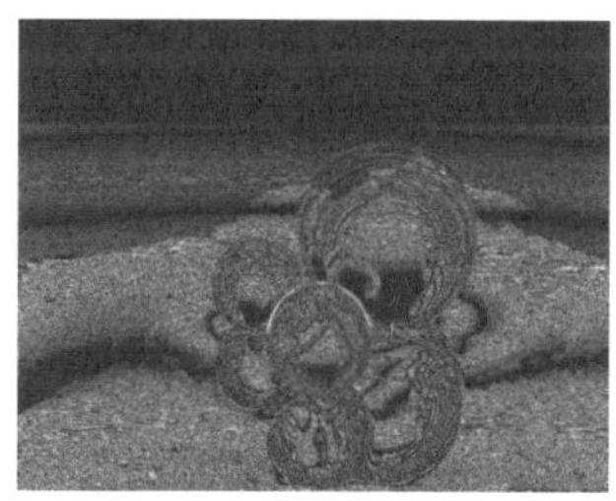

(i) $|O - F_3|$

Fig. 3. Application of SA to artificially blurred images (Gaussian blur).

caused by differences in reflections from the surfaces of the boxes. It seems that the initial setting values (in our case $n, m = 200$) did not play a significant role in this application.

5.1.2.2 Multichannel color input images

The application shows how the CA can be successfully used for the fusion of multi-focus color images. In our case, the fusion was performed separately for each color component. We assumed the RGB format for input color images and applied the CA with the same initial setting values three times on each R, G and B component. The final fused image was then composed from the fused individual color components.

The input images Fig. 5(a) and Fig. 5(b) depict a rather complicated scene with a lot of different smooth and glossy objects in the background. This observation forced us to choose the CA and not the simpler SA. The resulting (fused) toy in Fig. 5(c) and 5(d) seems to be perfect except for the one blurred area that is still blurred in all the input images. This blurred area is situated in a background area that contains both smooth and glossy elements and is thus

(a) C_1 – 1'st image (right box in focus) (b) C_2 – 2'nd image (left box in focus) (c) F – fused image by SA with $n, m = 200$

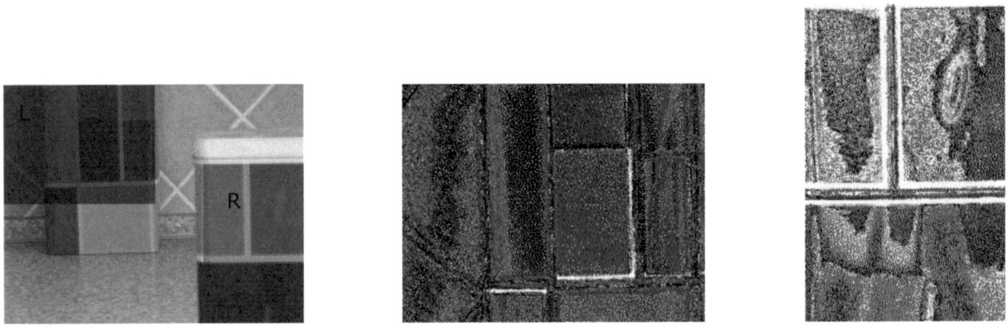

(d) Regions to compare (e) $|L - L_{C_2}|$ (f) $|R - R_{C_1}|$

Fig. 4. Application of SA to multi-focus images

very sensitive to any disturbances. Figs. 5(f) and 5(g) present graphs of the pointwise absolute differences (over the region of interest extracted from C_1) between the respective fused images and the first input image in Fig. 5(a). Obviously, the CA with a higher value of n_{start}, m_{start} gives a better fused image (compare Fig. 5(c) and 5(d)).

5.2 Multi-sensor images

This section presents two particular examples of multi-sensor images and their fusion using the F-transform technique.

5.2.1 Image fusion helps navigation

We start with a known benchmark, which can be downloaded from "http://www.metapix.de". It contains two input images taken by two sensors: a thermal imaging forward-looking infrared (FLIR) sensor, depicted in Fig. 6(a), and a low-light television (LLTV) sensor on Fig. 6(b). The sensors were used together in a helmet-mounted display intended for a helicopter pilot. The sensor input images help the helicopter pilot with orientation under poor-visibility conditions. However, they are not both simultaneously at the pilot's disposal. Therefore, image fusion is required. The goal here was to extract and fuse the most important characteristics of the scene, i.e., the paths and their localization in the landscape. In this case, a fast and efficient fusion method is highly desirable.
SA was deemed the most suitable for this application due to its low computational complexity. The results of the SA fusion (see Fig. 6(d)) were compared with the benchmark fusion (available on the same site) based on a multiresolution analysis (see Fig. 6(c)). The quality of our result, shown in Fig. 6(d), is visibly better. The main visual advantage lies in the part

(a) C_1 – 1'st input image (background in focus)

(b) C_2 – 2'nd input image (toy in focus)

(c) F_1 – fused image by CA with $n_{start}, m_{start} = 1, k_{\max} = 5, step = 2$

(d) F_2 – fused image by CA with $n_{start}, m_{start} = 10, k_{\max} = 4, step = 2$

(e) R – region of interest extracted from C_1

(f) $|R - R_{F_1}|$

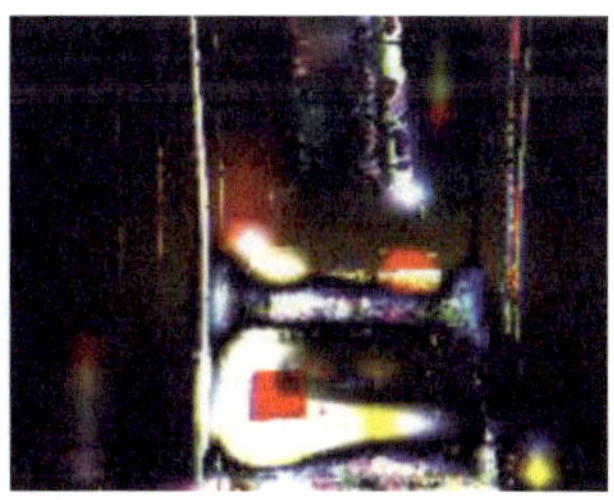

(g) $|R - R_{F_2}|$

Fig. 5. Application of CA to multi-focus color images

R marked by the red color in Fig. 6(e); it displays a field. In contrast to the output of the multiresolution analysis, the SA did not change this area. We note that the CA produced a fusion of even better quality (e.g. Fig. 6(f)), although at the cost of higher computational complexity.

5.2.2 Image fusion in medical diagnosis

An important field of applications for image-fusion methods is in medical diagnostics. Imaging methods such as computer tomography (CT), magnetic resonance imaging (MRI) or positron-emission tomography (PET) produce a multitude of images displaying particular information destined for further analysis and interpretation. The significant benefits of image fusion in this field are indisputable and widely sought.

For this application, we used brain MRI images, as in Bloch (2008). These images represent a slice of a dual-echo MRI image acquired with various parameters. As stated in Bloch (2008), the pathology (called adrenoleukodystrophy) is indicated by the bright area in Fig. 7(b) and is not visible in Fig. 7(a). There, the normal structure (ventricles) of a healthy brain is well delineated.

Initial experimental results with the original input images showed that the pure algorithms SA and CA could not be successfully applied. The reason is that Fig. 7(b) is almost uniformly smooth, and the F-transform components corresponding to this image are not within the values of the fusion operator. As can be deduced from the properties **S1** and **S2**, the contrast of an input image is very important for our F-transform-based fusion. Therefore, we modified the original input image in Fig. 7(b) by enhancing its contrast and obtained a new input image, depicted in Fig. 7(c). After this modification, the fusion was again applied to the input images in Fig. 7(b) and Fig. 7(c). The result is shown in Fig. 7(d). The pathological parts as well as the structure of the displayed brain are now nicely visible in the fused image.

6. Conclusion

This study focused on the application of the F-transform to the problem of image fusion. After a brief introduction to the theory of F-transform, detailed descriptions of two fusion algorithms were given. These algorithms are based on one-level and higher-level decompositions of input images. We then proposed an appropriate fusion operator and discussed several types of degradations that can be eliminated by its application.

In various examples, we showed that the proposed approach can be successfully applied in cases when input images are available as either:

1. multi-focus input images or
2. multi-sensor input images.

We examined input images that were artificially blurred and those blurred by inherent restrictions of the imaging tools. For the artificially blurred images, we estimated fusion quality by the Euclidean distance with the origin. For the others, we used the known benchmarks. Last, but not least, we discussed the influence of initial settings of the parameter values of the proposed algorithms on the quality of the resulting fusion.

7. Acknowledgement

Perfilieva, M. Daňková, P. Hod'áková acknowledge a partial support by projects: F-transfrom in Image Processing of the Univ. of Ostrava and 1M0572 of MŠMT ČR.

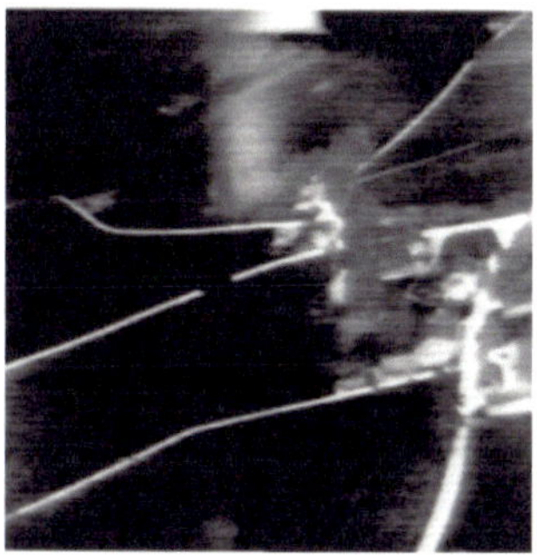

(a) FLIR image

(b) LLTV image

(c) Fusion by means of multiresolution analysis

(d) SA $n, m = 100$

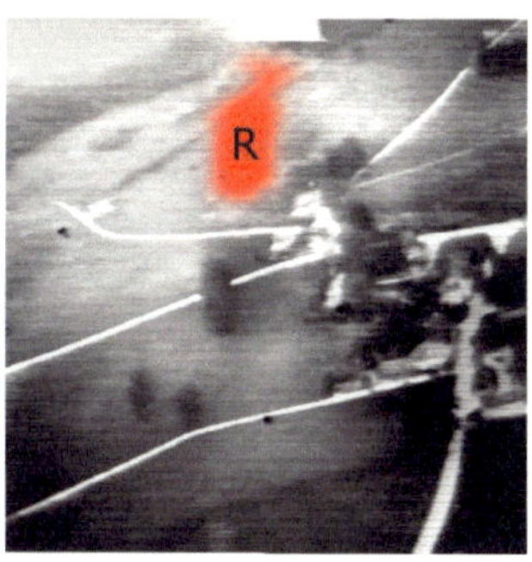

(e) Problematic part R

(f) CA with $n_{start}, m_{start} = 40, k_{\max} = 3, step = 2$

Fig. 6. Illustration of various initial setting values in SA and CA applied to multi-sensor images

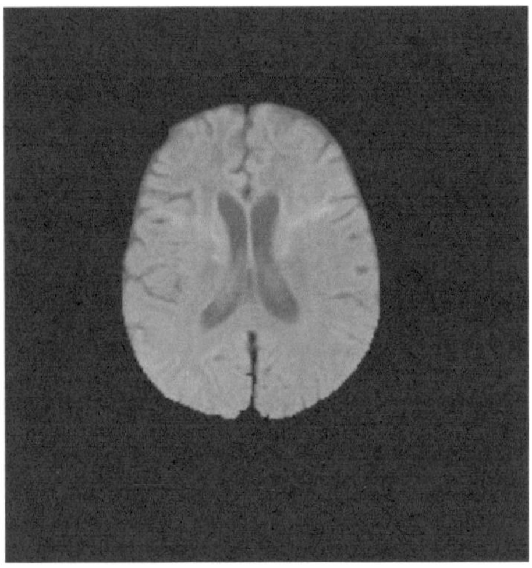

(a) 1'st MRI image

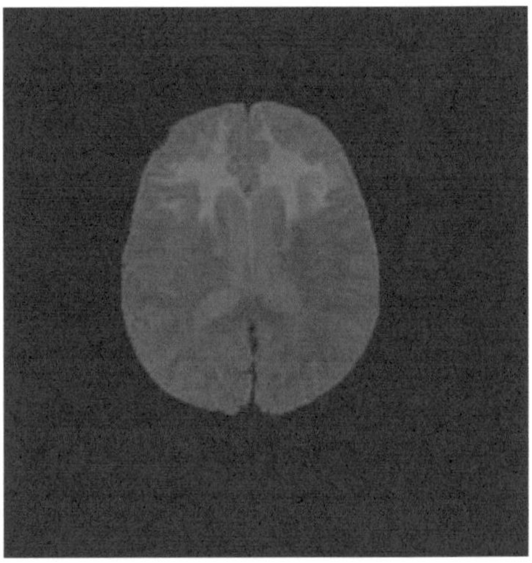

(b) 2'nd MRI image

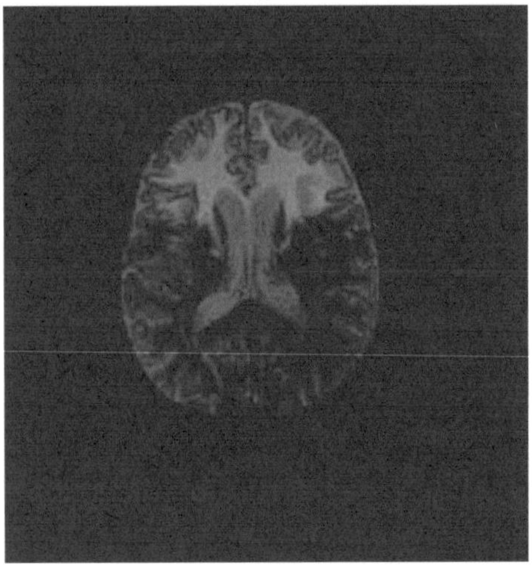

(c) 2'nd image with modified contrast

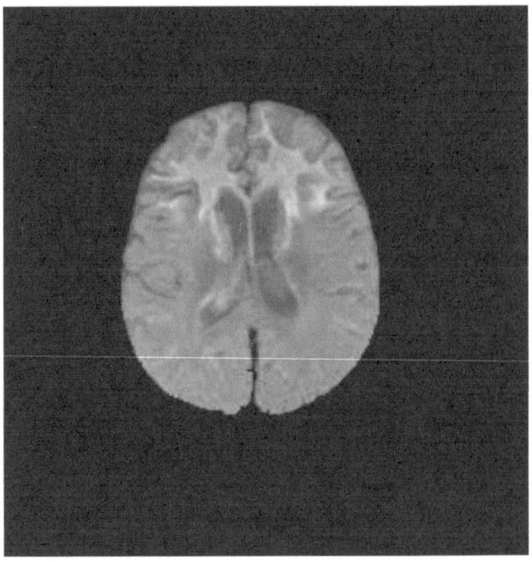

(d) CA with $n_{start}, m_{start} = 10, k_{max} = 5, step = 2$

Fig. 7. One axial slice of dual-echo magnetic resonance imaging acquisitions (pathological brain image), courtesy of Professor Catherine Adamsbaum, Saint Vincent de Paul Hospital, Paris.

8. References

Amolins, K., Zhang, Y. & Dare, P. (2007). Wavelet based image fusion techniques - an introduction, review and comparison, *ISPRS Journal of Photogrammetry and Remote Sensing* 62(4): 249 – 263.

Ashoori, A., Moshiri, B. & Setarehdan, S. (2008). Fuzzy image fusion application in detecting coronary layers in ivus pictures, *Communications, Control and Signal Processing, 2008. ISCCSP 2008. 3rd International Symposium on*, pp. 20 –24.

Bloch, I. (2008). Defining belief functions using mathematical morphology - application to image fusion under imprecision, *International Journal of Approximate Reasoning* 48(2): 437 – 465. In Memory of Philippe Smets (1938-2005).

Blum, R. S. (2005). Robust image fusion using a statistical signal processing approach, *Information Fusion* 6(2): 119 – 128.

Constantinos, S., Pattichis, M. & Micheli-Tzanakou, E. (2001). Medical imaging fusion applications: An overview, *Signals, Systems and Computers, 2001. Conference Record of the Thirty-Fifth Asilomar Conference on*, Vol. 2, pp. 1263 –1267 vol.2.

Daňková, M. & Valášek, R. (2006). Full fuzzy transform and the problem of image fusion, *Journal of Electrical Engineering* 12: 82–84.

Loza, A., Bull, D., Canagarajah, N. & Achim, A. (2010). Non-gaussian model-based fusion of noisy images in the wavelet domain, *Computer Vision and Image Understanding* 114(1): 54 – 65.

Mumtaz, A. & Majid, A. (2008). Genetic algorithms and its application to image fusion, *Emerging Technologies, 2008. ICET 2008. 4th International Conference on*, pp. 6 –10.

Perfilieva, I. (2006). Fuzzy transforms: Theory and applications, *Fuzzy Sets and Systems* 157: 993–1023.

Perfilieva, I. (2007). Fuzzy transforms: A challenge to conventional transforms, *in* P. W. Hawkes (ed.), *Advances in Images and Electron Physics*, Vol. 147, Elsevier Academic Press, San Diego, pp. 137–196.

Perfilieva, I. & Daňková, M. (2008). Image fusion on the basis of fuzzy transforms, *Proc. 8th Int. FLINS Conf.*, Madrid, pp. 471–476.

Perfilieva, I., De Meyer, H., De Baets, B. & Plšková, D. (2008). Cauchy problem with fuzzy initial condition and its approximate solution with the help of fuzzy transform, *Proc. of WCCI 2008, IEEE Int. Conf. on Fuzzy Systems*, Hong Kong, pp. 2285–2290.

Perfilieva, I., Novák, V., Pavliska, V., Dvořák, A. & Štěpnička, M. (2008). Analysis and prediction of time series using fuzzy transform, *Proc. of WCCI 2008, IEEE Int. Conf. on Neural Networks*, Hong Kong, pp. 3875–3879.

Perfilieva, I., Pavliska, V., Vajgl, M. & De Baets, B. (2008). Advanced image compression on the basis of fuzzy transforms, *Proc. Conf. IPMU'2008*, Torremolinos (Malaga), Spain, pp. 1167–1174.

Perfilieva, I. & Valášek, R. (2005). Fuzzy transforms in removing noise, *in* B. Reusch (ed.), *Computational Intelligence, Theory and Applications*, Springer, Heidelberg, pp. 225–234.

Piella, G. (2003). A general framework for multiresolution image fusion: from pixels to regions, *Information Fusion* 4(4): 259 – 280.

Ranjan, R., Singh, H., Meitzler, T. & Gerhart, G. (2005). Iterative image fusion technique using fuzzy and neuro fuzzy logic and applications, *Fuzzy Information Processing Society, 2005. NAFIPS 2005. Annual Meeting of the North American*, pp. 706 – 710.

Singh, H., Raj, J., Kaur, G. & Meitzler, T. (2004). Image fusion using fuzzy logic and applications, *Fuzzy Systems, 2004. Proceedings. 2004 IEEE International Conference on*,

Vol. 1, pp. 337 – 340 vol.1.

Šroubek, F. & Flusser, J. (2005). Fusion of blurred images, *in* L. Z. Blum R. (ed.), *Multi-Sensor Image Fusion and Its Applications*, Signal Processing and Communications Series, CRC Press, San Francisco.

Šroubek, Filip, F. J. & Zítová, B. (2006). Image fusion: a powerful tool for object identification, *Imaging for Detection and Identification* pp. 1–20.

Zhang, J. (2010). Multi-source remote sensing data fusion: status and trends, *International Journal of Image and Data Fusion* 1(1): 5 – 24.

2

Image Enhancement and Image Hiding Based on Linear Image Fusion

Cheng-Hsiung Hsieh[1] and Qiangfu Zhao[2]
[1]*Chaoyang University of Technology*
[2]*The University of Aizu*
[1]*Taiwan*
[2]*Japan*

1. Introduction

This chapter presents image enhancement and image hiding approaches based on linear image fusion (LIF). Most of materials presented here have been published in (Hsieh et al., 2008; Hsieh et al., 2010; Kondo and Zhao, 2006). Apparently, image enhancement, image morphing, and image hiding are completely different technologies for different applications, they can actually be unified under the core of LIF, and this unification can be helpful in other related researches. The reason we use LIF is its simplicity and low computational cost. By our observations, LIF generally has satisfactory performance provided that appropriate source images are used. This motivates the image enhancement approaches presented in this chapter. Note that the intermediate image generated by image morphing, in which LIF plays a fundamental role, can be a way to hide images, an LIF based approach to image hiding is presented in this chapter as well. This chapter consists of five sections. Section 1 gives introductions related to image enhancement and image hiding. Section 2 reviews LIF which is the core for the given applications. Then image enhancement approaches based on LIF are introduced in Section 3. Section 4 presents an image hiding approach based on LIF. Finally, conclusion and future work are mentioned in Section 5.

1.1 Image enhancement

1.1.1 High dynamic range imaging enhancement

Nowadays, CCD sensors have been extensively applied to capture an image in many scenarios such as digital camera and surveillance systems. In general cases, CCD sensors work well in automatic exposure mode. However, CCD sensors may fail to appropriately present pixels when they are saturated to the maximum or minimum values. One example is that an image is taken in a high contrast or high dynamic range situation. Though the automatic exposure control tries to determine an appropriate exposure value, the captured image still suffers from missing details in overexposed and underexposed areas. To deal with the cases when automatic exposure mode is not suitable, an image fusion approach is sought. Since a satisfactory image cannot be obtained in one shot, multiple images are used in image fusion generally. Recently, two approaches based on image fusion have been reported to get rid of high dynamic range imaging problem. In (Tang and Zhao, 2007), an image fusion approach to relieve the problem of overexposure and underexposure was presented which was based on wavelet-based contourlet transform. In (Kao, 2007), a real-time image fusion approach was proposed to solve exposure problem in an image with high dynamic range, where medians of source images were manipulated. In (Tang and Zhao, 2007; Kao, 2007), image fusion requires a mechanism to determine how the information is fused. In this chapter, an image fusion approach is proposed for the problem in high dynamic range imaging where no mechanism is needed to determine the way to fuse source images. Besides, two source images are taken with different exposures to benefit LIF since they are of detail-complementary property (DCP). The concept of DCP will be described later in Section 3. It will show that a pair of source images with DCP is appropriate for LIF and generally leads good results.

1.1.2 Contrast enhancement

An objective of image enhancement is to improve the visual quality of images. Among image enhancement schemes, contrast enhancement is a popular approach and has been widely used in many display related fields, such as consumer electronics, medical analysis, and so on. It is well-known that the contrast in an image is related to its dynamic range of histogram distribution. That is, an image with wider histogram dynamic range generally has better contrast. Consequently, to enhance the contrast in an image can be achieved by expanding its histogram distribution. Because of its simplicity, the conventional histogram equalization (CHE) is very popular which expands the histogram to its admissible extremes. Though the image contrast is enhanced, however a poor equalized image may be obtained because of the unsuitable histogram distribution for the CHE.

Note that the visual quality of histogram equalized image can be improved by restricting the dynamic range or by modifying the original histogram distribution. Recently, several HE-based approaches have been presented to improve the performance of the CHE. In (Kim, 1997), taking the brightness shift into account, the approach called mean preserving bi-histogram equalization (BBHE) was proposed to enhance image contrast while preserving the mean brightness. In the BBHE, the histogram was partitioned into two portions based on the mean brightness value of a given image. Then the CHE was performed on each of the two sub-histograms. In light of the BBHE, several variations were reported. In (Wan et al., 1999), the histogram was partitioned into two sub-histograms by the median, instead of the mean, of brightness in a given image. In (Chen and Ramli, 2003), a recursive mean-separate histogram equalization approach was reported where the histogram of a given image was partitioned into sub-histograms in a number of two's power. Note that the histogram spike generally causes visual problems in the CHE. In (Wang and Ward, 2007), the distribution of pixel values was modified through weighting and thresholding before histogram equalization. To consider the histogram spike, in (Ibrahim and Kong, 2007) a Gaussian filter was introduced to smooth the histogram distribution first. Then the smoothened histogram was partitioned and the partitioned histogram was equalized. In (Kim and Chung, 2008), the histogram of an image was weighted by a normalized power law function while the recursive partition was performed based on the mean or the median of the image brightness. In (Arici et al., 2009), a histogram modification approach based on an optimization scheme was proposed where the level of contrast enhancement, noise robustness, white/black stretching, and mean-brightness preservation were all under consideration. In (Ooi et al., 2009), the bi-histogram equalization with a plateau level was proposed. In the approach, two stages were involved: input histogram subdivision and sub-histogram clipping based on the plateau value. Generally speaking, HE-based approaches manipulated the histogram of input image by histogram partitioning, histogram modification with weighting or filtering, to improve the performance of the image contrast enhancement.

In (Chen et al., 2010), an image enhancement based on linear image fusion was presented where an adaptive weight was employed on a pixel-by-pixel basis. In our experiences on the approach of (Chen et al., 2010), it shows that the fused images is of good visual quality when source images are appropriate but anomaly pixels are found in homogenous area if source images are not suitable for the approach. A fixed weight may avoid the problem or a better adaptive way should be sought. In Section 3.2, a simple contrast enhancement approach will be presented which is based on detail-complementary property (DCP) and LIF. Though simple, the proposed approach will be justified effective in the improvement of image visual quality.

1.2 Image hiding with morphing technology

Image morphing is a technology for generating a sequence of images from a source image and a target image. This technology has been used mainly for producing moving pictures. In our study, it is noticed that the intermediate images generated by morphing can actually be used to hide the source or the target image. In image morphing, many intermediate images can be generated using different morphing rates. With LIF, the morphing rate, denoted by a, represents the contribution portion of the source image for synthesizing an intermediate image while the contribution portion of the target image is $(1-a)$. Therefore, image morphing is a variation of LIF where two input images, source image and target image, are different.

To generate images of natural looking, both source image and target image are first warped based on a common skeleton. This skeleton is usually determined by using a set of characteristic points or characteristic lines. The first step in morphing is to obtain the skeleton of the intermediate image. By sharing the same skeleton, the warped source image and the warped target image are found. With LIF, the warped images are then used to generate intermediate images with different morphing rates. Then intermediate images can be used to hide the source (or target) image. In other words, image hiding can be achieved by the morphing technology based on LIF.

To recover the source (or target) image from an intermediate image, the target (or the source) image, the skeletons, and the morphing rate are required. With those information, the source (or target) image can be found by the de-morphing. Though image warping is generally not reversible, and some information in input images may be lost in the warping process, the original images can be recovered almost perfectly in general.

With the morphing technology, an image hiding approach is developed and applied to steganography where the target (or the source) image, the feature vectors, e.g. skeletons, of the source and the target images, and the morphing rate are considered as the stego keys. A steganograhic approach based on image morphing will be proposed in Section 4.

2. Linear image fusion

The main objective of image fusion is to integrate information or details from different source images of a scene to form an image with better visual quality. A general expression to obtain a fused image $\boldsymbol{I}_f$ with two source images is given as

$$I_f = f(I_1, I_2) \tag{1}$$

where I_1 and I_2 are two source images and $f(.)$ is a function to fuse the source images. Eq. (1) suggests that the fused image I_f is significantly affected by function $f(.)$ and source images I_1 and I_2. Therefore, how to find an appropriate fusion function and source images is a fundamental issue for a successful image fusion.

In this chapter, we will employ the linear interpolation as $f(.)$ in Eq. (1). With I_1 and I_2, the fused image I_f by the linear interpolation is found as

$$I_f = aI_1 + (1-a)I_2 \tag{2}$$

where $0 \leq a \leq 1$ is a weighting factor.

The image fusion based on linear interpolation is called linear image fusion (LIF). Though simple, LIF generally has satisfactory performance if appropriate source images can be found. In Section 3, two ways to obtain appropriate source images are introduced.

Interesting enough, the fused image I_f can be considered as a morphed image when source images I_1 and I_2 are different object images, e.g. face images of different persons. Since I_f is somewhere between I_1 and I_2, and different from either I_1 or I_2, it thus can be used to hide I_1 or I_2. The idea will be described and applied to steganography in Section 4.

3. Image enhancement based on LIF

One of objectives in image enhancement is to improve visual quality of an image for human viewers. An image with better visual quality can be obtained by image fusion through combining information from different source images. Thus, in this section, LIF will be applied to image enhancement where source images play an important role. Two image enhancement approaches based on LIF are proposed in this section. The first approach is to deal with the problem in high dynamic range imaging while the second approach provides a way to enhance contrast of a given image. The two approaches based on LIF are described in Section 3.1 and Section 3.2, respectively.

3.1 Image enhancement based on LIF with two source images, IE/LIF_2

In this section, an approach to image enhancement based on LIF with two source images is proposed which is abbreviated IE/LIF_2. The motivation is given in Section 3.1.1 and the proposed IE/LIF_2 is described in Section 3.1.2. Then simulation results are provided to justify the IE/LIF_2 in Section 3.1.3.

3.1.1 Motivation of IE/LIF_2

As mentioned previously, LIF will have satisfactory performance if suitable source images can be found. It is observed that source images of detail-complementary property (DCP) are appropriate for LIF. In the proposed IE/LIF_2, source images of DCP are obtained through different exposure settings. As an example, two images taken with different exposures are shown in Fig. 2. In Fig. 2(a), the image is underexposed while the image in Fig. 2(b) is overexposed. Note that the details of both images are of a sort of complementary property. For instance, the details of sign board area can be found in Fig. 2(a) while other details found in Fig. 2(b). The example in Fig. 2 demonstrates the idea of DCP. In light of DCP, the fused image by LIF will combine details from Fig. 2(a) and Fig. 2(b). For example, the details of sign board area come from Fig. 2(a) and the details of building and road are from Fig. 2(b). This is verified by the result shown in Fig. 3(b). The proposed approach to image enhancement based on LIF with two source images is abbreviated as IE/LIF_2 whose illustration is depicted in Fig. 1 where $\boldsymbol{F}_{dark}$ and $\boldsymbol{F}_{light}$ denote the underexposed source image and the overexposed source image, respectively. And $\boldsymbol{F}_{fused}$ stands for the fused image. It will show that the IE/LIF_2 is able to deal with the problem in high dynamic range imaging.

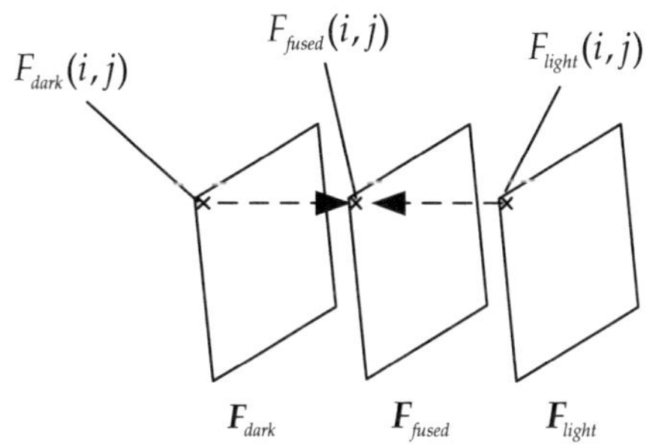

Fig. 1. An illustration of IE/LIF_2

3.1.2 The proposed IE/LIF_2 approach

In this section, the proposed IE/LIF_2 approach is introduced. In the proposed approach, LIF with two source images are employed. In practice, LIF is implemented on a pixel-by-pixel basis. That is, two pixels, one pixel from the first source image and the other form the second source image, are fused to find the corresponding pixel in the fused image. Fig. 1 shows the idea where $F_{dark}(i,j)$ and $F_{light}(i,j)$ denote elements of the underexposed source image and the overexposed source image, respectively. $F_{fused}(i,j)$ are elements of the fused image. Assume source images are of RGB format. With source images $\boldsymbol{F}_{dark}$ and $\boldsymbol{F}_{light}$, the implementation steps of IE/LIF_2 for each component are given as follows.

Step 1. Input a two-pixel pair from source images, $\boldsymbol{x} = \{F_{dark}(i,j), F_{light}(i,j)\}$, where $F_{dark}(i,j)$ and $F_{light}(i,j)$ denote the (i,j) pixel in $\boldsymbol{F}_{dark}$ and $\boldsymbol{F}_{light}$, respectively.

Step 2. By LIF described in Section 2, the fused pixel $F_{fused}(i,j)$ is found, where $\boldsymbol{F}_{dark}$ and $\boldsymbol{F}_{light}$ are considered as $\boldsymbol{I}_1$ and $\boldsymbol{I}_2$ in Eq. (2), respectively.

Step 3. On a pixel-by-pixel basis, continue Steps 1 and 2 until all fused pixels $F_{fused}(i,j)$ are found.

Note that in the IE/LIF_2 there is no mechanism to determine how to fuse the source images as in (Tang and Zhao, 2007; Kao, 2007). The weighting factor a in LIF is the only parameter needed to be determined in the IE/LIF_2. By our experiences, $a = 0.4$ is a good choice for most of cases. That is, more portion is taken from the overexposed source image in the fused image. Though simple, the proposed IE/LIF_2 approach will be shown effective in high dynamic range imaging in Section 3.1.3.

3.1.3 Simulation results for the IE/LIF_2

In this section, two high contrast examples are provided to justify the proposed IE/LIF_2 approach whose results are also compared with those from (Kao, 2007) which is abbreviated

as RTIF here. In the simulation, the parameter $a = 0.4$ is used in LIF. For the first example, source images $\boldsymbol{F}_{dark}$ and $\boldsymbol{F}_{light}$ of 7-11 are taken on some street at night which are shown in Fig. 2(a) and Fig. 2(b), respectively. In Figure 2(a), the image is underexposed. Therefore lots of areas cannot be seen but the details of bright area, like sign boards, are found. On the other hand, the image in Fig. 2(b) is overexposed where details of dark area, like building and road, can be seen and the bright parts lose their details because of saturation. The two source images $\boldsymbol{F}_{dark}$ and $\boldsymbol{F}_{light}$ reveal the DCP and it is expected that a good fused image can be obtained by LIF.
The fused images of 7-11 by the RTIF and the IE/LIF_2 are shown in Fig. 3(a) and Fig. 3(b), respectively. By the results, the fused image from the IE/LIF_2 is better than that from the RTIF since better visual quality with more details are found in the IE/LIF_2.

(a) Source image $\boldsymbol{F}_{dark}$ (b) Source image $\boldsymbol{F}_{light}$

Fig. 2. Source images of 7-11

(a) by the RTIF (b) by the IE/LIF_2

Fig. 3. Fused images of 7-11

For the second example, outdoor building images are taken from indoor through a window with different exposure settings. Two source images $\boldsymbol{F}_{dark}$ and $\boldsymbol{F}_{light}$ are given in Fig. 4(a) and Fig. 4(b). In this example, it is almost impossible to capture both building outside and textbook inside clearly in one shot. Once one is obtained, the other is lost. Thus two or more source images are required for different parts of details. Note that source image in Fig. 4(a) and Fig. 4(b) show the DCP and thus a good result is expected for LIF. The fused images for the RTIF and the IE/LIF_2 are given in Fig. 5(a) and Fig. 5(b), respectively. As one may see, better details of outside building are for the IE/LIF_2 while details of textbook are similar for both approaches. Consequently, the one from the IE/LIF_2 has better visual quality than that for the RTIF.

(a) Source image $\boldsymbol{F}_{dark}$ (b) Source image $\boldsymbol{F}_{light}$

Fig. 4. Source images of Building

(a) by the RTIF (b) by the IE/LIF_2

Fig. 5. Fused images of Building

In summary, the simulation results indicate that the proposed IE/LIF_2, though simple, is able to effectively deal with the problem of high dynamic range imaging and outperforms the RTIF in the given examples.

3.2 Image enhancement based on LIF with single source image, IE/LIF_1

In Section 3.1, the IE/LIF_2 is proposed to deal with the problem in high dynamic range imaging. This section will propose an approach to contrast enhancement based on LIF where only single source image is available. This approach is called image enhancement based on LIF with single source image and abbreviated as IE/LIF_1. Unlike the IE/LIF_2, the IE/LIF_1 is not for images of high dynamic range but provides a way to enhance contrast in a given image. When details in the given image are lost, it is impossible to make any enhancement in the IE/LIF_1 since only single source image is available. In other words, the IE/LIF_1 will use similar approach as in the IE/LIF_2 to enhance contrast in a given image. Since only single source image I_1 is available in the IE/LIF_1, the problem now is how to fine another source image, i.e., I_2 in Eq. (2), from the available source image. Moreover, images I_1 and I_2 should have the DCP for better result in LIF. These issues are going to be discussed later. This section is organized as follows. Motivation of IE/LIF_1 is described in Section 3.2.1 and its implementation steps are stated in Section 3.2.2. Then simulations to verify the proposed IE/LIF_1 are given in Section 3.2.3.

3.2.1 Motivation of IE/LIF_1

The motivation for the proposed IE/LIF_1 approach is based on the following observation. Note that the conventional histogram equalizaion (CHE) is able to enhance the contrast in a given image. Thus the details which are not obvious may be revealed after the CHE, though some other details may be lost because of over enhancement. That is, the CHE reveals the details hard to perceive in the original image while destroys some details in the original image. The revealed details in the equalized image are desired in the image fusion. Roughly speaking, the original image can be divided into two types of regions: the region with good details and the region with poor details. This is also true for its equalized image. Interesting enough, there is a kind of complementary between details in the original image and its equalized image by the CHE. In other words, when a region in one image is of poor details its counterpart shows good details in general. Thus, the DCP is revealed between the original image and its equalized image by the CHE. That is, the DCP is obtained through the CHE in the IE/LIF_1 while by exposure setting in the IE/LIF_2.

To show the DCP by the CHE, Airplane in Fig. 6 is given as an example. In Fig. 6(a), the original Airplane has good details around the airplane while with poor details in the field. On the other hand, as shown in Fig. 6(b) the equalized image by the CHE loses the details of airplane but has better details in the field. The images of Airplane in Fig. 6(a) and Fig. 6(b) demonstrates the DCP which motivates the proposed IE/LIF_1 approach. Since the details in the original image and its equalized image by the CHE are of DCP, it gives us a hope that LIF would be good to obtain a fused image with better visual quality than the original image. This idea is justified as follows.

(a) Original (b) by the CHE

Fig. 6. Images of Airplane

By Eq. (2), here the original image I_o takes the place of I_1 and the equalized image of I_o by the CHE, I_h, replaces I_2. With $a = 0.7$, the fused image I_f is shown in Fig. 7. As expected, both details in the original image and its equalized image are found in the fused image. That is, the fused image shows both details around the airplane and in the field. This justifies the idea just described.

Fig. 7. Fused Airplane by LIF

3.2.2 The proposed IE/LIF_1 approach

In this section, the proposed IE/LIF_1 approach is descried. Suppose the original image I_o is of bitmap format, i.e., in RGB color space. Since R-, G-, and B-component are processed similarly in the proposed IE/LIF_1, thus only one component, X_o, is considered in the following. The implementation steps for the IE/LIF_1 approach are described as follows.

Step 1. Input the original image X_o.

Step 2. Perform the CHE on X_o and the equalized image is denoted as X_h.

Step 3. With a user-defined a, obtain the fused image X_f as in Eq. (2).

The block diagram for the proposed IE/LIF_1 approach is depicted in Fig. 8.

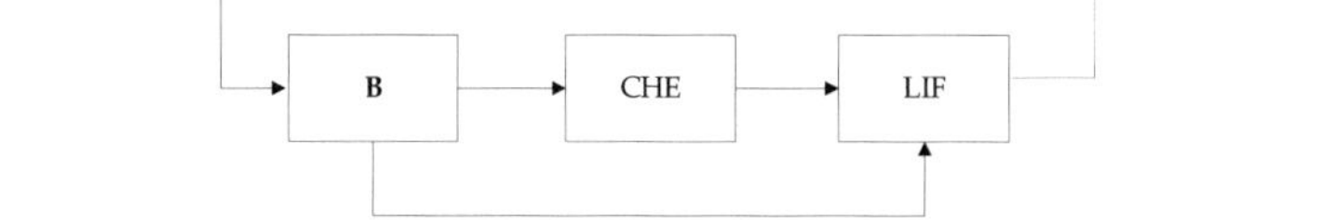

Fig. 8. The block diagram for the IE/LIF_1

Note that two stages involved in the proposed IE/LIF_1 approach are the CHE and the LIF. Both of them are of low computational complexity and easy to implement in the hardware. Thus, it is easy to apply the proposed IE/LIF_1 approach in the real-world applications where computational complexity and hardware cost are limited. Moreover, there is only one parameter a in the proposed IE/LIF_1 approach needed to be determined. Note that the overall visual quality of the original image is generally better than that in the equalized image. Thus, the value of a is set greater than 0.5 which takes more portion from the original image than that from the equalized image in LIF. By our experiences, weighting factor $a = 0.7$ works well for most of cases. This will be justified in the following section.

3.2.3 Simulation results for the IE/LIF_1

In this section, the proposed IE/LIF_1 approach is verified by two examples, images Girl and River. The parameter a in the proposed IE/LIF_1 approach is set to 0.7 for all simulations. The original images, the equalized images by the CHE, and the fused or enhanced images by the IE/LIF_1, are shown in Fig. 9 and Fig. 10, respectively. Moreover, to compare the results by the IE/LIF_1 with HE-based approach, one recently reported approach in (Wang and Ward, 2007) is employed to enhance the images as well. The enhanced images are also shown in Fig. 9 and Fig. 10 where the approach in (Wang and Ward, 2007) is denoted as WTHE. Discussions on the results are given in the following.
Image Girl in Fig. 9(a) was taken indoors under fluorescent light. By the CHE, the enhanced image is given in Fig. 9(b) where some details are revealed and some details, like the cake, are lost. Fortunately, the details lost in the equalized Girl by the CHE can be found in the original image. By fusing the two images, the fused Girl with better visual quality is obtained as shown in Fig. 9(c). Fig. 9(d) shows the enhanced images from the WTHE. As shown in Fig 9(d), the contrast is enhanced but the color fades and over enhancement, like the cake, results. By the results, the enhanced image by the proposed IE/LIF_1 is of better visual quality than the original Girl and that from the WTHE.

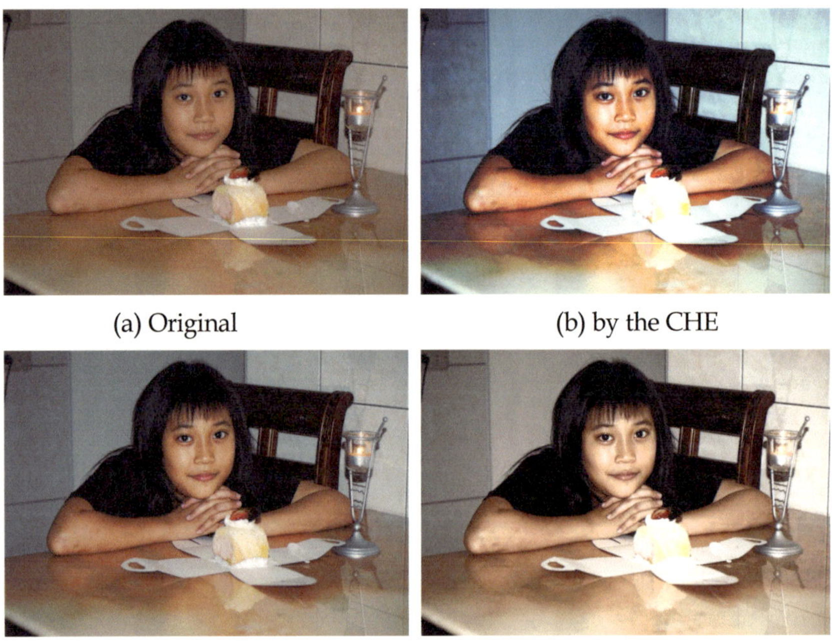

(a) Original (b) by the CHE

(c) by the IE/LIF_1 (d) by the WTHE

Fig. 9. Images of Girl

As the second example, image River was taken outdoors at night. In this example, the DCP is revealed as shown in Fig. 10(a) and Fig. 10(b). In the enhanced River by the IE/LIF_1, the original image provides the details of brighter area while the equalized River by the CHE contributes the details of darker area in general. This results in better visual quality of the enhanced River as shown in Fig. 10(c). On the other hand, the enhanced image shown in Fig. 10(d) is over enhanced in the light area and the color fading is found after the WTHE. Thus, better enhanced image is for the proposed IE/LIF_1 approach.

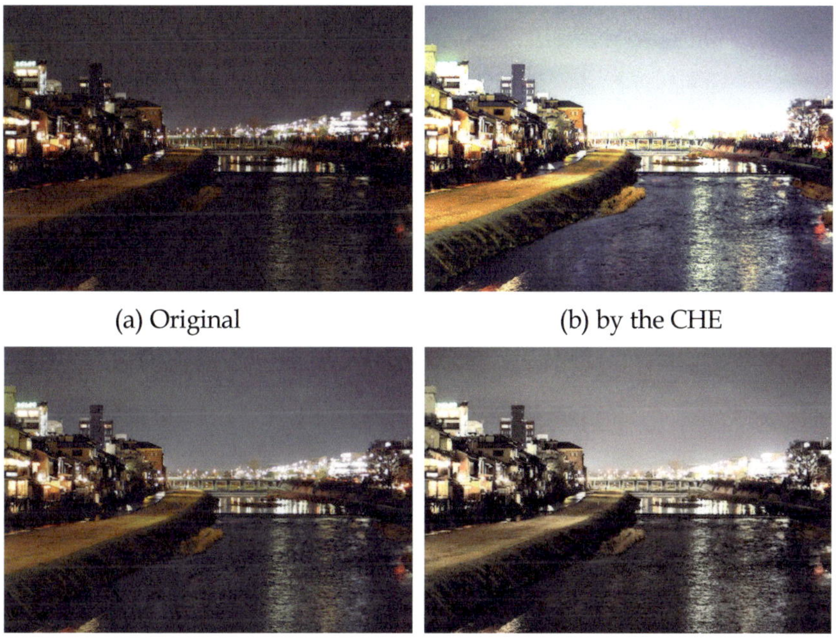

(a) Original (b) by the CHE

(c) by the IE/LIF_1 (d) by the WTHE

Fig. 10. Images of River

To sum up, simulation results suggest that the proposed IE/LIF_1 is able to enhance image contrast for the given examples and has better visual quality than those from the compared HE-based approach, i.e., the WTHE. Besides, there is a fundamental difference between the IE/IFLI_2 and the IE/IFLI_1. For the IE/IFLI_2, two source images are employed and thus more information can be found in the fused image. Consequently, the IE/IFLI_2 is able to deal with the problem in high dynamic range imaging. On the other hand, in the IE/IFLI_1 there is only one source image available and the second source image is derived from the available source image. Thus, only image contrast in the given image can be enhanced. In other words, the IE/LIF_1 gives a way to contrast enhancement for the given image. Even the IE/LIF_2 and the IE/LIF_1 both are based on LIF, they are fundamentally different from each other as described above.

4. Image hiding with morphing technology based on LIF, IH/LIF

This section presents an approach to image hiding with morphing technology based on LIF. The approach is abbreviated as IH/LIF. In Section 4.1, the IH/LIF is described. Then a way to apply the IH/LIF to steganography is given in Section 4.2 where motivation and a proposed steganographic approach are described. Finally, a scenario for the proposed steganographic approach is given in Section 4.3.

4.1 The proposed IH/LIF approach

The image morphing consists of two stages: warping and fusion. Two images are involved in the morphing process, i.e. a source image $\boldsymbol{I}_s$ and a target image $\boldsymbol{I}_t$. Based on $\boldsymbol{I}_s$ and $\boldsymbol{I}_t$, an intermediate image $\boldsymbol{I}_m$ is generated which is then used to hide the source image or target image. In the warping stage, a common skeleton is found based on characteristic points or characteristic lines in $\boldsymbol{I}_s$ and $\boldsymbol{I}_t$. Suppose $\boldsymbol{F}_s$ and $\boldsymbol{F}_t$ are the skeletons of the source image $\boldsymbol{I}_s$, and the target image $\boldsymbol{I}_t$, respectively. Then the skeleton of the intermediate image $\boldsymbol{I}_m$, which is considered as the common skeleton, is found as

$$\boldsymbol{F}_m = a\boldsymbol{F}_s + (1 - a)\boldsymbol{F}_t \tag{3}$$

where $0 < a < 1$ is a morphing rate. Based on $\boldsymbol{F}_m$ and $\boldsymbol{F}_s$, the source image $\boldsymbol{I}_s$ is warped to $\boldsymbol{I}_s^w$. Similarly, the target image $\boldsymbol{I}_t$ is warped to $\boldsymbol{I}_t^w$ through $\boldsymbol{F}_m$ and $\boldsymbol{F}_t$. After warping, $\boldsymbol{I}_s^w$, $\boldsymbol{I}_t^w$ and $\boldsymbol{I}_m$ share the same skeleton, and thus an intermediate image with natural looking can be obtained by LIF as

$$\boldsymbol{I}_m = a\boldsymbol{I}_s^w + (1 - a)\boldsymbol{I}_t^w \tag{4}$$

In Eq. (4), the morphing rate a represents the contribution of the source image to synthesizing intermediate image $\boldsymbol{I}_m$ and the contribution of the target image is (1- a). Note that image morphing can be considered as a variation of IE/LIF_2 where two input images, i.e. the warped source image and the warped target image, are different.
Fig. 11 shows an example of image morphing. In Fig. 11, the left image is the source image, the right image is the target image, and the small images are the intermediate images generated using different morphing rates, from 0 to 1. Note that in Fig. 11 the intermediate images, especially those close to the center, can be used to hide the source (or target) image. That is, image hiding can be achieved by morphing technology based on LIF.

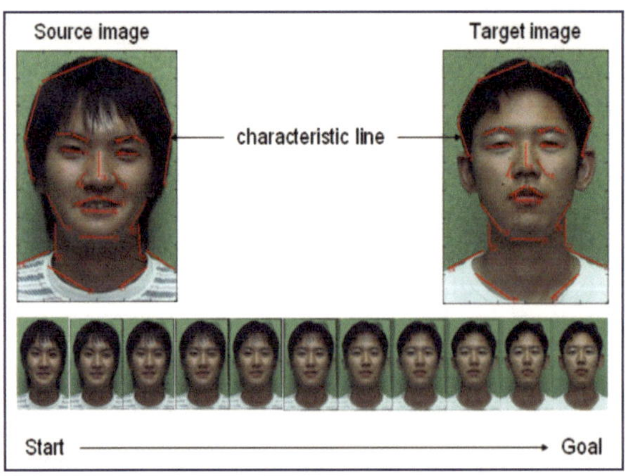

Fig. 11. An example of image morphing

To reconstructed the source (or target) image from the intermediate image, the target (or the source) image, the skeletons, and the morphing rate are required. The process to reconstruct the source (or target) image is called de-morphing, that is, inverse of morphing. The implementation steps of de-morphing to recontruct the source image are given as follows.

Step 1. Input the warped target image I_t^w.

Step 2. Obtain the warped source image I_s^w as

$$I_s^w = [I_m - (1-a)I_t^w]/a \tag{5}$$

Step 3. Calculate the skeleton of the source image as

$$F_s = [F_m - (1-a)F_t]/a \tag{6}$$

Step 4. Find the source image as

$$I_s = dewarp(I_s^w, F_m, F_s) \tag{7}$$

where $dewarp(.)$ is a function to de-warp the source image.

Fig. 12 shows an example of de-morphing. As described previously, the source image can be recontructed almost perfectly except the borders.

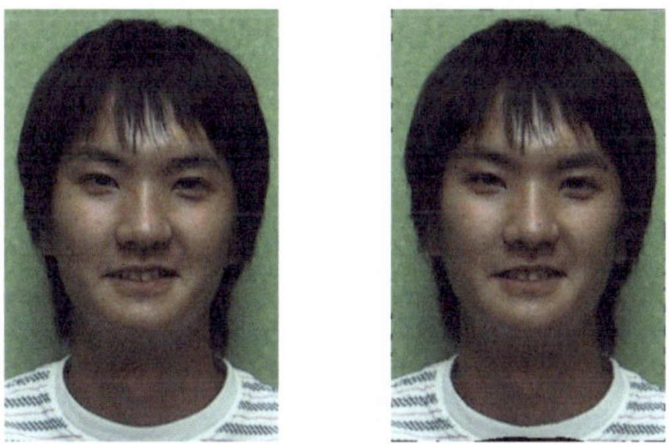

(a) Source image (b) Reconstructed image

Fig. 12. An example of image de-morphing

4.2 Application of IH/LIF to steganography

In light of the IH/LIF, a steganographic approach based on image morphing is proposed here. The motivation is given in Section 4.2.1 and the proposed steganographic approach is introduced in Section 4.2.2.

4.2.1 Motivation

Steganography is a technology to hide messages in such a way that no one except the authorized recipient knows the existence of the messages. The block diagram of steganography is shown in Fig. 13. In steganography, the secret message is often hidden in some cover message. In general, larger cover message relative to the secret message can hide the latter easier. For instance, an image in general contains more data than a text and thus an image is often used as the cover message to hide some text data. Usually, the cover image is not changed visually after hiding the secret data. By this doing, the objective of steganography is achieved.

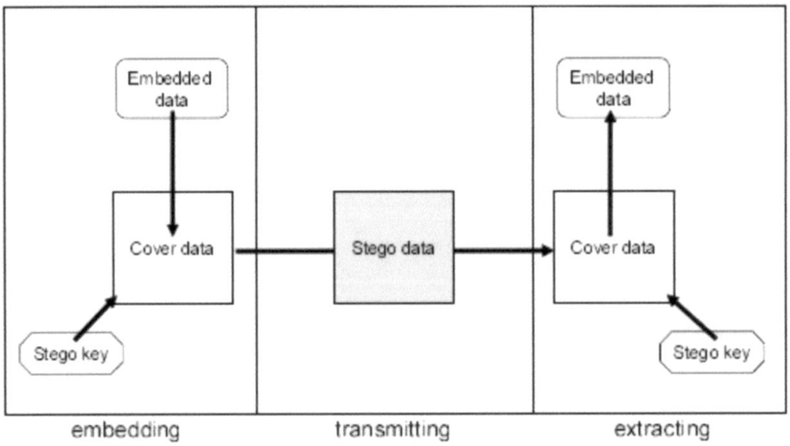

Fig. 13. The block diagram of steganography

Though the steganography is able to hide messages in cover messages, there are at least two problems in the framework of steganography. First, to hide an image using existing steganographic approaches is very difficult unless the size of the secret image is much smaller than that of the cover image. For example, a 1024×768 color image, with 3 bytes per pixel, has the potential to hide 294,912 bytes of information, if 3 bits are used for each pixel. In this case, the size of the secret image should be smaller than or equal to 1/8 of the size of the cover image. Consequently, in the framework of steganography, it is a challenge to embed a secret image into a cover image when both images of same size.

Another problem in existing steganographic approaches is that partial hiding of messages is not allowed. However, there are cases in which partial hiding is required. A scenario might be doctor's co-examination on medical images. In this case, one doctor may hide the patient's personal information (e.g., the patient's face image) while keeping the sickness information (e.g., face color) "readable" to other doctors. In the conventional steganographic approaches, the image data of the patient must be hidden completely in the cover data, and be recovered completely when the recipients want to see the data.

To solve the two problems just described, Section 4.2.2 proposes a steganographic approach based on image morphing. Morphing is a technology that transforms from a source image to a target image. So far, morphing is mainly used for producing animation movies or special TV programs. Here, morphing technology will be applied to image hiding where the two problems mentioned above can be solved as follows.

First, a morphed image, which is one of the intermediate images between the source image and the target image, can be used as the stego data. The source image here is the secret image to be hidden. Upon receiving the morphed image, the source image can be recovered through de-morphing based on four stego keys, that is, the morphing rate, the feature vector (skeleton) of the morphed image, the feature vector (skeleton) of the target image and the target image. Note that, the source image, the target image, and the morphed image are of the same size. Thus, the first problem is sovled by the proposed steganographic approach based on image morphing.

Second, the proposed steganographic approach is able to provide part of the information in the source image "readable", that is, visible on the stego data (the morphed image) while hiding other information. In the scenario of doctor's co-examination on medical images, the patient's personal information, i.e., face image, can be hidden through morphing, and keep the sickness information "readable" to doctors. Thus, partial hiding is achieved by the morphing based steganography. The proposed steganographic approach is described in the following section.

4.2.2 The proposed steganographic approach

In this section, we propose a steganographic approach based on morphing technology. The block diagram of the proposed approach is shown in Fig. 14. When compared, the followings are observed between the proposed steganographic approach and the steganography shown in Fig. 13.

a. The embedding algorithm: Morphing plays the role to embed the secret data.
b. The extracting algorithm: De-morphing corresponds to the algorithm to extract the secret data.
c. The embedded data: The source image is considered as the data to be embedded.
d. The cover data: There is no cover data in the proposed approach.
e. The stego data: the morphed image is considered as stego data.
f. The stego keys for embedding: The target image, the feature vector (skeleton) of the source image, the feature vector (skeleton) of the target image, and the morphing rate are considered as stego keys for embedding.
g. The stego keys for extraction: The target image, the feature vector (skeleton) of the morphed image, the feature vector (skeleton) of the target image, and the morphing rate are the stego keys for extraction.

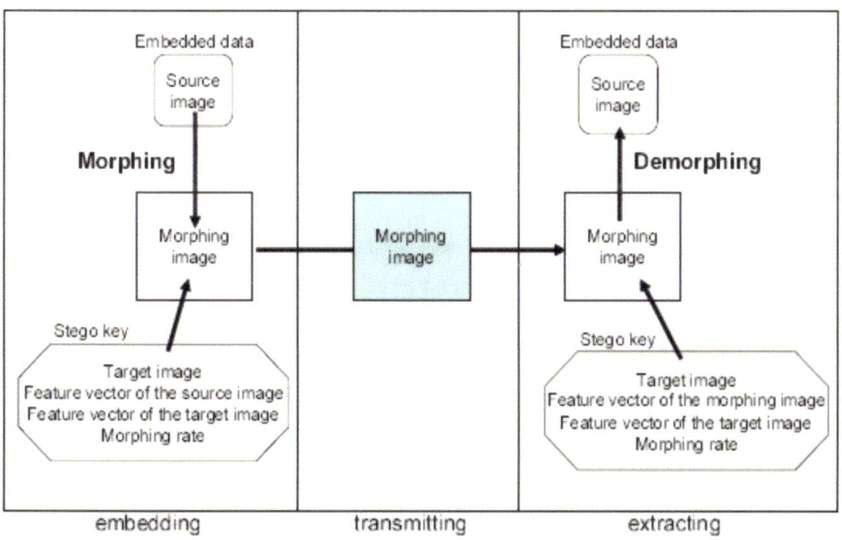

Fig. 14. The block diagram of the proposed steganographic approach

The correspondence between the proposed steganographic approach and the steganography shown in Fig. 13 is given Table 1.

Conventional information hiding	Information Hiding Based on Morphing Technology
embedding algorithm	morphing
extracting algorithm	demorphing
embedded data	source image
cover data	nothing
stego data	morphing image
stego key (embedding)	target image feature vector of the source image feature vector of the target image morphing rate
stego key (extracting)	target image feature vector of the morphing image feature vector of the target image morphing rate

Table 1. Correspondence between the proposed and conventional steganography

Two things should be noticed in the proposed steganographic approach. First, without cover data, the proposed approach is able to cover an image using much less data when compared with conventional steganographic approaches. In other words, the capacity of the proposed approach is very high. In the proposed approach, the morphed image plays the roles of cover data and stego data. To cover an image, only two images of same size and some morphing parameters are required. As described earlier, the stego keys for extraction include the target image, the feature vectors of the target image and the morphed image, and the morphing rate. The data amount of stego keys is relatively big which makes the morphing based steganography even securer than conventional approaches. In short, the proposed approach provides a way to embed an image into another image with same size where the conventional steganographic approaches fail to.

Second, in the conventional steganography the secret data is completely hidden in the cover data so that the stego data and the cover data look similarly. Only the recipient who has the stego key can extract the secret data. In the proposed morphing based steganography, the morphed image (the stego data) has certain similarity with the source image (the secret data) which is controlled by the morphing rate. This seems to be one defect of the morphing based steganography, but it is not. Even the morphed image has certain similarity with the source image, it is simply another natural image. For face images, the morphed image is just the face of another person who may not exist at all. Therefore, one is not able to extract the source image or even may not know the existence of the source image by the morphed image. This property of partial hiding or revealing in the propsed steganographic can be applied in the real world cases. One scenario to apply the partial hiding property is given in the following section.

4.3 A scenario for the proposed steganographic approach

A scenarios for the proposed steganographic approach is given in this section. The scenario related to doctor's co-examination is shown in Fig. 15. In this scenario, doctor A may share the sickness information of a patient to doctor B while hiding the individual information of the patient, i.e., face image. In Fig. 15, *S+sick* is the face image of the patient and *M+sick* is the corresponding morphed image. In this case, doctor B may examine the sickness of the patient without knowing who he/she is. This is impossible for conventional steganographic approaches. More details are given in the following.

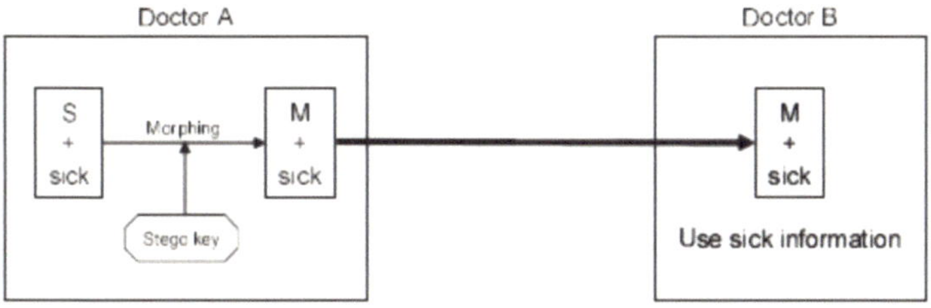

Fig. 15. Scenario to share sickness information while hiding the patient's face image

Fig. 16 shows the morphed images of a patient with different morphing rates. In the example, the painted part is considered as important clue for the sickness. While the morphing rate approaches to 1, the morphed image approaches to the target image in which there is no clue of sickness at all. That is, the individual information of the patient can be hidden completely with a morphing rate close to one. However, the sickness information on the face image is disappeared as well. The reason can be explained by Eq. (4). When the morphing rate is close to one, the morphed image is constructed almost from the target image alone.

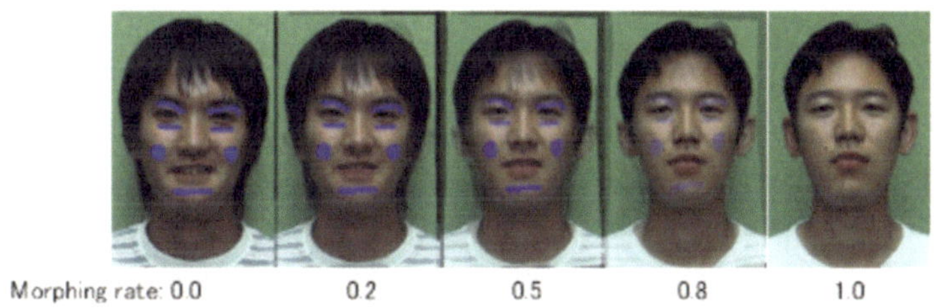

Fig. 16. Morphed image of a patient with different morphing rates

This problem can be solved by separating the sickness part from the face image of the patient. During morphing, the warped source image and the warped target are combined to form the morphed image for all pixels except the region of sickness part in the warped source image which is then added to the morphed image. Fig. 17 shows a way that sickness part is separated, warped and added to the morphed image. In Fig. 17, *Ssick* is the sickness part of the source image, and *Wsick* is the warped sickness part. In fact, the sickness part is warped in the same way as the source image. First of all, the sickness part is separated from

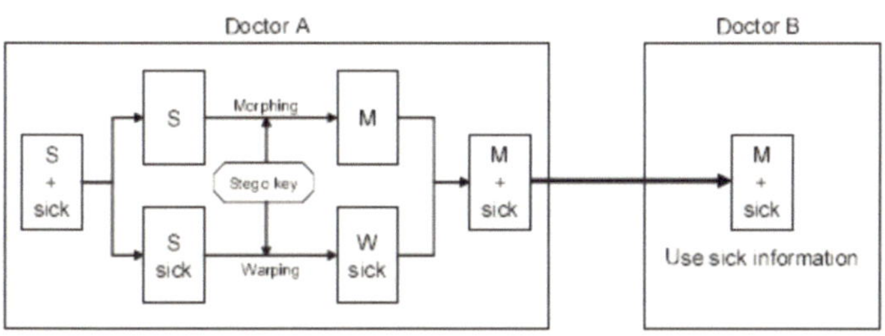

Fig. 17. A way that sick part is separated, warped and added to the morphed image

the image of the patient. Next, morphing is performed for all pixels except the sickness part. Then the sickness part is warped and added to the morphed image. By separating the sickness part, the morphed image can hide the face image of the patient and reveal the sickness part.
Fig. 18 shows several morphed images of a patient generated with various morphing rates by the way shown in Fig. 17. In Fig. 18, the patient's face is hidden by an appropriate morphing rate, say 0.8. Moreover, the sickness part can be retained in the morphed image since it is added directly to the morphed image after warping. In this way, a doctor can share the sickness information to another doctor while hiding the information of the patient.

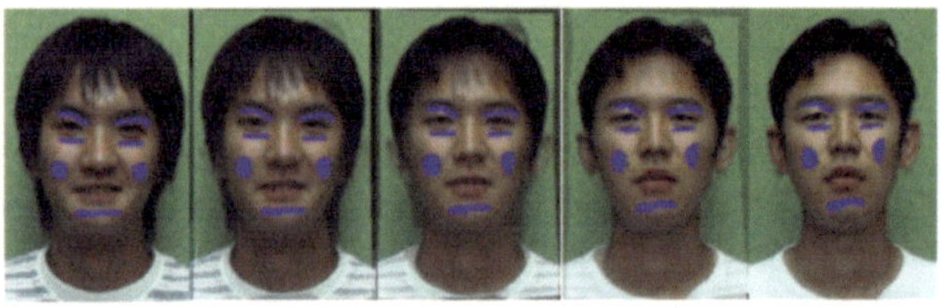

Fig. 18. Morphed images of a patient with separated sick part and different morphing rates

5. Conclusion and future work

This chapter presented approaches to image enhancement and image hiding based on linear image fusion (LIF). Though simple, LIF showed its effectiveness on image enhancement and image hiding. In image enhancement, LIF has been shown having good performance when source images are of detail-complementary property (DCP). In image hiding, a morphing technology based on LIF was given from which a stegnograhpic approach was developed. Conclusions and future works for the proposed image enhancement and image hiding approaches are described, respectively, in the following.
For image enhancement, the IE/LIF_2 and IE/LIF_1 were presented. Note that DCP benefits the result of LIF. By different exposure settings, two source images of DCP were obtained in the IE/LIF_2. Then LIF was applied to fuse the two source images with an appropriate weighting factor. It showed good results in the given examples and better visaul quality was for the proposed IE/LIF_2 when compared with the approach in (Kao, 2007). Simulation results suggested that the problem in high dynamic range imaging can be solved by the IE/LIF_2. When only a single source image was available, the IE/LIF_1 was applied to enhance contrast and therefore visual quality. In the proposed IE/LIF_1, a source image for LIF was derived from the available image by the conventional histogram equalization (CHE). The reason using the CHE was that the original image and the equalized image shows the DCP. In light of DCP, LIF may have good performance generally. As expected, simulation results of the given examples had justified the idea. When compared with the HE-based approach in (Wang and Ward, 2007), the IE/LIF_1 showed its supirority for better visual quality. Consequently, the IE/LIF_1 provides a good way to improve visual quality of images through contrast enhancement. No matter in the IE/LIF_2 or the IE/LIF_1, the weighting factor in LIF is fixed and determined by our rule of thumb. In the future, a mechanism to adaptively determine the weighting factor will be devised.

Note that the morphing technology based on LIF can be a way to hide images. The proposed image hiding approach called IH/LIF was developed. Then a steganographic approach based on IH/LIF was developed. When compared with conventional steganographic approaches, there are at least two advantages for the proposed approach. First, by morphing technology it is possible to embed a secret image whose size is same as the cover image in the framework of steganography where the stego keys are the morphing rate, the target image, the feature vector of the target image and the feature vector of the morphed image. With the stego keys, the secret imag can be extracted through de-morphing. Second, the proposed steganographic approach provides a way to partial hiding or revealing the secret image. The basic idea is to process the two kinds of information, separately. That is, perform morphing for the information to be hidden, and warping for the information to be revealed. A scenario was given for the proposed steganographic approach. In the future, the proposed approach will be extended to other types of data, like music and video, where a proper morphing or transformation should be sought.

6. Acknowledgement

This work was partially supported by National Science Council of the Republic of China under grant NSC 96-2221-E-324-044 and by the 2010 visiting researcher program in the University of Aizu, Japan, and as a part of cooperative research results with the System Intelligence Laboratory in the Universtiy of Aizu.

7. References

Arici, T.; Dikbas, S.; Altunbasak, Y. (2009). A Histogram Modification Framework and Its Application for Image Contrast Enhancement, *IEEE Transactions on Image Processing*, Vol. 18, No. 9, pp. 1921-1935, 2009, ISSN 1057-7149.

Chen, Q.; Xu, X.; Sun, Q.; Xia, D. (2010). A Solution to the Deficiencies of Image Enhancement, *Signal Processing*, Vol. 90, Issue 1, pp. 44-56, 2010, ISSN 0165-1684.

Chen, S.-D.; Ramli, R. (2003). Contrast Enhancement Using Recursive Mean-Separate Histogram Equalization for Scalable Brightness Preservation, *IEEE Transactions on Consumer Electronics*, Vol. 49, No. 4, pp.1301-1309, 2003, ISSN 0098-3063.

Hsieh, C.-H.; Chen, B.-C.; Lin, C.-M.; Zhao Q. F. (2010). Detail Aware Contrast Enhancement with Linear Image Fusion, *Proceedings of International Symposium on Aware Computing*, pp. 1-5, ISBN 978-1-4244-8312-9, Tainan, Taiwan, November 2010.

Hsieh, C.-H.; Chen, P.-W.; Lan, C.-W.; Hsiung, K.-C. (2008). Image Fusion Based on Grey Polynomial Interpolation, *Proceedings of International Conference on Intelligent Systems Design and Applications*, pp. 19-22, ISBN 978-0-7695-3382-7, Kaohsiung, Taiwan, November 2008.

Ibrahim, H.; Kong, N. S. P. (2007). Brightness Preserving Dynamic Histogram Iqualization for Image Contrast Enhancement," *IEEE Transactions on Consumer Electronics*, Vol. 53, No. 4, pp. 1752-1758, 2007, ISSN 0098-3063.

Kao, W.-C. (2007). Real-time Image Fusion and Adaptive Exposure Control for Smart Surveillance Systems, *Electronics Letters*, Vol. 43, No. 18, pp. 975-976, August 2007, ISSN 0013-5194.

Kim, M.; Chung, M. G. (2008). Recursively Separated and Weighted Histogram Equalization for Brightness Preservation and Contrast Enhancement, *IEEE Transactions on Consumer Electronics*, Vol. 54, No. 3, pp. 1389-1397, 2008, ISSN 0098-3063.

Kim,Y.-T. (1997). Contrast Enhancement Using Brightness Preserving Bi-Histogram Equalization, *IEEE Transactions on Consumer Electronics*, Vol. 43, No. 1, pp.1-8, 1997, ISSN 0098-3063.

Kondo, S.; Zhao Q. F.; (2006). A Novel Steganographic Technique Based on Image Morphing, *Proceedings of International Conference on Ubiquitous Intelligence and Computing*, pp. 806-815, ISBN 3-540-38091-4, Wuhan and Three Gorges, China, September 2006. (Lecture Notes in Computer Science 4159, Springer)

Ooi, C. H.; Kong, P.; Sia, N.; Haidi, I. (2009). Bi-Histogram Equalization with a Plateau limit for Digital Image Enhancement, *IEEE Transactions on Consumer Electronics*, Vol.55, No.4, pp. 2072-2080, 2009, ISSN 0098-3063.

Tang, L.; Zhao, Z.-G. (2007). The Wavelet-based Contourlet Transform for Image Fusion, *Proceedings of Eighth ACIS International Conference on Software Engineering, Artificial Intelligence, Networking, and Parallel/Distributed Computing*, pp. 59-64, ISBN 0-7695-2909-7, Qingdao, China, July 2007.

Wan, Y.; Chen, Q.; Zhang, B. (1999). Image Enhancement Based on Equal Area Dualistic Sub-Image Histogram Equalization Method, *IEEE Transactions on Consumer Electronics*, Vol. 45, No. 1, pp.68-75, 1999, ISSN 0098-3063.

Wang, Q.; Ward, R. K. (2007). Fast Image/Video Contrast Enhancement Based on Weighted Thresholded Histogram Equalization, *IEEE Transactions on Consumer Electronics*, Vol. 53, No. 2, pp. 757 – 764, 2007, ISSN 0098-3063.

A Multi Views Approach for Remote Sensing Fusion Based on Spectral, Spatial and Temporal Information

FARAH Imed Riadh
[1]*National school of computer science, Manouba University, Laboratory RIAD-GDL,*
[2]*Telecom-Bretagne, Department ITI, Brest,*
[1]*Tunisia*
[2]*France*

1. Introduction

Nowadays, operational earth observation satellites provide a large variety of multi-sensor, multi-temporal and multi-modal data. Signals generated by miscellaneous sensors needs to be sampled, filtered, fused, stored, and interpreted (Yu & Christakos, 2010). Each of these data-processing steps must be conducted in an efficient way to conserve data fidelity. Amidst these research areas, remote sensing community is notably interested in studying multi-source images fusion issues. Over last past decades, information fusion has emerged to manage large amounts of multi-source data in the military field (Mahler, 2007). Recently, substantial amount of research has been dedicated to data fusion techniques development and adaptation for signal and images processing applications. Therefore, data fusion is now largely adopted in several fields including, but are not limited to, satellite and aerial imaging, medical imaging, sonar and radar, robotics, etc. (Stathaki, 2008).

Until recently, images fusion has become a worthy tool in remote sensing image processing and received great attention for satellite image interpretation. Motivations for images fusion are numerous and predominantly justified by application issue (Farah et al., 2008b). Fusion techniques aim to produce an enhanced single view with extended information content by combining intelligently multi-modality data coming from different sources. However, remote sensing images are characterized by their unique spectral, spatial, temporal and directional dimensions depending fundamentally on the nature of the corresponding sensor (Farah et al., 2010). Thus, image fusion can be looked with different points of view; each one is designed to answer specific research requirements and to meet a particular need.

Typically, for an efficient fusion, some questions must been answered before deciding about the fusion approach: What is the objective of image fusion? Which types of data are the most useful? What is the most "appropriate" method of fusion to achieve study goals? What technique is used for results assessment? (Pohl & Van Genderen, 1998).

Moreover, numerous challenging research issues are related to developing new approaches for remotely sensed signals managing and interpretation. In most actual researches, sensors must operate in an unfriendly environment with many complications. Therefore, an image processing method must be able to deal effectively with limited resources and missing/noisy data (Yu & Christakos, 2010). Imperfections are inherent in all applications fields and arise from measurements errors, spatio-temporal variability and numerical approximation, etc. Therefore, the fusion procedure is associated, generally, with the calculation of uncertainties. In our case, we use the term imperfection to denote limitations associated with data. Here, we refer to one or more of the characteristics: imprecise, uncertain, incomplete, inconsistent and vague when using this term. In a remotely sensed context, we identified the following types of imperfection:

- Imperfections related to nature: it is a consequence of the spatio-temporal variability of the natural phenomena (precipitation, climate changes, etc.) which introduces a random function into the physical process.
- Imperfections related to data: most researchers agree that it is impossible to identify the variability and the local data complexity through some points of measurement.
- Uncertainty related to model parameters: influenced by data imprecision.

Difficulties in fusion process lie also with the problems of redundant information reducing and the large volume data managing. In addition, data specially extracted from each individual source are naturally incomplete (Farah et al., 2003). Hence, developing an efficient data fusion technique must take into account these factors. Some requirements to the images processing algorithms included:

- Tolerance to noise, un-calibrated data frequently associated with remote sensing data.
- Resource constrained computation.
- Robustness and reliability: if any data sources are missing
- Ambiguity reducing.

Having answered these requirements and questions, appropriate technique for data fusion may be chosen. Conjointly, specific data features must been taken into account at all fusion process stages. These features differ from one area to another typically including heterogeneous, large amount, and multi-objective data. Improving knowledge and providing a better description of the real world is the major goal of information fusion techniques. To achieve this ambition, remotely sensed images must be mapped to semantic level for data analysis, interpretation, and decision making (Bentabet et al., 2002). Such mapping requires further efforts and effective images processing tools (Gamba et al., 2005).
This chapter focuses on image fusion techniques for remotely sensed applications. Designing a fusion process requires a good assimilation of techniques foundations, a well-defined input data as well as an effective assessment metrics. The objectives of this chapter are to contribute to the apprehension of image fusion approaches including concepts definition, techniques ethics and results assessment. It is structured in five sections. Following this introduction, a definition of image fusion provides involved fundamental concepts. Respectively, we explain cases in which image fusion might be useful. Most existing techniques and architectures are reviewed and classified in the third section. In fourth section, we focuses heavily on algorithms based on multi-views approach, we compares and analyses the process model and algorithms including advantages, limitations and applicability of each view. The last part of the chapter summarized the benefits and limitations of a multi-view approach image fusion; it gives some recommendations on the effectiveness and the performance of these methods. These recommendations, based on a comprehensive study and meaningful quantitative metrics, evaluate various proposed views by applying them to various environmental applications with different remotely sensed images coming from different sensors. In the concluding section, we fence the chapter with a summary and recommendations for future researches.

2. Image fusion: definition and fundamentals

Data fusion is a formal framework defined by means and tools for heterogeneous data alliance (Wald, 1999). Image fusion (IF) has been used in many application areas especially in computer vision and remote sensing fields. Most popular applications concern multi-sensor fusion combining images from different engines to achieve a high spatial and spectral resolutions. Nowadays, Earth observation satellites provide data covering different portions of the electromagnetic spectrum at different spatial, spectral and temporal resolutions (Hemissi et al. 2009). Multi-source, multi-sensor and multi-temporal data often present complementary information about a surveyed scene, so image fusion appears as an effective way enabling efficient analysis of such data (Farah et al., 2008a). Therefore, data fusion from various sources aids in delineating objects with interest and comprehensive information thanks to complimentary data integration.

The list of image fusion techniques grows as new forms of sensors that are expanded and applied to data acquisition. Many definitions have been proposed from the remote sensing community, where fusion concepts and algorithms have been matured over several decades. Image fusion aims to integrate complementary heterogeneous data and/or multi-view information acquired in several domains. Hence, a multi-view fusion aims to generate an image with higher information degree by considering diverse aspects.

Image fusion means a very wide domain and it is very difficult to provide a precise definition. A number of earlier definitions of sensor, data, images and information fusion have been proposed in the literature (Gamba et al., 2005), among these we can cite:

Def 1: "Fusion … aims at obtaining information of greater quality; the exact definition of greater quality' will depend upon the application." (Wald, 1999)

Def 2: "…techniques combine data from multiple sensors, and related information from associated databases, to achieve improved accuracy and more specific inferences than what could be achieved by the use of a single sensor alone"(Hall & Llinas, 1990)

Def 3: "…a multilevel, multifaceted process dealing with the automatic detection, association, correlation, estimation, and combination of data and information from multiple sources" (US Department of Defense)

It was felt in all these definitions that several concepts appear around images fusion. First the term "data" is used in the definition 2, whereas the term "information" is preferred in definitions 1 and 3. Here, we choose to use the term information in order to designate the whole of what can be fused. Moreover, most definitions treat the term "information" in its entirety. However, several other authors assume that is possible to characterize information into two or three main types (Bloch, 1996). The first type relates to numerical information which may be signal intensity, pixel gray level, etc. The second type is the symbolic information which may be expressed in symbols, proposals (e.g. what is great is not small), rules (e.g. if it's big and it flies, c is a plane), etc. Recently, numerous researches propose a hybrid type of information (Bloch, 1996). We noticed also that the symbolic type has been a little studied in images fusion, although it can be an important source of information. The difficulty lies in formulation of expert knowledge on data and sensors (Stathaki, 2008).

We further denote that all these definitions delineate information fusion as a combination from several sources. So, it is important to clarify the purpose of the term "combination", allowing a new image with more valuable information and which quality cannot be achieved otherwise. Many writers from the computer scientist community understand the

fusion as the concatenation of multi-sources information. This does not exclude the possibility of obtaining information from a single source after specific treatment. Therefore, the proposal of image fusion is to create new images that are more suitable for further image-processing tasks usually allowing the data amount reducing.
Formally, suppose that we have m sources Sj with j € [1,...,m]. Each source S_j can be characterized by information provided by the ith source as a function of the observation X noted $s_j(X)$. For each observation X, these sources should take a decision in a set of n decisions $d_1,...,d_n$. Each source S_j provides information to decision d_i about observation X that we denoted $M_i^j(x)$. Thus the final decision on the observation x, E(x) will be taken from the combination of information contained in the matrix $(M_i^j(x))$ given by (1).

$$\begin{array}{c} S_1 \\ \vdots \\ S_j \\ \vdots \\ S_m \end{array} \overset{\begin{array}{ccccc} d_1 & \dots & d_i & \dots & d_n \end{array}}{\begin{bmatrix} M_1^1(x) & \dots & M_i^1(x) & \dots & M_n^1(x) \\ \vdots & \ddots & \vdots & \ddots & \vdots \\ M_1^j(x) & \dots & M_i^j(x) & \dots & M_n^j(x) \\ \vdots & \ddots & \vdots & \ddots & \vdots \\ M_1^m(x) & \dots & M_i^m(x) & \dots & M_n^m(x) \end{bmatrix}} \quad (1)$$

Most of these definitions were focusing too much on fusion techniques despite giving some attention to quality. Once the results of fusion process have been generated, quality evaluation provides convincing indicators about fusion contribution. However, meaning and measurement depend on the particular application. Thus, the effectively evaluation has been a challenging topic among the image fusion community (Gianinetto & Villa, 2007). Most common image fusion quality evaluation approaches can be classified into two main categories: qualitative approach which considers a visual comparison of results, and quantitative approach involving a set of predefined quality indicators.

3. Image fusion approaches

A variety of image fusion schemes have been proposed in the literature, concerning multi-sources data combination and support decision making. Each fusion method is designed for a specific problem resolution with disparate inputs, processing approach and outputs. This section aims to propose a state of art of images fusion approaches for remotely sensed applications, to study their main ideas and to sort algorithms into respective categories.

3.1 Data fusion architecture

Fusion architecture describes how to set and use information sources commonly with mathematical and images processing algorithms in order to perform an efficient fusion operation. Some studies tend to characterize image fusion architecture by data type (Dasarathy, 2001) or by the desired applications (Hall & Llinas, 1990). In remotely sensed studies, it is more interesting to characterize its structure which can be defined as a fusion cell. Wald (Wald, 1999) structured synthetically the fusion cell into several elementary operations shown in Figure 1.
Information sources, original data or sensors measurements are the main inputs of the fusion cell. Auxiliary information, providing additional data, can be obtained by a specific source processing or deriving out of another fusion operation. External knowledge is designed to support and assist the fusion process by imposing a priori information, which leads us to elect the adequate model for fusion process. In iterative processing, fusion results

can be used as auxiliary information, since it is not considered as original sources. Finally, it is interesting to get a quality index in addition to results after fusion process. This quality index serves to evaluate the chosen method and to adjust additional information.

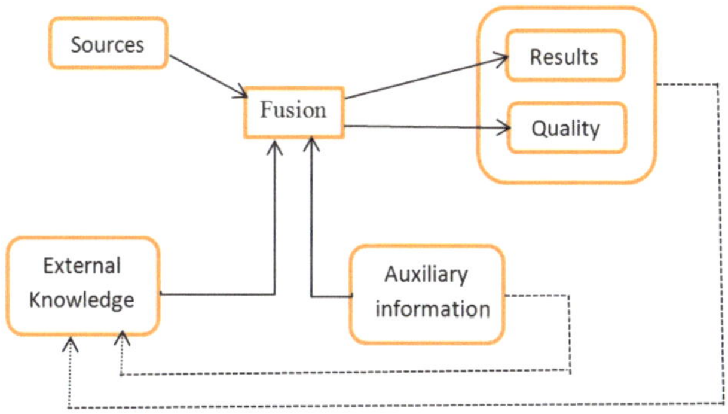

Fig. 1. Formalization of an elementary fusion operation as a fusion cell.

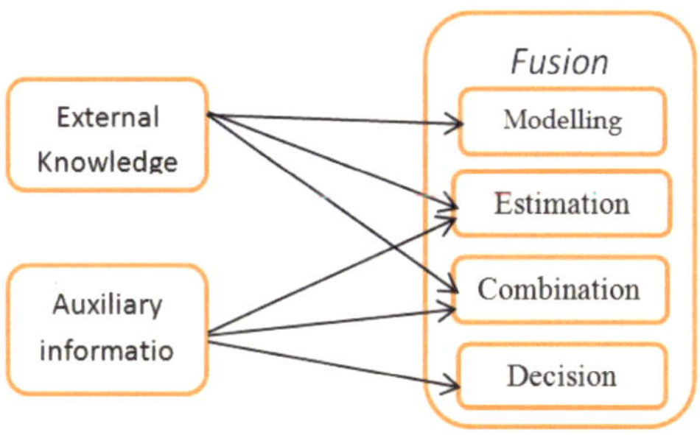

Fig. 2. Fusion process steps.

Three types of architectures are usually considered: centralised, decentralised and hybrid (Lawrence, 2004). The centralised architecture exploits, concurrently or not, input data in a single location. Since this architecture takes into account the whole available sources and knowledge, it provides theoretically an optimal result. Centralised architecture has some drawbacks such as rigidity and noise sensitivity. Therefore, if a particular source has a large error rate, the whole data set is affected which leads to the decrease in the decision quality. Satellite image properties severely limit the use of this type of architecture owing to noise, atmospheric conditions, sensor drifts, etc. Although, decentralised architecture is often adopted since it offers a large flexibility and modularity. Hybrid architectures, which are a combination of centralized and decentralised architectures, may be used recently.
According to fusion cell proposed by (Wald, 1999), numerous researches look to the fusion as a compound stage and a succession of several steps (cf. Figure 2); including generally:

- **Modelling**: the first step of fusion process formulation and it is particularly critical since it tend to choose the fusion formalism (i.e. information representation). It consists generally of determining M_i^j, which can be a distribution, a cost function, etc.
- **Estimation**: depends on previous step, it is necessary for most fusion formalism since it allows function initialization.
- **Combination**: The combination step is the heart of fusion operation allowing information consolidation. It meets to choose an appropriate fusion operator

conforming to the representation formalism defined in step one. Additional information can guide this choice. Most interesting properties of fusion operators are associativity, commutativity, idempotency and adaptability (Bloch, 1996).

- **Decision**: is final step of fusion operation. Usually, it consists of minimizing or maximizing the combination function. The same function can be also used to calculate a quality index.

3.2 Image fusion process

Images fusion techniques are usually conceived following a similar methodology. An overall processing workflow for remotely sensed images fusion is given in figure 3 (Pohl & Van Genderen, 1998). Later on data collection step, images should be corrected from system errors. Indeed, satellite imagery is influenced by atmosphere during data acquisition and therefore needs some corrections and/or other radiometric enhancements such as edge enhancement. Data are also further radiometrically processed. Following this, data are geometrically corrected due to the height variations in the contained images area.

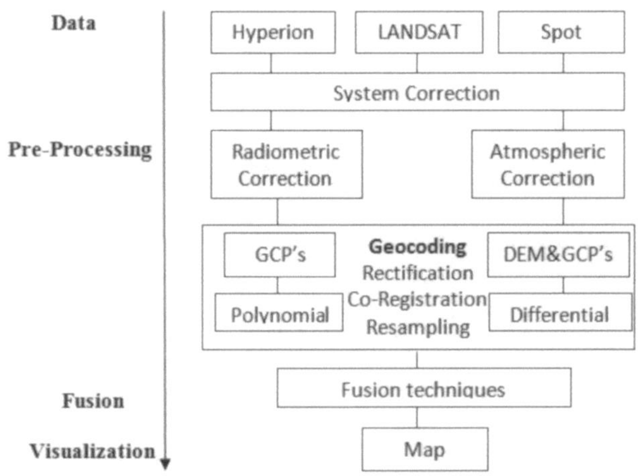

Fig. 3. Flowchart of image fusion process

According to several early studies, fusion techniques are generally grouped into three classes: (1) Colour related techniques, (2) Statistical/numerical methods and (3) combined approaches. The first comprises the colour composition techniques which slice original data into their respective layers, which can be RGB, IHS, HSV or more luminance-chrominance. Statistical approaches use a mathematical approach for data integration. They involve addition, multiplication, differencing and rationing treatments. Combined approaches involve integration of both statistical as well as colour related techniques (Mahler, 2007).

Otherwise, some other researches tend to classify techniques depending to their fusion level. It is often written that fusion takes place at three levels in data fusion: pixel, feature (attribute) and decision. In pixel-based fusion, the information associated with each pixel is obtained by fusing the set of corresponding pixels in source images. In the feature-level approach, each sensor generates a feature vector for a specific object in the scene, which are then fused. In the decision-level fusion, each sensor performs independent processing scheme, and then outputs from each sensor are thereafter combined via a fusion process.

Techniques referring to feature and decision level are generally deriving from a large range of areas including pattern recognition, artificial learning, artificial intelligence, etc.
Until recently, fusion levels are also discussed in their terminology and their number (Gamba et al, 2205). In several studies four analysis levels are preferred: symbolic, feature, pixel and signal level. The goal of the signal-based fusion is to improve the signal-to-noise ratio.
We can notice that there is confusion between information type and fusion level. Hence signal level can be considered as the pixel level for remote sensing applications. In addition, despite the laborious development of sensors, most images have a low spatial resolution. Recent researches (Farah et al., 2010) suggest analysing remote sensing data at sub-pixel level. Thus, we update in this chapter images fusion techniques classification by adding the sub-pixel level to standard above pixel, feature and decision levels. This new classification is summarized by figure 4. Figure 5 shows the various fusion inputs/outputs, to which we added the ability to have entrances at different levels. This figure is an illustrative example of all cases that we can meet by adding the sub-pixel level. We recall here that the fusion process can play the role of selection, transformation, extraction, and information classification i from multiple sources.
In the following sections, we propose to illustrate some fusion level by proposing a specific view. For each of them, we present application schema, used data and obtained results.

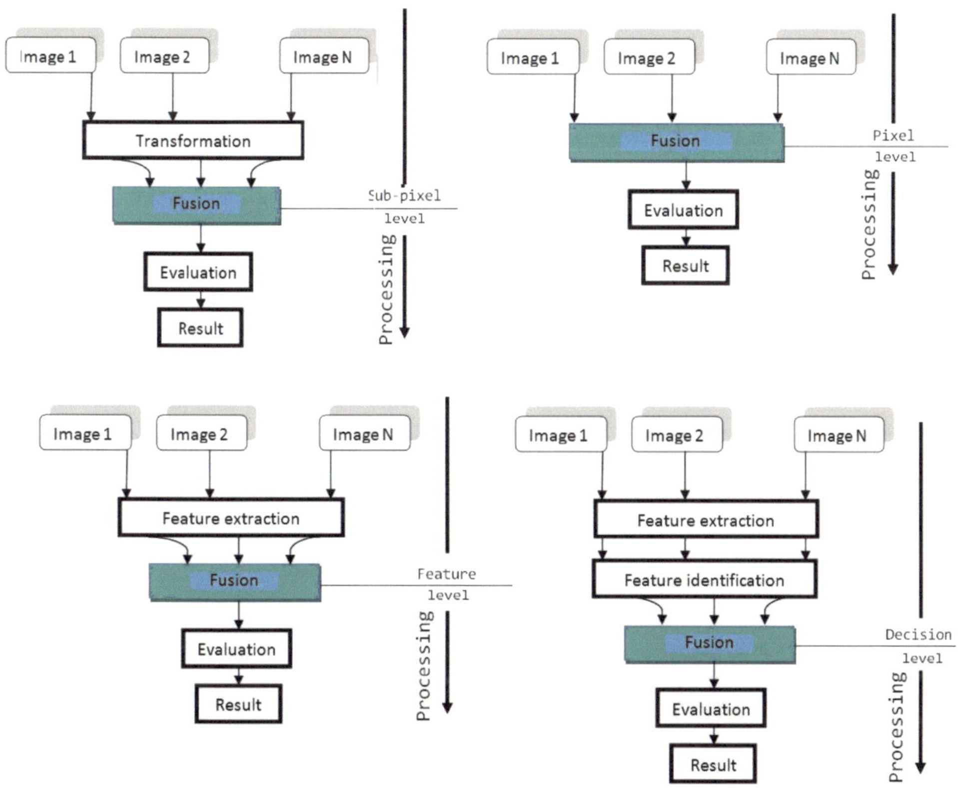

Fig. 4. Proposed classification of fusion techniques

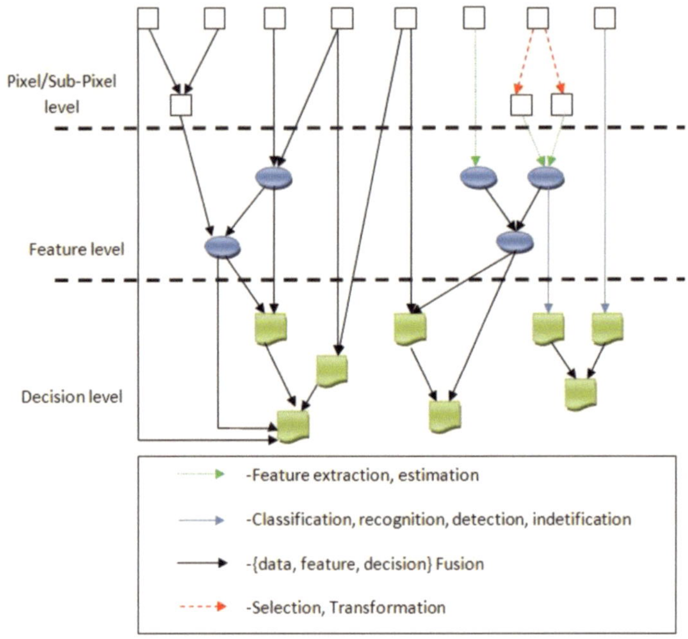

Fig. 5. Inputs/outputs of fusion process

Sub-pixel level	Specral unmixing, Mathematical morphology, Second Order Statistics, Iterative Back-Projection, Wavelet decomposition, Markov chain/MRF, etc.
Pixel level	Neural, fuzzy, neuro fuzzy approaches Voting Strategies, Wavelets, Regression fusion, Filters, Colour Normalized transformation, etc.
Feature level	Cluster Analysis, Neural Networks Bayesian Inference, Evidential Fusion Expert Systems, Logical Templates, etc.
Decision level	Classical Inference, Bayesian Inference Evidential fusion, Contextual Fusion Voting Strategies, Expert Systems Neural Networks, Fuzzy Logic Blackboard Syntactic Fusion, etc.

Table 1. Fusion approaches review depending on fusion level

4. Towards a multi-view approach of satellite images fusion

To overcome problems arising satellite images fusion, we propose a new mufti-view approach intended to enhance images fusion and interpretation. It is designed with diverse fusion schemes and dealing with multi-sources, multi-sensor data and symbolic information. Based on the fact that a unique fusion scheme is impossible to achieve today, we present in this chapter an approach declined on several multiform views. So, fusion practitioners and readers can easily adopt one of these views related to their own problems and application areas. Our contribution lies on a novel conception of fusion process offering more flexibility and providing a largest adaptation aptitude. In fact, the proposed approach is structured under several points of view, each designed to meet a specific need, to solve a peculiar problem. The first view tries to overcome the difficulties related to the presence of mixed pixels by performing a sub-pixel probability fusion. The purpose of the second view will be to fuse information extracted from the image with symbolic knowledge in the sub-pixel level. The last view aims to resolve the conflict related to choice of the optimal fusion technique by combining optimally several approaches. In the following sections, we outline in detail each point of view by emphasizing on its application criteria, proposed fusion process and outputs.

4.1 View 1: Towards an intelligent Sub-pixel multi-sensor satellite image fusion

4.1.1 Introduction

Recently, with the development of miscellaneous satellite sensors, a wide variety of remotely sensed data have become available for scientific studies. As the intensity of data acquisition grows, so does the need to combine multi-sensor images in order to extract the most useful information. However, most studies tend often to fuse multi-sensor images by combining straightly radiometric pixels values. This assumption suffers from pixels heterogeneity due to the low spatial resolution of most satellite images (figure6-a). In this view, we introduce a new multi-sensor fusion approach for land cover classification. The proposed approach is an exhibition of multi-sensor images fusion in the presence of mixed pixels considering that the fusion is performed in the sub-pixel level.

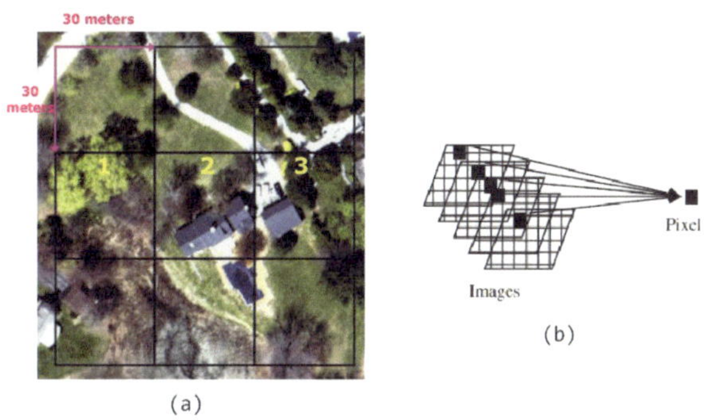

Fig. 6. (a): Satellite images heterogeneity, (b): mixed pixel representation

4.1.2 Proposed approach

The considered approach focuses on multi-sensor images fusion for land cover recognition. Outlined method is applied to both optical and radar images considering that each sensor is associated with a well-defined spectral band. If optical images are easier to interpret, SAR images are very interesting for land cover studies since they are not bound to the daylight constraint and cloudless conditions, allowing an image acquisition independently of weather conditions (Pohl & Van Genderen, 1998). Therefore, considering the well-known advantages and disadvantages of each sensor, it seems logical to combine optical and SAR data for an enhanced apprehension of land cover types.

The proposed approach includes various stages for multi-sensors images processing and fusion. Generic flowchart is summarized by figure7. After data collection and preprocessing, the proposed approach begins by extract source images thanks to Blind Source Separation methods. Under linearity assumption, the radiometric value of a given pixel can be seen as a mixture of physically independent sources (Farah et al., 2003) (c.f figure 6-b). Thereafter, we generate a set of source images and source signals, each outlining a specific land cover type. Extracted sources evaluation is performed in the next step, allowing additional knowledge discovering from most informative sources signals. To further improve images interpretation, the framework promises a source knowledge representation capabilities delineated as a set of decision rules. Hence, multi-source information fusion produce a valuable understanding of the observed site by decreasing the uncertainty related to single sources (Mansour et al., 2000). In our study, we assumed that multi-sensor adopted images have negligible registration problems, which implies that the objects in all images are geometrically aligned (Goshtasby, 2005). In the following sub-sections, we describe this knowledge representation, as well as the components of the architecture and the interpretation steps.

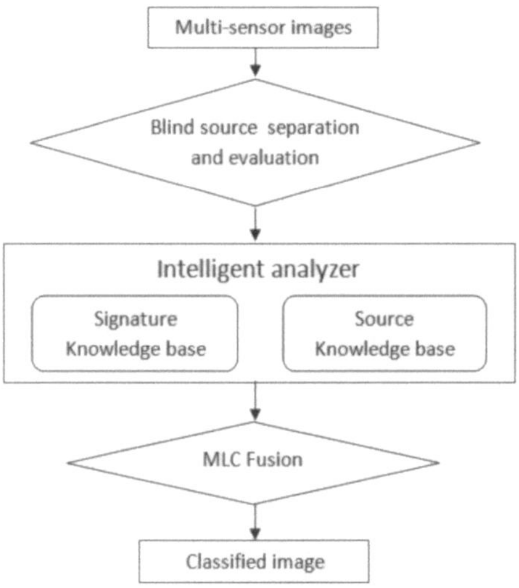

Fig. 7. Workflow of proposed approach

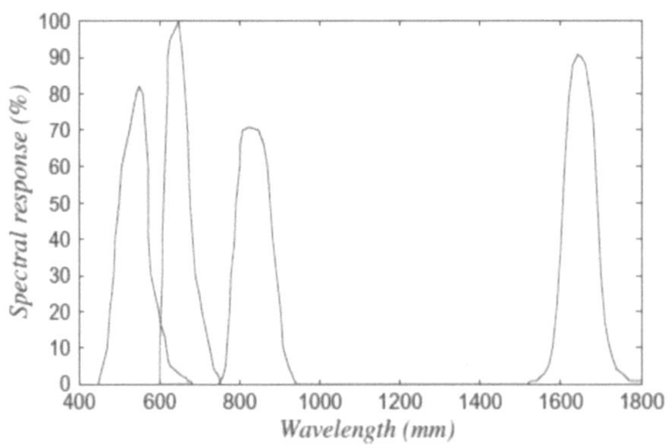

Fig. 8. Typical spectral sensitivity of SPOT4.

4.1.2.1 Blind source separation

The BSS problem aims to retrieve unknown original signals from their mixtures (measured signals). Its main assumptions are the mutual independence and non-Gaussianity of sources (Mansour et al., 2000). Thus, we attempt to separate observed signals into a set of other signals, such that the regularity of each resulting signal is maximized, and the regularity between the signals is minimized (i.e. statistical independence is maximized). If we admit the linearity of mixing process, the model of BSS can be expressed by:

$$X = A \times S + N \tag{2}$$

where X is an n×p observed image matrix; each of its rows determines the reflectance of the observed image according to a given spectral band. S is an m×p source images matrix; each of its rows determines the reflectance of one source image. A is an n×m mixing matrix; each of its columns is called the directional vector associated to the corresponding source. N is defined as an n×p matrix realized from a spatially additive white Gaussian noise considered as negligible.

Many approximate methods have been proposed in order to solve equation (2) (Cao & Liu, 1996). The adapted algorithms in our approach are approximate diagonalization of eigen-matrix (JADE-2D) (Cardoso & Souloumiac, 1993), second order blind identification (SOBI-2D) (Belouchrani, 1997) and fast-independent component analysis (Fast-ICA-2D) (Hyvärinen & Oja, 1997) algorithms. Source separation can be obtained by optimizing a contrast function that can be based on entropy, mutual independency, higher order statistics, etc. Each of these algorithms takes as an input a matrix X representing the set of multi-sensor images. The goal of all these BSS algorithms is to solve equation (2), in which A (mixing matrix) and S (source images) are the unknown components. After source images extraction, we propose to evaluate their information content using the following criteria, which help us to select just the most informative sources to the fusion process.

The entropy source: This criterion can be interpreted as the degree of information granted by each source image. We use the entropy source in order to assort source images and electing those having a maximum of information degree. Entropy source criterion is given by:

$$E(S) = -\sum_{n} P_s(n) \log_2 p_s(n) \tag{3}$$

where S and $p_s(n)$ denote respectively the source image and the probability of gray level value n of S.

Source mutual information (SMI): To evaluate the performances of BSS algorithms, we use the SMI criterion in order to quantify the separation rate between extracted sources. It's based on the concept of mutual information (Zadeh & Jutten 2005) and defined as:

$$E(S_1) = -\sum_{n} P_{s1}(n) \log_2 p_{s1}(n) \tag{4}$$

$$E(S_2) = -\sum_{n} P_{s2}(n) \log_2 p_{s2}(n) \tag{5}$$

where $p_{s1}(n)$ and $p_{s2}(n)$ are the probability of the pixel value n in sources S_1 and S_2, respectively. The entropy of the couple S_1 and S_2 is:

$$E(S_1,S_2) = -\sum_{n1,n2} p(n_1,n_2)\log_2 p(n_1,n_2) \quad (6)$$

where $p(n_1, n_2)$ is the joint probability of pixel value n_1 for S_1 and n_2 for S_2. If the sources are independent, the mutual information of a set of k sources is defined as follow:

$$I(S_1,...,S_n) = -\sum_{n_1,...,n_n} p(n_1,...,n_n)\log_2 \frac{p(n_1,...,n_n)}{p_{S1}(n_1 n_1)...p_{sn}(n_n)} \quad (7)$$

After entropy and MSI criterion computing, we choose the source images having the maximum of information degree. This will help us to extract a learning area that models the spectral characteristics of each land cover type. The knowledge about the land cover theme will be modelled by an intelligent tool based on decision rules.

4.1.2.2 Source signals

After source images extraction and evaluation, we propose to improve interpretation process by using filters called also sources signals (Farah et al., 2003). Thus, the sensitivity of each source image can be modelled by source filters, which consist of a physical representation of source images sensitivity according to the spectral bands (cf. figure 8).
The sensitivity of multispectral observations according to the wavelength λ is represented by $S(k,l,\lambda)$, which can be obtained by sampling and quantifying the spectral sensitivity of optical sensor. Each ith image for the (k,l) pixel represented by $X_i(k, l)$ is observed with a filter of reflectance $R_i(\lambda)$. Thus, these images can be written as follows:

$$X_i(k,l) = \int R_i(\lambda)S(k,l,\lambda)d\lambda \quad (8)$$

From equation (8), the $(k,l)^{th}$ pixel of the jth image source $S_j(k, l)$ can be modelled by:

$$S_j(k,l) = \sum_i c(i,j)X_i(k,l) \quad (9)$$

where c(i,j) is the unmixing coefficient A^{-1} of source j and image i. Combining equations (8) and (9), we obtain:

$$S_j(k,l) = \int U_i(\lambda)S(k,l,\lambda)d\lambda \quad (10)$$

$$\int U_i(\lambda) = \sum_i e(i,j)\int R_i(\lambda) \quad (11)$$

The source images can be regarded as observed images through filters $U_j(l)$, called the source signals. Therefore, the sensitivity of each source image extracted from the BSS can be modelled by the source signal.

4.1.2.3 Intelligent analyzer

This module performs the enhancement of source images extracted by multi-sensor BSS module by allowing semantics information assigning and improvement (Cf. Figure 9). For each source image, corresponding source signal will be depicted in terms of source knowledge, offering further information about land cover types. This relation will be expressed by a set of decision rules.

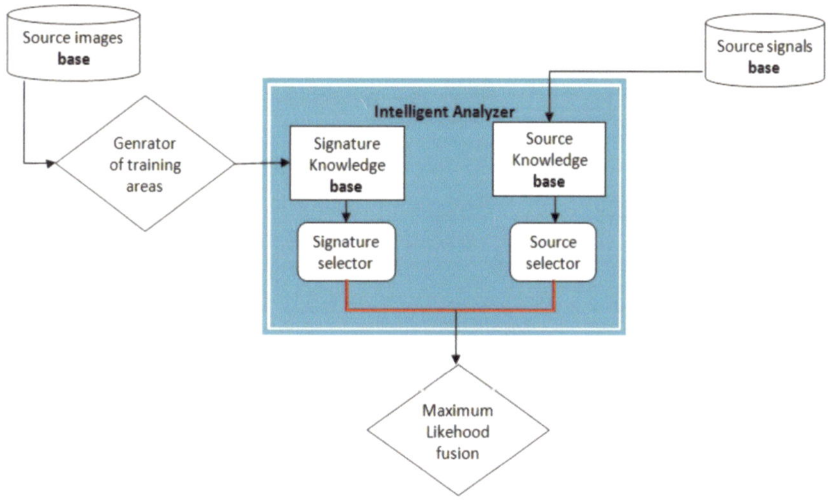

Fig. 9. Workflow of the intelligent analyzer module.

In order to perform a supervised multi-source image fusion, we choose the source image having the maximum information criterion. This operation is carried out by the "source selector" which retains sources with a maximum information degree. This allows us extract a learning area that models the spectral characteristics of each land cover type. The knowledge about the land cover themes will be modelled by an intelligent tool based on decision rules, which will be used by the multi-source image fusion in order to improve and enhance image analysis. Simultaneously, training zones are extracted by the "generator of training areas" module in order to assist satellite image classification and to maximize information extraction. Signatures Knowledge basis concedes semantics to each training zone. The "signature selector" module retains only the one with a maximum percentage of identification. We specify in the following sub-sections each of these sub-modules.

The sources knowledge base. Thanks to this base, land cover type can be recognized for the source images resulting from the multi-sensor BSS step. The base is constructed by using the parameters related to the source signals and the rate of identification of the land cover classes. The facets used to construct this basis are:

a. Parameters
   - *Interval of λ (Intervalλ)*. This parameter represents the wavelength interval corresponding to the maximum value of source signal.
   - *Maximum value (MaxV)*. This parameter gives the maximum value of the source signal, indicating that the source is sensitive to a particular type of soil occupation.

b. Decision rules

The production rules are formalized as follows:

$$If(MaxV(S_{i,j})_{i=1:3,j=1:5} \succ \sup(MaxV(S_{k,l})_{k=i,l=1:5,l\neq j}))\ \&\ Interval_{\lambda} \in (I_m)_{m=1:5} Then\_S_{i,j} isO_n$$

where MaxV is the maximum value, j is the number of the source, i is the used algorithm(1 = Fast-ICA-2D; 2 = JADE-2D; 3 = SOBI-2D), l is the number of the source test, and k is the algorithm used. Im denotes the wavelength interval tests:

The sources selector. This module selects more significant source images depending on their entropy values, sources are ranked in a descending order and significant ones are selected. Three sources were chosen from the set of sources affected by radar. From other sources, we choose two sources for each algorithm with maximum entropy criterion which is defined by:

$$MaxEntropy((S_{i,j,k})_{i=1:3,j=1:5,k=0:1}) \tag{12}$$

where j represents the number of the source, i represents the algorithm used (1 = Fast- ICA-2D; 2 = JADE-2D; 3 = SOBI-2D), and k indicates whether the source is affected by the radar (1 = radar; 0 if not).

The signatures knowledge basis. This knowledge basis is constructed by zones training and from expert knowledge. It includes two main stages:

a. *Generator of training zones*: this generator extracts a training zone from each source in order to assist the module of fusion and to give an improved classified image. This generation is accomplished by using histogram analysis of each image.
b. *Signatures knowledge basis*: allows determination of the nature of the training zones extracted from the generator of training zones (GTZ) module.

The multi-source fusion module. This module performs the fusion of selected sources. Maximum likelihood classification (MLC) was used for fusion process. In perform images classification and produce a thematic map.

4.1.3 Study areas and results

The proposed method will be illustrated using two different datasets located in central Tunisia. The images come from the ERS2 and SPOT4 satellites. Kairouan, our first selected zone, is situated at approximately 100 km south of Tunis. Corresponding images for this zone are as follows: (i) a synthetic-aperture radar image from ERS2 acquired on 24th of April 1998, presenting a spatial resolution of 12.5 m, and operating in band C centred on the value frequency 5.36 GHz, with a polarization VV and an incidence angle centred at 26°; and (ii) an optical image of SPOT4 acquired on 31st of May 1998, with a spatial resolution of 20×20m. The second selected zone is Tunis, centred over the gulf of Tunis. Respective images are as follows: (i) an ERS2 image acquired in June 2003 operating in band C, centred on the value frequency 5.36 GHz, with a polarization VV and an incidence angle centred at 26°; and (ii) an optical SPOT4 image acquired in June 2003, with a spatial resolution of 20×20.

After data correction and co-registration, blind source module is executed to extract sources images which will be evaluated in the next step. In order to choose the training data, a cartographic map has been used. After having determined the source images and the training and testing zones, we carried out fusion multi-source by MLC for selected zones. The source images used in our experiment are S2 and S4 from Fast- ICA-2D, S1 and S4 from JADE-2D, and S4 and S1 from SOBI-2D. The classification resulting from MLC is an image including five classes related to the various types of land cover (compartmental, humid, urban, lake and vegetation areas (figure 10 (B) (D)).

Confusion matrixes are used for classification evaluation. In order to prove the effectiveness of the proposed method in land cover classification over conventional methods, a thematic map was produced with a maximum likelihood classification (MLC) applied to multispectral imagery without a BSS treatment (Table 2). The overall classification accuracies are listed in tables 2(a) and 2(b), respectively. The improved land-use map is characterized with mixed pixels and more homogeneous regions. The overall accuracy increased considerably from 63% for MLC applied to multispectral imagery to 85% with the proposed approach.

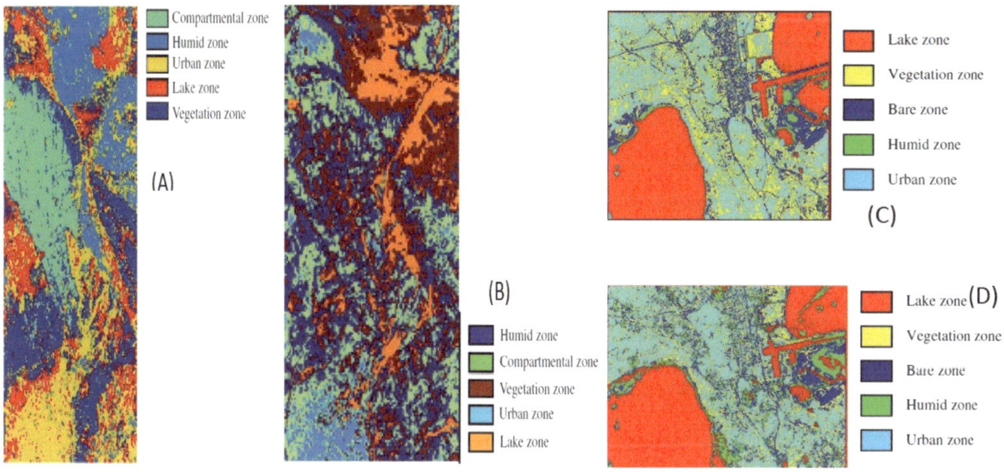

Fig. 10. Classified Kairouan image (A) and Tunis (C) issued from fusion of multi-source images; (B) and (D) are respectively Kairouan and Tunis zone classification with MLC applied to SPOT and ERS imagery.

Class	MLC	Proposed approach
Humid	81.96	100.00
Compartmental	61.76	99.44
Vegetation	58.51	99.40
Urban	52.53	97.80
Lake	75.27	95.73
Overall accuracy	66.01	98.47

Table 2(a). Classification accuracy for Kairouan zone,

Class	MLC	Proposed approach
Lake	80.60	98.53
Vegetation	52.98	83.93
Bare	58.31	82.67
Humid	54.04	80.76
Urban	73.88	83.80
Overall accuracy	63.96	85.93

Table 2(b). Classification accuracy for Tunis zone.

3.2 View 2: Towards Neuro-fuzzy approach image fusion

3.2.1 Introduction

Recently, the advent of hyperspectral data provides hundreds of relatively narrow and contiguous bands that may be useful for extracting land-use information. This new form of information can revolutionize the appliance of multisensory images fusion thanks to the wealth of spectral information. Thus, hyperspectral imaging has become a fruitful ally for land cover recognition and natural phenomena monitoring. However, the interpretation of hyperspectral imagery is confronted to several problems such as high data dimensionality,

spatio-temporal variability of natural phenomena, data imperfection and the requirement of a recurrent expert intervention. So the major dilemma with hyperspectral data interpretation bears upon knowledge integration and fusion flexibility.
As discussed in Section 2, very few studies have focused on an efficient integration of symbolic information in image fusion process. Therefore, we propose in this view a neuro-fuzzy approach for hyperspectral images interpretation at a sub-pixel level. This investigation serves to consolidate the alliance of the symbolic knowledge into images fusion process and takes advantage of the spectral information provided by hyperspectral imaging. Previous view address spatial and spectral dimensions of images by considering each pixel value as a mixture of several sources. In this view, we show how to analyze also the temporal aspect in satellite images fusion. This investigation is decidedly interesting if information coming from various sensor lack fidelity in the spectral or/and spatial domains.

4.2.2 Proposed approach

Our environment is subject to disturbances practiced on variables scales of space and time. On the attempt of natural risk prediction and management, we outline in this view a neuro-fuzzy fusion strategy for where data fusion is the combination of heterogeneous information from multiple data sources.
The proposed methodology in this view is mainly divided into two stages corresponding to the development of a predictive model of risk hazard monitoring. The first step is "spectral unmixing" allowing abundance maps generation. Each map is relative to a specific endmember in the image. Abundance map of a pure material (source) is a 2D image whose pixel values, ranged between 0 and 1, indicate the proportion of this material spectrum in each pixel vector. The second step is the fusion of these maps with In situ data using a neuro-fuzzy architecture. The choice of a fuzzy logic has been motivated by data and knowledge imperfection; neural networks have been preferred due to their learning ability allowing model calibration and adaptation (Hemissi et al., 2009).

4.2.2.1 Spectral unmixing

Hyperspectral imaging spectrometers collect images provided by spectral information reflected from surface materials. Each pixel in such image contains a resulting mixed spectrum from reflected sources radiation. Spectral unmixing techniques allow mapping of elements of the scene at the sub pixel level. The objective of this module is to achieve, for each pixel, a reliable extraction of pure spectral signatures and an accurate estimation of their fractional abundances (maps). This investigation should be done using only observed data (hyperspectral pixels), from which the interest of using blind separation of sources techniques, and particularly the independent component analysis (ICA). Formally, the spectral mixture model for a pixel is expressed by equation (2). Then using a BSS technique, mixing proportions of each ground cover material could be retrieved.
In order to obtain abundance maps, we use Independent Component Analysis (ICA) technique which is a blind source separation (BSS) method based on the hypothesis that the independent components (ICs) are statistically independent. Particularly, FAST-2D-ICA (Hyvärinen & Oja, 1997) algorithm has been adopted to achieve independent components (ICs) generation from hyperspectral images. After ICs computing, we calculate a Priority score for each of them based on higher order statistics (CSOs) (Wang & Chang, 2006). Since the number of materials in the hyperspectral scene is much less than the dimension of hyperspectral data; we used the Virtual Dimensionality algorithm (Chang, 2004) to estimate

the number of endmembers in the hyperspectral scene denoted p. We can then classify ICs in order of importance and select only, first p priority ICs. For each of them we elect the pixel with maximum radiometry which may be assumed to be a pure spectral signature (endmember). For endmembers labeling and identification, we use the Spectral Angle Mapper Technical (SAM) (Yuhas, 1992). Outputs of "spectral Unmixing" stage are a set of endmembers and their respective abundance maps. In the next section, we show how to integrate these maps with field (In-situ) data in order to increase fusion and prevision quality.

4.2.2.2 Neuro-fuzzy fusion

This module provides a neuro-fuzzy interpretation of abundance maps generated by BSS analysis. Its main purpose is to build a block of correspondence such as from a set of multi-source information (abundance maps and the in Situ data) describing the current situation, it is possible to obtain a prediction of future risks. Fundamentally, the interpretation is essentially seen as a predicting problem by neuro-fuzzy pattern recognition approach.

The use of a neuro-fuzzy model in the problem of hyperspectral images interpretation and for heterogeneous data fusion offers the possibility to model a priori knowledge and linguistic decision rules defined by experts. It also benefits the capabilities and advantages of the fuzzy inference modeled by a parallel neural architecture. Thus, the adjustment of fuzzy system parameters is achieved through neural learning (Lin, 1997). The overall objective of the proposed model is how to associate any new entry to a class of potential risk. For temporal dimension appending, the inputs of our fusion system can also be multi-temporal fractions extracted by unmixing a series of hyperspectral images. Therfore, the analysis of these fractions by the neuro-fuzzy model will lead us to analyze change efficentiely by spatial\temporel and spectral consolidation.

Adopted neuro-fuzzy architecture is the FALCON model (Fuzzy Adaptive Learning Control Network) (Lin, 1997), a connectionist model that can be contrasted with a traditional fuzzy logic and decision system into a connectionist structure in terms of its network structure and learning abilities. The FALCON is then a feed-forward multilayer network in which the input nodes represent the input states, the hidden layers work as membership functions and fuzzy logic rules, the output layers represent decision signals. The expert knowledge can be easily incorporated into the model and provides a human understandable meaning to the normal multilayer neural network, the structure avoids the rule-matching time of the inference engine in the traditional fuzzy control system.

The proposed model, shown in Figure 11, consists of five layers. Each node in layer 1 corresponds to one input variable. Each node in layer 2 corresponds to one linguistic label which acts as membership functions representing the terms of the respective linguistic variables. Nodes in layer 3 represent one fuzzy logic rule and perform precondition matching of a rule Layer 3 hence links define the preconditions of the rule. Layer 5 is the output layer. Nodes in layer 4 links define the consequences of rules. The links in layers 2 and 5 are fully connected between linguistic nodes and their corresponding terms nodes. The semantic meaning and function of the neurons are as below:

Layer 1: This layer transfers the input variable to the next layer. Therefore, there are p+q neurons in layer 1, each represents one input variable. For the ith neuron in this layer, the input (I_i^1) and output (O_i^1) are represented, respectively, as:

$$I_i^1 = X_i^1 \quad \text{and} \quad O_i^1 = I_i^1 \ (1) \tag{13}$$

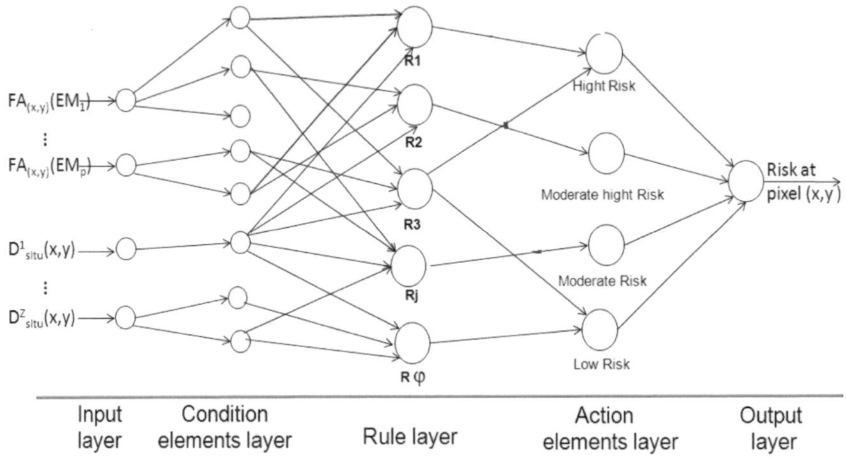

Fig. 11. Proposed neuro-fuzzy model

Where: $FA_{(x,y)}$ Emp : abundance fraction of endmember p in pixel with (x,y) coordinates,
$D_{(x,y)}^q$: value of the q In-Situ data, with q: the In-Situ data index
ф : the rules index

From Eq.(13), the link weight at layer 1 ($W_i^{(1)}$) is unity.

Layer 2: Each input feature x_i , i =1,2 is expressed in terms of membership values, where i corresponds to the input feature and j corresponds to the number of term sets for the linguistic variable x_i. We use a single node to perform a bell-shaped membership function Eq.(14):

$$I_{ij}^2 = -\frac{(O_i^1 - \mu_{ij})^2}{2\sigma_{ij}^2} \quad \text{and} \quad O_{ij}^2 = e^{I_{ij}^2} \tag{14}$$

where μ_{ij} and σ_{ij} are, respectively, the center (or mean) and the width (or variance) of the bell-shaped function of the jth term of the ith input linguistic variable x_i. Hence, the link weight at layer 2 ($W_i^{(2)}$) can be interpreted as μ_{ij}.

Layer 3: The links in this layer are used to perform precondition matching of fuzzy logic rules. Hence, the rule nodes perform the fuzzy AND operation:

$$I_i^3 = \begin{Bmatrix} O_{ij}^2 \cdots Si \cdots O_{ij}^2 = Min\{O_{ij}^2, ..., O_{ij}^2\} \\ 0 \cdots Sinon \end{Bmatrix} \quad \text{and} \quad O_{ij}^3 = I_{ij}^3 \tag{15}$$

The link weight in layer 3 ($W_i^{(3)}$) is then unity.

Layer 4: The nodes in this layer have two transmission modes, i.e., forward and backward. In forward transmission mode, the nodes in this layer perform the fuzzy OR operation to integrate the fired rules which have the same consequence. In the backward transmission mode, the links function exactly same as the layer 2 nodes:

$$I_i^4 = \begin{Bmatrix} O_i^3 \cdots Si \cdots O_i^3 = Max\{O_i^3, ..., O_i^3\} \\ 0 \cdots Sinon \end{Bmatrix} \quad \text{and} \quad O_i^4 = I_i^4 \tag{16}$$

Hence, the link weight ($W_i^{(4)}$) =1.

Layer 5: The nodes of the layer 5 links attached to them act as the defuzzifier. If μ_{ij} and σ_{ij} are, respectively, the center and the width of the membership function of the jth term of the its output linguistic variable, then the Eq.(17) can be used to simulate the center of area defuzzification method:

$$I_i^5 = \sum_i W_i^5 O_i^4 \text{ and } O_i^5 = I_i^5 \tag{17}$$

Here the link weight in layer 5 ($W_i^{(5)}$) is $\mu_{ij}\sigma_{ij}$.
Based on this connectionist structure, a supervised gradient-descent learning procedure is developed to determine the proper centers (μ_{ij}) and widths (σ_{ij}) of the term nodes in layers 2 and 4. To set up the neuro fuzzy model, a hybrid learning algorithm from a set of supervised training data was developed. It consists on a learning strategy based on two successive stages which combines unsupervised learning. A self-organized learning scheme (i.e., unsupervised learning) is used to detect the potential fuzzy logic rules and to locate initial membership functions, then a supervised gradient-descent learning procedures is used to optimally adjust the parameters of the membership functions for desired outputs.
The result of the fusion module is a predictive map of potential risks. This map can be regarded as a decision model alert. We mean by alert, the ability to get ahead of an event in time, space, or both. Indeed, the map produced provides the evolution of a phenomenon in medium and long-term consequences for each pixel. This leads to the definition of preventive strategies and policies depending on potential risk seriousness.

4.2.3 Results and validation

The validation of the proposed approach regards its application on the "Hydric erosion" risk affecting southern Tunisian region. To delimitate this risk, a case study was conducted using a subset of HYPERION hyperspectral dataset. In situ data include a slope and a lithofaçies maps describing soil properties. Interpretation and risk assessment consists to fuse abundances maps with in situ data using the proposed neuro-fuzzy model. As such, CNT's (Tunisian Remote sensing Center) experts have defined a set of 42 fuzzy rules defining the degree of risk as a function of slope value, lithofaçies class and the proportion of some materials in each pixel. Laterally, we defined the form of membership functions using sigmoidal function which is legitimately chosen to model data variability (Cox, 1999).
Learning neuro-fuzzy model has been developed on the basis of 568 pixels. This phase was used to calibrate the prediction model by adjusting the parameters of membership functions and refining the fuzzy rules base. Finally, neuro-fuzzy model generates the risk map shown by Figure 13.
In order to evaluate the results, the predicted risks were overlaid to the observed risks from 2000 to 2008 by the CNT experts. Performance on training and validation data are presented in Table 3 which indicates that about 87.54% of the training data which fell within the high category coincided with high category, about 85.53% of moderately high category coincided with moderately high category, 83.09% of moderate category coincided with moderate and 90.3% of the low category coincided with low. For the training data sets, correct classification was (94.2%) and number of misclassified entries about (5.8%). For the validation data sets (49% of the training sets), the correct classification was (97%) and number of misclassified entries about (3%). Some others methods of interpretation used were evaluated independently in terms of prediction accuracy. Table 4 summarizes the measurements of efficiency and quality obtained from confusion matrices.

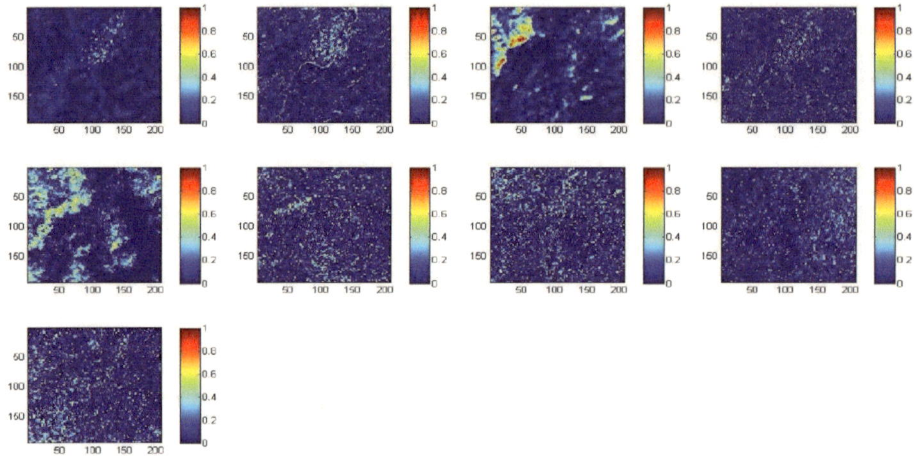

Fig. 12. Abundances maps,

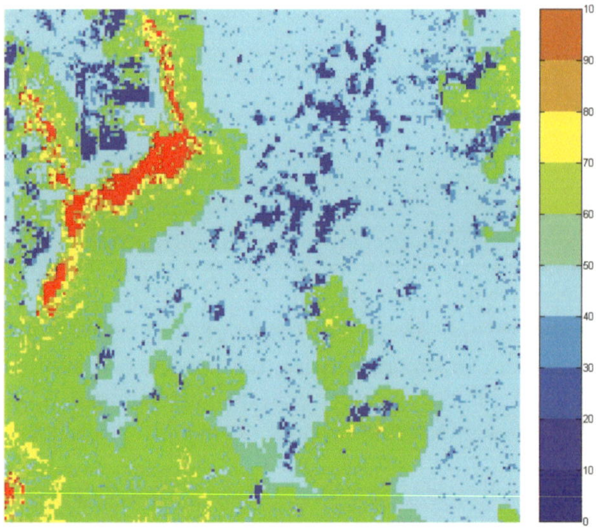

Fig. 13. Erosion risk map

Vulnerability Classes	High	Moderately High	Moderate	Low
High	87.54	10.64	4.75	0.00
Moderately high	9.77	85.53	8.94	3.27
Moderate	2.15	3.00	83.09	6.43
Low	0.54	0.83	3.22	90.3

Table 3. Performance of the training data (%) for erosion vulnerability

Table 4 allowed us to justify the choice of the neuro-fuzzy model. Indeed, comparing the average accuracy of the fuzzy approach (75.04%) with neuronal prediction (82.01%) and the maximum likehood (83.49%), we can see the remarkable improvements (91.9%) obtained by coupling these two techniques in one hybrid architecture. Furthermore, comparison of results obtained with the truth ground testifies the effectiveness of prevention diction of the approach proposed, this is expressed by a Kappa coefficient of about 0.7002 against 0.5847 for the fuzzy approach 0.6514 for neuronal prediction.

Vulnerability Classes	Neural networks	Fuzzy logic	MLC	Proposed approach
High	87,32	87,35	89,17	90,07
Moderately high	77,70	73.62	81.06	85.76
Moderate	75.61	63.19	73.37	88.57
Low	79,67	69.27	79.57	89.71

Table 4. Comparison several approaches

4.3 View 3: Towards a multi-approach image fusion

4.3.1 Introduction

We have shown, in previous sections, that combining multi-sensor information provides a greater recognition accuracy and improves analysis quality. However, we have also noticed that satellite images interpretation is frequently marked by several types of imperfection. To overcome these weaknesses, most commonly approaches are probability, possibility, and evidence theories. Frequently, the major matter arising most studies is the choice of the most appropriate method for a particular situation and application issue. This section aims to present a novel approach consolidating several fusion techniques in order to choose the most appropriate depending on application field. By choosing the optimum theory for a particular image context, our approach will lead to improve images classification. Developed Framework is performed in the pixel level and it is based on a multi-agent system and a case-based reasoning.

4.3.2 Proposed approach

Data as available for an interpretation system are always somehow imperfect. Hence, imperfection, be it imprecision, uncertainty or ignorance, affect strongly most remotely sensed data and must be incorporated into every interpretation process. The term "imperfection" is usually used as a most general label. Materially, it can be due to imprecision, inconsistency, ignorance, uncertainty, etc (Farah et al., 2008b). Imprecision arises from the existence of a value, which cannot be measured with suitable precision. These imprecision can be resulting from a noise affecting satellite images that should be treated by applying some filters. Uncertainty is a property that arises from a lack of information about application nature. The uncertainty is resulting from an unreliable sensor or from spatial or temporal constraints. Imprecision and inconsistency are essentially properties of the information itself whereas uncertainty is a property of the relation between the information and our knowledge about context. The incompleteness reflects the fact that information is unable to capture all relevant aspects of an observable event (Bloch, 1996).
Conventionally, data imperfection was fluently modeled by probability theory. Until recently, many new theories have been proposed to deal with this problem. The large number of theories reflects the recent acknowledgement that probability theory, as good as it is, is not the unique alternative and it is not able to take into account all aspects of data

imperfection (Mahler, 2007). Then, the use of inappropriate, unjustified, or purely one theory can lead to decline interpretation task and results. Moreover, the majority of interpretation systems do not hold into account the imperfection accompanying satellite images. Few systems use only one theory with very restricted parameters.

In this view, in order to handle data imperfection, we propose a new intelligent multi-approach for uncertain satellite images fusion combining three different data fusion methods, namely, the probability, possibility, and evidence methods. This system can provide a powerful framework for multi-sensor images fusion and decision-making. Therefore, the proposed architecture incorporates the information extracted by learning. It includes also some "structures detection" modules based on a set of agents; each of them is specialized in the detection of a specific object type.

Figure 14 summarized the proposed approach, which enclosed three levels of abstraction: the low level, the intermediate level and the high level. The three levels are independent and cooperate to build the whole image fusion and interpretation process. As shown, proposed approach is based on a multi-agent architecture. Interest for multi-agent approach is motivated by many factors (Tupin et al., 1999). Primary, as the fusion cell can be decomposed into several well-defined stages; each will be accountable of an independent processing agent. Second, agent's interaction, communication and cooperation induce a robust treatment process, allowing us to solve difficult situations and to reduce imperfection rate (Farah et al., 2006). Thus, a high performance of application can be achieved through parallelism between agents. Agents for each level communicate with their counterparts at other levels in order to answer requests and to transmit respective information. In our system, agent's knowledge will be stored in the fact basis, allowing a subsequent reasoning step using a set of rules. The learning process is necessary to initialize the multi-approach and images fusion. The agent of each abstraction level carries on and cooperates and generates information to the upper level in order to achieve interpretation task.

4.3.2.1 Low-level abstraction:

This level assures the extraction of symbolic information such as borders or homogeneous regions. Adopted techniques are intensely associated with data type, but they are independent of the application domain. In our approach, we choose to develop a set of agents allowing the extraction of useful information for interpretation and fusion tasks such as the learning agent, the structure detection agent (river detection, urban detection, etc.), the probability agent, the possibility agent, and the evidence agent. To better monitor imperfections, the process initializing our system emphasizes a learning process. Learning can be supervised or unsupervised allowing functions estimation.

4.3.2.2 Intermediate-level abstraction:

The intermediate level performs the designation of symbolic primitives extracted in previous level. This level is more sensitive and expresses a notable importance sense it provides an articulation component between low and high levels.

Depending on application's field, this level can be decomposed into several sub-levels; each of them is designed for specific kind of primitives and achieving to a particular transformation or a selection. In our case, we develop three types of intermediate-level agents, namely, the supervisor structure detection agent, the supervisor fusion agent, and the supervisor learning agent. The information gathered by the low-level agents is sent to the supervisor detection agent who must use knowledge about this information offered by the high level Decision support system (DSS). The DSS allows recognizing the type of the extracted zones through a set of rules stored in the rule basis. The rules are expressed in a language that is close to natural language, allowing DSS enrichment. We develop three types of rules:

1. Radiometric rules: modeling the shade level.
2. Geometric rules: concerning pixels arrangement.
3. Topologic rules: concerning the spatial relation and the position of the objects to detect.

These three kinds of rules do not have the same weight to all images objects. For example, to validate the presence of an urban zone, the geometric criterion is more relevant than the radiometric and the topologic one. Moreover, the structures' description is often imprecise. To detect structures from images, we develop a set of agents, each of them designed to detect a specific object type. We can find for example the humid detection agent, the river detection agent, the urban detection agent, and the road detection agent.

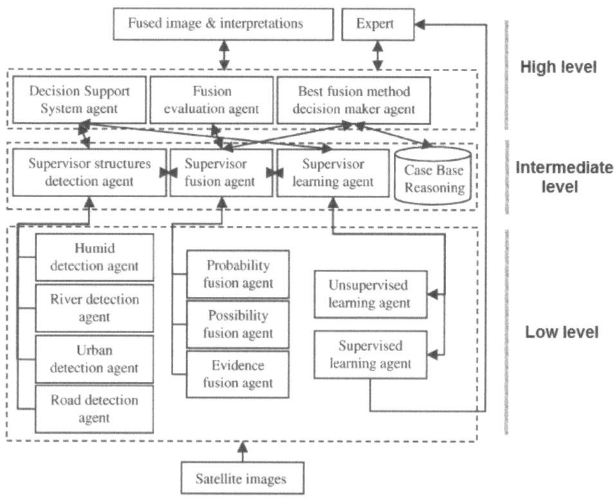

Fig. 14. Workflow of proposed multi-approach

4.3.2.3 High-level abstraction:

This level incorporates the interpretation mechanisms and symbolic representation of the scene. Information provided by learning and structure detection agents of intermediate level are used by the high-level fusion agents in order to build the resulting fused image.

In order to optimize the interpretation process, we have developed an agent called the best fusion method decision maker. This agent refers to case-based reasoning (CBR) module, which is particularly useful for applications where we lack sufficient knowledge either for formal representation or for parameter estimation (Bentabet et al., 2002). CBR presents cases related to similar previously handled problems; it suggests the solution adapted under similar situations and decides what order previous cases can provide for dealing with the current problem.

This module stores an archive about different fusion cases previously handled (Jurisica & Glasgow, 2004). In our approach, each case has three components:

- The features describing each case: including textual, shape, color, and texture features;
- Image fusion method: gives a solution to a given problem
- The case relevance: provided by an expert.

For a better characterization of problem, we have weighed each problem feature according to its importance. A communication is launched between the supervisor fusion agent and

the best fusion method decision-maker. For each image, we start by determining the features described above. Then we retrieve the best fusion method using a quadtree technique, allowing a multilevel structure representation of image features. Each level contains a set of nodes reserved for a specific feature (textual, color, texture, or shape).
The quadtree technique lets us to filter images by gradually increasing the detail level (Inglada & Mercier, 2007). Image retrieval can be done in two ways. Globally by comparing globally the query image with all case base images, or using a region-based image retrieval in which each image in the database is split into different regions by the fuzzy c-means method (Archambeau et al. , 2006); then, each region in the input image is compared with all regions in the image in the basis.
For similarity measurement, the Bhattacharyya distance has been adopted (Deb & Zhang, 2004). The distance between two images is computed using the distance between most resembling couples, excluding those having a distance less than a given threshold *th*.
After retrieving the closest image to the input one, the fusion method is deduced from the corresponding case. If the case basis does not contain a case similar to the current one, the three low-level fusion agents are launched.
The last step consists of evaluating the fusion method. The goal of the evaluation agent is to help the expert select the best fusion method for a given sequence of images. In order to accomplish that, we opted for a post-fusion analysis based on a confusion matrix.

4.3.3 Results and validation

In order to evaluate our multi-approcha fusion, we have used data presented in view 1. The possibility method with the T-norm operator was selected as the most suitable fusion method for the first example. For the second example, the possibility method with the mean operator is the most suitable. Tables 5 and 6 shows, respectively, confusion matrices for the possibility methods (T-norm and mean operators).
To evaluate the performance of the proposed approach, we compare CBR results with those obtained following methods: the probability method established on equiprobablity between the five images, the possibility method applied with three types of combination operators (T-norm, T-conorm, and mean). The last method is an unsupervised fusion by evidence theory. The images resulting from these fusion methods will be compared according to OK criteria.

	1	2	3	4	5
1	98.33	1.5	0.17	0.00	0.12
2	1.55	94.75	3.32	0.38	2.88
3	0.11	3.59	91.05	4.92	1.28
4	0.01	0.16	5.33	92.68	2.06
5	0.00	0.00	0.13	2.02	92.66

Table 5. Confusion matrix of the first example.

	1	2	3	4	5
1	93.11	1.03	3.73	2.01	0.12
2	1.02	93.16	2.07	0.87	2.88
3	3.75	1.91	89.05	4.01	1.28
4	2.01	0.82	2.22	92.89	2.06
5	0.11	3.08	2.93	0.22	92.66

Table 6. Confused matrix of the second example.
(1:Humid, 2:Parcel, 3:Cultivated, 4:Urban, 5:Sebkha)

Tables 7 and 8 present a comparison between the probability, possibility, and evidence fusion methods for examples 1 and 2, respectively, according to OK criteria.
As we can see, the possibility method with T-norm and mean operators has the best value for the assessment criteria of the two examples. This result, in perfect correspondence with CBR one, proves that our approach seems to be useful and effective. It allows interpretation process optimization by avoiding the call of the three fusion methods.

Assessment parameter	OK
Probability theory	0.891
Possibilty theory (1)	0.932
Possibilty theory (2)	0.748
Possibilty theory (3)	0.889
Evidence theory	0.921

Table 7. Evaluation of three fusion method for the fist example.

Assessment parameter	OK
Probability theory	0.882
Possibilty theory (1)	0.781
Possibilty theory (2)	0.866
Possibilty theory (3)	0.893
Evidence theory	0.849

Table 8. Evaluation of three fusion method for the second example.

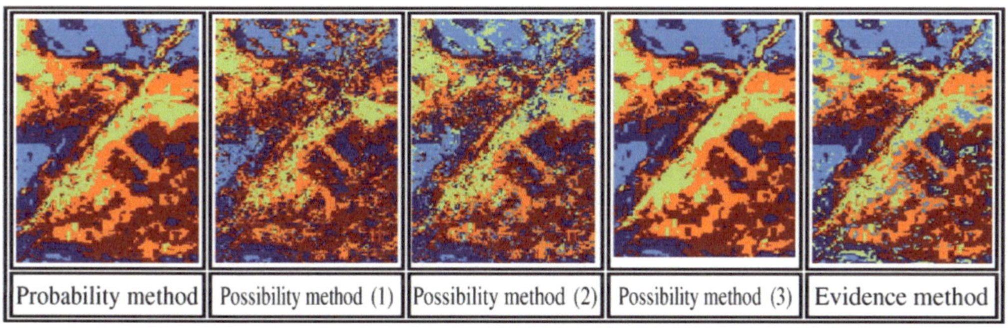

Fig. 15. Classified images for the second example.

5. Discussion

In this chapter, we have presented several views for satellite images fusion. As shown, several kinds of problems hamper and dampen the quality of a reliable images fusion. Images fusion, especially multi-sensor one, is limited by several factors. First, simultaneously acquired multi-sensor images are not always available for the same area and time. Moreover, interpretation is usually limited by spatial resolutions unconformity and data incompatibility. Since there is no common recognized procedure to do this, most studies are regularly forced to find empirically the best fusion scheme, the most useful data and optimal results. Numerous authors have agreed that the fusion should be done usually from separate and heterogeneous data sources. We have introduced, in this chapter, a different kind of fusion that is made at the sub-pixel

level. Thus, the transformation performed at each pixel attempt to provide additional fusion sources. This investigation leads us to overcome the assumption of pixels homogeneity in remotely sensed data. Therefore, newest sources, extracted by bind source separation, offers a new precise and detailed knowledge about land cover proprieties.
We have also addressed the dilemma related to an efficient combination of symbolic knowledge into fusion process in order to increase interpretation quality. We have thus proposed an appropriate framework for this fusion allowing an efficient fusion of both images (extracted additional sources) and In-situ data modelled by a fuzzy rule basis. A learning capability has been added to calibrate and adjust the model.
We also showed that the choice of a specific theory for fusion is a tedious task which must be done carefully; taking into account several parameters such as study context, available data etc. Proposed multi-view is an accomplished way for finest interpretation of large volumes data from multiple sources. Against feature or decision level fusion, all proposed views in this chapter operate in the pixel and sub-pixel have the opportunity to use all available original data. This leads us to reduce the loss of information occurring during the feature extraction process.

6. Conclusions

In this chapter, we reviewed some images fusion approaches on remote sensing field. We have shown, by exposing various interpretation views, that the sub-pixel fusion level has become a successful way to overcome difficulties related to multi-sensor and multi-source images fusion. Hence, the growth of signal processing techniques and symbolic knowledge enable a new fusion leading to an enhanced interpretation quality. Besides knowledge integration, the election of the optimum fusion approach and results evaluation of pixel and sub-pixel level image fusion have been well studied in this chapter, each view was designed to solve a specific fusion issue.
Obtained results show that the sub-pixel fusion level has been rapidly developing and gradually becoming mature. Therefore, fusion process issues and practical matters associated with the implementation of such image fusion strategy should be considered seriously. Challenges remain with regard to developing intelligent fusion methods adapting to vastly different situations. However, there still remain many issues that deserve to be studied further such as mathematic formulation and learning incorporation. In addition, the development of the sub-pixel level image fusion techniques urgently demands widely accepted, objective quality metrics.

7. References

Archambeau, C.; Valle, M.; Assenza, A. & Verleysen M. (2006). Assessment of probability density estimation methods: Parzen window and finite Gaussian mixtures, *In proceedings of IEEE ISCAS*, Vol.11, No.2, pp. 3245-3248, ISBN: 0-7803-9389-9, Septembre 2006.

Babaie-Zadeh, M.; & Jutten, C. (2005). A general approach for mutual information minimization and its application to blind source separation. *Signal Processing*, Vol. 85, No.5, (May 2005) (975-995), ISSN:0165-1684.

Belouchrani, A.; Abed-Meraim, K.; Cardoso J.-F.; & Moulines, E. (1997). A blind source separation technique using second-order statistics. *IEEE Transactions on signal processing*, Vol. 45, No.2, (February 1997) (434-444), ISSN:1053-587X.

Bentabet, L.; Jodouin, S.; & Boudraa, A. (2002). Iterative estimation of Dempster-Shafer's basic probability assignment: application to multisensor image segmentation. *Optical Engineering,* Vol. 41, No.4 , (April 2004)(760–770), ISSN:0091-3286.

Bloch, I. (1996). Information Combination Operators for Data Fusion : A Comparative Review with Classification. *IEEE Transactions on Man, and Cybernetics - Part A : Systems and Humans,* Vol. 26, No.1 , (Janvier 1996)(52-67), ISSN:0196-2892.

Cao, X.R. & Liu, R.-W. (1996). General approach to blind source separation. *IEEE Transactions on signal processing,* Vol. 44, No. , (1996) (562–571), ISSN: 1053-587X.

Cardoso, J.-F.; & Souloumiac, A. (1993). Blind beamforming for non Gaussian signals, *IEEE proceedings of Radar and Signal Processing,* Vol. 140, No.6, pp. 362 - 370, 0956-375X, Toulouse France, December 1993.

Chang, C.-I., & DU, Q. (2004). Estimation of the number of spectrally distinct signal sources in hyperspectral imagery. *IEEE Transactions on Geoscience and Remote Sensing,* Vol. 44, No.3 , (2004)(608-619), ISSN 0196-2892.

Cox, E. (1994). *The fuzzy systems handbook: a practitioner's guide to building, using, and maintaining fuzzy systems,* Academic Press Professional, ISBN:0-12-194270-8, San Diego, CA, USA.

Dasarathy, B.V. (2001). Information fusion - what, where, why, when, and how? *Information Fusion,* Vol. 6, No.4 , (December 2005)(75-76).

Deb, S. & Zhang, Y. (2004). An overview of content-based image retrieval techniques, *In proceedings of 18th Int. Conf. AINA,* Vol., No., pp. 59–64, 2004.

Farah, I.R; & Ahmed, M. B. (2010). Towards an intelligent multi-sensor satellite image analysis based on blind source separation using multi-source image fusion. *IJRS International Journal of Remote Sensing : Taylor & Francis* Vol. 31, No. 1, (10 January 2010)(13–38).

Farah(a), I.R; Boulila, W.; Saheb Ettabaâ, K.; Solaiman, B.; Ben Ahmed, M. (2008). Interpretation of multisensor remote sensing images: Multi-approach fusion of uncertain information. *IEEE Transactions on Geoscience and Remote Sensing,* Vol. 46, No.12 , (Decembre)(4142-4152), ISSN 0196-2892.

Farah(b), I.R; Boulila, W.; Saheb Ettabaâ, K.; Solaiman, B.; Ben Ahmed, M. (2008). Multi-approach system based on fusion of multi-spectral image for land cover classification. *IEEE Transactions on Geoscience and Remote Sensing,* Vol. 46, No.12 , (Decembre)(4153-4161), ISSN 0196-2892.

Farah, I.R.; Saheb Ettabaa, K. & Ben Ahmed M. (2006). A generic multi-agent system for analyzing spatial-temporal geographic information. *International Journal of Computer Science and Network Security,* Vol. 6, No.8 , (Aug 2006)(4–10).

Farah, I.R.; Ahmed, M.B.; & Boussema, M.R. (2003). Multispectral satellite image analysis based on the method of blind separation and fusion of sources, *Proceedings of IEEE International Geoscience and Remote Sensing Symposium,* pp. 3638–3640, ISBN, Toulouse France, May 2003.

Gamba, P.; Dell'Acqua, F.; V. Dasarathy, B.V. (2005). Urban remote sensing using multiple data sets: Past, present, and future. *Information Fusion,* Vol. 6, No.4 , (December 2005)(319-326).

Gianinetto, M. & Villa, P. (2007). Rapid response flood assessment using minimum noise fraction and composed spline interpolation. *IEEE Transactions on Geoscience and Remote Sensing,* Vol. 45, No.10 , (Octobre 2007)(3204–3211), ISSN: 0196-2892.

Goshtasby, A. (2005). *2-D and 3-D Image Registration for Medical, Remote Sensing, and Industrial Applications,* Wiley Publishers, ISBN: 0123725291.

Hall Dave L. & Llinas, J. (1997). Introduction to Multisensor Data Fusion, *Proc. of IEEE,* Vol.85, No.1, pp. 6 - 23, ISSN: 0018-9219, January 1997.

Hemissi, S.; Ben Rabah Z. B. ; Farah, I.R ; Mercier, G. & Solaiman B. (2009). Un modèle neuro-flou pour l'interprétation d'images hyperspectrales : application à la gestion des risques, *TAIMA 2009 Traitement et Analyse de l'Information : Méthodes et Applications,* May 2009, Hammamet Tunisia.

Hyvärinen, A. & Oja, O. (1997). A Fast Fixed-Point Algorithm for Independent Component Analysis. *Neural Computation,* Vol. 9, No., (1997) (1483--1492), ISSN:0899-7667.

Inglada, J. & Mercier, G. (2007). A new statistical similarity measure for change detection in multitemporal SAR images and its extension to multiscale change analysis. *IEEE Transactions on Geoscience and Remote Sensing,* Vol. 45, No.5, (May 2007)(1432–1445), ISSN:0196-2892.

Jurisica, I. & Glasgow, J. (2004). Applications of case-based reasoning in molecular biology. *Artificial Intelligence Magazine. – Special Issue on Bioinformatics,* Vol. 25, No.1 , (May 2004)(85–95), ISSN:0738-4602.

Lawrence A. Klein (2004). *Sensor and Data Fusion: A Tool for Information Assessment and Decision Making (SPIE Press Monograph Vol. PM138),* SPIE- International Society for Optical Engineering, ISBN: 0819454354.

Lin, C.J.; & Lin, C.T. (1997). An ART-based fuzzy adaptive learning control network. *IEEE Transactions on Fuzzy Systems,* Vol. 5, No.4 , (Novembre 1997)(477 - 496), ISSN:1063-6706.

Mahler Ronald P. S. (2007). *Statistical Multisource-Multi-target Information Fusion,* Artech House Inc, ISBN:9781596930926, Norwood MA USA.

Mansour, A.; Barros, A.K; & Ohnish, N. (2000). Blind separation of sources: methods, assumptions and applications. *IEICE Transactions on Fundamentals of Electronics, Communications and Computer Sciences, Special Section on Digital Signal Processing,* Vol. 83, No.A , (2000)(1498-1512).

Pohl, C.; Van Genderen, J.L. (1998). Review article: multisensor image fusion. In Remote sensing: concepts, methods and applications. *International Journal of Remote Sensing,* Vol. 19, No.5 , ()(823-854).

Stathaki, T. (2008). *Image Fusion: Algorithms and Applications,* Academic Press, ISBN: 0123725291.

Tupin, F.; Bloch, I.; & Maître. H. (1999). A first step toward automatic interpretation of SAR images using evidential fusion of several structure detectors. *IEEE Transactions on Geoscience and Remote Sensing,* Vol. 27, No.3 , (May 1999)(1327–1343), ISSN: 0196-2892.

Wald, L. (1999). Some terms of reference in data fusion. *IEEE Transactions on Geoscience and Remote Sensing,* Vol. 37, No.3 , (May 1999) (1190 - 1193), 0196-2892, ISSN: 0196-2892.

Wang, J.; & Chang, C.-I. (2006). Applications of independent component analysis in endmember extraction and abundance quantication for hyperspectral imagery. *IEEE Transactions on Geoscience and Remote Sensing,* Vol. 44, No.9 , (September 2006)(2601 - 2616), 0196-2892, ISSN: 0196-2892.

Yuhas, R.H.; Goetz, A.F.H.; & Boardman, J.W. (1992). Discrimination Among Semi-Arid Landscape Endmembers Using the Spectral Angle Mapper (SAM) Algorithm, *Summaries of the 4th JPL Airborne Earth Science Workshop,* Vol. 92, No.41, pp. 147-149.

Yu, H.-L.; Christakos, G. (2010). Modeling and Estimation of Heterogeneous Spatiotemporal Attributes Under Conditions of Uncertainty. *IEEE Transactions on Geoscience and Remote Sensing,* Vol. 48, No. 9, (Aout 2010) 11 (1 - 11).

4

Performance Evaluation of Image Fusion Methods

Vassilis Tsagaris, Nikos Fragoulis and Christos Theoharatos
Irida Labs
Greece

1. Introduction

The recent advances in sensor technology, microelectronics and multisensor systems have motivated researchers towards processing techniques that combine the information obtained from different sensors. For this purpose a large number of image fusion techniques [Mukhopadhyay & Chanda, 2001; Pohl & van Genderen, 1998, Tsagaris & Anastassopoulos, 2005; Piella, 2003] have been proposed in the fields of remote sensing, medical diagnostics, military applications, surveillance etc. The main goal of these image fusion techniques is to provide a compact representation of the multiple input images into a single grayscale one that contains all the important original features. Such an image provides improved interpretation capabilities but can also be used for further computer processing tasks, like feature extraction or classification.

The performance of image fusion techniques is sometimes assessed subjectively by human visual inspection. The reproduction of subjective tests is often time-consuming and expensive, while the exact same conditions for the test cannot be guaranteed. This has led to a rising demand for objective measures in order to rapidly compare the results obtained with different algorithms or to obtain optimal settings for a specific fusion algorithm. The objective evaluation of the performance of pixel level fusion methods is addressed in this book chapter. The image fusion processes can be classified in grayscale or color methods depending on the resulting fused image.

For this purpose the general framework of objective evaluation of image fusion is discussed and different fusion measures are discussed. Moreover, a global measure for grayscale image fusion schemes, *IFPM*, based on information theory is presented. The measure employs mutual and conditional mutual information in order to assess and represent the amount of information transferred from the source images to the final fused grayscale image. Accordingly, the common information contained in the source images is considered only once in the performance evaluation procedure. The experimental results clarify the applicability of the *IFPM* measure in comparing different fusion methods or in optimizing the parameters of a specific algorithm.

Moreover, a measure for objectively assessing the performance of color image fusion methods, *CIFM*, is presented in this chapter. Two different aspects are considered in establishing the measure, namely the amount of common information between the source images and the final fused image as well as the distribution of color information in the final image in order to achieve optimal color representation. Mutual information and conditional mutual information are employed in order to assess information transfer between the source images and the final fused image. Simultaneously, the distribution of colors in the final image is explored by means of the hue coordinate in the perceptually uniform CIELAB space. The proposed measure does not depend on the use of a target fused image for the objective performance evaluation. It is employed experimentally for objective evaluation of fusion methods in the cases of medical imaging and night vision data.

2. Image fusion measures

The problem of objective evaluation has not been addressed only in image fusion applications. A large number of metrics has been proposed over the years for assessing image and video fidelity. An informative overview on the topic can be found in [Avcibas et al, 2002]. These measures cannot be applied to evaluate image fusion methods since they require an ideal target image. Such an image is not always available as it happens in the field of remote sensing or medical imaging.

The performance of image fusion techniques is sometimes assessed subjectively by human visual inspection [Toet and Franken, 2003]. The reproduction of subjective tests is often time-consuming and expensive, while the exact same conditions for the test cannot be guaranteed. This has led to a rising demand for objective measures in order to rapidly compare the results obtained with different algorithms or to obtain optimal settings for a specific fusion algorithm.

In this context, [Xydeas & Petrovic, 2000] proposed a measure based on edge information that is probably the first objective image fusion measure. The authors associated the important visual information with the "edge" information that is present in each pixel of an image. The evaluation of the amount of edge information that is transferred from input images to the fused image is employed as a measure of fusion performance. The edge detection process is based on Sobel algorithm that is applied both horizontally and vertically. The edge strength and the orientation information for each pixel are comprised and for an input image A we calculate

$$g_A(n,m) = \sqrt{S_A^x(n,m)^2 + S_A^y(n,m)^2} \tag{1}$$

$$\alpha_A(n,m) = \arctan\left(\frac{S_A^y(n,m)}{S_A^x(n,m)}\right) \tag{2}$$

Relative values of edge strength and orientation are calculated for a source image A and a fused image F is

$$G^{AF}(n,m) = \begin{cases} \frac{g_F(n,m)}{g_A(n,m)} & \text{if } g_A(n,m) \geq g_F(n,m) \\ \frac{g_A(n,m)}{g_F(n,m)} & \text{otherwise} \end{cases} \tag{3}$$

These are used to derive the edge strength and orientation preservation values

$$Q_g^{AF}(n,m) = \frac{\Gamma_g}{1+e^{k_g(G^{AF}(n,m)-\sigma_g)}} \tag{4}$$

$$Q_{\alpha}^{AF}(n,m) = \frac{\Gamma_{\alpha}}{1+e^{k_{\alpha}(A^{AF}(n,m)-\sigma_{\alpha})}} \tag{5}$$

$Q_g^{AF}(n,m)$ and $Q_\alpha^{AF}(n,m)$ model perceptual loss of information in F, in terms of how well the strength and orientation values of a pixel in A are represented in the fused image. The constants Γ_g, k_g, σ_g and Γ_a, k_a, σ_a determine the exact shape of the sigmoid functions used to form the edge strength and orientation preservation values. Edge information preservation values are then defined as

$$Q^{AF}(n,m) = Q_g^{AF}(n,m)Q_\alpha^{AF}(n,m) \tag{6}$$

while Q^{AF} takes its values in the range zero to one. A value of zero corresponds to the complete loss of edge information, at location (n,m), as transferred from A into F. $Q^{AF} = 1$ indicates "fusion" from A to F with no loss of information. The authors have also proposed weighted versions of the Q^{AF} criterion. The main drawback of this approach is the loss of information related with texture since it is mostly based on edge detection.
Moreover, in [Piella & Heijmans, 2003], an image quality index proposed by [Wang & Bovik, 2002] has been used for image fusion assessment. This measure is based on the second order statistics of both the source images and the final fused image, in order to assess fusion performance. The Q_0 measure is calculated as:

$$Q_0 = \frac{4\sigma_{xy}\bar{x}\bar{y}}{(\bar{x}^2+\bar{y}^2)(\sigma_x^2+\sigma_y^2)} \tag{7}$$

but it can also be analyzed as:

$$Q_0 = \frac{\sigma_{xy}}{\sigma_x\sigma_y} \cdot \frac{2\bar{x}\bar{y}}{\bar{x}^2+\bar{y}^2} \cdot \frac{2\sigma_x\sigma_y}{\sigma_x^2+\sigma_y^2} \tag{8}$$

Each image is a random variable x, and its mean value and variance are $\bar{x}, \sigma_x^2$ respectively. The first term in (8) is the correlation coefficient between images x and y. The value of Q_0 ranges between -1 and 1 and is a measure of similarity between the two images. Piella and Heijmans, were based on the fact that image signals are generally non-stationary, thus it is more appropriate to measure the image quality index Q_0 over local regions and then combine the different results into a single measure. The fusion measure is given by

$$Q(a,b,f) = \frac{1}{|W|}\sum_{w\in W}\big(\lambda(w)\big)Q_0(a,f|w) + (1-\lambda(w))Q_0(b,f|w) \tag{9}$$

where $\lambda(w)$ are local weights in the range of zero to one.
The ERGAS measure [Wald et al, 1997] which is an error index that offers a global picture of the quality of a fused product. The index is called ERGAS after its name in French, means relative dimensionless global error and is given by

$$ERGAS = 100a\sqrt{\frac{1}{K}\sum_{k=1}^{K}\left(\frac{RMSE(k)}{\mu(k)}\right)^2} \tag{10}$$

where a is the ratio between pixel sizes in cases of pansharpened and multispectral images, $\mu(k)$ is the mean of the K band and K is the number of bands. According to the authors, an ERGAS value greater than 3 corresponds to fused products of low quality, while an ERGAS value lower than 3 denotes a product of satisfactory quality.

Especially for remote sensing applications, [Alparone et al, 2004] proposed the Q4 index that is suitable for MS imagery having four spectral bands. Both spectral and radiometric distortion measurements are encapsulated in a unique measurement, simultaneously accounting for local mean bias, changes in contrast, and loss of correlation of individual bands, together with spectral distortion.

More recently, the measures that have been proposed for objective evaluation of image fusion are based in information theory. These approaches provide a more general assessment of each image and have attracted the interest of a lot of researchers. A short discussion on basics of information theory is needed before presenting the *IFPM* and *CIFM* measures for grayscale and color image fusion respectively.

In [Qu et al, 2002], the authors introduced an information measure for image fusion assessment, which employs mutual information for representing the amount of information that is transferred from the source images to the final fused image. The overall fusion performance is the sum of mutual information between each source image and the final fused image. In this approach only the common information between each of the source images and the fused image is considered whereas no attention has been paid to the overlapping information of the source images. Additionally, the values of this measure are not bounded, e.g. in the range $[0-1]$, so the comparison between different fusion algorithms and data sets is not straightforward. The concepts of the overlapping information and comparable fusion performance are also considered in the following fusion measures.

3. Information theory basics

In this section the basic concepts from information theory, that are needed to describe the information and the common information between images, are provided. These concepts are used in different image fusion measures in order to evaluate and describe the amount of information in each image as well as common information between two or more images.

Each source image or the final grayscale image is considered as being a discrete random variable. The entropy or total information H(x) for a discrete random variable X, is defined as

$$H(X) = -\sum_x p(x) log p(x) \tag{11}$$

where $p(x)$ is the probability density function of the variable. Entropy is always a finite, positive number for discrete random variables and takes its maximum value in the case of a uniformly distributed variable. In the case of an image, entropy describes the total amount of information. The joint entropy $H(X,Y)$ for a pair of random variables X, Y with joint distribution $p(x,y)$ is defined as

$$H(X,Y) = -\sum_x \sum_y p(x,y) log p(x,y) \tag{12}$$

In addition the conditional entropy of a random variable X given the random variable Y is expressed as

$$H(X|Y) = -\sum_x \sum_y p(x,y) log p(x|y) \tag{13}$$

The chain rule for two variables is expressed as $H(X,Y) = H(X) + H(Y|X)$. The generalized entropy chain rule is

$$H(X_1, X_2, \dots, X_N) = H(X_1) + \sum_{i=2}^{N} H(X_i|X_{i-1}, \dots, X_1) \quad (14)$$

The common information shared between two random variables X, Y is expressed by the mutual information that is defined as

$$I(X;Y) = \sum_x \sum_y p(x,y) log \frac{p(x,y)}{p(x)p(y)} \quad (15)$$

It can be proved that mutual information is always a positive quantity that vanishes only if $p(x,y) = p(x)p(y)$. Therefore, it can be interpreted as a measure of the statistical dependence between X and Y. The relationship between mutual information and conditional entropy is given by

$$I(X_1, X_2, .., X_N; Y) = H(X_1, X_2, \dots, X_N) - H(X_1, X_2, \dots, X_N|Y) \quad (16)$$

The above quantities are schematically demonstrated by the Venn diagram of Figure 1.

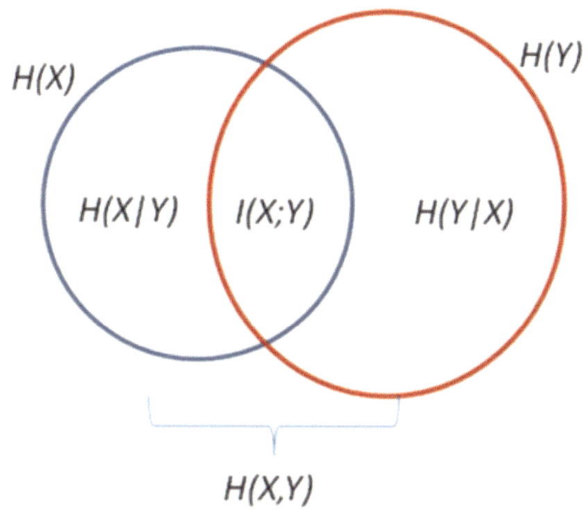

Fig. 1. The relationship between entropy and mutual information for two variables

The conditional mutual information of random variables X_1 and X_2 given Y is defined by

$$I(X_1; Y|X_2) = H(X_1|X_2) - H(X_1|Y, X_2) \quad (17)$$

and can be seen as the reduction in the uncertainty of X_1 due to the knowledge of Y when X_2 is given [Cover & Tomas, 1991]. The interpretation of conditional mutual information in a Venn diagram can be found in Figure 2. Apparently, conditional mutual information describes the shared information between two variables when a third variable has already been considered. Thus, conditional mutual information is employed to address the problem of overlapping information. The chain rule for mutual information is expressed as

$$I(X_1, X_2, \dots, X_n; Y) = I(X_1; Y) + \sum_{i=2}^{n} I(X_1; Y|X_{i-1}, \dots, X_2, X_1) \quad (18)$$

The $IFPM$ measure is based on mutual information in order to evaluate the amount of information that is transferred from the source images to the final fused representation. Moreover, the use of conditional mutual information guarantees that the overlapping information of the source images is considered only once.

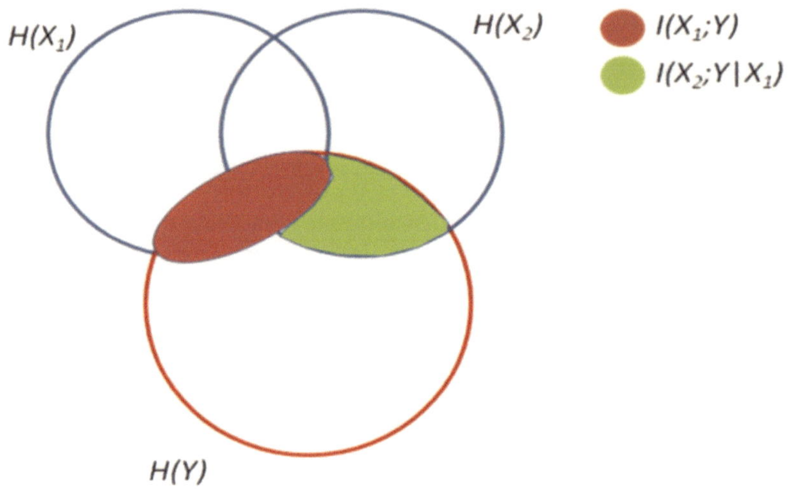

Fig. 2. The conditional mutual information for three variables

4. Grayscale image fusion evaluation

The purpose of an image fusion process is to combine a number of multimodal or multispectral images into a final entity that comprises the maximum possible information, which is present in the source images. The source images often exhibit a high degree of correlation since the same area is covered in different regions of the electromagnetic spectrum or with complementary imaging technologies. Thus, the same information can be found in more than one of the source images and is described as overlapping information. For example, in the case of multispectral imagery, each band reveals different aspects of the same scene but, at the same time, a large amount of overlapping information can be seen due to texture or spectral correlation. In an objective assessment of the effectiveness of a fusion algorithm the overlapping information should be considered only once and this problem has not been addressed in the existing measures.

4.1 The IFPM measure

The aim of the authors' work in [Tsagaris & Anastassopoulos, 2006] was to provide an information-based global measure for objective performance evaluation of image fusion schemes. The proposed Image Fusion Performance Measure (*IFPM*) employs mutual information as well as conditional mutual information in order to evaluate the amount of information transferred from the source images to the final fused image.
IFPM is based on information quantities in order to objectively evaluate the performance of a fusion method. These quantities are evaluated all over the image resulting in a measure that can be regarded as global or universal. Each source image X_i is treated as a discrete random variable with corresponding pdf (x_i), while all the information quantities, described in the previous section, are employed. The resulting fused image is denoted as Y while the corresponding probability density function as $p(y)$. Mutual information $I(X_1;Y)$ describes the common information between the source image X_1 and the final fused image Y. The conditional mutual information $I(X_2;Y|X_1)$ describes the common information between X_2 and Y given X_1. In this way, only the information that is present in X_2 is considered in the evaluation of the common information between X_2 and Y. In its general form the conditional

mutual information $I(X_n;Y|X_{n-1},..,X_2,X_1)$ guarantees that the overlapping information between the source images X_i is considered only once. The sum of all the conditional information represents the total amount of common information CI, transferred from the source images X_i to the final fused image Y and is expressed as

$$CI = I(X_1;Y) + I(X_2;Y|X_1) + \cdots + I(X_N;Y|X_{N-1},\dots,X_1) \tag{19}$$

On the other hand the joint entropy $H(X_1, X_2, \dots, X_n)$ represents the total amount of information that is present in the source images. The Image Fusion Performance Measure ($IFPM$) is defined as

$$IFPM = \frac{CI}{H(X_1,X_2,\dots,X_n)} \tag{20}$$

$IFPM$ takes values in the range $[0-1]$ where zero corresponds to total lack of common information between the source and the fused image and one corresponds to an effective fusion process that transfers all the information from the source images to the fused image (ideal case).

4.2 Evaluation of grayscale image fusion based on *IFPM*

In order to have a descriptive overview of objective evaluation we employ $IFPM$ in order to compare four different fusion methods applied to three different data sets. The first fusion method that will be further referred to as Method 1, is a simple averaging of the source images. Method 2 is the well-known principal component analysis (PCA) algorithm, which is applied to the source images and the first principal component is considered as the final fused image. An approach based on discrete wavelet transform (DWT) and specifically on DBSS(2,2) is considered as Method 3 [Piella, 2003]. Finally, a fusion approach based on multiscale morphological pyramid [Mukhopadhyay and Chanda, 2001] is employed as Method 4.

The first data set used in this work consists of four multispectral bands and has been acquired by IKONOS-2 sensor. The radiometric resolution of each band is 11 bits. The ground resolution provided by IKONOS-2 for the multispectral imagery is 4m. The spectral range of the sensor is in the visible and near infrared region of the EM spectrum. The area covered in this multispectral image is mainly an urban area with a structured road network, a forest, a stadium, a park etc. The natural color composite image is shown in Figure 3(a), while in Figure 3(b), the near-infrared band is depicted. For perceptual comparison of the four fusion methods, their output fused images are demonstrated in Figure 3(c) to 3(f) for the fusion methods 1 to 4 respectively. A comparison of the fusion results at this point, from a perceptual point of view, reveals that all fusion methods provide an improved representation with methods 2 and 3 (PCA and DWT) to perform superiorly.

The second data set is derived from the night vision research area and comprises a color image of a scene representing a sandy path, trees and fences (Fig. 4(a)) and a midwave infrared (3-5μm) image in which a person is standing behind the trees and close to the fence, as shown in Fig. 4(b). The data set has been provided by TNO, Human Factors and a more detailed description of the data acquisition procedure can be found in [Toet, 2003]. The results of the four fusion methods are available for subjective visual evaluation in Figure 4(c)-4(f). Similar comments regarding the performance of the four methods, from a perceptual point, are valid for this data set as well.

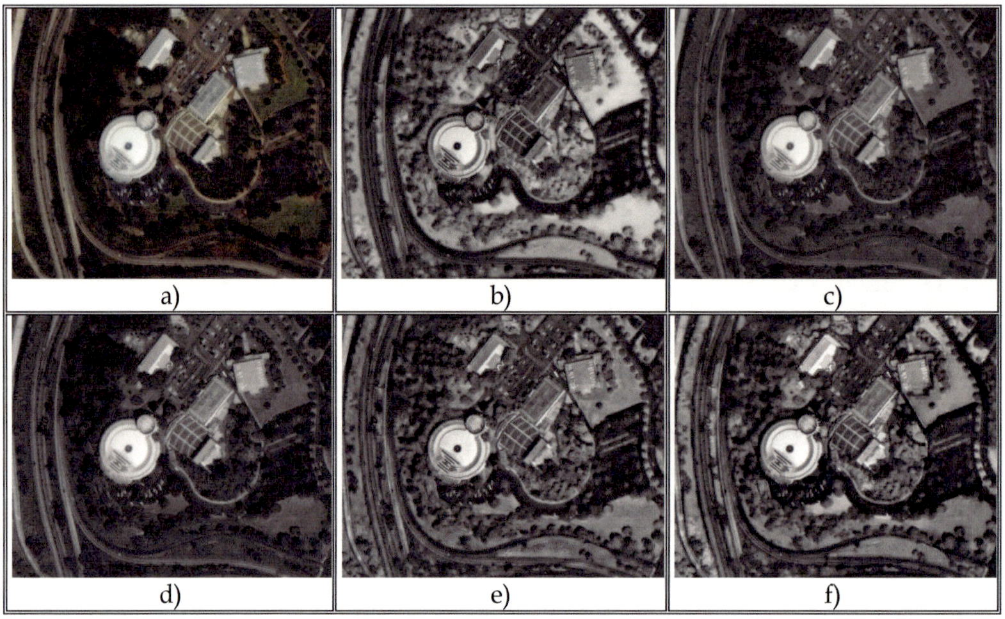

Fig. 3. Source images (a) Natural color composite of the first three bands (b) the near infrared band. Results for (c) averaging (d) PCA (e) DWT and (f) morphological fusion methods

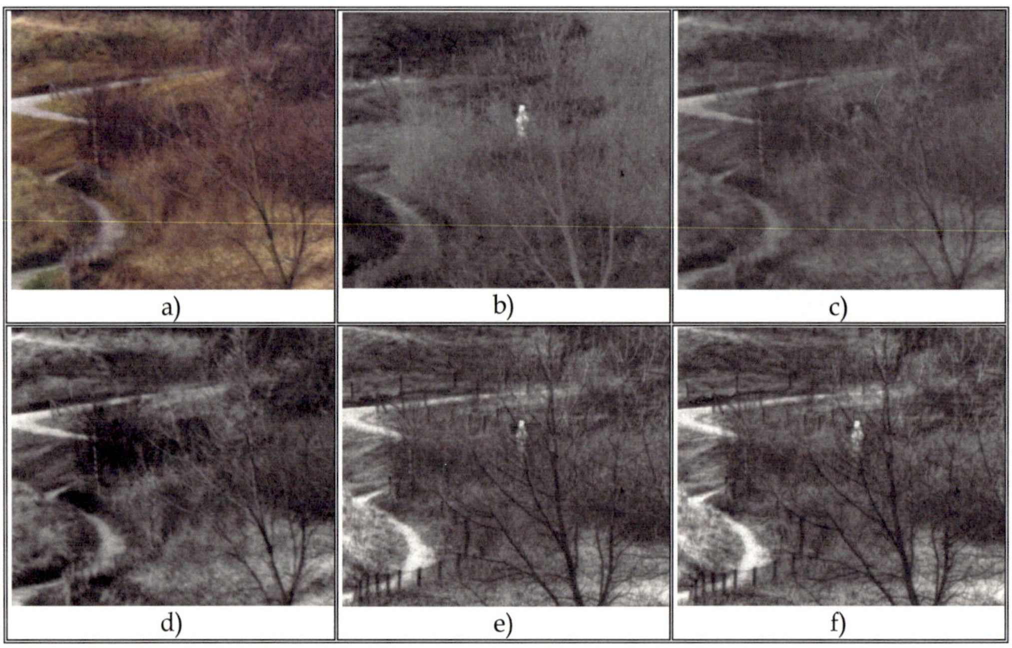

Fig. 4. Source images (a) Natural color composite of the first three bands (b) the near infrared band. Results for (c) averaging (d) PCA (e) DWT and (f) morphological fusion

The evaluation of the four fusion methods for two different data sets based on the information theory measures can be found in Table 1 and reveals some interesting aspects of image fusion. The first conclusion is that there is no superior or outperforming image fusion method that can be used regardless the application. This conclusion has also been reported in [Toet and Franken, 2003, Qu et al, 2002] and proves that evaluation of image fusion performance in a real application, without having an ideal target image, is a complicated issue. Moreover, the type of the data involved in the image fusion process plays an important role. For example, in the case of high resolution multispectral data the source images to be fused possess a lot of features or objects with high edge information content. On the other hand, if thermal imagery is to be fused the visual features that are to be merged have a rather coarse outline.

The authors of [Tsagaris and Anastassopoulos, 2006] have compared the two measures in order to reveal the concept of overlapping information with a trivial case in which overlapping information is present between the source images. The results demonstrated that *IFPM* measure is not affected by the overlapping information, while the same conclusion does not hold for *MI* measure. Moreover, *IFPM* provide largest percentages of differentiation between the fusion methods and gives comparable results.

	Dataset 1 Remote sensing		Dataset 2 Night vision	
	IFPM	*MI*	*IFPM*	*MI*
Method 1	0.2629	3.4755	0.3104	2.0684
Method 2	0.2993	3.9023	0.3247	3.2043
Method 3	0.3050	3.4318	0.3704	2.8024
Method 4	0.2434	1.7036	0.4063	3.5632

Table 1. Objective performance evaluation using *IFPM* and *MI* for the two datasets

5. Color image fusion

The objective measures discussed so far address the problem of grayscale image fusion that is fusion methods that result in grayscale representations. However, these measures cannot be trivially extended into color image fusion techniques.

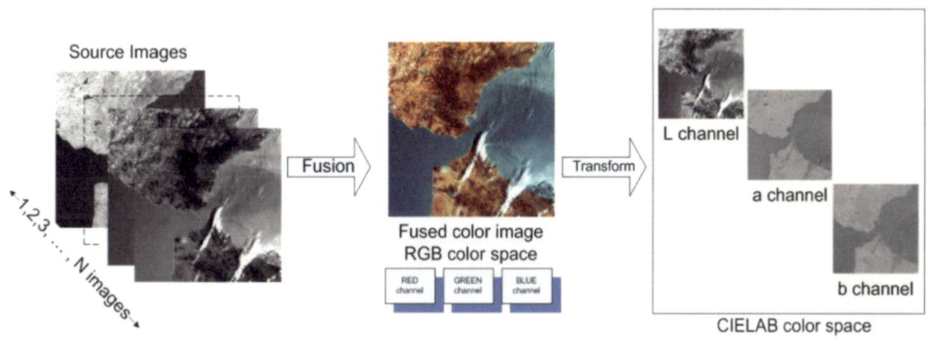

Fig. 5. Color image fusion process

In an ordinary fusion procedure, N multimodal or multispectral images are regarded as being the source images to be fused in order to produce a final color representation as shown in Figure 5. This color representation should perform as an ideal candidate for both detection and classification purposes and furthermore, be perceptually of high quality. Fusion methods that result in color images have to be assessed for the way they distribute the source information in the intensity, hue and saturation components since the main motivation behind color image fusion is the ability of the human vision system to distinguish thousands of colors. The fused color image is often formed in the RGB color space that is used in nowadays standard display devices and most computer vision tasks. However, the transformation of the color image in a uniform color space like CIELAB seems suitable in order to objectively evaluate the image fusion performance since in this color space the luminance component is independent of the chromaticity components.
Assessment of the effectiveness of a fusion method to result in a final image with maximum perceivable color information should be carried out in a perceptually uniform color space. The perceptually uniform CIELAB space consists of an achromatic luminosity component L^* and two chromatic values a^* and b^*, each one incorporating opponent colors [Malacara, 2002]. An alternative way to represent color characteristics is by transforming the $L^*a^*b^*$ components into cylindrical C^*_{ab} and h^*_{ab} coordinates on the a^*b^* plane, given by

$$C^*_{ab} = [a^{*2} + b^{*2}]^{1/2} \tag{21}$$

$$h^*_{ab} = arctan\left[\frac{b^*}{a^*}\right] \tag{22}$$

where C^*_{ab} correlates with chroma and h^*_{ab} is an angle correlating with hue. In this system, an average observer is more sensitive to hue than to chroma differences [Malacara, 2002]. The $IFPM$ measure employs the h^*_{ab} coordinate to evaluate the color distribution in the final fused color image.

5.1 The CIFM measure

An approach for objectively assessing the performance of image fusion methods resulting in color images should address two issues. The problem of transferring information from the sources images and in the same time the problem of distributing this information in a color image that is color distribution in the final representation. The sources images could be either several grayscale images or a color image and grayscale images. In the case of a RGB color image each channel is regarded as a grayscale image.
The Color Image Fusion Measure (*CIFM*) presented in [Tsagaris, 2009] takes into consideration the amount of information transferred to the final image and, at the same time, the variety of colors obtained. It is a two component vector and each component deals with one of the two issues of the objective color image fusion evaluation previously described. The first terms concerns the amount of common information CI, between the intensity component of the final fused color image in the CIELAB color space, denoted as L^* and the source images X_i expressed as

$$CI = I(X_1; L^*) + I(X_2; L^*|X_1) + \cdots + I(X_N; L^*|X_{N-1}, \ldots, X_1) \tag{23}$$

or equivalently

$$CI = I(X_1; L^*) + \sum_{i=2}^{N} I(X_i; L^*|X_{i-1}, \ldots, X_1) \tag{24}$$

The joint entropy $H(X_1, X_2, \ldots, X_n)$ represents the total amount of information that is present in the source images and is used in order to derive a normalized version of the amount of common information. The Image Fusion Performance Measure ($IFPM$) was defined as

$$IFPM = \frac{CI}{H(X_1, X_2, \ldots, X_{N})} \tag{25}$$

The angular coordinate h^*_{ab} is additionally employed in order to evaluate the distribution of colors and hues in the final image. In [Tsagaris & Anastassopoulos, 2005(b)] the concept of an image with Maximum Realizable Color Information (MRCI) and uniformly distributed information in the CIELAB color space and thus maximum perceivable information was proposed. The evaluation of the marginal distribution is carried out numerically using the uniformly distributed vector population in the CIELAB space for the MRCI image and it turns out that these marginal probabilities are not uniform [Tsagaris & Anastassopoulos, 2005(b)] mainly due to the non-cylindrical shape of the CIELAB color space. In order to evaluate the color distribution the authors employed the angular coordinate h^*_{ab} and its marginal probability density function $p(h^*_{ab})$ which is calculated using

$$p(h^*_{ab}) = \iint_{L,C} p(L^*, C^*_{ab}, h^*_{ab}) dL^* dC^*_{ab} \tag{26}$$

The color image resulting from the fusion process is considered in the CIELAB space and its h^*_{ab} coordinate has a marginal pdf denoted as $q(h^*_{ab})$. The Kullback-Leibler or relative entropy distance between the probability mass functions $p(h^*_{ab})$ and $q(h^*_{ab})$ is employed in order to quantify the similarity between the distribution of the color image resulted from the fusion process and the image with the maximum perceivable information. It is defined as

$$D(p^*_{ab} || q^*_{ab}) = \sum_h p(h^*_{ab}) h log \frac{p(h^*_{ab})}{q(h^*_{ab})} \tag{27}$$

If $q(h^*_{ab})$ is close to $p(h^*_{ab})$, the quantity $D(p^*_{ab} || q^*_{ab})$ is close to zero, which means that the image resulting from the fusion process, with histogram $q(h^*_{ab})$ has a an almost ideal distribution of color and hues in the CIELAB space. In order to have an easily comparable measure we propose the Hue Distribution (HD) is given by

$$HD = 1 - D(p^*_{ab} || q^*_{ab}) = 1 - \sum_h p(h^*_{ab}) h log \frac{p(h^*_{ab})}{q(h^*_{ab})} \tag{28}$$

The $CIFM$ is expressed as

$$CIFM = (IFPM, HD) \tag{29}$$

The two vector components deals with the two problems of the objective color image fusion evaluation discussed in the previous section. A large value of $IFPM$ indicates that a large amount of information is transferred from the source images to the luminance L^* of the final fused color image. The use of mutual information along with conditional mutual information guarantees that no overlapping information is considered in this objective evaluation. Simultaneously, the HD term measures the divergence of the hue coordinate in the CIELAB space of the fused color image from the hue coordinate of an image with uniform distribution in the CIELAB space. In this way, it provides an objective assessment of the variety of colors in the specially selected h^*_{ab} coordinate. Both vector components are calculated in the CIELAB color space in order to take advantage of the perceptual uniformity of this color space and the independency between the luminosity component L^* and the chromatic components.

5.2 Objective evaluation of color image fusion methods

The proposed $CIFM$ is experimentally used in this section in order to assess the performance of four different fusion methods resulting in color images. In the following paragraphs a short description of the tested fusion methods is provided. Moreover, the experimental data from three different application areas are presented. Then, the two components of the $CIFM$ measure, namely $IFPM$ and HD are calculated for all data sets and for each fusion method and the results are discussed in order to derive conclusions.

Method 1 - The first fusion scheme, will be referred to as Method 1, is the well known Karhunen-Loewe transform or equivalently principal components analysis (PCA). In this approach the source data are transformed into an orthogonal space and then the first three principal components corresponding to the largest eigenvalues of the covariance matrix, are mapped to the RGB channels in order to form a color image.

Method 2 - This color image fusion scheme is based on perceptual attributes [Tsagaris & Anastassopoulos, 2005]. The approach takes into consideration the inherent high correlation of the RGB bands in natural images. The resulting image is directly formed in the RGB color space and no further transformation is needed. The main advantage of the method is that it results in fused color images with adjustable covariance matrix.

Method 3 - A large variety of color image fusion methods based on wavelet methods has been proposed in the literature [Piella, 2003]. In these approaches the wavelet decomposition of the original images is merged using different fusion rules applied to the approximations coefficients and the details coefficients. Then inverse wavelet transform is applied to the merged coefficients in order to derive the final fused color image. Method 3 is based on the DBSS(2,2) wavelet and fusion is applied by taking the maximum for approximation and the minimum for the details coefficients.

Method 4 - Finally, Method 4 [Tsagaris & Anastassopoulos, 2005] is a fusion scheme based on non-negative matrix factorization [Lee & Seung, 1999] and the application of a color transfer technique. In this way an additive representation of the source features is obtained while inappropriate color mappings are avoided due to the use of color transfer. Simultaneously, the overall discrimination capabilities in the final fused color image are enhanced.

The source experimental data employed in this work are three data sets one derived from the field of medical imaging, the second from the area of night vision and the third from the field of remote sensing. These data sets originate from different research fields and are acquired with different imaging techniques in order to cover in the experimental results different source data and a variety of research challenges in image fusion.

Dataset 1 - The first data set is composed of multi-modal medical images selected from the Brain Atlas collection of the Medical Harvard School. A four-dimensional vector space is considered, where a greyscale magnetic resonance image (MRI) and the three components of a computed tomography (CT) pseudo-color image, shown in Figure 6 (a) and (b) respectively, define the axes of this space. The two images are registered and of the same size. Employing the aforementioned fusion methods, four different final color images are obtained as shown in Figure 6(c) – (f) respectively.

Dataset 2 - The second data set is from the research field of night vision and thermal imaging, and was also described in the case of grayscale image fusion. It comprises a color

image of a scene representing a sandy path, trees and fences and a midwave infrared (3-5μm) image in which a person is standing behind the trees and close to the fence.
Dataset 3 - The third data set originates from the field of remote sensing. It consists of multispectral data acquired from the ENVISAT satellite and specifically MERIS sensor. MERIS (MEdium Resolution Imaging Spectrometer Instrument) measures the solar radiation reflected by the Earth at a ground spatial resolution of 300m, in 15 spectral bands, programmable in width and position, in the visible and near infra-red region of the electromagnetic spectrum. The geographical area is in the South part of Greece and covers both sea and land. The results of the previously described fusion methods can be found in Figure 7.

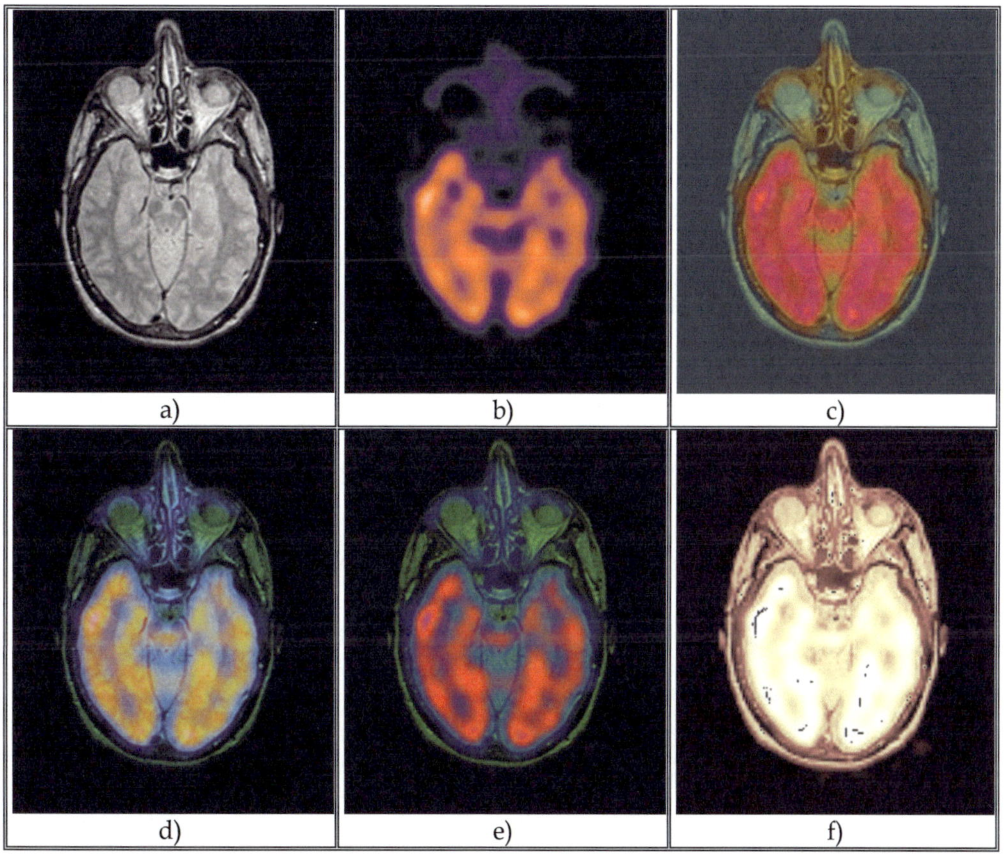

Fig. 6. Source data and fused color images. In (a) original MRI image and (b) the corresponding PET image (registered). (c) result of Method 1, (d) result of Method 2, (e) result of Method 3 and (f) result of Method 4

The proposed $CIFM$ vector measure is calculated for the above described color image fusion methods. The two components of the measure namely, $IFPM$ and HD are calculated and the results are summarized in Table 2 for the medical data. In the case of the medical data set Method 2 outperforms other methods for both $IFPM$ and HD vector components whilst

Method 4, based on NMF is having a comparable performance. The first method based on PCA is having a significant performance as derived from the IFPM measure but it achieves poor results in the color distribution since the final color image is dominated by red color (first principal component). The Method 3 based on wavelet approach provides a good solution but not the best one.

The same procedure for the calculation of the proposed measure is applied for the case of the night vision data. In the case of the second dataset Method 3 provides the best results in both *IFPM* and *HD* measures. Method 2 is the second best solution and demonstrates a comparable high performance since it merges all the important features of the source images in the final fused representation. The poor performance of Method 1 is mainly due to the statistical nature of the PCA approach that fails to transfer small details of the source images in the final fused color image.

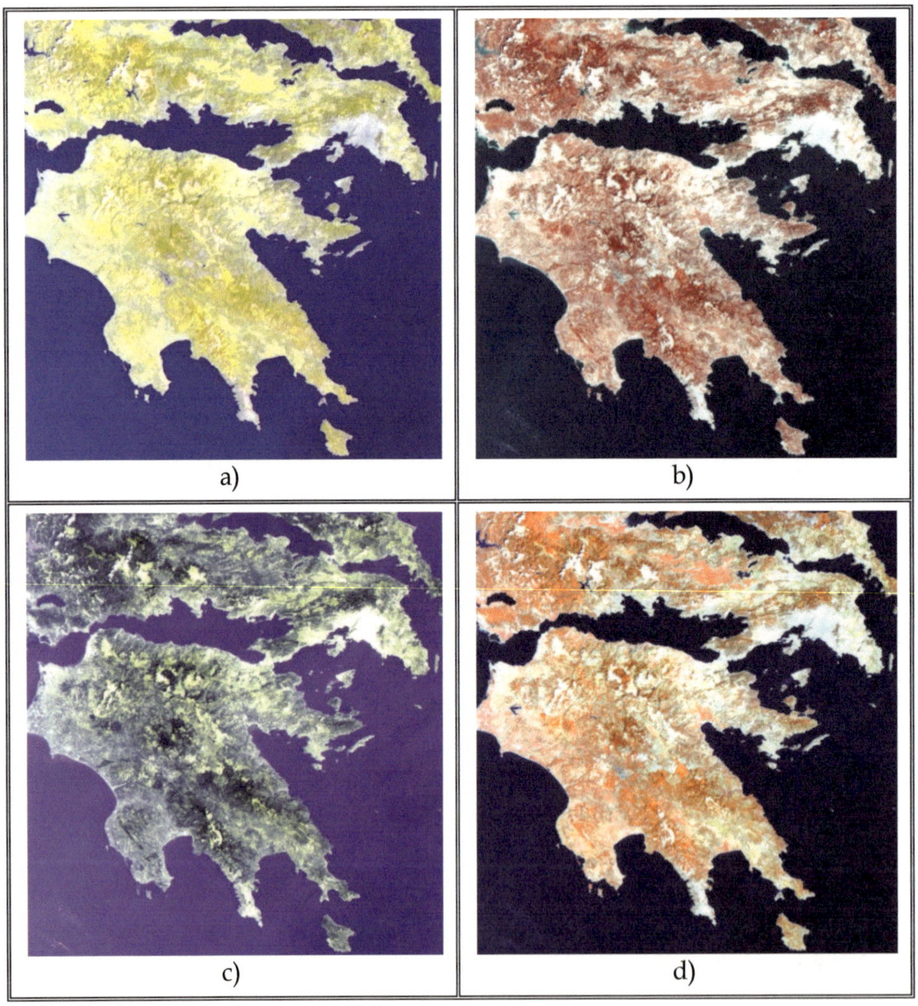

Fig. 7. Source Results of the fusion methods applied on MERIS data. In (a) result of Method 1, (b) result of Method 2, (c) result of Method 3 and (d) result of Method 4

The vector components of the $CIFM$ measure are also calculated for the case of the third dataset from the field of remote sensing. Method 2 achieves superior performance in both $IFPM$ and HD components for the case of the third dataset. The fusion method that is based on the wavelet approach is having a comparable performance especially in the color distribution expressed by HD measure. Method 4 achieves rather good but not optimal results in any measure whilst Method 1 fails to provide an efficient performance both in the information transfer but also in the color distribution.

These results are compliant with findings reported for the cases of grayscale image fusion [Toet & Franken, 2003, Xydeas & Petrovic, 2000, Qu et al, 2002, Tsagaris & Anastassopoulos, 2006] which state that there is no superior image fusion method that can be applied in all datasets. Thus, objective evaluation of fusion schemes should be employed in order to decide on the best available solution for the specific application. Moreover, image fusion measures are also useful in parameter calculation and optimization for a specific image fusion method.

	Dataset 1 Medical data		Dataset 2 Night vision		Dataset 3 Remote sensing	
	IFPM	*HD*	*IFPM*	*HD*	*IFPM*	*HD*
Method 1 - PCA	0.3601	0.0503	0.1912	0.4848	0.2466	0.2811
Method 2 - VTVA	0.4850	0.9201	0.2423	0.6418	0.4248	0.7758
Method 3 - DBSS	0.3562	0.6216	0.2805	0.9034	0.3709	0.7558
Method 4 - NMF	0.4485	0.8444	0.2085	0.5997	0.3687	0.5226

Table 2. Objective performance evaluation using $IFPM$ and HD for the different datasets

The two components of the $CIFM$ measure can also be used for a graphical representation in order to evaluate image fusion methods. The $CIFM$ vector components, namely $IFPM$ and HD provide an orthogonal base for a two dimensional vector space ($IFPM$, HD) where each fusion method is regarded as a single point. Each vector component can also be used independently in certain applications. For example, $IFPM$ could be employed if the amount of information transferred from the source images to the final image is important since further digital processing will be employed. On the other hand if the fused image will be used by visual experts then special attention should be given to the color distribution and thus HD provide a useful tool.

The results of Table 2 are depicted in a graphical representation in Figure 8. The same conclusions about the performance of the four different fusion methods can be derived from this figure. Based on this representation, one may try to describe the $CIFM$ measure in a scalar rather than a vector form, i.e. to use a distance expressed as $CIFM_{alternative} = \sqrt{(1 - IFPM)^2 + (1 - HD)^2}$. However, this or any similar approach fails to describe the two important issues in the color image fusion performance evaluation that is the assessment of information transferred to the final image and also the distribution of colors in the final fused color image and therefore should be employed in specific cases only.

These results demonstrate that *CIFM* measure is a useful tool that can either replace or assist subjective evaluation. The experimental findings of the comparison of the four fusion methods prove that the proposed measure provides similar conclusions as those already known from the case of grayscale image fusion methods. That means there is no superior image fusion method that can be used independently of the application. Thus, objective performance evaluation based on *CIFM* should be employed in order to compare and choose between different image fusion methods for the specific application.

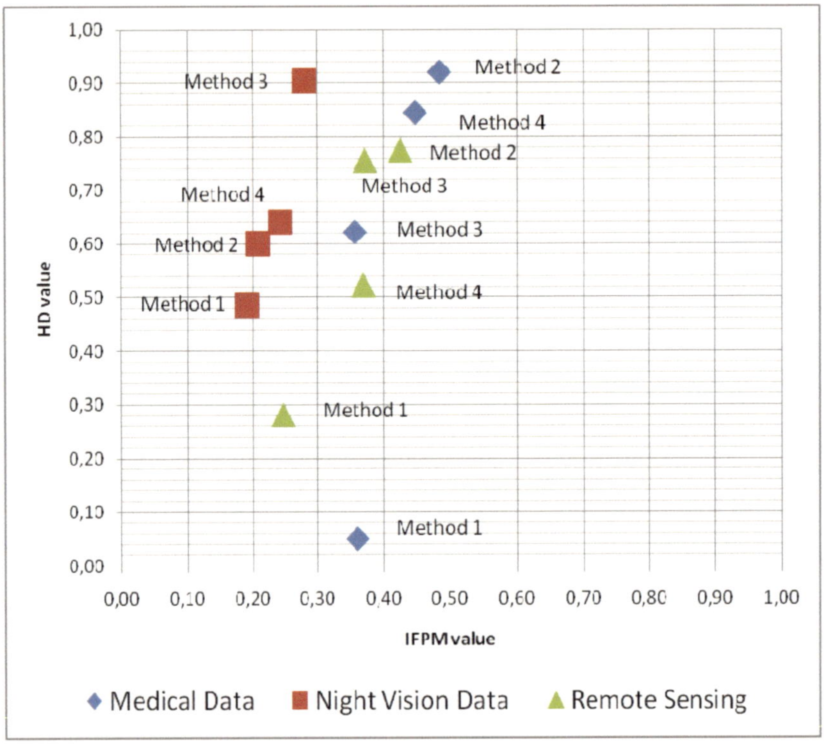

Fig. 8. Vector representation of image fusion performance for the different fusion methods and the three different data sets

6. Future research

The objective evaluation of image fusion methods is a challenging research problem that has attracted a lot of attention due to the new image fusion algorithms that are developed. The measures proposed up to now provide reliable objective evaluation based on information theory or other approaches. However, a thorough comparison of image fusion measures with subjective tests that can be easily reproduced would be very interesting.

Additionally, it is expected that in the near future the problem of dealing with regions instead of pixels will also affect the objective evaluation of image fusion methods.

Simultaneously, the evolution in color image fusion methods will result in new objective measures for these applications. Finally, the use of objective evaluation in real time applications leads to a new research field dealing with the development of dedicated software/hardware for real time objective evaluation of image fusion.

7. References

Alparone L., Baronti S., Garzelli A. and Nencini F., A global quality measurement of Pan-sharpened multispectral imagery, *IEEE Geoscience and Remote Sensing Letters*, vol. 1, issue 4, pp. 313–317, 2004.

Avcibas A., Sankur B. and Sayood K., Statistical evaluation of image quality measures, *Journal of Electronic Imaging*, vol. 11, no. 2, pp. 206-223, 2002.

Cover T. M. and Thomas J.A., Elements of information theory, Wiley Series, 1991.

Lee D.D. and Seung H.S., Learning the parts of an object by non-negative matrix factorization, *Nature,* vol. 401, pp. 788-791, 1999.

Malacara D., Color vision and colorimetry: theory and applications, SPIE Press, Washington 2002.

Mukhopadhyay S., Chanda B., Fusion of 2D Grayscale Images Using Multiscale Morphology, *Pattern Recognition*, vol. 34, no. 10, pp. 1939-1949, 2001.

Piella G., A general framework for multiresolution image fusion: from pixels to regions, *Information Fusion*, vol. 4, pp. 259-280, 2003.

Piella G. and Heijmans H., A new quality metric for image fusion, *Proceeding of the IEEE International Conference in Image Processing*, ICIP-2003, vol. 3, pp. 173-176, 2003.

Pohl C., van Genderen J.L., Multisensor image fusion in remote sensing: concepts, methods and applications, *Int. Journal of Remote Sensing*, vol. 19, no.5, pp. 823-845, 1998.

Qu G., Zhang D. and Yan P., Information measure for performance of image fusion, *Electronics Letters*, vol. 38, pp. 313-315, 2002.

Toet A., Natural color mapping for multiband night vision imagery, *Information fusion*, vol. 4, pp.155-166, 2003.

Toet A. and Franken E.M., Perceptual evaluation of different image fusion schemes, *Displays*, vol. 24, pp. 25-37, 2003.

Tsagaris V. and Anastassopoulos V., Multispectral image fusion for improved RGB representation based on perceptual attributes, *Int. Journal of Remote Sensing*, vol. 26, no. 15, pp. 3241-3254, 2005.

Tsagaris V. and Anastassopoulos V., Assessing information content in color images, *Journal of Electronic Imaging*, vol 14, no, 4, 043007, 2005.

Tsagaris V. and Anastassopoulos V., Fusion of visible and infrared imagery for night color vision, *Displays Journal*, vol. 26, no. 4-5, pp. 191-196, 2005.

Tsagaris V. and Anastassopoulos V., A Global Measure for Assessing Image Fusion Methods, *Optical Engineering* vol. 45, no2, 2006 DOI: 10.1117/12.683964.

Tsagaris V., Objective evaluation of color image fusion methods, *Optical Engineering* vol. 48, 066201, 2009 DOI:10.1117/1.3153331.

Wald L., Ranchin T. and Mangolini M., Fusion of satellite images of different spatial resolutions: assessing the quality of resulting images, *Photogrammetric Engineering and Remote Sensing*, vol. 63, no. 6, pp. 691-699, 1997.

Wang Z., Bovik A.C., A universal image quality index, *IEEE Signal Processing Letters*, vol. 9, no. 3, pp. 81-84, 2002.

Xydeas C.S. and Petrovic V., Objective image fusion performance measure, *Electronics Letters*, vol. 36, pp. 308-309, 2000.

5

Estimating 3D Surface Depth Based on Depth-of-Field Image Fusion

Marcin Denkowski[1], Paweł Mikołajczak[1] and Michał Chlebiej[2]
[1]*Faculty of Computer Science, Maria Curie-Sklodowska University, pl. Marii Curie-Sklodowskiej 5, 20-031 Lublin*
[2]*Faculty of Mathematics and Computer Science, Nicolaus Copernicus University, Chopina 12/18, 87-100 Toruń*
Poland

1. Introduction

Image fusion is a process of combining a set of images of the same scene into one composite image. The main objective of this technique is to obtain an image that is more suitable for visual perception. This composite image has reduced uncertainty and minimal redundancy while the essential information is maximized. In other words, image fusion integrates redundant and complementary information from multiple images into a composite image but also decreases dimensionality. There are many methods discovered and discussed in literature that focus on image fusion. They vary with the aim of application used, but they can be mainly categorized due to algorithms used into pyramid techniques (Burt (1984); Toet (1989)), morphological methods (Ishita et al. (2006); Mukopadhyay & Chanda (2001); Matsopoulos et al. (1994)), discrete wavelet transform (Li et al. (1995); Chibani & Houacine (2003); Lewiset al. (2007)) and neural network fusion (Ajjimarangsee & Huntsberger (1988)).
The different classification of image fusion involves pixel, feature and symbolic levels (Goshtasby (2007)). Pixel-level algorithms are low level methods and work either in the spatial or in transform domain. This kind of algorithms work as a local operation despite of transform used and can generate undesirable artifacts. These methods can be enhanced by using multiresolution analysis (Burt (1984)) or by complex wavelet transform (Lewiset al. (2007)). Feature-based methods use segmentation algorithms to divide images into relevant patterns and then combine them to create output image by using various properties (Piella (2003)). High-level methods combine image descriptions, typically, in the form of relational graphs (Wiliams et al. (1999)).
In this work we use image fusion algorithm to achieve first of our aims, i.e. to obtain the deepest possible depth-of-field in macro-photography using standard digital camera images. Macro photography is a type of close-up photography. In the classical definition it is described as photography in which the image on film or electronic sensor is at least as large as the subject. Therefore, on 35mm film, the camera has to have the ability to focus on an area at least as small as 24×36mm, equivalent to the image size on film (magnification 1:1). In other words, macro photography means photographing objects at extreme close-ups with magnification ratios from about 1:1 to about 10:1. There are some primary difficulties in macro photography; one of the most crucial is the problem of insufficient lighting. When using some

cameras to take photos in the macro-mode, the camera must be positioned so close to the object that it touches the front piece of glass in the lens. In this case it is impossible to place a light source between the camera and the subject, making extreme close-up photography impractical. 50mm is a typical focal-length lens used on a 35mm camera, and can focus so close that the lighting problem remains. The method of choice in such situations is usually to use a telephoto macro lenses. When using such devices in macro photography it is possible to increase the focal length to be grater than 100mm. But this implies second problem of macrophotography – very shallow Depth-of-Field (DOF) (see Figure 1(a)).
Because it is very difficult to obtain high values of DOF for extreme close-ups it is essential to focus on the most important part of the subject. Any other elements that are even a millimeter farther or closer may appear blurred in the acquired photo. For this reason, special devices like advanced tripods for a medium-scale objects or microscope stage for micro-scale objects are required for precise focusing. The depth of field can be defined as the distance in front of and behind the subject appearing in focus. Only a very short range of the photographed subject will appear in exact focus. This focus decreases rapidly on either side of this distance, but due to imperfections of the human eye the focused area seems to be much bigger. This focused area decreases more quickly in front of the focus point than behind as the angle of the light rays changes more rapidly when it is closer to the lens, while becoming parallel with increasing distance. It is for these reasons that there is no precise definition of what is focused; there are many factors that determine whether the subject appears in focus. The most important factor is how a single point is mapped onto the film area. If a given point is exactly at the focus distance it will be imaged as one point on the film, but if this point is farther or nearer it will produce a disk whose border is known as a "circle of confusion". These circles can be used to define the measure of focus and blurriness as they increase in diameter the further away they are from the focus point. For the most common size of 35mm camera negative (22x16mm), the acceptable "circle of confusion" diameter at which human eye is able to distinguish such a circle as a dot is usually set to 0.05mm. The film size is also important when considering the depth of field problem because, for a given scene, the larger the negative is then the longer the lens needed to capture it. Summarizing, for a specific film format, the depth of field is described as a function parameterized by: the focal length of the lens, the diameter of the lens opening (the aperture), and the distance between the subject and the camera. Let D be the distance at which the camera is focused, F the focal length (in millimeters) calculated for an aperture number f and k - the "circle of confusion" for a given film format (in millimeters), then depth of field (DOF) (Constant (2000)) can be defined as:

$$DOF_{1,2} = \frac{D}{1 \pm \frac{1000 \times D \times k \times f}{F2}} \tag{1}$$

where DOF_1 is distance from the camera to the far depth of field limit, and DOF_2 is the distance from the camera to the near depth of field limit. The aperture controls the effective diameter of the lens opening. Reducing the aperture size increases the depth of field, however, it also reduces the amount of light transmitted. Lenses with a short focal length have a greater depth-of-field than long lenses. Greater camera-to-subject distance results in a greater depth-of-field (see Figure 1(b)). We use this optical phenomenon to determine the distances from the camera to every point of the scene which gives as the height map field of this scene. The height map field allows us to achieve our second goal i.e. to create a three-dimensional model of the photographed scene.

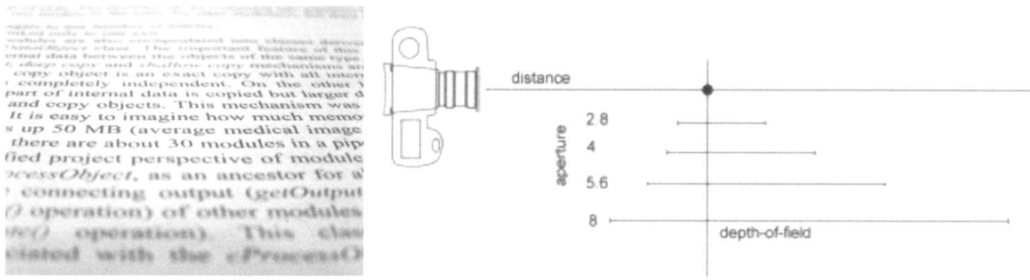

(a) (b)

Fig. 1. (a) An example of very shallow depth of field in macro-photography. (b) Example diagram of how the f-number (aperture) affects depth-of-field.

As an input we have created a series of macro photograph images of the same subject with different focus lengths and registered them to each other to create a properly aligned stack of images. The next step was to fuse them into a one composite image. Many of the methods mentioned above can do this perfectly, but our finall objective is to create a 3D visualization of that scene. And the main difficulty was to obtain the height map without spikes or noise, generally smooth but with sharp edges. Most of the fusing methods don't care about height map smoothness (if create it at all) beacuse its only goal is to create good fused image. Such an observation determined us to develop a new fusion algorithm.

Our method is based on discrete Fourier transform which copes with problem of height map smoothness. As an effect of fusing algorithm we obtain a height map field and the reconstructed focused image with a very deep depth-of-field. The height map field is a label map which determines the height of each part of the scene. From this map, we can construct a 3D model of the scene.

Generally, we limit our method to macro photography only and we assume that images were taken perpendicularly or almost perpendicularly to the scene. There is also a strong limitation of our method to scenes that can be represented as a height field. The whole method consists of several phases including: image segmentation, height map creation, image reconstruction and 3D scene generation.

2. Methodology

We capture our set of images using standard digital SLR camera mounted on a tripod with macro lenses attached. Our method works best when the photographed plan is perpendicular or almost perpendicular to the lens line. It is also good idea to avoid specularities and shinning surfaces. For better results gray background can be used. All images are taken in RAW format and then manually calibrated to one another to equalize their illumination, white ballans and exposure.

After that, all images are aligned to each other and the reconstruction process combines the image stack into the height map field and the fused image. We introduce a new method which employs discrete Fourier transform to designate sharp regions in the set of images and combines them together into an image where all regions are properly focused. From the created height map field and the fused image we can generate a 3D surface model of the scene. After that the mesh is created and textured with a plane mapping using the fused image.

The main difficulty is to obtain the height map field without spikes or noise, generally smooth but with sharp edges. It is not essential from the point of view of the image fusion, but it may

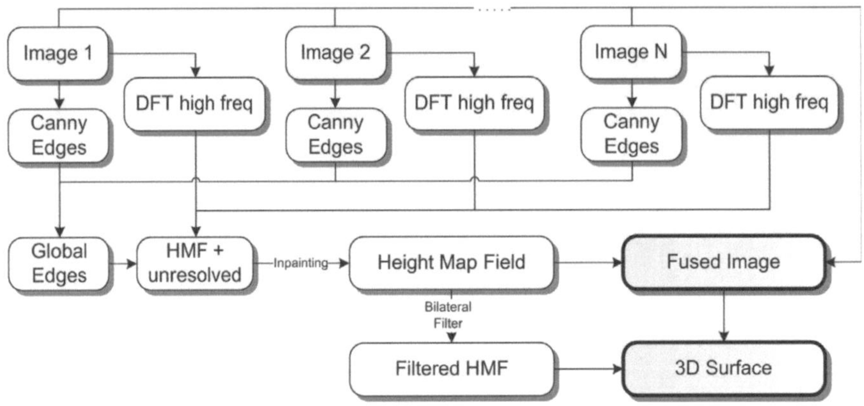

Fig. 2. Image Fusion scheme showing the steps in our method.

be crucial in three-dimensional reconstruction of the scene. Most of such peaks are generated in smooth regions, where noise in defocused region on one image from the stack is often more varied than in the corresponding region on sharp image. This leads to undesired deformations of reconstructed spatial surface. For that reason, we introduced a background plane. For now, we assumed that the background plane overlaps with the last image on the stack, but the user can choose it by hand.

2.1 Image fusion

In our work we use discrete Fourier transform methods combined with Canny edge detector and inpainting techniques to distinguish homogeneous regions. Our fusion method is also capable to work with color images. Color image fusion has been discussed in (Bogoni & Hansen (2001)). A naive approach to image fusion in color might include performing image fusion separately and independently on each color plane, then providing the resulting three color planes as a single color image. In practice, this does not work because color in three-dimmensional space is a vector and not just three independent components. Similar results gives conversion of RGB images to gray scales and processing them in one-dimmensional color space. But in this case a great number of information is lost and it generates another problem: how to map resulted grayscale image back to color space. And our assumption is that the result of the fusion process applied to color images should preserve colors and boundaries between colors. To maximize focus, fusion algorithm must emphasize structural details of the image while the color is preserved. To meet these constraints, from many possible choices for color image representations, we have chosen the CIE L*a*b color space, which separates luminance channel from chromatic channels. LAB also aspires to be perceptualy uniform and most complete color space, and its L component closely matches human perception of lightness. Therefore, L channel, which represents the luminance of the color space represent an edge energy itself.
At this stage we assume that images on the image stack are aligned to each other. The main objective is to create the focused image and the height map field (HMF). The whole algorithm diagram is shown in Figure 2.
First, the Discrete Fourier Transform for all images is calculated as follows:

$$F_z(u,v) = \frac{1}{NM} \sum_{x=0}^{N-1} \sum_{y=0}^{M-1} f_z(x,y) e^{-2\pi i(\frac{xu}{N} + \frac{yv}{M})} \tag{2}$$

Where N and M are dimensions of the image, $f_z(x,y)$ is value of the pixel at (x,y) position taken for $z - th$ image on the stack. This transform is multiplied with normalized two dimensional Gaussian distribution:

$$F'_z(u,v) = F_z(u,v) * G(u,v) \tag{3}$$

where

$$G(u,v) = \frac{1}{k} exp \frac{(u+v)^2}{2\sigma^2} \tag{4}$$

where k is normalization factor and σ is a free parameter determining degree of details preserved, which can be specified by the user. After that inverse transform $f(x,y) = F^{-1}(u,v)$ is calculated. This gives us an image where pixels with high local gradients are emphasised, see Fig. 5b). This transform is applied to to all L*, a* anb b* channels in case of color images, converted previously to CIE L*a*b* color space. These three channels compose one high frequency map by applying weighted sum operator, e.i.:

$$F'_z(u,v) = 0.8F_z^L(u,v) + 0.1F_z^a(u,v) + 0.1F_z^b(u,v) \tag{5}$$

Next, two metrices: local variance and entropy are calculated for every point of that map:

$$\sigma_z^2(u,v) = \frac{1}{ST} \sum_{j,k}^{S,T} (f_z(u+j, v+k) - \overline{f}_z)^2 \tag{6}$$

$$E_z(u,v) = -\sum_{j,k}^{S,T} f_z(u+j, v+k) \log(f_z(u+j, v+k)) \tag{7}$$

where S and T define the size of the local neighbourhood. In our case we use neigbourhood defined as disk-shaped structure with radius equal to $S/2$, and $S = T$. $f_z(u,v)$ is a value taken from (u,v) position in high frequency map F'_z for $z - th$ blurry image, $\overline{f}_z$ is a mean value of the whole neigbourhood for current (u,v) position.
These two metrices are used for creating height map field according to:

- For every point (u,v) for both σ_z^2 and E_z square $y(x) = ax^2 + bx + c$ function is fitted through $z - th$ dimension.
- Maximum for $y_\sigma(x)$ and $y_E(x)$ is calculated and x position of the maximum (Z) is designated as $Z = 0.5x_{y\sigma} + 0.5x_{yE}$
- Height Map Field at (u,v) position is equal to Z but only if range of σ_z^2 values at (u,v) position for all z is greater than k, otherwise $HMF(u,v)$ is designated as (-1):

$$HMF(u,v) = \begin{cases} Z, & \forall_z \text{range}(\sigma_z^2(u,v)) > k \\ -1, & \text{otherwise} \end{cases} \tag{8}$$

k is a free threshold value controlled by the user. All values equal to (-1) are treated as unresolved.

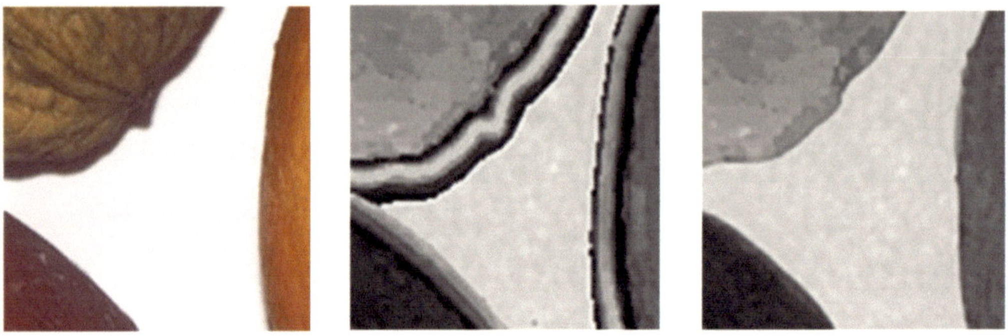

(a) (b) (c)

Fig. 3. Example of halo effect: (a) part of the original image, (b) the height map created only based on frequencies - visible halo effect, (c) edges in the height map with help of inpainting.

A base Heigh Map Field (HMF) created by these steps is filtered by hit and miss morphology operator to remove small islands, usually formed because of noise in original images.

The next step is optional but it highly improves the quality of the edges in a resulted image. Figure 3 shows usual problem with halo effect appearing on and nearby edges and where there is a large difference in lightness in local area.

To overcome this problem we use Canny Edge Detector filter which finds sharp edges in all input images. This edge line is localy dilated depending on the strength of the edge in local area. To achieve this we create distance to the edge map for whole edge image and then based on the strength of the edge, they are thickened. The strenght of the edge is determined on the basis of difference between original image and its version convolved with a Gaussian filter and the distance map secures that this thickness will only be applied to exact edges. From these edge images we form fused edge image with all edges by simply applying bitwise OR operator for all images. Figure 4 ilustrates steps of this edge designating procedure. This process also introduces two free parameters that control its efects: (1) standard deviation of the Gaussian filter and (2) maximum distance to edge. Both parameters are set to default values but much beter results are obtained when they are set by the user for a given set of images.

With this edges image we just mark all pixels in a nearby and on the edges in the height map field $HMF(x,y)$ as unresolved, see Figure 5f).

To classify all unresolved pixels in the height map field HMF we distinguish two cases:

1. Field of island formed by linked unresolved pixels in bigger than background factor B_f - these pixels are marked as backround.
2. Otherwise we employ image inpainting technique, described for example in (Bertalmo et al. (2001)) to fill remaining gaps. Inpainting is a technique for reconstructing lost or broken parts of image, widely used for image restoration or noise removing. Generally, the idea is to fill missing gaps using information from the surrounding area. In our work we use Bertalmo algorithm (Bertalmo et al. (2001)) which uses Navier-Stokes partial differential equations with boundary conditions for continuity. An example of inpainting technique is shown in Figure 5g.

Now, we have the height map field prepared to fuse blurry images into a fused one. A value of a fused image pixel $I_{fused}(x,y)$ is equal to the pixel $I_i^{(z)}(x,y)$ from $z-th$ input image on

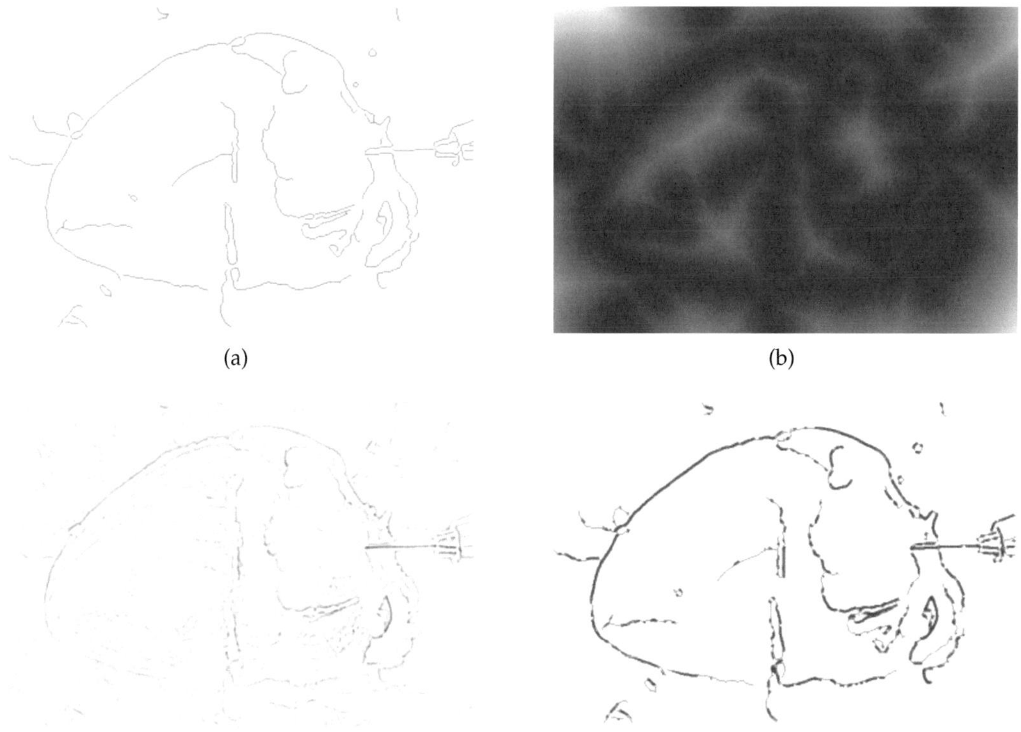

(a) (b)

(c) (d)

Fig. 4. (a) Canny edges acquired from all blurry images, (b) distance to edge map calculated for canny edge image (scaled in intensity), (c) gaussian strength of the edges (scaled in intensity), (d) finall edge map.

the stack, where z is a value interpolated form the height map field $HMF(x,y)$. Separately, regions marked as a background in the HMF in fused image I_{fused} are taken from a specific image selected by the user, but generally they can be taken from any image from the stack due to smoothness and not big differences between corresponding images in background regions.

2.2 Scene visualization

Before three-dimensional visualization the HMF is filtered by the median and bilateral filter (Tomasi & Manduchi (1998)) to smooth homogeneous regions while preserving edges beetwen objects (see Figure 8). Bilateral filtering is in details a simple, non-iterative scheme for edge-preserving smoothing, work in spatial and intensity domain and uses shift-invariant low pass Gauss filters. An output pixel's value is calculated according to:

$$h(x) = k \sum_{i \in R} f(x,i) C(x,i) (I(x,i) \tag{9}$$

where:

$$C(x,i) = exp\left(-\frac{1}{2}\left(\frac{d(x,i)}{\sigma_d}\right)^2\right) \tag{10}$$

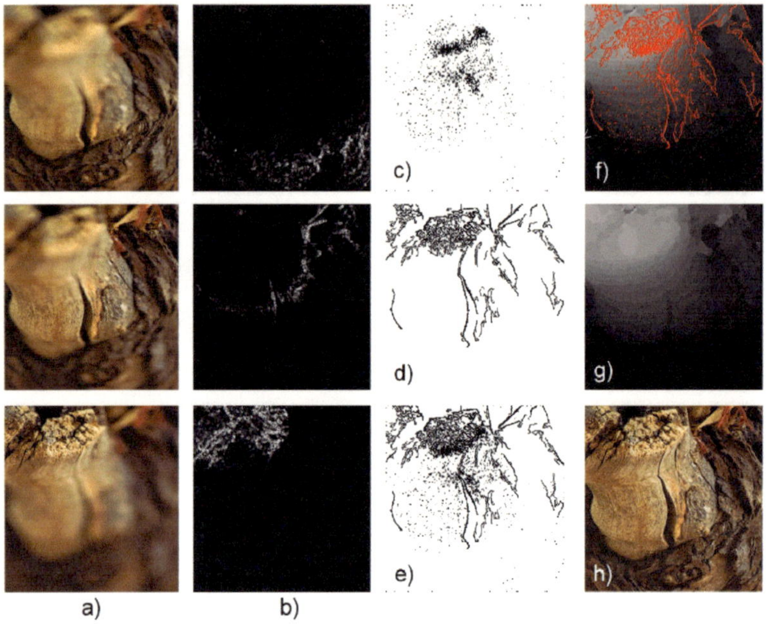

Fig. 5. Example of image fusion in steps; (a) input images; (b) high frequencies in images; (c) unresolved pixels; (d) edges pixels; (e) unresolved + edges pixels; (f) composed Height map field with unresolved pixels; (g) inpainted unresolved pixels in the HMF, (h) fused image.

is a closeness function, a typical Gaussian filter, where $d(x,i) = d(x-i) = \|x-i\|$is the Euclidian distance between x and i;

$$I(x,i) = exp\left(-\frac{1}{2}\left(\frac{\delta(f(x),f(i))}{\sigma_\delta}\right)^2\right) \tag{11}$$

is an intensity function, where $\delta(\phi,\theta) = \delta(\phi-\theta) = \|\phi-\theta\|$is a suitable measure of distance between the two intensity values ϕ and θ. An examples of different σ parameters for both closeness and intensity functions are shown in Figure 7.

Because the input images are taken from an analogue camera settings, the focus lengths in successive planes do not arrange in a constant or linear function. Thus the user can specify the distances between successive slices in the height map field and HMF is appropriately rescaled in intensities. Now, the *HMF* is prepared for creating three dimensional surface.

Generally, spatial scene can be visualized by any rendering technique which is able to show information contained in the height map field, where each pixel value represents z coordinate of appropriate mesh vertex. But, due to very high resolutions of tested images (up to 4096×4096) a regular triangle mesh (above 16 millions of triangles) can be not the very best choise. Thus, we decided to approximate a height field with an irregular triangle mesh using algorithm similar to (Garland & Heckbert (1995)). The input for this algorithm is a height field map represented by an image whose scalar values are heights and the output is polygonal data consisting of triangles. The algorithm uses a top-down decimation approach and starts with two triangles with vertices positioned at the corners of the height field and, on each pass, locates the point with the greatest error (difference between height field and interpolated mesh approximation) and injects it as a vertex into the mesh using the standard incremental

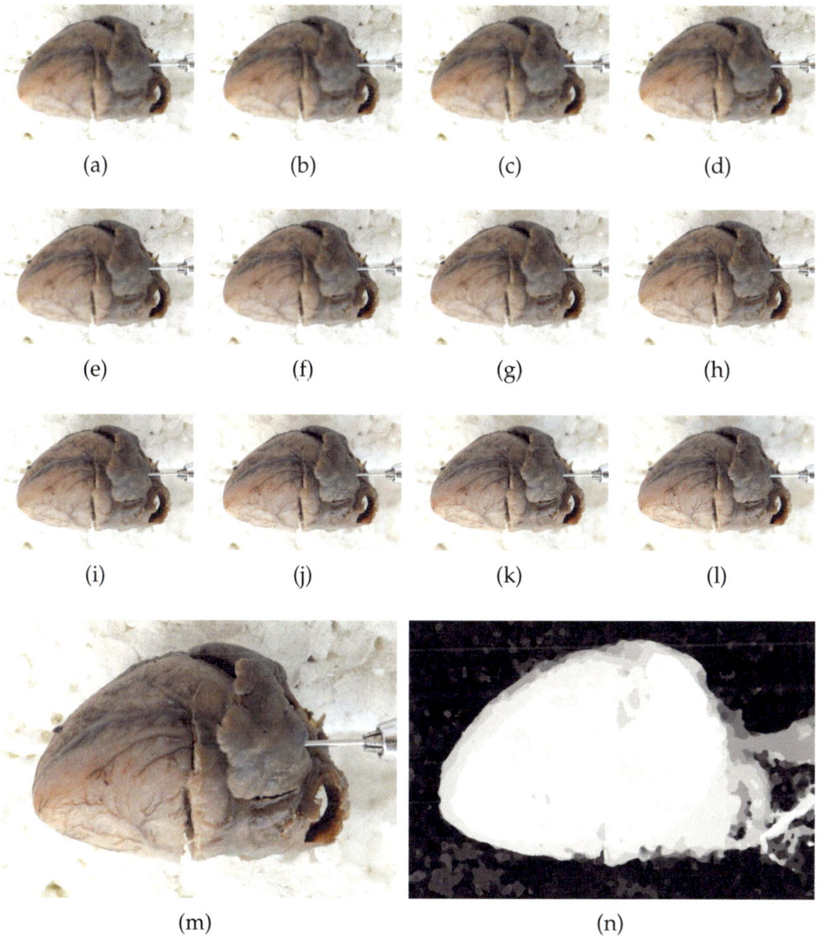

Fig. 6. (a-l) A series of macro photograph taken with different focus length, (m) reconstructed image by out algorithm, (n) the depth map for that series scaled in intensity to fit 8-bit depth. Images courtsey of Department of Anatomy, Medical Faculty, University of Varmia and Masuria in Olsztyn, Poland.

Delaunay point insertion algorithm. The mesh is modified in an iterative fashion until the specific error criterion is met. As a result the number of triangles in the output is reduced as compared to a naive tessellation of the input height field map. From our empirical tests, it seems that the reduction of triangles compared to the regular mesh while preserving good quality vary from 40% to 70% depending on the complexity of the approximated scene. See the differences between regular and irregular mesh if Figure 9.
Generated mesh is smoothed and resulted surface is textured with a plane mapping by the fused image. Additionally, the scene is lit by a directional light which is able to cast shadows to make bumpy surfaces more visible.

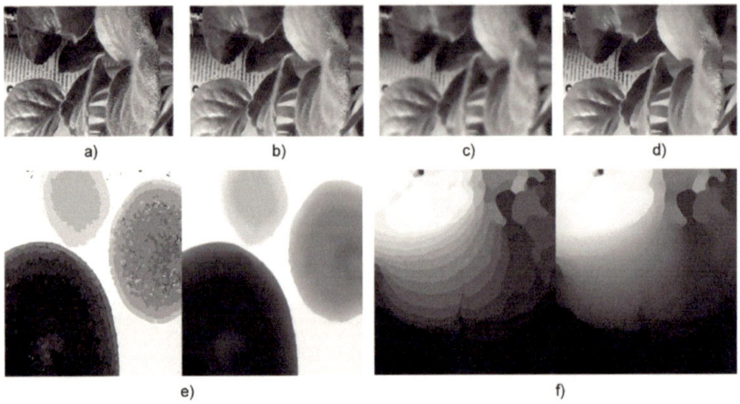

Fig. 7. Example images filtered by bilateral filter; (a) original image; (b) image filtered with radius $r = 24, \sigma = 20$; (c) $r = 24, \sigma = 96$; (d) $r = 12, \sigma = 12$, 8 iterations; (e, f) examples of the HMF from fusion algorithm (on left) and the HMF filtered by bilateral filter (on right).

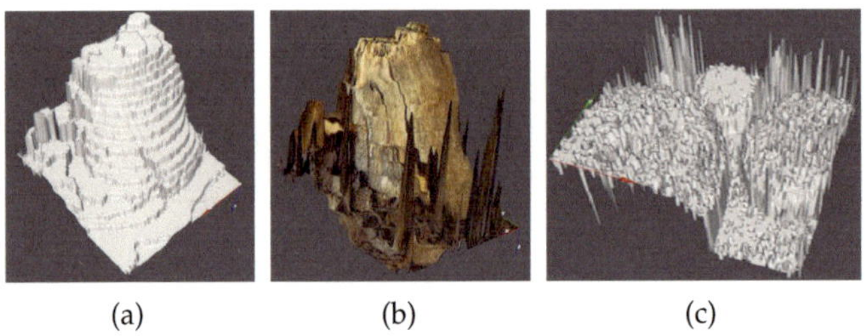

Fig. 8. (a) Surface of 3D model without bilateral smoothing, (b) and (c) examples of 3D model surfaces without removing spikes in fusing algorithm.

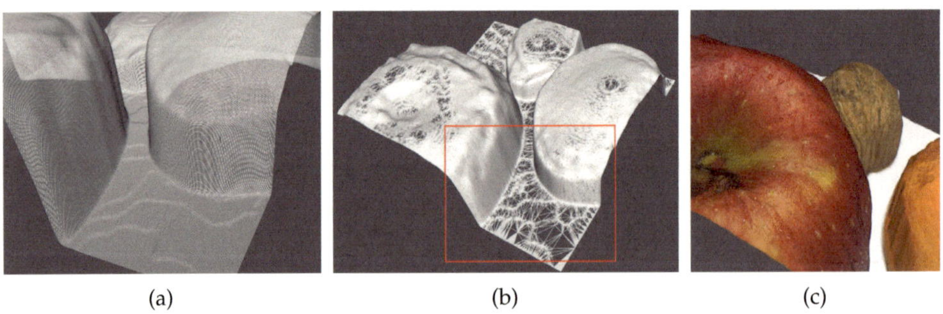

Fig. 9. (a) 3D model generated as a regular triangle mesh, (b) 3D model generated as decimated irregular triangle mesh – red rectangle covers the region visible in (a), (c) full textured 3D model rendered from the same point of view.

3. Experimental results

The proposed method has been implemented on Linux platform in C++ language using our Integrated Graphics and Modeling Environment (IGME) framework and Kitware VTK library for visualisation purposes.

To test whole reconstraction procedure we have prepared eight image stacks from macrophotography. Here, each image contains objects at different distances from the camera. Thus, one or more objects naturally become out-of-focus when the image is taken. Each stack containes six to twelve images taken with different depth-of-field. In all cases the procedure is performed in the following order. At first, we have manually equalize all images to each other, then the registration process aligns multifocus images to each other to minimize misregistration. Next, the reconstruction process combine image stack into the height map field and fused image. Finally, 3D scene was generated.

Reconstruction time strongly depends on the size of the images used in the fusion and the number of images on the stack. The fusion process takes about 45%, and generation of three dimensional mesh takes remaining 55% of all time needed for full reconstruction. For a typical set of images, containing ten images with resolution 512x512 the whole procedure lasts about 60 seconds.

3.1 Evaluating image fusion algorithm

Examples of multifocus images with height map fields and reconstructed fused images are shown in Figures 10(a,b) and 11(a,b). Quantitative measure that evaluates the quality of image fusion and produces single numerical score that indicates the success of the fusion process is hard to define and is often performed in impractical subjective trials. We have decided to use a metric $Q^{AB/F}$ proposed by Xydeas and Petrović in (Xydeas & Petrović (2000)). In this case, a per-pixel measure of information preservation is obtained between each input and the fused image which is aggregated into a single score $Q^{AB/F}$ using a simple local importance assignment. This metric is based on the assumption that fusion algorithm that transfers input gradient information into result image more accurately performs better. Furthermore, by evaluating the amount of edge information that is transferred from input images to the fused image, a measure of fusion performance can be obtained. $Q^{AB/F}$ is in range [0,1] where 0 means complete loss of information and 1 means perfect fusion. In our case we have modified this metric to calculate measure of quality for more than two images as it was in case of original $Q^{AB/F}$ metric:

$$Q^{AB/F} = \frac{\sum_z Q_z^{AF}(n,m)w_z(n,m)}{\sum_z w_z(n,m)} \tag{12}$$

where z is a number of image on the stack of blurry images and:

$$Q^{AF}(n,m) = Q_g^{AF}(n,m)Q_\alpha^{AF}(n,m) \tag{13}$$

$$Q_g^{AF}(n,m) = \frac{\Gamma_g}{1 + e^{\kappa_g(G^{AF}(n,m)-\sigma_g)}} \tag{14}$$

$$Q_\alpha^{AF}(n,m) = \frac{\Gamma_\alpha}{1 + e^{\kappa_\alpha(A^{AF}(n,m)-\sigma_\alpha)}} \tag{15}$$

where $A^{AF}(n,m)$ and $G^{AF}(n,m)$ are defined as in (Xydeas & Petrović (2000)) and describe the relative strength and orientation of the edges in an image using the Sobel operator. Constansts

	S1	S2	S3	S4	S5	S6	S7	S8
$Q^{AB/F}$	0.43	0.38	0.53	0.22	0.46	0.39	0.44	0.52

Table 1. The quality measure $Q^{AB/F}$ for all eight cases.

are: $\Gamma_g = 0.9994$, $\Gamma_g = 0.9879$, $\kappa_g = -15$, $\kappa_\alpha = -22$, $\sigma_g = 0.5$, $\sigma_\alpha = 0.8$. Table 1 contains velues of $Q^{AB/F}$ metric that measures quality of image fusion.

3.2 Evaluating 3D reconstruction

Figures 10 and 11 show qualitative results of our method for eight tested image sets. The biggest problem in this 3d reconstruction is to obtain a surface which is smooth enough in uniform regions and simultaneously has sharp edges on the objects boundaries. The best results are received when the photographs are taken perpendicularly to the background, objects are within the scene, and they are rough without smooth regions.

Because quantitative measure of the 3D reconstruction of real models is practically impossible we have created synthetic tests. Two simple scenes have been generated in 3D modeling application: (1) a flat surface inclined 15° to the perpendicular plane to camera axis, this surface has been textured and iluminated only with ambient light and (2) spherical surface, also textured and lit with ambient light. For both scenes analytical equation of the surface was known allowing to calculate quantities like volume or shape and to compare with other surface(s). These surfaces are presented in Figure 12.

Both scenes have been rendered with depth-of-field filters that simulates depth-of-field effect using Blender 3D graphic application. In both cases 10 images of partially sharp images have

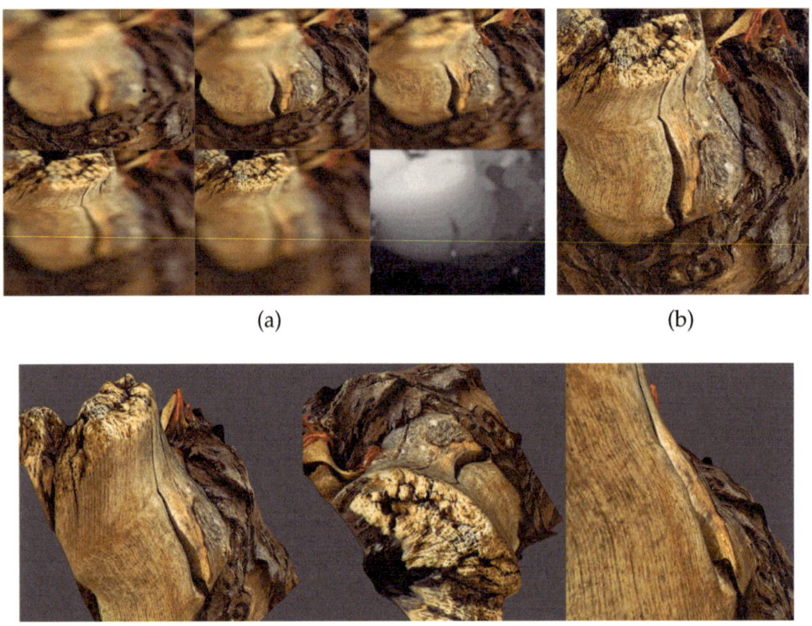

(a) (b) (c)

Fig. 10. (a) A few samples of blurry images with height map, (b) finall fused image, (c) reconstructed 3D model.

Fig. 11. (a) A few samples of blurry images with height map, (b) finall fused image, (c) reconstructed 3D model.

been created. For every image the focus length was set to different part of the scene covering a range from the farthest parts of the scene to the nearest ones with constant step between slices. These images were input images to test our fusing and 3D reconstruction method. After reconstruction, created scene was rescaled to match to bounding box of the original scene. We chose two quantites to compare 3D scene generated by 3D application and scene generated by our method:

1. Mean square difference of differences in meshes of reconstructed and original scene:

$$MSD = \frac{1}{R} \sum_{x,y \in R} (f(x,y) - g(x,y))^2 \tag{16}$$

2. Normalized cross-correlation between meshes of reconstructed and original scene:

$$XC = \frac{\sum_{x,y \in R} (f(x,y) - \overline{f}) \cdot (g(x,y) - \overline{g})}{\sqrt{\left(\sum_{x,y \in R} (f(x,y) - \overline{f})^2 \cdot \sum_{x,y \in R} (g(x,y) - \overline{g})^2 \right)}} \tag{17}$$

To calculate both quantities the space of the scene was quantitized in (X,Y) dimension to the size equal to the resolution of the height map field (marked as R). $f(x,y)$ is interpolated height

Fig. 12. Two test scenes: (a) flat surface inclined 15° to the perpendicular plane to camera axis, (b) spherical surface, (c) wireframe rendering of the reconstructed plane scene, (d) wireframe rendering of the reconstructed sphere scene.

(z axis) in the (x,y) position in reconstructed scene, $\overline{f}$ is the mean height of reconstructed scene, $g(x,y)$ is interpolated height in the (x,y) position in original scene, $\overline{g}$ is the mean height of original scene.

Mean square difference estimates the difference between the reconstructed surface and the original one and was equal $MSD = 0.018$ and $MSD = 0.031$ respectively for plane and sphere scenes. Cross correlation gives information about how this two surfaces are similar to each other. Two identical surfaces give value of XC equal to 1 or (-1), value equal to 0 means completely different surfaces. For plane scene XC was equal to 0.98 and for sphere scene XC was equal to 0.96. Obtained results indicate very good match for both surfaces. However, despite the use of mesh decimation algorithm the number of triangles is still much larger than original mesh. The problem is also "effect of blocks" which must be smoothed by very expensive algorithms for smoothing mesh of triangles. We also expect that synthetic tests would give better results than real tests. To estimate the quality of our procedure we plan to scan a simple but real micro-scene by a 3D laser scanner and then compare with a reconstructed mesh to acquire more precise results.

Figure 13 shows an example of a typical failure. Our method often fails when there are large smooth regions which don't belong to the background plane. The main difficulty in such cases is to distinguish between background and an object without any external spatial knowledge of the scene.

Fig. 13. Typical image that creates failed 3D model. This photograph presents a common child's spinning top. Reconstruction algorithms failed because of many smooth and uniform regions and a lack of background plane.

4. Conclusions

This paper presented a new attempt to the image fusion and estimation of surface depth based on multifocus images. We proposed the whole pipeline from raw photographs to the final spatial surface. Input multifocus images were fused by DFT method and the height map field was created. Based on the *HMF* the image with a greater depth-of-field was composed. Finally, further algorithms reconstructed the 3d surface of the photographed scene.
The presented results of generation of 3D models show that our method is a good tool for acquiring surfaces from a few photographs. However, future work should include automatic detection of the background plane. Second, there should be more complex methods used to identify smooth regions of objects. We think that in both cases pattern recognition algorithms should improve effectiveness of our method. Also Feature-based fusion methods such as (Piella (2003)) could generate more accurate height maps.

5. References

Ajjimarangsee, P. & Huntsberger, T. (1988). Neural network model for fusion of visible and infrared sensor outputs, Sensor Fusion, Spatial Reasoning and Scene Interpretation, *The International Society for Optical Engineering*, 1003, SPIE, Bellingham, USA pp. 152-160

Bertalmo, M., Bertozzi, A. & Sapiro, G. (2001). Navier-Stokes, Fluid Dynamics, and Image and Video Inpainting, *IEEE Computer Society Conference on Computer Vision and Pattern Recognition* (CVPR'01) - Volume 1

Bogoni, L. & Hansen, M. (2001). Pattern-selective color image fusion, *Pattern Recognition 34* pp. 1515-1526

Burt, P. (1984). The pyramid as a structure for efficient computation, *Multiresolution Image Processing and Analysis*, Springer-Verlag, Berlin pp. 6-35

Chibani, Y. & Houacine, A. (2003). Redundant versus orthogonal wavelet decomposition for multisensor image fusion, *Pattern Recognition 36* pp. 879-887

Constant, A. (2000). *Close-up Photography*, Butterworth-Heinemann (2000)

Goshtasby, A. (2007). Guest editorial: Image fusion: Advances in the state of the art, *Information Fusion 8*, pp. 114-118

Garland, M. & Heckbert, P. (1995). Fast Polygonal Approximations of Terrain and Height Fields, *Technical Report* CMU-CS-95-181, School of Computer Science, Carnegie Mellon University, Pittsburgh, PA 15213

Ishita, D., Bhabatosh, C. & Buddhajyoti, C. (2006). Enhancing effective depth-of-field by image fusion using mathematical morphology, *Image and Vision Computing 24*, pp. 1278-1287

Lewis, L., O'Callaghan, R., Nikolov, S., Bull, D. & Canagarajah, N. (2007). Pixel- and

region-based image fusion with complex wavelets, *Information Fusion 8*, pp. 119-130
Li, H., Manjunath, H. & Mitra, S. (1995). Multisensor image fusion using the wavelet transform, *Graphical Models and Image Processing 57 (3)*, pp. 235-245
Mukopadhyay, S. & Chanda, B. (2001). Fusion of 2d gray scale images using multiscale morphology, *Pattern Recognition 34*, pp. 1939-1949
Matsopoulos, G., Marshall, S. & Brunt J. (1994). Multiresolution morphological fusion of mr and ct images of the human brain, *IEEE Proceedings Vision, Image and Signal Processing 141 (3)*, pp. 137-142
Piella, G. (2003). A general framework for multiresolution image fusion: from pixels to regions, *Information Fusion 4*, pp. 259-280
Toet, A. (1989). Image fusion by rati of low-pass pyramid, *Pattern Recognition Letters 9 (4)*, pp. 245-253
Tomasi, C. & Manduchi, R. (1998). Bilateral Filtering for Gray and Color Images, *Proceedings of the 1998 IEEE International Conference on Computer Vision*, Bombay, India
Wiliams, M., Wilson, R. & Hancock, E. (1999). Deterministic search for relational graph matching, *Pattern Recognition 32*, pp. 1255-1516
Xydeas, C. & Petrović, V. (2000). Objective image fusion performance measure, *Electronics Letters 36 (4)*, pp. 308-309

6

EM-based Bayesian Fusion of Hyperspectral and Multispectral images

Yifan Zhang
Northwestern Polytechnical University
P. R. China

1. Introduction

During the last two decades, the number of spectral bands in optical remote sensing technology kept growing steadily going from multispectral (MS) to hyperspectral (HS) data sets. HS images employ hundreds of contiguous spectral bands to capture and process spectral information over a range of wavelenghts, compared to the tens of discrete spectral bands used in MS images (Chang, 2003). This increase in spectral accuracy is delivering more information, allowing a whole range of new and more precise applications. The detailed spectral information of HS images is helpful for interpretation, classification and recognition. However, in remote sensors, usually a trade-off exists between SNR, spatial and spectral resolutions due to physical limitations, data-transfer requirements and some other practical reasons. In most cases, high spatial and spectral resolutions are not available in a single image, which makes the spatial resolution of HS images usually lower than that of MS images (Gomez et al., 2001). In practice, many applications require high accuracy both spectrally and spatially, which inspires research on spatial resolution enhancement techniques for HS image (Gomez et al., 2001; Duijster et al., 2009; Zhang & He, 2007; Hardie et al., 2004; Eismann & Hardie, 2005; 2004).

When more than one observation of the scene is available, a popular technique dealing with this limitation is image fusion, a well studied field for more than ten years. As a prototype problem, usually an image of high spectral resolution is combined with an image of high spatial resolution to obtain an image of optimal resolutions both spectrally and spatially. Most fusion techniques for spatial resolution improvement were developed for the specific purpose of enhancing MS image by using a panchromatic (Pan) image of higher spatial resolution, also referred to as pansharpening. Principal component analysis (PCA) (Chavez et al., 1991; Shettigara, 1992) and Intensity-Hue-Saturation (IHS) transform (Carper et al., 1990; Edwards & Davis, 1994; Tu et al., 2001) based techniques are the most commonly used ones. The Pan image is applied to totally or partially substitute the 1*st* principal component or intensity component of the coregistered and resampled MS image. To generalize to more than three bands and to reduce spectral degradation, generalized IHS (GIHS) transforms (Tu et al., 2004) and generalized intensity modulation techniques (Alparone et al., 2004) were defined. High-pass filtering and high-pass modulation techniques were developed (Chavez et al., 1991; Shettigara, 1992; Liu & Moore, 1998), in which spatial high-frequency information is extracted and injected adequately into each band of the MS image. With the rise of multiresolution analysis, many researchers have proposed pansharpening techniques, using Gaussian and Laplacian pyramids as well as discrete decimated and undecimated wavelet transforms (WTs)

(Aiazzi et al., 2002; Núñez et al., 1999; Shi et al., 2003). A detailed description and comparison of these techniques is given in (Pohl & Van Genderen, 1998; Wang et al., 2005; Alparone et al., 2007).

In this work, a more general fusion is considered, in which an HS image of low spatial resolution and an MS image of high spatial resolution are observed and fused. Since the high spatial resolution MS image is multiband, the pansharpening techniques cannot be applied directly to the problem of HS and MS image fusion. Usually, a spatial high-frequency component of the MS image is extracted (by PCA, IHS, *etc.*) first and then injected to the HS image, which may lead to spectral distortion. Techniques using 2D and 3D WTs were also proposed (Gomez et al., 2001; Zhang & He, 2007), in which the MS and HS images were spectrally and spatially resampled a priori. These two approaches were both capable of improving the spatial resolution of the HS image effectively. However, the performance was highly dependent on the spectral resampling methods adopted. Some researchers proposed statistical estimation techniques for HS and MS image fusion. In (Hardie et al., 2004), MAP estimation based on a spatially varying statistical model is employed to enhance the spatial resolution of HS image. The framework developed was validated for pansharpening but allowed for any number of spectral bands in both the HS and MS images. Extensions of this work applied an extended stochastic mixing model (Eismann & Hardie, 2005; 2004).

In this work, we treat the problem of fusion of a low-spatial high-spectral resolution observation (HS image) with a high-spatial low-spectral resolution observation (MS image), for the purpose of spatial enhancement of the former. A Bayesian fusion framework is proposed, in which the fusion is accomplished by assuming an observation model for the HS image and a joint statistical model between the HS and MS images. Specifically, an *expectation-maximization* (EM) algorithm is employed for estimation optimization.

The rest of this work is arranged as follows. In Section 2, mathematical description of the problem concerned is introduced, as well as some related theoretical basis. In Section 3, the EM-based Bayesian fusion framework is elaborated and a practical implementation scheme is provided. In Section 4, simulation experiments with a reference are performed for validation and comparison. Finally, the conclusions are given in Section 5.

2. Problem description and theoretical basis

2.1 Problem description

The general problem discussed in this paper is to describe a scene $\mathbf{z}$ based on a series of observations, each with specific spatial and spectral resolutions. As a prototype problem, we will consider the case where a low-spatial high-spectral resolution observation $\mathbf{x}$ (HS image) is available together with a high-spatial low-spectral resolution observation $\mathbf{y}$ (MS image).

Although the two observations may be presented at different spatial and spectral sampling rates, in this paper, we will assume that all images are equally spatially sampled at a grid of N pixels, sufficiently fine to reveal the spatial resolution of $\mathbf{z}$. Since we will concentrate on the optimization of the spatial resolution and no spectral enhancement will be performed, the spectral sampling rate of $\mathbf{x}$ is sufficient. Each image is presented in band-interleaved-by-pixel lexicographical notation, that is, $\mathbf{z} = [\mathbf{z}_1^T, \mathbf{z}_2^T, \cdots, \mathbf{z}_N^T]^T$ with $\mathbf{z}_n = [z_n^1, z_n^2, \cdots, z_n^P]^T$ where P is the number of spectral bands. Similar notations are applied to all related images. Normally, a standard linear observation model is applied for $\mathbf{x}$:

$$\mathbf{x} = \mathbf{W}\mathbf{z} + \mathbf{n} \tag{1}$$

where the PSF $\mathbf{W}$ reflects the spatial blurring of the observation $\mathbf{x}$, and $\mathbf{n}$ is the additive Gaussian white noise with covariance $\mathbf{C_n}$.

2.2 Theoretical basis

2.2.1 EM algorithm

When only the observation $\mathbf{x}$ is available, one way to improve its spatial resolution would be image restoration. A possible treatment of the restoration is splitting it up into a deblurring and a denoising part as was done in (Figueiredo & Nowak, 2003), where the *expectation-maximization* (EM) algorithm was employed to solve the problem. In (Duijster et al., 2009), this procedure was extended for multiband images. The key concept in the EM-based restoration procedure is that the observation model for $\mathbf{x}$ is inverted by performing the deblurring and denoising in two separate steps. To accomplish this, the observation model is decomposed as:

$$\mathbf{x} = \mathbf{W}\mathbf{s} + \mathbf{n}'' \tag{2}$$

$$\mathbf{s} = \mathbf{z} + \mathbf{n}'. \tag{3}$$

In this way, the noise is decomposed into two independent parts $\mathbf{n}'$ and $\mathbf{n}''$, with $\mathbf{W}\mathbf{n}' + \mathbf{n}'' = \mathbf{n}$. The spatial-invariance of $\mathbf{W}$ guarantees a semi positive-definite covariance for $\mathbf{n}''$. If $\mathbf{W}$ would be not translation-invariant, a rescaling is required (see (Figueiredo & Nowak, 2003)). The splitting up leaves the option to divide the originally assumed Gaussian white noise $\mathbf{n}$ into two parts. Choosing $\mathbf{n}'$ to be white with $p(\mathbf{n}') = \phi(0, \mathbf{C_n})$ facilitates the denoising problem (3). However, $\mathbf{W}$ colors the noise so that $\mathbf{n}''$ becomes colored with $p(\mathbf{n}'') = \phi(0, \mathbf{C_n} - \mathbf{W}\mathbf{C_n}\mathbf{W}^T)$. When the largest part of the original noise appears into $\mathbf{n}'$, $\mathbf{n}''$ can be neglected, making (2) a pure deblurring problem.
The estimation problem concerned can be then described as:

$$\begin{aligned} \hat{\mathbf{z}} &= \arg\max_{\mathbf{z}} p(\mathbf{z}|\mathbf{x},\mathbf{s}) \\ &= \arg\max_{\mathbf{z}} p(\mathbf{x},\mathbf{s}|\mathbf{z})p(\mathbf{z}) \end{aligned} \tag{4}$$

which is solved using the iterative EM algorithm. At each iteration k, the EM algorithm involves two steps:

- The *E-step* computes the conditional expectation of the complete log-likelihood, the so-called Q-function, given the observation $\mathbf{x}$ and an estimate of $\mathbf{z}$ acquired in the previous iteration:

$$Q(\mathbf{z}, \hat{\mathbf{z}}^{(k-1)}) = \mathbb{E}[\log\left(p(\mathbf{x},\mathbf{s}|\mathbf{z})p(\mathbf{z})\right)|\mathbf{x}, \hat{\mathbf{z}}^{(k-1)}]. \tag{5}$$

- The *M-step* maximizes the Q-function and updates the estimate of $\mathbf{z}$:

$$\hat{\mathbf{z}}^{(k)} = \arg\max_{\mathbf{z}} Q(\mathbf{z}, \hat{\mathbf{z}}^{(k-1)}). \tag{6}$$

2.2.1.1 E-step

Conditioned on $\mathbf{s}$, $\mathbf{x}$ is independent of $\mathbf{z}$ (see (2)), therefore:

$$\begin{aligned} p(\mathbf{x},\mathbf{s}|\mathbf{z})p(\mathbf{z}) &= p(\mathbf{x}|\mathbf{s},\mathbf{z})p(\mathbf{s}|\mathbf{z})p(\mathbf{z}) \\ &= p(\mathbf{x}|\mathbf{s})p(\mathbf{s}|\mathbf{z})p(\mathbf{z}) \\ &\propto p(\mathbf{s}|\mathbf{z})p(\mathbf{z}). \end{aligned} \tag{7}$$

From Equation (3), one has $p(\mathbf{s}|\mathbf{z}) = \phi(\mathbf{z}, \mathbf{C_n})$. When a Gaussian prior is assumed for $\mathbf{z}$, one has

$$p(\mathbf{z}) = \phi(\boldsymbol{\mu}_\mathbf{z}, \mathbf{C_z}) \tag{8}$$

with

$$\begin{aligned} \boldsymbol{\mu}_\mathbf{z} &= \mathbb{E}[\mathbf{z}] \\ \mathbf{C_z} &= \mathbb{E}[(\mathbf{z} - \mathbb{E}[\mathbf{z}])(\mathbf{z} - \mathbb{E}[\mathbf{z}])^T] \end{aligned} \tag{9}$$

which can be estimated from an estimate of $\mathbf{z}$ obtained in the previous iteration ($\hat{\mathbf{z}}^{(k-1)}$). Hence, the complete log-likelihood can be expressed as:

$$\log(p(\mathbf{x},\mathbf{s}|\mathbf{z})p(\mathbf{x}|\mathbf{y})) \propto -\frac{1}{2}(\mathbf{z}-\mathbf{s})^T\mathbf{C_n}^{-1}(\mathbf{z}-\mathbf{s}) - \frac{1}{2}(\mathbf{z}-\boldsymbol{\mu}_\mathbf{z})^T\mathbf{C_z}^{-1}(\mathbf{z}-\boldsymbol{\mu}_\mathbf{z}). \tag{10}$$

Since the $\mathbf{z}$-dependent part of this expression is linear in $\mathbf{s}$, finding the Q-function or the expectation of (10) comes down to finding the expectation of $\mathbf{s}$, conditioned on the observation $\mathbf{x}$ and an estimate of $\mathbf{z}$ from last iteration. Denoting this expectation as $\hat{\mathbf{s}}^{(k)}$, the final expression for the Q-function becomes:

$$Q(\mathbf{z},\hat{\mathbf{z}}^{(k-1)}) \propto -\frac{1}{2}(\mathbf{z}-\hat{\mathbf{s}}^{(k)})^T\mathbf{C_n}^{-1}(\mathbf{z}-\hat{\mathbf{s}}^{(k)}) - \frac{1}{2}(\mathbf{z}-\boldsymbol{\mu}_\mathbf{z})^T\mathbf{C_z}^{-1}(\mathbf{z}-\boldsymbol{\mu}_\mathbf{z}). \tag{11}$$

2.2.1.2 Calculation of $\hat{\mathbf{s}}^{(k)}$

$\hat{\mathbf{s}}^{(k)}$ can be obtained from the conditional pdf of $\mathbf{s}$ given the observation $\mathbf{x}$ and an estimate of $\mathbf{z}$ from the previous iteration:

$$\begin{aligned} p(\mathbf{s}|\mathbf{x},\hat{\mathbf{z}}^{(k-1)}) &= \frac{p(\mathbf{x}|\mathbf{s},\hat{\mathbf{z}}^{(k-1)})p(\mathbf{s}|\hat{\mathbf{z}}^{(k-1)})}{p(\mathbf{x}|\hat{\mathbf{z}}^{(k-1)})} \\ &= \frac{p(\mathbf{x}|\mathbf{s})p(\mathbf{s}|\hat{\mathbf{z}}^{(k-1)})}{p(\mathbf{x}|\hat{\mathbf{z}}^{(k-1)})} \\ &\propto p(\mathbf{x}|\mathbf{s})p(\mathbf{s}|\hat{\mathbf{z}}^{(k-1)}) \end{aligned} \tag{12}$$

where the first pdf comes from (2) and the second from (3)

$$p(\mathbf{x}|\mathbf{s}) = \phi(\mathbf{W}\mathbf{s}, \mathbf{C_n} - \mathbf{W}\mathbf{C_n}\mathbf{W}^T) \tag{13}$$

$$p(\mathbf{s}|\hat{\mathbf{z}}^{(k-1)}) = \phi(\hat{\mathbf{z}}^{(k-1)}, \mathbf{C_n}). \tag{14}$$

As a result, the conditional expectation of $\mathbf{s}$ can then be obtained as:

$$\begin{aligned} \hat{\mathbf{s}}^{(k)} &= \mathbb{E}[\mathbf{s}|\mathbf{x},\mathbf{z}^{(k-1)}] \\ &= \int \mathbf{s}p(\mathbf{x}|\mathbf{s})p(\mathbf{s}|\hat{\mathbf{z}}^{(k-1)})d\mathbf{s} \\ &= \hat{\mathbf{z}}^{(k-1)} + \mathbf{W}^T(\mathbf{x} - \mathbf{W}\hat{\mathbf{z}}^{(k-1)}). \end{aligned} \tag{15}$$

2.2.1.3 M-step

In this step, the estimate of $\mathbf{z}$ is updated by maximizing the Q-function obtained in (11):

$$\begin{aligned}\hat{\mathbf{z}}^{(k)} &= \arg\max_{\mathbf{z}} Q(\mathbf{z},\hat{\mathbf{z}}^{(k-1)}) \\ &= \mathbf{C}_{\hat{\mathbf{z}}^{(k-1)}}(\mathbf{C}_{\hat{\mathbf{z}}^{(k-1)}}+\mathbf{C}_{\mathbf{n}})^{-1}\hat{\mathbf{s}}^{(k)}+\mathbf{C}_{\mathbf{n}}(\mathbf{C}_{\hat{\mathbf{z}}^{(k-1)}}+\mathbf{C}_{\mathbf{n}})^{-1}\boldsymbol{\mu}_{\hat{\mathbf{z}}^{(k-1)}}. \end{aligned} \tag{16}$$

Since no auxiliary information is used in the whole procedure, its performance in spatial enhancement is usually quite limited.

2.2.2 Bayesian fusion using MAP estimation

When the high-spatial low-spectral resolution observation $\mathbf{y}$ is also available, image fusion technique would be a solution for spatial enhancement of $\mathbf{x}$. In a Bayesian framework, an estimate of $\mathbf{z}$ can be obtained from the conditional pdf given both observations using MAP estimation (Hardie et al., 2004):

$$\begin{aligned}\hat{\mathbf{z}} &= \arg\max_{\mathbf{z}} p(\mathbf{z}|\mathbf{x},\mathbf{y}) \\ &= \arg\max_{\mathbf{z}} p(\mathbf{x}|\mathbf{z})p(\mathbf{z}|\mathbf{y}). \end{aligned} \tag{17}$$

The first pdf is obtained from the observation model for $\mathbf{x}$ (see (1)):

$$p(\mathbf{x}|\mathbf{z}) = \phi(\mathbf{W}\mathbf{z},\mathbf{C}_{\mathbf{n}}). \tag{18}$$

By assuming a jointly Gaussian distribution between $\mathbf{z}$ and $\mathbf{y}$, the conditional pdf $p(\mathbf{z}|\mathbf{y})$ would also be a Gaussian (Hardie et al., 2004):

$$p(\mathbf{z}|\mathbf{y}) = \phi(\boldsymbol{\mu}_{\mathbf{z}|\mathbf{y}},\mathbf{C}_{\mathbf{z}|\mathbf{y}}) \tag{19}$$

with

$$\begin{aligned}\boldsymbol{\mu}_{\mathbf{z}|\mathbf{y}} &= \mathbb{E}[\mathbf{z}]+\mathbf{C}_{\mathbf{z},\mathbf{y}}\mathbf{C}_{\mathbf{y}}^{-1}(\mathbf{y}-\mathbb{E}[\mathbf{y}]) \\ \mathbf{C}_{\mathbf{z}|\mathbf{y}} &= \mathbf{C}_{\mathbf{z}}-\mathbf{C}_{\mathbf{z},\mathbf{y}}\mathbf{C}_{\mathbf{y}}^{-1}\mathbf{C}_{\mathbf{z},\mathbf{y}}^{T}\end{aligned}$$

where

$$\mathbf{C}_{\mathbf{z},\mathbf{y}} = \mathbb{E}[(\mathbf{z}-\mathbb{E}[\mathbf{z}])(\mathbf{y}-\mathbb{E}[\mathbf{y}])^{T}]. \tag{20}$$

After some calculation, the following solution can be easily obtained:

$$\hat{\mathbf{z}} = \boldsymbol{\mu}_{\mathbf{z}|\mathbf{y}}+\mathbf{C}_{\mathbf{z}|\mathbf{y}}\mathbf{W}^{T}(\mathbf{W}\mathbf{C}_{\mathbf{z}|\mathbf{y}}\mathbf{W}^{T}+\mathbf{C}_{\mathbf{n}})^{-1}(\mathbf{y}-\mathbf{W}\boldsymbol{\mu}_{\mathbf{z}|\mathbf{y}}). \tag{21}$$

In this fusion approach, ideally, the fused result $\hat{\mathbf{z}}$ has the spectral resolution of $\mathbf{x}$ and the spatial resolution of $\mathbf{y}$. As a result, the spatial resolution of $\hat{\mathbf{z}}$ is limited to that of $\mathbf{y}$.

3. Bayesian fusion based on EM algorithm

In this section, a new Bayesian fusion approach for HS and MS images is proposed, which employs both the EM algorithm presented in Section 2.2.1 and Bayesian fusion framework explained in Section 2.2.2, for the purpose of performance improvement. Based on the splitting-up strategy ((2) and (3)), the objective of the fusion problem discussed is to find an estimate of $\mathbf{z}$ by:

$$\begin{aligned}\hat{\mathbf{z}} &= \arg\max_{\mathbf{z}} p(\mathbf{z}|\mathbf{x},\mathbf{y},\mathbf{s}) \\ &= \arg\max_{\mathbf{z}} p(\mathbf{x},\mathbf{s}|\mathbf{z})p(\mathbf{z}|\mathbf{y}).\end{aligned} \tag{22}$$

Employing the EM algorithm, the proposed fusion approach is an iterative procedure with two major steps in each iteration k:

- The *E-step* computes the conditional expectation of the complete log-likelihood, the so-called Q-function, given both observations ($\mathbf{x}$ and $\mathbf{y}$) and an estimate of $\mathbf{z}$ acquired in the previous iteration:

$$Q(\mathbf{z},\hat{\mathbf{z}}^{(k-1)}) = \mathbb{E}[\log(p(\mathbf{x},\mathbf{s}|\mathbf{z})p(\mathbf{z}|\mathbf{y}))|\mathbf{x},\mathbf{y},\hat{\mathbf{z}}^{(k-1)}]. \tag{23}$$

- The *M-step* maximizes the Q-function and updates the estimate of $\mathbf{z}$:

$$\hat{\mathbf{z}}^{(k)} = \arg\max_{\mathbf{z}} Q(\mathbf{z},\hat{\mathbf{z}}^{(k-1)}). \tag{24}$$

3.1 E-step

Since conditioned on $\mathbf{s}$, $\mathbf{x}$ is independent of $\mathbf{z}$ (see (2)), the following can be obtained:

$$\begin{aligned}p(\mathbf{x},\mathbf{s}|\mathbf{z})p(\mathbf{z}|\mathbf{y}) &= p(\mathbf{x}|\mathbf{s},\mathbf{z})p(\mathbf{s}|\mathbf{z})p(\mathbf{z}|\mathbf{y}) \\ &= p(\mathbf{x}|\mathbf{s})p(\mathbf{s}|\mathbf{z})p(\mathbf{z}|\mathbf{y}) \\ &\propto p(\mathbf{s}|\mathbf{z})p(\mathbf{z}|\mathbf{y}).\end{aligned} \tag{25}$$

From (3), one has $p(\mathbf{s}|\mathbf{z}) = \phi(\mathbf{z},\mathbf{C_n})$. As for $p(\mathbf{z}|\mathbf{y})$, we will assume that $\mathbf{z}$ and $\mathbf{y}$ are jointly normally distributed as in (Hardie et al., 2004), so that the conditional distribution is also a normal (see (19)). As a result,

$$\log(p(\mathbf{x},\mathbf{s}|\mathbf{z})p(\mathbf{z}|\mathbf{y})) \propto -\frac{1}{2}(\mathbf{z}-\mathbf{s})^T\mathbf{C_n}^{-1}(\mathbf{z}-\mathbf{s}) - \frac{1}{2}(\mathbf{z}-\boldsymbol{\mu}_{\mathbf{z}|\mathbf{y}})^T\mathbf{C}_{\mathbf{z}|\mathbf{y}}^{-1}(\mathbf{z}-\boldsymbol{\mu}_{\mathbf{z}|\mathbf{y}}). \tag{26}$$

Since the $\mathbf{z}$-dependent part of this expression is linear in $\mathbf{s}$, finding the Q-function or the expectation of (26) comes down to finding the expectation of $\mathbf{s}$, conditioned on both observations ($\mathbf{x}$ and $\mathbf{y}$) as well as $\hat{\mathbf{z}}^{(k-1)}$. We will denote this expectation as $\hat{\mathbf{s}}^{(k)}$, so that the final expression for the Q-function becomes:

$$Q(\mathbf{z},\hat{\mathbf{z}}^{(k-1)}) \propto -\frac{1}{2}(\mathbf{z}-\hat{\mathbf{s}}^{(k)})^T\mathbf{C_n}^{-1}(\mathbf{z}-\hat{\mathbf{s}}^{(k)}) - \frac{1}{2}(\mathbf{z}-\boldsymbol{\mu}_{\mathbf{z}|\mathbf{y}})^T\mathbf{C}_{\mathbf{z}|\mathbf{y}}^{-1}(\mathbf{z}-\boldsymbol{\mu}_{\mathbf{z}|\mathbf{y}}). \tag{27}$$

3.2 Calculation of $\hat{\mathbf{s}}^{(k)}$

The pdf of $\mathbf{s}$ given both observations and an estimate of $\mathbf{z}$ from the previous iteration is described as following:

$$\begin{aligned}p(\mathbf{s}|\mathbf{x},\mathbf{y},\hat{\mathbf{z}}^{(k-1)}) &= \frac{p(\mathbf{x}|\mathbf{s},\mathbf{y},\hat{\mathbf{z}}^{(k-1)})}{p(\mathbf{x}|\mathbf{y},\hat{\mathbf{z}}^{(\mathbf{k-1})})} \cdot p(\mathbf{s}|\mathbf{y},\hat{\mathbf{z}}^{(k-1)}) \\ &= \frac{p(\mathbf{x}|\mathbf{s},\mathbf{y},\hat{\mathbf{z}}^{(k-1)})}{p(\mathbf{x}|\mathbf{y},\hat{\mathbf{z}}^{(k-1)})} \cdot \frac{p(\hat{\mathbf{z}}^{(k-1)}|\mathbf{s},\mathbf{y})p(\mathbf{s}|\mathbf{y})}{p(\hat{\mathbf{z}}^{(k-1)}|\mathbf{y})}.\end{aligned}$$

Since conditioned on $\mathbf{s}$, $\mathbf{x}$ is independent of $\hat{\mathbf{z}}^{(k-1)}$ (see (2)), $\hat{\mathbf{z}}^{(k-1)}$ is independent of $\mathbf{y}$ (see (3)), besides $\mathbf{x}$ and $\mathbf{y}$ are independent, the conditional pdf can then be rewritten as:

$$\begin{aligned} p(\mathbf{s}|\mathbf{x},\mathbf{y},\hat{\mathbf{z}}^{(k-1)}) &= \frac{p(\mathbf{x}|\mathbf{s})p(\hat{\mathbf{z}}^{(k-1)}|\mathbf{s})p(\mathbf{s}|\mathbf{y})}{p(\mathbf{x}|\hat{\mathbf{z}}^{(k-1)})p(\hat{\mathbf{z}}^{(k-1)}|\mathbf{y})} \\ &\propto p(\mathbf{x}|\mathbf{s})p(\hat{\mathbf{z}}^{(k-1)}|\mathbf{s})p(\mathbf{s}|\mathbf{y}) \end{aligned}$$

with

$$\begin{aligned} p(\mathbf{x}|\mathbf{s}) &= \phi(\mathbf{W}\mathbf{s},\mathbf{C_n}-\mathbf{W}\mathbf{C_n}\mathbf{W}^T) \\ p(\hat{\mathbf{z}}^{(k-1)}|\mathbf{s}) &= \phi(\mathbf{s},\mathbf{C_n}) \\ p(\mathbf{s}|\mathbf{y}) &= \phi(\boldsymbol{\mu}_{\hat{\mathbf{z}}^{(k-1)}|\mathbf{y}},\mathbf{C}_{\hat{\mathbf{z}}^{(k-1)}|\mathbf{y}}+\mathbf{C_n}) \end{aligned}$$

where the first expression is derived from (2), the second from (3) and the third from the prior model assumption combined with (3). Thus, an estimate of the expectation of $\mathbf{s}$ leads to:

$$\begin{aligned} \hat{\mathbf{s}}^{(k)} &= \mathbb{E}[\mathbf{s}|\mathbf{x},\mathbf{y},\mathbf{z}^{(k-1)}] \\ &= \int \mathbf{s}p(\mathbf{x}|\mathbf{s})p(\hat{\mathbf{z}}^{(k-1)}|\mathbf{s})p(\mathbf{s}|\mathbf{y})d\mathbf{s} \\ &= \boldsymbol{\mu}+\mathbf{C}(\mathbf{x}-\mathbf{W}\boldsymbol{\mu}) \end{aligned} \tag{28}$$

with

$$\begin{aligned} \boldsymbol{\mu} &= \mathbf{B}[\mathbf{C_n}^{-1}\hat{\mathbf{z}}^{(k-1)}+(\mathbf{C}_{\hat{\mathbf{z}}^{(k-1)}|\mathbf{y}}+\mathbf{C_n})^{-1}\boldsymbol{\mu}_{\hat{\mathbf{z}}^{(k-1)}|\mathbf{y}}]. \\ \mathbf{C} &= \mathbf{B}\mathbf{W}^T[\mathbf{C_n}+\mathbf{W}(\mathbf{B}-\mathbf{C_n})\mathbf{W}^T]^{-1} \\ \mathbf{B} &= [\mathbf{C_n}^{-1}+(\mathbf{C}_{\hat{\mathbf{z}}^{(k-1)}|\mathbf{y}}+\mathbf{C_n})^{-1}]^{-1}. \end{aligned}$$

3.3 M-step

In this step, the estimate of $\mathbf{z}$ is updated by maximizing the Q-function in (27), which leads to:

$$\begin{aligned} \hat{\mathbf{z}}^{(k)} &= \arg\max_{\mathbf{z}} Q(\mathbf{z},\hat{\mathbf{z}}^{(k-1)}) \\ &= \mathbf{C}_{\hat{\mathbf{z}}^{(k-1)}|\mathbf{y}}(\mathbf{C}_{\hat{\mathbf{z}}^{(k-1)}|\mathbf{y}}+\mathbf{C_n})^{-1}\hat{\mathbf{s}}^{(k)}+\mathbf{C_n}(\mathbf{C}_{\hat{\mathbf{z}}^{(k-1)}|\mathbf{y}}+\mathbf{C_n})^{-1}\boldsymbol{\mu}_{\hat{\mathbf{z}}^{(k-1)}|\mathbf{y}}. \end{aligned} \tag{29}$$

3.4 Discussion

Remark that the obtained expression in the E-step (28) is a combination of the expressions obtained by a restoration of $\mathbf{x}$ and a fusion of $\mathbf{x}$ with $\mathbf{y}$. Indeed, when no high-spatial resolution image ($\mathbf{y}$) is available, (28) would reduce to (15) which is a deconvolution result of $\mathbf{x}$. On the other hand, if no EM algorithm would be applied, the MAP estimation of (22) would lead to (21) which is a Bayesian fusion of $\mathbf{x}$ and $\mathbf{y}$ using MAP estimation. The obtained expression in the M-step (29) makes use of both observations. Without the use of $\mathbf{y}$, the expression would reduce to (16), accounting for the interband correlation of $\hat{\mathbf{z}}^{(\mathbf{k-1})}$. While in (29), the correlation between $\hat{\mathbf{z}}^{(\mathbf{k-1})}$ and $\mathbf{y}$ are also accounted for. Therefore, the proposed approach is actually a combination of EM-based restoration and Bayesian fusion.

4. Experiments and analysis

4.1 Implementation

4.1.1 Noise covariance

The noise covariance $\mathbf{C_n}$ is required in the estimation. In this paper, instead of assuming it is known, it is estimated from $\hat{\mathbf{z}}^{(k-1)}$. The noise is assumed to be spectrally uncorrelated, so that $\mathbf{C_n}$ is diagonal:

$$\mathbf{C_n} = \begin{bmatrix} \mathbf{C_{n_1}} & \mathbf{0} & \cdots & \mathbf{0} \\ \mathbf{0} & \mathbf{C_{n_2}} & \cdots & \mathbf{0} \\ \vdots & \vdots & \ddots & \vdots \\ \mathbf{0} & \mathbf{0} & \cdots & \mathbf{C_{n_N}} \end{bmatrix} \text{ with } \mathbf{C_{n_n}} = \begin{bmatrix} \hat{\sigma}_1^2 & 0 & \cdots & 0 \\ 0 & \hat{\sigma}_2^2 & \cdots & 0 \\ \vdots & \vdots & \ddots & \vdots \\ 0 & 0 & \cdots & \hat{\sigma}_P^2 \end{bmatrix} \quad (n = 1, 2, \cdots, N).$$

The diagonal elements in the noise covariance can be estimated in several ways. In this work, we employ the well-known estimator by Donoho (Donoho & Johnstone, 1995):

$$\hat{\sigma}_p = \frac{\text{median}(|\hat{\mathbf{z}}_p^{(1,\text{diag})}|)}{0.6745} \tag{30}$$

where $\hat{\mathbf{z}}_p^{(1,\text{diag})}$ represents the wavelet diagonal subband at the first resolution scale of the pth $(p = 1, 2, \cdots, P)$ spectral band of $\hat{\mathbf{z}}^{(k-1)}$.

4.1.2 Spatial independence

Estimating the full size covariance matrix $\mathbf{C_{z|y}}$ (of size $NP \times NP$) is impractical for a typical size HS image. To keep the calculations feasible, we follow a similar strategy as employed in (Hardie et al., 2004). The pixels in $\mathbf{z}$ are assumed to be spatially conditionally independent, so that the conditional expectation and covariance can be estimated independently for each individual pixel:

$$\begin{aligned} \boldsymbol{\mu}_{\mathbf{z}|\mathbf{y}} &= [\boldsymbol{\mu}_{\mathbf{z}_1|\mathbf{y}_1}^T, \boldsymbol{\mu}_{\mathbf{z}_2|\mathbf{y}_2}^T, \cdots, \boldsymbol{\mu}_{\mathbf{z}_N|\mathbf{y}_N}^T]^T \\ \mathbf{C}_{\mathbf{z}|\mathbf{y}} &= \begin{bmatrix} \mathbf{C}_{\mathbf{z}_1|\mathbf{y}_1} & \mathbf{0} & \cdots & \mathbf{0} \\ \mathbf{0} & \mathbf{C}_{\mathbf{z}_2|\mathbf{y}_2} & \cdots & \mathbf{0} \\ \vdots & \vdots & \ddots & \vdots \\ \mathbf{0} & \mathbf{0} & \cdots & \mathbf{C}_{\mathbf{z}_N|\mathbf{y}_N} \end{bmatrix} \end{aligned}$$

where the individual conditional expectation and covariance is estimated as:

$$\begin{aligned} \boldsymbol{\mu}_{\mathbf{z}_n|\mathbf{y}_n} &= \mathbb{E}[\mathbf{z}_n] + \mathbf{C}_{\mathbf{z}_n,\mathbf{y}_n}\mathbf{C}_{\mathbf{y}_n}^{-1}(\mathbf{y}_n - \mathbb{E}[\mathbf{y}_n]) \\ \mathbf{C}_{\mathbf{z}_n|\mathbf{y}_n} &= \mathbf{C}_{\mathbf{z}_n} - \mathbf{C}_{\mathbf{z}_n,\mathbf{y}_n}\mathbf{C}_{\mathbf{y}_n}^{-1}\mathbf{C}_{\mathbf{z}_n,\mathbf{y}_n}^T. \end{aligned}$$

In this work, all related expectation as well as self- and cross-covariances are globally estimated, which denotes that they are constants for each pixel.

4.1.3 Block-by-block estimation strategy

Since $\mathbf{C_n}$ is diagonal and $\mathbf{C_{z|y}}$ is block-diagonal, $\boldsymbol{\mu} = [\boldsymbol{\mu}_1^T, \boldsymbol{\mu}_2^T, \cdots, \boldsymbol{\mu}_N^T]^T$ and $\mathbf{B}$ is also block-diagonal. However, because of the effect of $\mathbf{W}$ and matrix inversion, $\mathbf{C}$ is not block-diagonal. The calculation of **C** and thus the estimation in (28) cannot be implemented pixel by pixel. The matrix with size $NP \times NP$ is obviously too large to be practical. To solve this problem, we design a practical implementation scheme, in which **C** and thus $\hat{\mathbf{s}}^{(k)}$ are calculated block by block. The image is divided into non-overlapping blocks with an appropriate size (with M pixels, in this paper, a 16×16 square is used), which is sufficiently large for the PSF simulation and sufficiently small for keeping the calculations feasible. In this work, **W** models a space-invariant periodic convolution in the image domain. **W** is then a square block-circulant matrix (size $NP \times NP$) constructed from the convolution kernel. Using the same convolution kernel, we can construct $\mathbf{W}_b$ (size $MP \times MP$) in the same manner, which performs the blurring on each block in **z**, mimicking the way that **W** performs on **z**. The calculation of **C** and the estimation of **s** are then implemented block by block, using $\mathbf{W}_b$ instead of **W**.

4.2 Experimental setup

In this work, simulation experiments with a reference are employed for performance validation and comparison, so that the fused results can be compared to the reference. Performances of fusion techniques are usually difficult to be measured only based on observation, especially for multiband images. Objective and quantitative analysis can contribute to a more comprehensive evaluation. In this work, we employ the SNR in decibels between the result and the reference as the performance evaluation index:

$$\mathrm{SNR}(\mathbf{Z},\hat{\mathbf{Z}}) = 10\log_{10}\frac{\sum \mathbf{Z}^2}{\sum(\mathbf{Z}-\hat{\mathbf{Z}})^2}. \tag{31}$$

For the first set of experiments (Test 1), an AVIRIS HS image of NW Indiana's Indian Pine test site, USA in 1992 with 220 bands is employed. To construct the experimental data, we select 60 continuous bands (bands 11-70) and 128×128 pixels in each band, avoiding atmospheric water bands and bands with low SNR. To limit processing time, a 10-band HS reference image is constructed by averaging over 6 adjacent bands successively. It is then spatially smoothed by a Gaussian low-pass filter with a standard deviation of 1.2 and Gaussian noise is also added to acquire **x**. A 3-band image **y** is obtained by averaging the original 60-band image over 20 adjacent bands successively.

In the second set of experiments (Test 2), we apply the presented framework to a specific case of fusion, pansharpening, where an MS image of low spatial resolution is fused with a Pan image of high spatial resolution. For this, a set of color-composite Landsat images (3 bands, 30m resolution) and a SPOT Pan image (10m resolution) covering an area near London are used as test data. To be able to use the original Landsat image as a reference, we smooth it with a Gaussian low-pass filter with a standard deviation of 1.2 and Gaussian noise is also added to obtain **x**. A degraded SPOT Pan image to 30m is used as **y**.

For initialization of EM algorithm, we set $\hat{\mathbf{z}}^{(0)} = \mathbf{x}$.

4.3 Experimental results and analysis

4.3.1 Algorithm convergence

In this part, experiments are performed to validate the proposed fusion framework. In Test 1, general HS and MS image fusion is discussed, using **x** with noise level of 25dB. In Test 2, the proposed approach is validated for the specific case of pansharpening, using **x** with noise level of 20dB. In Fig. 1, the SNRs between the reference and fused images as a function of

Noise level	40	35	30	25	20
Test 1	35.4405	35.3011	34.7885	33.5456	29.0465
Test 2	25.3240	25.1845	24.9342	24.6979	24.2355

Table 1. SNR in fusion tests with different noise levels

the number of iterations of the EM algorithm involved are shown. It can be observed that the SNR increases sharply in the first several iterations and converges after around 10 iterations. The proposed approach is also validated for **x** with different noise levels (20-40dB) in both Test 1 and 2, and comparable results are observed. Fig. 2 shows **x** with specific noise levels and the corresponding fused results, as well as the reference from Test 2. The slight differences among all the fused images illustrate the excellent noise-resistance of the proposed fusion approach. The SNRs between the reference and fused images produced in different experiments are listed in Table 1, together with the original noise levels of **x**.

4.3.2 Knowledge about W

In the estimation of (28), the PSF **W** is required. Nevertheless, knowledge about the PSF is usually partly or totally unknown in practice. In this part, we will discuss the influence of (lack of) knowledge of **W** on the fused result. To address this problem, we arrange the following experiment. We employ the experimental data constructed in Section 4.2, while using Gaussian low-pass filters with standard deviation σ_1 to model **W**, with $\sigma_1 \in [0.3, 2.1]$ with a step of 0.1 (the actual $\sigma_1 = 1.2$). The SNRs between the fused and reference images as a function of σ_1 are shown in Fig. 3. It can be observed that a little underestimated or overestimated **W** ($\sigma_1 \in [1.0, 1.4]$) can still produce fairly good fused results. It seems that an overestimated **W** has even less influence on the fusion results than an underestimated **W**,

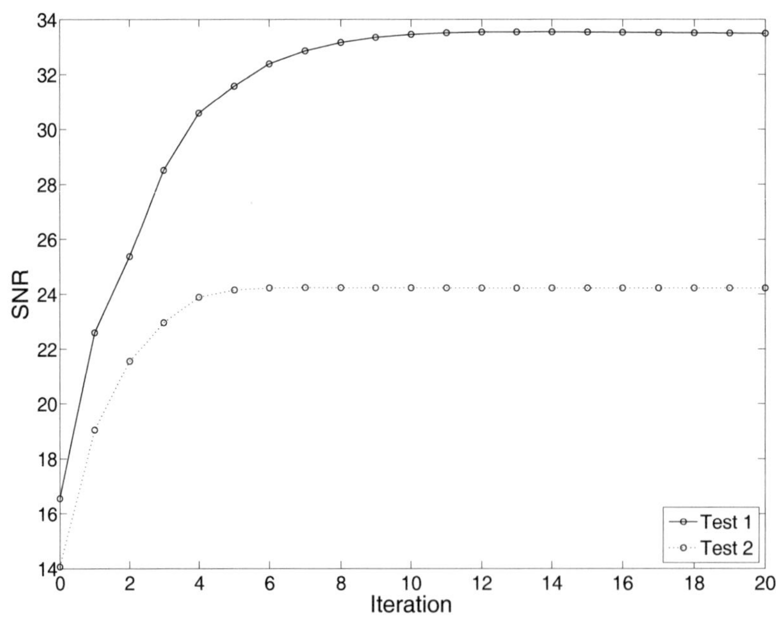

Fig. 1. SNR in function of number of iterations.

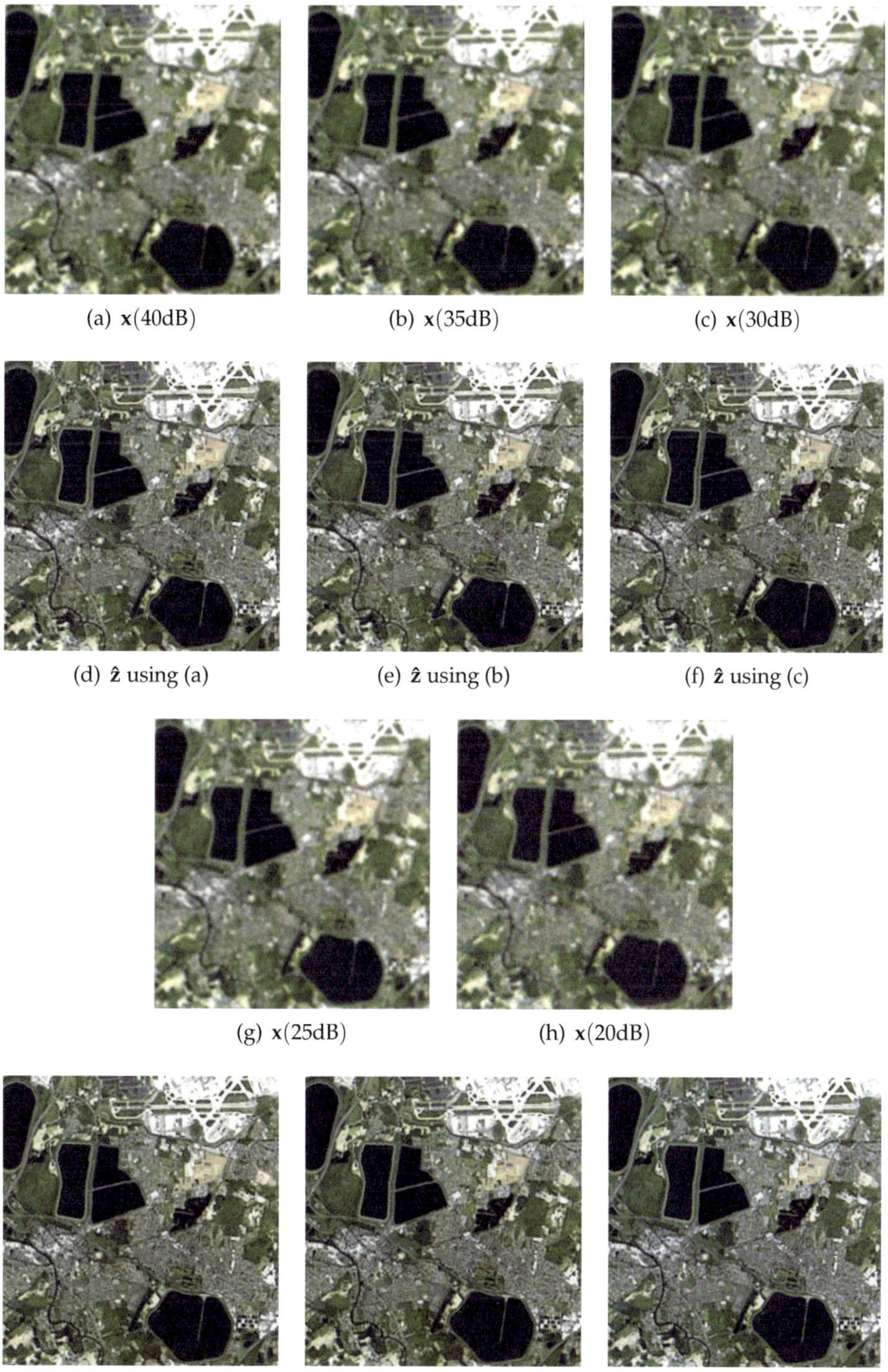

(a) $\mathbf{x}$(40dB) (b) $\mathbf{x}$(35dB) (c) $\mathbf{x}$(30dB)

(d) $\hat{\mathbf{z}}$ using (a) (e) $\hat{\mathbf{z}}$ using (b) (f) $\hat{\mathbf{z}}$ using (c)

(g) $\mathbf{x}$(25dB) (h) $\mathbf{x}$(20dB)

(i) $\hat{\mathbf{z}}$ using (g) (j) $\hat{\mathbf{z}}$ using (h) (k) Reference

Fig. 2. Experimental results in Test 2 using $\mathbf{x}$ with different noise levels.

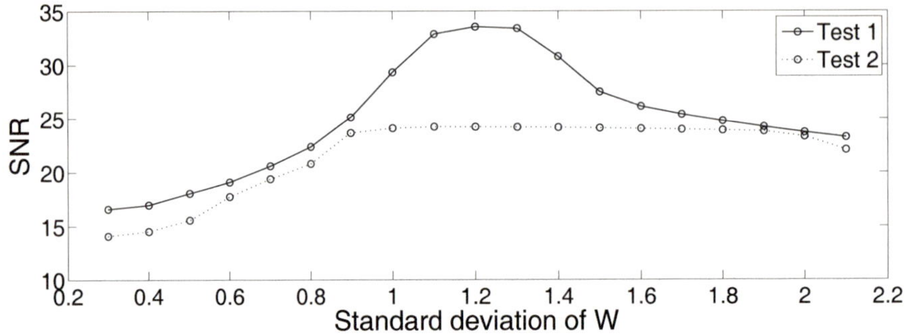

Fig. 3. Influence of **W** on fusion performance.

especially in Test 2 (dashed). It can be concluded that for the proposed fusion approach, the exact knowledge about **W** is not strictly required. By using a good approximation or estimation of **W**, fused results with fairly good quality can still be obtained.
In certain practical circumstances, ground truth (reference) may not be available as well, which means there is no prior knowledge about **W** at all. The proposed technique can still be applied, by applying Gaussian low-pass filters with increasing σ_1 as **W** and validating the results by users' observation. Some fused images from the pansharpening test with different underestimated as well as overestimated **W** are shown in Fig. 4.

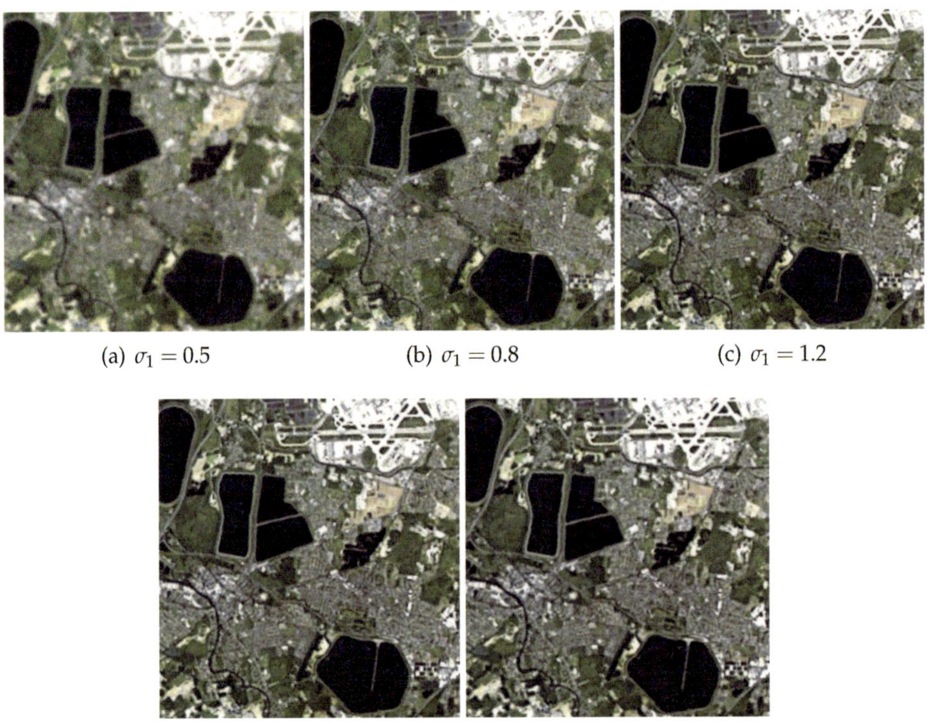

(a) $\sigma_1 = 0.5$ (b) $\sigma_1 = 0.8$ (c) $\sigma_1 = 1.2$

(d) $\sigma_1 = 1.7$ (e) $\sigma_1 = 2.0$

Fig. 4. Fused images using **W** with different σ_1.

4.3.3 Performance comparison

In this set of experiments we compare the proposed fusion technique with the EM-based restoration approach of (Duijster et al., 2009) as presented in Section 2.2.1 (denoted as EM-Res), and the Bayesian fusion approach of (Hardie et al., 2004) as presented in Section 2.2.2 (denoted as Bayes-F). To make a fair comparison, all three approaches employ the same statistical parameter estimation strategy.

When performing EM-Res, $\mathbf{W}$ denotes the imaging PSF and reflects the resolution difference between $\mathbf{x}$ and $\mathbf{z}$. Since no high-spatial resolution auxiliary information is utilized, its performance in spatial enhancement is usually quite limited. While in Bayes-F, $\mathbf{W}$ actually reflects the resolution difference between $\mathbf{x}$ and $\mathbf{y}$. Hence, the spatial resolution of $\mathbf{z}$ is limited to that of $\mathbf{y}$. It is notable that both resolution differences may be quite different in practice. However, either of the above two approaches only accounts for one of the resolution differences. The newly proposed fusion approach overcome this limitation, in which $\mathbf{W}$ describes the spatial resolution difference between $\mathbf{x}$ and $\mathbf{z}$, while the resolution difference between $\mathbf{x}$ and $\mathbf{y}$ is accounted for in the covariance estimation. In fact, it combines the advantages of the fusion and restoration techniques, obtaining a result which is actually a weighted result between the results produced by these two techniques. Depending on the spatial resolution differences and noise level in the observation model, it is capable of updating the weights adaptively. If the resolution difference between $\mathbf{x}$ and $\mathbf{y}$ is high, fusion is expected to contribute more to the result than restoration, while if it is low, the restoration part is expected to contribute more.

As a reminder, $\mathbf{W}$ is assumed to be known, but as shown in the first set of experiments, a fair estimation is sufficient. In the following experiments, we have used the knowledge of $\mathbf{W}$. The spatial resolution of $\mathbf{y}$ and thus knowledge about the spatial resolution difference between $\mathbf{x}$ and $\mathbf{y}$ is not required a priori and is estimated during the process.

In order to investigate the performance of different techniques, the following experiment is conducted. Gaussian low-pass filters $\mathbf{G}$ with standard deviation $\sigma_2 \in [0.3, 2.1]$ (with a step of 0.1) are applied to the original high-spatial low-spectral image, to generate $\mathbf{y}$ at different spatial resolution scales.

In Fig. 5, the SNRs as a function of σ_2 are shown, the original SNR of $\mathbf{x}$ and the reference is also depicted. The result produced by EM-Res is of course constant since it does not make use of $\mathbf{y}$, while the performance of Bayes-F decreases sharply with decreasing spatial resolution of $\mathbf{y}$ (increase of σ_2). For high spatial resolution of $\mathbf{y}$ ($\sigma_2 \in [0.3, 0.9]$), Bayes-F performs better than EM-Res. For higher values of σ_2, which implies the spatial resolution of $\mathbf{y}$ is only slightly higher or even lower than that of $\mathbf{x}$, EM-Res performs better than Bayes-F. When $\sigma_2 = 1.2$, the SNR of the result produced by Bayes-F is almost the same as the original SNR, which well explains the fact that no improvement can be expected by fusing two observations at the same spatial resolution scale. The slightly higher SNR over the original one can be attributed to the noise-resistance of Bayes-F. When the spatial resolution of $\mathbf{y}$ decreases further, Bayes-F does not make a contribution any more, it even deteriorates the $\mathbf{x}$ observation.

As for the proposed approach, three different regimes appear in Fig. 5. For low values of σ_2 ($\sigma_2 \in [0.3, 0.6]$), the result of the proposed technique is comparable to the Bayes-F result. For high values of σ_2 ($\sigma_2 \in [1.3, 2.1]$), restoration dominates the process and the result of the proposed technique seems to saturate to a value nearby the EM-Res result. This is more obvious in Test 1, in which general HS and MS image fusion is performed. The middle regime ($\sigma_2 \in [0.6, 1.3]$) is the most interesting one. In that regime, both restoration and fusion contribute to the result, leading to an improved fusion performance.

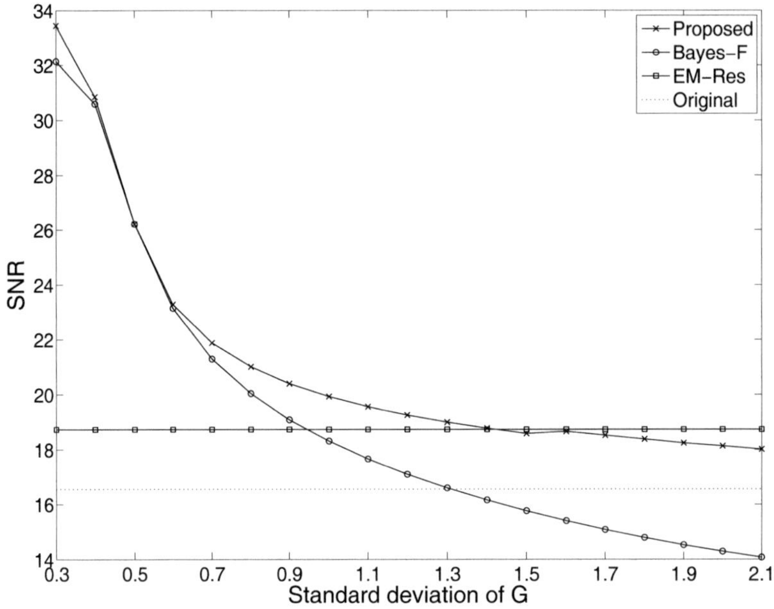

(a) Test 1

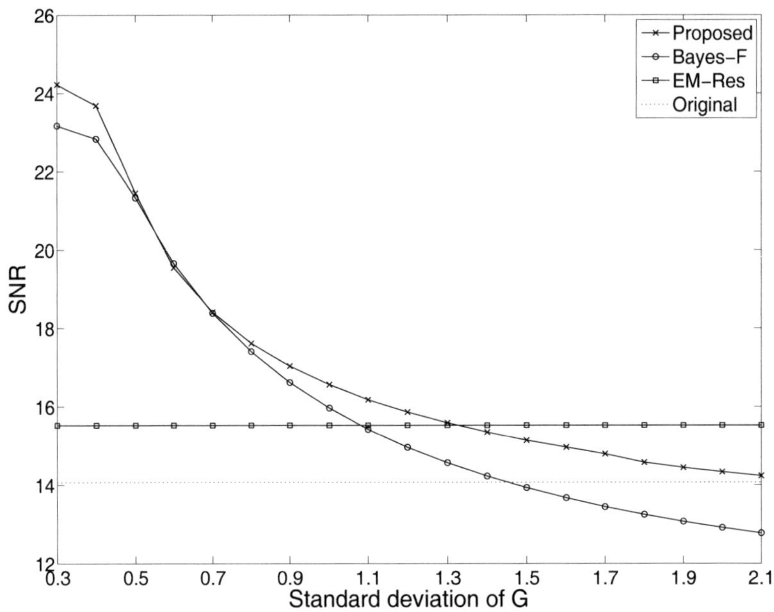

(b) Test 2

Fig. 5. Influence of the spatial resolution of **y** on performance.

(a) EM-Res (b) Bayes-F ($\sigma_2 = 0$) (c) Proposed ($\sigma_2 = 0$)

(d) Zoomed reference (e) Zoomed (a)

(f) Zoomed (b) (g) Zoomed (c)

Fig. 6. Experimental results from Test 2.

In Fig. 6, the experimental results of Test 2 are depicted, produced by EM-Res, Bayes-F and the proposed approach. Zoomed images of fusion results produced by Bayes-F and the proposed approach using $\mathbf{y}$ on different spatial resolution scales are also depicted in Fig. 7. It can be observed that for EM-Res, the spatial resolution improvement is limited and the result is quite noisy. The spatial resolution improvements of the results produced by Bayes-F and the proposed approach are comparable. When $\mathbf{y}$ is of lower spatial resolution, the spatial resolution improvement of the proposed approach is better than that of Bayes-F. However, severe spectral distortion (color difference with the reference) can be observed in Bayes-F result.

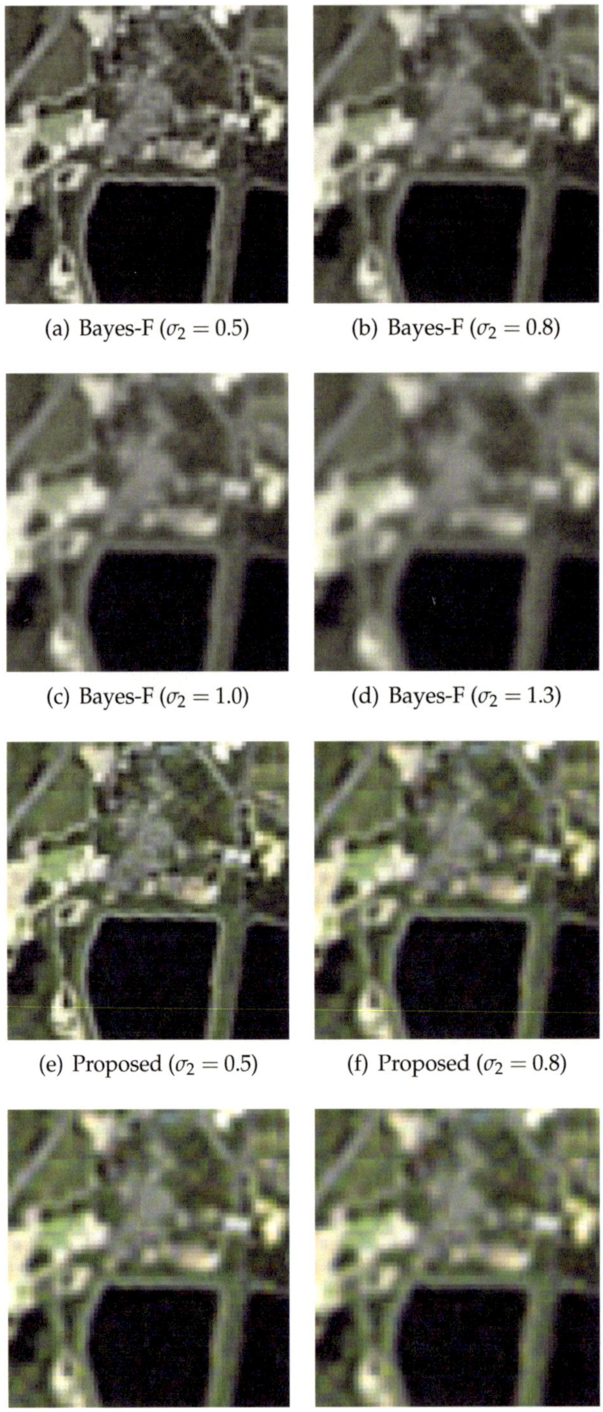

(a) Bayes-F ($\sigma_2 = 0.5$)

(b) Bayes-F ($\sigma_2 = 0.8$)

(c) Bayes-F ($\sigma_2 = 1.0$)

(d) Bayes-F ($\sigma_2 = 1.3$)

(e) Proposed ($\sigma_2 = 0.5$)

(f) Proposed ($\sigma_2 = 0.8$)

(g) Proposed ($\sigma_2 = 1.0$)

(h) Proposed ($\sigma_2 = 1.3$)

Fig. 7. Zoomed results in Test 2.

These findings reflect some weaknesses of EM-Res and Bayes-F approaches. EM-Res approach combines in each iteration a deconvolution step and a denoising step, the latter being a regularization step. It is known that such iterative processes sometimes overemphasize details and thereby tend to amplify the noise. On the other hand, the jeopardy with Bayes-F approach is that it may lose spectral fidelity of the low-spatial high-spectral resolution image by including spatial details from the high-spatial low-spectral resolution image. The proposed approach seems to be able to control both aspects by weighting of the contributions of restoration and fusion.

5. Conclusion

In this paper, a fusion approach for two observations (a low-spatial high-spectral resolution observation $\mathbf{x}$ and a high-spatial low spectral resolution observation $\mathbf{y}$) is proposed. The newly proposed fusion approach employs an iterative EM algorithm as well as a Bayesian fusion scheme, in which an image restoration process for $\mathbf{x}$ is applied in combination with a fusion of $\mathbf{x}$ and $\mathbf{y}$. In the simulation experiments, the proposed approach is validated and analyzed, as well as compared with some state-of-the-art techniques which clearly illustrates its advantages.

6. References

Aiazzi, B., Alparone, L., Baronti, S. & Garzelli, A. (2002). Context-driven fusion of high spatial and spectral resolution images based on oversampled multiresolution analysis, *IEEE Transaction on Geoscience and Remote Sensing* 40(10): 2300–2312.

Alparone, L., Baronti, S., Garzelli, A. & Nencini, F. (2004). Landsat ETM+ and SAR image fusion based on generalized intensity modulation, *IEEE Transaction on Geoscience and Remote Sensing* 42(12): 2832–2839.

Alparone, L., Wald, L., Chanussot, J., Thomas, C., Gamba, P. & Bruce, L. (2007). Comparison of pansharpening algorithms: outcome of the 2006 GRS-S data-fusion contest, *IEEE Transaction on Geoscience and Remote Sensing* 45(10): 3012–3021.

Carper, W. J., Lillesand, T. M. & Kiefer, R. W. (1990). The use of Intensity-Hue-Saturation transform for merging SPOT panchromatic and multispectral image data, *Photogrammetric Engineering and Remote Sensing* 56(4): 459–467.

Chang, C.-I. (2003). *Hyperspectral imaging: techniques for spectral detection and classification*, Kluwer Academic Publishers.

Chavez, P. S., Stuart, J., Sides, C. & Anderson, J. A. (1991). Comparison of three different methods to merge multiresolution and multispectral data: Landsat TM and SPOT panchromatic, *Photogrammetric Engineering and Remote Sensing* 57: 295–303.

Donoho, D. & Johnstone, I. (1995). Adapting to unknown smoothness via wavelet shrinking, *Journal of the American Statistical Association* 90(432): 1200–1224.

Duijster, A., Scheunders, P. & De Backer, S. (2009). Wavelet-based EM algorithm for multispectral-image restoration, *IEEE Transaction on Geoscience and Remote Sensing* 47(11): 3892–3898.

Edwards, K. & Davis, P. A. (1994). The use of Intensity-Hue-Saturation transform for producing color shaded-relief images, *Photogrammetric Engineering and Remote Sensing* 60(11): 1369–1374.

Eismann, M. T. & Hardie, R. C. (2004). Application of the stochastic mixing model to hyperspectral resolution enhancement, *IEEE Transaction on Geoscience and Remote*

Sensing 42(9): 1924–1933.

Eismann, M. T. & Hardie, R. C. (2005). Hyperspectral resolution enhancement using high-resolution multispectral imagery with arbitrary response functions, *IEEE Transaction on Geoscience and Remote Sensing* 43(3): 455–465.

Figueiredo, M. A. T. & Nowak, R. D. (2003). An EM algorithm for wavelet-based image restoration, *IEEE Transaction on Image Processing* 12(8): 906–916.

Gomez, R., Jazaeri, A. & Kafatos, M. (2001). Wavelet-based hyperspectral and multi-spectral image fusion, *Proceedings of SPIE* 4383: 36–42.

Hardie, R. C., Eismann, M. T. & Wilson, G. L. (2004). MAP estimation for hyperspectral image resolution enhancement using an auxiliary sensor, *IEEE Transaction on Image Processing* 13(9): 1174–1184.

Liu, J. G. & Moore, J. M. (1998). Pixels block intesnsity modulation: adding spatial detail to TM band 6 thermal imagery, *International Journal of Remote Sensing* 19(13): 2477–2491.

Núñez, J., Otazu, X., Fors, O., Prades, A., Palà, V. & Arbiol, R. (1999). Multiresolution-based image fusion with additive wavelet decomposition, *IEEE Transaction on Geoscience and Remote Sensing* 37(3): 1204–1211.

Pohl, C. & Van Genderen, J. L. (1998). Multi-sensor image fusion in remote sensing: concepts, methods and applications, *International Journal of Remote Sensing* 19(5): 823–854.

Shettigara, V. K. (1992). A generalized component substitution technique for spatial enhancement of multispectral images using a higher resolution data set, *Photogrammetric Engineering and Remote Sensing* 58: 561–567.

Shi, W. Z., Zhu, C. Q., Zhu, C. Y. & Yang, X. M. (2003). Multi-band wavelet for fusing SPOT panchromatic and multispectral images, *Photogrammetric Engineering and Remote Sensing* 69(5): 513–520.

Tu, T. M., Huang, P. S., Hung, C. L. & Chang, C. P. (2004). A fast intensity-hue-saturation fusion technique with spectral adjustment for IKONOS imagery, *IEEE Geoscience and Remote Sensing Letters* 1(4): 309–312.

Tu, T. M., Su, S. C., Shyu, H. C. & Huang, P. S. (2001). A new look at IHS-like image fusion methods, *Information Fusion* 2(3): 177–186.

Wang, Z., Ziou, D., Armenakis, C., Li, D. & Li, Q. (2005). A comparative analysis of image fusion methods, *IEEE Transaction on Geoscience and Remote Sensing* 43(6): 1391–1402.

Zhang, Y. & He, M. (2007). Multi-spectral and hyperspectral image fusion using 3-D wavelet transform, *Journal of Electronics(China)* 24(2): 218–224.

7

Pan-sharpening Methods based on ARSIS Concept

Mehran Yazdi and Arash Golibagh Mahyari
School of Electrical and Computer Engineering, Shiraz University, Iran

1. Introduction

Pan-sharpening aims to use image fusion techniques in the remote sensing field in order to synthesis the Multispectral (MS) images to higher resolution using spatial information of the Panchromatic (Pan) image. Up to now, several definitions for the image fusion have been suggested. Wald's definition (Wald, 1999) is one of these most celebrated definitions used commonly in the remote sensing community which defines image fusion as: "a formal framework in which are expressed means and tools for the alliance of data originating from different sources. It aims at obtaining information of a greater quality, although the exact definition of 'greater quality' will depend on the application". Many applications such as feature detection, change monitoring, urban analysis, and land cover classification recieve benefits of pan-sharpening. In fact, these applications need both high spectral and spatial resolution concurrently. Due to physical and technological constraints, creating a sensor which can provide high spectral and spatial resolution simultanously is not possible. So, the image fusion algorithms have been received increasingly attention to fuse MS and Pan images and to provide a new image including both spatial charachteristics of Pan and spectral charachteristics of MS images. Usually the pan-sharpening methods are categorized into three main sets (Wald, 2002; Thomas et al., 2008);projection substitution, relative spectral contribution, and methods that belong to the Amélioration de la Résolution Spatiale par Injection de Structures (ARSIS) concept.

The Projection–Substitution methods take advantage of a vectorial algorithm. In this kind of methods, all fused images corresponding to different MS images are synthesized simultaneously. These methods consider coincident pixels of MS images as spectral axes. Then, the spectral axes are projected into a new space to reduce the information redundancy. It results the decorrelated components. The structures of MS images, which are mainly related to color, are isolated by one of these components from the rest of the information. Actually these methods assume that the structures contained in this structural component are equivalent to those in the Pan image. Next, this structural component is replaced either partially or wholly with corresponding parts of Pan. Eventually, the inverse projection is performed to obtain the MS images in higher resolution, i.e. the fused images. The most famous methods of this category are those based on principal component analysis (PCA) (Ehlers, 1991; Chavez et al., 1991) and intensity hue saturation (IHS) (Haydn et al., 1982).

The Relative Spectral Contribution methods are also based on the linear combination of bands. The basic assumption of these methods is considering the low-resolution Pan as a

linear combination of original MS images. This assumption arises from the overlap of the spectral bands. Besides, a filtering operation applied on the Pan image is implicitly required. In addition, the fused MS product is a function of this linear combination and of the Pan image as well. Brovey (Gillespie et al, 1987) is the most important algorithm of this category.
The high correlation between the Pan and each MS images is the most important factor of the two mentioned categories which affects the fusion results. The higher the correlation between the Pan and each MS images is, the better the outcome of fusion will be. If the correlation of Pan and MS image is large, the MS image can be considered as an affine function of the Pan image. Moreover, the most characteristic of these two types of methods is their spectacular increase in visual impression with a good geometrical quality. So, they are well adapted to certain applications such as cartography or the localization of specific phenomena like target recognition (Vijayaraj et al, 2004; Yocky, 1996).Nevertheless, their major disadvantage is spectral distortion, called the color or radiometric distortion, characterized by inclining to present a predominance of a color on the others. However, their spectral distortion arises from the modification of the low frequencies of the original MS images (Shi et al, 2005). It means while no obvious relation exists between Pan and MS input modalities, creating the fused image as a function of the original MS and Pan images leads to this spectral distortion. Another disadvantage of these two types is that they apply the same model to the entire image (Thomas et al., 2008).
The third category is ARSIS concept which is the French acronym for "Amélioration de la Résolution Spatiale par Injection de Structures" meaning Improving Spatial Resolution by Structure Injection. The fundamental assumption of this type is that the missed spatial information in MS image can be derived from the high frequencies laying between orignial and low spatial version of the Pan, and possibly from external knowledge. This type is what would be discuused more in the following.
However, some other methods, called Hybrid methods, are possible which do not exclusively belong to one of the mentioned categories. They may include more than one category (Thomas et al., 2008). One of these renowned categories is projection-substitution combined with relative spectral contribution. Those methods which combine IHS method with spectral contribution assumption are the examples of this hybrid category. The relative spectral contribution combined with the ARSIS concept assumption is another famous category of hybrid methods. They are based on the minimization of energy functional. The third celebrated hybrid category is the projection-substitution combined with the ARSIS concept assumption. Many recent methods such as improved IHS method (González-Audícana et al, 2004), improved adaptive PCA method (Shah et al, 2008), etc can be put in this category.
In the following, more focuces will be placed on the ARSIS concept and it would be reviewed in more details. Then, some renowned methods based on ARSIS concept will be discussed. Finally, the simulation results of the described methods would be presented.

2. ARSIS concept

As mentioned in previous section, in ARSIS concept, synthesizing the MS image in higher resolution is seen as the inference of the information missing in the original MS image. The fundamental assumption of ARSIS concept is that the missing information is linked to the high frequencies of Pan and MS images. Indeed, finding this relationship between high frequencies in Pan and MS images is the thing that investigated in the ARSIS concept.

Methods based on ARSIS concept usually perform the following steps: at first, the required information should be elicited from Pan image; next, the missing information in MS image must be inferred using the extracted information; finally, the MS image in high resolution would be synthesized (Ranchin & Wald, 2000; Ranchin et al, 2003).

Although diverse algorithms for ARSIS concept are possible, the majority of recent algorithms apply multiscale or multiresolution transforms on both Pan and MS images to obtain a scale by scale description of the images content information. This description, called multiscale model (MSM), is usually represented by a pyramidal structure as shown in Figure 1 (Thomas et al., 2008).

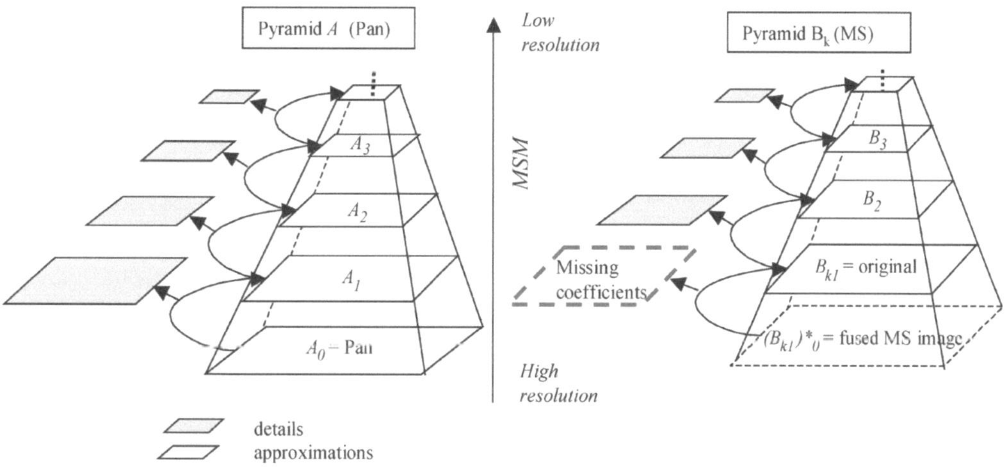

Fig. 1. Pyramidal structure of information (Thomas et al., 2008)

In this structure, the missing high frequency information of MS image, shown by dashed line in pyramid B, is extracted from the corresponding details in Pan image, which is displayed by gray parallelogram in pyramid A, to synthesize the MS image in higher resolution as indicated by dashed line in the bottom of pyramid B. However, if the extracted information from Pan is inserted directly into the missing high frequency information of MS image, the synthesized MS image may not be the same as "what would be seen if the MS image were taken by an especial sensor at Pan's resolution". Consequently, some adaption or transformation, called the intermodality model (IMM) (Wald, 2002) or the interband structure model (IBSM) (Ranchin et al, 2003), should be applied to adjust the extracted information to MS image. Figure 2 shows the ARSIS fusion procedure. Up to now, several IMM have been proposed (Ranchin et al, 2003; Aiazzi et al, 2002).

On the other hand, there are many methods like High Pass Filtering (HPF) method (Chavez et al., 1991) in which the extracted information are injected without any transformation into the low-resolution MS image. However, MSM might employ different transforms like Laplacian Pyramid (LP), Wavelet (Mallat, 1999), Curvelet (Starck et al, 2002), etc, to decompose and synthesize Pan and MS.

However, as the consistency property indicates (Thomas & Wald, 2004), if a fused product is downsampled to its original resolution, the original MS image must be restored. Since MSMs utilize mutiresolution algorithms to decompose input images into low and high frequency parts, they can isolate low frequencies from high frequencies and preserve the low frequencies while synthesizing high frequencies. Furthermore, in many papers it is

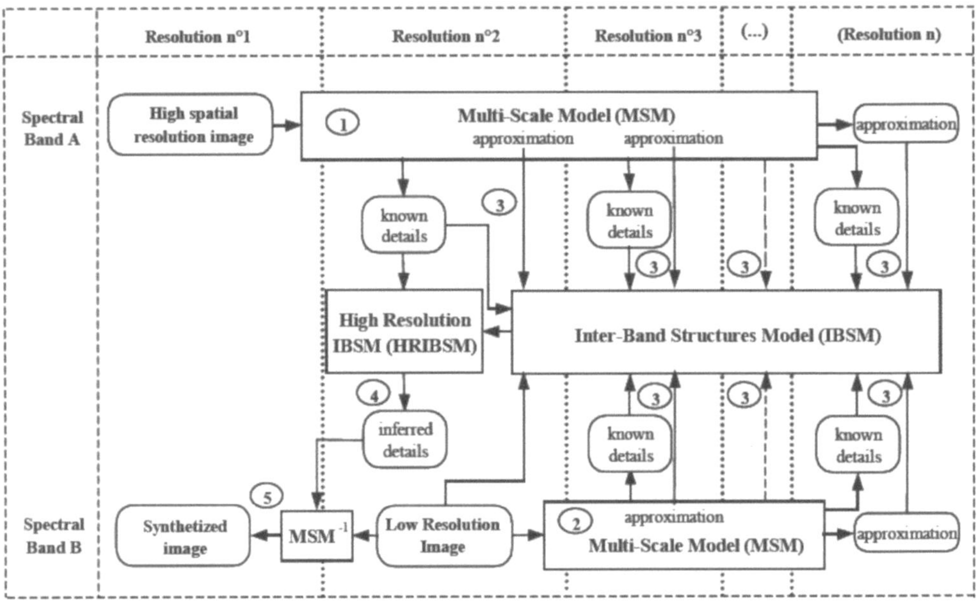

Fig. 2. General scheme for the application of the ARSIS concept (Ranchin et al, 2003)

mentioned that the multiresolution algorithms can provide a good trade off between preserving the low frequencies and injecting the high frequencies (Wald, 2002; Thomas et al., 2008; Ranchin et al, 2003). Nevertheless, multiscale algorithms should be selected in such a way that they do not produce artifacts affecting low frequencies like aliasing.

Likewise, many fusion methods are based on local estimation of parameters to take into account local dissimilarities between Pan and MS images. In these methods, the injection will be performed in such way that the local parameters meet certain demands. Although these methods assure good consistency with the original MS image, several experiments have demonstrated that it might decline the quality of the results and weakens image interpretation (Thomas et al., 2008).

However, the ARSIS concept is still being noticed by many researchers. We will discuss some of the famous ARSIS-based methods in more details in the following. Our discussion would concentrate on AABP model (Aiazzi et al, 2001), context driven method (Aiazzi et al, 2002) and the fusion method based on Linear Test Dependency (Golibagh Mahyar & Yazdi, 2010; 2009).

3. AABP model

The AABP (the model of Aiazzi, Alparone, Baronti and Pippi) proposed by Aiazzi *et al.* belongs to IBSM models (Aiazzi et al, 2001). As it was mentioned, IBSM models deal with the transformation of spatial structures with changes in spectral bands. Their model takes into account the relationship between the details or context of Pan and MS images.

In this method, the input images are decomposed into approximation and details coefficients by a multiresolution transform such as LP or wavelet. Let D_{MS}^{l} and D_{Pan}^{l} be the detail coefficients of MS and Pan images at certain resolution l, respectively. In addition, let C_{MS}^{l} and C_{Pan}^{l} be the approximation coefficients of input images. The AABP model tries to discover a local relationship between D_{MS}^{l} and D_{Pan}^{l}. This relationship is calculated by considering C_{MS}^{l} and C_{Pan}^{l}. In this model, it is assumed that the detail coefficients of MS can obtain by scaling the detail coefficients of Pan. This relation is defined as:

$$D_{MS}^{l} = \alpha \, . \, D_{Pan}^{l} \tag{1}$$

Where α is a coefficient representing the local relationship. Considering Figure 1, the missing coefficients in pyramid B are calculated by Eq. (1). In order to synthesize the MS image at a higher resolution, first Pan should be decomposed into a lower resolution. The obtained detail coefficients of Pan at this resolution are used to estimate the missing coefficients of the MS image in Eq. (1). Then, in order to acquire the proper value of α, the approximation coefficients of Pan and MS image are decomposed into a lower resolution. After calculating α, the missing coefficients of MS image can easily be anticipated by multiplying α at detail coefficients of Pan at the first level of decomposition. Finally, the synthesized MS image at a higher resolution can be created simply by computing the inverse multiresolution transform using original MS image as the approximation coefficients and estimated missing coefficients as the detail coefficients. This procedure is shown in Figure 3.

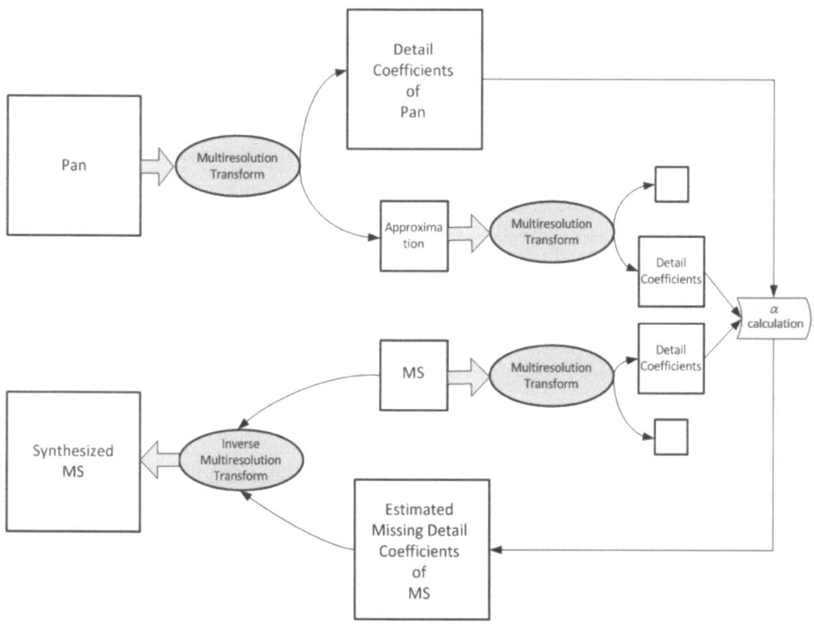

Fig. 3. Flowchart of AABP model

Furthermore, the calculation of α is performed in a $n \times n$ sliding window around each coefficient, typically 9×9 for IKONOS images. Let σ_{Pan} and σ_{MS} be the standard deviation of Pan's and MS's detail coefficient in this window. In addition, consider ρ as the local correlation coefficient between Pan's and MS's detail coefficient. Let also θ be a constant threshold. This threshold can have any value in the interval $[0.3 \, , 0.6]$; however the higher value of threshold is usually selected in condition that the correlation coefficient is not very large. According to these assumptions, α is chosen based on the below rule.

$$\alpha = \begin{cases} \min\left(\dfrac{\sigma_{MS}}{(1+\sigma_{Pan})}, 3\right) & if\ \rho \geq \theta \\ 0 & if\ \rho < \theta \end{cases} \tag{2}$$

To avoid numerical instabilities on homogenous areas of Pan, α is clipped above 3 in the first row of Eq. (2).

4. Context driven method

Similar to many methods in which the high frequencies of Pan are modified before injecting into MS, Context-driven method employs statistical measures in order to locally give weights to the high frequency coefficients of Pan. Moreover, this method uses a statistical criterion to make decision whether or not the high frequency coefficients obtained from Pan should be injected into the high frequency coefficients of MS. This decision rule is based on comparing the statistical criterion, which measures in turn the matching degree between the low-pass version of Pan and the expanded MS, using a specific threshold. Although the context-driven method can be implemented by any multiresolution transform, here we explain the algorithm based on wavelet transform.

In order to register the input images, original MS image should be upsampled by two and then passed into an 23-taps pyramid-generating lowpass filter. Next, Pan and upsampled MS are decomposed by wavelet transform. Let D_{MS}^{k} ; $k = H,V,D$ and D_{Pan}^{k} ; $k = H,V,D$ be the detail coefficients of MS and Pan images respectively where $k = H,V,D$ stand for Horizontal, Vertical and Diagonal coefficients. In addition, let C_{MS} and C_{Pan} be the approximation coefficients of input images. Firstly, the local correlation coefficient is calculated for every approximation coefficient. So, around $(i,j)th$ approximation coefficient in MS and Pan decomposed images, an $n \times n$-window is considered to compute the local correlation coefficient, named $LCC(i,j)$, between Pan and MS approximations; later during fusion process, $LCC(i,j)$ will be compared with the certain threshold θ. Furthermore, in order to create weighted Pan's detail coefficients before injecting into MS's detail coefficients, a local weight is calculated for $(i,j)th$ approximation coefficient; this weight is defined as the ratio of the standard deviation of MS image, which is locally computed in the $n \times n$ window among approximation coefficients of MS, to the standard deviation of Pan, locally computed in the $n \times n$ window among approximation coefficients of Pan. This weight for the $(i,j)th$ coefficient is $\gamma(i,j)$. Now, the $(i,j)th$ detail coefficient in all three subbands $k = H,V,D$ are injected, according to the rule in Eq. (3), into the corresponding location in MS's detail coefficient only if the $LCC(i,j)$ is greater than θ. The latter constraint is to avoid entering the unlikely unrelated details.

$$D_{MS}^{k} = \begin{cases} \gamma . D_{Pan}^{k} & if\ LCC \geq \theta \\ D_{MS}^{k} & Otherwise \end{cases} \quad ; \ k = H,V,D \tag{3}$$

Figure 4 shows the fusion procedure of this algorithm diagrammatically.

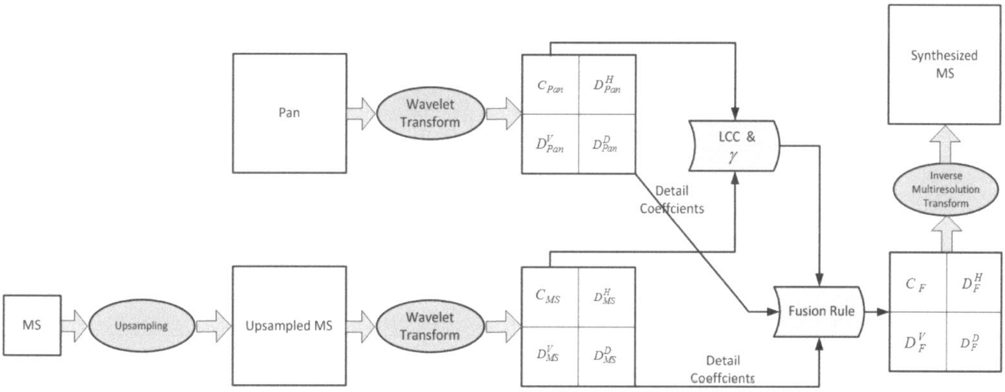

Fig. 4. Flowchart of fusion process based on context-driven method

5. GLP-SDM

Like other methods, the main goal of this method is to preserve the spectral information of MS images during the injection of high frequency details by means of selectively substituting the spatial-frequencies spectrum of Pan into MS image. In fact, the main idea of this method is based on minimizing the spectral distortion during fusion process which is performed by serving the Spectral Angle Mapper (SAM) as a criterion. However, the missing details are injected into the upsampled MS image after scaling them.

Suppose that h is the scaling ratio (e.g. $h = 2$ for Landsat images) between Pan and original MS images, namely the size of Pan is h times greater than that of original MS. Let MS be the original MS image, Pan be the Pan image and F be the fused image or enhanced MS image. In order to synthesize the MS image at higher resolution, first the original MS image is upsampled by h to create the upsampled MS image $M\tilde{S}$. Then $M\tilde{S}$ is passed into the h-expansion lowpass filter e_h whose cutoff frequency is equal to $1/h$ to prevent aliasing. On the other hand, in order to obtain the missing details, a low resolution version of Pan should be created. So, Pan is passed into the h-reduction lowpass filter r_h with cutoff frequency $1/h$ to avoid aliasing and then downsampled the results by h. Afterwards, the downsampled Pan is upsampled by h and passed into the h-expansion lowpass filter e_h with cutoff frequency $1/h$. This leads to the upsampled low resolution Pan image $\tilde{Pan}$. The difference between the upsampled low resolution Pan image and the original one is the missing details which must be injected into the upsampled MS image. Before injecting, the missing details must be rescaled. The proper gain, which can weigh the missing details appropriately, is defined as the ratio of the upsampled MS image ($M\tilde{S}$) over the upsampled low resolution Pan image; it means

$$\gamma = \frac{M\tilde{S}}{\tilde{Pan}} \tag{4}$$

Eventually, the final enhanced MS image is obtained by multiplying γ by the missing details and then adding the result to the upsampled MS image. The mentioned procedure is displayed in Figure 5.

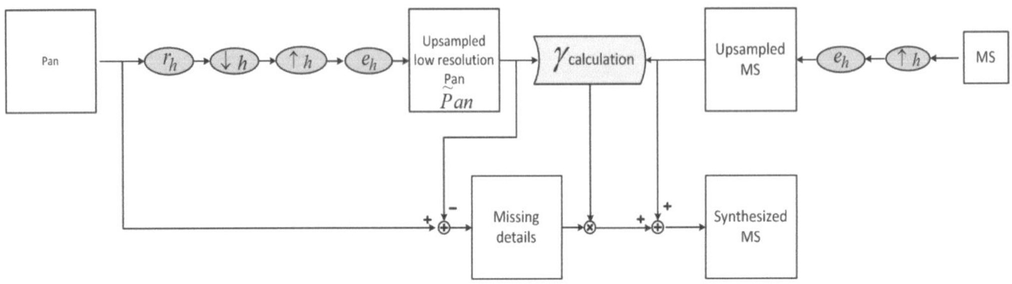

Fig. 5. Blockdiagram of GLP-SDM method

6. Fusion method based on linear dependency test

As it was pointed out, the MSMs use a multiresolution transform to decompose input images in order to efficiently represent their details. The choice of multiscale decomposing algorithm is crucial since it leads to improve the performance of fusion algorithm noticeably. Recently, beyond wavelets such as curvelet, contourlet, etc were proposed. The higher performance of these transforms in well representing details rather than LP and wavelet were proven (Starck et al, 2002). So, this method based on linear dependency test takes the advantages of curvelet transform (Starck et al, 2002). In addition, an appropriate fusion rule can increase the performance of fusion method significantly. Selecting the detail coefficients with the maximum absolute value is one of the simple fusion rules. However, fusion decision based on coefficient values alone can inject noise into the final image. As a result, not only the fusion algorithm won't enhance the spatial resolution of MS image, but also it will decline the spatial and spectral resolution of original MS image. So, in this method the detail coefficients are opted regionally. The outlandish details like lines are distributed among neighbouring detail coefficients. Therefore, in order to determine whether there is an outlandish feature in the vicinity of a detail coefficient, the linear dependency test is used in this method which is computed in a window centred on a certain coefficient detail. In the following, the basic concept of curvelet transform will be explained and then the fusion method based on the linear dependency test will be presented.

6.1 Discrete curvelet transform

Curvelets can be seen as an extension of wavelets for multidimensional data. The key difference between the wavelet and curvelet is that only curvelets are really directional. Curvelets satisfy the anisotropic scaling relation $width \approx length^2$ in the spatial domain (Candes & Donoho, 2000). For example, as shown in Figure 6(a), it would take many wavelet coefficients to accurately represent such a curve. Compared with wavelets, curvelets can represent a smooth contour with much fewer coefficients for the same precision (Figure 6(b)).

Curvelets are defined as a function of $x = (x_1, x_2)$ at scale 2^{-j}, orientations θ_l and positions $x_k^{(j,l)} = R_{\theta_l}^{-1}(k_1.2^{-j}, k_2.2^{-j})$ in the form of:

$$\varphi_{j,k,l}(x) = \varphi_j(R_{\theta_l}(x - x_k^{(j,l)})) \tag{5}$$

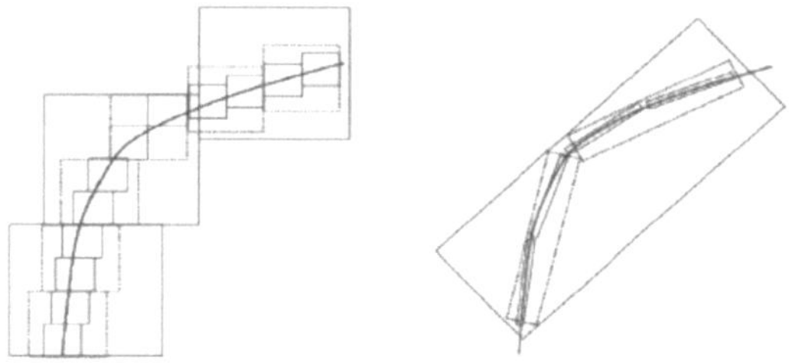
(a) (b)

Fig. 6. Comparison of non-linear approximation performance of wavelet and curvelet. (a) wavelet representation, (b) curvelet representation

where R_θ indicates amount of rotation by θ radians and for rotation angular we have $\theta_l = 2\pi.2^{-\lfloor j/2 \rfloor} l \ ; l = 0,1,2,\ldots,$ such that $0 \le \theta_l \le 2\pi$. $\varphi_j(x)$ is a waveform defined in the frequency domain as $\hat{\varphi}_j(\xi) = U(\xi)$ where $U(\xi)$ is defined in the polar coordinates as:

$$U_j(r,\theta) = 2^{-3j/4} W(2^{-j} r) V\left(\frac{2^{\lfloor j/2 \rfloor}\theta}{2\pi}\right) \tag{6}$$

where *W(r)* is the "radial window" supported on $r \in (0.5, 2)$ and *V(t)* is the "angular window" supported on $t \in [-1,1]$.

A curvelet coefficient is then simply the inner product between an element $f \in L^2(R^2)$ and a curvelet $\varphi_{j,l,k}$,

$$c(j,l,k) = < f, \varphi_{j,l,k} > = \int_{R^2} f(x) \cdot \overline{\varphi}_{j,k,l} dx \tag{7}$$

According to Plancherel's theorem, the above equation can be expressed as the integral over the frequency plane

$$\begin{aligned} c(j,l,k) &= \frac{1}{(2\pi)^2} \int \hat{f}(\xi) \overline{\hat{\varphi}}_{j,l,k}(\xi) d\xi \\ &= \frac{1}{(2\pi)^2} \int \hat{f}(\xi) U_j(R_{\theta_l} \xi) e^{i < x_k^{(j,l)}, \xi >} d\xi \end{aligned} \tag{8}$$

In (Candes et al, 2006), Candes *et al.* proposed two fast discrete curvelet transforms .The first one is a digital transformation which is based on unequally-spaced fast Fourier transforms (USFFT) and another is based on the wrapping of specially selected Fourier samples. We use the first fast discrete curvelet transform to decompose an image into its curvelet coefficients.

6.2 Fusion rule

At the first step, input images, Pan and MS, must be registered. It can be done by interpolating the MS image. Then, the registered images are decomposed by curvelet transform in order to set aside low frequencies for avoiding distortion. The low frequency part of MS image would be considered as the low frequency part of final image.

Furthermore, the linear dependency test is exerted to decide which detail coefficient should be injected into the MS detail coefficients. The linear dependency test can be performed based on either Wronskian determinant (Golibagh Mahyar & Yazdi, 2009) or Gramian (Golibagh Mahyar & Yazdi, 2010). For an $M \times N$ image I, Wronskian's determinant is calculated using Eq. (9)

$$D = \sum_{m=1}^{M} \sum_{n=1}^{N} C^2(m,n) - C(m,n) \tag{9}$$

In addition, the Gramian is defined as follows (Barth, 1999).

$$\begin{aligned} G(v_1, v_2, ..., v_N) &= \det\left(I^* I\right) \\ I &= \left(v_1 \; v_2 \; .... \; v_N\right) \end{aligned} \tag{10}$$

Where $C(m,n)$ is the $(m,n)th$ pixel and v_i is an M-dimensional vector of all pixels located in the ith column of the image.
In order to attain $(m,n)th$ detail coefficient of output image, an $W \times W$ window is considered around $(m,n)th$ detail coefficient of MS and Pan images. Then the linear dependency test is computed in this window based on either Eq. (9) or Eq. (10). The higher the value of Wronskian's determinant or Gramian is, the more prominent feature is inside the window. So this value can be compared between MS details and Pan ones to determine which input image has the stronger feature at the $(m,n)th$ detail coefficient. As a consequence, the detail coefficients of Pan will be injected to the final image only if this value in Pan details is greater than the value in MS details. Therefore, it will prevent the injection of noise and non-related details. The fusion rule in this method is defined as:

$$D_F(m,n) = \begin{cases} D_{Pan}(m,n) & if \;\; LD_{Pan}(m,n) \geq LD_{MS}(m,n) \\ D_{MS}(m,n) & if \;\; LD_{Pan}(m,n) < LD_{MS}(m,n) \end{cases} \tag{11}$$

Where $LD_{MS}(m,n)$ *and* $LD_{Pan}(m,n)$ are the value of linear dependency test which can be computed using either Eq. (9) or Eq. (10), respectively. In addition, $D_{Pan}(m,n)$, $D_{MS}(m,n)$, *and* $D_F(m,n)$ are the detail coefficients of Pan, MS and resulted fusion image, respectively. Figure 7 shows the flowchart of this algorithm.

7. Objective indicators

Generally, the quality of fusion process can be investigated either visually or quantitatively. Although a visual assessment gives better view about the quality of image fusion method owing to its dependence on human interpretation, it is not an appropriate way to compare different fusion methods. On the other hand, a quantitative assessment is more suitable to compare methods inasmuch since it is based on numerical values. However, some famous indicators are employed in this chapter in order to compare the mentioned fusion methods with each other. They are as follows.

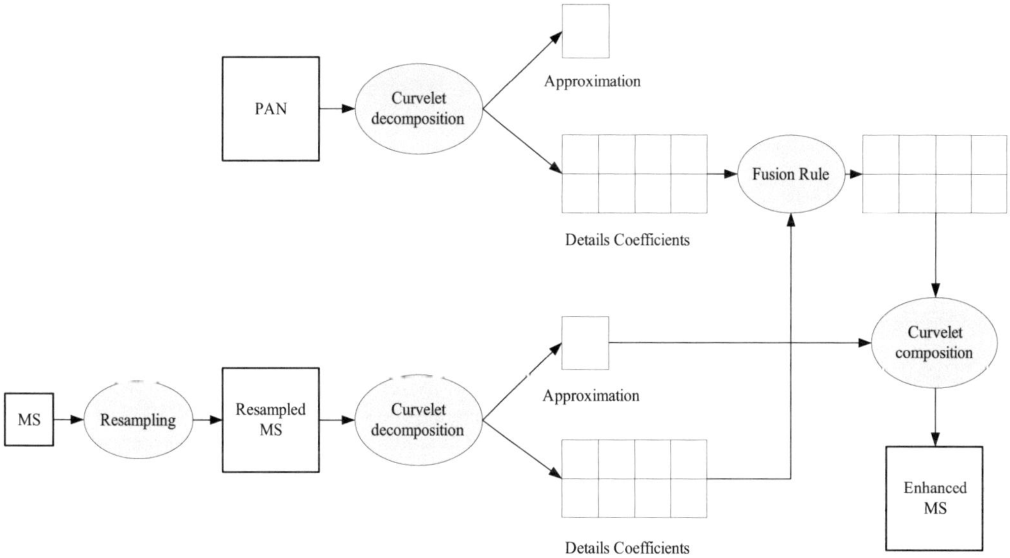

Fig. 7. Flowchart of fusion method based on linear dependency test

7.1 Erreur Relative Globale Adimensionnelle de Synthèse (ERGAS)

It means the relative global dimensional synthesis error and is defined as (Ranchin & Wald, 2000; Ranchin et al, 2003):

$$ERGAS = 100\frac{h}{l}\sqrt{\frac{1}{N}\sum_{i=1}^{N}\frac{RMSE^2(B_i)}{M_i^2}} \tag{4}$$

where h is the resolution of the high spatial resolution image, l is the resolution of the low spatial resolution image, M_i is the mean radiance of each spectral band involved in the fusion and RMSE is the root mean square error computed by:

$$RMSE^2(B_i) = bias^2(B_i) + SD^2(B_i) \tag{5}$$

The lower the value of the ERGAS is, the higher the spectral and spatial quality of the fused image will be.

7.2 Spectral Angle Mapper (SAM)

The spectral angle mapper for two given spectral vectors v and $\hat{v}$ is defined as (Ranchin & Wald, 2000; Ranchin et al, 2003):

$$SAM(v,\hat{v}) = \arccos\left(\frac{<v,\hat{v}>}{\|v\|_2\|\hat{v}\|_2}\right) \tag{6}$$

where $v = \{v_1, v_2, ..., v_L\}$ is the original spectral pixel vector $v_l = \tilde{G}^{(l)}(i,j)$ and $\hat{v} = \{\hat{v}_1, \hat{v}_2, ..., \hat{v}_L\}$ is the distorted vector obtained by applying the fusion process on the coarser resolution of

MS images, i.e. $\hat{v}_l = \hat{G}^{(l)}(i,j)$. SAM is calculated in degree for each pixel and is averaged on all pixels to obtain a single value.
The lower the value of the SAM is, the higher the spectral and spatial quality of the fused image will be.

7.3 Universal Image Quality Index (UIQI)

It is defined as (Wang & Bovik, 2002):

$$Q = \frac{\sigma_{\tilde{G}\hat{G}}}{\sigma_{\tilde{G}}\sigma_{\hat{G}}} \cdot \frac{2m_{\tilde{G}}m_{\hat{G}}}{m_{\tilde{G}}^2 + m_{\hat{G}}^2} \cdot \frac{2\sigma_{\tilde{G}}\sigma_{\hat{G}}}{\sigma_{\tilde{G}}^2 + \sigma_{\hat{G}}^2} \tag{7}$$

The UIQI is designed by modeling any image distortion as a combination of three factors: loss of correlation, radiometric distortion, and contrast distortion.
The greater the value of the UIQI is, the higher the spectral and spatial quality of the fused image will be.

7.4 Correlation Coefficient (CC)

It is defined as (Khan, 2008):

$$CC_{A,B} = \frac{1}{M \times N} \frac{\sum_{i=1}^{M}\sum_{j=1}^{N}(A(i,j)-\mu_A)(B(i,j)-\mu_B)}{\sqrt{\left(\sum_{i=1}^{M}\sum_{j=1}^{N}(A(i,j)-\mu_A)^2\right)\left(\sum_{i=1}^{M}\sum_{j=1}^{N}(B(i,j)-\mu_B)^2\right)}} \tag{8}$$

It is calculated between fused image and reference image.

8. Experimental results and discussion

A sample data set, which was obtained from LandSat ETM+, is used in order to evaluate the described methods. This satellite provides seven multispectral images in bands 1-7 and one panchromatic image in band 8. These bands are in three different resolution categories as follows.

- 30 m for bands 1–5 and 7;
- 60 m for band 6;
- 15 m for band 8.

According to the spectral range of these 8 bands, only three bands 2, 3 and 4 have overlap with spectral range of Pan which is why only these three bands are used to fuse with Pan and assess the fusion methods' performance. These three bands can be displayed as an RGB image.
The outcomes of applying AABP, context-driven, GLP-SDM and Fusion Method based on Linear Dependency Test methods are depicted in Figure 8.
In order to compare different methods, the original MS image in Figure 8(b) is set as the reference. AABP method (whose fusion result is shown in Figure 8(c)) not only did not enhance the resolution of the upsampled MS image (Figure 8(a)) but also injected noise and led the fusion result to become blurred. In addition, this method caused spectral distortion

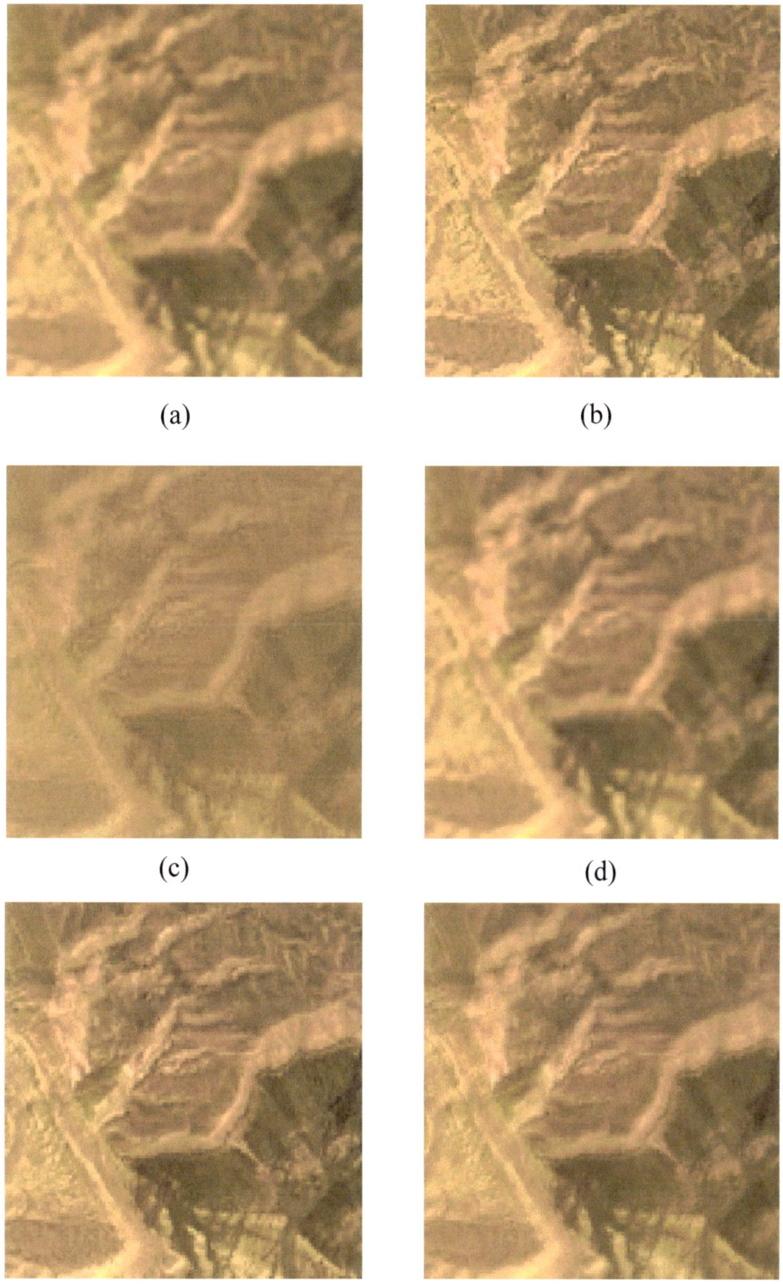

Fig. 8. Experimental results obtained using different methods; (a) upsampled low resolution MS; (b) original MS; Fusion results of (c) AABP model; (d) context-driven; (e) GLP-SDM; (f) Linear dependency test

in the final result which can be seen especially in the left-down corner of the image where mustered color was turned to bright brown. On the other hand, the context-driven method in the Figure 8(d) preserved the spectral content of MS image; it also enhanced the spatial resolution somehow but the image was still blurred. Unlike these two methods, the fusion results of GLP-SDM method was enhanced noticeably. Furthermore, visually comparison does not indicate any spectral distortion. Finally, the method based on linear dependency test provided enhancements in upsampled MS image. Moreover, no spectral distortion can be identified in the fusion outcome.
However, evaluation criteria can provide a better comparison among various methods. So that these four methods are compared numerically in Table 1 using described evaluation criteria in the previous section.

	ERGAS	SAM	UIQI	CC
AABP Model	3.73	1	0.29	0.73
Context-Driven	1.49	0.72	0.85	0.92
GLP-SDM	1.57	0.65	0.88	0.95
Linear Dependency Test	1.39	0.71	0.89	0.96

Table 1. Evaluation Criteria comparison

Sure enough, the AABP model has the worst performance among these four methods according to Table 1. On the other hand, although the evaluation criteria values of the other three methods are very close to each other, GLP-SDM and Linear Dependency Test methods have better outcomes in compare with context-driven method. Likewise, the performance of Linear Dependency Test method in spatial enhancement is little better than that of GLP-SDM method. Nevertheless, according to SAM, the GLP-SDM method preserves the spectral content better as it is clear from a visual comparison.

9. Conclusion

In this chapter, the ARSIS concept, one of the most important categories for the image fusion, was considered. The basic assumption of ARSIS concept is the existence of a relationship between high frequency components of Pan and MS images. So, the majority of fusion methods in this category incline to decompose input images by a multiresolution transform in order to separate high frequencies from low frequencies resulting in preservation of low frequencies during the fusion process.
Furthermore, four novel fusion methods were elaborated. Eventually, the methods were compared visually and assessed quantitatively based on some well-known criteria. However, further works on ARSIS concept would be appreciated by introducing newer multiresolution transform like ridgelet, surfacelet, etc.

10. References

Aiazzi, B.; Alparone, L.; Baronti, S.; & Pippi, I. (November 8-9th 2001). Quality assessment of decision-driven pyramid-based fusion of high resolution multispectral with panchromatic image data. *Proceedings of the IEEE/ISPRS Joint Workshop on Remote Sensing and Data Fusion over Urban Areas*, Rome, Italy, pp. 337-341.

Aiazzi, B.; Alparone, L.; Baronti, S.; & Garzelli, A. (Oct. 2002). Context-Driven Fusion of High Spatial and Spectral Resolution Images Based on Oversampled Multiresolution Analysis. *IEEE Transaction on Geoscience and Remote Sensing*, vol. 40, no. 10, pp. 2300-2312.

Barth, N.R. (1999). The Gramian and K-Volume in N-Space: Some Classical Results in Linear Algebra. *Journal of Young Invest. parallelograms by Frank Jones.*

Candes, E., Donoho, D.L. (2000): Curvelets: a surprisingly effective non-adaptive representation of objects with edges. Vanderbilt University Press, Nashville, TN. ISBN. 0-8265-1357-3.

Candes, E., Demanet, L., Donoho, D.L., Ying, L. (2006): Fast Discrete Curvelet Transform. www.curvelet.org.

Chavez, P. S.; Sides, Jr, S. C. & Anderson, J. A. (1991). Comparison of three different methods to merge multiresolution and multispectral data: Landsat TM and SPOT panchromatic, *Photogrammetric Engineering and Remote Sensing*, vol. 57, no. 3, pp. 295–303.

Ehlers, M. (1991). Multisensor image fusion techniques in remote sensing, *ISPRS Journal of Photogramm and Remote Sensing*, vol. 51, pp. 311–316.

Gillespie, A. R.; Kahle, A. B. & Walker, R. E. (Aug. 1987). Color enhancement of highly correlated images—II Channel ratio and 'chromacity' transformation techniques, *Remote Sensing of Environment*, vol. 22, no. 3, pp. 343–365.

Golibagh Mahyar, A. & Yazdi, M. (7-9March 2009). A Novel Image Fusion Method Using Curvelet Transform Based on Linear Dependency Test, *The 1nd International Conference on Digital Image Processing (ICDIP 2009)*, p.p. 351-354, Thailand.

Golibagh Mahyar, A. & Yazdi, M. (2010). Remote Sensing Image Fusion using Gramian as a Rule of Fusion, *accepted in International Journal of Electronics.*

González-Audícana, M.; Saleta, J. L.; Catalán, R. G. & García, R. (Jun. 2004). Fusion of multispectral and panchromatic images using improved IHS and PCA mergers based on wavelet decomposition, *IEEE Transaction on Geoscience and Remote Sensing*, vol. 42, no. 6, pp. 1291–1299.

Haydn, R.; Dalke, G. W.; Henkel, J. & Bare, J. E. (1982). Application of the IHS color transform to the processing of multisensor data and image enhancement, *Proceeding of International Symposium of Remote Sensing Arid, Semi-Arid Lands*, pp. 599–616, Cairo, Egypt.

Khan, M. M. ; Chanussot, J. ; Condat, L.; & Montanvert, A. (Jan 2008). Indusion: Fusion of Multispectral and Panchromatic Images Using the Induction Scaling Technique, *IEEE Geoscience and Remote Sensing Letters*, vol. 5, no. 1, p.p. 98-102.

Mallat , S. (1999). *A Wavelet Tour of Signal Processing*, Academic Press, 2nd Edition.

Ranchin, T. & Wald, L. (Jan. 2000). Fusion of high spatial and spectral resolution images: The ARSIS concept and its implementation, *Photogrammetric Engineering and Remote Sensing*, vol. 66, no. 1, pp. 49–61.

Ranchin, T.; Aiazzi, B.; Alparone, L.; Baronti, S.; & Wald, L. (Jun. 2003). Image fusion—The ARSIS concept and some successful implementation schemes, *ISPRS Journal of Photogrammetric and Remote Sensing*, vol. 58, no. 1/2, pp. 4–18.

Shah, V. P.; Younan, N. H.; & King, R. L. (May 2008). An Efficient Pan-Sharpening Method via a Combined Adaptive PCA Approach and Contourlets, *IEEE Transactions on Geoscience and Remote Sensing*, vol. 46, no. 5, pp. 1323–1335.

Shi, W.; Zhu, C.; Tian, Y. & Nichol, J. (Mar. 2005). Wavelet-based image fusion and quality assessment, *International Journal of Applied Earth Observation Geoinformation*, vol. 6, no. 3/4, pp. 241-251.

Starck , J.L., Candès, E.J., Donoho, D.L. (Jun. 2002). The Curvelet Transform for Image Denoising. *IEEE Transaction on Image Processing*, vol. 11, no. 6, pp.670-684.

Thomas, C. & Wald, L. (May 25-27, 2004). Assessment of the quality of fused products, *Proceeding of 24th EARSeL Symposium on New Strategies for European Association of Remote Sensing*, Dubrovnik, Croatia, Oluic, Ed. Rotterdam, The Netherlands: Millpress, pp. 317-325.

Thomas, C.; Ranchin, T,; Wald, L. & Chanussot, J. (May 2008). Synthesis of Multispectral Images to High Spatial Resolution: A Critical Review of Fusion Methods Based on Remote Sensing Physics, *IEEE Transaction on Geoscience and Remote Sensing*, vol. 46, no. 5, pp. 1301-1312.

Vijayaraj, V.; O'Hara, C. & Younan, N. (2004). Quality analysis of pansharpened images, *Proceeding of IEEE IGARSS*, vol. 1, pp. 85-88.

Wald, L. (May 1999). Some terms of reference in data fusion. *IEEE Transaction on Geoscience and Remote Sensing*, vol. 37, no. 3, pp. 1190-1193.

Wald, L. (2002). *Data Fusion: Definitions and Architectures. Fusion of Images of Different Spatial Resolutions*. Les Presses de l'école des Mines, ISBN: 978-2-911762-38-3, Paris, France.

Wang, Z.; & Bovik, A.C. (March 2002). A Universal Image Quality Index, *IEEE Signal Processing Letters*, vol. 9, no. 3, pp. 81-84.

Yocky, D. A. (1996). Multiresolution wavelet decomposition image merger of Landsat Thematic Mapper and SPOT panchromatic data, *Photogrammetric Engineering and Remote Sensing*, vol. 62, no. 9, pp. 1067-1074.

Image Fusion Using a Parameterized Logarithmic Image Processing Framework

Sos S. Agaian[1], Karen A. Panetta[2] and Shahan C. Nercessian[2]
[1]University of Texas at San Antonio
[2]Tufts University
USA

1. Introduction

Advances in sensor technology have brought about extensive research in the field of image fusion. Image fusion is the combination of two or more source images which vary in resolution, instrument modality, or image capture technique into a single composite representation (Hill et al., 2002). Thus, the source images are complementary in many ways, with no one input image being an adequate data representation of the scene. Therefore, the goal of an image fusion algorithm is to integrate the redundant and complementary information obtained from the source images in order to form a new image which provides a better description of the scene for human or machine perception (Kumar & Dass, 2009). Image fusion is essential for computer vision and robotics systems in which fusion results can be used to aid further processing steps for a given task. Image fusion techniques are practical and fruitful for many applications, including medical imaging, security, military, remote sensing, digital camera and consumer use. There are many cases in medical imaging where viewing a series of images individually is not convenient. For example, magnetic resonance imaging (MRI) and computed tomography (CT) images provide structural and anatomical information with high resolution. Positron emission tomography (PET) and single photon emission computed tomography (SPECT) images provide functional information with low resolution. Therefore, the fusion of MRI or CT images with PET or SPECT images can provide the needed structural, anatomical, and functional information for medical diagnosis, anomaly detection and quantitative analysis (Daneshvar & Ghassemian, 2010). Moreover, the combination of MRI and CT images can provide images containing both dense bone structure and soft tissue information (Yang et al., 2010). Similarly, the combination of MRI-T1 images provides greater details of anamotical structures while MRI-T2 images provides greater contrast between normal and abmormal tissue matter, and thus, their fusion can also help to extract the features needed by physicians (Wang, 2008). In security applications, thermal/infrared images provide information regarding the presence of intruders or potential threat objects (Zhang & Blum, 1997). For military applications, such images can also provide terrain clues for helicopter navigation. Visible light images provide high-resolution structural information based on the way in which light is reflected. Thus, the fusion of thermal/infrared and visible images can be used to aid navigation, concealed weapon detection, and surveillance/border patrol by humans or automated computer vision security systems (Qiong et al., 2008). In remote sensing applications, the fusion of multi-spectral low-resolution remote sensing images with a high-resolution panchromatic image can yield a high-resolution multispectral image with good spectral and spatial characteristics (Chibani, 2005). As a visible light image is taken by a CCR device at a given focal point, certain objects in the image may be in focus while others may be blurred and out of focus. For digital camera applications and consumer use, the fusion of images taken at different focal points can essentially create an image having multiple focal points in which all objects in the scene are in focus (Zhang, 1999).

The most basic of image fusion approaches include spatial domain techniques using simple averaging, Principal Component Analysis (PCA) (Chavez & Kwarteng, 1989), and the Intensity-Hue-Saturation (IHS) transformation (Tu et al., 2001). However, such methods do not incorporate aspects of the human visual system in their formulation. It is well known that the human visual system is particularly sensitive to edges at their various scales (Tabb & Ahuja, 1997). Based on this fact, multi-resolution image fusion techniques have been proposed in order to yield more visually accurate fusion results. These approaches decompose image signals into low-pass and high-pass coefficients via a multi-resolution decomposition scheme, fuse low-pass and high-pass coefficients according to specific fusion rules, and perform an inverse transform to yield the final fusion result. The use of different fusion rules for low-pass and high-pass coefficients provides a means of yielding fusion results inspired by the human visual system. Pixel-based image fusion algorithms fuse detail coefficients pixels individually based on either selection or weighted averaging. Motivated by the fact that applications requiring image fusion are interested in integrating information at the feature level, region-based image fusion algorithms use segmentation to extract regions corresponding to perceived objects from the source images, and fuse regions according to a region activity measure (Piella, 2003). Because of their general formulations, both pixel- and region-based fusion rules can be adopted using any multi-resolution decomposition technique, allowing for a convenient means of comparing the performance of multi-resolution decomposition schemes for image fusion while keeping the fusion rules constant. The most common of multi-resolution decomposition schemes for image fusion have been the pyramid transforms and wavelet transforms. Particularly, pixel- and region-based image fusion algorithms using the Laplacian Pyramid (LP) (Burt & Adelson, 1983), Discrete Wavelet Transform (DWT) (Mallat, 1989), and Stationary Wavelet Transform (SWT) (Rockinger, 1997) have been proposed.

Although much of the research in image fusion has strived to formulate effective image fusion techniques which are consistent with the human visual system, the mentioned multi-resolution decomposition schemes and their respective image fusion algorithms are implemented using standard arithmetic operators which are not suitable for processing images. Conversely, the Logarithmic Image Processing (LIP) model was proposed to provide a nonlinear framework for visualizing images using a mathematically rigorous arithmetical structure specifically designed for image manipulation (Jourlin & Pinoli, 2001). The LIP model views images in terms of their graytone functions, which are interpreted as absorption filters. It processes graytone functions using a new arithmetic which replaces standard arithmetical operators. The resulting set of arithmetic operators can be used to process images based on a physically relevant image formation model. The model makes use of a logarithmic isomorphic transformation, consistent with the fact that the human visual system processes light logarithmically. The model has also shown to satisfy Weber's

Law, which quantifies the human eye's ability to perceive intensity differences for a given background intensity (Pinoli, 1998). As a result, image enhancement, edge detection, and image restoration algorithms utilizing the LIP model have yielded better results (Deng et al., 2009; Debayle et al., 2006).

However, an unfortunate consequence of the LIP model for general practical purposes is that the dynamic range of the processed image data is left unchanged causing information loss and signal clipping. Moreover, specifically for image fusion purposes, the combination of source images in regions of vastly different mean intensity yield visually poor results even though their processing is motivated by a relevant physical model. It is therefore advantageous to formulate a generalized image processing framework which is able to effectively unify the LIP and standard processing frameworks into a single framework. Consequently, the Parameterized Logarithmic Image Processing (PLIP) model was formulated. The PLIP model is a generalization of the LIP model which attempts to overcome the mentioned shortcomings of the standard processing and LIP models and can yield visually more pleasing outputs (Panetta et al., 2008). A mathematical analysis shows that in fact LIP and standard mathematical operators are instances of the generalized PLIP framework. Adaptations of edge detection and image enhancement algorithms using the PLIP model have demonstrated the improved performance achieved by the parameterized framework (Panetta et al., 2007; Wharton et al. 2008). In this chapter, we investigate the use of the PLIP model for image fusion applications. New multi-resolution decomposition schemes and image fusion rules using the PLIP model are introduced, and consequently, new pixel- and region-based image fusion algorithms using the PLIP model are proposed.

The remainder of this chapter is organized as follows: Section 2 provides a brief overview of commonly used multi-scale image decomposition techniques. Section 3 provides background information for pixel-based image fusion algorithms, while Section 4 provides background information for region-based image fusion algorithms. Section 5 describes the LIP and PLIP models, and in particular, analyzes the advantageous properties of the proposed PLIP model. Section 6 subsequently introduces the proposed multi-scale image decomposition techniques and image fusion algorithms. Section 7 describes the quality metric used for quantitative assessment of image fusion quality. Section 8 compares the proposed image fusion algorithms with existing standards via computer simulations. Section 9 draws conclusions based on the presented experimental results.

2. Multi-resolution image decomposition schemes

2.1 Laplacian Pyramid (LP)

The LP uses the Gaussian Pyramid to provide a multi-resolution image representation for an image I (Burt & Adelson, 1983). Analysis and synthesis using the LP is illustrated in Figure 1. Each analysis stage consists of low-pass filtering, down-sampling, interpolating, and differencing steps in order to generate the approximation coefficients $y_0^{(n)}$ and detail coefficients $y_1^{(n)}$ at scale n. The approximation coefficients at a scale $n > 0$ are generated by

$$y_0^{(n)} = \left[w * y_0^{(n-1)} \right]_{\downarrow 2} \quad (1)$$

where $y_0^{(0)} = I$ and w is a 2D low-pass filter, usually defined as

$$w = \frac{1}{256}\begin{bmatrix} 1 & 4 & 6 & 4 & 1 \\ 4 & 16 & 24 & 16 & 4 \\ 6 & 24 & 36 & 24 & 6 \\ 4 & 16 & 24 & 16 & 4 \\ 1 & 4 & 6 & 4 & 1 \end{bmatrix} \quad (2)$$

The detail coefficients at scale n are consequently calculated as a weighted difference between successive levels of the Gaussian Pyramid, and is given by

$$y_1^{(n)} = y_0^{(n)} - 4w * \left[y_0^{(n+1)} \right]_{\uparrow 2} \quad (3)$$

The synthesis procedure begins from the approximation coefficient at the high decomposition level N. Each synthesis level reconstructs approximation coefficients at a scale $n < N$ by

$$y_0^{(n)} = y_1^{(n)} + 4w * \left[y_0^{(n+1)} \right]_{\uparrow 2} \quad (4)$$

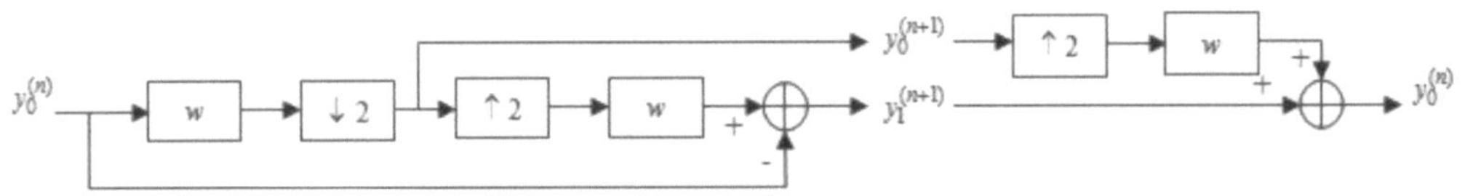

Fig. 1. Laplacian Pyramid analysis and synthesis

2.2 Discrete Wavelet Transform (DWT)

The 2D separable DWT uses a quadrature mirror set of 1D filters to provide a multi-resolution scheme for an image I with added directionality relative to the LP (Mallat, 1989). Analysis and synthesis using the DWT is illustrated in Figure 2. The DWT is able to provide perfect reconstruction while using critical sampling. Each analysis stage consists of filtering along rows, down-sampling along columns, filtering along columns, and down-sampling along rows in order to generate the approximation coefficient sub-band $y_0^{(n)}$ and detail coefficient sub-bands $y_1^{(n)}$, $y_2^{(n)}$, and $y_3^{(n)}$ at scale n. Given a 1D low-pass wavelet analysis filter g and a 1D low-pass wavelet analysis filter h, the approximation coefficients at a scale $n > 0$ are generated by

$$y_0^{(n)} = \left[g_C * \left[g_R * y_0^{(n-1)} \right]_{\downarrow 2_C} \right]_{\downarrow 2_R} \quad (5)$$

where $y_0^{(0)} = I$, and the subscripts R and C denote operations performed along rows and columns, respectively. Similarly, the detail coefficients at scale n are calculated by

$$y_1^{(n)} = \left[h_C * \left[g_R * y_0^{(n-1)} \right]_{\downarrow 2_C} \right]_{\downarrow 2_R} \quad (6)$$

$$y_2^{(n)} = \left[g_C * \left[h_R * y_0^{(n-1)} \right]_{\downarrow 2_C} \right]_{\downarrow 2_R} \quad (7)$$

$$y_3^{(n)} = \left[h_C * \left[h_R * y_0^{(n-1)} \right]_{\downarrow 2_C} \right]_{\downarrow 2_R} \quad (8)$$

and are oriented horizontally, vertically, and diagonally, respectively. The synthesis procedure begins from the wavelet coefficients at the highest decomposition level N. Filtering and up-sampling steps are performed in order to perfectly reconstruct the image signal. Each synthesis level reconstructs approximation coefficients at a scale $n < N$ by

$$\begin{aligned} y_0^{(n)} = \hat{g}_R * \left[\hat{g}_C * \left[y_0^{(n+1)} \right]_{\uparrow 2_R} + \hat{h}_C * \left[y_1^{(n+1)} \right]_{\uparrow 2_R} \right]_{\uparrow 2_C} + \\ + \hat{h}_R * \left[\hat{g}_C * \left[y_2^{(n+1)} \right]_{\uparrow 2_R} + \hat{h}_C * \left[y_3^{(n+1)} \right]_{\uparrow 2_R} \right]_{\uparrow 2_C} \end{aligned} \quad (9)$$

where $\hat{g}$ and $\hat{h}$ are 1D low-pass and high-pass wavelet synthesis filters, respectively.

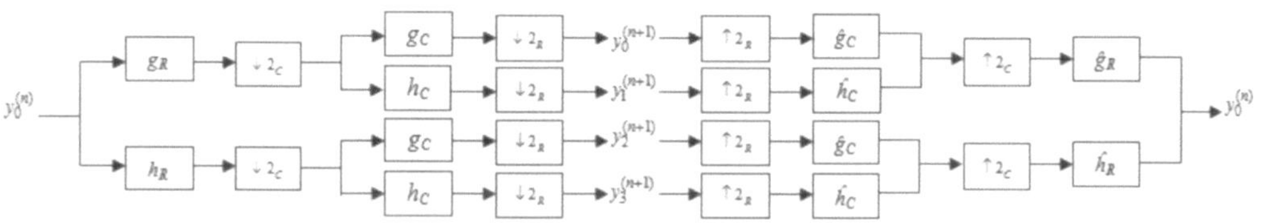

Fig. 2. Discrete Wavelet Transform analysis and synthesis

2.3 Discrete Wavelet Transform (SWT)

Both the DWT and LP are shift-variant due to the down-sampling step which they employ. Therefore, the alteration of transform coefficients may introduce artifacts when processed using the DWT and to a lesser extent, the LP. It can introduce artifacts into the fusion results particularly for cases in which source images are misregistered. The SWT is a shift-invariant, redundant wavelet transform which attempts to reduce artifact effects by up-sampling analysis filters rather than down-sampling approximation images at each level of decomposition (Fowler, 2005). Therefore, each analysis stage calculates the approximation coefficient sub-band $y_0^{(n)}$ and detail coefficient sub-bands $y_1^{(n)}$, $y_2^{(n)}$, and $y_3^{(n)}$ at scale n by

$$y_0^{(n)} = g_C^{(n)} * g_R^{(n)} * y_0^{(n-1)} \quad (10)$$

$$y_1^{(n)} = h_C^{(n)} * g_R^{(n)} * y_0^{(n-1)} \quad (11)$$

$$y_2^{(n)} = g_C^{(n)} * h_R^{(n)} * y_0^{(n-1)} \quad (12)$$

$$y_3^{(n)} = h_C^{(n)} * h_R^{(n)} * y_0^{(n-1)} \quad (13)$$

where

$$g^{(n)} = \left[g^{(n-1)} \right]_{\uparrow 2} \tag{14}$$

$$h^{(n)} = \left[h^{(n-1)} \right]_{\uparrow 2} \tag{15}$$

and $g^{(0)} = g$, $h^{(0)} = h$.

3. Pixel-based fusion using multi-resolution decomposition schemes

A generalized pixel-based multi-resolution image fusion algorithm is illustrated in Figure 3. The input source images are transformed using a given multi-resolution image decomposition technique *T*. One fusion rule is used to fuse the approximation coefficients at the highest decomposition level. A second fusion rule is used to fuse the detail coefficients at each decomposition level. The resulting inverse transform yields the final fused result. Although image fusion algorithms are expected to withstand minor registration differences, the source images to be fused are assumed to be registered.

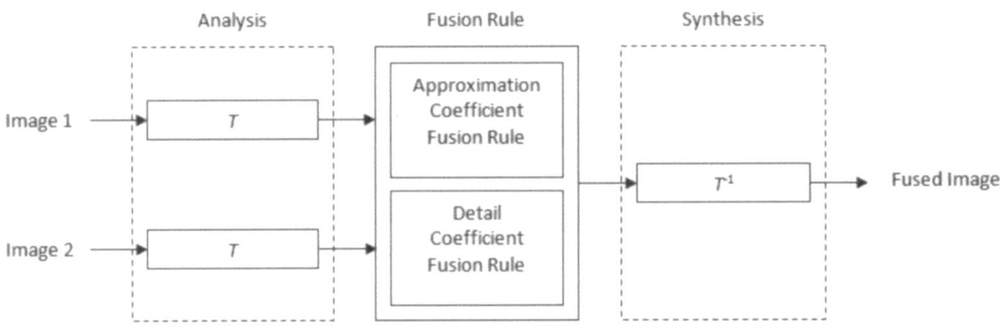

Fig. 3. A generalized pixel-based multi-resolution image fusion algorithm

Misregistered source images should be subjected to registration preprocessing steps independent to the image fusion algorithm. The approximation coefficients at the highest level of decomposition *N* are most commonly fused via uniform averaging. This is because at the highest level of decomposition, the approximation coefficients are interpreted as the mean intensity value of the source images with all salient features encapsulated by the detail coefficient sub-bands at their various scales (Piella, 2003). Therefore, fusing approximation coefficients at their highest level of decomposition by averaging maintains the appropriate mean intensity needed for the fusion result with minimal loss of salient features. Given $y_{I_1,0}^{(N)}$ and $y_{I_2,0}^{(N)}$, the approximation coefficient sub-bands of images I_1 and I_2, respectively, at the highest decomposition level *N*, the approximation coefficients for the fused image *F* at the highest level of decomposition is given by

$$y_{F,0}^{(N)} = \frac{y_{I_1,0}^{(N)} + y_{I_2,0}^{(N)}}{2} \tag{16}$$

Conversely, the detail coefficients of the source images correspond to salient features such as lines and edges detected at various scales. Therefore, fusion rules for detail coefficients at each decomposition level should be formulated in order to preserve these features. Such fusion rules are inspired by the human visual system, which is particularly sensitive to edges. Many pixel-based detail coefficient fusion rules have been proposed. In this work, two common detail coefficient fusion rules are considered.

3.1 Absolute maximum detail coefficient fusion rule

The absolute maximum (AM) detail coefficient fusion rule selects the detail coefficient in each sub-band with greatest magnitude (Piella, 2003). For each of the i high-pass sub-bands at each level of decomposition n, the multiplicative weights for fusion are given by

$$\lambda_i^{(n)}(k,l) = \begin{cases} 1 & \left|y_{I_1,i}^{(n)}(k,l)\right| > \left|y_{I_2,i}^{(n)}(k,l)\right| \\ 0 & \left|y_{I_1,i}^{(n)}(k,l)\right| \le \left|y_{I_2,i}^{(n)}(k,l)\right| \end{cases} \tag{17}$$

For each of the i high-pass sub-bands at each level of decomposition n, the detail coefficients of the fused image F are determined by

$$y_{F,i}^{(n)}(k,l) = \lambda_i^{(n)}(k,l)\, y_{I_1,i}^{(n)}(k,l) + \left(1 - \lambda_i^{(n)}(k,l)\right) y_{I_2,i}^{(n)}(k,l) \tag{18}$$

3.2 Burt and Kolczynski's detail coefficient fusion rule

Burt and Kolczynski's (BK) detail coefficient fusion rule combines detail coefficients based on an activity and match measure (Burt & Kolczynski, 1993). The activity measure for each wxw local window of each sub-band i is calculated for each source image, given as

$$a_{I,i}^{(n)}(k,l) = \sum_{(\Delta k,\Delta l)\in W} \left(y_{I,i}^{(n)}(k+\Delta k, l+\Delta l)\right)^2 \tag{19}$$

The local match measure of each sub-band measures the correlation of each sub-band between source images, and is given as

$$m_{I_1,I_2,i}^{(n)}(k,l) = \frac{2 \sum_{(\Delta k,\Delta l)\in W} \left(y_{I_1,i}^{(n)}(k+\Delta k, l+\Delta l)\right)\left(y_{I_2,i}^{(n)}(k+\Delta k, l+\Delta l)\right)}{a_{I_1,i}^{(n)}(k,l) + a_{I_2,i}^{(n)}(k,l)} \tag{20}$$

Comparing the match measure to a threshold th determines if detail coefficients are to be is combined by simple selection or by weighted averaging. The associated weights for fusion are given by

$$\lambda_i^{(n)}(k,l) = \begin{cases} 1 & m_{I_1,I_2,i}^{(n)}(k,l) \le th, a_{I_1,i}^{(n)}(k,l) > a_{I_2,i}^{(n)}(k,l) \\ 0 & m_{I_1,I_2,i}^{(n)}(k,l) \le th, a_{I_1,i}^{(n)}(k,l) \le a_{I_2,i}^{(n)}(k,l) \\ \dfrac{1}{2} + \dfrac{1}{2}\left(\dfrac{1 - m_{I_1,I_2,i}^{(n)}(k,l)}{1-T}\right) & m_{I_1,I_2,i}^{(n)}(k,l) > th, a_{I_1,i}^{(n)}(k,l) > a_{I_2,i}^{(n)}(k,l) \\ \dfrac{1}{2} - \dfrac{1}{2}\left(\dfrac{1 - m_{I_1,I_2,i}^{(n)}(k,l)}{1-T}\right) & m_{I_1,I_2,i}^{(n)}(k,l) > th, a_{I_1,i}^{(n)}(k,l) \le a_{I_2,i}^{(n)}(k,l) \end{cases} \tag{21}$$

For each of the i high-pass sub-bands at each level of decomposition n, the detail coefficients for the fused image F are again determined by (18).

4. Region-based fusion using multi-resolution decomposition schemes

Pixel-based image fusion approaches determine the detail coefficients of a fused image on a per pixel basis. Namely, they use the transform data at local neighborhoods to individually determine each detail coefficient of the ultimate fusion result. Applications which utilize image fusion schemes are by in large more interested in fusing the various objects found in the original source images. This suggests that information regarding feature instead of the pixels themselves should be incorporated into the fusion process. This provides the motivation for region-based image fusion algorithms (Piella, 2003). Region-based fusion algorithms use image segmentation to guide the fusion process. A generalized region-based multi-resolution fusion algorithm is illustrated in Figure 4. The source images are once again first transformed using a given multi-resolution decomposition scheme. They are segmented using a segmentation algorithm, yielding a shared region representation which is thereby used to aid the fusion of detail coefficients at each scale. The detail coefficients in each region at each scale are fused based on their level of activity in the given region. The fusion of approximation coefficients at the highest level of decomposition remains unchanged. The result is a more robust fusion approach which can overcome blurring effects and improve sensitivity to noise and misregistration known in pixel-based approaches. Moreover, region-based image fusion have allowed for a broader class of fusion rules to be formulated. The choice of segmentation algorithm used in region-based image fusion directly affects the fusion result. Segmentation algorithms which have been used in region-based image fusion algorithms include watershed (Lewis et al., 2004), K-means (Khan et al., 2007), texture-based (Li et al., 2003), pyramidal linking (Piella, 2003), and mean-shift segmentation (Shuang & Zhilin, 2008). In this paper, mean-shift segmentation is used for all region-based approaches because of its robustness and because it has previously been applied for image fusion purposes yielding promising results. It may be substituted with another segmentation algorithm. As this paper is primarily concerned with the use of the nonlinear frameworks and multi-resolution schemes for image fusion, a discussion of appropriate segmentation algorithms for image fusion is considered outside of the scope of this work. The main objective here is to ultimately extend the use of parameterized logarithmic image fusion to region-based approaches.

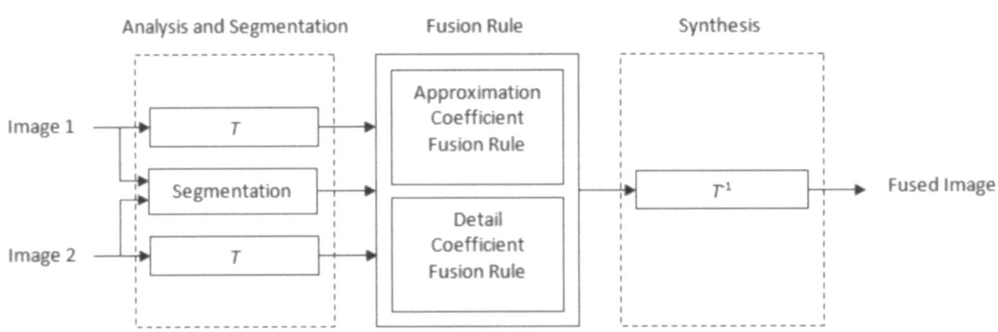

Fig. 4. A generalized region-based multi-resolution image fusion algorithm

4.1 Mean-shift segmentation

Mean-shift segmentation is a specific application of the mean-shift procedure (Comanicu & Meer, 2002). The mean shift procedure is an adaptive gradient ascent which can be used for mode detection, and is thus a nonparametric tool for feature space analysis. Given a radially symmetric kernel $K(x)$ with a monotonically decreasing profile function $k(x)$, the kernel $G(x)$ is defined as a kernel with profile function

$$g(x) = -k'(x) \tag{22}$$

For n data points x_i, $i = 1, \ldots, n$, the mean shift is defined by

$$m_{h,G}(x) = \frac{\sum_{i=1}^{n} x_i g\left(\left\| \frac{x - x_i}{h} \right\|^2\right)}{\sum_{i=1}^{n} g\left(\left\| \frac{x - x_i}{h} \right\|^2\right)} - x \tag{23}$$

where h is a bandwidth parameter and x is the center of the kernel G. The mean shift procedure iteratively calculates the center position of the kernel G by

$$y_{j+1} = \frac{\sum_{i=1}^{n} x_i g\left(\left\| \frac{y_j - x_i}{h} \right\|^2\right)}{\sum_{i=1}^{n} g\left(\left\| \frac{y_j - x_i}{h} \right\|^2\right)} \tag{24}$$

The procedure is guaranteed convergence, which is arrived when the estimate has a gradient of zero. By representing images as a 2D lattice of p-dimensional vectors, where p = 1 corresponds to grayscale, p = 3 corresponds to color, and p > 3 corresponds to multispectral images, the space of the lattice can be referred to as the spatial domain and the gray level, color, or spectral data can be referred to as the range domain. Accordingly, a multi-variate kernel K can be defined by

$$K_{hs,hr}(x) = \frac{C}{h_s^2 h_r^p} k\left(\left\| \frac{x^s}{h_s} \right\|^2\right) k\left(\left\| \frac{x^r}{h_r} \right\|^2\right) \tag{25}$$

where h_s is a spatial bandwidth parameter, h_r is a range bandwidth parameter, and C is a normalizing constant. Accordingly, a mean-shift filtering is proposed, where each pixel is mapped to its spatial and range convergence point. The mean-shift segmentation merges results from the mean-shift filtering algorithm by grouping pixels whose resulting convergence points are closer than h_s in the spatial domain and h_r in the range domain. Therefore, the h_s and h_r parameters are the only user selected parameters for the segmentation (Tao et al. 2007). A shared region representation for region-based image fusion purposes is yielded using mean-shift segmentation by individually segmenting each of the source images, and by then splitting overlapping regions into new regions. An example of a shared region representation yielded using mean-shift segmentation is shown in Figure 5. To maintain consistency in segmentation results across different scales, successive down-

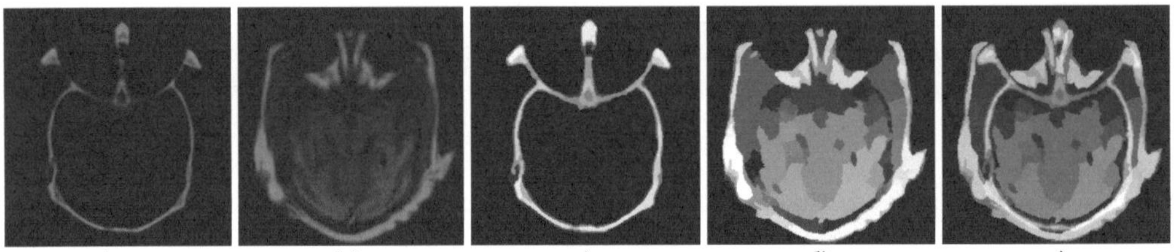

Fig. 5. (a)(b) Original "brain" source images, (c) mean-shift segmentation result of (a), (d) mean-shift segmentation result of (b), (e) shared region representation for region-based image fusion

sampling is performed to yield a shared region representation at each level of decomposition based on the image decomposition scheme used for image fusion.

4.2 Region-based detail coefficient fusion rules

Most any fusion rule formulated for pixel-based fusion can be easily formulated in terms of regions. The extension to regions merely involves calculating activity measures, match measures, and fusion weights for each region R instead of each pixel (Piella, 2003). For example, the activity measure for each region of each sub-band i of each source image can be defined by

$$a_{I,i}^{(n)}(R) = \sum_{(k,l)\in R} \left(y_{I,i}^{(n)}(k,l)\right)^2 \tag{26}$$

where $|R|$ is the area of the region R. Similarly, the match measure $m_{I_1,I_2,i}^{(n)}(R)$ and the multiplicative fusion weight $\lambda_i^{(n)}(R)$ for each region of each sub-band i can be defined. For each of the i high-pass sub-bands at each level of decomposition n, the detail coefficients of the fused image F in each region R are determined by

$$y_{F,i}^{(n)}(R) = \lambda_i^{(n)}(R)\, y_{I_1,i}^{(n)}(R) + \left(1 - \lambda_i^{(n)}(R)\right) y_{I_2,i}^{(n)}(R) \tag{27}$$

5. Parameterized logarithmic image processing (PLIP) model

5.1 Formulation

The LIP model was originally developed to provide a representation and processing framework for images in a bounded intensity range which is consistent with the physical laws of image combination and amplification. The model processes images as absorption filters known as graytones based on M, the maximum value of the range of I, and is characterized by its isomorphic transformation which mathematically emulates the relevant nonlinear physical model which the LIP model is based on. A new set of LIP mathematical operators, namely addition, subtraction, and scalar multiplication, are consequently defined for graytones g_1 and g_2 and scalar constant c in terms of this isomorphic transformation, thus replacing traditional mathematical operators with nonlinear operators which attempt to characterize the nonlinearity of image arithmetic (Jourlin & Pinoli, 2001). For example, LIP addition emulates the intensity image projected onto a screen when a uniform light source is filtered by two graytones placed in series. Subsequently, LIP convolution is also defined for a graytone g and filter w (Palomares et al., 2005). The framework is consistent with several properties of the human visual system, such as brightness range inversion, Weber's law, saturation characteristics, and the psychophysical notion. However, it has been shown that psychophysical laws can be context-dependent, and thus, the constants governing these psychophysical laws are indeed parametric (Krueger, 1989). Thus, the PLIP model generalizes the concept of nonlinear image processing frameworks initially proposed in the form of the LIP model by adding parameterization to the model.

Table 1 summarizes and compares the LIP and PLIP mathematical operators. In its most general form, the PLIP model generalizes graytone calculation, arithmetic operations, and the isomorphic transformation independently, giving rise to the model parameters μ, γ, k, λ, and β. To reduce the number of parameters needed for image fusion, this paper considers the specific instance in which $\mu = M$, $\gamma = k = \lambda$, and $\beta = 1$, effectively resulting in a single model parameter γ. In this case, The PLIP model generalizes the isomorphic transformation which defines the LIP model by accordingly choosing values for γ. Practically, for images in [0, M), the value of γ can either be chosen such that $\gamma \geq M$ for positive γ or can take on any negative value. The resulting PLIP mathematical operators based on the parameterized isomorphic transformation can be subsequently derived.

	LIP Model	PLIP Model
Graytone	$g = M - I$	$g = \mu - I$
Addition	$g_1 \overset{+}{\triangle} g_2 = g_1 + g_2 - \frac{g_1 g_2}{M}$	$g_1 \tilde{\oplus} g_2 = g_1 + g_2 - \frac{g_1 g_2}{\gamma}$
Subtraction	$g_1 \overset{-}{\triangle} g_2 = M \frac{g_1 - g_2}{M - g_2}$	$g_1 \tilde{\Theta} g_2 = k \frac{g_1 - g_2}{k - g_2}$
Scalar Multiplication	$c \overset{\times}{\triangle} g_1 = M - M\left(1 - \frac{g_1}{M}\right)^c$	$c \tilde{\otimes} g_1 = \gamma - \gamma\left(1 - \frac{g_1}{\gamma}\right)^c$
Isomorphic Transformation	$\varphi(g) = -M \ln\left(1 - \frac{g}{M}\right)$ $\varphi^{-1}(g) = -M\left[1 - \exp\left(-\frac{g}{M}\right)\right]$	$\tilde{\varphi}(g) = -\lambda \cdot \ln^{\beta}\left(1 - \frac{g}{\lambda}\right)$ $\tilde{\varphi}^{-1}(g) = \lambda\left[1 - \exp\left(\frac{-g}{\lambda}\right)^{\frac{1}{\beta}}\right]$
Graytone Multiplication	$g_1 \overset{\bullet}{\triangle} g_2 = \varphi^{-1}\left(\varphi(g_1)\varphi(g_2)\right)$	$g_1 \tilde{\bullet} g_2 = \tilde{\varphi}^{-1}\left(\tilde{\varphi}(g_1)\tilde{\varphi}(g_2)\right)$
Convolution	$u \overset{*}{\triangle} g = \varphi^{-1}\left(w * \varphi(g)\right)$	$w \tilde{*} g = \tilde{\varphi}^{-1}\left(w * \tilde{\varphi}(g)\right)$

Table 1. Summary of the LIP and PLIP operators

5.2 Properties

The PLIP properties to be discussed refer to the specific instance of the PLIP model in which $\mu = M$, $\gamma = k = \lambda$, and $\beta = 1$. Similar intuitions are deduced for the more general cases.

1. The PLIP model operators revert to the LIP model operators with $\gamma = M$.
2. It can be shown that

$$\lim_{|\gamma| \to \infty} \tilde{\varphi}(a) = \lim_{|\gamma| \to \infty} \tilde{\varphi}^{-1}(a) = a \tag{28}$$

Since $\tilde{\varphi}$ and $\tilde{\varphi}^{-1}$ are continuous functions, the PLIP model operators revert to arithmetic operators as $|\gamma|$ approaches infinity and therefore, the PLIP model approaches standard linear processing of graytone functions as $|\gamma|$ approaches infinity. Depending on the nature of the algorithm, an algorithm which utilizes standard linear processing operators can be found to be an instance of an algorithm using the PLIP model with $\gamma = \infty$.

3. The PLIP model can generate intermediate cases between LIP operators and standard operators by choosing γ in the range (M, ∞).
4. For input graytones in $[0, M)$, the range of PLIP addition and multiplication with γ in $[M, \infty]$ is $[0, \gamma]$.
5. For input graytones in $[0, M)$, the range of PLIP subtraction with γ in $[M, \infty]$ is $(-\infty, \gamma]$.
6. It can be shown that the PLIP operators obey the associative, commutative, and distributive laws and unit identities.
7. The operations satisfy the 4 requirements for image processing frameworks (Jourlin & Pinoli, 2001) and an additional 5th one. Namely, (1) the image processing framework must be based on a physically relevant image formation model; (2) The mathematical operations must be consistent with the physical nature of images; (3) The operations must be computationally effective; (4) The framework must be practically fruitful; (5) The framework must minimize the loss of information.

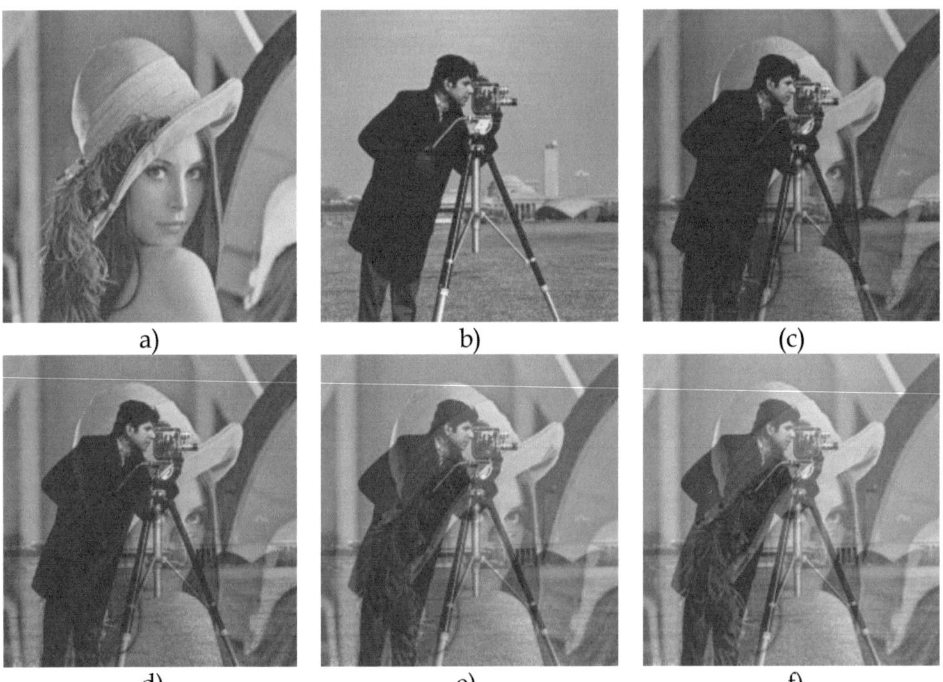

Fig. 6. (a) "Lena" image , (b) "Cameraman" image, image addition using (c) $\gamma = 256$ (LIP model case), (d) $\gamma = 300$, (e) $\gamma = 600$, (f) $\gamma = 10^8$

The 5th requirement essentially states that when visually "good" images are processed, the output must also be visually "good" (Panetta et al., 2008). The PLIP model satisfies the requirements by selecting values of γ which expands the dynamic range of outputs in order to minimize information loss while also retaining non-linear, logarithmic functionality according to a physical model. This property is illustrated in Figure 6. The LIP addition provides a good contrast between Lena and the cameraman, but there is also a loss of information in the output, namely in the area corresponding to the cameraman's coat. PLIP addition with γ = 300 is able to yield a good contrast while also minimizing loss of information. Thus, for positive γ, the PLIP model physically provides a balance between the standard linear processing model and the LIP model. Conversely, negative values of γ may be selected for cases in which added brightness is needed to yield more visually pleasing results.

6. Image fusion using the PLIP model

Adapting image fusion algorithms with the PLIP model require a mathematical formulation of multi-resolution decomposition schemes and coefficient fusion rules in terms of the model. The combination of the parameterized logarithmic image decomposition techniques with parameterized logarithmic fusion rules yields a new set of image fusion algorithms which are based on the PLIP model. The parameterized logarithmic multi-resolution decomposition schemes and fusion rules are defined for graytone functions. Therefore, images are converted to graytone functions before PLIP-based operations are performed and converted from graytone functions to images after PLIP-based operation are performed.

6.1 Parameterized logarithmic multi-scale image decomposition schemes

6.1.1 Parameterized Logarithmic Laplacian Pyramid (PL-LP)

The approximation coefficients for a graytone function g at a scale $n > 0$ are generated by

$$\tilde{y}_0^{(n)} = \left[w \,\tilde{*}\, \tilde{y}_0^{(n-1)} \right]_{\downarrow 2} \tag{29}$$

where $\tilde{y}_0^{(n)} = g$ and w is the low-pass filter defined in (2). The detail coefficients at scale n are then generated by

$$\tilde{y}_1^{(n)} = \tilde{y}_0^{(n)} \tilde{\Theta} (4w) \,\tilde{*} \left[\tilde{y}_0^{(n+1)} \right]_{\uparrow 2} \tag{30}$$

The inverse procedure begins from the approximation coefficient at the high decomposition level N. Each synthesis level reconstructs approximation coefficients at a scale $i < N$ by each synthesis level by

$$\tilde{y}_0^{(n)} = \tilde{y}_1^{(n)} \oplus (4w) \,\tilde{*} \left[\tilde{y}_0^{(n+1)} \right]_{\uparrow 2} \tag{31}$$

6.1.2 Parameterized Logarithmic Discrete Wavelet Transform (PL-DWT)

The PL-DWT at decomposition level n follows directly from (44) and (45). The PL-DWT for a graytone function g at a scale $n > 0$ is calculated by

$$\tilde{W}_{DWT}\left(\tilde{y}_0^{(n)}\right) = \tilde{\varphi}^{-1}\left(W_{DWT}\left(\tilde{\varphi}\left(\tilde{y}_0^{(n)}\right)\right)\right) \tag{32}$$

where $\tilde{y}_0^{(0)} = g$. Similarly, the inverse procedure begins from the discrete wavelet coefficients at the highest decomposition level N. Each synthesis level reconstructs approximation coefficients at a scale $i < N$ by each synthesis level by

$$\tilde{W}_{DWT}^{-1}\left(\tilde{W}_{DWT}\left(\tilde{y}_0^{(n)}\right)\right)=\tilde{\varphi}^{-1}\left(W_{DWT}^{-1}\left(\tilde{\varphi}\left(\tilde{W}_{DWT}\left(\tilde{y}_0^{(n)}\right)\right)\right)\right) \tag{33}$$

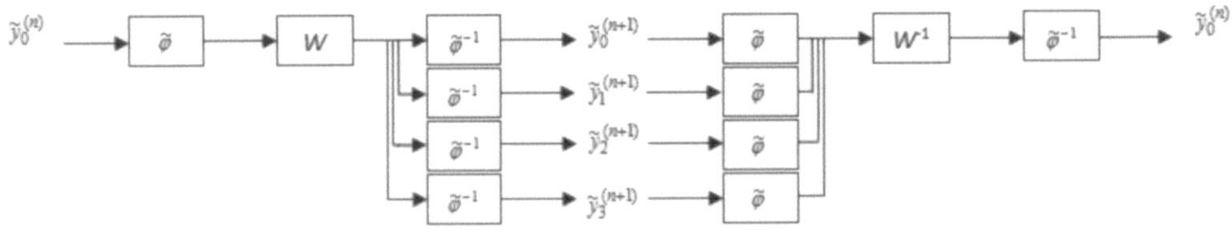

Fig. 7. Parameterized Logarithmic Wavelet Transform analysis and synthesis

6.1.3 Parameterized Logarithmic Stationary Wavelet Transform (PL-SWT)

The PL-SWT also follows directly from (44) and (45). The forward and inverse PL-SWT for a graytone function g at a scale $n > 0$ is calculated by

$$\tilde{W}_{SWT}\left(\tilde{y}_0^{(n)}\right)=\tilde{\varphi}^{-1}\left(W_{SWT}\left(\tilde{\varphi}\left(\tilde{y}_0^{(n)}\right)\right)\right) \tag{33}$$

$$\tilde{W}_{SWT}^{-1}\left(\tilde{W}_{SWT}\left(\tilde{y}_0^{(n)}\right)\right)=\tilde{\varphi}^{-1}\left(W_{SWT}^{-1}\left(\tilde{\varphi}\left(\tilde{W}_{SWT}\left(\tilde{y}_0^{(n)}\right)\right)\right)\right) \tag{34}$$

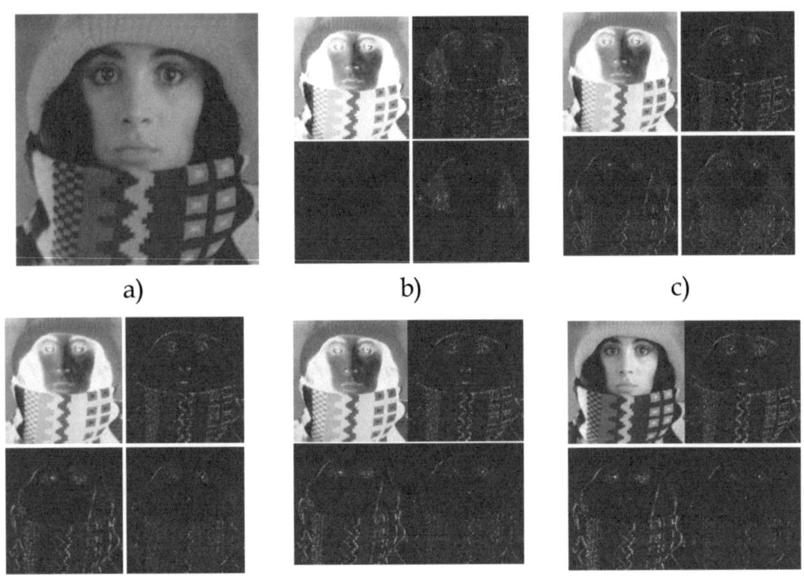

Fig. 8. (a) Original "Trui" image, top-left: approximation sub-band, magnitude of top-right: horizontal sub-band, bottom-left: vertical sub-band, bottom-right: diagonal sub-band magnitude of horizontal sub-band using the DWT and PLIP model operators with (b) $\gamma = 256$ (LIP model case), (c) $\gamma = 300$, (d) $\gamma = 500$, (e) $\gamma = 700$, (f) standard operators

Figure 7 illustrates the analysis and synthesis stages using PLIP wavelet transforms, where W is a type of wavelet transform (e.g. DWT, SWT, etc.) with a given set of wavelet filters (Courbebaisse, 2002). As the parameterized logarithmic decomposition approaches essentially makes use of standard decomposition schemes with added pre-processing and post-processing in the form of the isomorphic transformation calculations, they can be computed with minimal added computation cost.

Figure 8 illustrates the advantages yielded using parameterized logarithmic multi-resolution schemes. The wavelet decomposition using $\gamma = 256$ (LIP model case) predominantly extracts the hair features from the image. As γ increases, it is particularly apparent that the hair textures are less emphasized and that the scarf, hat, and facial edges and textures are more emphasized. The wavelet decomposition using standard operators extracts the most texture and edge information from the scarf, hat, and face in the image, and close to none of the texture of the hair. Visually, it is seen that the wavelet decomposition using the PLIP model operators with $\gamma = 300$ provides the best balance between extracting the hair, scarf, hat, and facial features in the image. Ultimately, the salient features which need to be extracted at each scale for further processing are task and image dependent, and thus, the PLIP model parameter can be tuned accordingly.

6.2 Parameterized Logarithmic image fusion rules

Both the approximation coefficient and detail coefficient fusion rules should also be adapted according to the PLIP model. For $\tilde{y}_{I_1,0}^{(N)}$ and $\tilde{y}_{I_2,0}^{(N)}$, the approximation coefficient sub-bands of images I_1 and I_2, respectively, at the highest decomposition level N yielded using a given parameterized logarithmic multi-resolution decomposition technique, the approximation coefficients for the fused image F at the highest level of decomposition using simple averaging is given by

$$\tilde{y}_{F,0}^{(N)} = \frac{1}{2} \tilde{\otimes} \left(\tilde{y}_{I_1,0}^{(N)} \tilde{\oplus} \tilde{y}_{I_2,0}^{(N)} \right) \tag{35}$$

In general, an approximation coefficient fusion rule can be adapted according to the PLIP model by

$$\tilde{y}_{F,0}^{(N)} = \tilde{\varphi}^{-1} \left(R_A \left(\tilde{\varphi}\left(\tilde{y}_{I_1,0}^{(N)} \right), \tilde{\varphi}\left(\tilde{y}_{I_2,0}^{(N)} \right) \right) \right) \tag{36}$$

where R_A is an approximation coefficient fusion rule implemented using standard arithmetic operators. An analysis of the PLIP operation in Table 1 and (35) yields a simple interpretation of the effect of γ on fusion results. Practically, γ can be interpreted as a brightness parameter, where negative values of γ yield brighter fusion results and positive values of γ yield darker fusion results. This is achieved while also maintaining the fusion identity that the fusion of identical source images is the source image itself. Therefore, improved visual quality is achieved within an image fusion context and not as a result of an independent image enhancement process. The influence of the parameterization on fusion results is not limited to this naïve observation, however, as γ also influences the multi-scale decomposition scheme and the detail coefficient fusion rule. The fusion rules for details coefficients at each decomposition level for pixel- or region-based approaches are similarly adapted according to the PLIP model via the parameterized isomorphic transformation. In general, a detail coefficient fusion rule can be adapted according to the PLIP model by

$$\tilde{y}^{(n)}_{F,i} = \tilde{\varphi}^{-1}\left(R_D\left(\tilde{\varphi}\left(\tilde{y}^{(n)}_{I_1,i}\right),\tilde{\varphi}\left(\tilde{y}^{(n)}_{I_2,i}\right)\right)\right) \tag{37}$$

where R_D is a pixel- or region-based detail coefficient fusion rule implemented using standard arithmetic operators.

7. Quantitative image fusion quality assessment

When an ideal fusion result is available, it can be used as a reference image to guide image fusion quality assessment. Measures such as the root mean square error (RMSE), normalized least square error (NLSE), peak signal-to-noise ratio (PSNR), correlation (CORR), difference entropy (DE), and mutual information (MI) can be used to relate the fusion result to the reference image, thus providing a means of assessing image fusion quality (Liu et. al, 2008). These measures are summarized in Table 2 for a fusion result F given a reference image I. However, an ideal reference image is usually not known, and thus, quality assessment becomes a non-trivial task. Blind objective performance assessment of image fusion quality is still an open problem requiring more research in order to provide valuable objective evaluation (Piella, 2003). The metrics proposed in (Xydeas & Petrovic, 2000) and (Piella & Heijmans, 2003) tend to favor fusion results which transfer more edge information into fusion results, and are therefore vulnerable to noisy test cases. Conversely, mutual-information-based metrics (Qu et al., 2002) tend to favor fusion approaches which

RMSE	$\sqrt{\dfrac{\sum_{k=1}^{K}\sum_{l=1}^{L}\left[I(k,l)-F(k,l)\right]^2}{KL}}$	M	Maximum pixel value
NLSE	$\sqrt{\dfrac{\sum_{k=1}^{K}\sum_{l=1}^{L}\left[I(k,l)-F(k,l)\right]^2}{\sum_{k=1}^{K}\sum_{l=1}^{L}\left[I(k,l)\right]^2}}$	$P_I(g)$	Probability of value g in I
PSNR	$10\log_{10}\dfrac{KLM^2}{\sum_{k=1}^{K}\sum_{l=1}^{L}\left[I(k,l)-F(k,l)\right]^2}$	$P_F(g)$	Probability of value g in F
CORR	$\dfrac{2\sum_{k=1}^{K}\sum_{l=1}^{L}I(k,l)F(k,l)}{\sum_{k=1}^{K}\sum_{l=1}^{L}\left[I(k,l)\right]^2+\sum_{k=1}^{K}\sum_{l=1}^{L}\left[F(k,l)\right]^2}$	h_{IF}	Normalized joint histogram
DE	$\left\lvert\sum_{g=0}^{M-1}P_I(g)\log_2 P_I(g)-\sum_{g=0}^{M-1}P_F(g)\log\right.$	h_I	Normalized histogram of I
MI	$\sum_{k=1}^{M}\sum_{l=1}^{M}h_{IF}(k,l)\log_2\dfrac{h_{IF}(k,l)}{h_I(k,l)h_F(k,l)}$	h_F	Normalized histogram of F

Table 2. Summary of the reference-based measure for image fusion quality assessment

transfer relatively less edge information but are less sensitive to noise, such as region-based and even simple averaging approaches. Nonetheless, to gain objective perspective not on the fusion rule or standard decomposition scheme of choice, but rather the improvement of fusion results using the PLIP model, fusion results are assessed quantitatively using the Piella and Heijmans image fusion quality metric. The metric measures fusion quality based on how much the fusion result reflects the original source images. Bovik's quality index (Wang, 2002) is used to relate the fused result to its original source images. The quality index Q_0 proposed by Bovik to measure the similarity between two sequences x and y is given by

$$Q_0 = \frac{\sigma_{xy}}{\sigma_x \sigma_y} \cdot \frac{2\mu_x \mu_y}{\mu_x^2 + \mu_y^2} \cdot \frac{2\sigma_x \sigma_y}{\sigma_x^2 + \sigma_y^2} \tag{38}$$

where σ_x and σ_y are the sample standard deviations of x and y, respectively, σ_{xy} is the sample covariance of x and y, and μ_x and μ_y are the sample means of x and y, respectively. For two images I and F, a sliding window technique is utilized to calculate the quality index $Q_0(I, F|w)$ at each local wxw window. The average of these quality indexes is used to measure the similarity between I and F, and is given by

$$Q_0(I,F) = \frac{1}{|W|} \sum_{w \in W} Q_0(I,F|w) \tag{39}$$

The resulting similarity index ranges from 0 to 1, with two identical images yielding a Q_0 equal to 1. Defining $s(I|w)$ as the saliency, and in this case, the variance of the image I in a local window wxw window, the quality of the fused result can be assessed by first calculating local weights $\lambda(w)$ for the source images I_1 and I_2, given by

$$\lambda(w) = \frac{s(I_1|w)}{s(I_1|w) + s(I_2|w)} \tag{40}$$

and then calculating the fusion quality index $Q(I_1,I_2,F)$ for the fused result F by

$$Q(I_1,I_2,F) = \frac{1}{|W|} \sum_{w \in W} \left(\lambda(w) Q_0(I_1,F|w) + (1-\lambda(w)) Q_0(I_2,F|w) \right) \tag{41}$$

a) b) c) d)

Fig. 9. (a)(b) Original "clock" source images, respective weights (c)$c{\cdot}\lambda$ (d) $c{\cdot}(1\text{-}\lambda)$ used for image fusion quality assessment

The metric assesses fusion quality by calculating the local quality indexes between the fused image and the two source images, and weighting them according to the local saliency between the source images. To better reflect the human visual system, another weight is added to give more weight to regions in which the saliency of the source images is greater. Defining the overall saliency of a window $C(w)$ by

$$C(w) = \max\left(s(I_1 \mid w), s(I_2 \mid w)\right) \tag{42}$$

The weighted fusion quality index $Q_W(I_1,I_2,F)$ is given by

$$Q_w(I_1, I_2, F) = \sum_{w \in W} c(w)\left(\lambda(w) Q_0(I_1, F \mid w) + \left(1 - \lambda(w)\right) Q_0(I_2, F \mid w)\right) \tag{43}$$

where

$$c(w) = \frac{C(w)}{\sum_{w' \in W} C(w')} \tag{44}$$

As Q_0 yields a maximum value of 1 for identical input images, higher fusion quality metric values indicate better fusion results. Figure 9 provides a graphical representation of the weights which are calculated by the quality metric in order to assess the quality of image fusion results.

8. Experimental results

The effectiveness of the proposed algorithms is illustrated via computer simulations. In general, three cases are considered for these experiments: 1) the extreme case in which the PLIP model operators yield the LIP model operators ($\gamma = M$), 2) standard operators, which are the extreme case of PLIP model operators with $\gamma = \infty$, 3) the case in which γ takes on a value other than M or ∞. For easy reference, we refer to these cases as the LIP model operator case, standard operator case, and PLIP model operator case, respectively, though in reality, all are cases of the proposed PLIP-based approach. It should be noted that image fusion algorithms employing LIP-based multi-resolution image decomposition schemes and fusion rules have not even been introduced to our knowledge. Thus, we refer to the LIP-LP, LIP-DWT, and LIP-SWT image fusion algorithms as the image fusion algorithms which use PLIP operators with $\gamma = M$ to implement the fusion rules and LP, DWT, and SWT, respectively. Consequently, the PL-LP, PL-DWT, and PL-SWT image fusion algorithms are compared to the traditional LP and LIP-LP; traditional DWT and LIP-DWT; and traditional and LIP SWT image fusion algorithms, respectively. The algorithms were tested over a range of different image classes, including out-of-focus, medical, surveillance, and remote sensing images. A portion of these results are presented here. It is assumed that the input source images are registered, although it is expected that image fusion algorithms be able to handle minor registration differences. There are many factors which influence image fusion using multi-resolution decomposition schemes, including the type of multi-resolution decomposition scheme, the number of decomposition levels, the choice of filter bank, and the fusion rule used to fuse coefficients at each scale. This paper emphasizes the transform which is used while keeping all other factors constant. In these experimental results, $N = 3$ for all methods, and both the pixel- and region-based fusion rules are examined. For the wavelet-based approaches, biorthogonal 2.2 filters are used. The fusion results are compared quantitatively by first normalizing source images and fused results to the range 0-255, and then using the Piella and Heijmans image fusion quality metric Q_W with $w = 7$. This metric is used to determine the optimal parameter value for γ, with the resulting fused image thereby taken to be the result for a given parameterized logarithmic image fusion algorithm. This demonstrates the ability to tune the PLIP model parameter in order to optimize results according to any metric used for quality assessment.

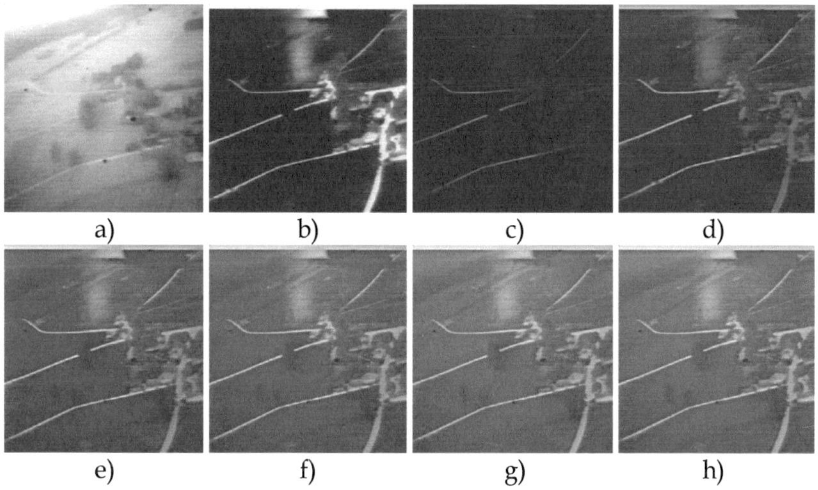

Fig. 10. (a)(b) Original "navigation" source images, image fusion results using the LP/AM fusion rule, and PLIP model operators with (c) $\gamma = 256$ (LIP model case), $Q_W = 0.3467$, (d) $\gamma = 300$, $Q_W = 0.7802$, (e) $\gamma = 430$, $Q_W = 0.8200$, (f) $\gamma = 700$, $Q_W = 0.8128$ (g) $\gamma = 10^8$, $Q_W = 0.7947$, (h) standard operators, $Q_W = 0.7947$

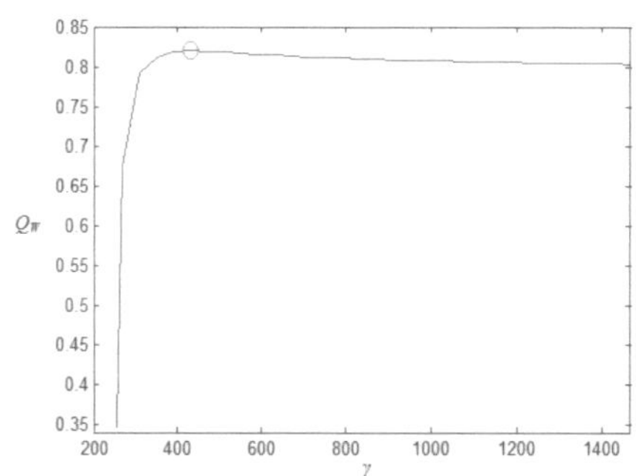

Fig. 11. Plot of Q_W vs. γ for image fusion results in Figure 9, indicating a maximum at $\gamma = 430$, $Q_W = 0.8200$

Figure 10 illustrates the fundamental themes which have been discussed so far, particularly highlighting the necessity for the added model parameterization. Figure 10.c shows that firstly, the PLIP model reverts to the LIP model with $\gamma = M = 256$, and secondly, that the combination of source images using this extreme case may still be visually unsatisfactory given the nature of the input images, even though the processing framework is based on a physically inspired model. Figure 10.d-f illustrates the way in which fusion results are affected by the parameterization, with the most improved fusion performance yielded by the proposed approach using parameterized multi-resolution decomposition schemes and fusion rules relative to both the standard processing extreme and the LIP model extreme with γ = 430. Namely, this result using the proposed approach has better visual contrast between roads and terrain, and provides the proper base luminance to effectively differentiate between the grass and bushes. Figure 11 plots the Q_W quality metric as a function of γ, and reflects the qualitative observation indicating Figure 10.e as the best fusion output. Lastly, Figure 10 also shows using the AM fusion rule that the PLIP operators revert to standard mathematical operators as γ approaches infinity.

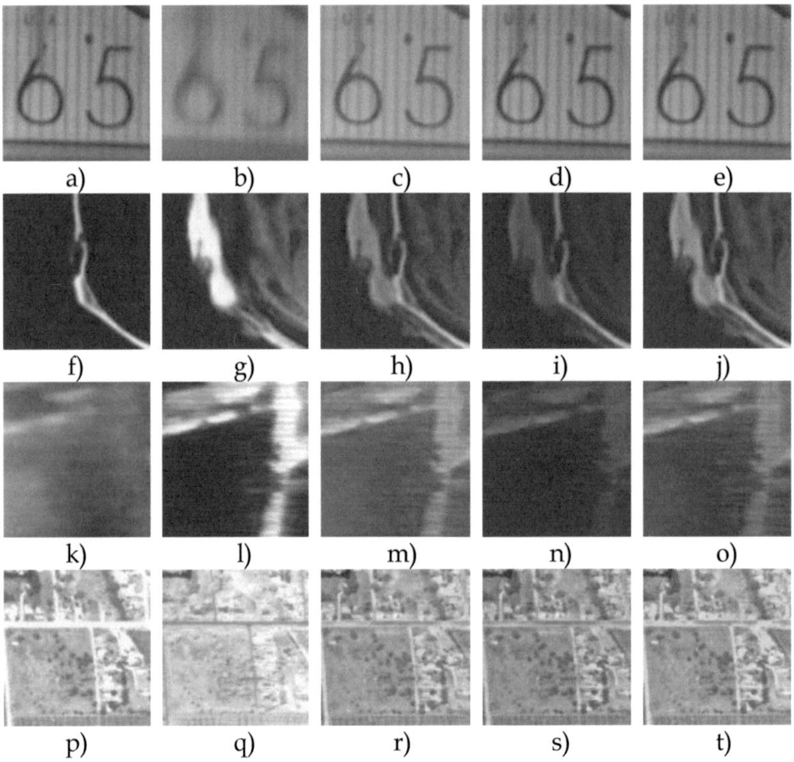

Fig. 12. Zoomed regions of (a)(b) Original "clocks" source images, image fusion results using (c)LP and RB, (d), LIP-LP and RB, (e) PL-LP and RB, (f)(g) original "brain" source images, image fusion results using (h) SWT and RB, (i) LIP-SWT and RB, (j) PL-SWT and RB (k)(l) original "navigation" source images, image fusion results using (m) DWT and AM, (n) LIP-DWT and AM, (o) PL-DWT and AM (p)(q) original "remote sensing" source images, image fusion results using (r) SWT and BK, (s) LIP-SWT and BK, (t) PL-SWT and BK

Zoomed details highlighting specific contrast differences of selected fusion results are shown in Figure 12. Selected image fusion results showing more global luminance differences can be found in Figure 13. Qualitatively, it is seen that the image fusion approaches using the PLIP model operator case yield more informative fusion results with more visually pleasing contrast. The zoomed details in the 1st row of Figure 12 show that the lines and numbers in the clock images are sharper and clearer in the fusion result using the PLIP model operator case. The 2nd row shows that the proposed method is able to better capture the terrain information and road information of the respective source images. The 3rd row shows the improved contrast of tissue information and dense bone structure yielded

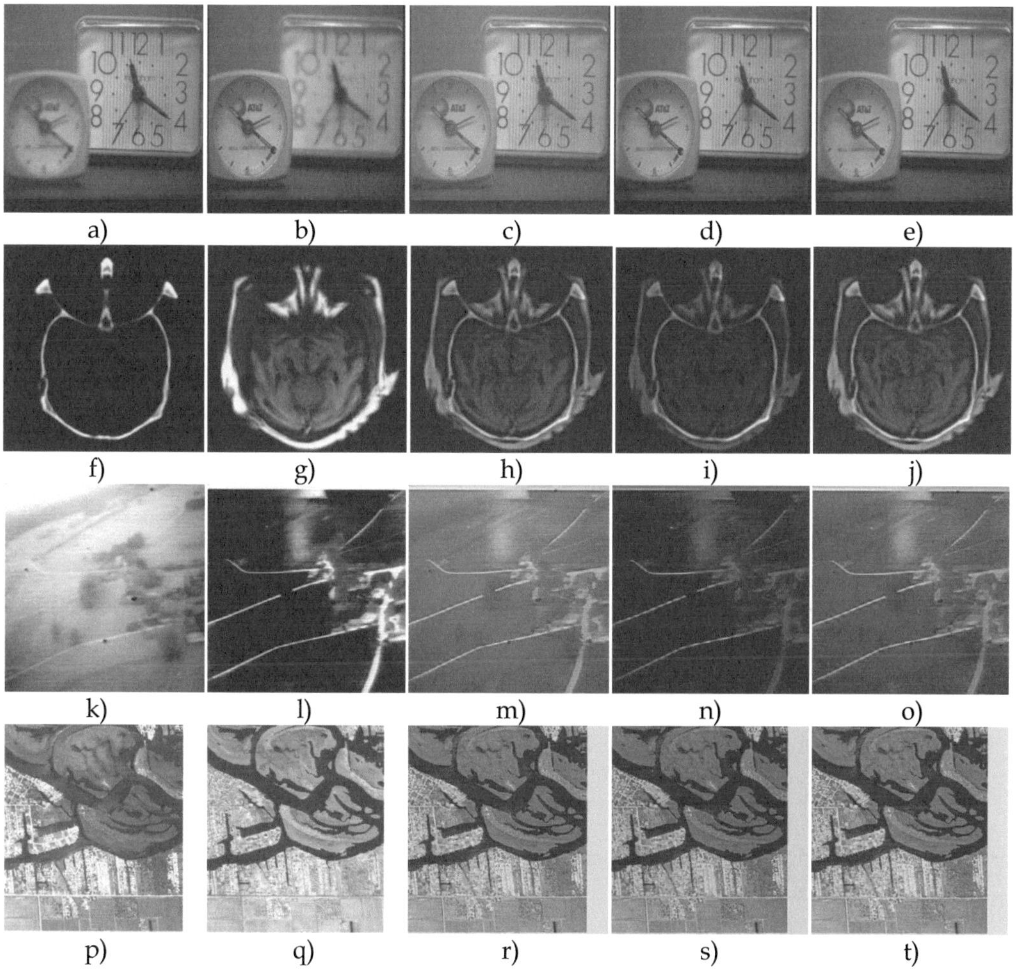

Fig. 13. (a)(b) Original "clocks" source images, image fusion results using (c)LP and RB, (d), LIP-LP and RB, (e) PL-LP and RB, (f)(g) original "brain" source images, image fusion results using (h) SWT and RB, (i) LIP-SWT and RB, (j) PL-SWT and RB (k)(l) original "navigation" source images, image fusion results using (m) DWT and AM, (n) LIP-DWT and AM, (o) PL-DWT and AM (p)(q) original "remote sensing" source images, image fusion results using (r) SWT and BK, (s) LIP-SWT and BK, (t) PL-SWT and BK

by the proposed method. Lastly, the 4th row shows that the proposed fusion approaches are able to better capture the subtle features at the point at which the roads intersect. Thus, the experimental results highlight the improvement of fusion results yielded using the PLIP model operators. While the standard operator extreme can often give adequate results, the contrast and luminance can be improved by choosing a value of γ which both reflects the human visual system and meets the dynamic range requirements of the input images. While the LIP model operator extreme can improve the performance of image fusion relative to standard operator extreme when the source images are similar in luminance (as in the case of the clocks images), it yields visually inadequate results for source images with greatly different local base luminance. This is particularly visible for input images in which one of the source images is predominantly dark as in the case of the "navigation" and "brain" images.

Decomposition Scheme	Fusion Rule	Clocks Standard	Clocks LIP	Clocks PLIP	Brain Standard	Brain LIP	Brain PLIP	Navigation Standard	Navigation LIP	Navigation PLIP	Remote Sensing Standard	Remote Sensing LIP	Remote Sensing PLIP
LP	AM	0.8914	0.9168	**0.9300**	0.7753	0.5256	**0.7760**	0.7947	0.3467	**0.8200**	0.8383	0.7842	**0.8404**
	BK	0.8851	0.9123	**0.9250**	0.7748	0.5349	**0.7762**	0.7933	0.3512	**0.8196**	0.8293	0.7627	**0.8300**
	RB	0.8849	0.9114	**0.9241**	0.7572	0.5327	**0.7576**	0.8051	0.3505	**0.8187**	0.8113	0.7424	**0.8120**
DWT	AM	0.8750	0.8979	**0.9002**	0.7124	0.5296	**0.7292**	0.7363	0.6011	**0.7607**	0.7672	0.7128	**0.7695**
	BK	0.8745	0.8891	**0.8918**	0.6701	0.4886	**0.6886**	0.7333	0.6064	**0.7600**	0.7378	0.6770	**0.7385**
	RB	0.8763	0.8955	**0.8972**	0.6872	0.5008	**0.7060**	0.7288	0.6052	**0.7589**	0.7162	0.6869	**0.7170**
SWT	AM	0.8879	0.9085	**0.9134**	0.7539	0.5581	**0.7718**	0.7460	0.7250	**0.7746**	0.8137	0.7954	**0.8150**
	BK	0.8926	0.9081	**0.9130**	0.7554	0.5714	**0.7647**	0.7382	0.7294	**0.7821**	0.8203	0.8045	**0.8238**
	RB	0.8877	0.9045	**0.9064**	0.7458	0.5557	**0.7684**	0.7542	0.6873	**0.7695**	0.8078	0.7882	**0.8080**

Table 3. Quantitative quality assessment of image fusion results using the Piella and Heijmans quality metric

The quantitative observations are reflected by their corresponding quality metric values in Table 3, in which rows correspond to the basic multi-resolution decomposition scheme and fusion rule employed and columns correspond to the image processing operators (LIP model operator case, standard operator case, or PLIP model operator case) used to implement the given decomposition scheme and fusion rule. It should be noted that a single, constant-size window is used in calculating the quality metric values. Thus, such an evaluation may be dependent on how well the window size reflects the scale of the objects of interest in the source images, and may not be able to effectively quantify differences in fusion results even when qualitative visual differences are seen. This provides a rationalization as to why the perceived visual improvement of the proposed methods may in some cases only translate to a small increase in the quality metric values, and continues to affirm the fact that objective image fusion quality assessment is still an open research topic. However, the rank of the scores are generally indicative of relative performance, and to standardize the testing procedure and to maintain the same formulation of the metric as it was originally proposed, the same parameters are used to calculate quality metric values for all test cases. Thus, the quantitative analysis serves as an objective means of validating subjective observations. The quality metric values in Table 2 show that in all cases, fusion algorithms using the parameterized logarithmic multi-resolution decomposition schemes and fusion rules outperform their respective general linear processing model counterparts.

9. Conclusions

This paper derived decomposition schemes and image fusion rules based on the PLIP model. The PLIP based multi-resolution decomposition schemes were developed and thoroughly applied for image fusion purposes. PLIP model properties were analyzed, and their implications for image fusion were verified by experimental means. The new multi-resolution decomposition schemes and fusion rules yields new image fusion tools which are able to provide visually more pleasing fusion results. A new class of image fusion algorithms, namely those based on the PL-LP, PL-DWT, and PL-SWT were proposed. The images are fused in the transform domain using novel pixel-based or region-based rules. Using a number of pixel-based and region-based fusion rules, one can combine the important features of the input images in the transform domain to compose an enhanced image. The proposed algorithms were tested and compared to traditional and LIP multi-resolution image fusion algorithms over a number of different image classes including out-of-focus, medical, surveillance, and remote sensing images, whose applications can make use of image fusion to improve perception for computer-aided or computer vision systems. These experimental results showed that the proposed image decomposition and image algorithms improved image fusion quality both qualitatively and quantitatively. The Qualitatively, the fusion results using the proposed algorithms provided better contrast and the necessary luminance needed for fusion purposes. Quantitatively, the proposed outperformed traditional and LIP multi-resolution image fusion algorithms using the Piella and Heijmans quality metric to objectively assess image fusion quality. The novelty of the proposed PLIP-based image fusion schemes lie in the combination of multi-resolution image fusion techniques with physically inspired proccessing models.

10. Acknowledgement

This work has been partially supported by NSF Grant HRD-0932339. The authors would like to thank Dr. Oliver Rockinger for kindly providing the registered images used for computer simulations.

11. References

Burt, P.J, & Adelson, E. (1983). The Laplacian pyramid as a compact image code. *IEEE Transactions on Communications,* Vol. 31, No. 4, pp. 532-540

Burt, P.J. & Kolczynski, R.J. (1993). Enhanced image capture through fusion, *Proceedings of the International Conference on Computer Vision*, pp. 173-1982.

Comanicu, D. & Meer, P. (2002). Mean shift: a robust approach toward feature space analysis, *IEEE Transactions on Pattern Analysis and Machine Intelligence*, Vol. 24, (May 2002) pp. 603-619

Courbebaisse, G.; Trunde. F., & Jourlin, M (2002). Wavelet transform and LIP model, *Image Anal Stereol*, Vol. 21, No. 2, (June 2002) pp. 121-125

Chavez, P.S. & Kwarteng, A.Y. (1989). Extracting spectral contrast in Landsat Thematic Mapper image data using selective component analysis, *Photogrammetric Engineering and Remote Sensing*, Vol. 55, No. 3, pp. 339-348

Chibani, Y. (2005). Selective synthetic aperture radar and panchromatic image fusion by using the a trous wavelet decomposition. *EURASIP Journal on Applied Signal Processing,* Vol. 2005, No. 14, pp. 2007-2214

Daneshvar, S. & Ghassemian, H. (2010). MRI and PET image fusion by combinging IHS and retina-inspired model. *Information Fusion*, Vol. 11, No. 2, (April 2010) pp. 114-123

Debayle, J.; Gavet, Y. & Pinoli, J.C. (2006). General adaptive neighbourhood image restoration, enhancement and segmentation, *Image Analysis and Recognition*, pp. 29-40

Deng G.; Cahill L.W., & Tobin, G.R. (2009). The study of logarithmic image processing model and its application to image enhancement. *IEEE Transactions on Image Processing*, Vol. 18, pp. 1135-1140

Fowler, J.E. (2005). The redundant discrete wavelet transform and additive noise. *IEEE Signal Processing Letters*, Vol. 12, No. 9, pp. 629-632

Hill, P.; Canagarajah, N. & Bull, D. (2002). Image fusion using complex wavelets, *Proceedings of the British Machine Vision Conference*, pp. 487-496

Jourlin, M. & Pinoli, J. (2001). Logarithmic image processing: the mathematical and physical framework for the representation and processing of transmitted images. *Advances in Imaging and Electron Physics*, Vol. 115, pp. 126-196

Khan, A.M.; Kayani, B. & Gillani, A.M. (2007). Feature level fusion of night vision images based on K-means clustering algorithm, *Innovations and Advanced Techniques in Computer and Inofrmation Sciences and Engineering*, pp. 73-76.

Lewis, J.J.; O'Callaghan, R.J., Nikolov, S.G., Bull, D.R. & Canagarajah, C.N. (2004). Region-based image fusion using complex wavelets, *Proceedings of the International Conference on Image Fusion*, pp. 2004, July 2004

Li., Z.; Jing, Z., Liu, G., Sun, S. & Leung, H. (2003). A region-based image fusion algorithm using multiresolution segmentation, *Proceedings of the IEEE International Conference on Intelligent Transportation Systems*, Vol. 1, pp. 96-101

Krueger, L. (1989). Reconciling Fechner and Stevens: toward a unified psychophysical law, *Behavioral and Brain Sciences*, Vol. 12, pp. 251-267

Kumar, M. & Dass, S. (2009). A total variation-based algorithm for pixel-level image fusion. *IEEE Transactions on Image Processing*, Vol. 18, No. 9, (September 2009) pp. 2137-2143

Mallat, S.G. (1989). A theory for multiresolution signal decomposition: the wavelet representation. *IEEE Transactions on Pattern Analysis and Machine Intelligence*, Vol. 11, (July 1989) pp. 674-693

Palomares, J.M.; Gonzalez, J. & Ros, E. (2005). Designing a fast convolution under the LIP paradigm applied to edge detection, *Proceedings of the International on Advances in Pattern Recognition*, pp. 560-569.

Panetta, K.; Wharton, E. & Agaian, S. (2008). Human visual system based image enhancement and logarithmic contrast measure. *IEEE Transactions on Systems, Man, and Cybernetics, Part B: Cybernetics*, Vol. 38, No. 1, (February 2008) pp. 174- 188

Piella, G. (2003). A general framework for multiresolution image fusion: from pixels to regions. *Information Fusion*, Vol. 4, pp. 259-280

Piella, G. & Heijmans, H. (2003). A new quality metric for image fusion, *Proceedings of the IEEE International Conference on Image Processing*, ISBN 1522-4880, September 2003

Pinoli, J.C. (1997). A general comparative study of the multiplicative homomorphic, log-ratio, and logarithmic image processing approaches, *Signal Processing*, Vol. 58, pp. 11-45

Qiong, Z.; Sheng, Z. & Zhao, Y. (2008). Dynamic infrared and visible image sequence fusion based on DT-CWT using GGD, *Proceedings of the IEEE International Conference on Computer Science and Information Technology*, Singapore, ISBN 978-0-7695-3308-7, August 2008

Qu, G.H.; Zhang, D.L. & Yan, P.F. (2002). Information measure for performance of image fusion, *Electronic Letters*, Vol. 38, No. 7, pp. 313-315

Rockinger, O. (1997). Image sequence fusion using a shift-invariant wavelet transform, *Proceedings of the IEEE International Conference on Image Processing*, pp. 288-291

Shuang, L. & Zhilin, L. (2008). A Region-based technique for fusion of high-resolution images using mean shift segmentation, *International Archives of the Photogrammetry, Remote Sensing, and Spatial Information Sciences*, Vol. 38, pp. 1267-1272

Tabb, M.& Ahuja, N. (1997). Multiscale image segmentation by integrated edge and region detection, *IEEE Transactions on Image Processing*, Vol. 6, No. 5, (May 1997) pp. 642-655

Tao, W.; Jin, H. & Chang, Y. (2007). Color image segmentation based on mean shift and normalized cuts, *IEEE Transactions on Systems, Man, and Cybernetics, Part B: Cybernetics*, Vol. 37, No. 5, (October 2007) pp. 1382-1389

Tu, T.M.; Su, S.C., Shyu, H.C. & Huang, P.S. (2001). Efficient intensity-hue-saturation-based image fusion with saturation compensation, *SPIE Optical Engineering*, Vol. 40, No. 720.

Wang, Z. (2008). Medical image fusion using m-PCNN, *Information Fusion*, Vol. 9, No. 2, (April 2008) pp. 176-185.

Wang, Z. & Bovik, A.C. (2002). A universal image quality index, *IEEE Signal Processing Letters*, Vol. 9, No. 3, pp. 81-84.

Wharton, E.; Agaian, S. & Panetta, K. (2006). Comparative study of logarithmic enhancement algorithms with performance measure, *Proceedings of SPIE Conference on Electronic Imaging: Algorithms and Systems, Neural Networks, and Machine Learning,* Vol. 6064

Wharton, E.; Panetta, K. & Agaian S. (2007). Logarithmic edge detection with applications, *Proceedings of IEEE International Conference on Systems, Man, and Cybernetics,* pp. 3346-3351, October 2007.

Xydeas C.S. & Petrovic, V. (2000). Objective image fusion performance measure, *Electronic Letters,* Vol. 36, No. 4, (February 2000) pp. 308-309

Yang, Y.; Park D.S., Huang S. & Rao N. (2010). Medical image fusion via an effective wavelet-based approach. *EURASIP Journal on Advances in Signal Processing,* Vol. 2010, No. 10115

Zhang, Z. & Blum, R. (1999). A categorization of multiscale-decomposition-based image fusion schemes with a performance study for a digital camera application. *Proceedings of the IEEE,* Vol. 87, No. 8, (August 1999) pp. 1315-1326

Zhang, Z. & Blum, R. (1997). Region-based image fusion scheme for concealed weapon detection, *Proceedings of the Conference on Information Sciences and Systems,* pp. 168-173.

Zheng, L.; Forsyth, D. & Laganiere, R. (2008). A feature-based metric for the quantitative evaluation of pixel-level image fusion, *Computer Vision and Image Understanding,* Vol. 109, No. 1, (January 2008) pp. 56-68

9

A Perceptive-oriented Approach to Image Fusion

Boris Escalante-Ramírez[1], Sonia Cruz-Techica[1],
Rodrigo Nava[1] and Gabriel Cristóbal[2]
[1]*Facultad de Ingeniería, Universidad Nacional Autónoma de México,*
[2]*Instituto de Óptica, CSIC*
[1]*Mexico,*
[2]*Spain*

1. Introduction

At present time image fusion is widely recognized as an important tool and has attracted a great deal of attention from the research community with the purpose of searching general formal solutions to a number of problems in different applications such as medical imaging, optical microscopy, remote sensing, computer vision and robotics.
Image fusion consists of combining information from two or more images from the same sensor or from multiple sensors in order to improve the decision making process.
Fused images from multiple sensors, often called multi-modal image fusion system, include at least, two image modalities ranging from visible to infrared spectrum and they provide several advantages over data images from a single sensor (Kor & Tiwary, 2004). An example of this can be found in medical imaging where it is common to merge functional activity as in single photon emission computed tomography (SPECT), positron emission tomography (PET) or magnetic resonance spectroscopy (MRS) with anatomical structures such as magnetic resonance image (MRI), computed tomography (CT) and ultrasound, which helps improve diagnostic performance and surgical planning (Guihong et al., 2001, Hajnal et al., 2001).
An interesting example of single sensor fusion can be found in remote sensing, where pansharpening is an important task that combines panchromatic and multispectral optical data in order to obtain new multispectral bands that preserve their original spectral information with improved spatial resolution.
Depending on the merging stage, common image fusion schemes can be classified into three categories: pixel, feature and decision levels (Pohl & van Genderen, 1998). Many fusion schemes usually employ pixel level fusion techniques but since features, that are sensitive to human visual system (HVS), are bigger than a pixel and they exist in different scales, it is necessary to apply multiresolution analysis which improves the reconstruction of relevant image features (Nava et al., 2008). Moreover, the image representation model used to build the fusion algorithm must be able to characterize perceptive-relevant image primitives.
In the literature several methods of pixel level fusion have been reported using a transformation to perform data fusion, some of these transformations are: intensity-hue-saturation transform (IHS), principal component analysis (PCA) (Qiu et al., 2005), the

discrete wavelet transform (DWT) (Aguilar et al., 2007, Chipman et al., 1995, Li et al., 1994), dual-tree complex wavelet transform (DTCWT) (Kingsbury, 2001, Hill & Canagarajah, 2002), the contourlet transform (CW) (Yang et al., 2007), the curvelet transform (CUW) (Mahyari & Yazdi, 2009), and the Hermite transform (HT) (Escalante-Ramírez & López-Caloca, 2006, Escalante-Ramírez, 2008). In essence, all these transformations can discriminate between salient information and constant or non-textured background.

Of all these methods, the wavelet transform has been the most used technique for the fusion process. However, this technique presents certain problems in the analysis of signals of two or more dimensions, examples of these are the points of discontinuity that cannot always be detected, and its limitation to capture directional information. The contourlet and the curvelet transforms have shown better results than the wavelet transform due to their multi-directional analysis, but they require an extensive orientation search at each level of the decomposition. In contrast, the Hermite transform provides significant advantages to the process of image fusion. First, this image representation model includes some of the more important properties of the human visual system such as the local orientation analysis and the Gaussian derivative model of primary vision (Young, 1986), it also allows multiresolution analysis, so it is possible to describe the salient structures of an image at different spatial scales, and finally, it is steerable, which allows efficiently representing oriented patterns with a small number of coefficients. The latter has the additional advantage of reducing noise without introducing artifacts.

Hereinafter, we assume the input images have negligible registration problems, thus the images can be considered registered. The proposed scheme fuses images at the pixel level using a multiresolution directional-oriented Hermite transform of the source images by means of a decision map. This map is based on a linear dependence test of the Hermite coefficients within a fixed windows size; if the coefficients are linearly dependent, this indicates the existence of a relevant pattern that must be present in the final image.

The proposed algorithm has been tested on both multi-focus and multi-modal image sets producing results that ovecome results achieved with other methods such as wavelets (Li et al., 1994), curvelets (Donoho & Ying, 2007), and contourlets (Yang et al., 2008, Do, 2005). In addition to this, we used other decision rules proving that our scheme best characterized important structures of the images at the same time that the noise was reduced.

2. The Hermite transform as an image representation model

The Hermite transform (HT) (Martens 1990a, Martens 1990b) is a special case of polynomial transform, which is used to locally decompose signals and can be regarded as an image description model. The analysis stage involves two steps. First, the input image $L(x,y)$ is windowed with a local function $\omega(x,y)$ at several equidistant positions in order to achieve a complete description of the image. In the second step the local information of each analysis window is expanded in terms of a family of orthogonal polynomials. The polynomials $G_{m,n-m}(x,y)$ used to approximate the windowed information are determined entirely by the window function in such a way that the orthogonality condition is satisfied:

$$\int_{-\infty}^{+\infty}\int_{-\infty}^{+\infty}\omega^2(x,y)G_{m,n-m}(x,y)G_{l,k-l}(x,y)dxdy = \delta_{nk}\delta_{ml} \tag{1}$$

for $n, k=0,1,\ldots,\infty$; $m=0,\ldots,n$ y $l=0,\ldots,k$; where δ_{nk} denotes the Kronecker function.

The polynomial transform is called Hermite transform if the windows used are Gaussian functions. The Gaussian window is isotropic (rotationally invariant), separable in Cartesian coordinates and their derivatives mimic some processes at the retinal or visual cortex of the human visual system (Martens, 1990b, Young, 1986). This window function is defined as follows

$$\omega(x,y)=\frac{1}{2\pi\sigma^2}\exp\left(-\frac{x^2+y^2}{2\sigma^2}\right) \tag{2}$$

In a Gaussian window function, the associated orthogonal polynomials are the Hermite polynomials, which are defined as

$$G_{n-m,m}(x,y)=\frac{1}{\sqrt{2^n(n-m)!m!}}H_{n-m}\left(\frac{x}{\sigma}\right)H_m\left(\frac{x}{\sigma}\right) \tag{3}$$

where $H_n(x)$ denotes the nth Hermite polynomial.
The original signal $L(x,y)$, where (x,y) are the pixel coordinates, is multiplied by the window function $\omega(x-p,y-q)$ at the positions (p,q) that conform the sampling lattice S. By replicating the window function over the sampling lattice, we can define the periodic weighting function as

$$W(x,y)=\sum_{(p,q)\in S}\omega(x-p,y-q) \tag{4}$$

This weighting function must be a number other than zero for all coordinates (x,y). Therefore,

$$L(x,y)=\frac{1}{W(i,j)}\sum_{(p,q)\in S}L(x,y)\omega(x-p,y-q) \tag{5}$$

In every window function, the signal content is described as the weighted sum of polynomials $G_{m,n-m}(x,y)$ of m degree in x and $n-m$ in y. In a discrete implementation, the Gaussian window function may be approximated by the binomial window function and in this case, its orthogonal polynomials $G_{m,n-m}(x,y)$ are known as Krawtchouck's polynomials.
In either case, the polynomial coefficients $L_{m,n-m}(p,q)$ are calculated convolving the original image $L(x,y)$ with the analysis filters $D_{m,n-m}(x,y) = G_{m,n-m}(-x,-y)\omega^2(-x,-y)$, followed by subsampling at position (p,q) of the sampling lattice S. That is,

$$L_{m,n-m}(p,q)=\int_{-\infty}^{+\infty}\int_{-\infty}^{+\infty}L(x,y)D_{m,n-m}(x-p,y-q)\,dxdy \tag{6}$$

The recovery process of the original image consists of interpolating the transform coefficients with the proper synthesis filters. This process is called inverse transformed polynomial and is defined by

$$\hat{L}(x,y)=\sum_{n=0}^{\infty}\sum_{m=0}^{n}\sum_{(p,q)\in S}L_{m,n-m}(p,q)P_{m,n-m}(x-p,y-q) \tag{7}$$

The synthesis filters $P_{m,n-m}(x,y)$ of order m and $n-m$, are defined by

$$P_{m,n-m}(x,y)=\frac{G_{m,n-m}(x,y)\omega(x,y)}{W(x,y)} \tag{8}$$

for m=0,…,n , and n=0,…,∞

2.1 The steered Hermite transform

The Hermite transform has the advantage of high-energy compaction by adaptively steering the HT (Martens, 1997, Van Dijk, 1997, Silván-Cárdenas & Escalante-Ramírez, 2006). Steerable filters are a class of filters that are rotated copies of each filter, constructed as a linear combination of a set of basis filters. The steering property of the Hermite filters explains itself because they are products of polynomials with a radially symmetric window function. The N +1 Hermite filters of Nth-order form a steerable basis for each individual Nth-order filter. Because of this property, the Hermite filters at each position in the image adapt to the local orientation content.

Thus, for orientation analysis, it is convenient to work with a rotated version of the HT. The polynomial coefficients can be computed through a convolution of the image with the filter functions $D_m(x)D_{n\_m}(y)$. They are separable in spatial and polar domains, and their Fourier transform can be expressed as $\omega_x=\omega cos\theta$ and $\omega_y=\omega sin\theta$, in polar coordinates, then

$$d_m(\omega_x)d_{n-m}(\omega_y)=g_{m,n-m}(\theta)d_n(\omega) \tag{9}$$

where $d_n(\omega)$ is the Fourier transform for each filter function expressed in radial frequency, given by

$$d_n(\omega)=\frac{1}{\sqrt{2^n n!}}(-j\omega\sigma)\exp\left(-\frac{\omega\sigma^2}{4}\right) \tag{10}$$

and the orientation selectivity for the filter is expressed by

$$g_{m,n-m}(\theta)=\sqrt{\binom{n}{m}}\cos^m\theta sen^{n-m}\theta \tag{11}$$

In terms of orientation frequency functions, this property of the Hermite filters can be expressed by

$$g_{m,n-m}(\theta-\theta_0)=\sum_{k=0}^{n}c^n_{m,k}(\theta_0)g_{n-k,k}(\theta) \tag{12}$$

where $c^n_{m,k}(\theta_0)$ is the steering coefficient.

The Hermite filter rotation at each position over the image is an adaptation to local orientation content. Fig. 1 shows the HT and the steered HT over an image. For the directional Hermite decomposition, first, a HT was applied and then the coefficients were rotated toward the estimated local orientation, according to a criterion of maximum oriented energy at each window position. This implies that these filters can indicate the direction of one-dimensional pattern independently of its internal structure.

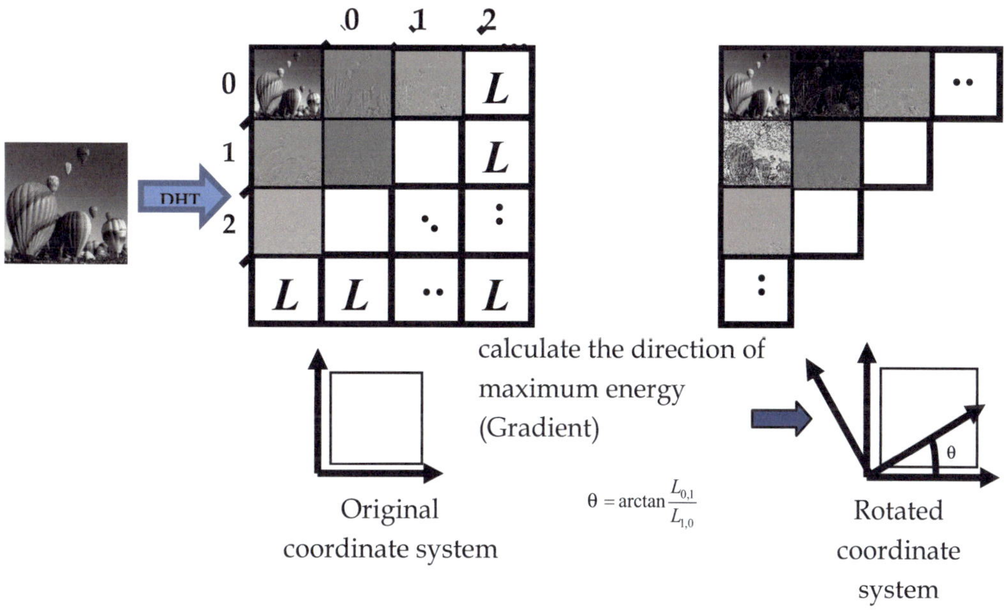

Fig. 1. The discrete Hermite transform (DHT) and the steered Hermite transform over an image

The two-dimensional Hermite coefficients are projected onto one-dimensional coefficients on an axis that makes an angle θ with the x axis, this angle can be approximated as $\theta = L_{01}/L_{10}$, where L_{01} and L_{10} are a good approach to optimal edge detectors in the horizontal and vertical directions respectively.

2.2 The multiresolution directional oriented HT

A multiresolution decomposition using the HT can be obtained through a pyramid scheme (Escalante-Ramírez & Silván Cárdenas 2005). In a pyramidal decomposition, the image is decomposed into a number of band-pass or low-pass subimages, which are then subsampled in proportion to their spatial resolution. In each layer the zero order coefficients are transformed to obtain -in a lower layer- a scaled version of the above. Once the coefficients of Hermite decomposition of each level are obtained, the coefficients can be projected to one dimension by its local orientation of maximum energy. In this way we obtain the multiresolution directional-oriented Hermite transform, which provides information about the location and orientation of the structure of the image at different scales.

3. Image fusion with the Hermite transform

Our approach aims at analyzing images by means of the HT, which allows us to identify perceptually relevant patterns to be included in the fusion process while discriminating spurious artifacts. As we have mentioned, the steered HT allows us to focus energy in a small number of coefficients, and thus the information contained in the first-order rotated

coefficient may be sufficient to describe the edge information of the image in a particular spatial locality. If we extend this strategy to more than one level of resolution, then it is possible to obtain a better description of the image. However, the success of any fusion scheme depends not only on the image analysis model but also on the fusion rule, therefore, instead of choosing for the usual selection operators based on the maximum pixel value, which often introduce noise and irrelevant details in the fused image, we seek a rule to consider the existence of a pattern in a region defined by a fixed-size window.
The general framework for the proposed algorithm includes the following stages. First a multiresolution HT of the input images is applied. Then, for each level of decomposition, the orientation of maximum energy is detected to rotate the coefficients, so the first order rotated coefficient has most edge information. Afterwards, taking this rotated coefficient of each image we apply a linear dependence test. The result of this test is then used as a decision map to select the coefficients of the fused image in the multiresolution HT domain of the input images. If the original images are noisy, the decision map is applied on the multiresolution directional-oriented HT. The approximation coefficients in the case of HT are the zero order coefficients. In most multifocal and multimodal applications the approximation coefficients of the input images are averaged to generate the zero order coefficient of the fused image, but it always depends on the application context. Finally the fused image is obtained by applying the inverse multiresolution HT. Fig. 2 shows a simplified representation of this method.

3.1 The fusion rule

The linear dependence test evaluates the pixels inside a window of w_s x w_s, if those pixels are linearly independent, then there is no relevant feature in the window. However, if the pixels are linearly dependent, it indicates the existence of a relevant pattern. The fusion rule selects the coefficient with the highest dependency value. A higher value will represent a stronger pattern. A simple and rigorous test for determining the linear dependence or independence of vectors is the Wronskian determinant. The dependency of the window centered at a pixel *(i,j)* is described in

$$D_A(i,j) = \sum_{m=i-w_s}^{i+w_s} \sum_{n=j-w_s}^{j+w_s} L_A^2(m,n) - L_A(m,n) \tag{13}$$

where $L_A(m, n)$ is the first order steered Hermite coefficient of the source image A with spatial position *(m,n)*. The fusion rule is expressed in (14). The coefficient of the fused HT is selected as the one with largest value of the dependency measure.

$$L_F(i,j) = \begin{cases} L_A(i,j) & si \ D_A(i,j) \geq D_B(i,j) \\ L_B(i,j) & si \ D_A(i,j) < D_B(i,j) \end{cases} \tag{14}$$

We apply this rule to all detail coefficients and in the most of the cases average the zero order Hermite coefficients as (15).

$$L_{00_F}(i,j) = \frac{1}{2}\left[L_{00_A}(i,j) + L_{00_B}(i,j)\right] \tag{15}$$

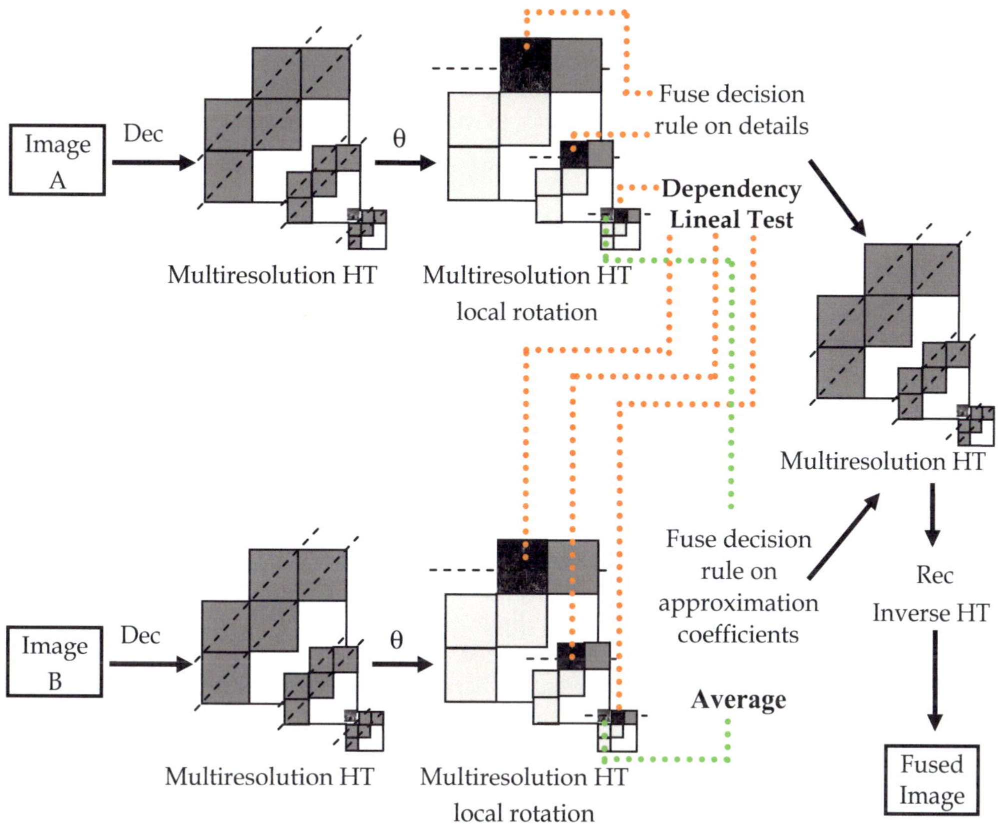

Fig. 2. Fusion scheme with the multiresolution directional-oriented Hermite transform

4. Image fusion results

The proposed algorithm was tested on several sets of multi-focus and multi-modal images, with and without noise degradation. Fig. 3 shows one of the multi-focus image sets used and the results of image fusion achieved with the proposed method using different decision rules. In these experiments, we used a Gaussian window with spread $\sigma=\sqrt{2}$, a subsampling factor T=2 between each pyramidal level and four decomposition levels. The window size for linear dependence test, maximum with verification of consistency and saliency and match measurement (Burt & Kolczynski, 1993), was 3 x 3.

Fig. 4 shows other multi-focus image sets that uses synthetic images. The results of image fusion were achieved with different fusion methods using linear dependence as decision rule. In these experiments, we used a Gaussian window with spread $\sigma=\sqrt{2}$, a subsampling factor T=2 between each pyramidal level and three decomposition levels; the wavelet transform used was db4 and in the case of the contourlet transform, the McClellan transform of 9-7 filters were used as directional filters and the wavelet db4 was used as pyramidal filters. The window size for the fusion rule was 3 x 3. The results were zoomed with the purpose to better observe the different methods performance.

On the other side, Figs. 5, 6 and 7 show the application in medical images comparing with other fusion methods, all of them using the linear dependence test with a window size of 3 x

3. All the transforms have two decomposition levels; the wavelet transform used was db4 and in the case of the contourlet transform, the McClellan transform of 9-7 filters were used as directional filters and the wavelet db4 was used as pyramidal filters.
In Fig. 7, Gaussian noise with σ=0.001 was introduced to the original images in order to show the efficiency of our method in noisy images.

5. Quality assessment of image fusion algorithms

Digital image processing involves many tasks, such as manipulation, storing, transmission, etc., that may introduce perceivable distortions. Since degradations occur during the processing chain, it is crucial to quantify degradations in order to overcome them. Due to their importance, many articles on the literature are dedicated to develop methods for improving, quantifying or preserving the quality of processed images. For example, Wang and Bovik (Wang, et al, 2004) describe a method based on the hypothesis that the HVS is highly adapted for extracting structural information, and they proposed a measure of structural similarity (SSIM) that compares local patterns of pixel intensities that have been normalized for luminance and contrast. In (Nava, et al, 2010; Gabarda & Cristóbal, 2007) two quality assessment procedures were introduced based on the expected entropy variance of a given image. These methods are useful in scenarios where there is no reference image, therefore they can be used in image fusion applications.
Quality is an image characteristic, it can be defined as ``the degree to which an image satisfies the requirements imposed on it'' (Silverstein & Farrell, 1996) and it is crucial for most image processing applications, because it can be used to compare the performance of the different systems and to select the appropriate processing algorithm for any given application. Image quality (IQ) can be used in general terms as an indicator of the relevance of the information presented by an image. A major part of research activity in the field of IQ is directed towards the development of reliable and widely applicable image quality measure algorithms. Nevertheless, only limited success has been achieved (Nava, at al, 2008).
A common way to measure IQ is based on early visual models but since human beings are the ultimate receivers in most applications, the most reliable way of assessing the quality of an image is by subjective evaluations. There are several different methodologies for subjective testing which are based on the idea how a person perceives the quality of images, and so it is inherently subjective (Wang, et al, 2002).
The subjective quality measure, mean opinion score (MOS), provides a numerical indication of the perceived quality. It has been used for many years, and it is considered the best method for image quality. The MOS metric is generated by averaging the results of a set of standard, subjective tests, where a number of people rate the quality of image series based on the recommendation ITU-T J247 (Sheikh, el al, 2006). MOS is the arithmetic mean of all the individual scores, and can range from 1 (worst) to 5 (best).
Nevertheless, MOS is inconvenient because it demands human observers, it is expensive and usually too slow to apply in real-time scenarios. Moreover, quality perception is strongly influenced by a variety of factors that depend on the observer. For these reasons, it is desirable to have an objective metric capable of predict image quality automatically. The techniques developed to assess image quality must depend on the field of application because it determines the characteristics of the imaging task we would like to evaluate. Practical image quality measures may vary according to the field of application and they should evaluate overall distortions. However, there is no single standard procedure to measure image quality.

Fig. 3. Results of image fusion in multi-focus images, using multiresolution directional-oriented HT. a) and b) are the source images, c) fused image using absolute maximum selection, d) fused image using maximum with verification of consistency, e) fused image using saliency and match measurement and f) fused image using the linear dependency

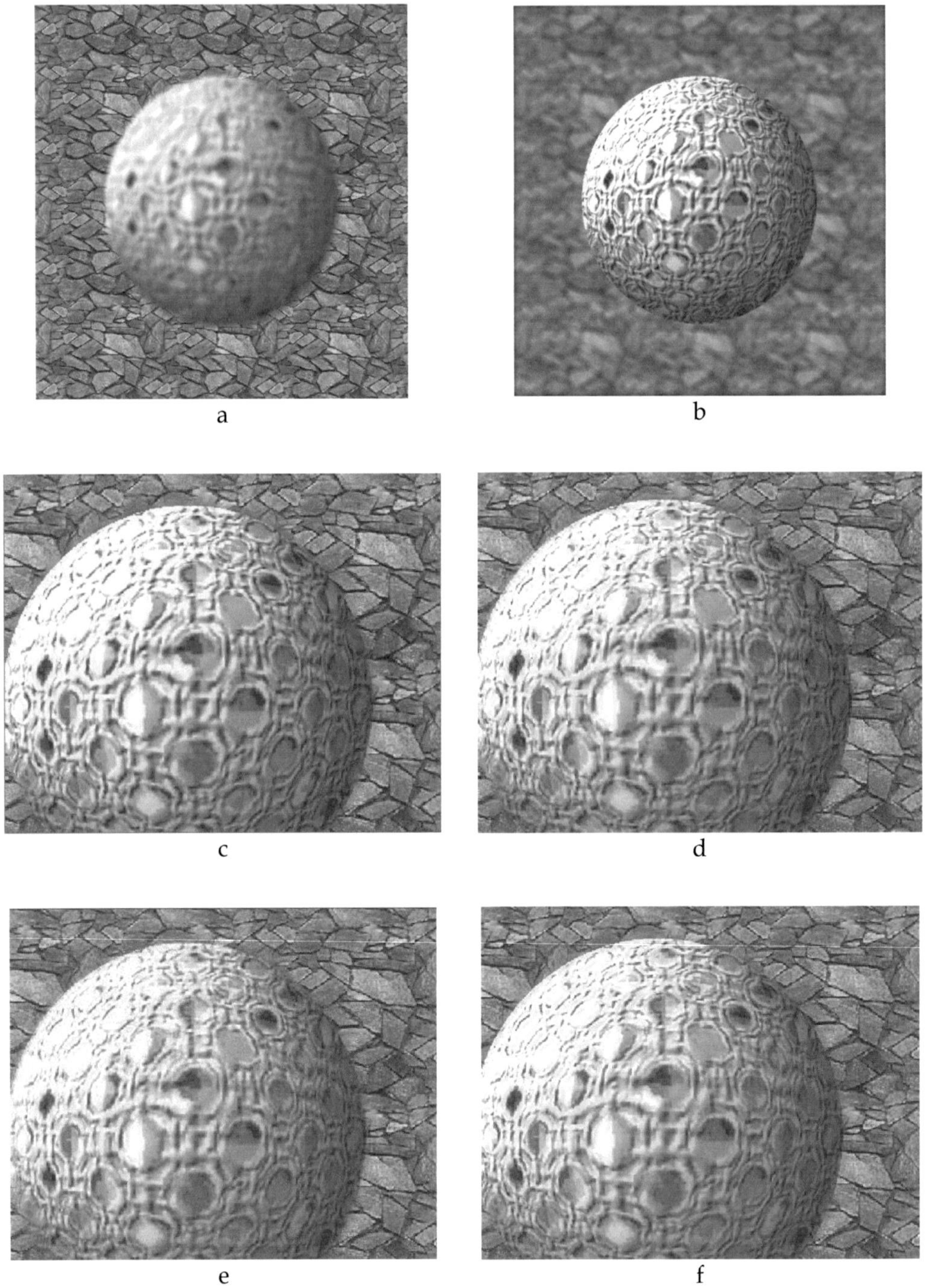

Fig. 4. Results of image fusion in synthetic multi-focus images, using the dependency test rule and different analyze techniques. a) and b) are the source images, c) HT, d) wavelet transform, e) contourlet transform and f) curvelet transform

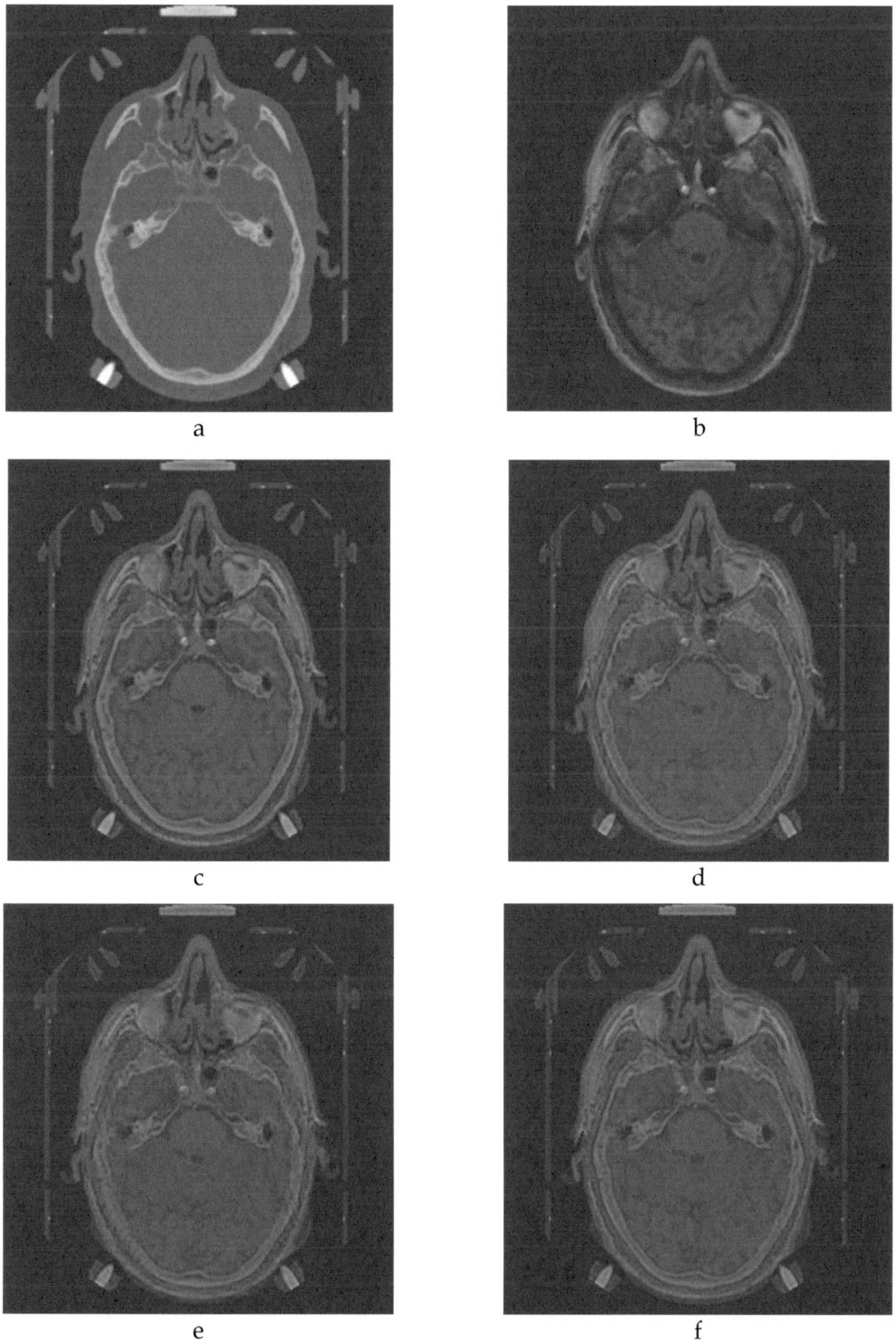

Fig. 5. Results of image fusion in medical images, using the dependency test rule and different analyze techniques. a) CT, b) MR, c) HT, d) wavelet transform, e) contourlet transform and f) curvelet transform

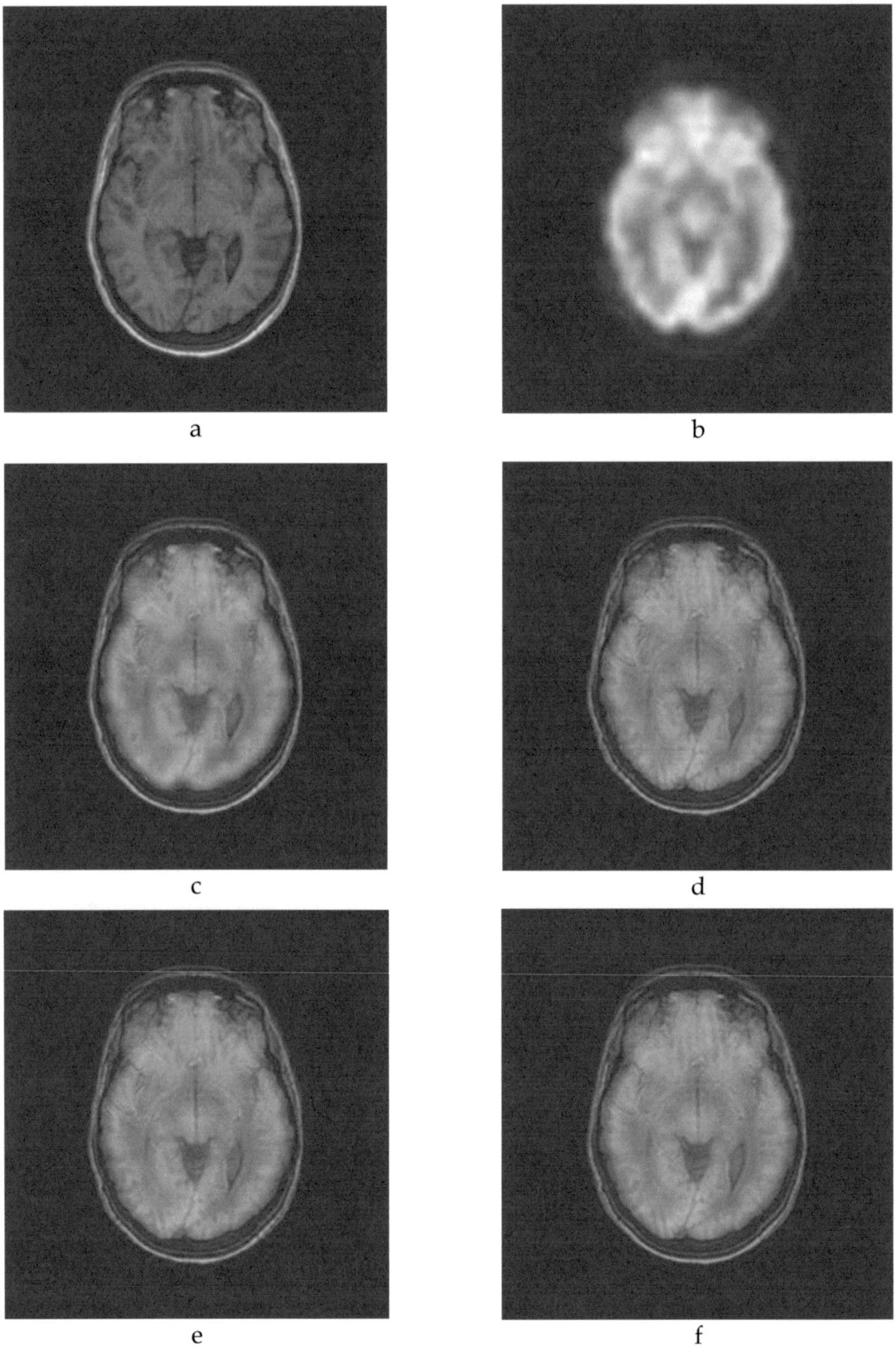

Fig. 6. Results of image fusion in medical images, using the dependency test rule and different analyze techniques. a) RM, b) PET, c) HT, d) wavelet transform, e) contourlet transform and f) curvelet transform

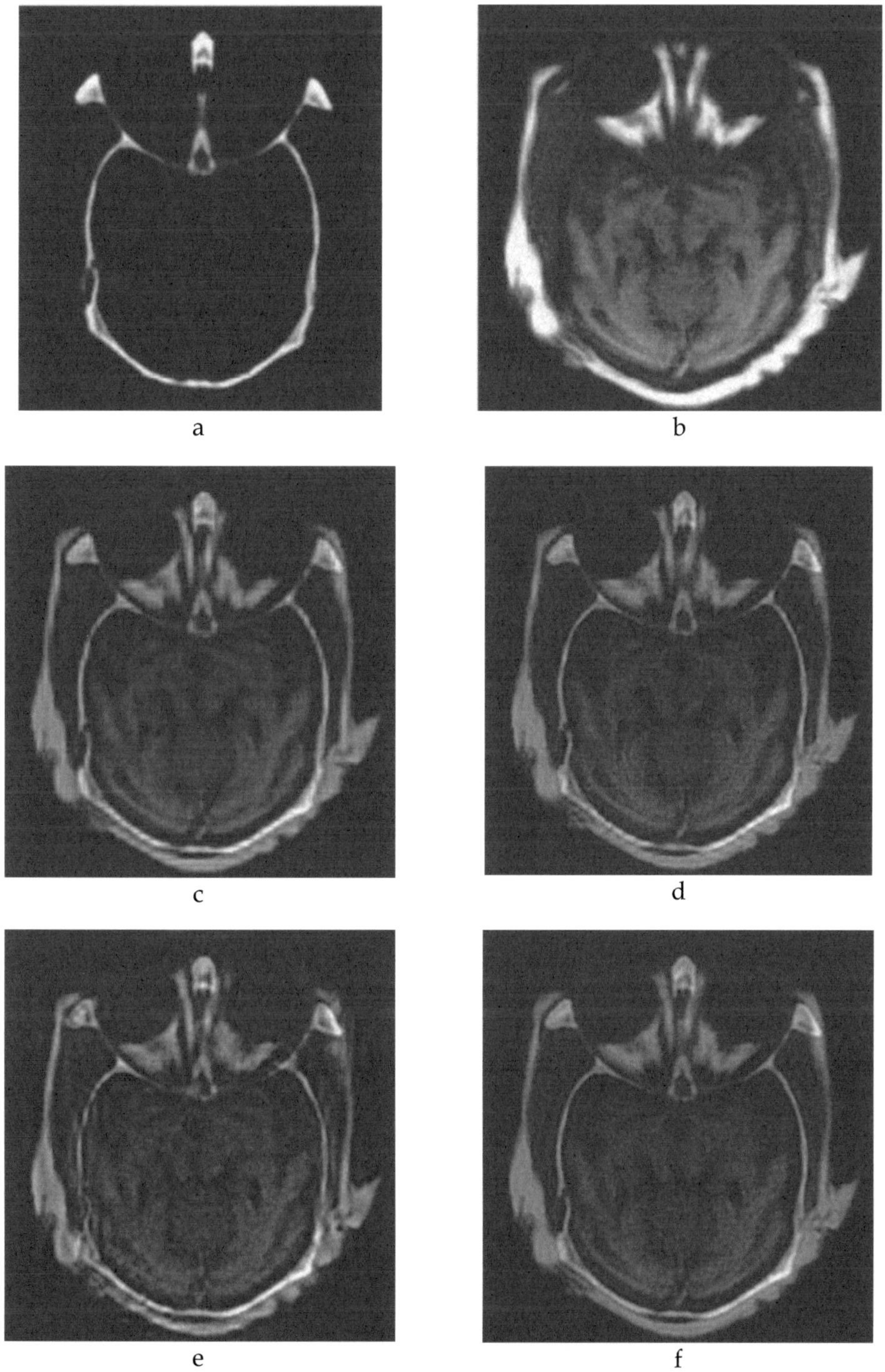

Fig. 7. Results of image fusion in medical images, using the dependency test rule and different analyze techniques. a) CT, b) MR, c) HT, d) wavelet transform, e) contourlet transform and f) curvelet transform. Images provided by Dr. Oliver Rockinger

Objective image quality metrics are based on measuring physical characteristics and they intend to predict perceived quality accurately and automatically. It means, that they should predict image quality that an average human observer will report. One important fact on this issue is the availability of an "original image", which is considered to be distortion-free or perfect quality. Most of the proposed objective quality measures assume that the reference image exists and they attempt to quantify the visibility error between a distorted image and a reference image.

Among the available ways to measure objective image quality, the mean squared error (MSE) and peak signal-to-noise ratio (PSNR) are widely employed because they are easy to calculate and usually they have low computational cost, but such measures are not necessarily consistent with human observer evaluation (Wang & Bovik, 2009). Both MSE and PSNR reflect the global properties of the image quality but they are inefficient in predicting structural degradations. Ponomarenko in (Ponomarenko, et al, 2009) evaluated correspondence of HVS with MSE and PSNR (0.525) where ideal value is 0.99. This shows that the widely used metrics PSNR and MSE have very low correlation with human perception (correlation factors are about 0.5).

In many practical applications, image quality metrics do not always have access to a reference image. However, it is desirable to develop measurement approaches that can evaluate image quality blindly. Blind or non--reference image quality assessment turns out to be a very difficult task, because metrics are not related to the original image (Nava, et al, 2007).

In order to quantitatively compare the different objective quality metrics, we evaluated our fusion results with several methods, including the traditional as well as some of the more recent ones that may correlate better with the human perceptive assessment. Among the first ones, we considered the PSNR and the MSE, and for the second group we used the measure of structural similarity (SSIM), the Mutual information (MI) and the Normalized Mutual Information (NMI) based on Tsallis entropy (Nava et al, 2010). In experiments with no reference image (ground truth) was available, metrics based on mutual information were used.

PSNR is a ratio between the maximum possible power of the reconstructed image and the power of the noise that affects the fidelity of the reconstruction, this is

$$PSNR = 10\log_{10} \frac{255^2(MN)}{\sum_{i=1}^{M}\sum_{j=1}^{N}\left[F(i,j)-R(i,j)\right]^2} \tag{16}$$

where $F(i,j)$ denotes the intensity of the pixel of the fused image and $R(i,j)$ denotes the intensity of the pixel of the original image.

The MSE indicates the error level between the fused image and the ideal image (ground truth), the smaller value of MSE indicates the better performance of the fusion method.

$$MSE = \frac{\sum_{i=1}^{M}\sum_{j=1}^{N}\left[F(i,j)-R(i,j)\right]^2}{MN} \tag{17}$$

The SSIM (Wang et al., 2004) compares local patterns of pixel intensities that have been normalized for luminance and contrast and it provides a quality value in the range [0,1].

$$SSIM(R,F)=\frac{\sigma_{RF}}{\sigma_R\sigma_F}\frac{2\mu_R\mu_F}{(\mu_R)^2+(\mu_F)^2}\frac{2\sigma_R\sigma_F}{\sigma_R^2\sigma_F^2} \tag{18}$$

Where μ_R is the original image mean and μ_F the fused image mean; σ is the variance and σ_{RF} is the covariance.

MI has also been proposed as a performance measurement of image fusion in the absence of a reference image (Wang et al., 2009). Mutual information is a measurement of the statistical dependency of two random variables and the amount of information that one variable contain about the other. The amount of information that belongs to image A contained in the fused image is determined as follows:

$$MI_{FA}(I_F,I_A)=\sum P_{FA}(I_F,I_A)\log\left[\frac{P_{FA}(I_F,I_A)}{P_F(I_F)P_A(I_A)}\right] \tag{19}$$

where P_F and P_A are the marginal probability densisty functions of images F and A respectively, and P_{FA} is the joint probability density funtion of both images.Then, mutual information is calculated by

$$MI_F^{AB}=MI_{FA}(I_F,I_A)+MI_{FB}(I_F,I_B) \tag{20}$$

Another performance measurement is the Fusion Symmetry (FS) defined in equation (21), it denotes the symmetry of the fusion process in relation to the two input images. The smaller the FS is, the better the fusion process performs.

$$FS=abs\left(\frac{MI_{FA}(I_F,I_A)}{MI_{FA}(I_F,I_A)+MI_{FB}(I_F,I_B)}-0.5\right) \tag{21}$$

The NMI (Nava et al 2010) is defined as

$$NMI^q(F,A,B)=\frac{M^q(F,A,B)}{MAX^q(F,A,B)} \tag{22}$$

where

$$M^q(F,A,B)=I^q(F,A)+I^q(F,B) \tag{23}$$

and

$$I^q(F,A)=\frac{1}{1-q}\left(1-\sum_{f,a}\frac{P(F,A)^q}{(P(F)P(A))^{q-1}}\right) \tag{24}$$

$MAX^q(F,A,B)$ is a normalization factor that represents the total information.

At first glance, the results obtained in Fig. 3 were very similar, thought quantitatively it is possible to verify the performance of the proposed algorithm. Table 1 shows the HT fusion performance using a ground truth image and different fusion rules, while that Table 2 compares the performance of different fusion methods with the same reference image and the same fusion rule.

Fusion Rule	MSE	PSNR	SSIM	MI
Absolute maximum	4.42934	41.6674	0.997548	5.535170
Maximum with verification of consistency	0.44076	51.6886	0.999641	6.534807
Saliency and match measurement	4.66043	41.4465	0.996923	5.494261
Linear dependency test	0.43574	51.7385	0.999625	6.480738

Table 1. Performance measurement of Fig. 3 using a ground truth image by the multiresolution directional-oriented HT using different fusion rules

Fusion Method	MSE	PSNR	SSIM	MI	NMI
Hermite Transform	0.43574	51.7385	0.999625	6.480738	0.72835
Wavelet Transform	0.76497	49.2944	0.999373	6.112805	0.72406
Contourlet Transform	1.51077	46.3388	0.998464	5.885111	0.72060
Curvelet Transform	0.88777	48.6478	0.999426	6.083156	0.72295

Table 2. Performance measurement of Fig. 3 using a ground truth image applying the fusion rule based on linear dependency with different methods

Tables 3 and 4 correspond to tables 1 and 2 for the case of Fig. 4.

Fusion Rule	MSE	PSNR	SSIM	MI
Absolute maximum	54.248692	30.786911	0.984670	3.309483
Maximum with verification of consistency	35.110012	32.676494	0.989323	3.658905
Saliency and match measurement	38.249722	32.304521	0.989283	3.621530
Linear dependency test	33.820709	32.838977	0.989576	3.659614

Table 3. Performance measurement of Fig. 4 using a ground truth image by the multiresolution directional-oriented HT with different fusion rules

Fusion Method	MSE	PSNR	SSIM	MI	NMI
Hermite Transform	33.820709	32.838977	0.989576	3.659614	0.23967
Wavelet Transform	128.590240	27.038724	0.953244	2.543590	0.24127
Contourlet Transform	156.343357	26.190009	0.945359	2.323243	0.23982
Curvelet Transform	114.982239	27.524496	0.952543	2.588358	0.24024

Table 4. Performance measurement of Fig. 4 using a ground truth image applying the fusion rule based on linear dependency with different methods

From Figs. 5, 6 and 7, we can notice that the image fusion method based on the Hermite transform preserved better the spatial resolution and information content of both images. Moreover our method shows a better performance in noise reduction.

Fusion Method	MI_{FA}	MI_{FB}	MI_{FAB}	FS
Hermite Transform	1.937877	1.298762	3.236638	0.098731
Wavelet Transform	1.821304	1.202295	3.023599	0.102363
Contourlet Transform	1.791008	1.212183	3.003192	0.096368
Curvelet Transform	1.827996	1.268314	3.096310	0.090379

Table 5. Performance measurement of Fig. 5 (CT/RM) applying the fusion rule based on linear dependency with different methods

Fusion Method	MI_{FA}	MI_{FB}	MI_{FAB}	FS
Hermite Transform	1.617056	1.766178	3.383234	0.022038
Wavelet Transform	1.626056	1.743542	3.369598	0.017433
Contourlet Transform	1.617931	1.740387	3.358319	0.018232
Curvelet Transform	1.589712	1.754872	3.344584	0.024691

Table 6. Performance measurement of Fig. 6 (RM/PET) applying the fusion rule based on linear dependency with different methods

6. Conclusions

We have presented a multiresolution image fusion method based on the directional-oriented HT using a linear dependency test as fusion rule. We have experimented with this method for multi-focus and multi-modal images and we have obtained good results, even in the

presence of noise. Both subjective and objective results show that the proposed scheme outperforms other existing methods.
The HT has proved to be an efficient model for the representation of images because derivatives of Gaussian are the basis functions of this transform, which optimally detect, represent and reconstruct perceptually relevant image patterns, such as edges and lines.

7. Acknowledgements

This work was sponsored by UNAM grants IN106608 and IX100610.

8. References

Aguilar-Ponce, R.; Tecpanecatl-Xihuitl, J.L.; Kumar, A.; & Bayoumi, M. (2007). Pixel-level image fusion scheme based on linear algebra, *IEEE International Symposium on Circuits and Systems, 2007. ISCAS 2007*, pp. 2658–2661, May 2007.

Burt, P.J. & Kolczynski, R.J. (1993). Enhanced image capture through fusion, *Proceedings of the Fourth International Conference on Computer Vision, 1993*, pp. 173 -182, 11-14.

Chipman, L.J.; Orr, T.M. & Graham, L.N. (1995). Wavelets and image fusion, *Proceedings of the International Conference on Image Processing*, Vol. 3, pp. 248 -251, Oct. 1995.

Do, M (2005). Contourlet toolbox. http://www.mathworks.com/matlabcentral/fileexchange/8837, (Last modified 27 Oct 2005).

Donoho, D. & Ying, L. (2007). The Curvelet.org team: Emmanuel Candes, Laurent Demanet. Curvelet.org. http://www.curvelet.org/software.html, (Last modified 24 August 2007).

Escalante-Ramírez, B. & López-Caloca, A.A. (2006). The Hermite transform: an efficient tool for noise reduction and image fusion in remote sensing, In: *Signal and Image Processing for Remote Sensing*, C.H. Chen, (Ed.), 539–557. CRC Press, Boca Raton.

Escalante-Ramírez, B. (2008). The Hermite transform as an efficient model for local image analysis: an application to medical image fusion. *Computers & Electrical Engineering*, Vol. 34, No. 2, 99–110, 2008.

Escalante-Ramírez, B & Silván-Cárdenas, J.L. (2005). Advanced modeling of visual information processing: A multi-resolution directional-oriented image transform based on gaussian derivatives. *Signal Processing: Image Communication*, Vol. 20, No. 9-10, 801 - 812.

Gabarda, S., & Cristóbal, G. (2007). Blind image quality assessment through anisotropy. Journal of the Optical Society of America A, Vol. 24, No. 12, B42--B51.

Guihong, Q.; Dali, Z. & Pingfan, Y. (2001). Medical image fusion by wavelet transform modulus maxima. *Optics Express*, Vol. 9 No. 4, 184–190.

Hajnal, J.; Hill, D.G. & Hawkes, D. (2001). *Medical Image Registration*. CRC Press, Boca Raton.

Hill, P; Canagarajah, N. & Bull, D. (2002). Image fusion using complex wavelets, *Proceedings of the. 13th British Machine Vision Conference*, pp. 487–496, 2002.

Kingsbury, N (2001). Complex wavelets for shift invariant analysis and filtering of signals. *Applied and Computational Harmonic Analysis*, Vol. 10, No. 3, 234 - 253.

Kor, S. & Tiwary, U. (2004) Feature level fusion of multimodal medical images in lifting wavelet transform domain, *Proceedings of the IEEE International Conference of the Engineering in Medicine and Biology Security*, Vol. 1, pp. 1479–1482, 2004.

Li, H; Manjunath, B.S. & Mitra, S.K. (1994). Multi-sensor image fusion using the wavelet transform, *Proceedings of the IEEE International Conference on Image Processing, ICIP-94,* Vol. 1, pp. 51 -55, Nov. 1994.

Mahyari, A.G. & Yazdi, M. (2009). A novel image fusion method using curvelet transform based on linear dependency test, *Proceedings of the International Conference on Digital Image Processing 2009,* pp. 351–354, March 2009.

Martens J.B. (1990a). The Hermite transform-applications. *IEEE Transactions on Acoustics, Speech and Signal Processing,* Vol. 38, No. 9, 1607–1618.

Martens, J.B. (1990b). The Hermite transform-theory. *IEEE Transactions on Acoustics, Speech and Signal Processing,* Vol. 38, No. 9, 1595–1606.

Martens, J.B. (1997). Local orientation analysis in images by means of the Hermite transform. *IEEE Transactions on Image Processing,* Vol. 6, No. 8, 1103–1116.

Nava, R., Cristóbal, G., & Escalante-Ramírez, B. (2007). Nonreference image fusion evaluation procedure based on mutual information and a generalized entropy measure, *Proceedings of SPIE conference on Bioengineered and Bioinspired Systems III.* Vol. 6592. Maspalomas, Gran Canaria, Spain, 2007.

Nava, R.; Escalante-Ramirez, B. & Cristobal, G (2008). A novel multi-focus image fusion algorithm based on feature extraction and wavelets, *Proceedings of SPIE,* vol. 5616800, 2008, pp. 700028-10.

Nava, R., Escalante-Ramírez, B., & Cristóbal, G. (2010). Blind quality assessment of multi-focus image fusion algorithms, *Proceedings of Optics, Photonics, and Digital Technologies for Multimedia Applications.* 7723, p. 77230F. Brussels, Belgium, Apr. 2010, SPIE.

Pohl, C. & Van Genderen, J.L.(1998). Multisensor image fusion in remote sensing: concepts, methods and applications, *International Journal of Remote Sensing,* Vol. 19, No. 5, 823–854.

Ponomarenko, N., Lukin, V., Zelensky, A., Egiazarian, K., Carli, M., & Battisti, F. (2009). TID2008 - A Database for Evaluation of Full-Reference Visual Quality Assessment Metrics. *Advances of Modern Radioelectronics* Vol. 10, No. 4, 30-45.

Qiu, Y; Wu, J; Huang, H.; Wu, H.; Liu, J. & Tian, J. (2005). Multi-sensor image data fusion based on pixel-level weights of wavelet and the PCA transform, *Proceedings of the IEEE International Conference Mechatronics and Automation,* Vol. 2, 653 - 658, Jul. 2005.

Sheikh, H. R., Sabir, M. F., & Bovik, A. C. (2006). A Statistical Evaluation of Recent Full Reference Image Quality Assessment Algorithms. *IEEE Transactions on Image Processing* , 15 (11), 3440-3451.

Silván Cárdenas, J.L. & Escalante-Ramírez, B. (2006). The multiscale hermite transform for local orientation analysis, *IEEE Transactions on Image Processing,* Vol. 15, No. 5, 1236-1253.

Silverstein, D. A., & Farrell, J. E. (1996). The relationship between image fidelity and image quality, *Proceedings of the International Conference on Image Processing,* 1, pp. 881-884, 1996.

Van Dijk, A.M. & Martens, J.B. (1997). Image representation and compression with steered Hermite transforms. *Signal Processing,* Vol. 56, No. 1, 1 - 16.

Wang, Z., & Bovik, A. C. (2009). Mean squared error: Love it or leave it? A new look at Signal Fidelity Measures. *IEEE Signal Processing Magazine* , 26 (1), 98-117.

Wang, Z., Bovik, A. C., & Lu, L. (2002). Why is image quality assessment so difficult?, *Proceedings of the IEEE International Conference on Acoustics, Speech, and Signal Processing*, pp. IV-3313-IV-3316), 2002.

Wang, Z.; Bovik, A.C.; Sheikh, H.R. & Simoncelli, E.P. (2004). Image quality assessment: from error visibility to structural similarity, *IEEE Transactions on Image Processing*, Vol. 13, No. 4, 600 -612.

Wang, Q.; Yu, D, & Shen Y. (2009). An overview of image fusion metrics, *Proceedings of the Instrumentation and Measurement Technology Conference, 2009. I2MTC '09. IEEE*, pp. 918–923, May 2009.

Yang, L.; Guo, B.L. & and Ni, M. (2008). Multimodality medical image fusion based on multiscale geometric analysis of contourlet transform. *Neurocomputing*, Vol. 72, No. 1-3, 203 - 211, 2008. Machine Learning for Signal Processing (MLSP 2006) / Life System Modelling, Simulation, and Bio-inspired Computing (LSMS 2007).

Young, R. (1986). The gaussian derivative theory of spatial vision: analysis of cortical cell receptive field line-weighting profiles. Technical Report GMR-4920, General Motors Research, 1986.

10

Image Fusion Based on Muti-directional Multiscale Analysis and Immune Optimization

Fang Liu, Jing Bai, Shuang Wang, Biao Hou and Licheng Jiao
Key Laboratory of Intelligent Perception and Image Understanding of Ministry of Education of China,
Institute of Intelligent Information Processing Xidian University, Xi'an, P.R. China

1. Introduction

Image fusion is a process by combining two or more source images from different modalities or instruments into a single image with more information. The successful fusion is of great importance in many applications, such as military, remote sensing, computer vision and medical imaging, et al. Image fusion can be performed at signal, pixel, feature and symbol levels depending on the representation format at which image information is processed. The pixel-level image fusion can provide the fine information by fusing the pixels of the source images and the fused images. In this chapter, we only consider the fusion technique on pixel-level. To the pixel-level fusion, some generic requirements can be imposed on the fused on the fusion results (Rockinger, O., 1996):

a. The fused image should preserve all relevant information contained in the source images as closely as possible;
b. The fused process should not introduce any artifacts or inconsistencies, which can distract or mislead the human observer, or any subsequent image processing steps;
c. In the fused image, irrelevant features and noise should be suppressed to a maximum extent.

The visible light sensor and the infrared sensor are in common use sensors acting on different bands. The infrared imaging sensor is sensitive to the radiation of object scene, but not to the brightness change of scene. The visible light imaging sensor is sensitive and decided by the reflectivity and the shadow of the object sensor and has the higher contrast degree, but independent to the heat contrast. The image features of the two kinds of sensors have the different gray values and have the complement information. The fusion of the infrared images and the low visible light images can be in favor of integrating the good object denote character of the infrared images and the clear scene information of the visible light images.

Panchromatic (PAN) images of high spatial resolution can provide detailed geometric information, such as shapes features, and structures of objects of the earth's surface. While multispectral(MS) images with usually lower resolution are used to obtain spectral information necessary for environmental applications. The different objects within images of high spectral resolution are easily identified. Data fusion methods aim to obtain the images with high spatial and spectral resolution, simultaneously. The PAN and MS remote sensing image fusion is different in military missions or computer-aided quality control. The specificity is to preserve the spectral information for subsequent classification of ground cover. The classical fusion methods are principle component analysis (PCA), intensity-hue-saturation (IHS) transform, etc. In recent years, with the development of wavelet transform (WT) theory and multiresolution analysis, two-dimensional separable wavelets have been widely used in image fusion and have achieved good results(Nunez, J., 1999; Gonzalez-Audicana. M., 2004; Wang, Z. J., 2005). Thus, the fusion algorithms mentioned above can hardly make it by themselves. They usually cause some characteristic degradation, spectral loss, or color distortion. The WT can preserve spectral information efficiently but cannot express spatial characteristics well. Furthermore, the isotropic wavelets are scant of shift-invariance and multidirectionality and fail to provide an optimal expression of highly anisotropic edges and contours in image.

Image decomposition is an important link of image fusion and affects the information extraction quality, even the whole fusion quality. In recent years, along with the development and application to express local signal makes wavelet a candidate in multisensor image fusion. However, wavelet bases are isotropy and of limited directions and fail to represent high anisotropic edges and contours in images well. The MGA emerges, which comes form wavelet, but beyond it. The MGA can take full advantage of the geometric regularity of image intrinsic structures and obtain the asymptotic optimal representation. As an MAG tool, the contourlet transform (CT) has the characteristics of localization, mulitdirection, and anisotropy (Do, M. N., 2005). The CT can give the asymptotic optimal representation of contours and has been applied in image fusion effectively. However, the CT is lack of shift-invariance and results in artifacts along the edges to some extend. The nonsubsampled contourlet transform (NSCT) is in virtue the nonsubsampled filter banks to meet the shift-invariance(da Cunha, 2006). Therefore, the NSCT is more suitable for image fusion, which is explained in section II together with the immune clonal selection (ICS) optimization algorithm.

Considering of the characteristics of low visible light images and infrared images and combining with the human visual system, a novel image fusion technique is presented in section III. The fusion technique is based on ICS in the natural immune selection and the NSCT. The NSCT can give the asymptotic optimal representation of the edges and contours in image by virtue of the characteristics of good multiresolution, shift-invariance and multi-directionality. And then the ICS is introduced into the NSCT domain to optimize the fusing weights adaptively. Numerical tests show that this algorithm provides improvements both in visual effects and quantitative analysis. And the fused images hold more edge and texture information and have stronger contrast and definition.

The fusion of multispectral and panchromatic remote sensing images is discussed in section IV. An NSCT-based panchromatic and multispectral image fusion method is presented after analyzing the basic principles of remote sensing image system and fusion purpose. An intensity component addition strategy based on LHS transform is introduced into NSCT domain to preserve spatial resolution and color content. Experiments show that the fusion method proposed can improve spatial resolution and keep spectral information simultaneously.

A novel image fusion scheme is presented based on multiscale decomposition and multiwavelet transform (MWT) in section V. First, contrast pyramid (CP) decomposition is used to each level of each original image. Then, each image are decomposed by WT.

Furthermore, a kind of evolution computation method-ICS algorithm is introduced to optimize the fusion coefficients for better fusion products. Applying this technique to fusion of multisenor images, simulation results clearly demonstrate the superiority of this new approach. Fusion performance is evaluated through subjective inspection, as well as objective performance measurements. Experimental results show that the fusion scheme is effective and the fused images are more suitable for further human visual or machine perception.

2. NSCT and ICS

2.1 Contourlet transform and NSCT

Do and Vetterli proposed a "true" 2-D transform called contourlet transform, which is based on nonsubsampled filter banks and provides an efficient directional multiresolution image representation. However, because of downsampling and upsampling, CT lacks shift-invariance and results in artifacts. In order to get rid of the frequency aliasing of contourlets and enhance directional selectivity and shift-invariance, nonsubsampled contourlet transform based on nonsubsampled pyramid decomposition and nonsubsampled filter banks (NSFB) is proposed (Jianping, Zhou, 2005). The NSCT provides not only mulitresolution analysis but also geometric and directional representation.

Multiscale decomposition step of the NSCT is realized by shift-invariant filter banks satisfying Bezout identical equation (perfect reconstruction (PR)), not LP of CT. Because of no downsampling in pyramid decomposition, there is no frequency aliasing in low-pass subband, even the band width is larger than π/2. Hence, the NSCT has better frequency characteristic than CT. The two-level NSCT decomposition is shown in Figure 1.

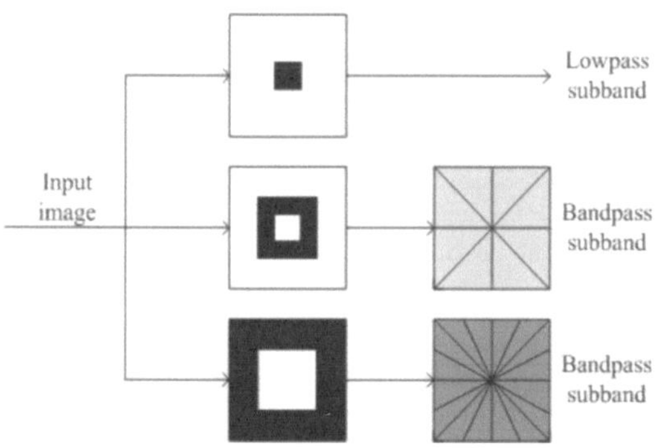

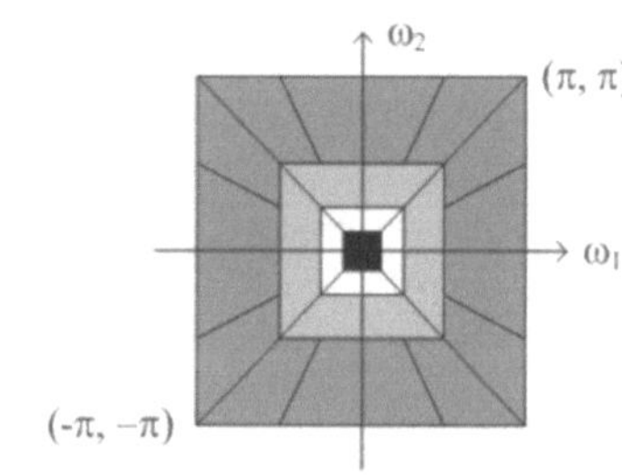

Fig. 1. Two-level NSCT decomposition. (a) NSCT structure that implements the NSCT (b) Frequency partitioning obtained with the proposed structure

The core of the NSCT is the nonseparable two-channel NSFB. It is easier and more flexible to design the needed filter banks that lead to an NSCT with better frequency selectivity and regularity when compared to the corresponding CT. Based on mapping approach and ladder structure fast implementation, the NSCT frame elements are regular and symmetric, and the frame is close to a tight frame. The multiresolution decomposition of NSCT can be realized by nonsubsampled pyramid (NSP), which can reach the subband decomposition structure similar to LP. On j -th decomposition, the desired bandpass support of the low-pass is $[-\pi/2^j,\pi/2^j]^2$. And then the corresponding band-pass support of the high-pass is the complement set of the low-pass, that is $[-\pi/2^{j-1},\pi/2^{j-1}]^2 \backslash [-\pi/2^j,\pi/2^j]^2$. The filters of subsequent scales can be acquired through upsampling that of the first stage, which gives the mulitscale property without the need of additional filters desigh. From the computation complexity, on bandpass image is produced at each stage resulting in $J+1$ redundancy. By contrast, the corresponding NSWT produces three directional images at each stage and resulting in $3J+1$ redundancy.

The NSFB is built form a lowpass analysis filter $H_0(z)$ and $H_1(z)=1-H_0(z)$. The corresponding synthesis filter $G_0(z)=G_1(z)=1$. The perfect reconstruction (PR) condition is given as

$$H_0(z)G_0(z)+H_1(z)G_1(z)=1 \tag{1}$$

2.2 ICS optimization

As a novel artificial intelligent optimization technique, the artificial immune system (AIS) aim at using ideas gleaned from immunology in order to develop systems capable of performing different tasks in various areas of research. The clonal selection functioning of the immune system can be interpreted as a remarkable microcosm of Charles Darwin's law of evolution, with the three major principles of diversity, variation and natural selection.

The clonal selection algorithm is used by the natural immune system to define the basic features of an immune response to an antigenic stimulus (De Castro, L. N. 2000). The main features of the clonal selection theory are: generation of new random genetic changes subsequently expressed as diverse antibody patterns by a form of accelerated somatic mutation; phenotypic restriction and retention of one pattern to one differentiated cell (clone); proliferation and differentiation on contact of cells with antigens. It establishes the idea that only those cells that recognize the antigens are selected to proliferate. The selected cells are subject to an affinity maturation process, which improves their affinity to the selective antigens. Random changes are introduced and will lead to an increase in the affinity of the antibody. It is these high-affinity variants which are then selected to enter the pool of memory cells. Those cells with low affinity receptors must be efficiently eliminated become anergic or be edited, so that they do not significantly contribute to the pool of memory cells.

Evolutionary strategy (ES) is an optimization technique based on group, which considers the feasible solutions as the group and as the operation object. The individual in the group is defined as a real value vector $Y=(y_0,y_1,\cdots,y_n)$, which measures the advantage and disadvantage by the fitness function. The optimization object is to search an optimal individual $Y^*=(y_0^*,y_1^*,\cdots,y_n^*)$ with the largest fitness $Fit(f^*)$. The basic process of the ES is as follows:

a. Produce initial parent-off springs $\{Y_i, i=, \ 1,2,\cdots,\mu\}$ where μ is the number of individuals and uniform distribution on $[0,1]$.
b. Aberrance: Producing subgroup individuals $\{Y_i^j=Y_i+N(0,\delta_j^2)\}$, where $i=1,2,\cdots,\mu$, $j=1,2,\cdots,\lambda$. And $N(0,\delta_j^2)$ denotes the Gaussian noise with mean 0 and variance δ^2, where the variance can be fixed or change adaptively.

c. Reselection: we can adopt the fixed or random selection methods. In this chapter, we adopt the fixed selection and avoid loosing in the local optimal, which means selecting the optimal μ individuals from the $\mu + \mu\lambda$ individuals and composing new parent group.
d. Repeating the (b) and (c) steps until the fitness function satisfy the end requirement or the iterated run time reach the maximum permissible run time. The terminal resolution is the optimal individual of the last generation group.

The definition of antigen, antibody, and antigen is as follows:

Antigen: it denotes the question and the corresponding constraint and like to the fitness function of evolution algorithm. For detail, it is the function of the object function $f(x)$ and denoted as $g(f(x))$, which is the important weighted index of starting factor and the algorithm performance in the artificial immune system However, the determination of the antigen g usually needs considering the intrinsic characteristics of the question, that is to say, needs to combine with the prior knowledge. Generally, for simple disposal and under the unspecified case, we adopt $g(x) = f(x)$.

Antibody: It denotes the candidate solutions of the question in the artificial immune system, which is the same to the evolution algorithm.

Antigen—antibody affinity, Avidity: reflects the whole adhesion between the molecular antibody and antigen. In the artificial immune system, the avidity denotes the object function values or the fitness of the candidate solutions to question.

a. **Clonal oprating** T_c^C

The essence of the clonal operating is that the producing of new sub-group around candidate solutions based on the values of the affinity during the immune process. The colnal process enlarges the search range. The definition of clonal is as follows:

$$\begin{aligned} A'(k) &= [A_1'(k)\ A_2'(k)\ \cdots\ A_n'(k)] = \mathrm{T}_c^C(A(k)) \\ &= [\mathrm{T}_c^C(A_1(k))\ \mathrm{T}_c^C(A_2(k))\ \cdots\ \mathrm{T}_c^C(A_n(k))]^{\mathrm{T}} \end{aligned} \tag{2}$$

In equation (2), $A_i'(k) = \mathrm{T}_c^C(A_i(k)) = I_i \times A_i(k)$ is called the clonal of antibody A_i, which show that the antibody realizes the increase of biologic induced by antigen, where $i = 1,2,\cdots,n$, and I_i is the row vector of element I.

b. **Immune gene operating** T_m^C

The immune gene operating has the crossover and aberrance. Based on the distribution of information exchange diversity characteristics of biological monoclonal antibody and polyclonal antibody, the ICS only adopted aberrance is called monoclonal Selection Algorithm (MCSA), and the ICS adopted crossover and aberrance is called Polyclonal Selection Algorithm (PCSA). Immunology believes that the generation of the affinity maturation and the antibody diversity depend mainly on the high frequency mutation of antibody, not crossover or regroup. In this chapter, we adopt the MCSA only including aberrance and denote the ICS. The individual after mutation is $A''(k) = T_m^C(A'(k))$.

c. **Clone selection operating** T_s^C

Immune selection operator T_s^C indicates the process selecting the optimal individual from the sub-group of antibody after clone and come into being new groups, which denotes as $A(k+1) = T_s^C(A''(k) \cup A(k))$. Therefore, the ICS is described as follows:

$$C_s : A(k) \xrightarrow{T_c^C} A'(k) \xrightarrow{T_m^C} A''(k) \xrightarrow{T_s^C} A(k+1)$$

The ICS enlarges the search range and is helpful to prevent evolution premature and search fall into the local minimum. In other words, the clone is a process changing a low-dimensional space into a higher-dimensional space to solve and mapping the solution into the low-dimensional space.

The basic ICS algorithm is described as the mathematics model of Markov Chain. As the encoding mode is determined, the ICS process likes the random walk with memory from a state to another.

3. Low visible light and infrared image fusion based on the NSCT and the ICS

3.1 Fusion strategy

In this section, we propose the fusion algorithm based on NSCT and the ICS optimization fusion algorithm. We consider the characteristics of coefficients on each multiresolution decomposition level and each subband, and adopt different fusion rules to lowpass subband and detail subbands. Figure 2 illustrates a single analysis/synthesis stage of NSCT processing.

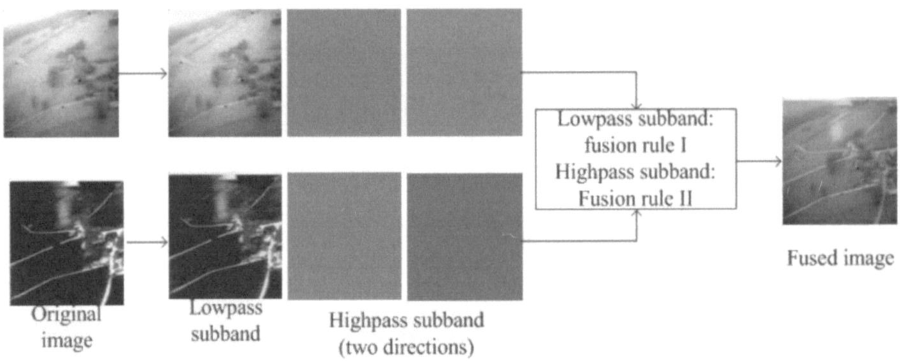

Fig. 2. Image fusion processing based on the one-level NSCT

Because the remote sensing image has no desired contrast image and we expect the image with more detail information and texture information. Therefore, the cost function is defined as the values of the Edge-dependent fusion qualidity index (EFQI) maximax and as the affinity function of ICS. During the process of searching optimization weights, we introduce the elitist preserved definition to keep the weights corresponding to the current best affinity function and save the memory space.

Definition (Elitist preserved) Suppose that $S^* = \{S^* : f(S_l^*) = \min(f(S_l^*)), l = \lg 2(N),\ ,\cdots,2,1\}$ where S_l^*, S_{l-1}^* are the sets (memory population) of optimal directions on l level and $l+1$ level, $f(S_l^*)$ and $f(S_{l-1}^*)$ are the corresponding values of object function. If $f(S_l^*),\ > f(S_{l-1}^*)$ then $S_l^* := S_{l-1}^*$ and $f(S_l^*) := f(S_{l-1}^*)$.

Without of generalization, we only focus on two source image. There is the same to many source images. Suppose all the source images are registrated, that is, each image being aligned to the same pixel position. If the sensors to be fused are not perfectly aligned, any corrections to the alignment can be made through a low-latency image warp function. The fusion algorithm is as follows:

Step 1. Loading source images;

Step 2. Performing multi-level NSCT. Suppose that the source images are I_1 and I_2, we have the approximation sub-band on the last decomposition level and the subimage series of detail sub-band on each decomposition level;

Step 3. Performing the fusion rule of absolute-values maximum to combine corresponding detail sub-band images;

Step 4. Performing the ICS to search the optimal fusion weights to the corresponding approximation sub-images on the last decomposition level adaptively,

$$F_{cA} = \alpha cI_1 + (1-\alpha)cI_2 \tag{3}$$

where cI_1, cI_2 and F_{cA} denote the approximation subimages of source images I_1, I_2 and the synthesis image, $\alpha(0 \le \alpha \le 1)$ is the resulting weights. The corresponding ICS sub-algorithm as following and shown in Figure 3:

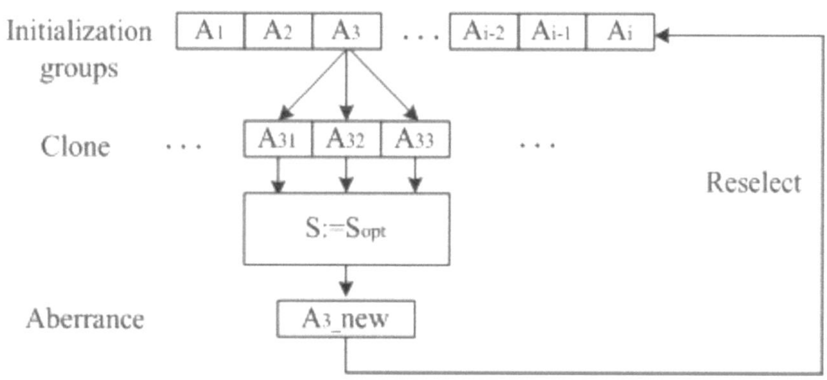

Fig. 3. Block diagram of the clonal selection algorithm

Step 4.1. Initialization. Pre-select the weights in [0, 1] and denoting them initial group individuals with the size of $i = 9$. Let the clone generations is ten.

Step 4.2. Calculating the affinity values of the initial group individuals and storing them in memory cell in sort;

Step 4.3. Clone. Cloning the initial group. Suppose the clone size is three, that is, each individual is cloned to three child individuals by random changes around the father individual. And then we calculating the affinity values of the child individuals;

Step 4.4. Aberrance. Compare the three child individuals with the corresponding father individual, based on an affinity measure. If the affinity value of the child is larger than its father counterpart, then the former replaces the latter and be kept to the memory cell $S := S_{opt}$. Otherwise, the father individual is kept;

Step 4.5. Reselection. Return to step4.3 and repeat the optimization procedure until satisfy the stop condition;

Step 5. Substitute the resulting optimal weights to equation (3) and fusion the appreciation subimages;

Step 6. Performing inverse NSCT to obtain the fused image.

3.2 Experiments and results

Subjective visual perception gives the direct comparison. However, it is easily influenced by Visual Psychological Factors. Therefore, the effect of image fusion must base on subjective vision and combined with objective quantitative valuation criterions. For the remote sensing images, the desired standard image cannot be acquired. Hence, the index such as root mean square error and peak value of signal to noise is unusable. In this section, we adopt the following statistic index to performance the fusion results entirely, such as mean value, standard deviation, entropy, mutual information, cross-entropy, weighted fusion quality index and edge-dependent fusion quality index, et al.

a. **Mean value (MV)**: The MV is the gray mean value of the pixels in a image and the average brightness reflecting to human eye. Suppose the size of the image is MN, $I(i,j)$ is the pixel in the image, then the MV is defined as:

$$MV = \frac{1}{NM}\sum_{i=0}^{N-1}\sum_{j=0}^{M-1} I(i,j) \tag{4}$$

b. **Standard deviation (STD)**: The variance of image reflects the dispersion degree between the gray values and the gray mean value. The STD is the square root of the variance. The large the STD is, the more disperse the gray level. The definition of the STD is:

$$STD = \sqrt{\frac{\sum_{i=0}^{N-1}\sum_{j=0}^{M-1}[I(i,j)-MV]^2}{NM}} \tag{5}$$

c. **Information entropy (IE)**: The IE of the image is an important index to measure the abound degree of the image information. Based on the principle of Shannon information theory, the IE of the image is definition as:

$$E = -\sum_{i=0}^{255} P_i \log_2 P_i \tag{6}$$

where P_i is the ratio of the number of the pixels, which the gray equals to i, and the total number of the pixels. IE reflects the capacity of the information carried by images. The large the IE is, the more information the image carries.

d. **Weighted fusion quality index (WFQI) and Edge-dependent fusion qualidity index (EFQI)**: WFQI and EFQI are evaluation indexes without standard referred image and consider some aspect of the human visual system. Suppose y_A', y_B', y_F' are edge images of the source images y_A, y_B and fused image y_F, respectively. WFQI is introduced to weight feature information of the fused images comes from source images. EFQI focuses on human visual system sensitivity to the edge information. The two measures have a dynamic range of [-1, 1]. The closer the value to 1, the higher the quality of the composite image is.

$$Q_{WFQI}(y_A, y_B, y_F) = \sum_{\omega \in Q} c(\omega)(\rho_A(\omega)Q_0(y_A, y_F, | \omega) + (1-\rho_A(\omega))Q_0(y_B, y_F, | \omega)) \tag{7}$$

$$Q_{EFQI}(y_A, y_B, y_F) = Q_{WFQI}(y_A, y_B, y_F)^{1-\alpha} \cdot Q_{WFQI}(y_A', y_B', y_F')^{\alpha} \tag{8}$$

where $c(\omega) = C(\omega) / [\sum_{\omega \in Q} C(\omega')]$,and $C(\omega) = \max(\eta((y_A | \omega), \eta(y_B | \omega))$ denotes the overall saliency of a window, $\rho_A(\omega) = \eta(y_A | \omega) / (\eta(y_A | \omega) + \eta(y_B | \omega)), \eta(y_A | \omega)$ is some salient features of image y_A in the window ω . In this chapter, we select the energy as the salient feature and the size of the window is 3×3 . Q is the summation of the total windows and Q_0 is the general image quality index. The parameter α in equation (8) expresses the contribution of the edges images compared to the original images, and its variation range is [0, 1]. Here we select $\alpha = 0.2$. LOG operator was adopted to obtain the edge image. However, the LOG operator cannot provide the edge directional information and sensitive to noise. Therefore, we select canny operator to detect the edge information, which detect the edges by searching the local maximum of image gradient. Canny operator detects the strong edges and weak edges with the two thresholds, respectively, where the thresholds are system automatic selection. Just when the weak edges and strong edges are jointed and the weak edges may be combined in the output. The canny operator is not sensitive to noise and can detect the true weak edges.

e. **Mutual Information (MI)**: MI of source images A 、 B and the fused image F is defined:

$$MI((A,B);F) = \sum_{i=0}^{L-1} \sum_{j=0}^{L-1} \sum_{k=0}^{L-1} p_{BAF}(i,j,k) \ln \frac{p_{BAF}(i,j,k)}{p_{BA}(i,j) p_F(k)} \tag{9}$$

where $p_{BAF}(i,j,k)$ is the normalized grey-level histogram of images A , B and F . MI denotes how much the information of fused image extracts from source images. The larger the MI is, the more information the fused image from source images.

f. **Cross-entropy (CE) and Root mean square cross entropy (RCE)**: Let $P = \{p_1, p_2, \cdots, p_i, \cdots, p_m\}$, $Q = \{q_1, q_2, \cdots, q_i, \cdots, q_m\}$, the CE of P and Q is

$$CE(P,Q) = \sum_{i=1}^{m} p_i \ln(p_i / q_i) \tag{10}$$

CE directly reflects the difference of the corresponding pixels between two images. The smaller the CE is, the smaller the difference is. The RCE denotes the comprehensive difference by considering the two CE and denoted as

$$RCE = \sqrt{\frac{CEN_1^{\ 2} + CEN_2^{\ 2}}{2}} \tag{11}$$

To allow helicopter pilots navigate under poor visibility conditions (such as fog or heavy rain) helicopters are equipped with several imaging sensors, which can be viewed by the pilot in a helmet mounted display. A typical sensor suite includes both a low-light-television (LLTV) sensor and a thermal imaging forward-looking-infrared (FLIR) sensor. In the current configuration, the pilot can choose on of the two sensors to watch in his display. A possible improvement is to combine both imaging sources into a single fused image which contains the relevant image information of both imaging devices.

The two source images are geometric adjustment and with the size of 256×256. This group images have uniform area, point informatiomn, linear information and texture information. The fusion methods are WT and ICS-based (WT-ICS), CT and ICS (CT-ICS), and NSCT and ICS-based (NSCT-ICS). Without of generality, the decomposition level of the adopted transform is all three. The WT adopts the 9-7 biorthogonal wavelet. The corresponding LP filter banks of CT and NSCT are all adopted 9-7 filter banks obtained from 9-7 1-D prototypes. And the DFB are adopted 'pkva' ladder filters proposed by Phong et al [15], which are with the decomposition 0, 0, 0, 3, 4 corresponding to the five levels LP decomposition, respectively. The decomposition values of DFB correspond to the directions decomposition number, such as "3" denote the direction decomposition number is $2^3 = 8$, and so on.

From the human visual system (as shown in Figure 4), we can see that our fusion technique based on NSCT-ICS is superior to any other fusion methods. The fusion image has the clear edges information, texture information and good definition and contrast than that of based on WT-ICS, NWST-ICS and CT-ICS.

The comparisons of fusion results are shown in Table 1. From the table I, we can see that the quantitative evaluation indexes are in accord with the visual effect. The fusion results based on our proposed adaptive fusion technique are superior to WT-ICS, NSWT-ICS and CT-ICS based fusion methods, which embody in the moderate brightness and the dispersion degree between the gray values, the larger entropy, the larger mutation information, the smaller difference to the source images and the more edge information. From the whole effects, and by virtue of our proposed adaptive fusion technique, the NSCT-based fused result is better than that of the WT-based, nonsubsample wavelet transform-based, and the CT-based, respectively.

Fusion methods	Fusion results						
	MV	STD	IE	WFQI	EFQI	MI	RCE
Visible image	157.75	50.25	5.27	–	–	–	–
Infrared image	41.45	64.55	4.11	–	–	–	–
WT-ICS	162.70	69.09	5.14	0.44	0.39	2.27	2.37
NSWT-ICS	175.14	70.63	4.94	0.55	0.49	2.79	0.34
CT-ICS	162.70	65.12	5.08	0.44	0.39	2.27	4.12
NSCT-ICS	175.14	70.65	4.94	0.56	0.50	2.80	0.32

Table 1. Comparison of the two algorithms by reconstruction precision and runtime

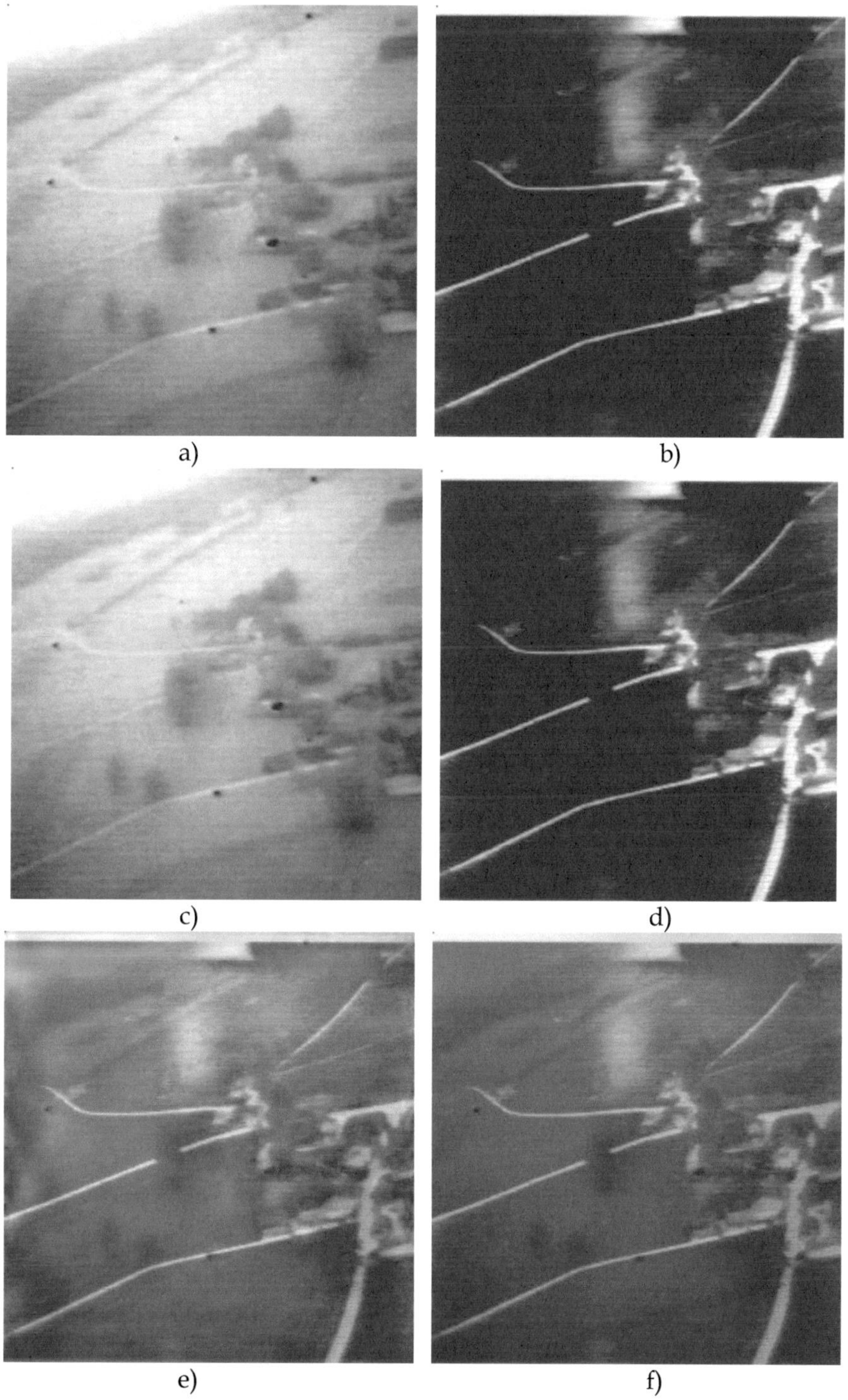

a) b) c) d) e) f)

Fig. 4. Compaison of fused images based on different transforms (a) Visible source image (b) Infrared source image (c) WT-ICS based fused image (d) NSWT-ICS based fused image (e) CT-ICS based fused image (f) NSCT-ICS based fused image

4. High resolution and multispectral remote image fusion based on the LHS and the NSCT

4.1 Fusion strategy

In this section, an adaptive panchromatic and multispectral remote sensing image fusion technique is presented based on the NSCT and the LHS transform after analyzing the basic principles of PAN image and MS image and fusion purpose. Here, we adopt an intensity (brightness) component addition method, that is, the detail information of the high-resolution PAN image is added to the corresponding intensity component of the low-resolution image's high frequency subbands to preserve some spectral information.

An image can be represented by RGB color system in computer. However, the RGB color system disagrees with the comprehensive and cognition habits of the human visual system. Human always recognize the color with three features, that is, intensity (I), hue (H), and saturation (S), called IHS system. I component is decided by the spectral main wave length and denotes the nature distintion. S component symbolizes the proportion of the main wave length of the intensity. I component means the brightness of the spectral. In the IHS space, spectral information is mostly reflected on the hue and the saturation. From the visual system, we can conclude that the intensity change has little effect on the spectral information and is easy to deal with.

For the fusion of the high-resolution and multispectral remote sensing images, . the goal is ensuring the spectral information and adding the detail information of high spatial resolution, therefore, the fusion is even more adequate for treatment in IHS space.

IHS color space transform means the change of image from RGB space components to IHS spatial information I component and spectral information H and S components. However, the general IHS color system has the disadvantage that neglects two components when computing the brightness values. The IHS system results in that the brightness of pure color is the same as the achromatic color. Therefore, we adopt the LHS color system to solve the paoblem. The LHS color system generates the brightness with the value of 255 to achromatic color pixel and the value of 85 to pure color pixel.

The detailed process of this fusion algorithm is as follows:

Step 1. Perform polynomial interpolation to keep the edges of the linear landmark and make the PAN and SPOT images with the same sizes.

Step 2. Transform the RGB representation of the multispectral image by LHS transformation into the intensity, hue, and saturation(L. H. S)components.

$$L = \frac{r+g+b}{3} \tag{12}$$

$$S = 1 - 3 \times \frac{\min(r,g,b)}{r+g+b} \tag{13}$$

$$H = \frac{arc\cos\{0.5 \times [(r-g)+(r-b)]\}}{\sqrt{(r-g)^2 + (r-b)(g-b)}} \tag{14}$$

The corresponding matrix expression is as follows

$$\begin{bmatrix} I \\ v_1 \\ v_2 \end{bmatrix} = \begin{bmatrix} 1/3 & 1/3 & 1/3 \\ 1/\sqrt{6} & 1/\sqrt{6} & -2/\sqrt{6} \\ 1/\sqrt{2} & -1/\sqrt{2} & 0 \end{bmatrix} \begin{bmatrix} R \\ G \\ B \end{bmatrix} \tag{15}$$

$$H = \tan^{-1}(\frac{v_1}{v_2}) \tag{16}$$

$$S = \sqrt{v_1^2 + v_2^2} \tag{17}$$

Step 3. Apply histogram matching between the original panchromatic image and multispectral intensity component to get new panchromatic high-resolution(PAN HR) image and multispectral intensity(MSI) component image.
Step 4. Decompose the matched MSI image and PAN HR image to get the NSTC decomposition coefficients.
Step 5. Fuse the detail and approximate coefficients of the MSI and PAN HR according to (25)and(26), respectively.

$$Fuse_{low} = MSI_{low} \tag{18}$$

$$Fuse_{high} = \sum MSI_{details} + \sum PANHR_{details} \tag{19}$$

Step 6. Apply the inverse NSCT transform to the fused detail and approximate coefficients to reconstruct the new intensity component I_{new}
Step 7. Perform the inverse LHS transform to the new intensity component, new I, together with the hue and saturation components to obtain the fused RGB images.

$$\begin{bmatrix} R \\ G \\ B \end{bmatrix} = \begin{bmatrix} 1 & 1/\sqrt{6} & 1/\sqrt{2} \\ 1 & 1/\sqrt{6} & -1/\sqrt{2} \\ 1 & -2/\sqrt{6} & 0 \end{bmatrix} \begin{bmatrix} I \\ v_1 \\ v_2 \end{bmatrix} \tag{20}$$

4.2 Experiments and results

The test source images are the SPOT PAN image and LANDSAT TM5, 4, 3 bands image of the same area. The TM image was acquired on February 17, 1993, and the SPOT PAN images were obtained on May 28, 1995. The two source images were after geometric adjustment and with the size of 256×256.

The fusion methods are traditional PCA and IHS, WT-based weighted fusion(WT-W), WT and LHS transform-based(WT-LHS), CT and LHS transform-based(CT-LHS), NSCT and LHS transform-based (NSCT-LHS). Without loss of generality, the decomposition levels of the adopted transforms are all three. The WT adopts the 9-7biorthogonal wavelet. The corresponding LP filter banks of CT and NSCT are all adopted 9-7 filter banks obtained from 9-7 1-D prototypes. And the DFB are adoped "pkva" ladder filters proposed by phong et al., which are with the decomposition 0, 3, 4 corresponding to the three levels of LP decomposition, respectively. The fusion results are shown in Fig. 5.

a)

b)

c)

d)

e)

f)

g) h)

Fig. 5. (a) SPOT image (b) TM image (c) PCA fusion image (d) IHS fusion image (e)WT-W fusion image (f) WT-LHS fusion image (g) CT-LHS fusion image (h)NSCT-LHS fusion image

From the human visual system, we can see that our fusion technique based on the NSCT-LHS can improve spatial resolution and at the same time hold spectral information well. Our intensity added fusion technique based on LHS transform is superior to classical PCA fusion method and IHS transform fusion method, and the WT-W fusion method. The fused image has more information of the source images, which is demonstrated in spatial resolution, definition, micro-detail difference, and contrast. The adaptive intensity component addition method preserves the whole spatial information, which has the advantage of the utilization of the detail information of the two source images. The fusion method only uses high-resolution information to adjust intensity component and better holds the multispectral information and texture information and introduces the high-resolution characteristic in multispectral image. Moreover, the fusion algorithm based on NSCT-LHS has more outstanding detail information than those based on WT-LHS and CT-LHS.

In this section, we adopt the following statistic index to performance the fusion results entirely, such as mean value, standard deviation, information entropy, weighted fusion quality index, average gradient, correlation coefficient, bias index, spectrum distoration and et al.

a. **Average gradient(AG)**:AG is the index to reflect the expression ability of the little detail contrast and texture variation, and the definition of the image. The calculation formula is

$$g = \frac{1}{(M-1)(N-1)} \sum_{i=1}^{(M-1)(N-1)} \sqrt{[(\frac{\partial f}{\partial x})^2 + (\frac{\partial f}{\partial y})^2]/2} \tag{21}$$

Generically, the larger g, the more the hierarchy, and the more definite the fused image.

b. **Correlation coefficient(CC)**:The CC denotes the degree of correlation of two images. The more the CC close to 1, the higher the correlation degree is. The definition is denoted as

$$corr(\frac{A}{B}) = \frac{\sum_{j=1}^{n}\sum_{i=1}^{m}(x_{i,j} - \mu(A))(x'_{i,j} - \mu(B))}{\sqrt{\sum_{j=1}^{n}\sum_{i=1}^{m}(x_{i,j} - \mu(A))^2(x'_{i,j} - \mu(B))^2}} \quad (22)$$

where A and B are two images, $x_{i,j}$ and $x'_{i,j}$ denote the pixels of A and B, respectively, $\mu(A)$ and $\mu(B)$ are the corresponding mean values of the two images.

c. **Spectrum distortion (SD)**: SD means the distortion degree of a multispectral image and is defined as follows:

$$W = \frac{1}{M \times N}\sum_{j=1}^{N}\sum_{i=1}^{M}| I_f(i,j) - I(i,j) | \quad (24)$$

where I(i, j) and If(i, j) are the pixels of the source and fused images, respectively. The larger value of W, the higher the distortion.

d. **Bias index**: This is an index of the deviation degree between fused image and low-resolution multispectral image:

$$Bias = \frac{1}{M \times N}\sum_{i=1}^{M}\sum_{j=1}^{N}\frac{| I_f(i,j) - I(i,j) |}{I(i,j)} \quad (25)$$

From Table 2, we can see that the quantitative evaluation indexes are in accord with the visual effect. The fusion results based on our adaptive fusion technique are superior to the traditional PCA and IHS fusion methods, which embody the moderate brightness and the dispersion degree between the gray values, the larger entropy , the stronger correlation degree. From the whole effects, and by virtue of our proposed adaptive fusion technique, the NSCT-based fused results are better than those of the WT-based, and the CT-based, respectively, especially for the spectral holding. The better values are underlined.
The comparison of the histogram images of R, G, B components of the TM multispectral images and the NSCT-based fusion image are shown in Figure 6, respectively.
From the comparison of the R, G, and B components histograms, we can conclude that the dynamic range of fused image is larger than that of the source image, that is , the fused image has more detail information and higher special resolution than that of the source image.

Fusion methods	MV	STD	IE	AG	CC	SD	Bias	Q_W	Q_E
SPOT PAN	92.45	9.55	7. 30	12.75	-	-	-	-	-
TM	102.82	47.68	4.96	9.50	-	-	-	-	-
PCA	94.08	46.62	5.08	18.74	0.52	58.40	0.58	0.53	0.51
IHS	92.45	80.80	5.24	13.85	0.66	38.24	0.36	0.52	0.50
WT-W	102.88	37.55	5.00	8.86	0.85	32.23	0.27	0.52	0.43
WT-LHS	112.66	54.37	5.33	16.21	0.92	14.79	0.14	0.51	0.44
CT-LHS	112.66	53.23	5.31	16.80	0.92	15.02	0.14	0.52	0.45
NSCT-LHS	112.72	52.66	5.30	16.76	0.93	14. 22	0.13	0.54	0.47

Table 2. Comparison of fusion results

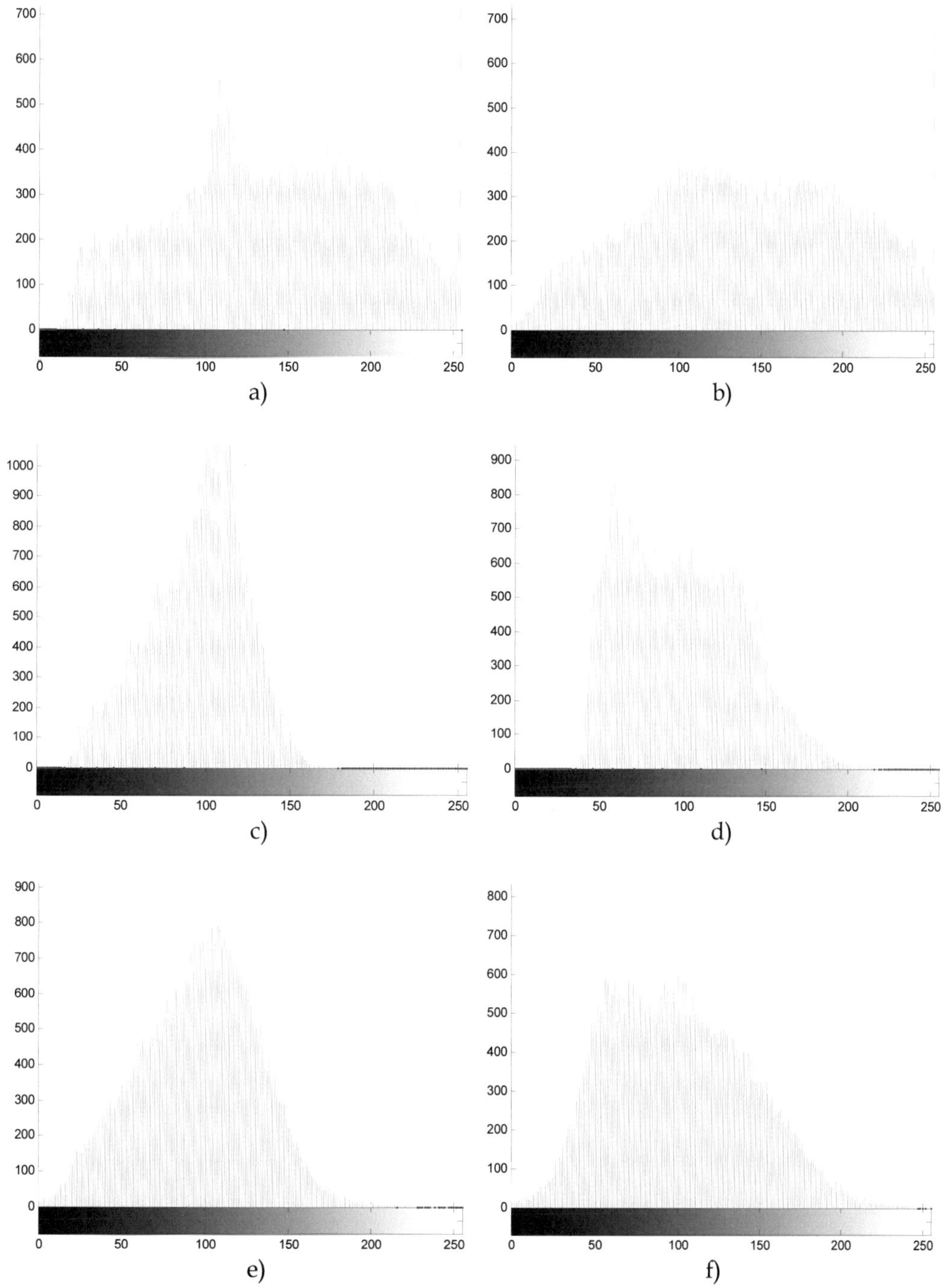

Fig. 6. The R, G, and B components histograms of TM source image and the NSCT-LHS fusion image (a)R component of TM source image (b)R component of NSCT-LHS fusion image (c)G component of TM source image (d) G component of NSCT-LHS fusion image (e)B component of TM source image (f) B component of NSCT-LHS fusion image

5. Multisensor image fusion based on the CP and MW-HMT

5.1 CP decomposition and HMT model

The construction of CP structure is as follows (A. Toet 1990): Firstly, a Gaussian pyramid is constructed. This is a sequence of images in which each image is lowpass filtered and subsampling copy of its predecessor. We denote original images as $I(i,j), i \le m, j \le n$, when m and n are the number of row and column of images, respectively. Let G_l present the level l of the Gaussian pyramid decomposition and array G_0 contains the original image. This array G_0 becomes the bottom or zero level of the pyramid structure. Each node of pyramid level l ($1 \le l \le N$, where N is the index of the top level of the pyramid) is obtained as a Gaussian weighted average of the nodes at level $l-1$ that are positioned within a 5x5 window centered on that node. Convolving an image with a Gaussian-like weighting function is equivalent to applying a lowpass filter to the image. Gaussian pyramid construction generates a set of lowpass-filtered copies of the input image, each with a bandlimit one octave lower than that of its predecessor. Because of the reduction in spatial frequency content, each image in the sequence can be represented by an array that is half as large as that of its predecessor in both directions. The process that generates each image in the sequence from its predecessor is called REDUCE operation since both the sampling density and the resolution are decreased. Thus, for $1 \le l \le N$ we have

$$G_l = REDUCE(G_{l-1})$$
$$G_l = \sum_{m=-2}^{2} \sum_{n=-2}^{2} w(m,n) G_{l-1}(2i+m, 2j+n), 0 < l \le N, 0 \le i < C_l, 0 \le j < R_l. \tag{26}$$

where N is the total levels of the pyramid, C_l and R_l are the number of column and row of the level l, respectively, and $w(m,n)$ is a weighted function, which satisfies some conditions. We can choose the weighting function:

$$w = \frac{1}{256} \begin{bmatrix} 1 & 4 & 6 & 4 & 1 \\ 4 & 16 & 24 & 16 & 4 \\ 16 & 24 & 36 & 24 & 6 \\ 4 & 16 & 24 & 16 & 4 \\ 1 & 4 & 6 & 4 & 1 \end{bmatrix} \tag{27}$$

CP analysis scheme is based on local luminance contrast. This scheme computes the ratio of the lowpass images at successive levels of the Gaussian pyramid. Since these levels differ in sample density, it is necessary to interpolate new values between the given values of the lower frequency image before it can divide the higher frequency image. Interpolation can be achieved simply by defining the EXPAND operation as the inverse of the REDUCE operation.

Let $G_{l,k}$ be the image obtained by applying EXPAND to G_l k times. Then

$$\left. \begin{aligned} G_{l,0} &= G_l \\ G_{l,k} &= EXPAND(G_{l,k-1}) \end{aligned} \right\} \tag{28}$$

meaning

$$G_{l,k}(i,j) = 4\sum_{m=-2}^{2}\sum_{n=-2}^{2} w(m,n)G_{l,k-1}(\frac{i+m}{2},\frac{j+n}{2}) \tag{29}$$

where only integer coordinates $(\frac{i+m}{2},\frac{j+n}{2})$ contribute to the sum. A sequence of ratio images R_i is defined by

$$\left.\begin{array}{c} R_i = \dfrac{G_i}{EXPAND(G_{i+1})}, for\ 0 \le i \le N-1 \\ R_N = G_N \end{array}\right\} \tag{30}$$

Thus, every level R_i is a ratio of two successive levels in the Gaussian pyramid.
Luminance is defined as

$$C = (L - L_b)/L_b = L/L_b - I \tag{31}$$

where L denotes the luminance at a certain location in the image plane, and L_b represents the luminance of the local background, and I is the unit gray image, that is $I(i,j)=1$, for all i,j. When C_i is defined as

$$C_i = \frac{G_i}{Expand(G_{i+1})} - I \quad 0 \le i \le N$$

$$C_N = G_N \tag{32}$$

Combining with formula (36), we have

$$R_i = C_i + I \tag{33}$$

Therefore, we refer to the sequence as CP. G_0 can be recovered exactly by reversing the above steps as formula (40)

$$\left.\begin{array}{c} G_N = R_N \\ G_i = (C_i + I)Expand(G_{i+1}) = R_i Expand(G_{i=1}) \qquad 0 \le i \le N-1 \end{array}\right\} \tag{34}$$

Hidden Markov models (M. S. Crouse, 1998) can capture the correlation of multiscale of images effectively, it is a very practical operation and the probability model can depict coefficient between the statistical characteristics of joint effectively. Figure 7 shows a multiwavelets hidden markov tree(HMT) model for one subhand. We model each coefficient(black node) as a Gaussian mixture controlled by a hidden state variable(white node). To capture the persistence across scale property of multiwavelets (Salesnick, I. 1998), we connect the states vertically across scale in Markov-1 chains. We agreed on the following: an indicator of the quadtree between different nodes, the root node, the coefficient of mw1 shall state for S1, p(i) represent the parent node of i. We do the following description for this model.

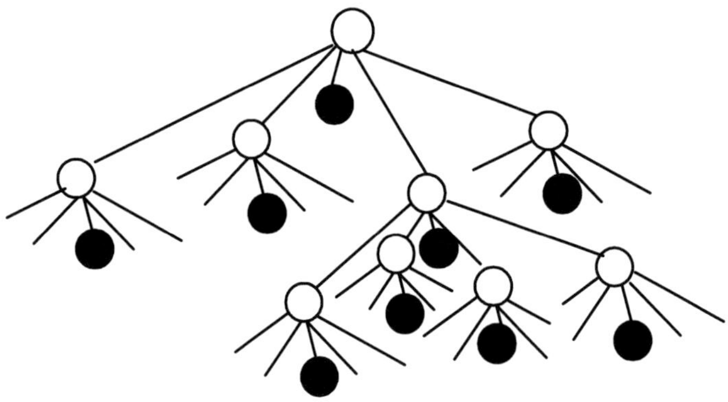

Fig. 7. Multiwavelets coefficient and HMT modle for one subband

5.2 Fusion strategy

a. **Iterated Algorithm Based CP and GHM**

Step 1. Initialization. Suppose the number of CP decomposition level is 4. The two original; images to be fused are denoted as "m_1" and "m_2", respectively;

Step 2. CP decomposition. According to the number of decomposition level pre-supposed;

Step 3. decompose each original image using window function and obtain two images with size of $(N/2^4)\times(N/2^4)$ denoted as "M_1" and "M_2", respectively.

b. **The iterative algorithm combining with HMT model**

Step 1. Initialize: Set the initial model to estimate for θ 0, and set l =0;

Step 2. E step. Train the two multiwavelets M1' and M2' separately, which got from step 3 of algorithm 3.3. Calculate each child coefficient P(S | mw, θ l), which is the weighting function of the state probability, and the maximum value of $E_S\left[\ln f(\text{mw},S|\theta)|\text{mw},\theta^l\right]$;

Step 3. M step. Updata $\theta^{l+1} = \arg\max_\theta E_S\left[\ln f\left(\text{mw},S|\theta\right)|\text{mw},\theta^l\right]$;

Step 4. Set the constringency threshold for 10^{-5}. Iterative can be termination, when two iterative convergence error is less than 10^{-5}. Establishment HMT model for the last $l = l + 1$, and can get two group train coefficient $c1$ and $c2$;

Step 5. According to the modulus maxima of fusion rules, get new coefficient c by taking coefficients corresponding maxima modulus position $c1$ and $c2$.

c. **Iterated Algorithm Combining with ICS Optimizing**

Step 1. Initialization. Taking the coefficient matrix obtained from step 5 in above algorithm as the original population $A(0)$, in which each element can be regarded as chromosome. The original number of generation is k=1, and the maximal number of iterated generation G_S=20;

Step 2. Terminating condition judgment. Judge whether the terminating condition is satisfied or not. That is, if the pre-supposed times of iteration is finished, stop and determine the current population composed by current individual as the optimized solution population and turn to step 8; else turn to step 3;

Step 3. Clone operation. Clone operation is performed to the *k*-th generation parent population A (k) to obtain A'(k);

Step 4. Mutation operation. Gaussian mutation with square error 0.1 is performed to A′(k) to obtain A″(k) ;

Step 5. Affinity function computation;

Step 6. Clonal selection operation. In child population, if exist muted antibody $b = \max\{a_{ij} | j = 2,3,...,q_i - 1\}$ making $Q(a_i) < Q(b)$, $a_i \in A(k)$, then choose b to enter the new parent population;

Step 7. k=k+1, turn to step 2;

Step 8. Obtaining a group of optimized fusion coefficients denoted as "result-coefficient" and reconstruction in light of this group of coefficients;

Step 9. CP reconstruction according to the parameter "result-coefficient" from step 8;

Step 10. Output the final fusion result;

5.5 Experiments and results

The test source images are two bands of mutisensor images. The fusion methods are traditional and multiwavelet transform. Without loss of generality, the decomposition levels of the adopted transforms are all three. The WT adopts the "db8" wavelet. The fusion results are shown in Fig. 8 and Fig. 9. In the experiments, Fig.8 (a), (b) and Fig.9 (a), (b) are satellite images of two different sensor respectively.

From the visual effect, the resulting images fused by WT-based method (Fig.8(c) and Fig. 9(c)), MWT-based method (Fig.8(d) and Fig. 9(d)) are fairly well, but our proposed method (Fig.8 (e) and Fig.9 (e)) is more clear and contains structural details, which contain richer structure content and spatial information and reconstruct the interesting targets. In a word, compared with the results of the fusion obtained by the other techniques, the results of the ICS-CPMWHMT fusion have better visual effect.

In addition to visual analysis, we conducted a quantitative analysis. We based our analysis of the experimental results on the many factors; namely, the information entropy (IE), the average grads (AG) and the standard deviation (STD). Using these factors such as IE, AG and STD, Table 3 to Table 4 compares the experimental results of image fusion for the ICS-CPMWHMT method and the other methods.

IE refers to the change of information capability. The more the information included in the image, the better the fused image. AG can reflect the capability to represent the detail contrast of images sensitively and can be used to assess the definition of images. STD is an index to measure the contrast value of images. But for the fusion of infrared and visual image, if IE value is too high, maybe over smooth the image; if STD value is too high, maybe lose too much spectral information. So when we assess fused image using these factors, combine with visual effect in general.

IE value of the fused image by ICS-CPMWHMT method keeps at a high level. AG value and STD value of fused images are also moderate, which show that fused images not only reflect the detail features also retain plenty detail information better. It is benefit and significant for following target automatic recognition and classification.

a)

b)

c)

d)

e)

Fig. 8. (a) The image of sensor 1 (b) the image of sensor 2 (c) WT fusion image (d) MWT fusion image (e) ICS-CPMWHMT fusion image

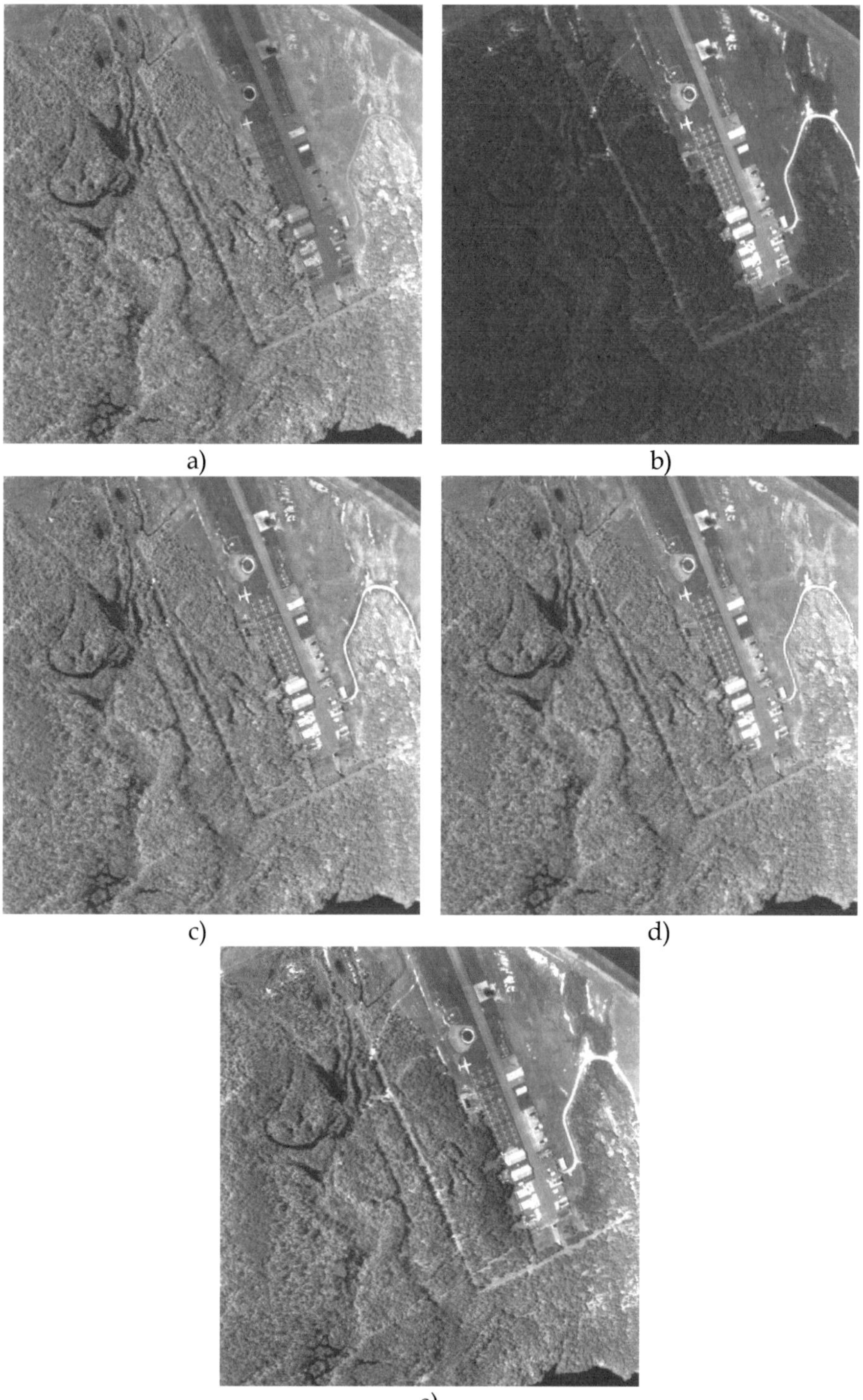

Fig. 9. (a) The image of sensor 1 (b) The image of sensor 2 (c) WT fusion image (d) MWT fusion image (e) ICS-CPMWHMT fusion image

Image 1	IE	AG	STD
Sensor 1	4.59	9.92	48.80
Sensor 2	4.10	8.43	50.00
WT	4.82	12.35	52.22
MWT	4.76	11.56	51.71
ICS-CPMWHMT	5.08	13.30	61.71

Table 3. Comparison of fusion performance on image 1

Image 2	IE	AG	STD
Sensor 1	5.13	12.23	41.96
Sensor 2	4.63	6.08	39.09
WT	4.93	13.30	43.64
MWT	5.13	11.95	42.47
ICS-CPMWHMT	5.13	14.86	50.14

Table 4. Comparison of fusion performance on image 2

6. Conclusion

The multiscale geometry analysis tool and ICS algorithm are adopted to three remote sensing images fusion in this chapter, including the multi-sensor images, the lower spatial resolution multispectral image and the higher spatial resolution panchromatic image, the infrared image and visible light image.

Fristly, we propose a panchromatic high-resolution image and multispectral image fusion technique, which is based on NSCT and LHS transform. We take full advantage of the NSCT, including good multiresolution,shift-invariance, and multidirectional decomposition. And an intensity compenent addition technique is introduced into the NSCT domain to better improve the spatial resolution and hold the spectral information and texture information,simultaneously. Experiments that the proposed fusion technique is more effective than other traditional fusion methods and has some improvements,especially for holding of spectral information,texture information,and contour information.

Secondly, based on NSCT and ICS strategy, we take full advantage of the NSCT with the good shift-invariance and multi-directional decomposition. And the ICS in introduced into the NSCT domain to optimize the fusion weights adaptively. From quantitative analysis, we can hold the conclusion that our fusion technique can take full advantage of the low light image and infrared image and have improvements both in vision and in quantitative index.

From the subjectivity and objectivity, we can conclusion that our proposed fusion technique is more effective than other traditional fusion methods and has improvements, especially for the holding of more clear texture and contour information. Experiments show that the proposed fusion technique is a preferred and effective remote sensing image fusion method. Thirdly, based on multiwavelet-domain HMT models and ICS optimization, we explain a novel intelligence optimization technique. The immune clonal selection technique is introduced into image fusion to obtain the optimal fusion weights adaptively. Experimental results show that the proposed approach has improvements in visual fidelity and quantitative analysis.
Finally, in the ICS algorithm optimizing fusion coefficients, iterative times need to be preinitialized or experientially selected; also it decides the runtime of whole the technique. So it is our further work to study self-adaptive ICS algorithm to apply in the fusion processing. How to solve the fusion problem of remote images without desired compared images is our future work.

7. References

A. Toet (1990). Hierarchical image fusion, *Machine Vision and Applications*, Vol. 3, No. 1, (1999) pp. 1-11, 19900932-8092

da Cunha, A. L.; Jianping Zhou & Do, M. N. (2006). The nonsubsampled contourlet transform: theory,design and applications, *IEEE Transactions on Image Processing*, Vol. 15, No.10, (Oct. 2006) pp.3089-3101, 3089-3101

De Castro, L. N., Von Zuben, F. J.(2000). The Clonal Selection Algorithm with Engineering Applications. Procedings of GECCO'00, Workshop on Artificial Immune Systems and Their Applications. (July 2000) pp. 36-37, Las Vegas, USA

Do, M. N. & Vetterli, M. (2005). The contourlet transform:an efficient directional multiresolution image representation, *IEEE Transactions on Image Processing*, Vol. 14, No. 12, (Dec. 2005) pp. 2091-2106, 2091-2106

Gonzalez-Audicana. M.; Saleta, J. L.; Catalan, R. G. & Garcia, R. (2004). Fusion of multispectral and panchromatic images using improved HIS and PCA mergers based on wavelet decomposition, *IEEE Transactions on Geoscience and Remote Sensing*, Vol. 42, No. 6, (June 2004) pp. 1291-1299, 0196-2892

Jianping, Zhou; Cunha, A. L. & Do, M. N. (2005). Nonsubsampled contourlet transform: construction and application in enhancement, *Proceedings of IEEE International Conference on Image Processing*, pp.469-472, 0-7803-9134-9, 11-14 Sept. 2005, Dept. of Electr. & Comput. Eng., Illinois Univ., Champaign, IL, USA

M. S. Crouse, R. D. Nowak, R. G. Baraniuk (1998). Wavelet-based statistical signal processing using hidden Markov models. *IEEE Transactions on Signal Processing*, (Apr 1998), Vol. 46, No. 4, pp. 886-902, 1053-587X

Nunez, J.; Otazu, X.; Fors, O.; Prades, A.; Pala,V.&Arbiol,R. (1999). Multiresolution-based image fusion with additive wavelet decomposition, *IEEE Transaction on Geoscience and Remote Sensing*, Vol. 37, No.3, (May 1999) pp.1204-1211, 0196-2892

Rockinger, O. (1996). Pixel-level fusion of image aequences using wavelet frames, *Proceedings of Image Fusion and Shape Variability Techniques*. pp. 149-154, July 3-5, UK:Leeds University Press, Leeds

Salesnick, I. (1998). Multiwavelet bases with extra approximation properties. *IEEE Transactions on Signal Processing*, Vol. 46, No. 11, (Nov 1998) pp. 2898-2908, 1053-587X.

Wang, Z. J.; Ziou, D.; Armenakis, C.; Li, D. & Li, Q. G. (2005). A comparative analysis of image fusion methods, *IEEE Transactions on Geoscience and Remote Sensing*, Vol. 43, No. 6, (June 2005) pp.1391-1402, 0196-2892

11

Image Fusion Based Enhancement of Nondestructive Evaluation Systems

Ibrahim Elshafiey, Ayed Algarni and Majeed A. Alkanhal
King Saud University
Saudi Arabia

1. Introduction

Advantages and limitations associated with each nondestructive evaluation (NDE) modality raises a tradeoff in which no single modality can be identified for a particular application. Techniques are presented here that can be used to enhance inspection process based on multi-spectral, multi-temporal, and multi-resolution image fusion. The necessary elements for building an intelligent NDE system based on image fusion are introduced. An application is presented considering the fusion of optical and eddy current images. Developed image evaluation measures (quality metrics) are adopted to cross the gap between subjective and objective evaluation, which is essential to automate NDE systems in industrial environments.

2. Multimodal NDE

NDE methods involve the application of a suitable form of energy to the specimen under test. Wide variety of testing methods exists, where each method has certain properties and offers advantages, while having its drawbacks. The basic categories of NDE methods are: visual and optical testing (VT), radiography (RT) magnetic particle testing (MT), ultrasonic testing (UT), penetrant testing (PT), leak testing (LT) acoustic emission testing (AE), and electromagnetic testing (ET). Electromagnetic testing modalities are attractive for NDE applications due to the maturity and robustness of use of these techniques. The adopted ranges of the operating frequency cover almost the entire electromagnetic spectrum. Techniques employing the static operation, such as the magnetic flux leakage, and the quasi-static frequency range such as eddy current methods are commonly used more in industry than higher frequency (Lord, 1983). However, attention is being made to the higher end of the spectrum. Examples include application of microwave imaging techniques in inspecting civil structures (Cantor, 1984). Thermal waves are being used in characterization coating adhesion (Jaarinen et al., 1989), and optical methods are implemented in evaluating concrete and composite materials (Ansari, 1992). Ionizing radiation frequency ranges such as x-ray techniques are famous in tomographical reconstruction of defects and in assessing residual stresses. Among the ET modalities, the EC techniques get considerable attention, since they do not require hazard precautions as in the case of ionization radiation, in addition to the fact that they do not lack time information as for the static range.

NDE systems that are capable of extracting and fusing complementary segments of information from collected NDE data offer additional insight relative to the conventional systems. Fusion techniques are expected to play a major role in the next-generation NDE systems (Algarni et al., 2009). Fusion can make use of data collected from various NDE modalities, or even from the same technique operated at different points of time or using various parameter values (Elshafiey et al., 2008).

3. NDE signal fusion

NDE data fusion can be traced back to early 90s (Gros & Takahashi, 1998). Data fusion algorithms in NDE can be broadly classified as phenomenological or non-phenomenological. Phenomenological algorithms utilize knowledge of the underlying physical processes as a basis for deriving the procedure for fusing data. However, such methods are likely to be difficult to derive and cumbersome to implement (Simone & Morabito, 2001). Non-phenomenological approaches, in contrast, tend to ignore the physical process and attempt to fuse information based on the statistics associated with individual segments of data. The later methods can be classified into three different categories: pixel level, feature level and symbol level fusion, according to the stage at which fusion takes place as illustrated in Fig. 1.

Pixel based fusion requires accurate registration of the images to each other. Feature level fusion operate on mapped versions of original images. Decision (symbol) level fusion represents a method that implements value-added data obtained from processing the input images individually for information extraction, before applying decision rules.

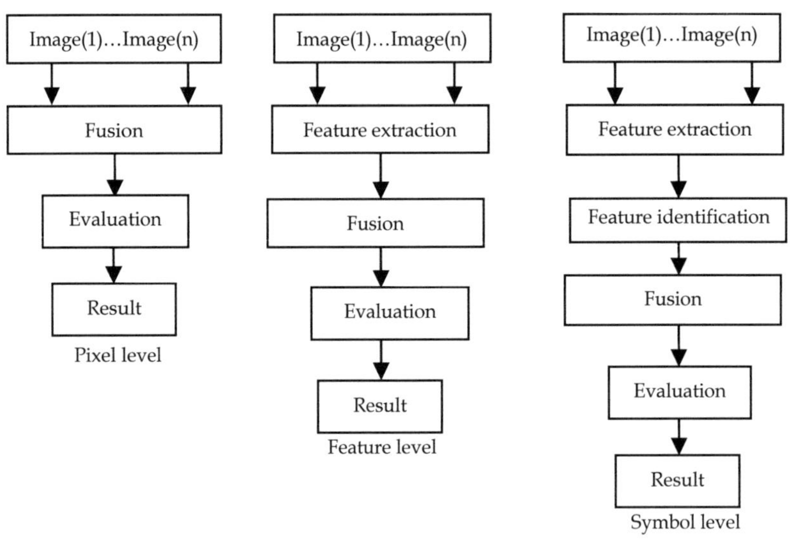

Fig. 1. NDE image fusion categories

4. NDE fusion algorithms

Various algorithms have been developed for NDE data fusion to improve the reliability and the performance of testing. The most widely applied are summarized next.

4.1 Linear minimum mean square error (LMMSE)

This optimal approach uses a LMMSE filter to fuse multiple images, which was proposed in (Yim, 1995). The architecture of the fusion algorithm is given in Fig. 2. From system point of view, $s(u,v)$ is the input signal to the system with the degradation transfer function $H_i(u,v)$ associated with i^{th} stage, $1 \leq i \leq N$. From NDE point of view, $s(u,v)$ is the perfect response of the original signal in the inspection process. The measurement system acquires signal $x_i(u,v)$ with additive noise $n_i(u,v)$. Applying a controller filter $G_i(u,v)$, the output signal $\tilde{s}(u,v)$ is controlled to have a minimum mean square error with the input signal. $G_i(u,v)$ can be constructed from the spectra of the acquired images as follows:

$$G_j(u,v) = \frac{\sqrt{S_s(u,v)S_{xj}(u,v)}}{\sum_{i=1}^{N} S_{xi}(u,v)} \qquad 1 < j < N \tag{1}$$

$G_j(u,v)$ is the jth filter, $S_s(u,v)$ is the Laplace transform of the original signal $s(u,v)$, and $S_{xj}(u,v)$ is the Laplace transform of the jth acquired image.
The spectrum of the original signal is approximated as (Yim, 1995)

$$G_j(u,v) = K\frac{\sqrt{S_{xj}(u,v)}}{\sum_{i=1}^{N} S_{xi}(u,v)} \qquad 1 \leq j \leq N \tag{2}$$

Where, K is estimated spectrum which can be estimated by using the coefficients of Fourier decomposition of the signal.

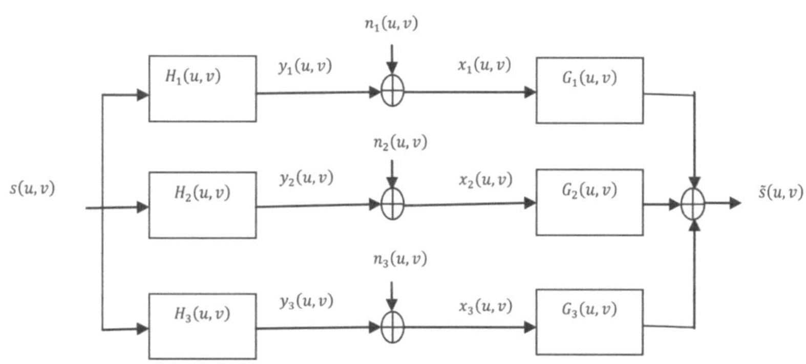

Fig. 2. Model for linear signal fusion

4.2 Neural networks (NN) fusion

An attempt to fuse eddy current and ultrasonic images, and the other to fuse multi-frequency eddy current images are proposed as in (Yim et al., 1996), and (Udpa, 2001). Networks types implemented in fusion algorithms include multilayer perceptron (MLP) as well as radial basis function (RBF). The MLP network consists of a set of simple nonlinear processing elements that are arranged in layers and connected via adjustable weights. The network is usually trained using an appropriate algorithm such as back-propagation algorithm to estimate the interconnection weights. In RBF networks, the output nodal values are a linear combination of the basis functions that are calculated by the hidden layer nodes. A variety of basis functions can be employed, and Gaussian function is the most common type. The MLP-based algorithm is sensitive to the choice of data used during the training phase. The RBF-based system fuses the image inputs smoothly reflecting information from input images.

4.3 Multi-resolution analysis (MRA) fusion

In this approach, the input NDE image is decomposed into a set of spatial frequency band pass sub-images. The sub-band images are computed by convolving and sub-sampling operations, as presented in (Gros et al., 2000); (Liu et al., 1999) and (Matuszewski et al., 2000). The multi-resolution analysis fusion techniques include the image pyramid approaches and wavelet based approaches. Different implementations of multi-resolution fusion are presented in Table 1, and are discussed next.

4.3.1 Gaussian and Laplacian pyramid

Image pyramid consists of a set of low pass (Gaussian pyramid) or band pass (Laplacian pyramid) copies of an image, representing pattern information of a different scale. Burt and Adelson proposed Laplacian pyramid in 1983 (Gonzalez & Woods, 2007). The pyramid can be used for image compression and processing. Two operation involved are the EXPAND and REDUCE. The relation between two sub-images at level *l* and *l-1* is:

$$G_l = REDUCE\left(G_{l-1}\right) \tag{3}$$

EXPAND is defined as the reverse of REDUCE function and its effect is to expand an $(M + 1)$ by $(N + 1)$ array into a $(2M + 1)$ by $(2N + 1)$ array.

4.3.2 Ratio of low pass pyramid

This is also based on the Gaussian pyramid, and the ratio of low pass pyramid is defined is introduced in (Toet, 1992) as:

$$R_l = \frac{G_l}{EXPAND\left(G_{l+1}\right)} \; for\, 0 \le l \le K \;\; \& \; R_K = G_K \tag{4}$$

The perceptually important details are revealed by this kind of representation.

4.3.3 Wavelet fusion

Multi-resolution analysis using wavelet transforms allows decomposing images into a set of new images with coarser and coarser spatial resolution (approximation images). The discrete approach of the wavelet transform mainly can be performed using two algorithms: discrete wavelet transform (DWT) also called decimated algorithm, and shift invariant discrete wavelet transform (SIWT), un-decimated discrete wavelet transform:

Decimated Algorithm: It is a fast DWT algorithm based on a multi resolution dyadic scheme that allows to decompose an image A^i, into an approximation image CA^{i+1} and three detail coefficient images, CV^{i+1}, CH^{i+1}, and CD^{i+1}, where i is the level of the decomposition. If the original image A^i has *C* columns and *R* rows, the approximation and the wavelet coefficient images obtained applying this multi-resolution decomposition have C/2 columns and R/2 rows. The computation of the approximation and the detail coefficients is accomplished with a pyramidal scheme based on convolutions along rows and columns with one-dimensional filters followed by a sub-sampling or decimation operation. When the multi-resolution wavelet decomposition process is inverted, the original image A^i can be reconstructed exactly from an approximation and detailed images, applying an up-sampling or oversampling process followed by filtering. To get an image fusion, wavelet decomposition is applied for input images, followed by integration of these decomposition coefficients to produce a composite representation. An inverse discrete wavelet transform is applied to get the fused image. The wavelet base fusion technique can reduce color distortion. Furthermore, the down sampling process may cause shift variation, which increases the distortion in the fused images.

Un-decimated Algorithm: This algorithm is based on the idea of no decimation. It is a redundant wavelet transform algorithm based on a multi-resolution dyadic scheme accomplished not with a pyramidal scheme but with a parallelpipedic scheme. The original image is decomposed as into four coefficients as in DWT but without decimation. All the approximation and wavelet coefficient images obtained by applying this algorithm have the same number of columns and rows as the original image thus such decomposition is highly redundant. Based on (Li et al., 2002) the performance of the SIWT based algorithm outperforms the DWT based fusion algorithms.

MRA Method	Algorithm	Rule of fusion
Gaussian and Laplacian Pyramid	Sequence of images in which each member of the sequence is a low pass filtered or band pass version of its predecessor	-Coefficient selection based on maximum absolute value. -Coefficient selection or average based on salience and match measure.
Ratio of Low Pass Pyramid	Every level the image is the ratio of two successive levels of the Gaussian pyramid	Coefficient selection based on maximum absolute contrast.
Discrete Wavelet Transform (DWT)	Images are decomposed via wavelet transform, after applying the rule of fusion, then inverse discrete wavelet transform is found	Selection based on choosing the maximum absolute values, or an area based maximum energy
Shift Invariant Discrete Wavelet Transform (SIDWT)	SIDWT is obtained using à trous algorithm so the process of fusion is independent of the location of an object in the image	

Table 1. MRA based image fusion algorithms

Wavelet Image Fusion Rules

Several rules can be used for selecting the wavelet packet coefficients for image fusion. The most frequently used fusion rules are:

- **Maximum frequency rule.** The coefficients with the highest absolute value indicating salient features are selected.

- **Weighted average rule.** It generates a coefficient via a weighted average of the two images' coefficients, where the weighting coefficients are based on the correlation between the two images.
- **Standard deviation rule.** It calculates an activity or energy measure associated with a pixel. A decision map is created, which indicates the source image from which the coefficient has to be selected.
- **Window based verification rule.** It creates a binary decision map to choose between each pair of coefficients using a majority filter.

5. Implementation examples of NDE signal fusion

Implementation examples of fusion methods in some of the NDE applications are presented next, along with by a brief summary of related literature listed in Table 2.

5.1 Fusion of eddy current signals

A fusion algorithm is proposed using the data from both real and imaginary image components using artificial cracks around rivet holes in an aluminum specimen in (Mina et al., 1997). The operation is implemented in the transform domain with the discrete Fourier transform. The fusion process is based on the spectrum of the acquired signal, where the linear minimum mean square error (LMMSE) approach was adopted to fuse the images using a weighting scheme. Multi-frequency eddy current testing (MF-ET) is implemented in (Mina et al., 1996) to enhance SNR. Two ET scan images obtained at 6 and 20 KHz, with radial basis function (RBF) neural networks. A relatively clear display of subsurface flows is achieved after the fusion process. Pixel level fusion technique using a multi-resolution image pyramid was proposed in (Liu et al., 1999). Signals from two different ET systems in weld inspection, are fused using the Dempster-Shafer (DS) combination rule in (Gros et al., 1995), achieving accurate estimation of crack size.

5.2 Fusion of ultrasonic signals

Amplitude, frequency, or time of flight of the echo signals provides information about the nature and position of flaws. Ultrasonic testing produces high resolution measurements but the signal is affected by the surface roughness of the specimen and grain structure of metals. Ultrasonic image is fused with eddy current images using the AND operation in (Song & Udpa, 1996) in order to take advantage of both methods. Experiments were carried out on an aluminum plate where a simulated defect was present. The boundary of the defect was extracted from the UT image, whereas the depth information could be characterized from an ET image. Another way to fuse UT and ET data is the use of RBF NNs or multilayer perceptron (MLP). The experiments were carried out in (Simone & Morabito, 2001) to fuse eddy current and ultrasonic images showed that the fusion operation improves the process of defect classification.

5.3 Fusion of other NDE modalities

Infrared (IR) thermographic testing and ET C-scan is fused using wavelet-based methods, where an impacted carbon fiber reinforced plastic composite panel is used in (Gros, Liu, Tsukada, & Hanaski, 2000) (Gros et al., 2000) and (Liu et al., 1999). Application of multiple inspection techniques for NDE fusion is presented in increasing (Tian et al., 2005); (Volponi et al., 2004) and (Kaftandjian et al., 2005).

6. Image visualization of NDE signals

Data visualization is an effective and intuitive method for understanding the results of inspection. An effective data visualization stage helps improve the evaluation, especially in quantitative evaluation of types, locations, sizes and shapes of the defects. On the other hand, imaging reduces the necessity for highly qualified inspector for interpretation of the results. Imaging also gives the ability to use the advanced image processing techniques for further improvements as image. Casting NDE data on image format allows also application of image fusion techniques. Image registration however is essential in this process to allow robust fusion results. Image registration is discussed next followed by the techniques which are used to present eddy current data, normally presented as one-dimensional signal form in two-dimensional c-scan image format.

6.1 Image registration

Registration is the process, which determines the best match of two or more images acquired at the same or various times by different or identical sensors. One image is used as the reference image, and all the other images are matched relative to this reference data. Match can be performed at the one-dimensional level, the two-dimensional level and the three-dimensional level. The majority of the registration methods consist of the following four steps (Zitova & Flusser, 2003):

Selection of feature points. Salient and distinctive objects (closed-boundary regions, edges, contours, line intersections, corners, etc.) are manually or, preferably, automatically detected. These points are called control points.

Feature matching. In this step, the correspondence between the features detected in the input image and those detected in the reference image is established.

Transform model estimation. The type and parameters of the so-called mapping functions, aligning the input image with the reference image, are estimated. The parameters of the mapping functions are computed by means of the established feature correspondence.

Image re-sampling and transformation. The input image is transformed by means of the mapping functions. Image values in non-integer coordinates are computed by the appropriate interpolation technique.

6.2 Eddy current imaging

Various techniques have been developed to present eddy current inspection data in the form of C-scan images. Probe impedance values acquired in two dimensional surface scans provide a set of ranges (Udpa & Elshafiey, 2001). Magnetic flux maps could also be presented in image format using techniques such as magneto-optic eddy current technology (Lee & Song, 2005) or giant magneto-resistive sensors GMR field scanning (Chalastaras et al., 2004).

6.3 Pulsed eddy current imaging

Pulsed eddy current sensing is an emerging technique that has been particularly developed for subsurface flow. These techniques can work at some distance below the surface (up to 100 mm in aluminum) (Tian et al., 2005). In PEC techniques the probe's excitation coil is excited with a repetitive broadband pulse, usually a rectangular wave. The resulting transient current through the coil induces transient eddy currents in the test object, which are associated with highly attenuated magnetic pulses propagating through the material.

Reference	Fusion Technique	Modality
(Tai & Pan, 2008)	Physical interaction / Human fusion	EC / photo inductive imaging
(Liu, Abbas, & Nezih, 2006)	Dempester-Shafer	EC / PEC
(Kaftandjian et al., 2005)	Evidence Theory / Fuzzy logic	X-Ray / Ultrasonic
(Chady et al., 2005)	Barkhausen noise method	EC / Flux leakage
(Djafari, July, 2002)	Bayesian	X-ray / Geometrical data
(Francois & Kaftandjian, 2003)	Dempester-Shafer	X-ray/ Ultrasonic
(Simone & Morabito, 2001)	Feed-forward Neural Networks (NN)	EC/Ultrasonic
(Udpa, 2001)	NN	EC/Ultrasonic
(Matuszewski et al. 2000)	Wavelet	Ultrasonic / radiographic
(Brassard et al., 2000)	Image subtraction	Edge of light / PEC
(Liu et al., 1999)	Multiresolution Analysis (MRA)	Multi-frequency EC
(Mina et al., 1996)	Image Pyramid	Multi-frequency EC
(Mina et al., 1997)	DFT/LMMSE	Real/imaginary of Z
(Song & Udpa, 1996)	Image Pyramid	Ultrasonic/EC
(Yim et al., 1996)	NN	Multi-frequency EC
(Yim et al., 1995)	NN	Ultrasonic/EC
(Yim, 1995)	LMMSE	Ultrasonic/EC
(Liu et al., 1999)	MRA	Multi-frequency EC

Table 2. Fusion algorithms applied to NDE applications

The probe provides a series of voltage-time data pairs as the induced field decays, and since the produced pulses consist of a broad frequency spectrum, the reflected signal contains important depth information, physically, the field is broadened and delayed as it travels deeper into the highly dispersive material. Flaws or other anomalies close to the surface affect the eddy current response earlier than deeper flaws. Peak values, time to maximum values, and time to minimum values have been used for flow detection and identification. Features are selected based on knowledge about the possible crack that might be most probably happened. In surface cracks the amplitude feature gives better resolution, while the time feature gives more information about the subsurface cracks.

7. Fusion performance evaluation

In many applications, a human observer is the end user of the fused image. Therefore, the human perception and interpretation of the fused image is very important. Consequently, one way to assess the fused images is to use subjective tests. Although the subjective tests are typically accurate whenever performed correctly, they are inconvenient, expensive, and time consuming. Hence, an objective performance measure that can accurately predict human perception would be a valuable complementary method. However, it is difficult to find a good, easy to calculate, objective evaluation criterion which matches favorably with visual inspection and is suitable for a variety of different application requirements. In the literature, there are two broad classes of objective performance measures. One class requires a reference image, while the other does not (Wang et al., 2004).

7.1 Evaluation measures requiring a reference image

For certain applications, it is possible to generate an ideal fused image, which is then used as a reference to compare with the experimental fused results. The five quality metrics used for these comparisons are given next, where *R* denotes the reference image, *F* denotes the fused image, *(i, j)* denotes a given pixel, *L* denotes the number of gray levels, and $N \times M$ is the size of the input image.
denotes the reference image, *F* denotes the fused image, *(i, j)* denotes a given pixel, and $N \times M$ is the size of the image.
The root mean square error (RMSE)

$$RMSE = \sqrt{\frac{1}{NM}\sum_{i=1}^{N}\sum_{j=1}^{M}\left|R(i,j) - F(i,j)\right|^2} \tag{5}$$

The correlation (CORR)

$$CORR = \frac{2C_{R,F}}{C_R + C_F} \tag{6}$$

Where $C_R = \sum_{i=1}^{N}\sum_{j=1}^{M} R(i,j)^2, C_F = \sum_{i=1}^{N}\sum_{j=1}^{M} F(i,j)^2$ and $C_{R,F} = \sum_{i=1}^{N}\sum_{j=1}^{M} R(i,j)F(i,j)$.

The peak signal to noise ratio (PSNR)

$$PSNR = 10log_{10}\left(\frac{L^2}{\frac{1}{NM}\sum_{i=1}^{N}\sum_{j=1}^{M}\left|R(i,j)-F(i,j)\right|^2}\right) \tag{7}$$

The mutual information (MI)

$$MI = \sum_{i_1=1}^{L}\sum_{i_2=1}^{L} h_{R,F}(i_1,i_2)log_2\frac{h_{R,F}(i_1,i_2)}{h_R(i_1)h_F(i_2)} \tag{8}$$

where $h_{R,F}$ denotes the normalized joint gray level histogram of images R and F while h_R, h_F are the normalized marginal histograms of the two images.
Structure information, structural similarity (SSIM)
This image quality assessment is proposed as (Wang et al., 2004) (Wang, Bovik, Sheikh, & Simoncelli, 2004)

$$SSIM = \frac{(2\mu_R\mu_F + C_1)(2\sigma_{RF} + C_2)}{(\mu_R^2 + \mu_F^2 + C_1)(\sigma_R^2 + \sigma_F^2 + C_2)} \tag{9}$$

where C_1 is a constant that is included to avoid the instability when sum of mean of reference image R, and mean of fused image F is close to zero (i.e. $\mu_R^2 + \mu_F^2 \approx 0$), and C_2 is a constant that is included to avoid the instability when standard deviations is close to zero (i.e. $\sigma_R^2 + \sigma_F^2 \approx 0$)
The objective image quality measures: RMSE, PSNR, CORR and MI, are widely employed due to their simplicity. However, they have been found sometimes not correlate well with human evaluation when sensors of different types are considered (Blum & Liu, 2006) and the SSIM measure can be used.

7.2 Evaluation measures not requiring a reference image

It is generally difficult to access the ideal reference images. Several simple quantitative evaluation methods which do not require a reference image are listed below.
The standard deviation (SD)

$$\sigma = \sqrt{\sum_{i=0}^{L}\left(i-\bar{i}\right)^2 h(i)} \tag{10}$$

where h is the normalized histogram of image and $\sum_{i=0}^{L} ih(i)$.
The entropy (H)

$$H = -\sum_{i=0}^{L} h(i)log_2h(i) \tag{11}$$

Petrovic quality index (QI)
An objective performance metric is proposed in (Petrovic, 2000), which measures the amount of information that is transferred from the input images into the fused image. Their

approach is based on the assumption that important visual information is related with edge information. A Sobel edge operator is applied to yield edge strength $g(i,j)$ and orientation $\alpha(i,j) \in [0,\pi]$ for each pixel of the image. The relative strength and orientation values, $G^{AF}(i,j)$ and $\Phi^{AF}(i,j)$, of input image A with respect to fused image F are defined as:

$$G^{AF}(i,j) = \begin{cases} \dfrac{g_F(i,j)}{g_A(i,j)} & \text{if } g^F(i,j) > g^A(i,j) \\ \dfrac{g_A(i,j)}{g_F(i,j)} & \text{otherwise} \end{cases} \quad (12)$$

$$\Phi^{AF}(i,j) = 1 - \frac{|\alpha_A(i,j) - \alpha_F(i,j)|}{\pi / 2} \quad (13)$$

The edge preservation values Q^{AF} from input image A to fused result F is formed by the product of a sigmoid mapping function of the relative strength and orientation factors. Some constants as defined in (Petrovic, 2000) κ, σ and Γ determine the shape of the sigmoid mapping as

$$Q^{AF}(i,j) = \frac{\Gamma_g \Gamma_a}{\left(1 + exp^{\kappa_g\left(G^{AF}(i,j) - \sigma_g\right)}\right)\left(1 + exp^{\kappa_\alpha\left(\Phi^{AF}(i,j) - \sigma_\alpha\right)}\right)} \quad (14)$$

In equation (14), there are 6 parameters ($\kappa_g, \sigma_g, \kappa_a, \sigma_a, \Gamma_g$, and Γ_a), where the first four parameters are determined via an optimization process that maximizes a correspondence measure between objective and subjective image fusion assessment results. Furthermore the constant Γ_g and Γ_a are selected such that for optimal values of $\kappa_g, \sigma_g, \kappa_a, \sigma_a$ and G^{AF}, Φ^{AF} equal to 1, the Q^{AF} will also be equal to 1 (Chen & Blum, 2005). The overall objective quality quantity measure $QI^{AB/F}$ is obtained by weighting the normalized edge preservation values of both input images A, and B as:

$$QI^{AB/F} = \frac{\sum_{i=1}^{N}\sum_{j=1}^{M} Q^{AF}(i,j) w^A(i,j) + Q^{BF}(i,j) w^B(i,j)}{\sum_{i=1}^{N}\sum_{j=1}^{M} (w^A(i,j) + w^B(i,j))} \quad (15)$$

In general the weights $w^A(i,j)$ and $w^B(i,j)$ are a function of edge strength. The range of QI is between 0 and 1, where 0 indicates the complete loss of source information and 1 means the ideal fusion.

8. Proposed NDE fusion systems

Three proposed fusion systems based on IHS transformation, PCA, and multi-resolution wavelet decomposition (MWD) are presented next.

8.1 Intensity-hue-saturation (IHS) transform fusion

The IHS technique is a standard procedure in image fusion, and has fast computing capability for fusing images (Tania, 2008). The widespread use of the IHS transform to merge remote sensing images is based on the ability to separate the spectral information of the RGB image into its two components (H) and (S), while isolating most of the spatial information in the (I) component. The fusion steps can be summarized as:

Register three input images defined as R, G, and B to the same size as the high resolution image defined as HR.

Transform the R, G, and B false color image into the IHS component using one of the different transformations that have been developed to transfer a color image from the RGB space to the IHS space. The most common RGB- IHS conversion system is based on the following linear transformation (Gonzalez-Audicana et al., 2006), for each pixel p.

$$\begin{bmatrix} I^p \\ V_1^p \\ V_2^p \end{bmatrix} = \begin{bmatrix} \frac{1}{3} & \frac{1}{3} & \frac{1}{3} \\ \frac{-\sqrt{2}}{6} & \frac{-\sqrt{2}}{6} & \frac{-\sqrt{2}}{6} \\ \frac{1}{\sqrt{2}} & -\frac{1}{\sqrt{2}} & 0 \end{bmatrix} \begin{bmatrix} R^p \\ G^p \\ B^p \end{bmatrix} \tag{16}$$

$$H^p = tan^{-1}\left(\frac{V_1^p}{V_2^p}\right) \tag{17}$$

$$S^p = \sqrt{\left(V_1^p\right)^2 + \left(V_1^p\right)^2} \tag{18}$$

Modify the HR image to accounts for differences related to acquisition techniques, this is usually performed by conventional histogram matching between the HR image and the intensity component I of the IHS representation (Nunez, 1999), i.e. after computing the histogram of both HR image and the intensity component I of the IHS representation, the histogram of the intensity component I is used as reference to which HR image histogram was matched, the new HR image defined as NHR.

Replace the intensity component I by the NHR image.

Perform the inverse transformation to obtain the merged $R'G'B'$ fused image using the relations

$$\begin{bmatrix} R'^p \\ G'^p \\ B'^p \end{bmatrix} = \begin{bmatrix} 1 & \frac{-1}{\sqrt{2}} & \frac{1}{\sqrt{2}} \\ 1 & \frac{-1}{\sqrt{2}} & \frac{-1}{\sqrt{2}} \\ 1 & \sqrt{2} & 0 \end{bmatrix} \begin{bmatrix} NHR^p \\ V_1^p \\ V_2^p \end{bmatrix} \tag{19}$$

The generated fused image provides the full details of the HR image but introduces color distortion. This is because of the low correlation between the HR image and the intensity component I.

8.2 Principal component analysis PCA fusion

PCA provides a powerful tool for data analysis which is often used in signal and image processing (Gonzalez & Woods, 2007) as a technique for data compression, data dimension reduction, and data fusion. Original images constitute the input data, and the result of this transformation is to obtain non-correlated new bands, called the principal components. PCA in signal processing can be described as a transform of a given set of n input vectors (variables) with the same length K formed in n-dimensional vector $x = [x_1, x_2, \ldots x_n]^T$ into a vector y according to

$$y = P(x - m_x) \tag{20}$$

The vector m_x is the vector of mean values of all input variables defined by the relation

$$m_x = E\{x\} = \frac{1}{K}\sum_{k=1}^{K} x_k \tag{21}$$

Matrix P is determined by the covariance matrix C_x, where rows in P are formed from the eigenvectors e of C_x ordered according to corresponding eigenvalues in descending order. The evaluation of the C_x matrix is possible according to relation

$$C_x = E\left\{(x - m_x)(x - m_x)^T\right\} = \frac{1}{K}\sum_{k=1}^{K} x_k x_k^T - m_x m_x^T \tag{22}$$

For n-dimensional input vector x, the size of C_x is $n \times n$. The elements $C_x(i,i)$ lying in its main diagonal are the variances of x, and the other values $C_x(i,j)$ determine the covariance between input variables x_i, x_j. The rows of P are orthonormal so the inversion of PCA is possible.

Both IHS and PCA mergers are based on the same principle: to separate most of the spatial information of multispectral image from its spectral information by means of linear transforms. The IHS transform separates the spatial information of the multispectral image as the intensity (I) component. In the same way, PCA separates the spatial information of the image into the first principal component PC1. PCA allows synthesizing the original bands creating new bands, the principal components, which pick up and reorganize most of the original information. In general, the first principal component PC1 collects the information that is common to all the bands used as input data in the PCA, i.e., the spatial information, while the spectral information that is specific to each band is picked up in the other principal components (Kwarteng & Chavez, 1989).

The proposed PCA method is similar to the described IHS method, with the main advantage that an arbitrary number of bands can be used as shown in Fig. 3. If more than three images to be fused using *IHS*, PCA is used as a first step. PC1 is replaced by the HR image, whose histogram has previously been matched with that of PC1. Finally, the inverse transformation is applied to the whole dataset formed by the modified HR image and the PC2, ... PCn.

8.3 Improved IHS based on multi-resolution wavelet decomposition (MWD) fusion

The IHS fusion method usually can integrate color and spatial features smoothly. If the correlation between the IHS intensity image and the HR image is high, the IHS fusion can well preserve the color information. However, the color distortion can be significant for low correlation values, between the intensity image and the HR image, especially when the input images and HR images originally from different sensors.

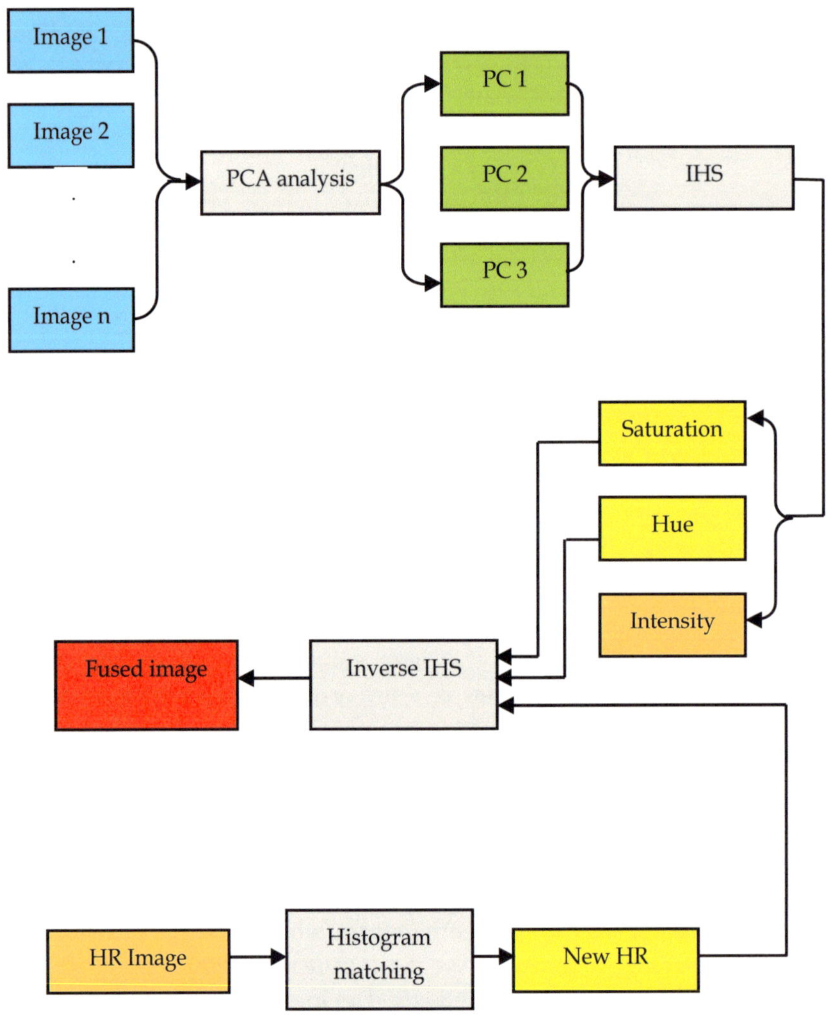

Fig. 3. Arbitrary number of inputs IHS fusion system

On the other hand, the discrete wavelet transform (DWT) image fusion can usually preserve color information better than other fusion methods, since the high-resolution spatial information from HR image is injected into all the three low-resolution multispectral bands. However, the spatial detail from HR image is often different from that of a multispectral band having the same spatial resolution. This difference may introduce some color distortion into the wavelet frame fusion results. To better utilize the advantages of the IHS and the DWT fusion techniques, and to overcome the shortcomings of the two techniques, an integrated IHS and wavelet frame fusion approach is proposed here as shown in Fig. 4. The shift invariant wavelet transform obtained using á trous (with holes) algorithm overcomes image artifacts (Wang et al., 2005) and (Fowler, 2005), the un-decimated multi-resolution wavelet decomposition (MWD) or shift invariant discrete wavelet transform (SIDWT) was used for the IHS fusion improvement.

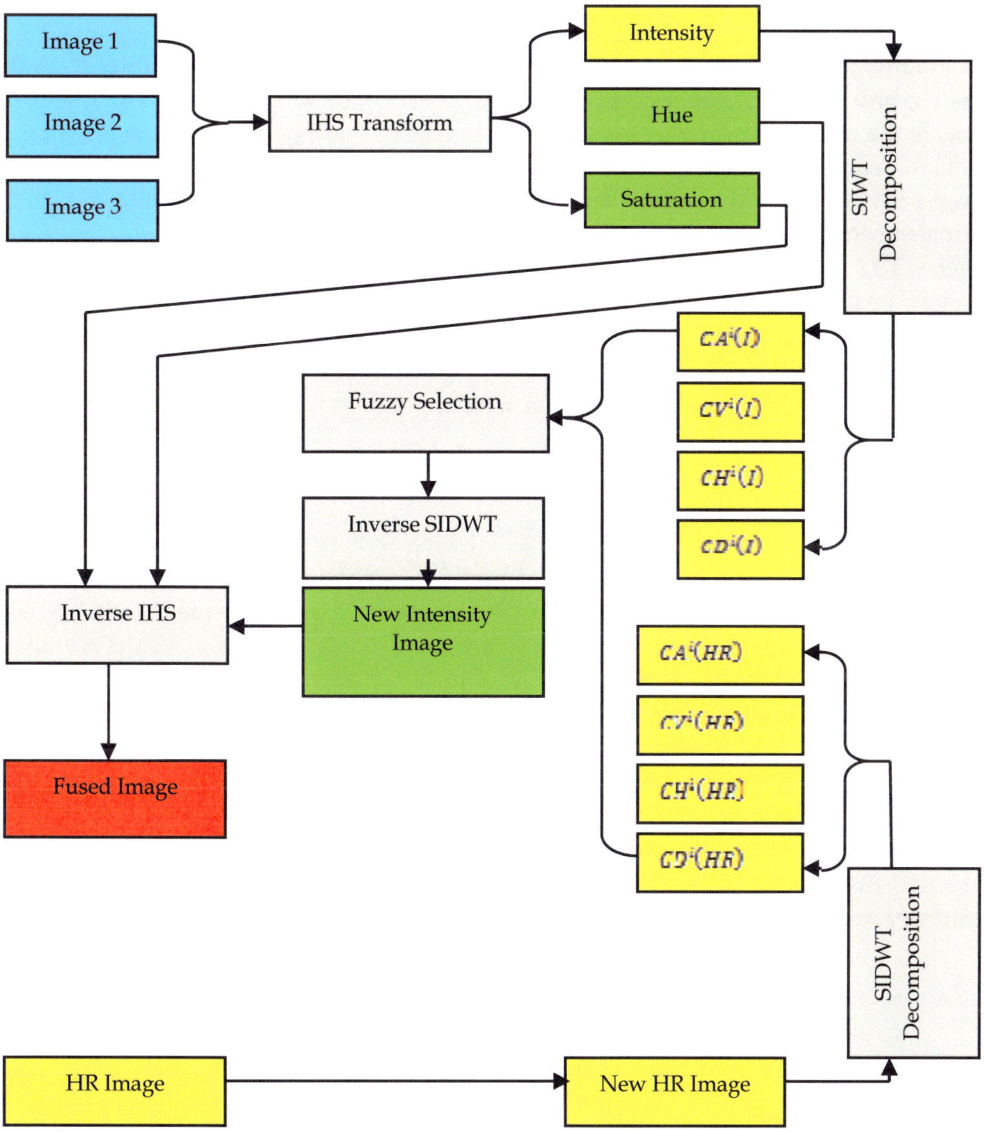

Fig. 4. Improved IHS fusion based on MWD

The steps of this approach are summarized as:

Registration. All images are first registered.

IHS Transform. the multispectral image is transformed into IHS components as illustrated before.

Histogram match. The histogram of the HR image and the intensity component *I* of the IHS color space are matched and a new HR image (*NHR*) is obtained.

SIDWT Decomposition: Apply the un-decimated wavelet decomposition, to the intensity component *I* and to the corresponding histogram matched *NHR* image using the Daubechies four coefficient wavelet.

Fuzzy selection: after the decomposition has been made a selection based on the application needed should be made. For example one possible application is to fuse optical image that has information about the rivets and joints for example with inspection EC images, in this case the best selection would be to take the approximation of the optical image and the detail of the EC images. Another application is to replace high spatial resolution information with low spatial resolution of the fused images, in this case the detail of the *NHR* is selected.
Inverse SIWT: the shift invariant reconstruction transform applied to the selected wavelet coefficients to form the new intensity image.
Inverse IHS transform: The final fused image is generated by transforming the new intensity image together with the hue and saturation components back into RGB space.

8.4 NDE fusion results

The evaluation of the IHS proposed fusion with application to NDE were peformred using simulation as well as experimental signals.

8.4.1 Simulation results

Fig. 5 presents ten images generated with 128x128 resolution, representing probe resistance values (images R_1-R_5) on the top row, and probe inductance values (images L_1-L_5) on the bottom row. Images R_1 and L_1 on the left side correspond to lowest frequency while R_5 & L_5 on the right side correspond to the highest frequency. First some of fusion results presented, before the presentation of a comparison of various fusion algorithms. Fig. 6 is based on IHS fusion with high frequency high-resolution PEC image generated at 256x256. Fig. 7 presents the first four principal components images computed from R_1-R_5 (the first row of Fig. 5). Examples of image fusion with shift invariant wavelet decomposition are presented in Fig. 8, where Daubechies wavelets of order 4 are used. Four images were selected to make the comparison of fusion algorithms that have been applied to the NDE technology with the proposed fusion algorithms. The selected simulation images presented in Fig. 9 were two frequency domain images, and two time domain images.

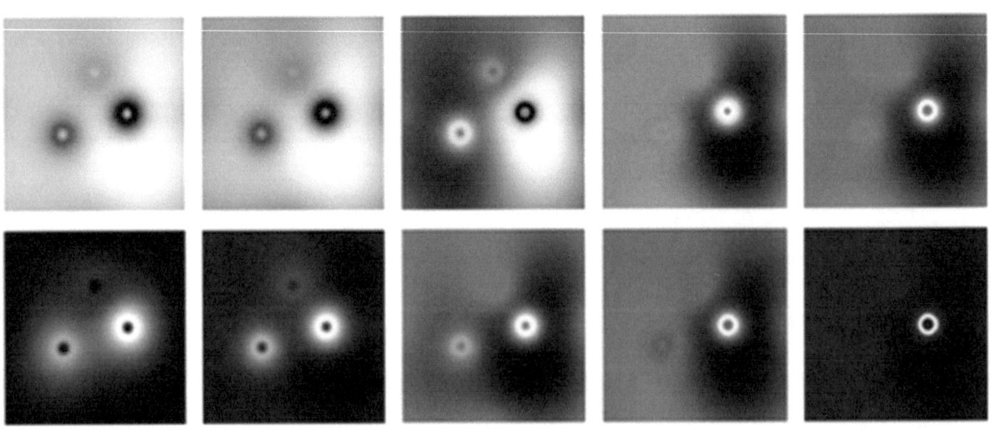

Fig. 5. Ten images representing probe resistance values R1-R5 (top row, left to right) and inductance values L1-L5 (bottom row, left to right) corresponding to five different frequency values: 100 Hz, 1 kHz, 10 kHz, 100 kHz, and 1M Hz

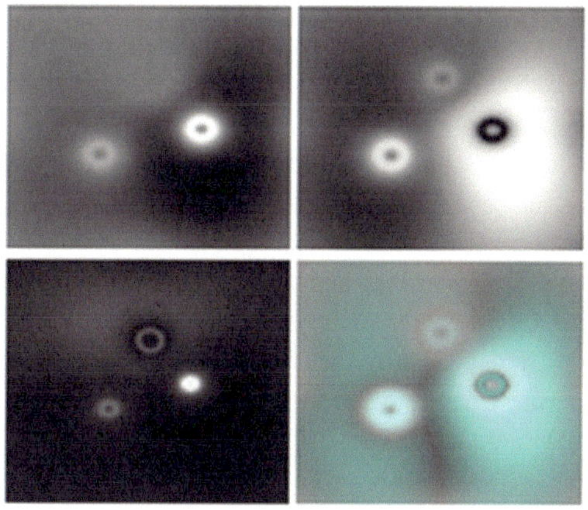

Fig. 6. Fusion obtained with IHS transformation. Top-left is L_3(10 kHz) image, top-right is R_3(10 kHz) image, down-left is PEC image and down-right is fused image

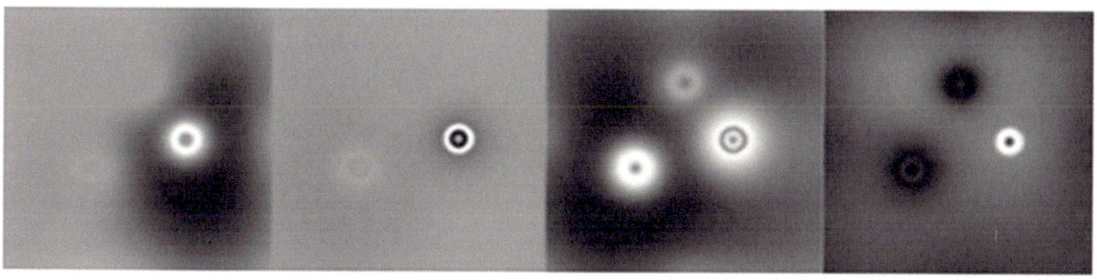

Fig. 7. The first four principal components images computed from R_1-R_5

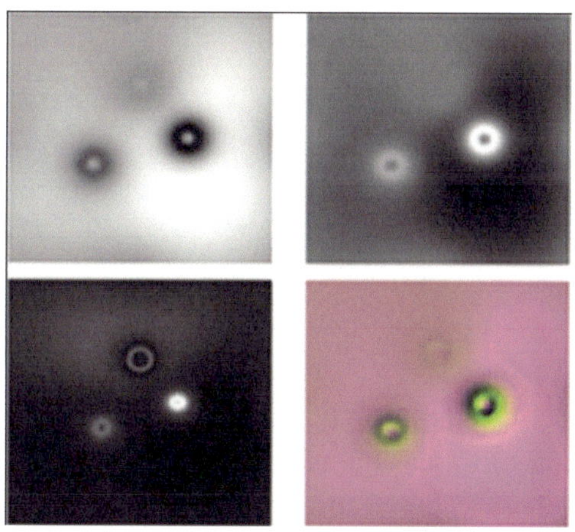

Fig. 8. Fusion obtained with wavelet decomposition, where the high spatial resolution image was taken as R_5. Top-left is R_2(1 kHz) image, top-right is L_3(10 kHz) image, down-left is PEC image and down-right is fused image

The proposed IHS based fusion algorithms, and the improved IHS based on MWD fusion termed as IHSW were compared with three fusion algorithms mostly presented in literature with application to NDE i.e. the Laplacian pyramid (LAP), the discrete wavelet transform (DWT), and the shift invariant discrete wavelet transform (SIDWT). The maximum frequency rule was used which selects the coefficients with the highest absolute value for LAP, DWT, and SIDWT fusion methods.

Fig. 10 presents the fusion results of the compared fusion algorithms where the input images for all were shown in Fig. 9. Table 3 shows the estimated quality measure for these fused images. Notice that the standard deviation (SD) and the entropy (H) illustrated that the IHS based methods are better in performance, while .IHS based methods are not. There are six parameters in the QI performance measure that are determined via optimization process to maximize the correspondence measure between objective and subjective image fusion assessment. It is not thus a relabile performance measure for genral application. Investegating these quality measure revealed that, a small change in these constant highly affect the performance.

Fusion method	Standard deviation (SD)	Entropy (H)	quality index (QI)
Laplacian pyramid (LAP)	30.1900	6.8695	0.7565
Discrete wavelet transform (DWT)	35.1318	6.8822	0.8077
Shift invariant discrete wavelet transform (SIDWT)	27.7046	6.7731	0.7588
Intensity hue saturation (IHS)	45.8145	7.1791	0.6008
Intensity hue saturation with wavelet (IHSW)	33.3772	7.3190	0.5484

Table 3. Comparison of the quality measures for the fused images shown in Fig. 10

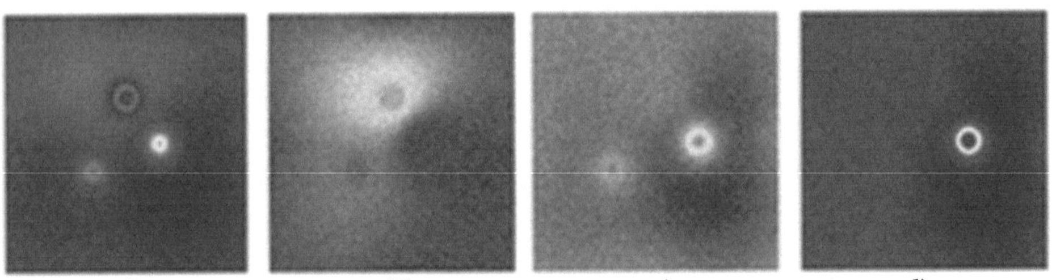

a) b) c) d)

Fig. 9. Images used to evaluate the fusion algorithms, (a) maximum amplitude feature PEC image, (b) time to maximum PEC image, (c) probe-L image at 10 kHz, (d) probe-L at 1MHz as a HR

With the Gaussian noise added to the input images according to a predefined signal to noise ratio SNR, the performance of the fusion methods were compared with standard deviation SD, and entropy H, the results plotted in Fig. 11. It is clear from the results that the IHS based methods perform better. Also it is noticed out that the SD of the IHS based methods increases with the increase of SNR of input images. Entropy is used to measure the amount of uncertainty or information of an image, but it is sensitive to noise (Naidu & Raol, 2008). The dynamic range of SD and H are very small when the SNR exceed 20 dB which is typically the acceptable image SNR. Subjectively, IHS based fusion methods ranked higher than the other fusion methods.

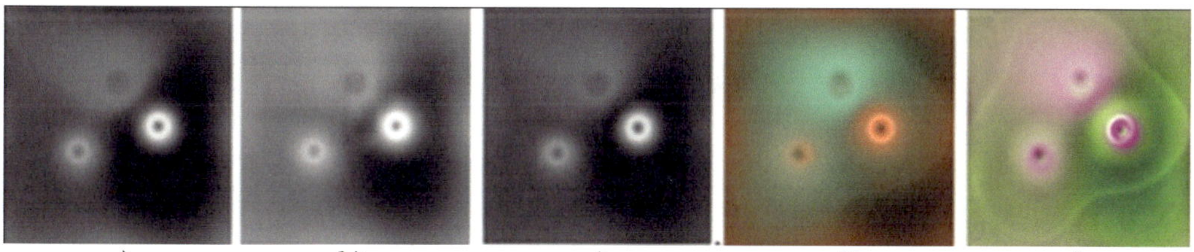

a) b) c) d) e)

Fig. 10. Fusion results of the images shown in Fig. 7 using LAP (a), DWT (b), SIDWT (c), IHS (d), IHSW (e) techniques

8.4.2 Experimental eddy current images

Experimental EC images produced employing EC measurement device measurement system (Rohmann B300) (Rohmann Documentation), connected to a scanning system, based on six degree of freedom robot arm manufactured by Staubli (Staubli Documentation) which can gives a resolution of 0.1. The main parts of the system are shown in Fig. 12. The output of the EC measurement system for both scanning systems was connected to a data acquisition system manufactured by National Instruments (National Instruments Documentation). The data was then stored for future processing. The standard sample used for experimental measurements is shown in Fig. 13. This plate was manufactured by Olympus NDT (Olympus NDT, Documentation), and it has been chosen because of the artificial cracks have different sizes, shapes, and orientation with respect to the scanning direction.

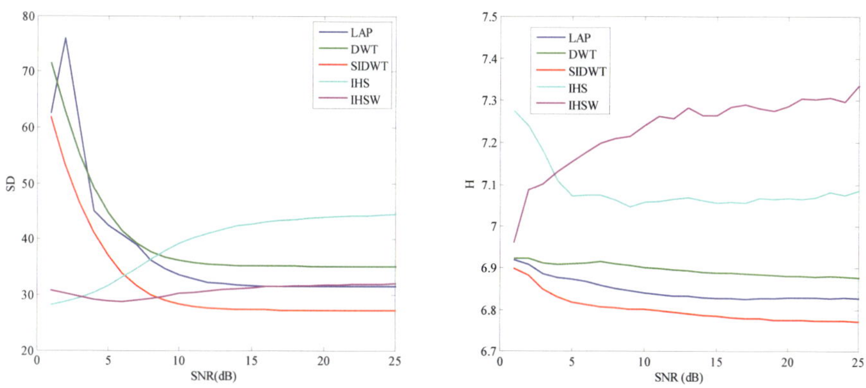

Fig. 11. Performance of fusion with standard deviation and entropy quality metric

Four experimental images at frequencies 10 kHz, 100 kHz, 300 kHz, and 800 kHz, respectively are shown in Fig. 14. These images represent the amplitude of the vertical component after the rotation of the axes to reduce the effect of liftoff noise.

After the registration of EC to the optical image, three of the EC images of Fig. 14 and the optical image were used as input to the fusion algorithms. IHS and IHSW use three EC images as input to the IHS transform, and optical image as the HR image, while the other fusion methods LAP, DWT, and SIDWT normally accept two input images only, so a multi-stage fusion process were conducted for the comparison. A comparison using the three lowest frequency value images and the three highest frequency images of Fig. 12 are shown in Fig. 15 and Fig. 16 respectively. Notice that with high frequency images used, the good resolution of the fused images is noticeable.

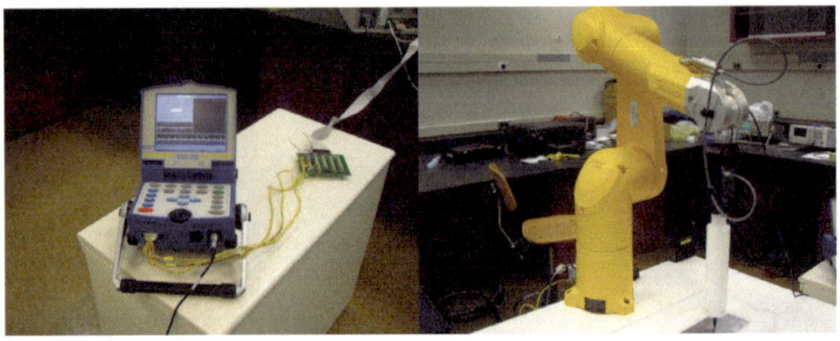

Fig. 12. Eddy current measurement system (Rohmann B 300) (left) and Staubli robot (right), which are the main parts of the scanning system

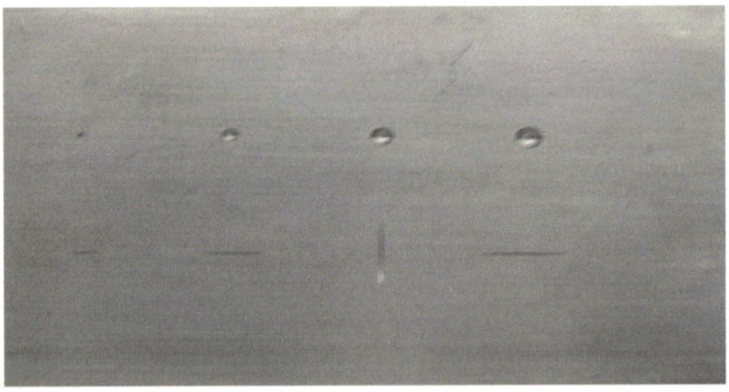

Fig. 13. Optical photo of the plate used in experimental measurements

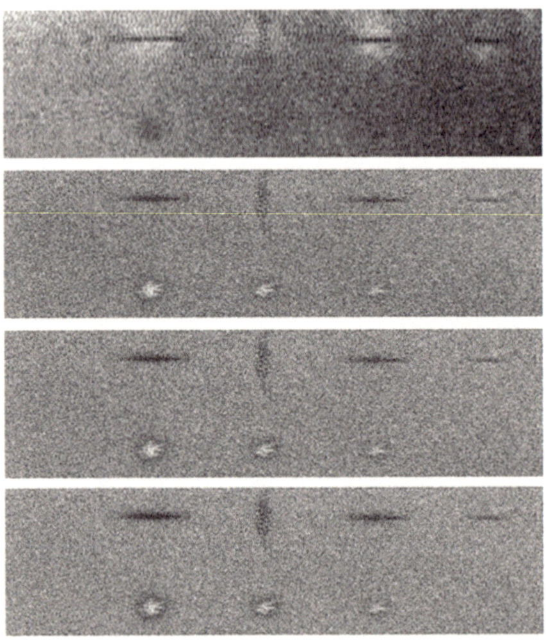

Fig. 14. Measured EC images at 10 kHz, 100 kHz, 300 kHz, and 800 kHz, top to bottom, respectively

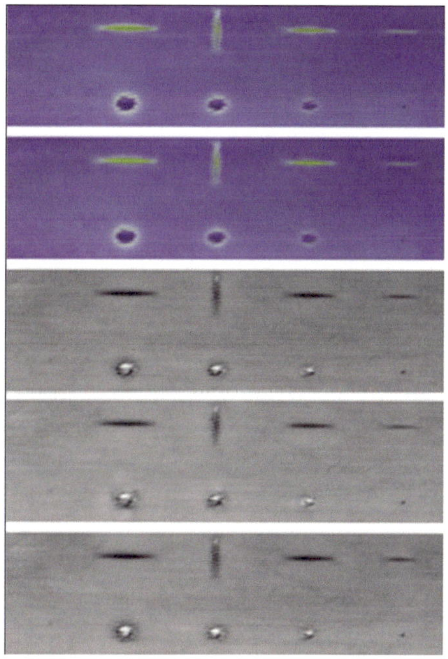

Fig. 15. Fusion results with the first three lowest frequency value images shown in Fig. 14, along with the optical image. Results reveal IHS, IHSW, SIDWT, DWT, LAP fusion, top to bottom, respectively

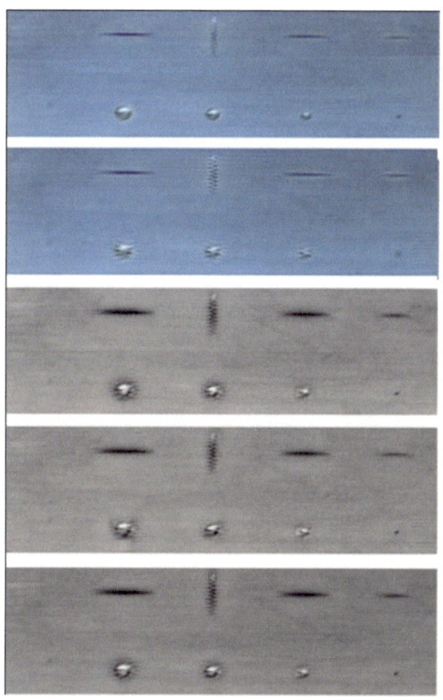

Fig. 16. Fusion results with the last three highest frequency value images shown in Fig. 14, along with the optical image. Results reveal IHS, IHSW, SIDWT, DWT, LAP fusion, top to bottom, respectively

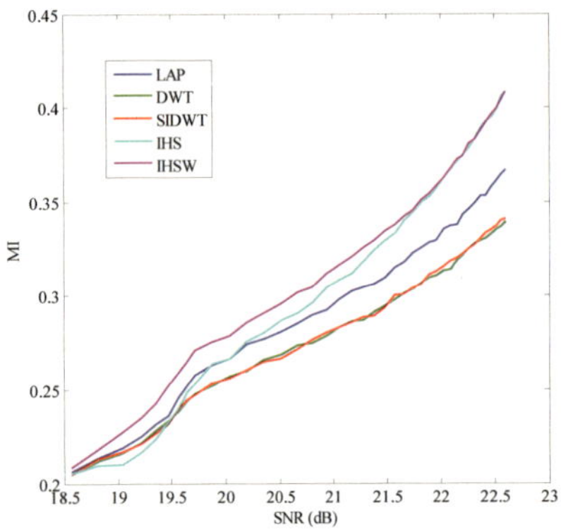

a)

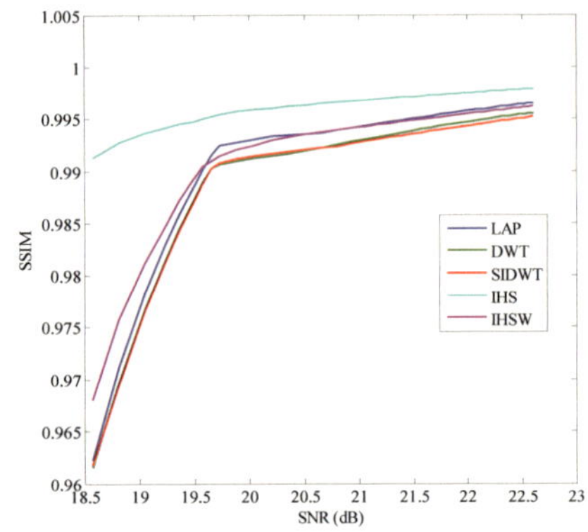

b)

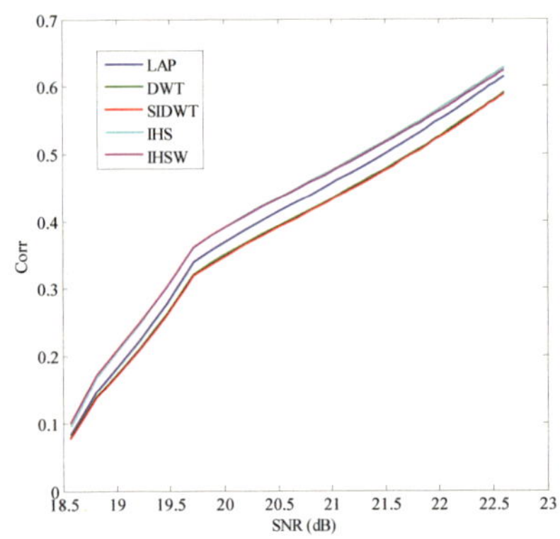

c)

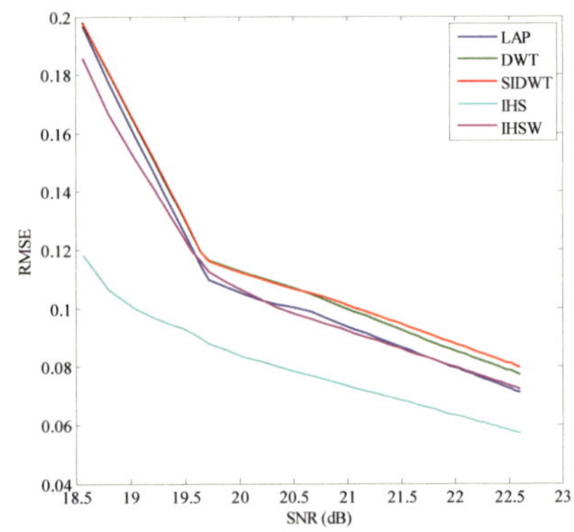

d)

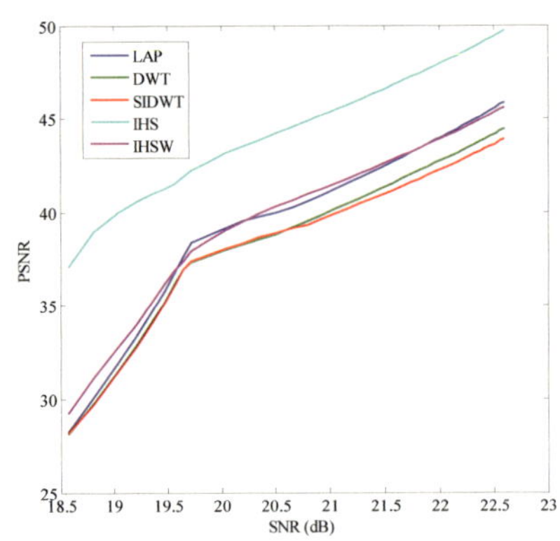

e)

Fig. 17. Performance of fusion with mutual information metric (a), structure information, structural similarity metric (b), correlation metric (c), root mean square error metric (d), and peak SNR quality metric (e)

Gaussian noise added to the experimental images used as inputs to the fusion methods according to a predefined signal to noise ratio SNR, and the performance of the fusion methods were compared with five objective evaluation measures that require reference image, namely, mutual information (MI), structure information, structural similarity (SSIM), correlation coefficient (Corr), root mean square error (RMSE), and peak signal to noise ratio (PSNR). The reference image was produced depending on the standard sample used. Fig. 17 shows the results of the five mentioned metrics and how these metrics are affected by noise. Results illustrate that the IHS based methods perform better than the others three fusion methods for all performance measures used in the range of acceptable image SNR.

9. Conclusions and future work

The emerging concept of data fusion, particularly in NDE image fusion is used to develop robust NDE systems, which can easily be adapted in industrial applications. Novel systems are introduced implementing image fusion in electromagnetic NDE applications. The focus is directed toward the emerging techniques based on eddy current (EC) inspection methods, which are among the most promising electromagnetic inspection modalities, due to their simplicity, versatility, high sensitivity, and high speeds of testing. Results are presented for fusing conventional as well as pulsed eddy current images. EC scanning of sample under test is done based on automatic robotic system to obtain c-scan images.

Image fusion algorithms exploit both the redundancy and complementary information to enhance the robustness of the resulting image. Redundant information is used to improve the SNR and complementary information is used to augment the overall information content, which increases the accuracy and reliability of inspection systems. The developed systems can be used to fuse multi-spectral, multi-temporal, and multi-spatial information in EC images. Results reveal that the proposed fusion system performs better than conventional fusion system applied to NDE, according to the performance quality measures. Various image metrics are used to assess the quality of resulting fusion images. Effective quality metrics help automate NDE fusion systems in industrial environments. The obtained results of the objective evaluation metrics are found to be almost consistent with the subjective evaluation.

10. Acknowledgments

This research is funded by King Abdulaziz City for Science and Technology (KACST), Research Grant: 122-28.

11. References

Algarni, A., Elshafiey, I., & Alkanhal, M. A. (2009). Multimodal Image Fusion for Next Generation NDE Systems. *IEEE International Symposium on Signal Processing and Information Technology*, (pp. 219-224).

Ansari, F. (1992). Real Time Condition Monitoring of Conctere Structures by Embadded Optical Fibers Sensors. *Nondestructive Testing of Concrete Elements and Structures proceedings of sessions sponsored by the Engineering Mechanics Division of the American Society of Civil Engineers.*

Blum, R. S., & Liu, Z. (2006). Multi-sensor image fusion and its applications. Boca Raton: CRC Press, Taylor & Francis Group.

Brassard, M., Chehbaz, A., Pelletier, A., & Forsyth, D. S. (2000). Combined NDT inspection techniques for corrosion detection of aircraft structures. *Proc. 15th World Conf. Nondestructive Testing*. Rome, Italy.

Cantor, T. R. (1984). Review of Penetrating Radar as Applied to Nondestructive Evaluation of Concrete. In V. M. Malhotra (Ed.). In *Situ/Nondestructive Testing of Concrete*. Detroit: American Concrete Institute.

Chady, T., Sikora, R., Psuj, G., Enokizono, M., & Todaka, T. (2005). Fusion of electromagnetic inspection methods for evaluation of stress-loaded steel samples. *IEEE Trans. Magn.* , 41 (10), pp. 3721-3723.

Chalastaras, A., Malkinski, L., Jung, J.-S., Oh, S.-L., Lee, J.-K., Ventrice, C. J., et al. (2004). GMR Multilayers on a New Embossed Surface. *IEEE Trans. Magn.* , 40, pp. 2257 - 2259 .

Chen, Y., & Blum, R. S. (2005). Experimental Tests of Image Fusion for Night Vision. *8th International Conference on Information Fusion*,ECE Dept., Lehigh Univ.

Djafari, A. M. (July, 2002). Fusion of X-ray and geometrical data in computed tomography for nondestructive testing applications. *Proceedings of the Fifth Int. Conf. Inf. Fusion* , pp. 309–316.

Elshafiey, I., Alkanhal, M., & Algarni, A. (2008). Image Fusion Based Enhancement of Eddy Current Nondestructive Evaluation. *International Journal of Applied Electromagnetics and Mechanics* (IJAEM) , 28 (1-2), pp. 291-296.

Fowler, J. E. (2005). The Redundant Discrete Wavelet Transform and Additive Noise. *IEEE Signal Processing Letters* , 12, pp. 629-632.

Francois, V., & Kaftandjian, N. (2003). Use of data fusion methods to improve reliability of inspection: Synthesis of the work done in the frame of a European thematic network. *Journal of Nondestructive Testing* , 8, pp. 1-8.

Gonzalez, R., & Woods, R. (2007). Digital Image Processing. (3rd, Ed.) Prentice Hall.

Gonzalez-Audicana, M., Otazu, X., Fors, O., & Alvarez-Mozos, J. (2006). A Low Computational-Cost Method to Fuse IKONOS Images Using the Spectal Response Function of Its Sensors. *IEEE Trans. Geosci. Remote Sens.* , 44, pp. 1683-1691.

Gros, X. E., & Takahashi, K. (1998). Fusion of NDT Data Improve Inspection of Composite Materials. *Proceedings of 1998 Japanese Society of Nondestructive Inspection Spring Conference*, (pp. 265–268).

Gros, X. E., Strachan, P., & Lowden, D. W. (1995). Theory and Implementation of NDT Data Fusion. *Res. Nondestruct. Eval.* , 6 (4), pp. 227–236.

Gros, X., Liu, Z., Tsukada, K., & Hanasaki, K. (2000). Experimenting with Pixel-level NDT Data Fusion Techniques. *IEEE Trans. Instrumentation and Measurement* , 49, pp. 1083 - 1090 .

Jaarinen, J., Hartikainen, J., & Luukkala, M. (1989). Quantitative Thermal Wave Characterization of Coating Adhesion Defects. In *Review of Progress in Quantitative NDE*. D. O. Thompson, & D. Chimenti (Eds.): Plenum Press.

Kaftandjian, V., Zhu, Y. M., Dupuis, O., & Babot, D. (2005). The Combined Use of the Evidence Theory and Fuzzy Logic for Improving Multimodal Nondestructive Testing Systems. *IEEE Trans. Instrumentation and Measurement* , 54 (5), pp. 1968-1977.

Kwarteng, P. S., & Chavez, A. Y. (1989). Extracting spectral contrast in Landsat Thematic Mapper image data using selective principal component analysis. *Photogramm. Eng. Remote Sens.*, 55, pp. 339–348.

Lee, S. J., & Song, S. H. (2005). Magnetooptic Sensor for Remote Evaluation of Surfaces. *IEEE Trans. Magn.*, 41, pp. 2257-2259.

Li, S., et al. (2002). Using the discrete wavelet frame transform to Merge Landsat TM and SPOT Panchromatic Images. *Information Fusion*, 3, pp. 17-23.

Liu, Z., Abbas, F., & Nezih, M. (2006). Application of Dempster-Shafer Theory for Fusion of Lap Joints Inspection Data7. *Proceedings of SPIE, the International Socity for Optical Engineering*, 6176.

Liu, Z., Gros, X. E., Tsukada, K., Hanasaki, K., & Takahashi, K. (1999). The use of wavelets for pixel level NDT data fusion. *Proc. 2nd Jpn.-US Symp. Advances NDT*, (pp. 474-477). Kahuku, HI.

Liu, Z., Tsukada, K., Hanasaki, K., & Kurisu, M. (1999). Two-Dimensional Eddy Current Signal Enhancement via Multifrequency Data Fusion. *Res. Nondestruct. Eval.*, 11 (3), pp. 165-177.

Lord, W. (1983). Application of Numerical Field Modeling to Electromagnetic Methods of nondestructive Testing. *IEEE Trans. on Magnetics*, 19, pp. 2437-2442.

Matuszewski, B. J., Shark, L. K., & Varley, M. R. (Oct., 2000). Region-based wavelet fusion of ultrasonic, radiographic and shearographic nondestructive testing images. *Proceedings of the 15th World Conf. Nondestructive Testing*. Rome, Italy.

Mina, M., Udpa, S. S., Udpa, L., & Yim, J. (1997). A new approach for practical two dimensional data fusion utilizing a single eddy current probe. *Review of Progress in QNDE*, 16, pp. 749–755.

Mina, M., Yim, J., Udpa, S. S., & Udpa, L. (1996). Two dimensional multi-frequency eddy current data fusion, (pp. 2125–2132).

Naidu, V. P., & Raol, J. R. (2008). Pixel-level Image Fusion using Wavelets and Principal Component Analysis. *Defence Science Journal*, 58, pp. 338-352.

National Instruments Documentation. Retrieved from www.ni.com/dataacquisition.

Nunez, J. O. (1999). Multiresolution based image fusion with additive wavelet decomposition. *IEEE Trans. Geosci. Remote Sens.*, 37 (3), pp. 1204 - 1211.

Olympus NDT, Documentation. Retrieved from www.OlympusNDT.com

Petrovic, C. X. (2000). Opjective pixel level image fusion performance measure. *Proc. SPIE*, 4051, pp. 88-99. Orlando, FL.

Rohmann Documentation. Retrieved from www.rohmann.de.

Simone, G., & Morabito, F. C. (2001). NDT image fusion using eddy current and ultrasonic data. *Int. J. Comput. Math. Elect. Electron. Eng.*, 20 (3), pp. 857-868.

Song, Y. W., & Udpa, S. S. (1996). A New Morphological Algorithm for Fusing Ultrasonic and Eddy Current Images. *Proc. IEEE Ultrason. Symp*, (pp. 649–652).

Staubli Documentation. Retrieved from www.staubli.com/en/robotics

Tai, C.-C., & Pan, Y.-L. (2008). A Novel Multiphysics Sensing Method Based on Thermal and EC Techniques and its Application for Crack Inspection. *Proceedings of the 2008 IEEE International Conference on Sensor Network*, Ubiquitous, and Trustworthy Computing, pp. 475-479.

Tania, S. (2008). Image Fusion: Algorithms and applications. London: Academic Press.

Tian, G. Y., Sophian, A., Taylor, D., & Rudlin, J. (2005). Multiple sensors on pulsed eddy-current detection for 3-D subsurface crack assessment. *IEEE Sensors Journal* , 5, pp. 90-96.

Toet, A. (1992). Multiscale Contrast Enhancement with Application to Image Fusion. *Optical Engineering* , 31 (5), pp. 1026-1031.

Udpa, L. (2001). Neural Networks for NDE. Proc. IV Int. Workshop: Advances Signal Process. *Nondestructive Eval. Mater.* Quebec City, QC, Canada.

Udpa, L., & Elshafiey, I. (2001). WINSAS: A New tool for Enhancing the Performance of Eddy Current Inspection of Aging Aircraft Wheels. Hyatt-Orlando, Orlando, Florida.

Volponi, A. J., Brotherton, T., Luppold, R., & Simon, D. L. (2004). Development of an Information Fusion System for Engine Diagnostics and Health Management. NASA.

Wang, Z., Bovik, A. C., Sheikh, H. R., & Simoncelli, E. P. (2004). Image Quality Assessment: From Error Visibility to Structural Similarity. *IEEE Transactions on Image Processing* , 13, pp. 600 - 612.

Wang, Z., Ziou, D., Armenakis, C., Li, D., & Li, Q. (2005). A Comparative Analysis of Image Fusion Methods. *IEEE Transactions on Geoscience and Remote Sensing* , 43, pp. 1391-1402.

Yim, J. (1995). Image Fusion Using Multiresolution Decomposition and LMMSE Filter. Ph.D. dissertation, Iowa State Univ.

Yim, J., Udpa, S. S., Mina, M., & Udpa, L. (1996). Optimum Filter Based Techniques for Data Fusion. *Review of Progress in Quantitative NDE*. D. O. Thompson, & D. Chimenti (Eds.): Plenum Press. pp. 773–780.

Yim, J., Udpa, S. S., Udpa, L., & Lord, W. (1995). Neural Network Approaches to Data Fusion. In D. O. Thompson, & D. E. Chimenti (Ed.), *Review of Progress in QNDE*. 14, pp. 819–826. New York: Plenum.

Zitova, B., & Flusser, J. (2003). Image registration methods: a survey. *Image and Vision Computing* , 21, pp. 977–1000.

Part 2

Advanced Application and Utility of Image Fusion Technology

12

Fusion of Infrared and Visible Images for Robust Person Detection

Thi Thi Zin, Hideya Takahashi, Takashi Toriu and Hiromitsu Hama
Graduate School of Engineering, Osaka City University,
Osaka 558-8585
Japan

1. Introduction

In the current context of increased surveillance and security, more sophisticated and robust surveillance systems are needed. One idea relies on the use of pairs of video (visible spectrum) and thermal infrared (IR) cameras located around premises of interest. To automate the system, a robust person detection algorithm and the development of an efficient technique enabling the fusion of the information provided by the two sensors becomes necessary and these are described in this chapter.

Recently, multi-sensor based image fusion system is a challenging task and fundamental to several modern day image processing applications, such as security systems, defence applications, and intelligent machines. Image fusion techniques have been actively investigated and have wide application in various fields. It is often a vital pre-processing procedure to many computer vision and image processing tasks which are dependent on the acquisition of imaging data via sensors, such as IR and visible. One such task is that of human detection. To detect humans with an artificial system is difficult for a number of reasons as shown in Figure 1 (Gavrila, 2001). The main challenge for a vision-based pedestrian detector is the high degree of variability with the human appearance due to articulated motion, body size, partial occlusion, inconsistent cloth texture, highly cluttered backgrounds and changing lighting conditions.

Fig. 1. Typical dangerous situation – A child suddenly crossing the street

Moreover, the applications, to protect pedestrians, define hard real-time requirements and rigid performance criteria. In night-time environment, only limited visual information can be captured by CCD cameras under poor lightning conditions, thus making it difficult to do surveillance only by visual sensor. Meanwhile IR camera, that is IR sensor, captures thermal image of object. Thermal image of pedestrian in night-time environment can be seen clearly in IR video sequence used for this work. IR video provides rich information for higher temperature objects, but poor information for lower temperature objects. Visual video, on the other hand, provides the visual context to the objects. Thus, the fusion of the two videos will provide good perceptibility to human vision under poor lightning condition. This will help detect the moving objects (pedestrian) during night-time (Chen & Han, 2008). Combining visible and thermal infrared images is advantageous since visible images are much affected by lighting conditions while IR images provide enhanced contrast between human bodies and their environment. However in outdoor conditions, it was noticed that IR images are somewhat sensitive to wind and temperature changes. Nevertheless, these limitations for both modalities are independent and usually do not occur simultaneously. In the person detection and tracking literature, many approaches have been proposed to combine the information from multiple sources, in order to provide more accurate and robust detection and tracking. Probabilistic methods are commonly used to fuse information sources (Malviya & Bhirud, 2009).

The term fusion in general means an approach to extract information acquired in several domains. Image fusion is the process of combining relevant information from two or more videos into a single image. The resulting image will be more informative than any of the input image. The goal of image fusion is to integrate complementary multi-sensor, multi-temporal and/or multi-view information into one new image containing information, the quality of which cannot be achieved otherwise. An intelligent fusion of the information provided by both sensors reduces detection errors, thereby increasing the performance of tracking and the robustness of the surveillance system. A literature search reveals a few interesting papers on the exploitation of near-infrared information to track humans (Bertozzi et al., 2003). These papers generally deal only with the face of observed people and a few are concerned with the whole body. However, when looking to the efforts in the visible part of the spectrum for the same task, many papers are available such as (Masoud & Papanikolopoulos, 2003). Surprisingly, the idea to couple visible and thermal infrared is not yet seen as a popular research field for this application. One reason explaining this is probably due to the still high cost of the thermal infrared cameras versus their visible counter parts. Moreover outdoor scenarios are obviously more challenging to visible imagery due to shadows, light reflections, levels of darkness and luminosity. However, on the other hand, moving leaves and grass, cooling winds, moving shadows with clouds, reflecting snow, etc., are challenging for IR imagery too.

Thus, fusion of IR and visual image is a potential solution to improve person detection, tracking, recognition, and fusion performance (Wang et al., 2007). Tracking and recognition using the visual image is sensitive to variations in illumination conditions. On the other hand, tracking and recognition of targets based on IR images has become an area of growing interest. Thermal IR imagery is nearly invariant to changes in ambient illumination, and provides a capability for identification under all lighting conditions including total darkness. IR sensors are routinely used in remote sensing applications. Coupling an IR sensor with a visual sensor - for frame of reference or for additional spectral information - and properly processing the two information streams has the potential to provide valuable information in night and/or poor visibility conditions (Park et al., 2008).

In a review of video surveillance and sensor networks research (Cucchiara, 2005), it is said that the integration or fusion of video technology with sensors and other media streams will constitute the fundamental infrastructure for new generations of multimedia surveillance systems. Also reviewing surveillance research (Hu et al., 2004), it is worth to note on future developments in surveillance that surveillance using multiple different sensors seems to be a very interesting subject. Moreover, image fusion in multi-sensors has two advantages. First, multi-sensor image has inherent redundancy for each sensor because it can be fused each image from a various multi sensor. Second, multi-sensor differs from a single sensor because it is included information of each sensor and is separated information of object easily in real environments. The main problem is how to make use of their respective merits and fuse information from such kinds of sensors.
The challenge remains whether using stationary or moving imagery system. This is due to a number of key factors like lighting changes (shadow vs. sunny day, indoor/night vs. outdoor), cluttered backgrounds (trees, vehicles, animals), artificial appearances (clothing, portable objects), non-rigid kinematics of pedestrians, camera and object motions, depth and scale changes (child vs. adult), and low video resolution and image quality. In this chapter, we shall propose a new approach to person detection that combines both thermal and visible information and subsequently models the motion in the scene using the multi-slit method and movement of Gravity Center (GC) patterns. Example images are shown in Figure 2 (Alex et al., 2007).

Fig. 2. Thermal image of the scene (left), visual image of the same scene (right)

To be specific, we shall briefly describe the problems, motivation, approach, challenges, and applications as follows.

1.1 Problems

The detection of the moving persons has become more and more important over the past few years. Numerous applications in the area of security and surveillance are emerging. The objective of this chapter is to develop a new prototype system which combines an IR and visible sensor to enable the detection and surveillance of pedestrians over a period of time. More specifically, we will focus the problems in an environment where pedestrians are moving in a range of specified distances within an area affected by various lighting and atmospheric conditions.

1.2 Motivation

The addition of an IR sensor will provide information which complements the images obtained in the visible range. Visible images offer a rich content where the detection of people can however be limited by a change in lighting conditions. IR images generally allow a better contrast to be obtained between a person and the environment, but these images are not as robust to changes in temperature and wind conditions. An intelligent fusion of the information provided by both sensors could reduce false alarms and the advent of non detected pedestrians, thereby increasing the performance of a pedestrian detection and surveillance system.

1.3 Approach

The detection of pedestrians is a process involving several interdependent steps. The quality of the steps involving data acquisition, locating zones of movement, classification and monitoring over time is crucial for a more robust detection. Data acquisition requires the constitution of a database which combines sequences of visible and IR images obtained under difference climatic and lighting conditions. The extraction of each region of interest makes use of movement and is carried out independently for each sequence. A new methodology for matching of the nominated regions of interest is developed using multi-slits method and GC movement patterns .Finally, for the step involving the classification, critical parameters indicating the presence of people are determined on the basis of characteristics such as temperature, geometry and ratios compared to the rest of the environment.

1.4 Challenges

The detection and tracking of people in interior and exterior environments involves numerous challenges. Systems treating the detection of people already exist in the Computer Vision and Systems Laboratory and perform well for visible images (extraction of regions of interest, geometric calibration). One of the challenges is to adapt these systems for the treatment of IR images. Then, the respective limitations of the two sensors must be clearly identified so as to extract the complementary information. The greatest challenge involves the development of a method of intelligent fusion which will enable the robustness of human detection to be improved while reducing false alarms and the advent of non detected pedestrians. In this chapter, we will make some significant contributions to tackle these challenges.

1.5 Applications

The applications of a visible sensor for pedestrian detection and monitoring are already numerous and can be applied to many public areas such as airports, train stations ,shopping malls, parking lots, and etc.. With the addition of an IR sensor, these systems will become more robust and will be able to function under varying lighting and climatic conditions, both day and night, in summer as well as in winter.

2. Fusion of infrared and visible images

In many modern multi-sensor systems, fusion algorithms significantly reduce the amount of raw data that needs to be presented or processed without loss of information content as well as provide an effective way of information integration. Over the years there has been numerous image fusion algorithms developed to address the growing need for image fusion. The algorithms can be roughly divided into two groups; Multi-Scale-Decomposition

(MSD)-based fusion methods, and Non-Multi-Scale-Decomposition (NMSD)-based fusion methods (Blum, 2006). The basic idea of a MSD based fusion method is that a multi-scale transform is performed on the source images, and then a composite multi-scale representation of these images is constructed based on a predetermined selection rule. The fused image is obtained by taking the inverse of the original multi-scale transform. The most common MSD methods include pyramid transforms and Wavelet Transforms (WT). All NMSD are not based on multi-scale transforms. Most common NMSD fusion methods include, Principal Component Analysis (PCA), Weighted Average technique, Estimation Theory methods, and Artificial Neural Networks.

Image fusion techniques can also be classified based on the level of processing where the fusion takes place (Hall, 2001). There are three main levels where image fusion may take place and they include:

- Pixel Level,
- Feature Level and
- Decision Level.

Universal fusion system structure that illustrates them is shown in Figure 3.

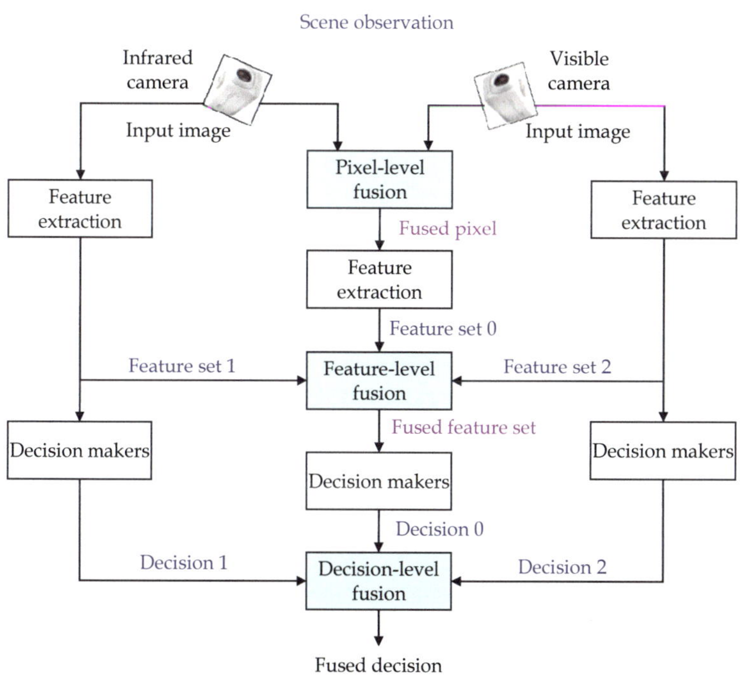

Fig. 3. Universal fusion system architecture

Main difference between the levels is in the amount of processing that is performed on the image prior to fusion and hence the format in which this information is fused and the type of fusion techniques applied. The information is captured from an observation of the scene by the sensors, which present it to the system in form of two digital image signals (Input Images). These images can be combined directly (pixel-level fusion) into a fused image that represents the information present in the input images in a single signal. Alternatively, input images (and potentially the fused) can be processed (e.g. edge detection, segmentation) to extract information about the basic features present in them. This information is of a more descriptive nature and can be combined from all cues into a single feature description set (fused feature set) by applying feature-level fusion techniques. This information then forms a basis for reaching decisions about (evaluating) the observed scene. Local decision makers produce probabilistic inferences about the scene from the feature sets provided by the lower level and these can be fused using decision level fusion techniques into a final evaluation (of the state) of the observed scene. This structure is important in the context of the concepts presented in this chapter since it illustrates well the one directional flow of information to obtain a more reliable and visually acceptable fused image.

2.1 Pixel level image fusion

Image fusion at the pixel level means fusion at the lowest processing level referring to the merging of the physical parameters of the source images. Among the three fusion levels, pixel level fusion is the most mature and encompasses the majority of image fusion algorithms in the literature today. Figure 4 illustrates a schematic of pixel level fusion process.

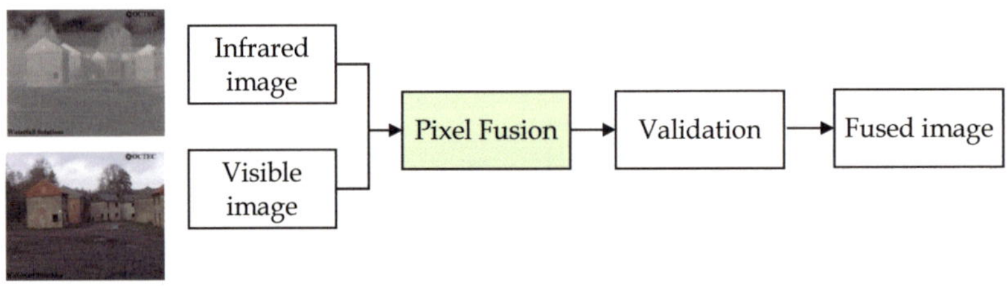

Fig. 4. A schematic of pixel level fusion process

All input images are aligned first and then the algorithm is performed across the pixels of all the input images. Therefore, to perform pixel level fusion all input images need to be spatially registered exactly to all other input images, so that all pixel positions of all the input images correspond to the same location in the real world. There can be some generic requirements imposed on the fusion result from pixel level fusion:

- The fusion process should preserve all relevant information on the input imagery in the composite image (pattern conservation);
- The fusion scheme should not introduce any inconsistencies which would distract the human observer or following processing stages and
- The fusion scheme should be shift and rotational invariant, i.e. the fusion result should not depend on the location or orientation of an object in the input imagery.

The most common pixel level fusion algorithms are (i) a simple averaging technique, (ii) principle components analysis, (iii) pyramid fusion schemes and (iv)wavelet transforms (Discrete Wavelet Transform and Shift Invariant Discrete Wavelet Transform) etc.

2.2 Feature level image fusion

Feature level methods are the next stage of processing where image fusion may take place. Fusion at the feature level requires extraction of objects (features) from the input images. These features are then combined with the similar features present in the other input images through a predetermined selection process to form the final fused image. Since, one of the essential goals of fusion is to preserve the image features, feature level methods have the ability to yield subjectively better fused images than pixel based techniques (Samadzadegan, 2004). Common algorithms that fuse images at the feature level include edge detection methods and artificial neural networks. Figure 5 illustrates a schematic of feature level fusion process.

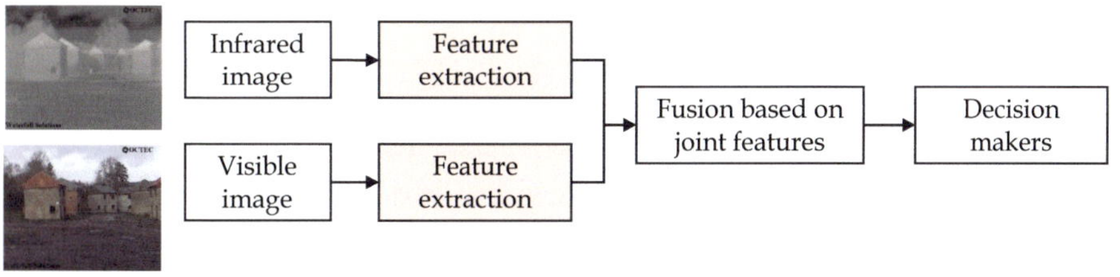

Fig. 5. A schematic of feature level fusion process

2.3 Decision level image fusion

Decision level methods are at the highest level of processing where image fusion can take place. Fusion at the Decision level takes Feature level fusion one step further by declaring identities to the objects recognized, by the individual input images, and then assigning a quality measure to the extracted features - See Figure 6. The obtained information is then combined by applying decision rules to reinforce common interpretation and resolve differences of the observed objects.

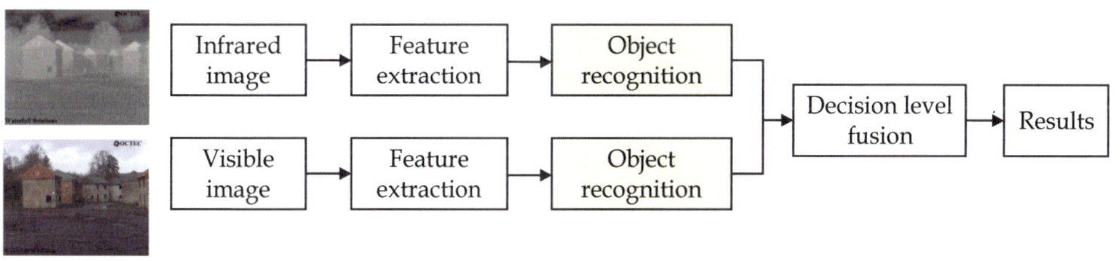

Fig. 6. A schematic of decision level fusion process

Due to fact that decision level fusion methods rely on the object recognition by all sensors in order to produce a valid representation of the input images, if an object is not recognized by all the sensors (via input images) then the output image will not utilize the full benefits of image fusion (Gunatilaka & Baertlein, 2001). Decision level fusion also creates another source of possible error when compared to the other fusion levels. If there is an error in recognition of objects from one of the sensors this error will be transferred to the output fused image. Some common algorithms used in decision level fusion include Fuzzy Logic, Rule-based Fusion, and Bayesian Networks.

2.4 Fusion evaluation methods

The ultimate aim of image fusion is to create a faithful and composite image that retains the important information from the source images while minimizing the noise caused by fusing the images. For the application, these images will be typically viewed and interpreted (perceived) by an operator. A number of evaluation approaches and metrics have been proposed to quantify and qualify image fusion performance: Fusion performance has been investigated using subjective and objective approaches.

2.4.1 Subjective evaluation approaches

Two basic subjective evaluation approaches were noted in the literature, active or task related (quantitative) and descriptive (qualitative). Quantitative approaches were utilized by (Toet, 2001), (Dixon, 2006) where subjects assessed different fusion approaches on target detection and recognition, as well as subject perception of situational awareness. Quantitative fusion assessment has focused on the target detection, recognition and situational awareness. Target detection and recognition assessment has been assessed in naturalistic and in laboratory settings. By their nature, real time assessments are difficult to duplicate, instead most fusion assessment experiments have focused on the capture of still or live video of targets in operational settings. The fusion community has captured and shared a number of multi-spectra reference images for algorithm development and assessment. In addition to quantitative subjective tests, a large number of qualitative evaluations have been undertaken to rate or rank the quality of fusion images evaluated both target detection performance and fused image quality generated from four fusion approaches. A variety of scales and methods have been used to evaluate the quality of fusion images, typically a subject is asked to rank or rate the quality of the image on a linear or ordinal scale. Three approaches are discussed in the literature (Petrovic, 2007), (Chen & Varshney, 2005) simple ranking, Single Stimulus Continuous Quality Evaluation (SSCQE) and Double Stimulus Continuous Quality Evaluation (DSCQE).

2.4.2 Objective evaluation approaches

Objective measures utilize input images and the fusion image to develop a numerical score of the success of the fusion process (Petrovic, 2007). And unlike subjective assessments which have significant organizational and logistic requirements, objective measures can be computed automatically. Objective metrics have also been developed to assess fusion performance. Unlike traditional image quality metrics which use a "ground truth" image, ideal fusion images are not available. Adjusting fusion filter bands, decomposition levels, weighting parameters, window sizes, etc. will affect fusion performance.

A large number of objective measures have been proposed to evaluate fusion performance, these include Root Mean Square Error (RMSE), Image Quality (QW), Fusion Quality Measure (Q) to name a few. The objective measure can be classified into four categories:

- Methods based on statistical characteristics,
- Methods based on definition,
- Methods based on information theory and
- Methods based on important features.

For image fusion, researchers have suggested a variety of objective measures to assess the success of the fusion. Ideally the researcher has developed a theory upon which to base the validity of their measure (theoretical constructs). Construct validity is the assessment of how well the researcher translated their theories into actual measures. The limited review of the literature did not identify theoretical constructs for many of the older statistical objective measures. Given the limitations of simple metrics, researchers have focused on developing metrics based on information theory and human perception (important features). Moreover, leading investigators in the image fusion community have indicated that they are now or soon will be, investigating task-specific fusion performance and the characterization of video fusion performance. The timing of the proposed fusion study in this chapter is thus occurring at an opportune time.

3. Potential applications of image fusion in surveillance

The objective of this section is to present a new robust pedestrian detection and tracking system which will exploit the information provided by a visible spectrum sensor and an IR sensor, while functioning within a complex environment. To-date, few detection and tracking systems have made use of IR information to track people (Xu & Fujimura, 2002). However, many researchers have addressed the same task using the visible part of the spectrum (Thi Thi Zin, 2009). The addition of an IR sensor will provide information which complements that obtained with visible images. The latter offer a rich content where the detection of pedestrians can however be limited by a change in lighting conditions. IR images generally enable a better contrast to be achieved between the pedestrian and his environment, but they are less robust to temperature and wind changes. Exploiting the complementary information obtained and improving the precision and robustness of tracking requires the development of an efficient technique allowing the fusion of this complementary information.

Fusion of visible and IR information can be done at different levels in the image processing. Sensor fusion has become an increasingly important direction in computer vision and in particular human detection and tracking systems in recent years. In this section, we have considered a strategy where information from both channels is fused at the highest level. Obviously, the main part of the work concerns image processing. An important hypothesis is that cameras do not move during the recording of one given sequence. Figure 7 presents the overall image processing algorithm. After the image acquisition, moving regions are extracted with a newly developed background subtraction algorithm. Detection processing is performed at two levels: blob and object.

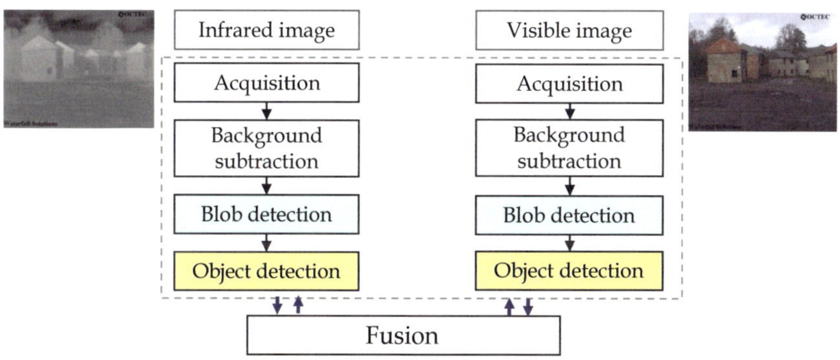

Fig. 7. Image processing flowchart

3.1 Two-level detection process

The algorithms of the first segmentation often provide data where the people are detected in the form of several blobs surrounded by noise and lacking certain body parts. The detection algorithm presented here supports the incomplete and noisy data provided by the first segmentation. In order to do this, the processing is continued on two levels. While the first level of the algorithm consists in following the blobs in an image sequence (both visible and IR), the second level builds on the first and tracks a combination of one or more blobs, i.e. objects. The output results of this two level processing can illustratively described as shown in Figure 8.

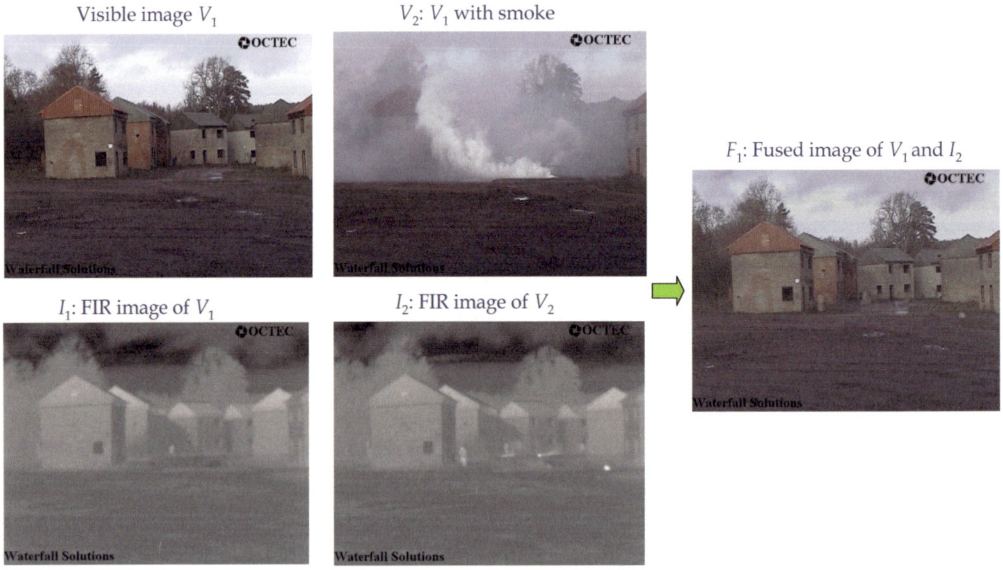

Fig. 8. Image fusion for visibility improvement (Source of image: http://www.imagefusion.org)

3.2 Robust person detection in far infrared images

Here, we propose two novel methods for robust person detection in Far Infrared (FIR) images. The first one is a generalized method to be branded as a multi-slit method for person detection with various standing postures at near and far distances. It is based on body parts detection by using multi-slits to extract head region. Among many things, the special feature of this multi-slit method using only a single camera is a key component and provides monocular vision. This is a significant and advantageous step to move forward for advances in person detection while other existing methods use more than one camera for stereo vision. In our method, the combined approach of multi-slits with vanishing line is also a new concept. The second one is a simplified method that is very useful at near distances which is a sequential decision method using GC movement patterns. Moreover, the simplified method makes a significant progress in differentiating person and non-person in almost all environments. This is due to the use of GC movement patterns which has been never seen in the existing literature. In both methods, we focus on a single frame person detection algorithm using step-by-step approach. Figure 9 shows two proposed methods.

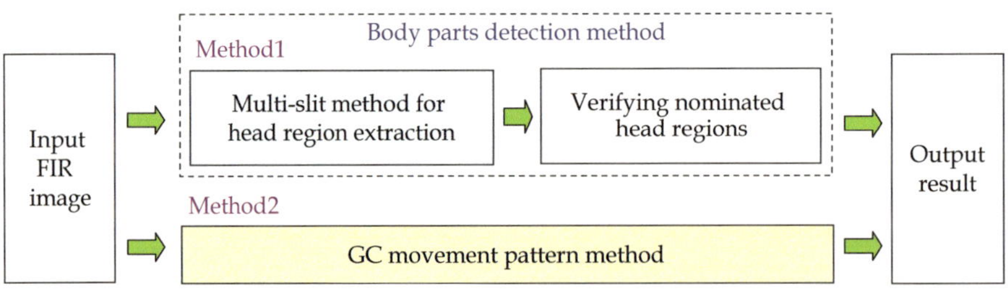

Fig. 9. Two novel methods for person detection

3.2.1 Multi-slit method using vanishing line

This method consists of two major steps: (i) extracting head nominators by multi-slits and (ii) verifying nominated head regions. The multi-slit method utilizes y-position of vanishing line as the scale factor. The block diagram is shown in Figure 10(a).

3.2.2 Extracting head nominators by multi-slit method

Each horizontal slit with height $h(d)$ for a distance d is considered, for example, d = 5m, 6m, 7m, ... Our method can determine the position and height of each slit from the vanishing line in an input FIR image. This aspect is shown in Figure 10(b). For distance d, we use the following parameters which are the coordinates on an input FIR image.

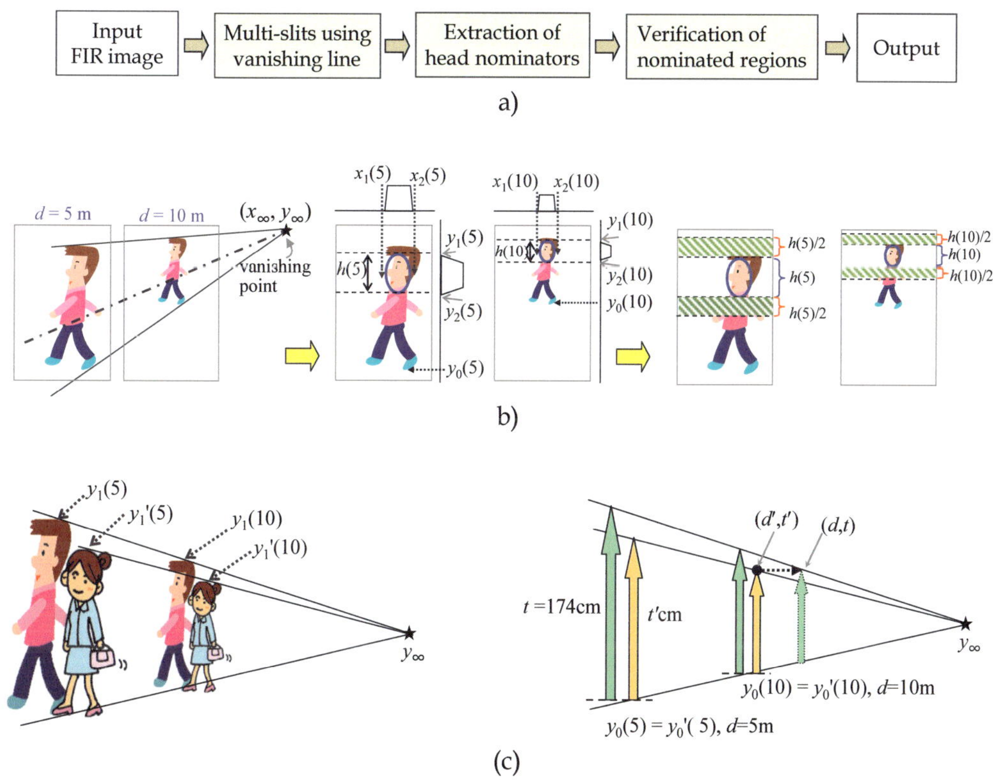

Fig. 10. Multi-slit method: (a) block diagram, (b) multi-slits using vanishing line, (c) relation between $y_i(d)$ and $y_i'(d)$, i = 0,1

$x_1(d)$ and $x_2(d)$: x-positions of left and right side of head, respectively,
$y_0(d)$: y-position of ground level,
$y_1(d)$, and $y_2(d)$: y-positions of top and bottom of a head (a matched slit for a distance d),
y_∞: y-position of vanishing line.

For reference, we adopt a person 174cm tall standing at a distance of 5m. The parameters $x_1(5)$, $x_2(5)$, $y_0(5)$, $y_1(5)$, $y_2(5)$, and y_∞ are manually obtained:

$$x_1(5)=331,\ x_2(5)=362,\ y_0(5)=341,\ y_1(5)=102,\ y_2(5)=140, \text{ and } y_\infty=195.$$

If the camera position and angle are not changed, then it is not necessary to update them. Under perspective projection, we can obtain the following equation for a distance d:

$$y_i(d) = y_\infty + 5\,(y_i(5) - y_\infty)/d, \quad i=0,1,2, \tag{1}$$

when $y_i(d) \neq y_\infty$, we get

$$d = 5\left(\frac{y_i(5) - y_\infty}{y_i(d) - y_\infty}\right). \tag{2}$$

The above equation means that distance d can be computed after getting $y_i(d)$ by monocular camera. In our experiments, $y_1(d)$ and $y_2(d)$ are used, and $y_0(d)$ is not used. If a head is detected at a distance d using these reference parameters, we can consider a person t' cm tall standing at a distance d' instead of a person 174cm tall standing at a distance d, for t' and d' which satisfy the following conditions.

$$\frac{t'}{t} = \frac{y_i'(5) - y_0'(5)}{y_i(5) - y_0(5)} = \frac{y_i'(d) - y_0'(d)}{y_i(d) - y_0(d)}, \; t = 174, \; i = 1,2. \tag{3}$$

Thus,

$$y_i'(5) = t'/t\,(y_i(5) - y_0(5)) + y_0'(5) = t'/t\,(y_i(5) - y_0(5)) + y_0(5), \tag{4}$$

where $y_0(d) = y_0'(d)$, and $y_i(d)$ and $y_i'(d)$ are y-positions of persons 174cm and t'cm tall at a distance d, respectively. It is noted that the distance between the camera and a person with height 174cm can be computed by Eq.(2), but some error is caused for a person with different height t'cm. From Eq.(1), we obtain

$$y_i'(d') = y_\infty + 5\left(y_i'(5) - y_\infty\right) / d'. \tag{5}$$

Setting $y_i'(d') = y_i(d)$ in Eq.(1) and Eq.(5) and substituting Eq.(4), we obtain

$$d = d'\left(\frac{y_i(5) - y_\infty}{y_i'(5) - y_\infty}\right) = d'\left(\frac{t(y_i(5) - y_\infty)}{t(y_0(5) - y_\infty) + t'(y_i(5) - y_0(5))}\right) \tag{6}$$

This means that it is possible to find a person t' cm tall standing at a distance d' m using data of a person 174cm tall standing at a distance dm as long as Eq.(6) is satisfied. If $y_0(d)$ or "$y_1(d)$ and $y_2(d)$" is obtained with satisfactory accuracy, then the distance d' and the height t' are uniquely determined. But it is not straightforward calculation in practice because of using low resolution images. For simplicity, here we suppose $t'/t \approx \left(y'(d) - y_\infty\right)/\left(y_1(d) - y_\infty\right)$.

We can extract head regions from vertical histogram (summation of pixel values) within each slit. Then to find the Local Maximum (LM) of the vertical histogram, some operations using morphological dilations with line shape Structuring Element (SE) are applied. Dilation D_j using SE_j are defined as:

$$D_j = SE_j \oplus V, \;\; j = 1, 2, \tag{7}$$

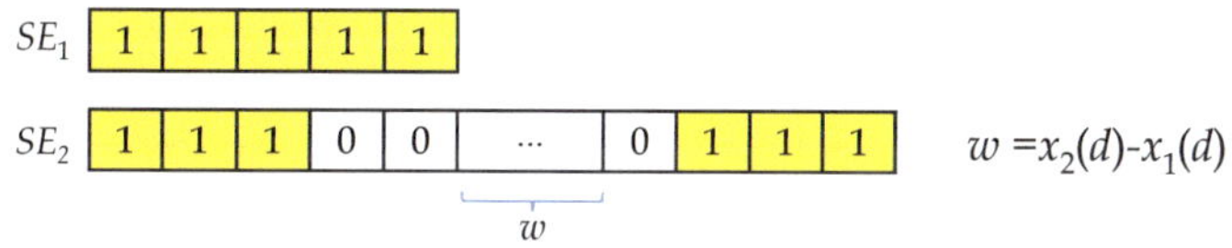

where V is the vertical histogram of the slit and $\oplus$ is morphological dilation. We can extract nominated head regions from D_1-D_2 by thresholding using Th_1. An example is shown in Figure 11 (a-i, a-ii, a-iii).

In the next step, we set two slits with height $h/2$ at both upper and lower sides of the original slit with height h, as shown in Figure 11(b-i). In Figure 11(b-ii), we then compute V-V_u-V_l, where V_u and V_l are the vertical histograms of the upper and lower slits, respectively. By using some thresholds, the system nominates the head region from Figure 11(a-iii, b-ii), as shown in Figure 11 (c). One can see that this method is very simple, robust, effective, and does not require any complex computational procedures. Moreover, this method can extract not only the person head, but also can give approximate distance from the camera position, that is, where and how tall the person is.

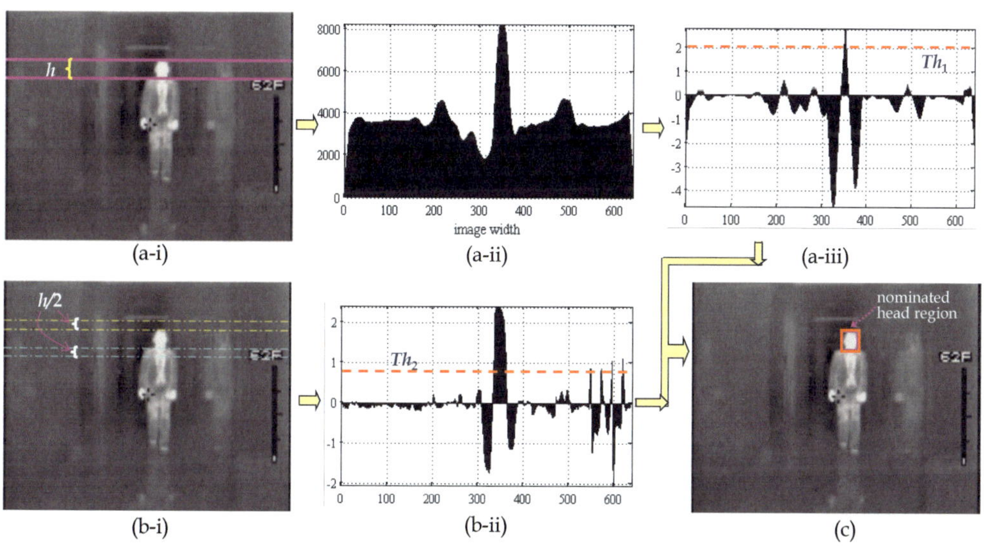

Fig. 11. Head region extraction by multi-slit method: (a-i) original slit for 5m distance with height h, (a-ii) vertical histogram V for the slit, (a-iii) LM from D_1-D_2, (b-i) two slits with height $h/2$ in both upper and lower sides of the original slit, (b-ii) V-V_u-V_l, and (c) nominated head region

3.2.3 Verifying nominated head regions

For each nominated region, the person body and legs region are roughly estimated. To verify and segment person regions, the system will check whether or not the following conditions are satisfied.

1. The values m_1 and m_2 of LMB and LML must be higher than a predetermined threshold, i.e. $m_1 > Th$, $m_2 > Th$, where LMB and LML are LM of histogram of body and legs region, respectively.

2. $1.2\,w_h < w_b < 3\,w_h$, where w_b and w_h are widths of body and head regions, respectively.
3. two x-positions of LMB and LML: one must be in the left side of the center of head region, another in the right side.

Although the conditions are defined as a whole, they are used as conditions for body detection and legs detection separately. The roughly estimated rectangular regions are determined as a person body and legs when all conditions for both body and legs are satisfied. But, if all conditions for body or legs only are satisfied, then we will say that a person is detected. These aspects are illustrated in Figure 12(a). In Figure 12(b), one example of correct nominator is shown. The proposed algorithm is able to detect person regions for various standing poses at near and far distances.

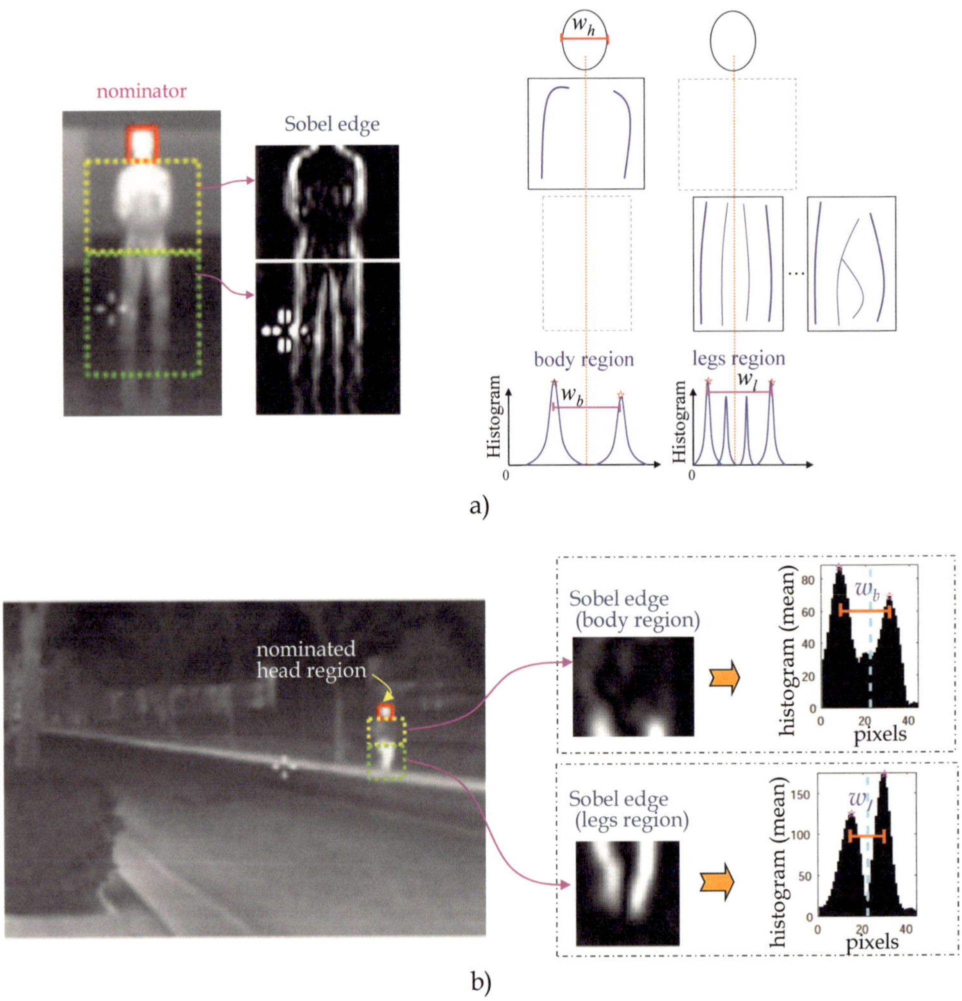

Fig. 12. Head Verification using histograms of body and legs regions: (a) Illustration of body and legs region, (b) example of correct nominator

3.3 Method using GC movement patterns

In this section, we present a person detection method using GC movement patterns which can segment by using appropriate threshold and differentiate human and other objects from the inputs. This approach based on sequential decision process. The GCs of enlarging connected regions have special movement patterns, if they are real head regions. By a binarized image using an appropriate threshold Th_l being changed in descending order, the regions are obtained. So, the regions become larger and larger. These aspects are shown in Figure 13. The GC movement patterns on each connected region for person are absolutely different from the others (non-person). This fact is the key point of our approach. More precisely, the GC of person moves slowly downward from the head regions and then goes to the legs region rapidly after passing body region. Finally, the regions spread widely including surrounding areas. In Figure 13(d), the red one is person region. Since this method utilizes the GC movement patterns, it is able to recognize the gradual changes which occur only in human body parts. Thus, this method can differentiate significantly human head region and artificially made human-like head region as shown in Figure 14.
Generally, the temperature of person regions is higher than that of the environment and their heat radiation is sufficiently high compared to the background. Therefore FIR imagery is particularly suited to person localization. Obviously, other objects that actively radiate heat, such as automobiles, trucks, busses, and motorcycles, heater, table lamp, have a similar behavior. But, our simplified approach demonstrates to be able to differentiate person and non-person from the GC movement patterns.

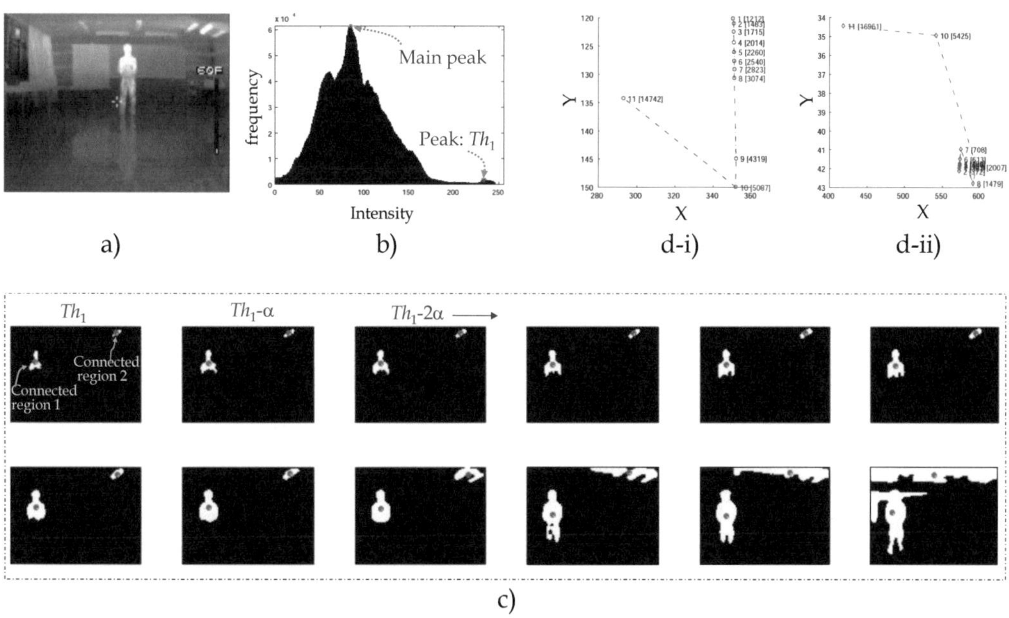

Fig. 13. GC movement pattern method: (a) input image, (b) smoothed histogram, (c) thresholding (thresholds are changing in descending order), (d-i) GC movement pattern (a person), and (d-ii) GC movement pattern (heater: non-person)

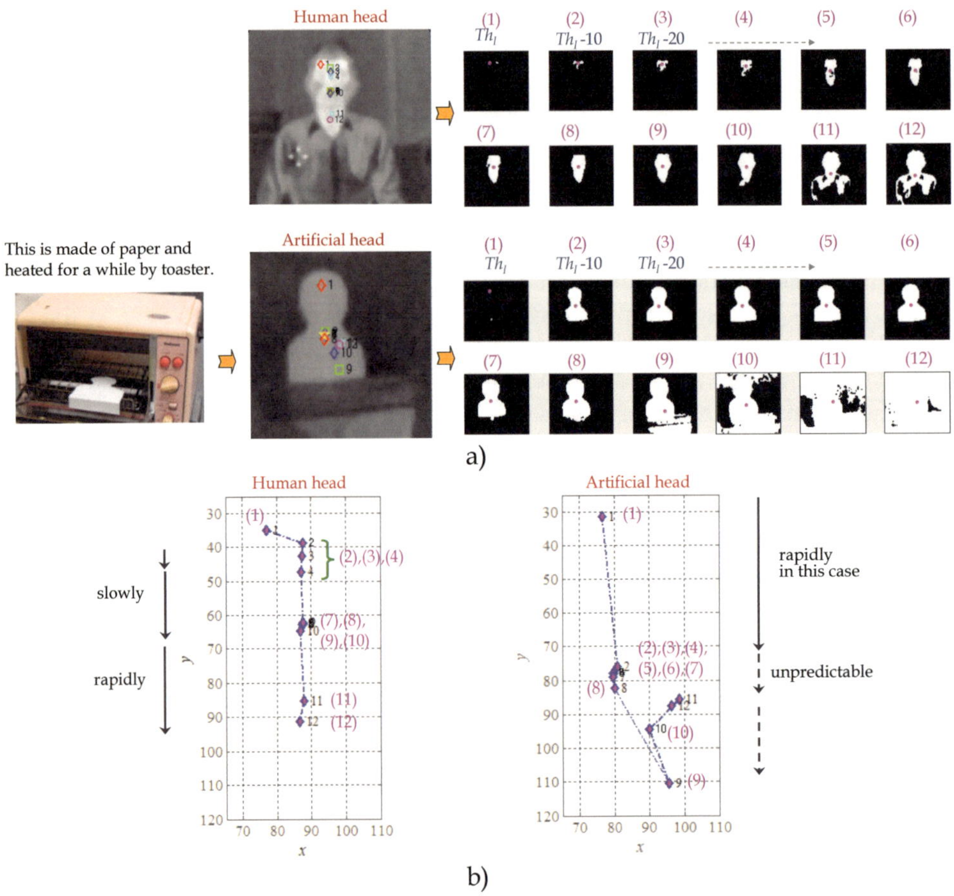

Fig. 14. Comparison of human head and artificial head: (a) enlarged regions due to changing threshold, (b) comparison of GC movement patterns

3.4 Image fusion algorithm for person detection

The fusion or merging algorithm improves the precision of the size and position of the predicted or nominated area computed during the first level processing. It is driven by three goals. The first one consists in establishing a correspondence between the objects detected in the visible and the IR images. For each pair of objects, the identification of the best object detected (in visible or IR images) describes our second goal. The objects with the best detection are called *master* and the second one *slave*. The confidence is used as a criterion for better detection and is computed for all the objects of each frame in the sequence. In this manner the identification of the master and the slave will change rapidly for an object when fast light illumination or temperature variation is present. Our last goal consists in using the information of the *master* object to help in tracking the *slave* one. The merging process is done independently for each pair of objects. For example, if at time t, three objects can be detected in the visible and IR images, two objects can be *master* in the IR image, and one object can be a *master* in the visible image. The merging algorithm has to determine situations where the position and the size of the predicted area need to be modified. These situations only occur when a great difference between the primitive area of the master object

and the slave object is detected. In this case we enter in the "enslavement" mode where the *master* predicted area controls the *slave* predicted area. For example, if a pedestrian has a green T-shirt and walks in front of a green hedge, this person's trunk will tend to disappear and the *slave* object will be put in the enslavement mode. The IR object will maintain a good detection and will help in tracking the pedestrian in the visible image because the body temperature is higher than the temperature of the green hedge.
The fusion algorithm is very useful in cases where two objects disappear and will allow objects to stay present in the system and allow the position of the predictive area to be assessed using the mean speed of the predictive area in the last frame. For example, if a pedestrian passes behind a tree, the objects will disappear in both images. If the pedestrian maintains his speed and direction, the object will be recovered when it appears on the other side of the tree. But, if the pedestrian stopped behind the tree and returns to the same side, the algorithm will create a new object.

3.4.1 Multi-slit HOG fusion innovation

In addition to general fusion approach, we shall explore a new hybrid-based feature level fusion method to fuse multi-slit features and Histograms of Oriented Gradients (HOG) features for pedestrian detection from Near Infrared (NIR) images. The fused feature set utilizes both the multi-slit method's capability of accurately capturing the local spatial layout of body parts (head, torso, and legs) in individual frames and the HOG's capability in region information relevant to higher frequency components. The hybrid feature vector describing various types of poses is then constructed and used for detecting the pedestrians. The part based pattern matching analysis indicates that the fused features have much higher feature space separation than the pure features. Experiments with a database of NIR images show that proposed method achieves a substantial improvement in tackling some difficult cases such as side view, back view which the conventional HOG method cannot handle. Detection and recognition performance is less computationally expensive than existing approaches. Specifically, an overview of our fusion method is described as shown in Figure 15.

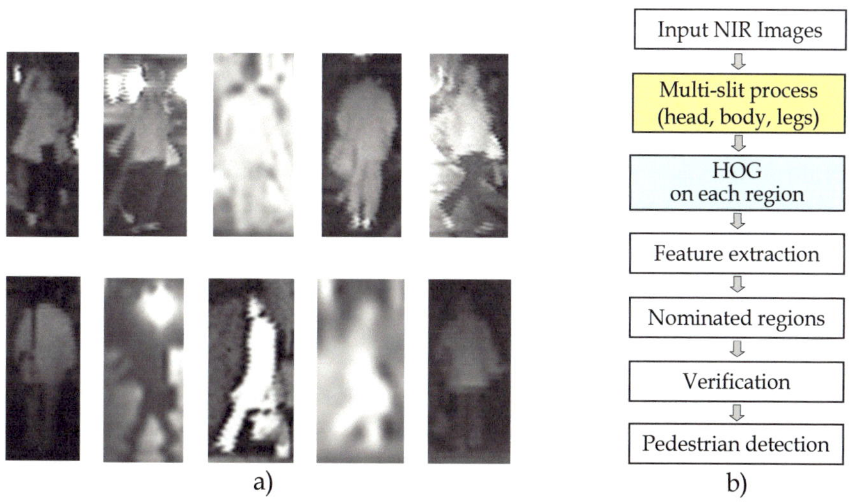

Fig. 15. Multi-slit HOG Fusion: (a) various poses of pedestrians, (b) system overview

The basic idea is that local object appearance and shape can often be characterized rather well by the distribution of local intensity gradients or edge directions, even without precise knowledge of the corresponding gradient or edge positions. In our system, these appearances will be described in a series of multi-slits for head, torso, and legs regions. The corresponding regions are extracted based on the properties of coplanar plane structures and distances. More precisely, vanishing line concepts are to be used for these purposes. We then divide the multi-slit into small spatial regions (cells), for each cell accumulating histogram of gradient directions or orientations over the pixels of the cell. The combined histogram entries form the representation. For better invariance to illumination, shadowing, etc., it is also useful to contrast-normalize the local responses before using them. This can be done by accumulating a measure of local histogram energy over somewhat larger spatial regions (blocks) and using the results to normalize all of the cells in the block. We will refer to the normalized descriptor blocks as Multi-slit HOG descriptors. The use of orientation histograms has been developed in many aspects, but it can only be reached maturity when combined with local spatial histograms and normalization in multi-slit approach to wide baseline image matching. So far our experiments show that even the best current approaches are likely to have false positive rates higher than our Multi-slit HOG approach for pedestrian detection.

The procedure for the complete system starts detecting people in images by selecting a suitable sub-window from the top left corner of the image as an input for head, the second sub-window of different size for torso and the third for legs. These inputs are then independently classified by appropriate similarity measure as either a respective body parts or a non-body part and finally those are fused into a proper geometrical configuration in a full window as a person. All of these nominated regions are processed by the respective component features to find the strongest candidate components. The component detectors process the candidate regions by applying the modified HOG features and then these features become fusion data vector for respective classifications.

In order to investigate the robustness and effectiveness of our proposed methods, experiments are carried out under various environments such as indoor, outdoor at daytime, outdoor at nighttime with distance variations. The results will be presented in the next section.

4. Experimental works and results

4.1 For FIR images

The algorithms described in the previous sections was tested on several sequences under various environments such as indoor, outdoor at daytime, outdoor at nighttime with distance variations. Input images are taken originally by FIR camera 3600 AS by L3 Co. Ltd.. The horizontal view angle is 50° and the image resolution is 160×120. In this experimental setting, the selection of parameters is quite general even though we have used a particular type of camera. However, it is worthwhile to point out that using the particular type of camera can not be considered as a. limitation of our methods. Higher resolution cameras with more acute view angle will increase the precision and recall rate at further distances. Since the original image is captured through NTSC (National Television Standards Committee), the digitized input image has the resolution 640×480. Some examples of head regions extracted by multi-slit method and our previous head shape-based method (Thi Thi Zin, 2007) for comparison are shown in Figure 16 and Figure 17, respectively.

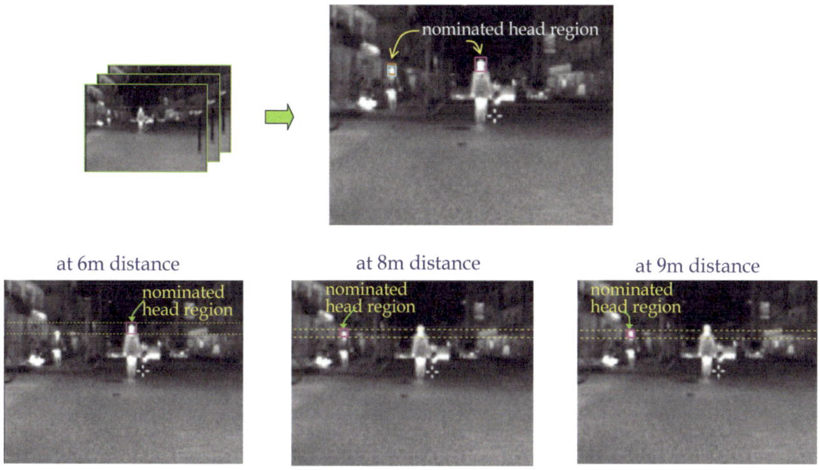

Fig. 16. Head regions extracted by multi-slit method at (6m, 8m, 9m) distances

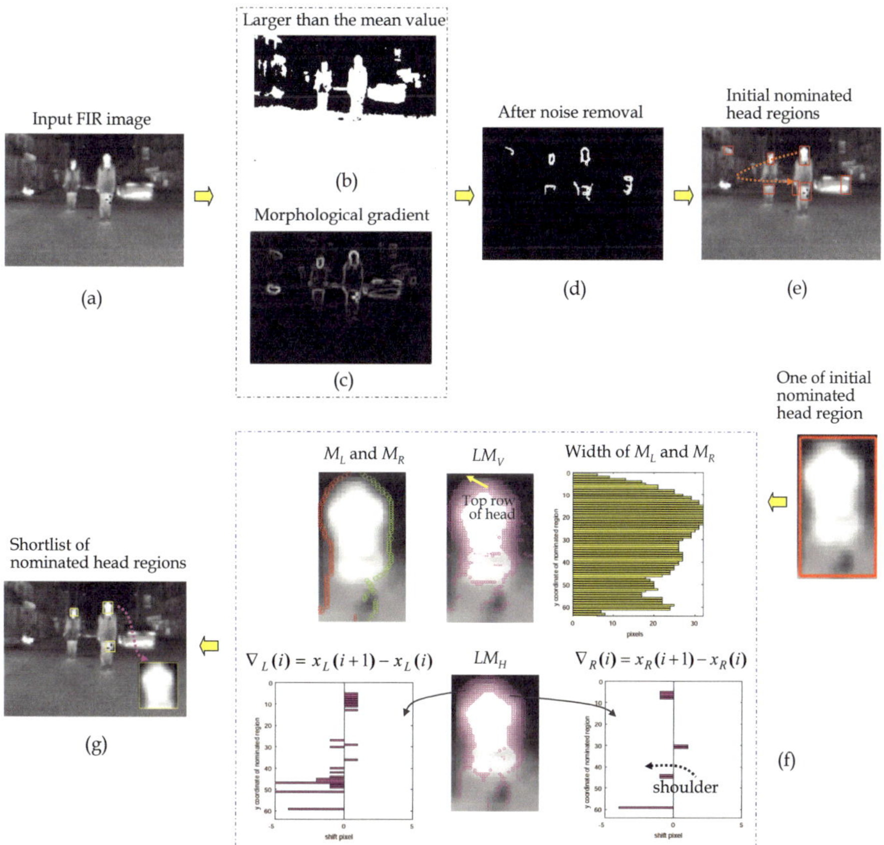

Fig. 17. Head regions extracted by head shape-based method: (a) input FIR image, (b) thresholding, (c) MG using disk shape SE, (d) after noise removal, (e) initial nominated regions, (f) narrow down process on initial nominators, and (g) shortlist of nominated head regions

Concerning with head region extraction, it would be appropriate to present a brief outlines of our previous head shape-based method. The initial nominators of head regions are extracted using the intensity information in the process of thresholding and Morphological Gradient (MG). The pixels larger than the mean value of the whole image region are shown with white pixels in Figure 17(b). Generally, person heads close to ellipse shape, so we adopt MG using disk shape SE shown in Figure 17(c). In Figure 17(e), the initial nominated head regions are described with red rectangles. Among the extracted initial nominators of head regions, the next process will remove the incorrect nominators as many as possible. Figure 17(f) shows the narrow down process on Sobel edge of each nominator. To confirm the performance of the proposed method, the experiments are conducted in outdoor and indoor scenes including various postures at near and far distances. Some of images used in our experiment are shown in Figure 18.

Fig. 18. Example of images used in our experiments

To compare the performance of two methods, the precision rate (the ratio of number of correct detected regions to the total number of detected regions) and recall rate (the ratio of number of correct detected regions to the number of relevant correct regions) are shown in Figure 19. For method using GC movement patterns, a variety of experiments have been carried out to show wide range of applications. We conduct experiments on standing and sitting postures in indoor and outdoor together with experiments to differentiate real and artificial heads. According to our experiments, this method is highly stable under various conditions and postures at near distances. The results based on various environments are summarized in Figure 20. From Figure 19 and Figure 20, under almost all conditions, multi-slit method gives so high precision rates that the noise removal and verification processes are virtually unnecessary. The precision rate and recall rate for head shape-based method can be increased when the complete three processes (stage1 through stage3), initial nominator extraction, noise removal, and verification are applied. As a result, the multi-slit method is more effective for person detection than head shape-based method. In addition, by multi-slit method, we can obtain the height of the detected person and the camera distance. The statement is also strengthened by calculations done from the geometrical point of view. Suppose that a person 174cm tall is standing at a distance 5m, the person with shorter height (say 165cm) standing at the same distance of 5m is detected at the distance of approximately 6m. This aspect is shown in Figure 21 with the relation between height and distance.

Here, it would be appropriate to make a few remarks on the input of FIR camera resolution. Nowadays, FIR cameras with image resolutions 320×240 and 640×480 are available at relatively low cost. Using such cameras with more acute view angle will increase the precision and recall rates at farther distances than 30m which we used in our experiment.

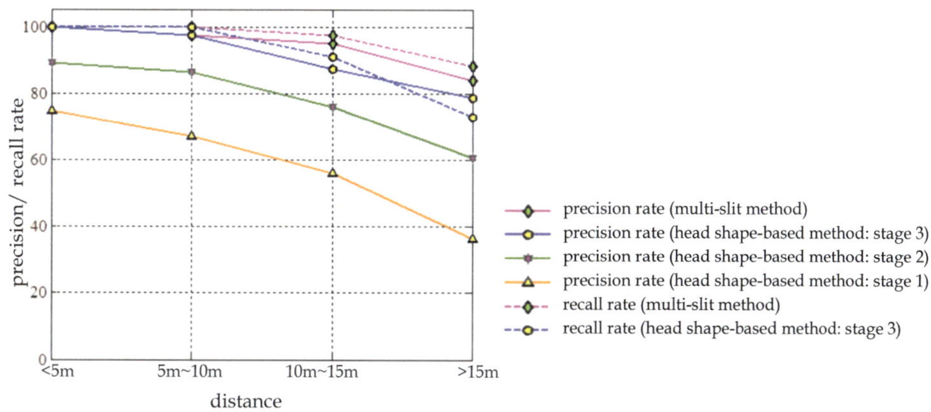

Fig. 19. Precision and recall rates based on distances for multi-slit and head shape-based methods

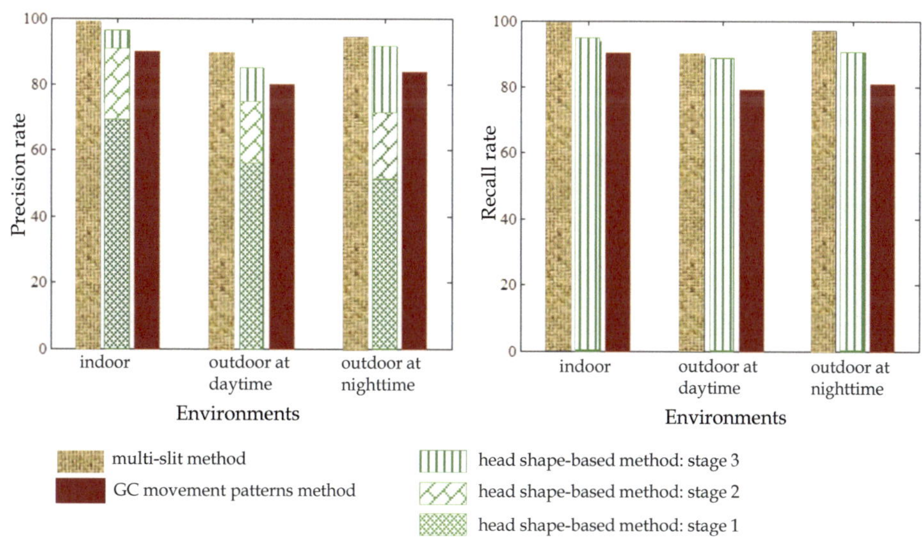

Fig. 20. Precision and recall rates based on environments for three methods

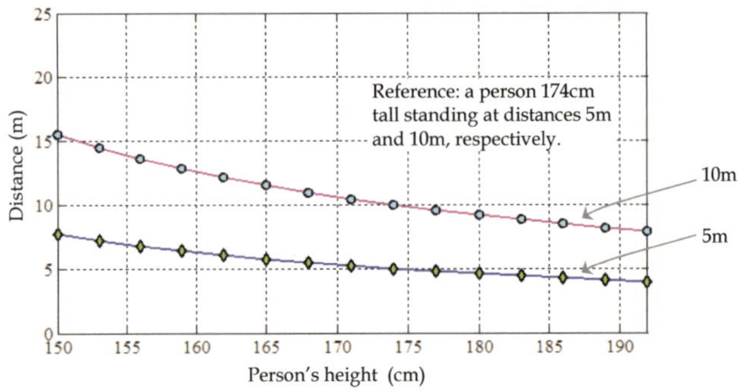

Fig. 21. The relation between person's height (cm) and distance (m)

4.2 For fused images

The fusion algorithms described in the previous sections was tested on several sequences. Various cases are illustrated in Figure 22 and Figure 23. It is obviously not possible to render the dynamics of these sequences in a paper and thus, some interesting situations were selected. In Figure 22, an indoor situation of multiple pedestrians standing in an office is presented. While the blob of one pedestrian is not well detected in visible image but it can be successfully detected in the IR image. In Figure 23 multiple outdoor pedestrians are shown where the blobs of some pedestrians at far distance are not well detected in visible images. It can be seen that those pedestrians are detected in the IR image. The fusion algorithm improved detection for the predicted area of this pedestrian.

4.2.1 Multi-slit HOG fusion experimental results

We tested our detector on the well-established pedestrian database, containing 4 types of training sets and 100 test images of pedestrians. It contains various views with a relatively wide range of poses. Our detectors give essentially perfect results on this data set, so we produced a new and significantly more challenging detector, Figure 24 shows some samples. The people are usually standing, but appear in any orientation and against a wide variety of background image including crowds. We have confirmed the effectiveness of our proposed method under difficult illumination such as the influence of flare and also various views of pedestrians including side view, back view, pedestrian carrying bag and so on.

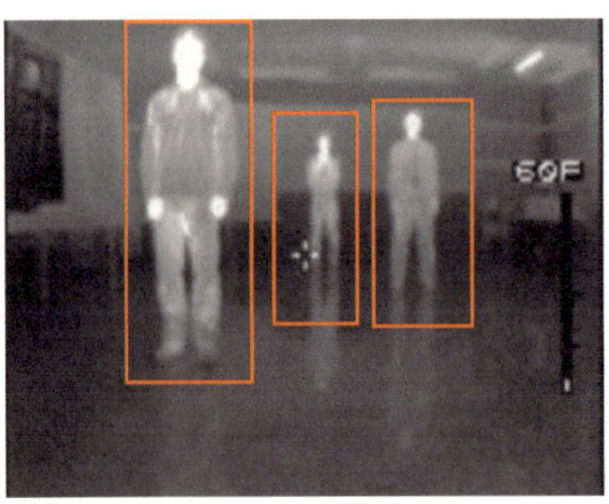

(a)

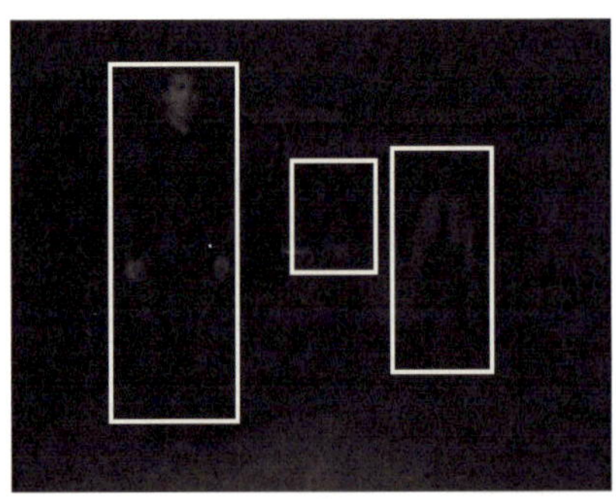

(b)

Fig. 22. Outdoor scene illustrating pedestrian extraction: (a, b) representation of the blob detected for both IR and visible images

(a) (b)

Fig. 23. Night scene showing pedestrian extraction: (a, b) representation of the blob detected for both IR and visible images

The people are usually standing, but appear in any orientation and against a wide variety of background image including crowds. We have confirmed the effectiveness of our proposed method under difficult illumination such as the influence of flare and also various views of pedestrians including side view, back view, pedestrian carrying bag and so on. Moreover, we can see that our fusion method (multi-slit & HOG) has better accuracy compared to HOG of the conventional method. With a false positive rate of one digit percentages, our method has 25% lower false negative rate than the HOG. This means that the appearance and spatiotemporal features are suitable for people detection.

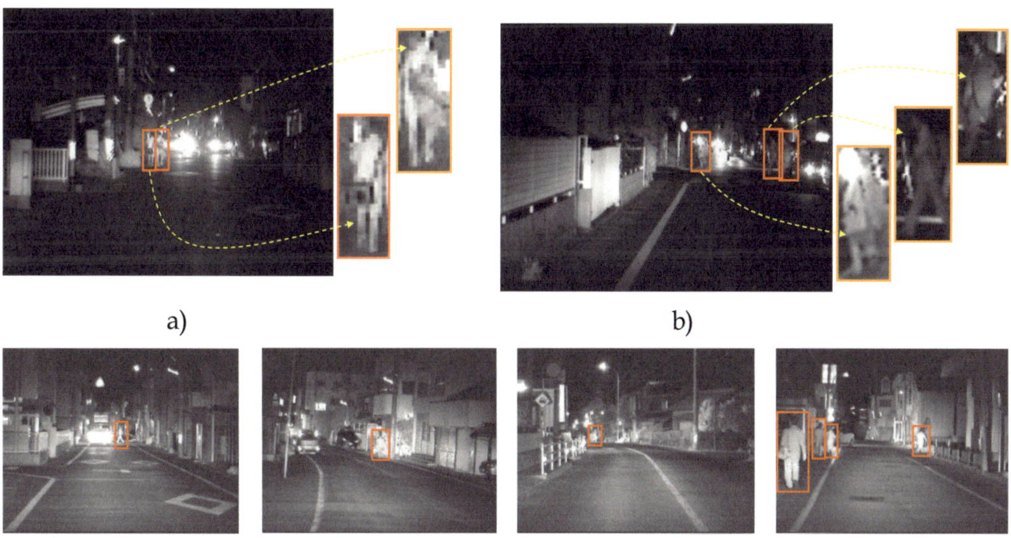

a) b) c) d) e) f)

Fig. 24. Example of detected pedestrians: (a) the image is influenced by flare and pedestrian with bags from back view, (b) pedestrians are in the dark and from side view, (c) side view pedestrian, (d) back view pedestrian, (e) pedestrian in far distance, and (f) multiple pedestrians

5. Conclusion and image fusion research challenges

In this chapter, we presented person detection methods in FIR images and outlined image fusion approach for person detection. The implementation has been done to detect near and faraway persons. Among the proposed methods, the multi-slit method is easy to apply and does not require any complex computational techniques for head region detection. Moreover, we can state that multi-slit method is more robust than head shape-based method. On the other hand, the GC movement patterns method can detect the targeted regions with high accuracy especially at near distances. In addition, this approach has versatile application for various poses. Moreover, it can differentiate person and non-person. It is worthwhile to note that these methods would lead to further steps for person detection research by using FIR images.

On the whole, through the proposed person detection methodology is by no means perfect for real world applications and it is still needed to further improve the detection performance. It has made much progress, considering the current research stages, and it presents encouraging results. Also, our approach collaborates with one another. Future work includes region-based image fusion for visibility improvement. The development of a visibility improvement is essential for poor vision at night, in bad weather, under smoke and so on. We also expect to consider for distance estimation of the person using FIR and visible images. Additional issues rise for future research widen application areas not only for night vision but also for finding people under smoke, flame, and for rescue at disaster site, and so on.

Therefore, horizon of our proposed person detection algorithm can be widen and applied to the tasks of region-based fusion method using FIR and visible images. In this aspect, both thermal infrared and visible spectrum video have some fundamental, as well as technological differences. In certain scenarios, one modality might have particular advantages over the other. The challenge, therefore, is to develop techniques to automatically decide on which modality is best to use at any one time, or how best to combine them to play on their strengths and allow them to compensate for each other's weaknesses.

Presently, visible spectrum technology is far more developed than thermal infrared, which has only recently come to the consumer market, after years of military development. Therefore visible spectrum cameras have a superior resolution to thermal cameras. The standard visible spectrum camera has roughly six times more pixels than a thermal camera. The visible spectrum allows robust tracking of objects using their color and texture, when there is good lighting.

However, there are many benefits to using thermal infrared. When an object has a temperature that is outside the background temperature distribution, it will have a very sharp edge around it in the thermal image. Thermal infrared video is also almost completely immune to lighting changes, as it depends primarily on emitted radiation. It can operate in total darkness when visible spectrum analysis would fail completely. The decimation/ saturation effect mentioned earlier can be very beneficial depending on the task at hand. If a segmentation mask is required, a simple thresholding of the thermal image can suffice.

Future work will focus on further development of both low-level algorithms for modality fusion in a computer vision system and the use of these algorithms in an application. Low-level algorithms such as change-detection and segmentation have been extensively researched for single modality. The future challenge now is to understand how the current state-of the- art can be used to benefit multimodal analysis, or whether new algorithms and fusion techniques are necessary to fully exploit the extra benefits of multiple modalities. Research into whether current methods of representational fusion can benefit analytical fusion is also of interest. Finally, the use of these low-level techniques in an application, such as people detection and tracking, will be the true test of their usefulness.

6. References

Anjali Malviya; Bhirud, S. G. (2009). Image Fusion of Digital Images, *International Journal of Recent Trends in Engineering*, Vol. 2, No. 3, Nov. 2009, pp.146-148, ISSN 1797-9617

Bertozzi, M.; Broggi, A.; Grisleri, P.; Graf, T.; Meinecke, M. (2003). Pedestrian Detection in Infrared Images, *Proceedings of IEEE Intelligent Vehicles Symposium*, pp. 662-667, ISBN, Columbus, USA, Jun. 2003

Blum, R. S.; Xue, Z.; Zhang, Z. (2006). An Overview of Image Fusion, *Multi-Sensor Image Fusion and Its Applications*, In Blum, R. S., & Liu, Z (1 ed.), pp. 1-36, Boca Raton: Taylor & Francis

Chen, H.; Varshney, P. K. (2005). A perceptual quality metric for image fusion based on regional information, *Proceedings of the SPIE: Multisensor, Multisource Information Fusion: Architectures, Algorithms, and Applications*, 2005, Vol. 5813, pp. 24-45

Chen, Y.; Han, C. (2008). Night-time Pedestrian Detection by Visual-Infrared Video Fusion, *Proceedings of 7th World congress on Intelligent Control and Automation*, pp. 5079 - 5084, ISBN 978-1-4244-2113-8, Chongoing, China, Jun. 2008

Cucchiara, R. (2005). Multimedia surveillance systems, *Proceedings of the 3rd ACM International Workshop on Video Surveillance & Sensor Networks*, New York, NY, USA, pp. 3-10, 2005

Dixon, T. D.; Canga, E. F.; Noyes, J. M.; Troscianko, T.; Bull, D. R. (2006). Methods for the assessment of fused images, *ACM Transactions on Applied Perception*, Vol. 3, No. 3, pp. 309-332

Gavrila, D. M. (2001). Sensor-based Pedestrian Protection, *IEEE Intelligent Systems*, Vol. 16, No. 6, pp. 77-81

Gunatilaka, A.; Baertlein, B. (2001). Feature-Level and Decision-Level Fusion of Noncoincidently Sampled Sensors for Land Mine Detection, *IEEE Transactions on Pattern Analysis and Machine Intelligence*, Vol. 23, No. 6, pp. 577 - 589, ISSN 0162-8828

Hall, D.; Llinas J. (2001). *Handbook of Multisensor Data Fusion*, CRC Press, 2001

Hu, W.; Tan, T.; Wang, L.; Maybank, S. (2004). A survey on visual surveillance of object motion and behaviors, *IEEE Transactions on Systems, Man and Cybernetics*, Vol. 34, No. 3, Aug. 2004, pp. 334- 350

Leykin Alex, Ran Yang, Hammoud Riad. (2007). Thermal-Visible Video Fusion for Moving Target Tracking and Pedestrian Classification, *IEEE Conference on Computer Vision and Pattern Recognition*, pp. 1-8

Masoud, O.; Papanikolopoulos, N. (2003). A method for human action recognition, *Image and Vision Computing*, Vol. 21, pp. 729-743, ISSN 0262-8856

Park, C.; Bae, K. H.; Choi, S.; Jung, J. H. (2008). Image fusion in infrared image and visual image using normalized mutual information, Signal Processing, Sensor Fusion, and Target Recognition, *Proceedings of SPIE*, Vol. 6968, 69681Q, 2008

Petrovic, V. (2007). Subjective tests for image fusion evaluation and objective metric validation, *Information Fusion*, Vol. 8, No. 2, pp. 208-216, ISSN 1566-2535

Samadzadegan, F. (2004). Data Integration Related to Sensors, Data and Models, *Proceedings of International Society for Photogrammetry and Remote Sensing*

Thi Thi Zin, Pyke Tin, Hama, H. (2009). Bundling Multislit-HOG Features of Near Infrared Images for Pedestrian Detection, *Proceedings of 4th Intl. Conf. on Innovative Computing, Information and Control* (*ICICIC2009*), Kaohsiung, Taiwan, pp.302-305, 2009

Thi Thi Zin, Takahashi, H.; Hama, H. (2007), Robust Person Detection using Far Infrared Camera for Image Fusion, *Proceedings of the 2nd Intl. Conf. on ICICIC 2007*, Kumamoto, Japan, Sep. 2007.

Toet, A.; Ijspeert, J. K.; Kadar, I. (2001). Perceptual evaluation of different image fusion schemes, *International Society for Optical Engineering Proceedings Series*, 4380, pp. 427-435

Wang, J.; Liang, J.; Hu, H.; Li, Y.; Feng, B. (2007). Performance evaluation of infrared and visible image fusion algorithms for face recognition, *Proceedings of International Conf. Intelligent Systems and Knowledge Engineering* (ISKE2007), pp. 1-8, 2007

Xu, F.; Fujimura, K. (2002). Pedestrian Detection and Tracking with Night Vision, *IEEE Transactions on Intelligent Transportation Systems*, Vol. 6, No. 1, Mar. 2005, pp. 67-71, ISSN 1524-9050

13

Remote Sensing Image Fusion for Unsupervised Land Cover Classification

Chaabane Ferdaous
University of 7th November at Carthage, Higher school of Communications of Tunis
Sup'Com, URISA
Tunisia

1. Introduction

1.1 Context

With the development of new satellite systems and the accessibility of data from public through web services like Google Earth, remote sensing imagery, knows today an important growing which advanced and still advances researches in this area on different aspects. Especially in cartography, many studies have been conducted for multi-source satellite images classification. These studies aim to develop automatic tools in order to facilitate the interpretation and provide a semantic land cover classification.

Classical tools based on satellite images deal essentially with one category of satellite images which allows a partial interpretation. Multi-sensor or multi-source image fusion have been applied in the field of remote sensing since 20 years and continues today to provide efficient solutions to problems related to detection and classification. The work presented in this chapter is a part of multi-source fusion research efforts to have reliable and automatic satellite image interpretation. We propose to apply the new fusion concepts and theories for multi-source satellite images. Our main motivation is to measure the real contribution of multi-source image fusion according to the exploitation of satellite images separately.

Recent studies suggest that the combination of imagery from satellites with different spectral, spatial, and temporal information may improve land cover classification performance. The use of multi-source satellites images fully take into account the complementary and supplementary information provided by different data sources and considerably optimize the classification of cartographic objects. Particularly, combination of optical and radar remote sensing data may improve the classification results because of the complementarities of these two sources. Spectral features extracted form optical data may remove some difficulties faced when using only radar images. However, radar images present the following massive advantage: the possibility of penetrating the clouds. Thus, data fusion technique is applied to combine these two kinds of information.

1.2 Proposed approach

In literature, there is a huge variety of fusion theories mainly probabilistic and Bayesian theory [Mitchell, 2007], fuzzy and possibility theory [Milisavljevi'C & Bloch, 2009], Dumpster and Shafer theory, etc. [Milisavljević & Bloch, 2008]. However, most of them are investigated in four steps which are: modeling, estimation, combination and decision (cf.

Fig. 1.). For radar and optical images fusion, we choose to apply a Bayesian fusion framework in order to take into account the speckle radar texture which can be better represented by a Markovian gamma distribution [Rui-hui et al., 2009].
The originality of the proposed method is on one hand, the introduction of spatial and contextual information in fusion process using Markovian modeling with an optimal neighborhood order. Indeed, it has been shown [Meddeb et al., 2007] that the optimal neighborhood order allows a better representation of the speckle radar texture in terms of contrast, homogeneity, isotropy, etc. On the other hand, the given approach characterizes the radar texture data with a Markovian gamma auto-model. The radar texture is being usually modeled by a Gaussian model in probabilistic fusion processes.
Fig. 1. presents the main steps for multi-source image classification. As we can see, before applying fusion processing, some pretreatments must be applied to both satellites data due to the different nature of optical and radar images. The first pretreatment is the geometric correction which allows the superposition of the two remote sensing images [Zitova & Flusser, 2003]. The second pretreatment is the single image classification applied to both radar and optic images using a Fuzzy C-Means (FCM) algorithm [Wang, 1990]. Radar images are gamma MAP [Hosomura & Jayasekera, 1993] filtered before classification in

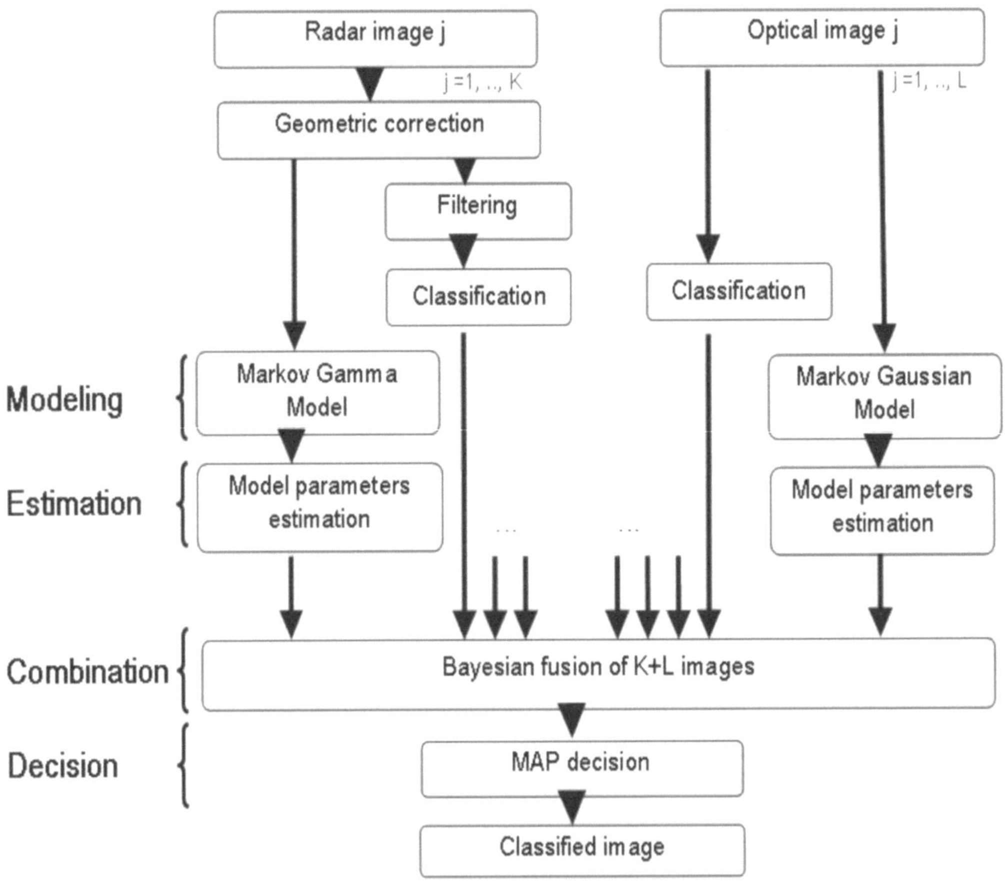

Fig. 1. Multi-source probabilistic fusion approach for land cover classification: main steps.

order to smooth the granular texture and reduce speckle noise. For each pixel, we model its posterior probability by a Besag Markov Gaussian auto-model in optical case and a Besag Markov gamma auto-model in radar case [Besag, 1974]. Parameters models are estimated using Expectation Maximization (EM) algorithm [Hogg et al., 2005]. Then the posterior probabilities are combined by the way of Bayesian fusion theory [Bloch, 2008].
This chapter is organized as follows. First, we describe briefly the three pretreatments phases. Secondly, the posterior probability modeling is presented for both radar and optical images. These probabilities are then used to present the Bayesian fusion process. Finally, pretreatments and fusion results are exposed in order to show land cover classification performances. Qualitative and Quantitative evaluations of the obtained results are also presented.

2. Fusion preprocessing

The exploitation of multi-source satellite images allows the obtaining of new signatures. However, these images are generated from various sensors, have different features (geometric, resolution, lighting, etc.) and are mainly not associated to the pixel level. Fusion process appears then complex and very sensitive to these data. To deal with this problem, some pretreatments must be done before combination step in order to correct images and prepare them for a simultaneous exploitation.
These preprocessing steps are essentially:

- Geometric correction
- Filtering
- Single image classification
- Data representation or modeling.

2.1 Geometric correction

The first pretreatment is the geometric superposition and geocoding [Hong & Schowengerdt, 2005]. For both optical and radar images, acquisition process is not the same and the measured data have different natures. Because of sampling and oblique geometric acquisition in radar imagery, there is no direct transformation from radar to optical image and inversely. Several registration techniques exist. Each registration method is characterized by four criteria that are essentially:

- The attributes: these are features extracted from both images to guide the transformation. There are extrinsic attributes (e.g. fixed external markers) and intrinsic attributes (e.g. the grayscale or extracted geometric primitives).
- The similarity criterion: it sets a certain distance between images attributes to quantify the notion of similarity.
- The deformation model: it determines how the image is geometrically changed. It can be local or global, and is characterized by a certain number of degrees of freedom.
- The optimization strategy: it determines the best processing within the meaning of a certain similarity criteria and a deformation model.

Depending on the type of deformation model, there are two types of registration: rigid and elastic registration [Shabou et al., 2007]. Among rigid registration family, there are linear or nonlinear transformations. The control points based registration is a non linear approach for which the geometric correction is determined according to a polynomial model (deformation model). The polynomial coefficients are calculated by minimizing the geometric errors between two sets of control points selected manually in both images (optimization strategy). These points should be visible on the two images. The quality of the geometric correction depends on the precision of these points's localization, their distribution in the image and their number. More, are the marked points, better is the correction. The polynomial transformation is then performed projecting one image onto another.

2.2 Radar texture filtering

The exploitation of radar images in terms of land cover classification presents some difficulties mainly because of the speckle noise.
The Synthetic Aperture Radar (SAR) is a coherent imaging system where backscattered signals coming from multiple distributed targets may interfere in any point of the space. If the interference is constructive, it results a brilliant point otherwise a dark point. The speckle noise, which gives the SAR image a granular character, reduces the correlation between pixels increasing thus the variance and the mean radar reflectivity of a local area. This phenomenon is a serious problem that degrades the quality of SAR images and causes difficulties for targets detection thus image interpretation. It is often compared to a multiplicative noise i.e. in direct proportion of the radar reflectivity which increases the difficulty of completely eliminating it.
It appears therefore necessary to reduce the speckle noise before using SAR images. Many techniques exist in the literature. Two techniques are often used: the multi-look processing, usually done at acquisition time, averages out the speckle noise by taking several "looks" at a single pixel of the radar image and the spatial filtering technique which includes adaptive and non-adaptive filters, is applied locally on a neighborhood around each pixel. The optimal choice of a filter depends on the ability of this filter to reduce speckle noise when preserving radiometric and radar texture information. The non-adaptive filters apply the same weights uniformly across the entire image thus they do not take into account backscattered signal local properties (example, the median and simple mean filters).
The adaptive filters adapt their weights across the image to the speckle level. They explicitly take account of the speckle and integrate local backscattering properties in their mathematical models. There are many forms of adaptive speckle filtering [Lee et al., 1994], including the Lee filter, the Frost filter, and the Gamma Maximum-A-Posteriori (GMAP) filter [Baraldi & Panniggiani, 1995]. The last one is based on the assumption that the radar intensity follows a gamma distribution. This filter, relatively to other filters, improves detection of edges and details in high-texture areas using second order spatial statistics and without losing information. Many other filters have been recently introduced [Maître, 2000] [Lee et al., 1994] but they have all comparable smoothing effects.

2.3 Single image classification

A critical step of multi-source satellite images processing is classification, whose objective is to identify all land cover types. There are mainly two categories of classification techniques:

- The supervised classification: it relies on prior information knowledge to search for classes. Training areas corresponding to sample pixels that are representative of specific classes, are selected manually by the user who also designates the outputs. The classification system is then used to develop a statistical characterization of each class basing on the training samples. The image is then classified by examining each pixel and making a decision about which of the signatures it is closest to. The most known supervised classification methods include neuronal network [Benediktsson et al., 1990] and SVM based approaches [Bazi & Melgani, 2006].

- The non-supervised classification: it uses data discriminating features to separate pixels in different classes as homogeneous as possible. The number of classes is often unknown by the user. These automatic methods are usually iterative and construct gradually classes basing on distances or pseudo-distances. Among these methods, we can mention the K-means algorithm [Philips, 2002] which has been largely used. Then, the "ISODATA (Iterative Self Organizing Data Analysis) clustering" algorithm [Philips, 2002], the FCM (Fuzzy C-means) method [Wang, 1990] [Bezdek et al., 1984], the "Competitive Learning" technique [Tang, 1998], etc. In the presented work, we focused on two non-supervised classification methods which have been used for satellite images: "ISODATA clustering" and FCM algorithm. The ISODATA algorithm is similar to the k-means algorithm with the distinct difference that the number of clusters is not previously known. It minimizes the distance to the mean as method of clustering and iterates through the data until user specified thresholds are reached and the optimal set of output classes is obtained. The ISODATA algorithm is very sensitive to initial starting values. Another commonly used unsupervised classification method is the FCM algorithm which is very similar to K-Means, but fuzzy logic is incorporated and recognizes that class boundaries may be imprecise or gradational. The FCM classification method creates an initial set of prototype classes and then determines a membership grade for each class for every pixel. The grades are used to adjust the class assignments and calculate new class centres, and the process is repeated until the iteration limit is reached. The FCM algorithm is more adaptive than other hard clustering methods and performs extremely well in situations of large variability of cluster shapes, densities and number of data points in each cluster.

Each optical and filtered radar image is classified using an automatic unsupervised FCM algorithm [Wang, 1990] to allow cartographic objects detection and classification. The results of FCM algorithm classification constitute the input of the fusion process.

2.4 Data representation

The exploitation of spatial information is fundamental for image processing, more particularly in image fusion. We often require specific developments to adapt the methods for each application. In the context of this work, we aim to introduce spatial information at the level of combination in fusion processing. Probabilistic Markov Random Fields (MRF) offer a natural framework to this. Markovian modelling implies that the probability that a random variable, in a pixel takes a given value knowing the entire image is equal to the probability in this pixel knowing its neighbours. It allows thus describing spatial interaction between level's pixels, by their neighbor's graph which coverage is quantified by a field order.

Previous works [Decombes et al., 1999] [Lorette et al., 2000] show Markov models effectiveness for texture and region characterization. Besag Markovian auto-models [Besag, 1974] form a class of Markov Random fields particularly simple and useful for spatial statistics. They are based on conditional distributions which are assumed to belong to an exponential family.

A Besag auto-model is defined as a Markovian field associated to Gibbs energy by:

$$U(x) = \sum_{s \in S} \phi_1(x_s) + \sum_{(s,r) \in C_2} \phi_2(x_s, x_r) \qquad (1)$$

Where x_s is the current pixel, S is the whole set of pixels in the image, C_2 represents the set of all possible order 2 cliques, x_r are order 2 neighborhood pixels of pixel x_s. Both Φ_1 and Φ_2 characterize totally the Markovian field:

$\phi_1(x_s)$ is the data description potential.

$\phi_2(x_s, x_r)$ is the interaction potential between x_s and x_r.

Order 2 is the lowest order to convey contextual information. It is widely used because of its simple formulation and low computational cost. However, previous works [Meddeb et al., 2007] show that superior orders neighborhoods allow a better representation of the optical and the radar texture. The optimal neighborhood order is determined basing on descriptors such as contrast, homogeneity, isotropy, entropy, texture coefficients, etc. Experimental results (cf. Fig. 2.) showed a convergence of descriptors majority to order 4. However, the obtained curves show a small loss of performances between order 3 and 4. For this reason and due to calculation complexity, we choose the third order neighborhood.

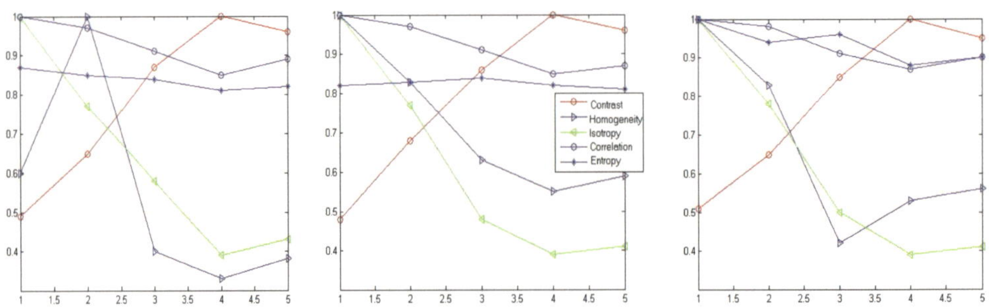

Fig. 2. Radar texture features versus neighborhood order for three region of interest: Left (water area), middle (Urban area), right (vegetation area) [Meddeb et al., 2007]

The auto-models can be classified according to the energy potential Φ_1 i.e. to assumptions made about x_s probability laws. Among these models, we can distinguish the auto-logistic, the auto-binomial, the auto-normal and the auto-gamma models. The following describes briefly the two last MRF models for representing respectively optical and radar image textures.

2.4.1 Auto-normal model

An auto-normal model also called Gaussian MRF is much used in the literature especially for segmentation, restoration and regularization problems. The corresponding energy is of the following form:

$$U(x) = \alpha \sum_{s \in S} \left\| x_s - \mu_s \right\|^2 + \beta \sum_{(s,r) \in C} \left\| x_s - x_r \right\|^2 \qquad (2)$$

Where C is the set of cliques around the pixel x_s, μ_s is the local mean and:

- $\alpha \sum_{s \in S} \left\| x_s - \mu_s \right\|^2$ is the potential describing the data,

- $\beta \sum_{(s,r)\in C} \|x_s - x_r\|^2$ is the regularization term describing interaction between pixels.

The conditional probability density function (pdf) of the site s, is given by:

$$P(X_s = x_s / X_r = x_r, r \in V_s) = N(\mu_s, \sigma_s^2) \tag{3}$$

Where X_s, X_r represent respectively the random variables associated to sites s with value x_s and r of value x_r and V_s is the neighbourhood of the site s.
The mean and the variance of the site s are defined by:

$$\begin{cases} \mu_s = E\{x_s / x_r, r \in V_s\} = m_s + \sum_{r\in V_s} \beta_{sr}(x_r - m_r) \\ \sigma_s^2 = Var\{x_s / x_r, r \in V_s\} \end{cases} \tag{4}$$

Where m_s and m_r are respectively the means around the site s and r and β_{sr} is the interaction parameter between sites s and r.
Thus the conditional probability becomes:

$$P(X_s = x_s / X_r = x_r, r \in V_s) = \frac{\exp(-\frac{1}{2\sigma^2}(x_s - m_s - \sum_{r\in V_s} \beta_{sr}(x_r - m_r))^2)}{\sum_{s\in S} \exp(-\frac{1}{2\sigma^2}(x_s - m_s - \sum_{r\in V_s} \beta_{sr}(x_r - m_r))^2)} \tag{5}$$

Where μ_s, σ_s and β_{sr} are the normal auto-model parameters to be estimated.
Several works [Descombes et al., 1999] demonstrate that Gaussian MRF shows better representation of optical images mainly because of texture homogeneity of the most cartographic objects. Other works [Belhadj et al. 2000] showed that the auto-gamma model is more adapted to radar images than auto-normal one because of the granular nature of radar texture.

2.4.2 Auto-gamma model

The auto-gamma model takes into account simultaneously the radar and speckle texture which guarantees to this model a considerable advantage [Belhadj et al., 2000]. Indeed, it makes it possible to be free from the pretreatment step which is speckle filtering. However, filtering is necessary before single radar image classification to limit the number of classes and to regularize their contours.
The auto-gamma model law is given by:

$$P(X_s = x_s / X_r = x_r, r \in V_s) = \gamma(a, (\alpha_s + \sum_{r\in V_s} \beta_{sr} x_r)) \tag{6}$$

Where a and α_s are the auto-gamma model parameters.
The local conditional probability becomes starting from this expression by:

$$P(X_s = x_s / X_r = x_r, r \in V_s) = \frac{x_s^{a-1} \exp(-x_s(\alpha_s + \sum_{r\in V_s} \beta_{sr} x_r))}{\sum_{s\in S} x_s^{a-1} \exp(-x_s(\alpha_s + \sum_{r\in V_s} \beta_{sr} x_r))} \tag{7}$$

Where a, α_s and β_{sr} are the gamma auto-model parameters to be estimated.

2.4.3 Parameter estimation

One of the main tasks of Bayesian classification is parameters estimation. In order to estimate the auto-models parameters by the maximum likelihood method we use the Expectation-Maximizing (EM) algorithm. Proposed by Dumpster et al. [Dumpster et al., 1977], the EM algorithm is an iterative algorithm for the calculation of the estimator of the maximum likelihood parameter of a model. The EM algorithm proceeds in two steps: an expectation step, followed by a maximization step which are iterated until convergence.
Parameters estimation algorithm was applied on both auto-normal and auto-gamma simulated images in order to validate the estimation process.

3. Probabilistic fusion model

In this section, we present a definition of data fusion in the field of image processing as well as the principal fusion steps applied to multi-source images. We will especially focus on the Bayesian probabilistic approach which has been adopted in this work.

3.1 Fusion steps

In the literature, there are several definitions for data fusion. Most of them are quoted in [Bloch, 2008] [Klein, 2004]. The definition that we adopt here was introduced by Bloch in [Bloch, 2008] and is adapted to the case of multi-source images: "The information fusion consists in combining heterogeneous information resulting from several sources in order to improve the decision." This definition is sufficiently general to include the diversity of fusion problems in signal and image processing.
Fusion is not usually a simple task. It can be investigated into four steps. We describe them briefly here, because they will be used for the presentation of fusion Bayesian theory. Let us consider a general fusion problem for which one has K sources, S_1, S_2,..., S_K and for which the goal is to make a decision chosen from N possible decisions d_1, d_2,..., d_N. The principal steps necessary to build fusion process are as follows [Bloch, 2008]:

- Modelling
- Estimation
- Combination
- Decision.

1. **Modelling**: this step includes the formalism choice and the mathematical expressions to be connected to this formalism. This step can be guided by additional or prior information about the context or the field of study. Let us suppose that each source S_j provides information represented by the model M_{ij} for the decision d_i. The shape of M_{ij} depends of course on the selected formalism.
2. **Estimation**: the majority of modelling techniques require a parameters estimation phase (for example all the distributions based methods). Here also additional information can be used.
3. **Combination:** this step relates on the choice of a compatible operator to the modelling formalism. It is also guided by additional information.
4. **Decision**: it represents the crucial fusion step, which makes it possible to change the information (provided by the sources) to the choice of a decision d_i.

The way in which these stages are arranged defines the fusion system and its architecture. In the literature, there are several fusion approaches. We focus here on probabilistic fusion theory and describe in details its main steps.

3.2 Bayesian fusion theory

The probabilistic fusion theory is the most useful fusion tool which is associated to Bayesian decision theory. This approach treats information uncertainty and is based on solid mathematical tools.

- **Modelling**

Information in probabilistic theory is modelled by a conditional probability. For example, the probability that a pixel x belongs to a particular class C_i, given the available image I_j has the following form [Bloch, 2008]:

$$M_i^j(x) = p(x \in C_i / I_j) \tag{8}$$

This probability is calculated starting from the information extracted from the image features $f_j(x)$. In the simplest case, it can be the considered pixel grey level, or more complex information requiring some pretreatments. The previous equation does not then depend any more on the entire image I_j and is written in the simplified form as:

$$M_i^j(x) = p(x \in C_i / f_j(x)) \tag{9}$$

- **Estimation**

In absence of strong functional modelling of the observed phenomena, probabilities $M_i^j(x) = p(f_j(x) / x \in C_i)$ or more generally $M_i^j(x) = p(I_j / x \in C_i)$ represents the conditional probability according to class C_i, of the information provided by the image I_j. They are learned or estimated by enumeration on test areas (the simplest case) or by training on these areas the parameters of a given probabilistic law.

- **Combination within a Bayesian framework**

Once information resulting from each sensor, represented by a convenient model, they can be combined according to specific rules according to the selected theoretical framework. The probabilistic and Bayesian fusion can be carried out by two equivalent ways and at two different levels [Bloch, 2008]:

- The fusion can be done at the modelling step. Then we calculate probabilities for l images sources as $p(x \in C_i / I_1,...,I_l)$. Using the Bayes rule:

$$p(x \in C_i / I_1,...,I_l) = \frac{p(I_1,...,I_l / x \in C_i)p(x \in C_i)}{p(I_1,...,I_l)} \tag{10}$$

The different terms are estimated by training.

- The fusion can also be done using Bayes rule itself. The information resulting from a source comes to update the information estimated according to the preceding sources:

$$p(x \in C_i / I_1,...,I_l) = \frac{p(I_1 / x \in C_i)...p(I_l / x \in C_i, I_1,...I_{l-1})p(x \in C_i)}{p(I_1)p(I_1 / I_2)...p(I_l / I_1,...,I_{l-1})} \tag{11}$$

Very often, known the complexity of the training starting from several sensors and the difficulty of obtaining sufficient statistics, these equations are simplified under the independence assumption. Several criteria were proposed to check the validity of this assumption. The previous formula becomes then:

$$p(x \in C_i / I_1, ..., I_l) = \frac{\prod_{j=1}^{l} p(I_j / x \in C_i) p(x \in C_i)}{p(I_1, ..., I_l)} \quad (12)$$

The equation (12) revealed clearly the type of information combination as a product. We can notice also that the prior probability $p(x \in C_i)$ plays the same role as the sources in the combination. Let us mention here that the Bayesian combination has a conjunctive character [Bloch, 2008] by the means of multiplication.

- **Decision**

The last fusion step is the decision. For example, the choice of the class to which a point belongs. This binary decision can be weighted with a quality measurement, allowing its acceptance or its rejection. The most used rule for the probabilistic and Bayesian decision is the maximum a posteriori:

$$x \in C_i \; si \; p(x \in C_i / I_1, ..., I_l) = \max\{p(x \in C_k / I_1, ..., I_l), 1 \le k \le N\} \quad (13)$$

Several other criteria were developed to adapt the user needs and the decision context as well as possible. Especially, we cite: the maximum probability, the maximum entropy, the maximum hope, the minimal risk, etc.
The next section presents the results corresponding to each processing step and the final fusion results.

4. Results

4.1 Pretreatments results

4.1.1 Data description

The proposed Bayesian fusion approach was applied using seven satellite images covering Tunis City area, North Africa: three ERS images acquired at three different dates (acquisitions relatively close, cf. Fig. 3.) and one Spot4 image containing four spectral bands (cf. Fig. 4.).

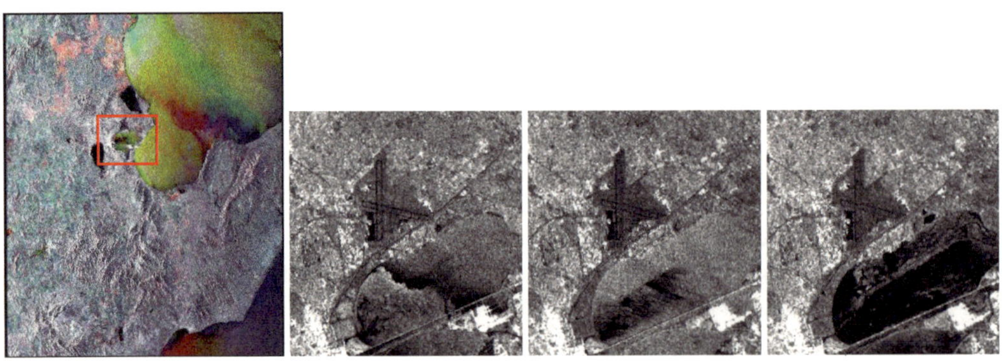

Fig. 3. The multi-temporal radar ERS image composed of three images acquired at three different dates.

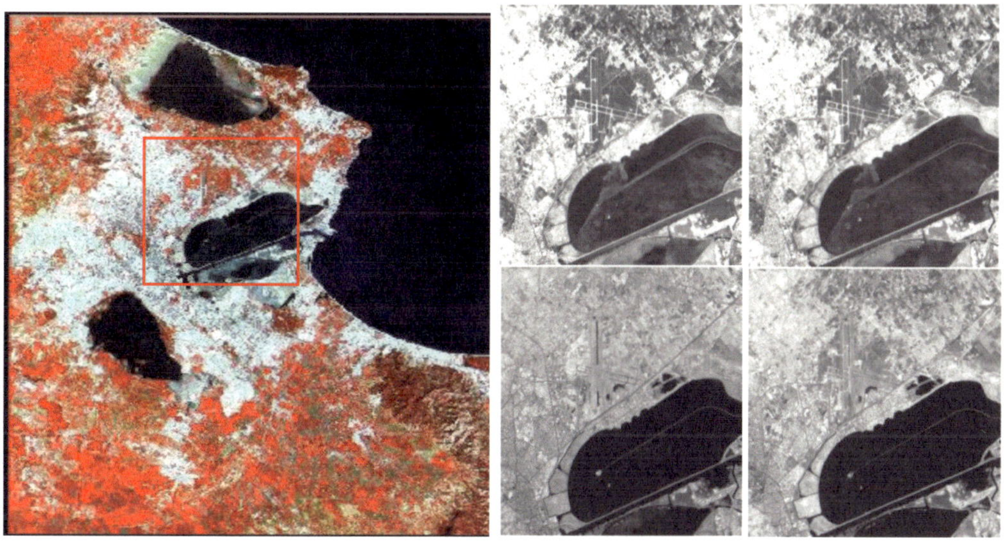

Fig. 4. The Spot4 image composed of four spectral bands.

4.1.2 Geometric correction

There are two types of geometric corrections:

- The correction of distortions due to the geometry variations between the ground and the sensor,
- The transformation of the data into true coordinates i.e. into ground geometry coordinates.

We firstly identify several clearly distinct points on the image to be corrected i.e. the radar image. The Spot4 image is geo-referenced (ground known reference). Then, these points are connected to another set of points selected on the optical image.

Fig. 5. illustrates the geometric correction result applied to the seven images. This preprocessing step is very delicate since its accuracy disturbs fusion results. Registration errors are chosen less than 10^{-2}.

Fig. 5. Result of geometric correction applied between optical and radar images.

4.1.3 Speckle filtering

The proposed fusion approach does not require radar images filtering phase since the radar texture model takes into account the speckle. However, we need filtering for single image classification since it necessitates a strong homogeneity degree inside the classes to be able to distinguish between them.

As explained in paragraph 2.2, the gamma Map filter was retained because it makes it possible to smooth the scene and reduce the speckle noise while preserving the radiometric and textural radar features.

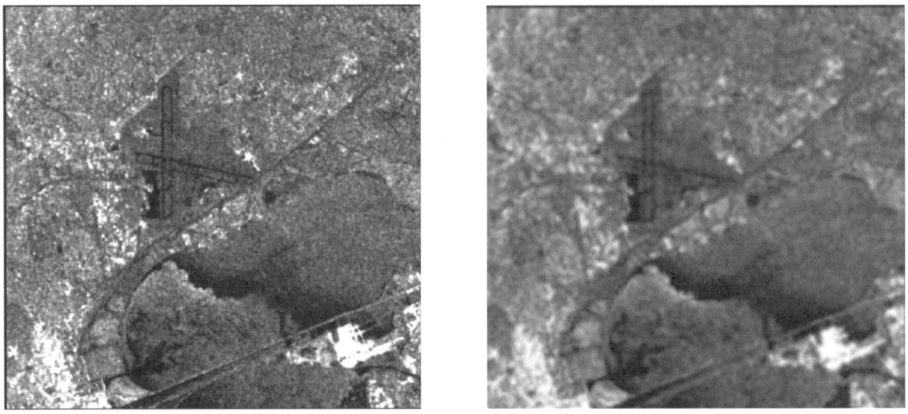

Fig. 6. Filtering results: original radar image (left). Radar image obtained after gamma MAP filtering (right).

The window size of the gamma MAP filter is fixed at 5x5. Fig. 6. shows the radar texture before and after speckle filtering. Radar filtering improves classification results.

4.1.4 Single image classification results

FCM classification algorithm was applied on both radar and optical images. To choose the classes number, we study auxiliary data such as maps and High Resolution (HR) images. We identify six classes. For the considered region, there are two types of vegetation: small trees and vegetation under water that we call humid area. There are also two types of urban areas: dense and disperse agglomeration regions.

Fig. 7. and 8. show Fuzzy classification results for the Spot4 four spectral bands and the three ERS radar images. As we can notice the single classification results vary from one image to another. This is due to differences between spectral features and speckle noise. Single classification results give good reason to combine all this kind of information in order to improve land cover classification.

4.1.5 Parameter estimation results

EM algorithm (cf. paragraph 2.4.3) was applied for Markovian parameters estimation. Both auto-normal and auto-gamma models parameters exposed in 2.4 are estimated for each classified area.

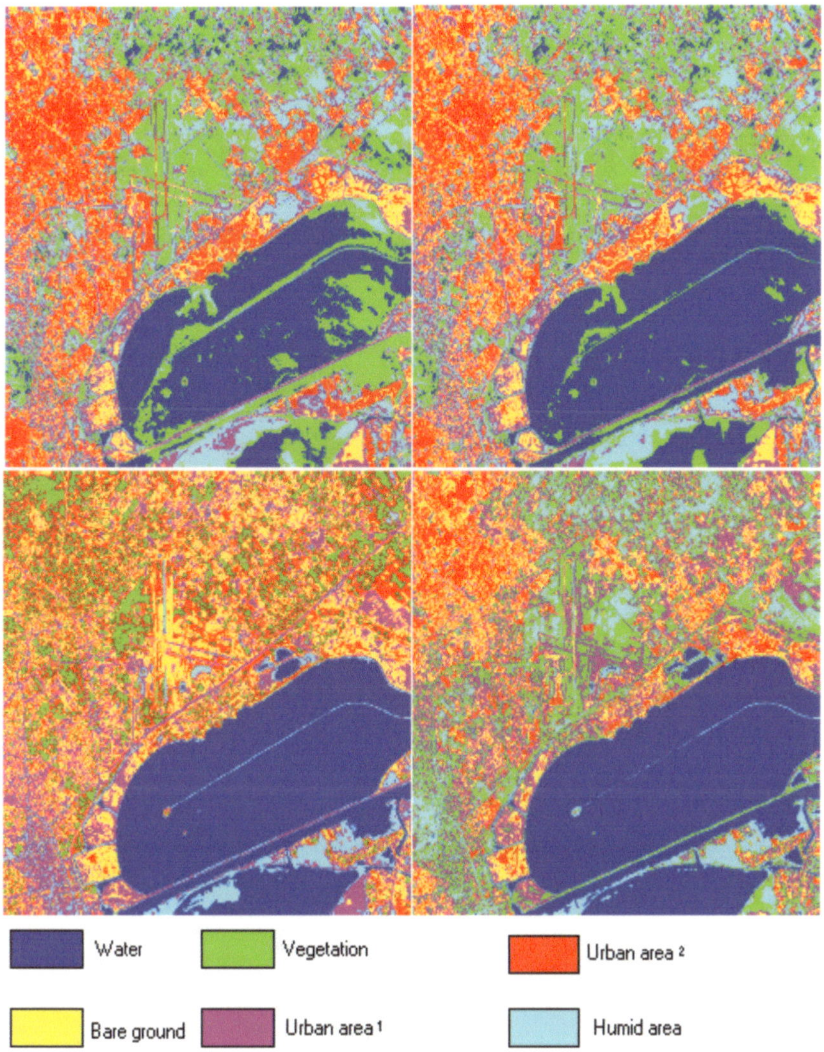

Fig. 7. FCM classification results for Spot4 XS1, XS2, XS3 and XS4 bands (from left to right).

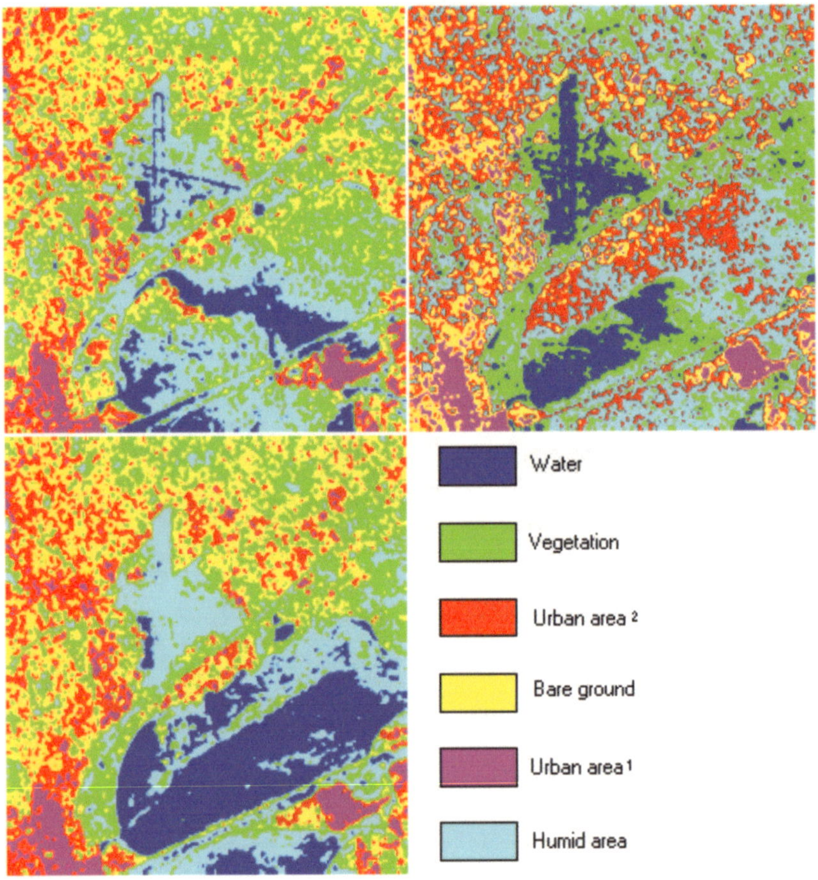

Fig. 8. FCM classification results for ERS images.

4.2 Fusion results

In order to highlight the contribution of spatial and contextual information introduced at the modelling level, we will present and compare fusion results obtained with and without spatial information exploitation. The four principal fusion steps are then investigated one by one in both cases.

4.2.1 Fusion without spatial information

First, we combine the optical and radar images without taking into account the pixel neighbourhood using Bayesian fusion. The expression of the posterior probability is given by the equation (12). In the case of radar and optical images, it becomes:

$$p(x \in C_i / I_{radar_{j=1,..Nr}}, I_{optiacl_{j=1,..,No}}) = \frac{\prod_{j=1}^{Nr} p(I_{radar_j} / x \in C_i) \prod_{j=1}^{No} p(I_{optical_j} / x \in C_i) p(x \in C_i)}{p(I_{radar_{j=1,..,Nr}}, \ldots, I_{optical_{j=1,..,No}})} \tag{14}$$

The modelling step consists in representing the conditional probability related to optical image by a Gaussian distribution and the one related to the radar image by a gamma distribution. The two probabilities are thus written:

$$p(I_{radar_j} / x \in C_i) = N(\mu_i, \sigma_i^2) \tag{15}$$

Where μ_i and σ_i^2 represent the Gaussian distribution parameters for the optical image I_j and the class C_i, they correspond respectively to the average and the variance.

$$p(I_{optical_j} / x \in C_i) = \gamma(a_i, \alpha_i) \tag{16}$$

Where, a_i and α_i represent the gamma distribution parameters for the radar image radar I_j and the class C_i.

Let us notice here, that we assume the sources independence which is justified by different nature of sensors.

Concerning the choice of the prior probability $p(x \in C_i)$, we fixed the same probability for each class. Indeed, since we do not have prior information about the real percentage of each class in the studied zones, one of the prior probabilities can be considered as equally probable.

Other choices can be carried out for the prior probability such as the occupation percentage of each class according to the most reliable image source, the Markovian modelling, etc.

The second step which is the estimation consists in determining for each class C_i, μ_I, σ_i^2, a_i and α_i by likelihood maximization. The combination is done using the Bayesian rule and the decision criterion is the posterior maximum.

4.2.1.1 *Qualitative evaluation*

We can notice here that the multi-source image fusion allows the characterization of humid and small vegetation dispersed areas inside Tunis City Lake. The fusion of two set of images of different nature highlights the presence of these zones. As we can see from high resolution Google earth image (cf. Fig. 9.), these areas have already existed and are not selected by a single image classification which underline the need of multi-source image classification.

The fusion of the seven images also characterizes better the urban zones and the road network. Indeed, we can observe the good detection of linear and fine structures at the level of the airport crossing raising thus confusion with vegetation areas. Moreover, the bare ground class is not too present after fusion; there is a certain confusion with urban classes, especially around Tunis City Lake.

4.2.1.2 *Quantitative evaluation*

Beside qualitative results, a manual classified image delimited by the help of higher resolution images, is used to evaluate quantitatively results accuracies. Thus we calculate

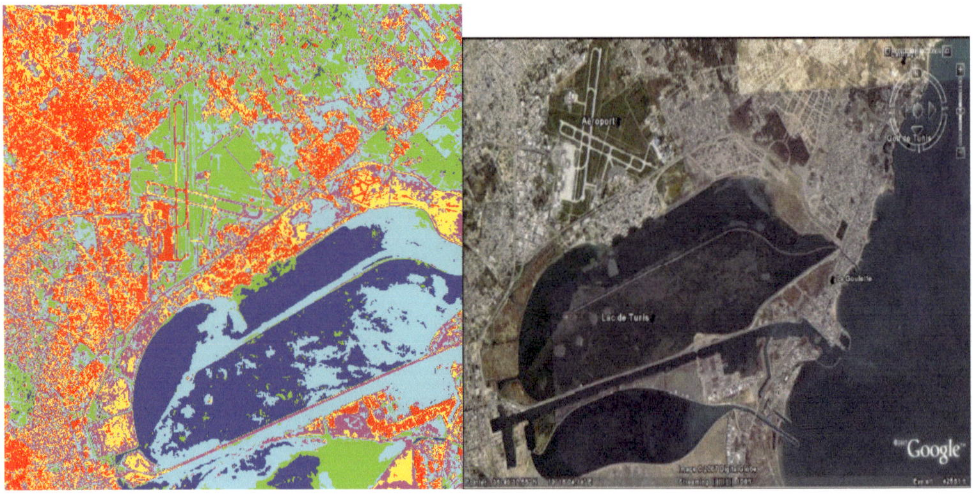

Fig. 9. The fist image corresponds to Bayesian fusion results without spatial information and the second image represents a high resolution Google Earth image.

the confusion matrix [Bloch, 2008] according to the manual classified image (table1). This quantitative measure expresses the good detection and false alarms rates according to each class. As we can see, without taking into acount spatial information, we obtain suffisent results.

Water	Vegetation	Urban 1		Bare ground	Urban 2	Humid zone
Water	97.50%	0.00%	1.70%	0.00%	0.00%	2.61%
Vegetation	0.00%	91,65%	1.00%	1.50%	3.10%	0.35%
Urban 1	0.00%	1.50%	89%	3.40%	2.67%	3.36%
Bare ground	0.00%	2.55%	4.98%	91.55%	0.10	0.15
Urban 2	0.00%	3.00%	1.32%	3.20%	92.44	1.13%
Humid zone	2.50%	1.30%	2%	0.35%	0.79%	92.40%

Table 1. The resulted Bayesian fusion confusion matrix. Case of the non exploitation of spatial information.

For the second step, we introduce space information into the fusion process.

4.2.2 Fusion with spatial information

The introduction of spatial information is done using the Markovian modelling of each class conditional probability. Besag auto-models are attributed to each source of information. We used auto-normal model for optical images because of optical texture homogeneity and auto-gamma model for non filtered radar images (cf. paragraph 2.4). Indeed, it has been shown that radar speckle texture follows a gamma distribution which has different features compared to a Gaussian distribution. Comparisons between Gaussian and gamma modeling are carried out to highlight the efficiency of gamma modeling in case of radar texture. Thus for optical texture the conditional probability is defined as:

$$P(I_{optical_j} / x_s \in C_i) \propto \frac{1}{\sqrt{2\pi\sigma_i}} \exp((-\frac{1}{2\sigma_i^2}(x_s - \mu_i - \sum_{r \in V_s} \beta_i (x_r - \mu_i)))^2) \quad (17)$$

Where μ_i, σ_i and β_i are the Markov Gaussian model parameters for each class and V_s is the neighborhood of each site s in the image. As for non filtered radar texture the conditional probability is defined by the following equation:

$$P(I_{radar_j} / x_s \in C_i) \propto \gamma(a_i, (\alpha_i + \sum_{r \in V_s} \beta_i x_r)) \propto x_s^{a_i - 1} \exp(-x_s(\alpha_i + \sum_{r \in V_s} \beta_i x_r)) \quad (18)$$

Where a_i, α_i and β_i are the gamma auto-model parameters for each considered class. V_s is the neighborhood of each site s. We remind here that radar images are not filtered for fusion process as for classification, because the gamma model takes into accounts the speckle granular texture [Belhadj et al., 2000].

The prior probability is chosen as a uniform probability to avoid FCM initial classifications influence in fusion process. The second step of the proposed fusion process consists in Markovian auto-models parameters estimation. Therefore, the parameters $(\hat{\mu}_i, \hat{\sigma}_i, \hat{\beta}_i)$ for Gaussian model and $(\hat{a}_i, \hat{\alpha}_i, \hat{\beta}_i)$ for gamma model are estimated using an EM algorithm.

The neighborhood order is fixed at 3 [Meddeb et al., 2007] for both radar and optical images. The fusion combination step is done by multiplying the modeled posterior probability of each source of information following the Bayesian fusion theory. We refer to equation (14) to replace the conditional probability term by its corresponding expression, equation (17) for optical data and equation (18) for non filtered radar texture. Class decision is the last step of the fusion process. It is assured for each pixel using the Maximum A Posteriori probability (MAP) method.

4.2.2.1 *Qualitative evaluation*

Comparing to single FCM classification and fusion by introducing spatial information results, we point out a clear improvement of class distribution. Indeed, on the one hand, urban zones are better delimited (cf. fig. 10.). On the other hand, humid and vegetation

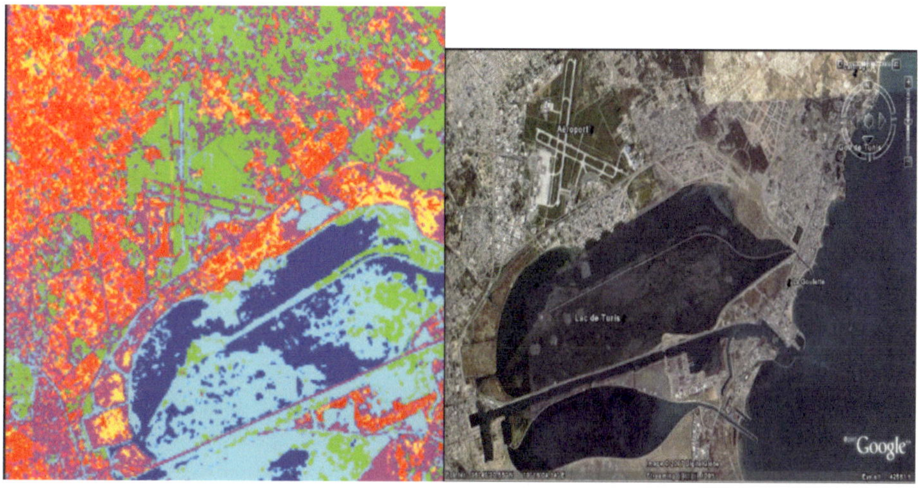

Fig. 10. The fist image corresponds to Bayesian fusion results by introducing the spatial information and the second image represents a high resolution Google Earth image.

areas in the middle of Tunis City Lake are refined. However, there are some false alarms especially for vegetation areas and missed detections for urban areas.
The urban zones 1 and 2 are quite present on the image with some confusion with the bare ground class which is less present after fusion. Also, the false alarm water areas selected away from Tunis City Lake are not present any more, and confusion with the vegetation was raised.

4.2.2.2 *Quantitative evaluation*

Looking at the obtained confusion matrix, we notice that diagonal values corresponding to good classification rates are sufficiently important. Besides, false alarm water areas outside Tunis City Lake are removed (comparing to single classification) reducing confusion with vegetation areas. However, there are still confusions between humid and vegetation areas, urban and bare ground areas.
By comparing tables 1 and 2, we notice an improvement for the good classification rate. On the other hand, it is noted that certain false alarms are less important. The introduction of spatial information is then quantitatively justified.

Water	Vegetation	Urban 1		Bare ground	Urban 2	Humid zone
Water	98.10%	0.00%	1.71%	0.00%	0.00%	1.23%
Vegetation	0.00%	92,00%	1.00%	1.50%	2.10%	0.00%
Urban 1	0.00%	1.50%	93.88%	1.78%	0.55%	1.20%
Bare ground	0.00%	2.55%	2.33%	94.22%	0.10	1.35
Urban 2	0.00%	3.00%	0.15%	2.15%	96.40	0.12%
Humid zone	1.90%	1.30%	1.54%	0.35%	0.85%	96.10%

Table 2. The resulted Bayesian fusion confusion matrix.

5. Conclusion

Two Besag Markovian auto-models are used to characterize remote sensing data issued from two different sensors. Gaussian model is applied on optical images whereas gamma model is used to represent radar images. For both models, an optimal Markov neighborhood order is used. Confusion matrix rates show that the proposed Bayesian fusion approach gives sufficient results according to single FCM classification. For future works and in order to improve the obtained results, we can introduce a reliability degree to each source of information in a fuzzy Bayesian fusion framework.

6. References

Baraldi, A.; Panniggiani, F. (1995). *A refined gamma MAP SAR speckle filter with improved geometrical adaptivity*, IEEE Transaction on Geoscience and Remote Sensing, pp. 1245 - 1257, Sep 1995.

Bazi, Y. & Melgani, F. (2006). *Toward an Optimal SVM Classification System for Hyperspectral Remote Sensing Images*, IEEE Transaction on Geoscience and Remote Sensing, pp. 3374-3385, Vol. 44, Issue 11, Nov. 2006.

Benediktsson, J., Swain, P. & Ersoy, O. (1990). *Neural network approaches versus statistical methods in classification of multisource remote sensing data,* IEEE Transaction on Geoscience and Remote Sensing, Vol. 28, N°4, pp. 540-552, july 1990.

Besag, J. (1974). Spatial *interaction and the statistical analysis of lattice systems,* Journal of the Royal Statistical Society, Series B, Vol. 36, pp.192-236.

Bloch, A. (2008). Information fusion in signal and image processing major probabilistic and non-probabilistic numerical approaches, ISTE John Wiley & Sons Ed., ISBN: 1-8482-1019-1, Janvier 2008.

Bezdek, J.C.; R. Ehrlich & Fall W. (1984). *FCM: the fuzzy c-means clustering algorithm,* Computers and Geoscience, Vol. 10, pp. 191-203.

Dempster, A. P.; Laird N. M. & Rubin D. B. (1977). *Maximum Likelihood from Incomplete Data via thc EM Algorithm,* Journal of the Royal Statistical Society, B, Vol.. 39, N° 1, pp. 1-38.

Descombes, X.; Sigelle, M. & Préteux F.(1999). *Estimating Gaussian Markov random field parameters in a nonstationary framework : application to remote sensing imaging.* IEEE Trans. on Image Processing, Vol. 8, N° 4, pp. 490–503.

Hogg, R.; McKean, J. & Craig, A. (2005). *Introduction to Mathematical Statistics,* 5th Edition, Upper Saddle River, NJ: Pearson Prentice Hall, 2005.

Hong, T. D.; Schowengerdt, R. A. (2005). *A Robust Technique for Precise Registration of Radar and Optical Satellite Images,* Photogrammetric Engineering & Remote Sensing, Vol. 71, No. 5, pp. 585–593, May 2005.

Hosomura, T. & Jayasekera, C.W. (1993). Speckle filtering and texture analysis in SAR images, *Geoscience and Remote Sensing Symposium, Better Understanding of Earth Environment.,* Vol. 3, pp. 1423 - 1425, Aug 1993.

Klein, L. A. (2004). *Sensor and Data Fusion: A Tool for Information Assessment and Decision Making,* SPIE Press, 342pp, ISBN: 0819454354, July 2004.

Lee, J. S.; Jurkevich, L.; Dewaele, P.; Wambacq, P. & Oosterlinck, A. (1994). *Speckle filtering of synthetic aperture radar images: A review,* Remote Sensing Reviews, Vol. 8, Issue 4, pp. 313 - 340, January 1994.

Lorette, A.; Descombes, X. & Zerubia J. (2000). *Urban areas extraction based on texture analysis through a Markovian modelling,* Int. Journal of Computer Vision, Vol. 36, N° 3, pp. 219–234.

Maitre, H. (2000). *Traitement des images de RSO,* Traité IC2, série traitement du signal et de l'image, ISBN: 2-7462-0155-0, Editions hermes-sciences 2000.

Meddeb, A.; Chaabane, F. & Belhadj, Z. (2007). Réflexion sur le choix de l'ordre de voisinage pour la modélisation par les champs de Markov de la texture SAR, *Traitements et Analyse d'Images, Méthodes et Applications, TAIMA'07,* Hammamet, Mai 2007.

Milisavljevi'C, N.; Bloch, I.& Acheroy, M. (2008). *Multi-Sensor Data Fusion Based on Belief Functions and Possibility Theory: Close Range Antipersonnel Mine Detection and Remote Sensing Mined Area Reduction,* in Humanitarian Demining: Innovative Solutions and the Challenge of Technology, chap. 4, pp. 392-418, M. K. Habib Ed., ARS I-Tech Education and Publishing, Vienna, Austria.

Milisavljevi'C, N. & Bloch, I. (2009). *Possibilistic and fuzzy multi-sensor fusion for humanitarian mine action,* in Advances in Geoscience and Remote Sensing, chap. 23, pp. 491-504, Gary Jedlovec Ed., InTech Croatia.

Mitchell, H.B. (2007). *Multi-Sensor Data Fusion,* springer Verlag, ISBN: 3540714634, jully 2007.

Phillips, S. (2002). Reducing the computation time of the Isodata and K-means unsupervised classification algorithms, *IEEE International Geoscience and Remote Sensing Symposium, IGARSS '02*, Vol. 3, pp. 1627 - 1629, Nov. 2002.

Rui-hui, P.; Shu-zong, W.; Xiang-wei, W. & Yong-sheng, L. (2009). Modelling of correlated gamma-distributed texture based on spherically invariant random process, *IEEE International Conference on Intelligent Computing and Intelligent Systems, ICIS*, pp. 53 - 58, Shanghai, Nov. 2009.

Shabou, A. & Tupin F. & Chaabane, F. (2007). Similarity measures between SAR and optical data, *IEEE International Geoscience and Remote Sensing Symposium (IGARSS'07)*, Barcelona, Spain, July 2007.

Tang, X.O. (1998). *Multiple Competitive Learning Network Fusion for Object Classification*, SMC-B, Vol. 28, N° 4, pp. 532-543, August 1998.

Wang, F. (1990). *Fuzzy Supervised Classification of remote Sensing Images*, IEEE Transaction on Geoscience and Remote Sensing. Vol. 28, No. 2, Mars 1990.

Zitova, B.; Flusser, J. (2003). *Image Registration Methods: A Survey*, Image and Vision Computing, Vol. 21, pp. 977-1000, Elsevier, June 2003.

14

Region-Based Fusion for Infrared and LLL Images

Junju Zhang, Yiyong Han, Benkang Chang and Yihui Yuan
Institute of Electronic Engineering and Optic-electronic Technology, Nanjing University of Science and Technology, Nanjing
China

1. Introduction

Thermal cameras and image intensifiers are common night vision (NV) cameras, which enable operations during night and in adverse weather conditions. NV cameras deliver monochrome images that are usually hard to interpret and may give rise to visual illusions and loss of situational awareness. The two most common NV imaging systems display either emitted infrared radiation or reflected low level light (LLL). In this way the different imaging modalities give complementary information about the objects or area under inspection. Thus, techniques for fusing infrared and LLL images should be employed in order to provide a compact representation of the scene with increased interpretation capabilities.

Image fusion can be classified into two types based on pixel-level: pixel-based and region-based. The pixel-based image fusion is characterized by simplicity and highest popularity. Because pixel-based methods fail to take into account the relationship between points and points, the fused image with either of them might lose some gray and feature information. However, for most image fusion applications, it seems more meaningful to combine objects rather than pixels. The region-based fusion, on the contrary, can obtain the best fusion results by considering the nature of points in each region altogether. Therefore, region-based fusion has advantages over the other two counterparts. At present, region-based methods use some segmentation algorithm to separate an original image into different regions, and then design different rules for different regions.

During the last decade, a number of gray fusion algorithms have been proposed, and the fusion methods based on the multiscale transform (MST) are the most typical. The commonly used MST tools include the Laplacian pyramid and the wavelet transform (DWT). In general, due to the perfect properties of the DWT such as multi-resolution, spatial and frequency localization, and direction, the DWT-based methods are superior to the pyramid-based methods. However, the DWT also has some limitations such as limited directions and non-optimal-sparse representation of images. Thus, some artifacts are easily introduced into the fused images using the DWT-based methods, which will reduce the quality of the resultant image consequently. The Dual-Tree Complex Wavelet Transform (DT-CWT) has been introduced by Nick Kingsbury, which has the following properties: Approximate shift invariance; Good directional selectivity in 2-D with Gabor-like filters also true for higher dimensionality; Perfect reconstruction using short linear-phase filters; Limited redundancy: independent of the number of scales. Therefore, the Dual-Tree Complex Wavelet Transform is more suitable for image fusion.

In the context of NV imaging, a number of color fused-based representations have been proposed. A simple mapping of infrared and visual bands into the three components of an RGB image can provide an immediate benefit, since the human eye can discriminate several thousands of colors but only a few dozens of gray levels. On the other hand, inappropriate color mappings may hinder situational awareness due to lack of color constancy. Hence, an image fusion method for night vision imagery must result in color images with natural appearance and a high degree of similarity with the corresponding natural scenes. To make the coloration of false-color images appear more natural, Reinhard recently introduced a method that enabled the transfer of colors from one image to another. Subsequently, Toet demonstrated that Reinhard's method could be adapted to transfer the natural color characteristics of daylight imagery into multi-band infrared and LLL images. Essentially, Toet's natural color mapping method matches the statistical properties of the NV imagery to that of a natural daylight color image. However, this particular color mapping method colors the image regardless of scene content, weights all regions of the source image by the "global" color statistics, and thus the accuracy of the coloring is very much dependent on how well the target and source images are matched.

In this chapter, we present a region-based gray fusion method using the DT-CWT and a region-based color fusion method for infrared and LLL images. Segmentation is very important because segmentation precision has a great influence on the following fusion process. Here, we adopt two segmentation methods: the morphologic mehod and the nonlinear diffusion method. In the gray fusion method, the infrared and LLL images are decomposed by DT-CWT, the segmentation regions are mapped into each level, and fusion is carried out region by region in terms of some fusion rules. The region-based color fusion method is based on Toet's global-coloring framework.

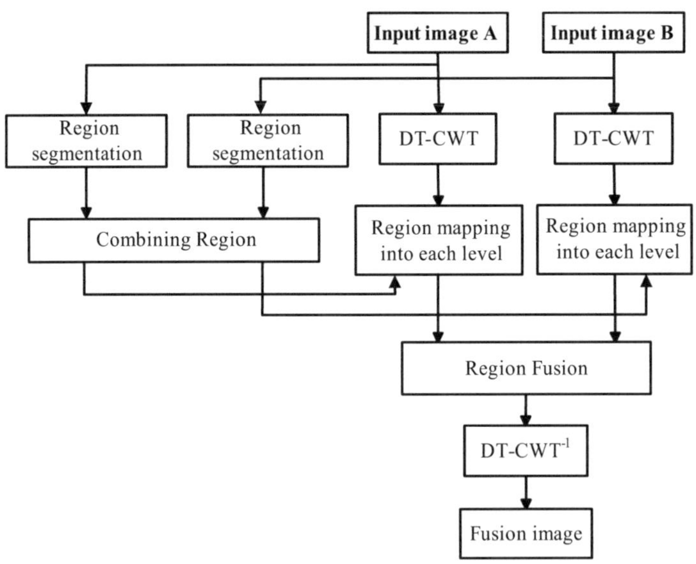

Fig. 1. Diagram of the proposed region-based method with DT-CWT

2. Image fusion based on region segmentation and complex wavelets

The region-based fusion method for infrared and LLL images adopts the DT-CWT because of its approximate shift invariance and limited redundancy. Diagram of the proposed region-based method with DT-CWT is shown in Fig. 1. Segmentation is firstly performed on the infrared image and LLL images respectively with top-bottom-hat filtering and the threshold method, consequently, the DT-CWT coefficients from the different regions are merged separately. Finally the fused image is obtained by performing inverse DT-CWT.

2.1 Image segmentation using morphology

The morphologic filters have been proven as powerful methods in the denoising and smoothing of image intensities while retaining and enhancing edges. The combination of different morphologic filters makes the segmentation flexible. The top-hat transform and the bottom-hat transform are all the combination of open operation, close operation and the original image.

The top-hat transform means subtracting a morphologically opened image from the original image and it can be used to enhance contrast in an image. The bottom-hat transform means subtracting the original image from a morphologically closed version of the image and it can be used to find intensity troughs in an image. The formula of the top-hat transform and bottom-hat transform are given by respectively

$$H_{top} = f - (f \circ p) \tag{1}$$

$$H_{bottom} = (f \bullet p) - f \tag{2}$$

Here f is the original image, "$\circ$" and "$\bullet$" are open operation and close operation, H_{top} and H_{bottom} are results of the top-hat transform and bottom-hat transform. Add the original image f to the top-hat filtered image H_{top}, and then subtract the bottom-hat filtered image H_{bottom}, we can obtain the enhanced image. At the same time, noises of the original image f are eliminated. The enhanced image H_E is given by

$$H_E = H_{top} - H_{bottom} + f \tag{3}$$

Then the threshold method is used to segment the enhanced image H_E. We can get the binary segmentation image based on this method. Because the physical significance of the pixel at the same location of the heterogeneous source images is different, the shapes of segmentation regions obtained by the former method are also different. So we must deal the segmentation region with the associate methods. The information of segmentation region should be added to the associated-segmentation image and is used to guide the fusion rules.

The following steps are used to generate the associated-segmentation image:

1. If there is no overlapping area between the region $R^{(1)}$ and the region $R^{(2)}$, then the associated- segmentation image is mapped into two regions, $R_1^{(j)} = R^{(1)}$, $R_2^{(j)} = R^{(2)}$;
2. If there is some overlapping area between the region $R^{(1)}$ and the region $R^{(2)}$, then the associated- segmentation image is mapped into three regions, $R_0^{(j)} = R^{(1)} \cap R^{(2)}$; $R_1^{(j)} = R^{(1)} \cap R_0^{(j)}$; $R_2^{(j)} = R^{(2)} - R_0^{(j)}$;

3. If region $R^{(1)}$ overlaps the region $R^{(2)}$ completely, the associated-segmentation image is mapped into the same region, $R^{(j)} = R^{(1)} = R^{(2)}$;
4. If one region completely contains the other region, for example, $R^{(1)} \subset R^{(2)}$, then the associated- segmentation image is mapped into two regions, $R_1^{(j)} = R^{(1)}$, $R_2^{(j)} = R^{(2)} - R^{(1)}$. Here, $R^{(1)}$ is presented a part of one source image, $R^{(2)}$ is presented a part of the other source image. $R^{(j)}$ is presented a part of associated-segmentation image. Fig. 2 is some typical examples of the associated region maps. There are some small regions in the associated-segmentation image, and they don't contain enough region information, which will cause false image in the fused image. We may merge these small regions using morphological operators.

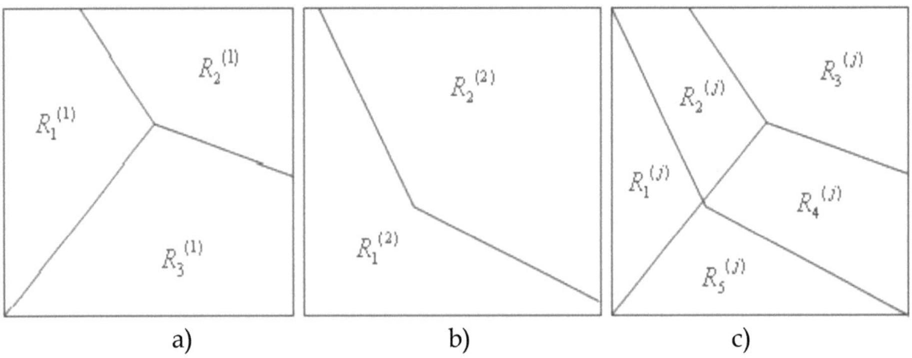

Fig. 2. Associated region maps for the fused image. (a) region map1, (b) region map2, (c) associated region map

2.2 Pixel fusion with complex wavelets

The dual-tree complex wavelet transform (DT-CWT) is a relatively recent enhancement to the discrete wavelet transform (DWT), with important additional properties: It is nearly shift invariant and directionally selective in two and higher dimensions. It achieves this with a redundancy factor of only 2d for d-dimensional signals, which is substantially lower than the undecimated DWT. The multidimensional (M-D) DT-CWT is non-separable but is based on a computationally efficient, separable filter bank (FB).

For 2-D signals, we can filter separately along columns and then rows by the way like 1-D. Kingsbury figured out in that, to represent fully a real 2-D signal, we must filter with complex conjugates of the column and row filters. So it gives 4:1 redundancy in the transform. Furthermore, it remains computationally efficient, since actually it is close to a classical real 2-D wavelet transform at each scale in one tree, and the discrete transform can be implemented by a ladder filter structure. The quad-tree transform is designed to be, as much as possible, translation invariant. It means that if we decide to keep only the details or the approximation of a given scale, removing all other scales, shifting the input image only produces a shift of the reconstructed filtered image, without aliasing. The most important property of DT-CWT is that it can separate more directions than the real wavelet transform. The 2-D DWT produces three band-pass subimages at each level, which are corresponding to LH, HH, HL, and oriented at angles of 0°, ± 45 °, 90 °. The 2-D DT-CWT can provide six subimages in two adjacent spectral quadrants at each level, which are oriented at angles of ±15 °, ±45 °, ±75 °. The strong orientation occurs because the complex filters are asymmetry responses. They can separate positive frequencies from negative ones vertically and horizontally. Therefore, positive and negative frequencies will not be aliasing.

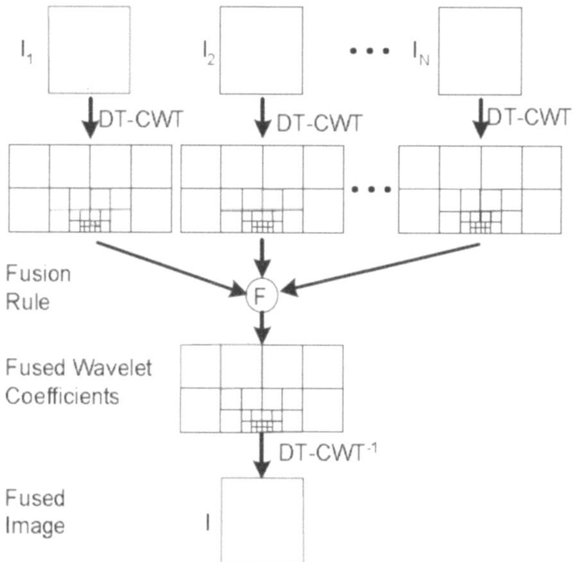

Fig. 3. The pixel-based image fusion scheme using the DT-CWT

The pixel-level fusion scheme used here employs the DT-CWT to obtain a MR decomposition of the input images. The wavelet coefficients are then combined, using a maximum-selection fusion rule to produce a single set of coefficients corresponding to the fused image. This process is shown in Fig. 3. The maximum-selection scheme selects the largest absolute wavelet coefficient at each location from the input images as the coefficient at that location in the fused image. As wavelets tend to pick out the salient features of an image, this scheme works well producing good results.

2.3 Image fusion based on region segmentation and complex wavelet

Decomposed by the multi-resolution DT-CWT, low-frequency part of the images denotes their approximate components, which contains spectral information of the source image. High-frequency part of the images denotes their detail components, which contains edge detail information of the source images. So, fusion algorithms after the source images decomposed are very important for the quality of fusion. At present, the fusion rules are commonly that average operator or weighted average operator is used in low-frequency domain, max absolute operator is used in high-frequency domain. For the two fused heterogeneous source images of the same scene, spectral information of one image is usually much richer than the other. For example, spectral information of visible light image is much richer than the infrared image. If the fusion rules of weighted average is adopted, part of spectrum information of visible light images will be lost, which results in that the spectrum information of fused image is less than visible light image.

To overcome these problems, we adopt spatial frequency to guide region-based fusion. The spatial frequency, which originated from the human visual system, indicates the overall active level in an image. The human visual system is too complex to be fully understood with present physiological means, but the use of spatial frequency has led to an effective objective quality index for image fusion. The spatial frequency of an image block is defined as follows: Consider an image, the row (R_F) and column (C_F) frequencies of the image block are given by

$$R_F = \sqrt{\frac{1}{M}\sum_{(i,j)\in\Omega}(F(i,j)-F(i,j-1))^2} \tag{4}$$

$$C_F = \sqrt{\frac{1}{M}\sum_{(i,j)\in\Omega}(F(i,j)-F(i-1,j))^2} \tag{5}$$

Here Ω is a certain segmentation region. The total spatial frequency S_F of the image is

$$S_F = \sqrt{R_F^2 + C_F^2} \tag{6}$$

We use the fusion of two registration source images A and B as an example, the image fusion process based on region segmentation and DT-CWT is accomplished by the following steps:

Step 1: Partition the source images A and B, then we get the region segmentations named R_A and R_B, using associated processing, then we can get the associated-segmentation image R_J. Calculate S_F of each region in the associated-segmentation image.

Step 2: Compare the spatial frequency of the corresponding regions of the two source images to decide fusion coefficients:

$$R_i^F = \begin{cases} \frac{S_{Fi}^{A}}{S_{Fi}^{A}+S_{Fi}^{B}}\bullet R_i^A + \frac{S_{Fi}^{B}}{S_{Fi}^{A}+S_{Fi}^{B}}\bullet R_i^B & \frac{1}{k} < S_{Fi}^{A} / S_{Fi}^{B} < k \\ R_i^A & S_{Fi}^{A} / S_{Fi}^{B} > k \\ R_i^B & S_{Fi}^{A} / S_{Fi}^{B} < \frac{1}{k} \end{cases} \tag{7}$$

Here R_i^F is the i th region of the fused image, S_{Fi}^{A} and S_{Fi}^{B} are the spatial frequencies of the i th region of image A and B, respectively, k is a threshold.

Step 3: Multi-level DT-CWT transform on the source images A and B, then we can get DT-CWT coefficients at different scale Layers, which contain low-frequency coefficient and high-frequency coefficient at different scale layers.

Step 4: Deal low-frequency and high-frequency part with fusion rules and fusion operators, then we get low-frequency coefficient and high-frequency coefficient at different scale Layers after fusion.

Step 5: Deal low-frequency coefficient and high-frequency coefficient at different scale Layers with DT-CWT inverse transform, then the reconstruction image is to be fused image.

2.4 Experiment results

To evaluate the presented fusion algorithm, we fuse the infrared and visible images of the same scene with this algorithm, and compare the fusion image with the fusion images with the DWT method (method 1) and SIDWT method (method 2). Fig. 4(a) is an infrared image, which presents the clear shapes such as a human being, trees and some high-temperature objects; Fig. 4(b) is a visible light (low light level) image, which provides more details than the infrared image. Besides this, it also shows some light sources. Fig. 4(c) is the segmentation region of the infrared image and Fig. 4(d) is the segmentation region of the visual image. Fig. 4(e) is associated region map of infrared/visible images, Fig. 4(f) is fused image with method 1 and Fig. 4(g) is fused image with method 2; Fig. 4(h) is fused image with the presented method.

According to the fusion images, the presented fusion algorithm has better effectiveness, which preserves not only the spectral information of the visible light image, but also the thermal target information of the infrared image. The details of the fusion image with the presented algorithm is clear, which shows that region segmentation has a function of extracting targets, also shows that the DT-CWT has the capability of capturing edge information. Though the fusion images with method 1 and 2 also reserve main scene information of the two images, they lose some details slightly. Edge of objects looks blurry slightly.

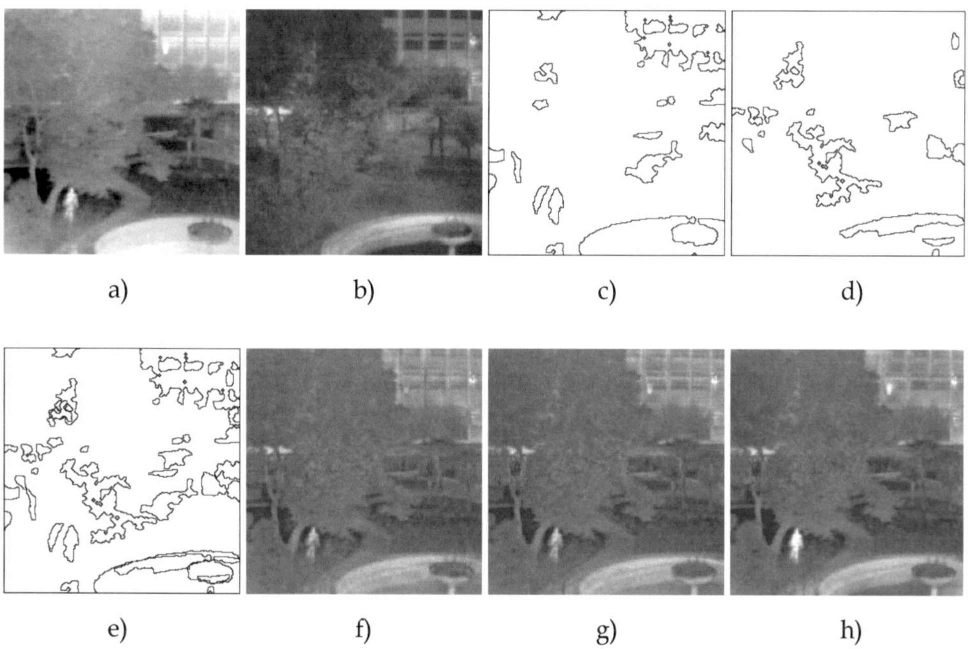

Fig. 4. Source images and fused results with different methods. (a) infrared image, (b) visible light image, (c) region map of the infrared image, (d) region map of the visible light image, (e) associated region map of infrared/visible light images, (f) fused image with method 1, (g) fused image with method 2, (h) fused image with the presented method

We use entropy, standard deviation, average gradient, structural similarity (SSIM) and $Q^{AB/F}$ to objectively evaluate the fusion images. Entropy reflects the average information of the image; standard deviation reflects the gray contrast of the fusion images and average gradient reflects the capability of expressing details of images; $SSIM(x,y,f)$ is an efficient metric of image fusion performance assessments. Given two images x and y of size $M \times N$, let μ_x denote the mean of x, let σ_x^2 and σ_{xy} be the variance of x and covariance of x and y. The SSIM index between signals x and y is :

$$\mathrm{SSIM}(x,y) = l(x,y)c(x,y)s(x,y) = \frac{(2\mu_x\mu_y + C_1)(2\sigma_{xy} + C_2)}{(\mu_x^2 + \mu_y^2 + C_1)(\sigma_x^2 + \sigma_y^2 + C_2)} \tag{8}$$

In this paper, we use an 11×11 circular-symmetric Gaussian weighting function to modify μ_x, μ_y, σ_{xy}, σ_x and σ_y. With such a windowing approach, the quality maps exhibit a locally isotropic property. In practice, one usually requires a single overall quality measure of the entire image. We use a mean SSIM index to evaluate the overall image quality.

$$\mathrm{SSIM(X,Y)} = \frac{1}{M}\sum_{j=1}^{M}\mathrm{SSIM}(x_j, y_j) \tag{9}$$

where X and Y are the reference and the distorted images, respectively; x_j and y_j are the image contents at the jth local window; and M is the number of local windows of the image.

We use the Wang-Bovik SSIM index in Eq. (9) to define a quality measure $SSIM(x,y,f)$ for image fusion. Here x, y are two input images and f is the composite image resulting from the fusion of x and y. The measure $SSIM(x,y,f)$ should express the "quality" of the composite image given the inputs x, y.

We denote by $s(x|w)$ some saliency of image x in window w. It should reflect the local relevance of image x within the window w, and it may depend on, e.g. contrast, variance, or entropy. Given the local saliencies $s(x|w)$ and $s(y|w)$ of the two input images x and y, we compute a local weight $\lambda_x(w)$ between 0 and 1 indicating the relative importance of image x compared to image y: the larger $\lambda_x(w)$, the more weight is given to image x. A typical choice for $\lambda_x(w)$ is

$$\lambda_x(w) = \frac{s(x|w)}{s(x|w) + s(y|w)} \tag{10}$$

In a similar fashion we compute $\lambda_y(w)$. Note that in this case $\lambda_y(w) = 1 - \lambda_x(w)$. Now we define the fusion quality measure $SSIM(x,y,f)$ as

$$SSIM(x,y,f) = \frac{1}{|W|}\sum_{w \in W}(\lambda_x(w)SSIM(x,f|w) + \lambda_y(w)SSIM(y,f|w)) \tag{11}$$

Thus, in regions where image x has a large saliency compared to y, the quality measure $SSIM(x,y,f)$ is mainly determined by the "similarity" of f and input image x. On the other hand, in regions where the saliency of y is much larger than that of x, the measure $SSIM(x,y,f)$ is mostly determined by the "similarity" of f and input image y.

$Q^{AB/F}$ is based on the idea that a fusion algorithm that transfers input gradient information into the fused image more accurately performs better. For the fusion of input images A and B resulting in a fused image F, gradient strength g and orientation $\alpha(\in[0,\pi])$ are extracted at each location (n,m) from each image using the Sobel operator and used to define relative strength and orientation "change" factors G and A, between each input and the fused image:

$$(G_{n,m}^{AF}, A_{n,m}^{AF}) = \left(\frac{g_{n,m}^{F}}{g_{n,m}^{A}}^{M}, 2\pi^{-1}\left\|\alpha_{n,m}^{A} - \alpha_{n,m}^{F}\right| - \pi/2\right|\right) \tag{12}$$

where M is 1 for $g^F > g^A$ and -1 otherwise. An edge information preservation measure Q^{AF} models information loss between A and F with respect to the 'change' parameters with sigmoid functions defined by constants Γ, κ_g, σ_g, κ_α, and σ_α:

$$Q_{n,m}^{AF} = \frac{\Gamma}{\sqrt{(1+e^{\kappa_g(G_{n,m}^{AF}-\sigma_g)})(1+e^{\kappa_\alpha(A_{n,m}^{AF}-\sigma_\alpha)})}} \tag{13}$$

Total fusion performance $Q^{AB/F}$ is evaluated as a sum of local information preservation estimates between each of the inputs and fused, Q^{AF} and Q^{BF}, weighted by local perceptual importance factors w^A and w^B usually defined as local gradient strength:

$$Q^{AB/F} = \frac{\sum_{\forall n,m} Q_{n,m}^{AF} w_{n,m}^{A} + Q_{n,m}^{AF} w_{n,m}^{B}}{\sum_{\forall n,m} w_{n,m}^{A} + w_{n,m}^{B}} \tag{14}$$

Table 1 gives the evaluation results of the three former algorithms. The evaluation results show the validity of the presented algorithm.

	Entropy	Average gradient	Standard deviation	$SSIM(x,y,f)$	$Q^{AB/F}$
Method 1	6.8313	0.0218	32.2700	0.6133	0.4282
Method 2	6.8774	0.0221	33.4626	0.6012	0.5010
The presented algorithm	6.9329	0.0226	34.1770	0.6304	0.5090

Table 1. Evaluation results of entropy, average gradient, standard deviation, $SSIM(x,y,f)$ and $Q^{AB/F}$

3. Region-based color fusion for infrared and LLL images

Toet demonstrated that transfer of colors could be adapted to transfer the natural color characteristics of daylight imagery into multi-band infrared and LLL images. However, this particular color mapping method colors the image regardless of scene content, weights all regions of the source image by the "global" color statistics, and thus the accuracy of the coloring is very much dependent on how well the target and source images are matched. Based on Toet's global-coloring framework, we present a new region-based method that the image segmentation is firstly carried out and then region coloring is realized.

3.1 Review of global-coloring method

The aim of the global-coloring is to give NV images the appearance of normal daylight color images. A false-color image (source image) is first formed by assigning multi-band NV images to three RGB channels. The false-color images usually have an unnatural color appearance. Then, a true-color daylight image (reference image) is manually selected with similar scenery (e.g., syntactic content and color appearance) to the NV images. Both source and reference images are transformed into a Luminance-Alpha-Beta ($l\alpha\beta$) color space, followed by calculating the global mean and standard deviation for each $l\alpha\beta$ plane. Next, a "statistic- matching" procedure is carried out between the source and reference image. The mapped source image is then transformed back to RGB space. Finally, the mapped source image is transformed into YCbCr space and the "value" component (similar to the luminance component in $l\alpha\beta$ decomposition) of the mapped source image is replaced with the "fused NV image", which is a grayscale image made with multi-band NV images (e.g., image intensified and infrared image). This fused image replacement is necessary to make the colorized image have a proper and consistent contrast. Notice that the "luminance" component in $l\alpha\beta$ space cannot be used directly for this replacement because its dynamic range is very different from that of the fused image, whereas the "value" component in YCbCr space has the same gray-level range as the fused image. The lab space is utilized for color mapping because of its decorrelation property of three channels, whereas the YCbCr space is suitable for human interface.

The fusion process can be summarized in the following steps:

1. Set the R channel with the infrared image data, G and B channel with low-light-level image data and generate the rough color fusion image. Choose a reference image with good contrast

$$\begin{bmatrix} R_S \\ G_S \\ B_S \end{bmatrix} = \begin{bmatrix} IR \\ LL \\ LL \end{bmatrix} \tag{15}$$

2. The RGB values can be converted to LMS space by using the following equation

$$\begin{bmatrix} L \\ M \\ S \end{bmatrix} = \begin{bmatrix} 0.3811 & 0.5783 & 0.0402 \\ 0.1967 & 0.7244 & 0.0782 \\ 0.0241 & 0.1288 & 0.8444 \end{bmatrix} \begin{bmatrix} R \\ G \\ B \end{bmatrix} \tag{16}$$

3. A logarithmic transform is employed here to reduce the data skew that existed in the above color space

$$\begin{aligned} \boldsymbol{L} &= \log L \\ \boldsymbol{M} &= \log M \\ \boldsymbol{S} &= \log S \end{aligned} \tag{17}$$

4. $l\alpha\beta$ space can decorrelate the three axes in the LMS space

$$\begin{bmatrix} l \\ \alpha \\ \beta \end{bmatrix} = \begin{bmatrix} 0.5774 & 0.5774 & 0.5774 \\ 0.4082 & 0.4082 & -0.8165 \\ 1.4142 & -1.4142 & 0 \end{bmatrix} \begin{bmatrix} \boldsymbol{L} \\ \boldsymbol{M} \\ \boldsymbol{S} \end{bmatrix} \tag{18}$$

5. A simple technique, termed "statistic matching", used to transfer the color characteristics from natural daylight imagery to false-color night-vision imagery is formulated as

$$\boldsymbol{I}_C^k = (\boldsymbol{I}_S^k - \mu_S^k) \bullet \frac{\sigma_T^k}{\sigma_S^k} + \mu_T^k, \ for \quad k = \{l, \alpha, \beta\} \tag{19}$$

where I_C is the colored image, I_S is the source (false-color) image in $l\alpha\beta$ space; μ denotes the mean and σ denotes the standard deviation; the subscripts 'S' and 'T' refer to the source and reference images, respectively; and the superscript 'k' is one of the color components $\{l, \alpha, \beta\}$.After this transformation the pixels comprising source image have means and standard deviations that conform to the reference daylight color image in $l\alpha\beta$ space.

6. The inverse transform from the lab space to the LMS space can be expressed by

$$\begin{bmatrix} \boldsymbol{L} \\ \boldsymbol{M} \\ \boldsymbol{S} \end{bmatrix} = \begin{bmatrix} 0.5774 & 0.4082 & 0.3536 \\ 0.5774 & 0.4082 & -0.3536 \\ 0.5774 & -0.8165 & 0 \end{bmatrix} \begin{bmatrix} l \\ \alpha \\ \beta \end{bmatrix} \tag{20}$$

7. The transform depicted above can be inverted by raising the LMS pixel values to the tenth order back to linear LMS space, and then using the inverse transform of Eq. (10) to RGB space

$$\begin{bmatrix} R \\ G \\ B \end{bmatrix} = \begin{bmatrix} 4.4679 & -3.5873 & 0.1193 \\ -1.2186 & 2.3809 & -0.1624 \\ 0.0497 & -0.2439 & 1.2045 \end{bmatrix} \begin{bmatrix} L \\ M \\ S \end{bmatrix} \tag{21}$$

8. Transfer the fusion image data from RGB space to YC_BC_R space

$$\begin{bmatrix} Y \\ C_B \\ C_R \end{bmatrix} = \begin{bmatrix} 0.2990 & 0.5870 & 0.1140 \\ -0.1687 & -0.3313 & 0.5000 \\ 0.5000 & -0.4187 & -0.0813 \end{bmatrix} \begin{bmatrix} R \\ G \\ B \end{bmatrix} \tag{22}$$

9. The brightness Y_f acquired by transforming the fusion image and reference image from RGB space to $l\alpha\beta$ space is not usually appropriate, because Y_f is the weight sum of the infrared and low-light-level images. Thereby, we adopt the fusion image by laplacian pyramid fusion method replacing Y_f.
10. Transfer the adjusted rough fusion image data from YC_BC_R space back to RGB space, and we can get the ultimate re-staining rough fusion image.

$$\begin{bmatrix} R \\ G \\ B \end{bmatrix} = \begin{bmatrix} 1.0000 & 0.0000 & 1.4020 \\ 1.0000 & -0.3441 & -0.7141 \\ 1.0000 & 1.7720 & 0.0000 \end{bmatrix} \begin{bmatrix} Y \\ C_B \\ C_R \end{bmatrix} \tag{23}$$

3.2 The region-based coloring fusion method

Based on the framework of the global-coloring method as described in Section 3.1, we present a region-based coloring fusion method (see Fig. 5.) that makes the fusion images appear more like daylight imagery. The major points for this new method are as follows. (a) The infrared and LLL images are rendered segment-by-segment. (b) The segmented regions of the two images are combined and form a new segmented map. (c) These regions are classified according to the target types and the spatial frequencies, and some valuable targets are extracted according to the luminance of the infrared images or the motion trend of the infrared and LLL video. At present, our classification is still carried out manually. (d) The infrared and LLL images are mapped into the RGB space. A lot of mapping color methods has been provided, but the simplest mapping method is still suitable. For example, the infrared image is mapped into the R channel and the LLL image is mapped into the G channel and the average of the infrared and LLL images is mapped into the B channel. (e) Some typical scene images must be chosen as the reference images. These images should include some features similar to a certain segmented region. (f) Transfer of color is run region by region in the $l\alpha\beta$ space according to Reinhard's method. (g) The gray fusion image is used to replace the Y of the color fusion image in the YCbCr space. Here, the gray fusion method may be the fusion method in Section 2 or some other classical ones.

Image segmentation is quite challenging because image contents vary greatly from image to image. We adopt two segmentation methods. One is the morphologic method in Section 2, the other is the nonlinear diffusion method. The two methods have been proven as powerful methods in the denoising and smoothing of image intensities while retaining and enhancing edges. Such an image smoothing process can be summarized as a successive coarsening of any given image while certain structures in that image are retained on a fine scale.

Basically, diffusion is a PDE (partial differential equation) method that involves two operators, smoothing and gradient, in 2D image space. The nonlinear diffusion equation is

$$\frac{\partial I(x)}{\partial t} = \vec{\nabla} \cdot \left(\omega(x) \vec{\nabla} I(x) \right) \tag{24}$$

Where $\vec{\nabla}$ is a vector containing gradients taken at different neighboring configurations (i.e., nearest-neighbors, second-neighbors, etc.) and $\omega(x)$ are the nonlinear diffusion coefficients.

The diffusion process smoothes the regions with lower gradients whereas stops smoothing at region boundaries with higher gradients. Nonlinear diffusion means the smoothing operation depends on the region gradient distribution. In other words, the diffused result is a nonlinear function of local gradients. Diffusion must be used with clustering and region merging techniques together, which make the segmentation flexible.

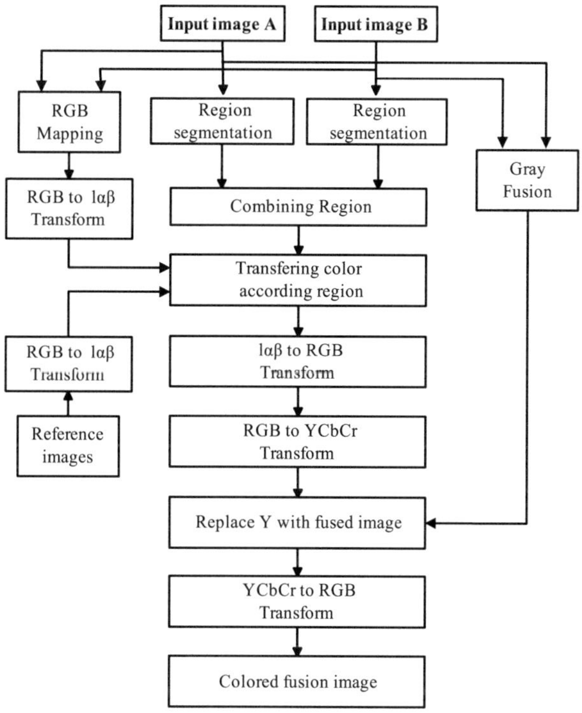

Fig. 5. Diagram of the proposed local-coloring method

3.3 Experiment result

Here two experiments have been carried out with the region-based coloring fusion method. The only difference is that the morphologic method is adopted in experiment 1 and the nonlinear diffusion method is adopted in experiment 2.

3.3.1 Experiment 1

To evaluate the region-based coloring fusion method, we fuse the infrared and LLL images of the same scene, and compare the fusion images with the presented method and the global-coloring method. Fig. 6(a) is an infrared image, which presents the clear shapes such as a human being, trees, building, pool and some high-temperature objects; Fig. 6(b) is a LLL image, which provides more details than the infrared image. Besides this, it also shows some light sources. Fig. 6(c) is the fusion image acquiring by Section 2. Fig. 6(e), (g), (i) and (k) are the fusion images with global-coloring method separately using Fig. 6(d), (f), (h) and (j) as reference image. Fig. 6(l) is the segmentation region of the infrared image with morphology method and Fig. 6(m) is the segmentation region of the visual image with morphology method. Fig. 6(n) is associated region map of infrared/ visible images. In the region image, that "person" was perfectly partitioned. The backgrounds such as road, building and so on are also well segmented. Fig. 6(o) is fused image with local-coloring method using Fig. 6(d), (f), (h) and (j) as reference images. Compared to Fig. 6(e), (g), (i) and (k), Fig. 6(o) has a clear color distinction between tree, person, building, pool and lawn. From Fig. 6(o) we can see that region-based coloring fusion method result can significantly improve observers' performance and reaction time.

Fig. 6. Source images, reference images and fused results with different methods. (a) infrared image, (b) LLL image, (c) fusion image using method in Section 2, (e), (g), (i) and (k) fusion images with global-coloring method separately using (d), (f), (h) and (j) as reference image, (l) region map of the infrared image, (m) region map of the LLL image, (n) associated region map of (l) and (m), (o) fused image with the region-based coloring fusion method using (d), (f), (h) and (j) as reference color images

3.3.2 Experiment 2

To evaluate the presented region-based coloring fusion method, we fuse the infrared and visible light images of the same scene with this algorithm, and compare the fusion image with the fusion images with global-coloring method. Fig. 7(a) is an infrared image, which presents the clear shapes such as trees, building, sky and some high-temperature objects; Fig. 7(b) is a visible light image, which provides more details than the infrared image.

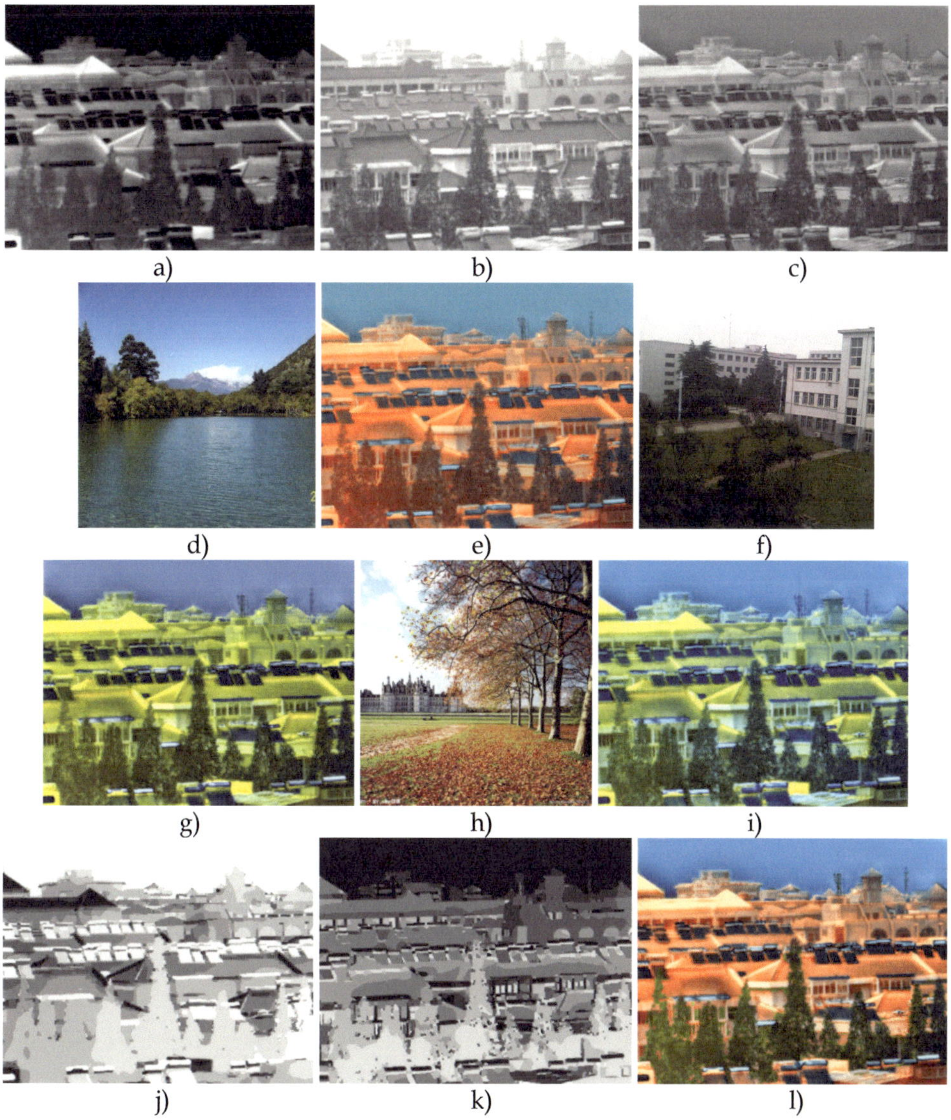

Fig. 7. Source images, reference images and fused results with different methods. (a) infrared image, (b) visible light image, (c) fusion image using gradient pyramid method, (e), (g) and (i) fusion images with global-coloring method separately using (d), (f) and (h) as reference image, (j) region map of the infrared image, (k) region map of the visible light image, (l) fused image with the region-based coloring fusion method using (d), (f) and (h) as reference images

Besides this, it also shows some light sources. Fig. 7(c) is the fusion image using gradient pyramid method. Fig. 7(e), (g) and (i) are the fusion images with global-coloring method separately using Fig. 7(d), (f) and (h) as reference image. Fig. 7(j) is the segmentation region of the infrared image with clustering method and Fig. 7(k) is the segmentation region of the visual image with clustering method. Fig. 7(l) is fused image with local-coloring method using (d), (f) and (h) as reference color images. Compared to Fig. 7(e), (g) and (i), Fig. 7(l) has a clear color distinction between tree, building and sky. From Fig. 7(i) we can see that local-coloring method result can significantly improve observers' performance and the colors are more nature than global-coloring method result.

4. Conclusion

This chapter presents a gray image fusion method and a color image fusion method based on the region segmentation. The region-based fusion methods use the different feature regions of original image and compound the pixel level and feature level of image fusions. The effective way to separate target and background proves crucial for the quality of image fusion. The proposed method preserves the details of the LLL image and the legible target of the infrared image, therefore, the fused image enables the exact location of the target to be easily observed and provides all-around information for further processing tasks.

In the gray method, segmentation is firstly performed on the IR image and LLL images with top-bottom-hat filtering and the threshold method, consequently, the DT-CWT coefficients from the different regions are merged separately. Finally the fused image is obtained by performing inverse DT-CWT. This method keeps the approximate shift invariance and the limited redundancy. Region segmentation performs us to using different rules for each region of each level. Experimental results evidence this method which could provide better fusion than classical fusion methods in terms of objective fusion metric values such as entropy, average gradient, standard deviation, $SSIM(x,y,f)$ and $Q^{AB/F}$

In the color fusion method, segmentation is firstly performed on the IR image and LLL image with the morphologic method or the diffusion method. At the same time, the IR image and LLL image are mapped into the RGB space, and the gray fusion of the two images is conducted. Here, the color map rule and the gray fusion method are not very important. The false-color images usually have an unnatural color appearance, but a chance of region by region color transferring is given to ensure the fusion image similar to natural images. The fusion images are transformed into YC_BC_R space and the brightness is replaced by the gray fusion images. Experimental results evidence this method which could provide better sense of hierarchy than the global color fusion method in terms of subjective evaluation.

5. Reference

A. Toet, New false color mapping for image fusion, *Opt. Eng.* 1996, 35(3).

A. Toet, et al. Fusion of visible and thermal imagery improves situational awareness, in: J.G. Verly (Ed.), Enhanced and Synthetic Vision 1997, *International Society for Optical Engineering, Bellingham,* WA, USA, 1997, pp. 177–188.

A. Toet, J.K. IJspeert, Perceptual evaluation of different image fusion schemes, in: I. Kadar (Ed.), Signal Processing, Sensor Fusion, and Target Recognition X, *The International Society for Optical Engineering*, Bellingham, WA, 2001, pp. 436–441.

A. Toet, and E.M. Franken. Perceptual evaluation of different image fusion schemes. *Displays*, 2003, 24.
Alexander Toet. Natural color mapping for multiband night vision imagery. *Information Fusion*, 2003, 4:155-166.
A.M. Waxman, et al. Color night vision: opponent processing in the fusion of visible and IR imagery. *Neural Networks*, 1997, 10(1):1-6.
A.M. Waxman. Solid-state color night vision: fusion of lowlight visible and thermal infrared imagery, *MIT Lincoln Laboratory Journal* 11 (1999) 41-60.
C. Wang, and Z.F. Ye. Perceptual contrast-based image fusion: A variational approach, *Acta Automatica Sinica*. 2007, 33(2).
Cvejic N, Lewis J, Bull D, et al. Region-based multimodal image fusion using ICA bases. *IEEE Sensors Journal* 2007, 7(5): 743-751.
D. Barash, D. Comaniciu. A common framework for nonlinear diffusion, adaptive smoothing, bilateral filtering and mean shift. *Image Vision Computing*, 2004, 22(1): 73-81.
D. Fay, et al. Color night vision: Opponent processing in the fusion of visible and IR imagery. *Neural Networks*, 1997, 10(1): 1-6.
D. Malacara. Color Vision and Colorimetry: Theory and Applications. *SPIE Press*, Bellingham, 2002.
D.A. Fay, et al. Fusion of multi-sensor imagery for night vision: color visualization, target learning and search. *Proceedings of the Third International Conference on Information Fusion*, Paris, France, 2000.
E. Reinhard, et al. Color transfer between images. *IEEE Computer Graphics and Applications*, 2001, 21(5):34-41.
Hill P, Canagarajah N, Bull D. Image fusion using complex wavelets, in *Proc. of British Machine Vision Conference*, 2002: 487-496
J. Bezdek. Pattern Recognition with Fuzzy Objective Functions. Plenum, New York, 1981.
J. Schuler, et al.. Infrared color vision: An approach to sensor fusion. *Optics and Photonics News*, August 1998.
J. Weickert, B.M. ter Haar Romeny, M.A. Viergever. Efficient and reliable schemes for nonlinear diffusion filtering. *IEEE Transactions on Image Processing*, 1998, 7:398-410.
J.S. Shi, et al. Objective evaluation of color fusion of visible and IR imagery by measuring image contrast, in *Proceedings of SPIE*, 2005, p.594.
Kingsbury N.G. Complex wavelets for shift invariant analysis and filtering of signals. *Applied and Computational Harmonic Analysis*, 2001, 10(3):234-253.
Kingsbury N.G. Image processing with complex wavelets. *Philosophical Transactions of the Royal Society of London*, 1999, 357: 2543-2560.
Krebs, et al. An evaluation of a sensor fusion system to improve drivers' nighttime detection of road hazards. *Proceedings of the 43 rd Annual Meeting Human Factors and Ergonomics Society*, 1999, p.1333.
Krista Amolins, Yun Zhang, Peter Dare. Wavelet based image fusion techniques—an introduction, review and comparison. *Journal of Photogrammetry & Remote Sensing*, 2007, 62:249-263
L.X. Wang, et al. Color fusion algorithm for visible and infrared images based on color transfer in YUV color space. *Proceedings of SPIE*, 2007, p. 67870S.

M. Aguilar, et al. Field evaluations of dual-band fusion for color night vision, in: J.G. Verly (Ed.), Enhanced and Synthetic Vision 1999, *The International Society for Optical Engineering*, Bellingham, WA, 1999, 168-175.

M. Nielsen, et al. Scale-Space Theories in Computer Vision, *Lecture Notes in Computer Science*, 1999, vol. 1682.

M.D. Fairchild. Color Appearance Models, Addison Wesley Longman. Inc., Reading, MA, 1998.

N. Otsu. A threshold selection method from gray-level histograms, *IEEE Trans. System, Man and Cybernetics*. 1979, 9(1).

O. Scherzer, J. Weickert. Relations between regularization and diffusion filtering. *Journal of Mathematical Imaging and Vision*, 2000, 12:43-63.

P. Hill, N. Canagarajah, D. Bull. Image fusion using complex wavelets. *Proceedings of the 13th British Machine Vision Conference*, Cardiff, UK, 2002.

Piella G. A general framework for multiresolution image fusion: from pixels to regions. *Information Fusion*, 2003, 4(4): 259-280.

Piella G. A region-based multiresolution image fusion algorithm. *Proceedings of the Fifth International Conference on Information Fusion*. 2002, 1557-1564.

R. O_Callaghan, D.R. Bull. Combined morphological–spectral unsupervised image segmentation. *IEEE Transactions on Image Processing*. 2005, 14(1):49–62.

Ranchin, T., Wald, L. Fusion of high spatial and spectral resolution images: the ARSIS concept and its implementation. *Photogrammetric Engineering & Remote Sensing*, 2000, 66(1):49–61.

S G Mallat, A theory for multiresolution signal decomposition: The wavelet representation, *IEEE Trans. PAMI*, 1989, 11(7):674-693

S. Li, J.T. Kwok, Y. Wang. Combination of images with diverse focuses using the spatial frequency, *Information Fusion*, 2001, 2(3):169–176.

Toet A, van Ruyven J J, Valeton J M. Merging thermal and visual images by a contrast pyramid. *Optical Engineering*, 1989, 28(7): 789-792.

V. Tsagaris, V. Anastassopoulos. Fusion of visible and infrared imagery for night color vision. *Displays*. 2005, 26:191–196.

V. Tsagaris and V. Anastassopoulos. A global measure for assessing image fusion methods. *Opt.Eng*. 2006, 45(2).

V. Tsagaris. Objective evaluation of color image fusion methods. *Opt.Eng*. 2009, 48(6).

W. Pedrycz. Conditional fuzzy c-means, *Pattern Recognition Letters*. 1996, 17:625- 631.

Wu, J. et al. Remote sensing image fusion based on average gradient of wavelet transform. *IEEE International Conference on Mechatronics and Automation*, 2005:1817–1821.

Yufeng Zheng, Edward A. Essock. A local-coloring method for night-vision colorization utilizing image analysis and fusion. *Information Fusion*, 2008, 9:186–199.

Z. Wang, et al. Image quality assessment: From error visibility to structural similarity. *IEEE Transactions on Image Processing*, 2004, 13(4):600-612.

Z.H. Xie, and T. G. Jr. Stockham.Toward the unification of three visual laws and two visual models in brightness perception, *IEEE Trans. System, Man and Cybernetics*. 1989, 19(2).

Zhang Junju, et al. An Image Fusion Method based on Region Segmentation and Complex Wavelets. *Proc. of SPIE*. Vol. 7384, 2009, 738421-1—738421-8.

Zhang Junju, et al. Real-time Color Image Fusion for Infrared and Low-light-level Cameras. *Proc. of SPIE*. Vol. 7383, 2009, 73833B-1—73833B-7.

15

Cognitive Image Fusion and Assessment

Alexander Toet
TNO Human Factors
The Netherlands

1. Introduction

The increasing availability and deployment of imaging sensors operating in multiple spectral bands has led to a requirement for methods that combine the signals from these sensors in an effective and ergonomic way for presentation to the human operator. Effective combinations of complementary and partially redundant multispectral imagery can provide information that is not directly evident from the individual input images.

Image fusion for human inspection should combine information from two or more images of a scene into a single composite image that is more informative than each of the input images alone, and that requires minimal cognitive effort to understand. The fusion process should therefore maximize the amount of relevant information in the fused image, while minimizing the amount of irrelevant details, uncertainty and redundancy in the output. Thus, image fusion should preserve task relevant information from the source images, prevent the occurrence of artifacts or inconsistencies in the fused image, and suppress irrelevant features (e.g. noise) from the source images (Smith & Heather, 2005). The representation of fused imagery should optimally agree with human cognition, so that humans can quickly grasp the gist and meaning of the displayed scenes. For instance, the representation of spatial details should effortlessly elicit the recognition of known Gestalts, and the color schemes used should be natural (ecologically correct) and thus agree with human intuition. Irrelevant details (clutter) should be suppressed to minimize cognitive workload and to maximize recognition speed.

Some potential benefits of image fusion are: wider spatial and temporal coverage, decreased uncertainty, improved reliability, and increased robustness of the system. Image fusion has applications in defense for situation awareness (Toet et al., 1997b), surveillance (Riley & Smith, 2006), target tracking (Zou & Bhanu, 2005), intelligence gathering (O'Brien & Irvine, 2004), and person authentication (Kong et al., 2007). Other important applications are found in industry and medicine (for a recent survey of different applications of image fusion techniques see Blum & Liu, 2006).

The way images are combined depends on the specific application and on the type of information that is relevant in the given context (Smith & Heather, 2005). By examining the effects of several image fusion methods on different cognitive tasks, Krebs et al. (Krebs & Ahumada, 2002) showed that the benefits of sensor fusion are task dependent. However, until now the human end user has not been involved in the design process and the development of image fusion algorithms to any great extent. Mostly, image fusion algorithms are developed in isolation, and the human end-user is little more than an afterthought, so that separate follow-up evaluation studies are usually required to assess to what extent humans benefit from these methods (Aguilar et al., 1999; Dixon et al., 2005; Dixon et al., 2006a; Dixon et al., 2006b; Essock et al., 1999; Essock et al., 2005; Krebs & Sinai, 2002; Smith et al., 2002; Toet & Franken, 2003; Waxman et al., 2006). Recently has it been realized that the only way to guarantee the ultimate effectiveness of image fusion methods for human observers is to include human evaluation as an integral part of the design process (Muller & Narayanan, 2009).

In this chapter we present some image fusion techniques and assessment methods that are based on the principles of cognitive engineering. Cognitive image fusion is based on concepts derived from neural models of visual perception and pattern recognition. Here we focus on the intuitive representation of spatial structures (outlines) and image color. We will argue that cognitive fusion leads to fused image representations that are optimally tuned to the human information processing capabilities.

1.1 The representation of spatial detail in fused imagery

Human visual image recognition performance depends on the amount of informative spatial features (like edges, corners, and lines) that are available in the image (Ullman, 2007). Hence, for optimal interpretation a fusion scheme should maximize the number of meaningful details in the resulting fused image. However, there is still a large semantic gap between computer image representations and human image understanding (Vogel & Schiele, 2007). This is a significant obstacle for the development of effective image fusion schemes. For instance, image segmentation and decomposition schemes still lead to undesirable over- and under- segmentation of semantically contiguous boundaries. Edge representations of images still yield incomplete object boundaries or numerous spurious (noise related) edges. As a result most image representation schemes do not correspond to human perception. It has been suggested to use cognitive principles to bridge the gap between human and computer image understanding (Jakobson et al., 2004). Some first attempts to apply concepts derived from neural models of visual processing and pattern recognition to image fusion and interpretation have been quite successful (Chiarella et al., 2004; Fay et al., 2004; Waxman et al., 2003).

1.2 Color representation of fused imagery

Fused imagery has traditionally been represented in graytones. However, the increasing availability of fused and multi-band vision systems has led to a growing interest in color representations of fused imagery (Li & Wang, 2007; Shi et al., 2005a; Shi et al., 2005b; Tsagiris & Anastassopoulos, 2005; Zheng et al., 2005). In principle, color imagery has several benefits over monochrome imagery for human inspection. While the human eye can only distinguish about 100 shades of gray at any instant, it can discriminate several thousands of colors. As a result, color may improve feature contrast, thus enabling better scene segmentation and object detection (Walls, 2006). Color imagery may yield a more complete mental representation of the perceived scene, resulting in better situational awareness. Scene understanding and recognition, reaction time, and object identification are indeed faster and more accurate with color imagery than with monochrome imagery (Cavanillas, 1999; Gegenfurtner & Rieger, 2000; Goffaux et al., 2005; Oliva & Schyns, 2000; Rousselet et al., 2005; Sampson, 1996; Spence et al., 2006; Wichmann et al., 2002). Also, observers are able to selectively attend to task-relevant color targets and to ignore non-targets with a task-irrelevant color (Ansorge et al., 2005; Folk & Remington, 1998; Green & Anderson, 1956). As a result, simply producing a fused image by mapping multiple spectral bands into a three dimensional color space already generates an immediate benefit, and provides a method to increase the dynamic range of a sensor system (Driggers et al., 2001).

However, the color mapping should be chosen with care and should be adapted to the task at hand. Although general design rules can be used to assure that the information available in the sensor image is optimally conveyed to the observer (Jacobson & Gupta, 2005), it is not trivial to derive a mapping from the various sensor bands to the three independent color channels, especially when the number of sensor bands exceeds three (e.g. with hyperspectral imagers; Jacobson et al., 2007). In practice, many tasks may benefit from a representation that renders fused imagery in natural colors. Natural colors facilitate object recognition by allowing access to stored color knowledge (Joseph & Proffitt, 1996). Experimental evidence indicates that object recognition depends on stored knowledge of the object's chromatic characteristics (Joseph & Proffitt, 1996). In natural scene recognition paradigms, optimal reaction times and accuracy are obtained for normal natural (or diagnostically) colored images, followed by their grayscale version, and lastly by their (nondiagnostically) false colored version (Goffaux et al., 2005; Oliva, 2005; Oliva & Schyns, 2000; Rousselet et al., 2005; Wichmann et al., 2002).

When sensors operate outside the visible waveband, artificial color mappings inherently yield false color images whose chromatic characteristics do not correspond in any intuitive or obvious way to those of a scene viewed under natural photopic illumination (e.g. Fredembach & Süsstrunk, 2008). As a result, this type of false color imagery may disrupt the recognition process by denying access to stored knowledge. In that case, observers need to rely on color contrast to segment a scene and recognize the objects therein. This may lead to a performance that is even worse compared to single band imagery alone (Sinai et al., 1999a). Experiments have indeed convincingly demonstrated that a false color rendering of fused night-time imagery which resembles natural color imagery significantly improves observer performance and reaction times in tasks that involve scene segmentation and classification (Essock et al., 1999; Sinai et al., 1999b; Toet et al., 1997a; Toet & IJspeert, 2001; Vargo, 1999; White, 1998), whereas color mappings that produce counterintuitive (unnaturally looking) results are detrimental to human performance (Krebs et al., 1998; Toet & IJspeert, 2001; Vargo, 1999). One of the reasons often cited for inconsistent color mapping is a lack of physical color constancy (Vargo, 1999). Thus, the challenge is to give nightvision imagery not merely an intuitively meaningful ("naturalistic") color appearance, but also one that is stable for camera motion and changes in scene composition and lighting conditions. A natural and stable color representation serves to improve the viewer's scene comprehension and enhance object recognition and discrimination (Scribner et al., 1999).Several techniques have been proposed to render night-time imagery in color (e.g. Sun et al., 2005; Toet, 2003; Tsagiris & Anastassopoulos, 2005; Wang et al., 2002; Zheng et al., 2005). Simply mapping the signals from different nighttime sensors (sensitive in different spectral wavebands) to the individual channels of a standard color display or to the individual components of perceptually decorrelated color spaces, sometimes preceded by principal component transforms or followed by a linear transformation of the color pixels to enhance color contrast, usually results in imagery with an unnatural color appearance (e.g. Howard et al., 2000; Krebs et al., 1998; Li et al., 2004; Schuler et al., 2000; Scribner et al., 2003). More intuitive color schemes may be obtained through opponent processing through feedforward center-surround shunting neural networks similar to those found in vertebrate color vision (Aguilar et al., 1998; Aguilar et al., 1999; Fay et al., 2000a; Fay et al., 2000b; Huang et al., 2007; Warren et al., 1999; Waxman et al., 1995; Waxman et al., 1997; Waxman et al., 1998). Although this approach produces fused nighttime images with appreciable color contrast, the resulting color schemes remain rather arbitrary and are usually not strictly related to the actual daytime color scheme of the scene that is registered. We recently developed a color transform that can give fused multisensor imagery a natural color appearance (Hogervorst & Toet, 2008a; Hogervorst & Toet, 2008b; Hogervorst & Toet, 2010). The method derives an optimal color mapping by optimizing the match between a set of corresponding samples taken from a daytime color reference image and a multi-band nighttime image. Once the mapping has been determined, it can be implemented as a color lookup-table transform. As a result, the color transform is extremely simple and fast, and can easily be applied in real-time with standard hardware. Moreover, it yields fused images with a natural color appearance and provides object color constancy, since the relation between sensor output and colors is fixed. Since the mapping is sample-based, it is highly specific for different types of materials in the scene and can therefore easily be adapted for the task at hand, such as optimizing the visibility of camouflaged objects.

1.3 The need for image fusion quality metrics

Because the number of image fusion techniques and systems available is steadily increasing, there is a growing need for metrics to evaluate and compare the quality of fused imagery. Clearly, the ultimate image fusion scheme should use semantically meaningful image representations, and should use fusion rules that give higher priority (weights) to regions with semantically higher importance to the operator. Generally the ideal fused image (reference) is not available. In applications where the fused images are intended for human observation, the performance of fusion algorithms can be measured in terms of improvement in user performance in tasks like detection, recognition, tracking, or classification. This approach requires a well defined task that allow quantification of human performance (e.g. Toet et al., 1997b; Toet & Franken, 2003). However, this usually means time consuming and often expensive experiments involving a large number of human subjects. In recent years, a number of computational image fusion quality assessment metrics have therefore been proposed (e.g. Angell, 2005; Blum, 2006; Chari et al., 2005; Chen & Varshney, 2005; Chen & Varshney, 2007; Corsini et al., 2006; Cvejic et al., 2005a; Cvejic et al., 2005b; Piella & Heijmans, 2003; Toet & Hogervorst, 2003; Tsagiris & Anastassopoulos, 2004; Ulug & Claire, 2000; Wang & Shen, 2006; Xydeas & Petrovic, 2000; Yang et al., 2007; Zheng et al., 2007; Zhu & Jia, 2005). Although some of these metrics agree with human visual perception to some extent, most of them cannot predict observer performance for different input imagery and scenarios. Metrics that accurately describe human performance are of great value, since they can be used to optimize image fusion systems and to predict human observer performance for different scenarios. However, since reliable human performance related metrics are extremely difficult to design, they are not yet available at present.

1.4 Overview of this chapter

In the rest of this chapter we investigate how different grayscale and color image fusion methods affect the perception of scene layout, object recognition, and the detection of camouflaged objects. We assessed the different fusion techniques by quantifying the performance of human observers using the fused imagery.

2. Scene layout recognition

In this section we investigate the effects of grayscale and color image fusion on a spatial localization task. We assess the different fusion techniques by quantifying the (objective) localization accuracy and the (subjective) confidence of human observers performing the task using the fused imagery.

2.1 Imagery

We recorded spatially registered visible light and mid-wave (3-5 μm) thermal motion sequences representing three military surveillance scenarios (for details see Toet et al., 1997b). The individual images used in this study correspond to successive frames from these time sequences. Corresponding visual and thermal frames were fused using an opponent color fusion technique developed by the MIT Lincoln Laboratory (Waxman et al., 1995; Waxman et al., 1996a; Waxman et al., 1996b; Waxman et al., 1996c; Waxman et al., 1997; Waxman et al., 1999). Grayscale fused images were obtained by taking the luminance component of the corresponding color fused images. The MIT color fusion method provides images with a semi natural color appearance, and enhances image contrast by filtering the input images with a feedforward center-surround shunting neural network (Grossberg, 1988).

In all three scenarios, the thermal images provide a poor representation of the scene layout, whereas they clearly show the presence of a person in the scene (Fig. 1). In contrast, the visible images clearly show the scene structure, whereas they poorly represent the person. In the fused images, both the background details and the person are clearly visible. Situational awareness is tested by asking observers to report the perceived position of the person relative to characteristic details in the scene. Because the relevant information is distributed over the individual image modalities (the images are complementary), this task cannot be performed with any of the individual image modalities. We used schematic (cartoon-like) representations of the actual scenes to obtain a baseline performance and to register the observer responses. Fig. 1 shows an example of a scenario in which the reference features are the poles that support the fence. These poles are clearly visible in the CCD images but not represented in the IR images because they have nearly the same temperature as the surrounding terrain. In the (graylevel and color) fused images the poles are again clearly visible.

2.2 Experiment

Each image was briefly (2s) shown on a CRT display, followed by the presentation of a corresponding schematic reference image. The subject's task was to indicate the perceived location of the person in the scene by placing a mouse controlled cursor at the corresponding location in this reference image. When the left mouse button was pressed the computer registered the coordinates corresponding to the indicated image location (the mouse coordinates) and computed the distance in the image plane between the actual position of the person and the indicated location. The subject pressed the right mouse button if the person in the displayed scene could not be detected. The subject could only perform the localization task by memorizing the perceived position of the person relative to the reference features in the scene.

The schematic reference images were also used to determine the optimal (baseline) localization accuracy of the observers. Baseline test images (Fig. 1) were created by placing a binary (dark) image of a walking person at different locations in the reference scene. In the resulting set of schematic images both the reference features and the person are highly visible. Also, there are no distracting features in these images that may degrade localization performance. Therefore, observer performance for these schematic test images should be optimal and may serve as a baseline to compare performance obtained with the other image modalities.

A total of 6 subjects, aged between 20 and 30 years, served in the experiments reported below (for details see Toet et al., 1997b).

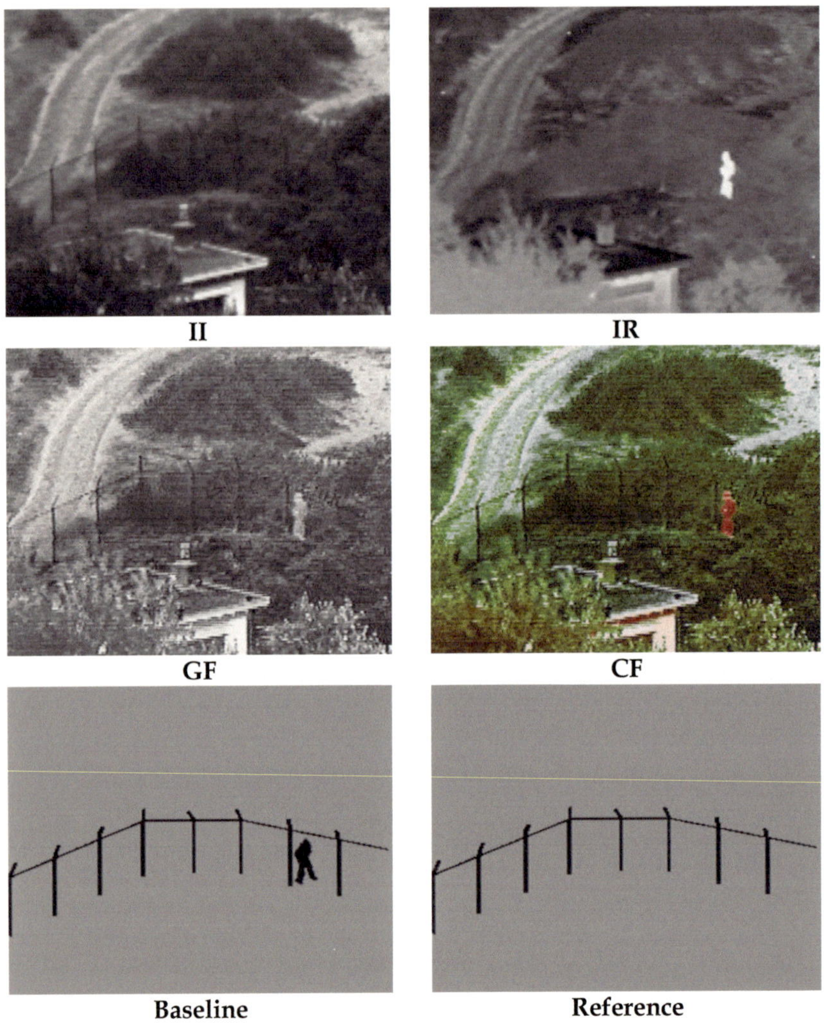

Fig. 1. Original intensified visual image (II), original thermal image (IR), graylevel fused (GF) image, color fused (CF) image, baseline test image (Baseline), and reference (Reference) image.

2.3 Results and discussion

Fig. 2 shows that subjects are uncertain about the location of the person in the scene for about 20% of the visual image presentations and 22% of the thermal image presentations.

The (graylevel and color) fused images result in a smaller fraction of about 13% "not sure" replies. The lowest number of "not sure" replies is obtained for the baseline reference images: only about 4%. This indicates that the increased amount of detail in fused imagery does indeed improve an observer's subjective situational awareness.

Fig. 3 shows the mean weighted distance between the actual position of the person in each scene and the position indicated by the subjects (the perceived position), for the visual (CCD) and thermal (IR) images, and for the graylevel and color fusion schemes. This Figure also shows the optimal (baseline) performance obtained for the schematic test images representing only the segmented reference features and the walking person. A low value of this mean weighted distance measure corresponds to high observer accuracy and a correctly perceived position of the person in the displayed scenes relative to the main reference features. High values correspond to a large discrepancy between the perceived position and the actual position of the person.

Fig. 3 shows that the localization error obtained with the fused images is significantly lower than the error obtained with the individual thermal and visual image modalities ($p=0.0021$). The smallest errors in the relative spatial localization task are obtained for the schematic images. This result represents the baseline performance, since the images are optimal in the sense that they do not contain any distracting details and all the features that are essential to perform the task (i.e. the outlines of the reference features) are represented at high visual contrast. The lowest overall accuracy is achieved for the thermal images. The visual images appear to yield a slightly higher accuracy. However, this accuracy is misleading since observers are not sure about the person in a large percentage of the visual images, as shown by Fig. 2. The difference between the results for the graylevel fused and the color fused images is not significant ($p=0.134$), suggesting that spatial localization of targets (following detection) does not exploit color contrast as long as there exists sufficient brightness contrast in the gray fused imagery.

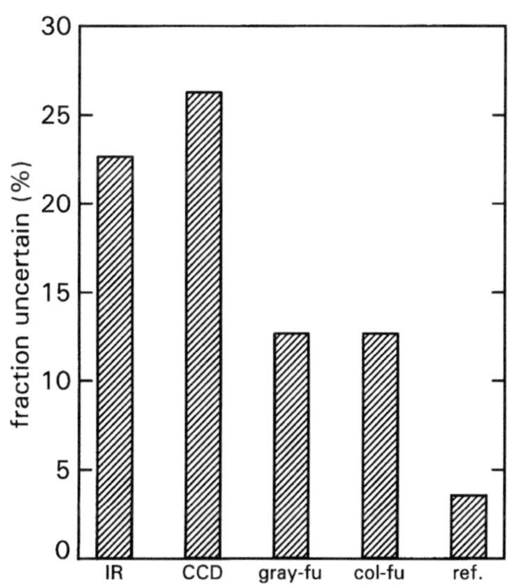

Fig. 2. Percentage of image presentations in which observers are uncertain about the relative position of the person in the scene, for each of the 5 image modalities tested (IR, intensified CCD, graylevel fused, color fused, and schematic reference images).

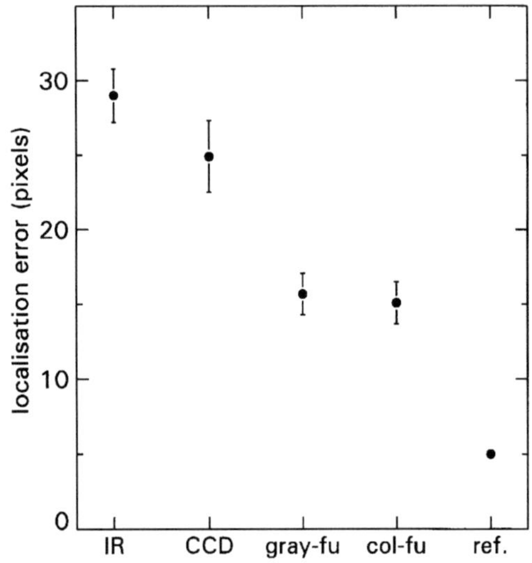

Fig. 3. The mean weighted distance between the actual position of the person in the scene and the perceived position for each of the 5 image modalities tested (IR, intensified CCD, graylevel fused, color fused, and schematic reference images). The error bars indicate the size of the standard error in the perceived location.

Summarizing, for the scenarios investigated here, we conclude that fused images provide a better representation of the layout of the scene, but color does not help to localize the targets.

3. Scene gist recognition

In this section we investigate the effects of grayscale and color image fusion on the perception of detail and the global structure of scenes. We assess the different fusion techniques by quantifying the sensitivity of human observers performing the task using the fused imagery.

3.1 Imagery

A variety of outdoor scenes, displaying several kinds of vegetation (grass, heather, semi shrubs, trees), sky, water, sand, vehicles, roads, and persons, were registered at night with a dual-band visual intensified (DII) camera (see below), and with a middle wavelength band (3-5 μm) infrared (IR) camera (Radiance HS). An example is shown in Fig. 4.

The DII camera provided a two-color registration of the scene, applying two bands covering the part of the electromagnetic spectrum ranging from visual to near infrared (400-900 nm). The crossover point between the bands of the DII camera lies approximately at 700 nm. The short (visual) wavelength part of the incoming spectrum is mapped to the R channel of an RGB color composite image. The long (near infrared) wavelength band corresponds primarily to the spectral reflection characteristics of vegetation, and is therefore mapped to the G channel. This approach utilizes the fact that the spectral reflection characteristics of plants are distinctly different from other (natural and artificial) materials in the visual and near infrared range (Onyango & Marchant, 2001). The spectral response of the

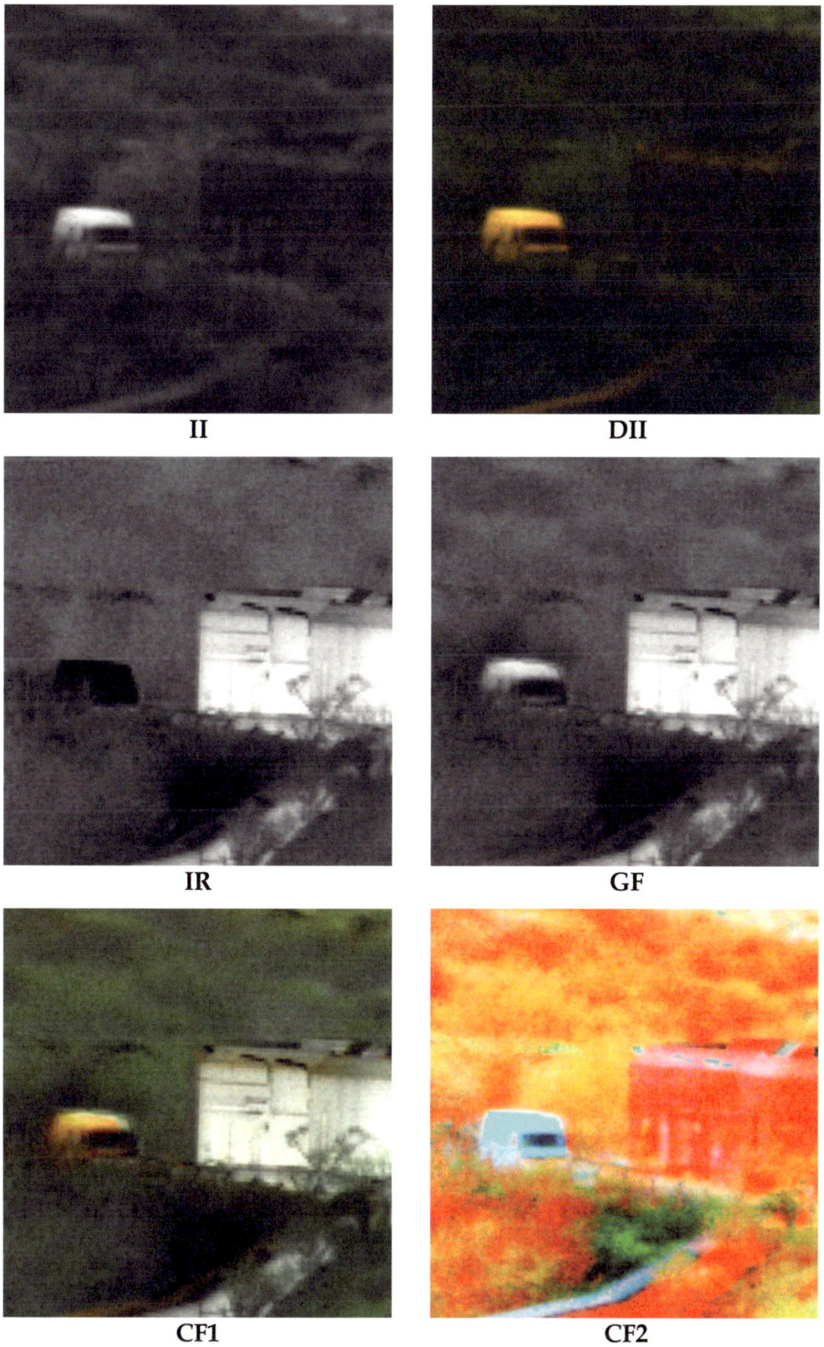

Fig. 4. Example of the different image modalities used in this study. II and DII: the long wavelength band and both bands of the false color intensified CCD image. IR: the thermal 3-5 μm IR image. GF: the greylevel fused image and CF1(2) and color fused images produced with Method 1(2). This image shows a scene with a road, a house, and a vehicle.

long-wavelength channel ('G') roughly matches that of a Generation III image intensifier (II) system, and is stored separately.

The images were registered, and patches displaying different types of scenic elements were selected and cut out from corresponding images in the different spectral bands. These patches were deployed as stimuli in the pyschophysical tests. The signature of the target items (i.e. buildings, persons, vehicles etc.) in the image test sets varied from highly distinct to hardly visible.

To test the *perception of detail*, small patches were selected that display either buildings, vehicles, water, roads, or humans. To investigate the *perception of global scene structure*, larger patches were selected, that represent either the horizon (to perform a horizon perception task), or a large amount of different terrain features (to enable the distinction between an image that is presented upright and one that is shown upside down).

Grayscale fused (GF) images were produced by combining the IR and II images though a pyramidal image fusion scheme (Burt & Adelson, 1985; Toet et al., 1989; Toet, 1990b). Color fused imagery was produced by the following two methods.

- *Color Fusion Method 1* (CF1): The short and long wavelength bands of the DII camera were respectively mapped to the R and G channels of an RGB color image. The resulting RGB color image was then converted to the YIQ (NTSC) color space. The luminance (Y) component was replaced by the corresponding aforementioned grayscale (II and IR) fused image, and the result was transformed back to the RGB color space (note that the input Y from combining the R and G channel is replaced by a Y which is created by fusing the G channel with the IR image). This color fusion method results in images in which grass, trees and persons are displayed as greenish, and roads, buildings, and vehicles are brownish.
- *Color Fusion Method 2* (CF2): First, an RGB color image was produced by assigning the IR image to the R channel, the long wavelength band of the DII image to the green channel (as in Method 1), and the short wavelength band of the DII image to the blue channel (instead of the red channel, as in Method 1). This color fusion method results in images in which vegetation is displayed as greenish, persons are reddish, buildings are red-brownish, vehicles are whitish/bluish, and the sky and roads are most often bluish.

The multiresolution grayscale image fusion scheme employed here, selects the perceptually most salient contrast details from both of the individual input image modalities, and fluently combines these pattern elements into a resulting (fused) image. As a side effect of this method, details in the resulting fused images can be displayed at higher contrast than they appear in the images from which they originate, i.e. their contrast may be enhanced (Toet, 1990a; Toet, 1992). To distinguish the perceptual effects from contrast enhancement from those of the fusion process, observer performance was also tested with contrast enhanced versions of the individual image modalities, using a multiresolution local contrast enhancement scheme. This scheme enhances the contrast of perceptually relevant details for a range of spatial scales, in a way that is similar to the approach used in the hierarchical fusion scheme (for details see Toet, 1990a; Toet, 1992).

3.2 Experiment

A computer was used to briefly (400ms) present the images on a CRT display, measure the response times and collect the observer responses. A total of 12 subjects, aged between 20 and 55 years, served in the experiments reported below. All subjects have corrected to normal vision, and no known color deficiencies.

The perception of the global structure of a depicted scene was tested in two different ways. In the first test, scenes were presented that had been randomly mirrored along the horizontal, and the subjects were asked to distinguish the orientation of the displayed scenes (i.e. whether a scene was displayed right side up or upside down). In this test, each scene was presented twice: once upright and once upside down. In the second test, horizon views were presented together with two horizontally aligned short markers on the left and right side of the image. In this test, each scene was presented twice: once with the markers located at the true position (height) of the horizon, and once when the markers coincided with a horizontal structure that was opportunistically available (like a band of clouds) and that could be mistaken for the horizon. The task of the subjects was to judge whether the markers indicated the true position of the horizon. The perception of the global structure of a scene is likely to determine situational awareness.

The capability to discriminate fine detail was tested by asking the subjects to judge whether a presented scene contained an exemplar of a particular category of objects. The following categories were investigated: buildings, vehicles, water, roads, and humans. The perception of detail is relevant for tasks involving visual search, detection and recognition.

3.3 Results and discussion

For each visual discrimination task the numbers of hits (correct detections) and false alarms (fa) were recorded to calculate $d' = Z_{hits}-Z_{fa}$, an unbiased estimate of sensitivity (Macmillan & Creelman, 1991).

The effects of contrast enhancement on human visual performance is similar for all tasks. Fig. 5 shows that contrast enhancement significantly improves the sensitivity of human observers performing with II and DII imagery. However, for IR imagery, the average sensitivity decreases as a result of contrast enhancement. This is probably a result of the fact that the contrast enhancement method employed in this study increases the visibility of irrelevant detail and clutter in the scene. Note that this result does *not* indicate that (local) contrast enhancement in general should not be applied to IR images.

Fig. 6 shows the results of all scene recognition and target detection tasks investigated here. As stated before, the ultimate goal of image fusion is to produce a combined image that displays more information than either of the original images. Fig. 6 shows that this aim is only achieved for the following perceptual tasks and conditions:

- the detection of roads, where CF1 outperforms each of the input image modalities,
- the recognition of water, where CF1 yields the highest observer sensitivity, and
- the detection of vehicles, where three fusion methods tested perform significantly better than the original imagery.

These tasks are also the only ones in which CF1 performs better than CF2. An image fusion method that always performs at least as good as the best of the individual image modalities can be of great ergonomic value, since the observer can perform using only a single image. This result is obtained for the recognition of scene orientation from color fused imagery produced with CF2, where performance is similar to that with II and DII imagery. For the detection of buildings and humans in a scene, all three fusion methods perform equally well and slightly less than IR. CF1 significantly outperforms grayscale fusion for the detection of the horizon and the recognition of roads and water. CF2 outperforms grayscale fusion for both global scene recognition tasks (orientation and horizon detection). However, for CF2 observer sensitivity approaches zero for the recognition of roads and water.

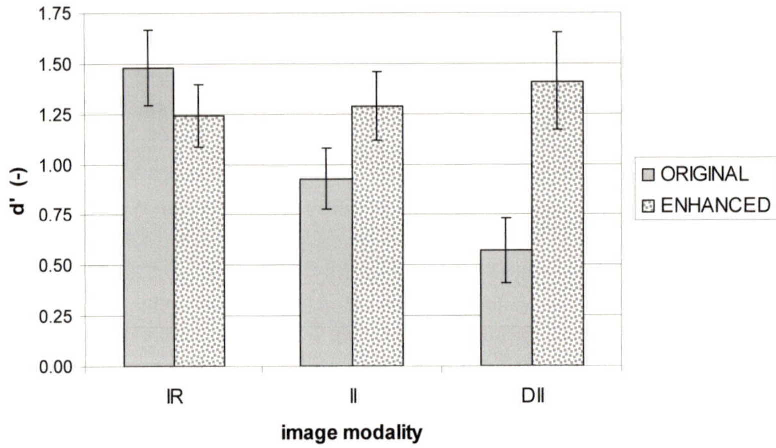

Fig. 5. The effect of contrast enhancement on observer sensitivity d'.

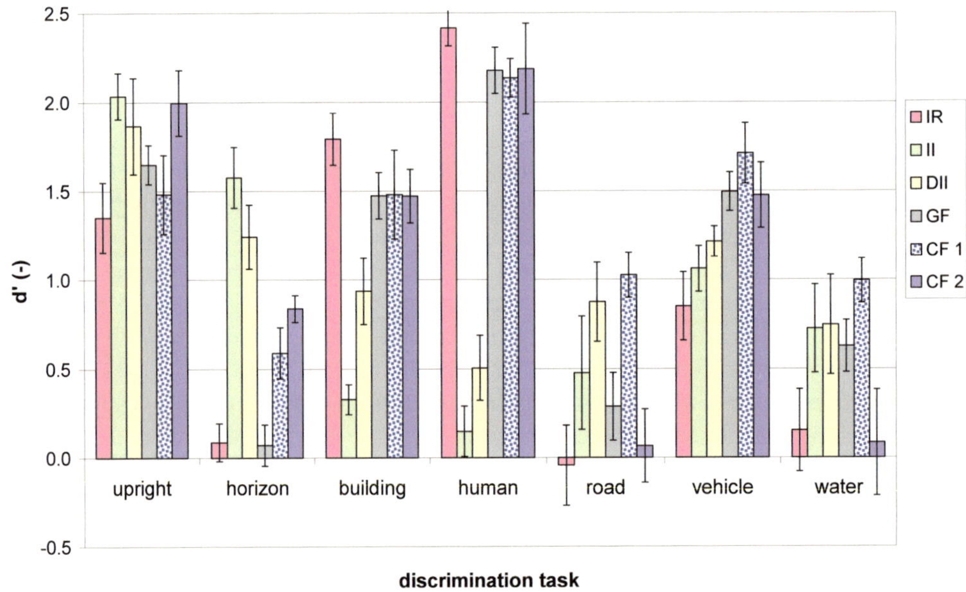

Fig. 6. Observer sensitivity d' for discrimination of global layout (orientation and horizon) and local detail (buildings, humans, roads, vehicles, and water), for six different image modalities. These modalities are (in the order in which they appear in the labeled clusters above): infrared (IR), single-band or grayscale (II) and double-band or color (DII) intensified visual, grayscale (GF) and color fused (CF1, CF2) imagery.

Table 1 summarizes the main findings of this study. IR has the lowest overall performance of all modalities tested. This results from a low performance for both large scale orientation tasks, and for the detection and recognition of roads, water, and vehicles. In contrast, intensified visual imagery performs best in both orientation tasks. The perception of the horizon is significantly better with II and DII imagery. IR imagery performs best for the perception and recognition of buildings and humans- DII has the best overall performance of the individual image modalities. Thus, IR on one hand and (D)II images on the other hand contain *complementary* information, which makes each of these image modalities suited for performing different perception tasks.

	IR	II	DII	GF	CF1	CF2
Upright	-1	2	1			2
Horizon	-1	2	1			
Building	2	-1		1	1	1
Human	2	-1		1	1	1
Road	-1		1		2	
Vehicle	-1			2	2	1
Water	-1				2	
Overall	-1	2	3	4	8	5

Table 1. The relative performance of the different image modalities for the seven perceptual recognition tasks. Rank orders -1,1, and 2 indicate respectively the worst, second best, and best performing image modality for a given task. The tasks involve the perception of the global layout (orientation and horizon) of a scene, and the recognition of local detail (buildings, humans, roads, vehicles, and water). The different image modalities are: infrared (IR), greyscale (II) and dual band false-color (DII) intensified visual, grayscale fused images (GF) and two different color fusion (CF1, CF2) schemes. The sum of the rank orders indicates the overall performance of the modalities.

CF1 has the best overall performance of the image fusion schemes tested here. The application of an appropriate color mapping scheme in the image fusion process can indeed significantly improve observer performance compared to grayscale fusion. In contrast, the use of an inappropriate color scheme can severely degrade observer sensitivity. Although the performance of CF1 for specific observation tasks is below that of the optimal individual sensor, for a combination of observation tasks (as will often be the case in operational scenarios) the CF1 fused images can be of great ergonomic value, since the observer can perform using only a single image.

4. Object recognition

In this section we will show how manual segmentations of a set of corresponding input and fused images can be used to evaluate the perceptual quality of image fusion schemes. Human visual perception is mostly concerned with object detection and boundary discrimination. The method is therefore based on the hypothesis that fused imagery should provide an optimal representation of the object boundaries that can be determined from the individual input image modalities. To compute the quality of the different image fusion schemes we formulate boundary-detection as a classification problem of discriminating non-boundary from boundary pixels, and apply the precision-recall framework, using reference contour images derived from the human-marked boundaries as a reference standard.

4.1 Imagery

Seven sets of IR and visible images, including noisy, clean, cluttered and uncluttered images, were used in this study (Fig. 7). These multi-sensor images are part of the Multi-

Sensor Image Segmentation Data Set (Lewis et al., 2006), and are publicly available through the ImageFusion.org website (ImageFusion.Org, 2007). These images were fused with three different pixel-based fusion algorithms: Contrast Pyramid (PYR); Discrete Wavelet Transform (DWT); and the Dual-Tree Complex Wavelet Transform (CWT; see Lewis et al., 2007).

4.2 Experiment

A group of 63 subjects with normal or corrected to normal vision manually segmented both the individual and the fused images. The average subject's age was 21.3 years (standard deviation = 2.7 years). A mixture of CRT (37) and TFT (26) screens were used. The segmentation instructions quite general, in order not to bias the subject to produce a specific type of segmentation. Thus, variations in segmentations were due to differences in perception and not to some other aspect of the experimental set up.

4.3 Results and discussion

Fig. 8 shows the annotated union of the human segmentations of each of the 7 scenes used in this study. In general the manual segmentations represent the actual scene layout quite well. Typical examples of human segmentations are shown in Fig. 12.

To compare the performance of subjects with the different individual (visual and infrared) and (CWT, DWT, and Pyramid) fused image modalities we adopted the following approach. For all features marked by the human subjects, we computed the percentage of subjects that completely delineated them. Then we defined the relevant features in the different scenes as those features that were fully segmented in either the visual or infrared images by more than half of the number of subjects. In previous studies we found a clear distinction in the performance of human observers using the different individual and fused image modalities for the detection of respectively terrain features, persons and man-made objects like buildings and cars (Toet et al., 1997b; Toet & Franken, 2003). In this study, we therefore classify the relevant features in three categories: terrain features, living creatures, and man-made objects. Typical terrain features are roads, trees, hills, and clouds. Typical man-made objects are houses, fences, poles, chimneys, boats, and buoys. Living creatures are for instance people and dogs. Then we computed the average percentage of subjects that fully segmented image features, for each feature category and for all image modalities.

The results are shown in Fig. 9. It appears that terrain features are best detected in the visual image modality, which yields the worst performance for the detection of living creatures. For the set of images tested in this study, human performance for the detection of man-made objects is quite similar for all image modalities. The CWT fusion scheme appears to yield the best overall performance. Each of the fused image modalities performs similar to the infrared image modality for the detection of living creatures, indicating that these schemes correctly include details from the infrared images in the resulting fused images. However, the performance of the fused image modalities for the detection of terrain features is below the performance with the visual image modality. This suggests that the representation of the visual details is not optimal in the fused images. Finally, for each of the fused image modalities we computed the mean percentage of objects that were segmented by a percentage of the human subjects that was larger than the percentage that segmented the same objects in either of the input image modalities. This number represents the percentage of cases in which a fused image is more than the sum of its parts: subjects can perceive details better in the fused image than in each of the individual input images.

Scene	Visual	Infrared	Features
UNCamp			Man-made: fence poles roof chimney Terrain : road hill with shrubs trees left trees right Living creatures: man
Dune_7404		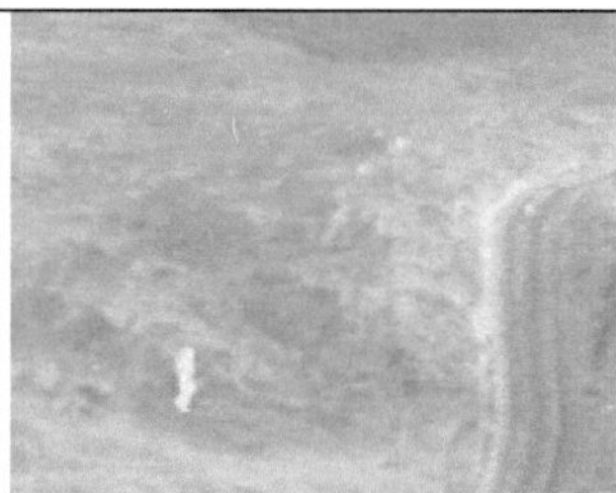	Terrain : crater hill small path road Living creatures: man
Octec02			Man-made: house 1-6 Terrain : trees left trees right road Living creatures: man
Octec21			Man-made: house 1-6 Terrain : trees left trees right smoke cloud Living creatures: man
Trees_4906	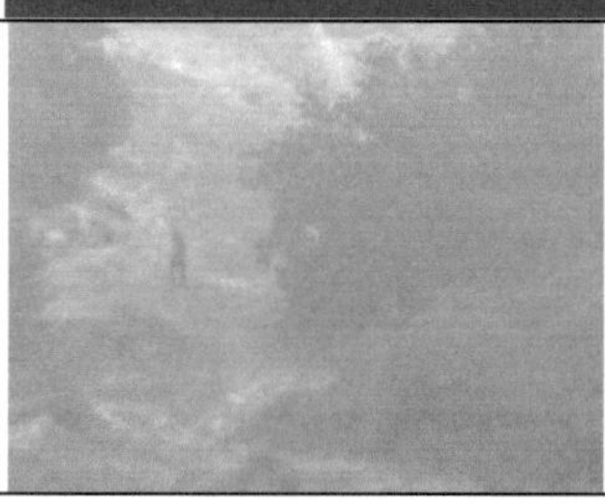		Terrain : trees left trees upper right trees lower right border between trees Living creatures: man

Fig. 7. The visual (2nd column) and infrared (3rd column) images of each of the 7 different scenes used in this study, with a list of the characteristic man-made and terrain features, as well as people or animals that were used to score subject performance.

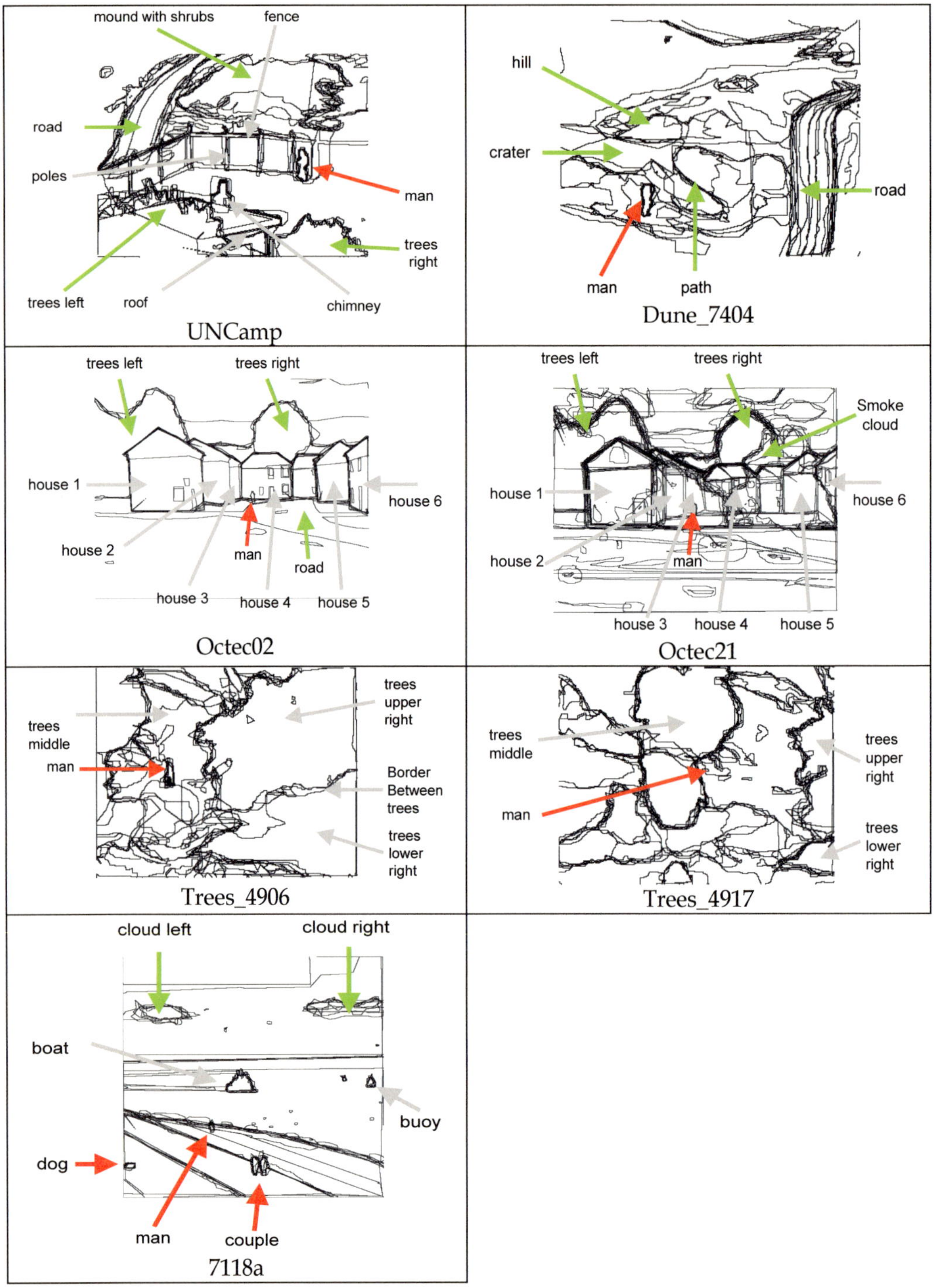

Fig. 8. Annotated union of all human segmentations of each of the 7 scenes used in this study. Indicated and labeled are the terrain features (green), man-made objects (gray) and living creatures (red) used to score the subject performance.

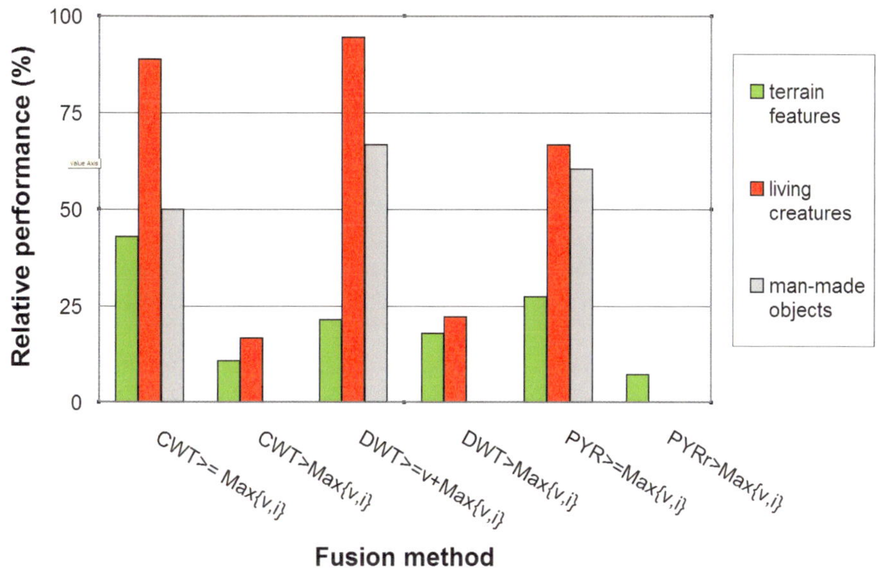

Fig. 9. Performance of subjects with the (CWT, DWT, and Pyramid) fused image modalities, expressed as the mean percentage of objects segmented by a fraction of subjects that was equal to or larger than the fraction of subjects that segmented these objects in either the visual (v) or infrared (i) image modalities.

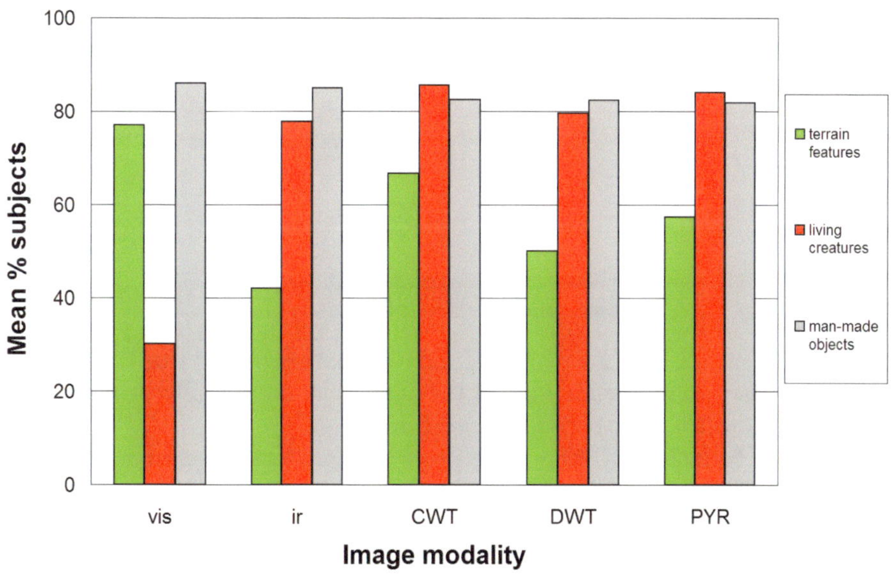

Fig. 10. The mean percentage of subjects that detected relevant features, for each class of objects (terrain, living creatures and man-made objects) and for each of the individual (visual and infrared) and (CWT, DWT, and Pyramid) fused image modalities.

Fig. 10 shows the percentage of cases in which the performance with fused imagery was both equivalent to (equal or larger than) or better (larger) than the performance with each of the input image modalities. This figure confirms the results in Fig. 9 by showing that most image modalities yield a performance for the detection of living creatures that is equivalent to that obtained with the input image modalities. The performance for the detection of man-made objects is below the performance with the input images. The performance for the detection of terrain features is considerably reduced, suggesting that the details from the visual images are not optimally represented in the fused images. There are only a few cases in which the performance with fused imagery exceeds the performance with the individual image modalities. This only occurs for the detection of living creatures and of terrain features.

Currently no well-established methods for objective image segmentation quality evaluation are available (Correia & Pereira, 2002; Correia & Pereira, 2006; Correia & Pereira, 2003). We will therefore use the boundary precision-recall measure, which has become a standard evaluation procedure in the information retrieval community (van Rijsbergen, 1979), as the evaluation criterion in the comparison of the human segmentation boundaries for the different image modalities. Precision is the fraction of detections that are true positives rather than false positives, while recall is the fraction of true positives that are detected rather than missed. Precision and recall are traditionally used to measure the performance of information extraction and information retrieval systems (van Rijsbergen, 1979), and have more recently also been applied to measure the performance of edge detection and image segmentation schemes (Martin et al., 2004), and the efficacy of multimodal image fusion schemes (Davis & Sharma, 2007). In the context of boundary detection, two types of errors arise. Type-I errors occur if a true object boundary has not been detected by the segmenter (boundary deletion). Type-II errors occur if a detected object boundary does not correspond to a segment boundary in
the reference (false alarm, or boundary insertion). Precision and recall can then be expressed by the Type-I and Type-II error rates as follows:

$$R = \frac{\text{number of correctly detected reference boundary pixels}}{\text{total number of reference boundary pixels}} \tag{1}$$

and

$$P = \frac{\text{number of correctly detected reference boundary pixels}}{\text{total number of detected boundary pixels}} \tag{2}$$

Thus, precision is the fraction of detected boundaries that are indeed true boundaries, while recall is the fraction of true boundaries in the image that are actually detected. Note that both precision and recall are bounded between 0 and 1.

In the context of boundary detection, the precision and recall measures are particularly meaningful in applications that make use of boundary maps, such as stereo or object recognition. It is reasonable to characterize this type of higher level processing in terms of how much true signal is required to succeed (recall), and how much noise can be tolerated (precision). A particular application can define a relative cost α between these quantities. The *F*-measure (van Rijsbergen, 1979), defined as

$$F = PR/(\alpha R + (1-\alpha)P) \tag{3}$$

captures this trade off as the weighted harmonic mean of the precision P and the recall R. Like R and P the F-measure is bounded between 0 and 1. In a precision-recall graph, higher F-measures correspond to points closer to $(P,R) = (1,1)$, representing maximal precision and recall for a given α. In our present experiments we choose the neutral parameterization and set α equal to 0.5, so that precision and recall are weighted equally, and (3) becomes

$$F = 2PR/(R+P) \quad (4)$$

Here we propose to use a combination of the manual segmentations of each of the individual image modalities to construct a reference contour image that can be used to evaluate the different fusion schemes. The segmentation data set provides multiple human segmentations for each image. Simply constructing a reference contour image by taking the union of individual manual boundary maps is not effective because of the localization errors present in the data set itself. Localization errors are inherent in a human image segmentation task, since human subjects are limited in the accuracy with which they can draw the edges they observe in the images. Evidently, some objects simply have no well defined boundaries (grass, trees, clouds). Moreover, for the type of imagery used in this study, the object representations are often not sharp. As a result, there is an inherent positional uncertainty in the manually drawn boundaries for the imagery used in this study. In the rest of this study we will use procedures to match different boundary representations. Simply matching corresponding coincident boundary pixels and declaring all unmatched pixels either false positives or misses would not tolerate any localization error. Therefore, we permit a controlled amount of localization error, by adopting a distance tolerance region with a radius of 20 pixels (this value was found to yield appreciable results throughout the entire procedures presented in this study). Any boundary pixel detected within this tolerance region around the location of a true (reference) boundary pixel is regarded as a correct detection.

Now we will discuss the steps taken in the construction of a reference contour image. First, the individual boundary maps resulting from the human segmentations are converted into binary mask images. For a given object boundary, a boundary mask image represents all pixels that are within a given tolerance distance of this boundary. These boundary masks are introduced to allow for small localization errors in the human segmentation data. The binary boundary mask image is obtained by first computing the exact squared two-dimensional Euclidean distance transform of the binary contour image (Figure 6a) using a square 3x3 structuring element (Lotufo & Zampirolli, 2001). The result of this transform is a graylevel image in which the value of each background pixel represents the Euclidian distance to the nearest boundary pixel (Fig. 11b; e.g. http://en.wikipedia.org/wiki/Distance_transform). Thresholding this distance image at the aforementioned distance threshold level of 20 pixels gives the binary mask image (Fig. 11).

Next, for each image modality, the corresponding binary boundary mask images from all subjects are summed. The summed mask image represents the number of subjects that have marked each individual pixel as a boundary pixel. The summed mask image is then thresholded at a level corresponding to half the number of subjects that contributed to the sum. Thus we obtain a binary mask image that represents the consensus among at least half of the subjects about the boundary status of each pixel (i.e. a pixel has value 1 if at least half of the subjects have marked this pixel as a boundary pixel; Fig. 12 lower left).

Then, we compute the morphological skeleton (Maragos & Schafer, 1986) of the binary consensus mask image (Fig. 12 lower right). This is done by a morphological thinning operation (Serra, 1982) that successively erodes away pixels from the boundary (while preserving the end points of line segments) until no more thinning is possible, at which point what is left represents the skeleton.

Finally, a joined binary mask for the combination of visual and infrared boundaries is produced as the logical union of the corresponding individual binary consensus mask images (Fig. 13 lower left). From the resulting binary mask image a joined skeleton image is then constructed (Fig. 13 lower right). In the following we will refer to the joined binary consensus mask and its morphological skeleton as respectively the *reference mask* and the *reference contour image*. Note that the reference contour image represents the combination of the maximal amount of object boundary information that was extracted by human visual inspection from each of the individual image modalities.

For each of the fused image modalities precision and recall measures are then computed as follows. First, we count the number of non-zero (object) pixels in the reference contour image (*n*_ref) and those in the corresponding boundary image manually drawn by a human subject (*n*_subject). To compute the number of pixels in the boundary image drawn by the subject that are accounted for by the reference mask (the number of hits: *na*_subject) we take the intersection of the subject's boundary image and the reference mask, and count the number of non-zero pixels. Similarly, to compute the number of pixels in the reference contour image that are accounted for by the subject's boundary drawing (*na*_reference) we

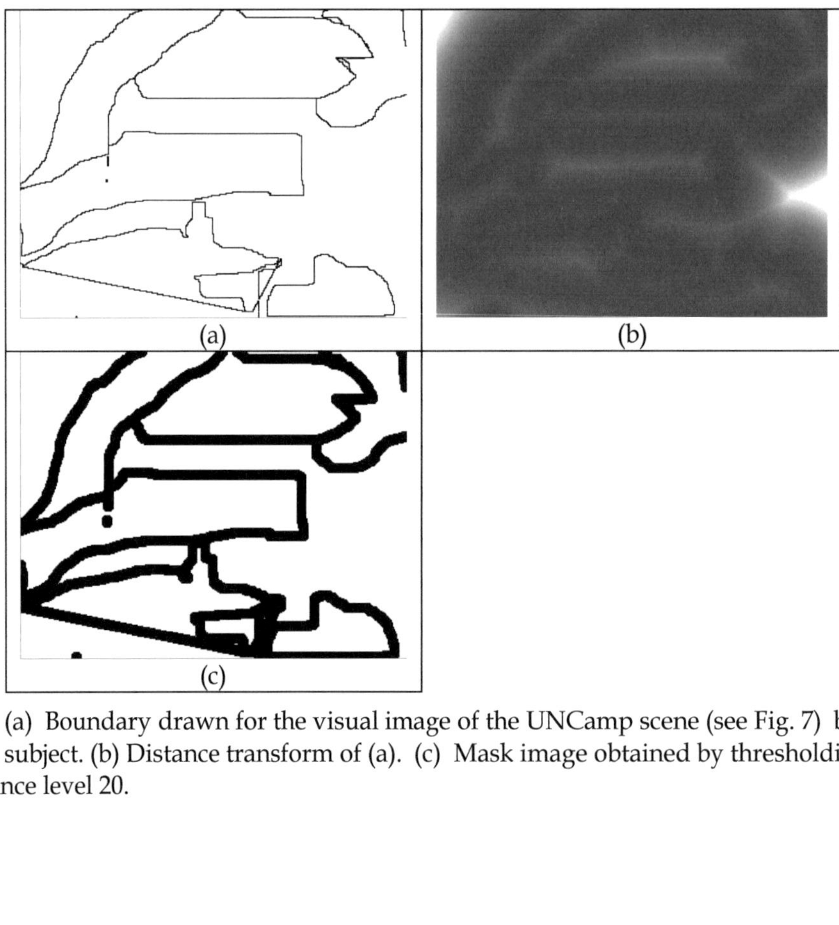

Fig. 11. (a) Boundary drawn for the visual image of the UNCamp scene (see Fig. 7) by a human subject. (b) Distance transform of (a). (c) Mask image obtained by thresholding (b) at distance level 20.

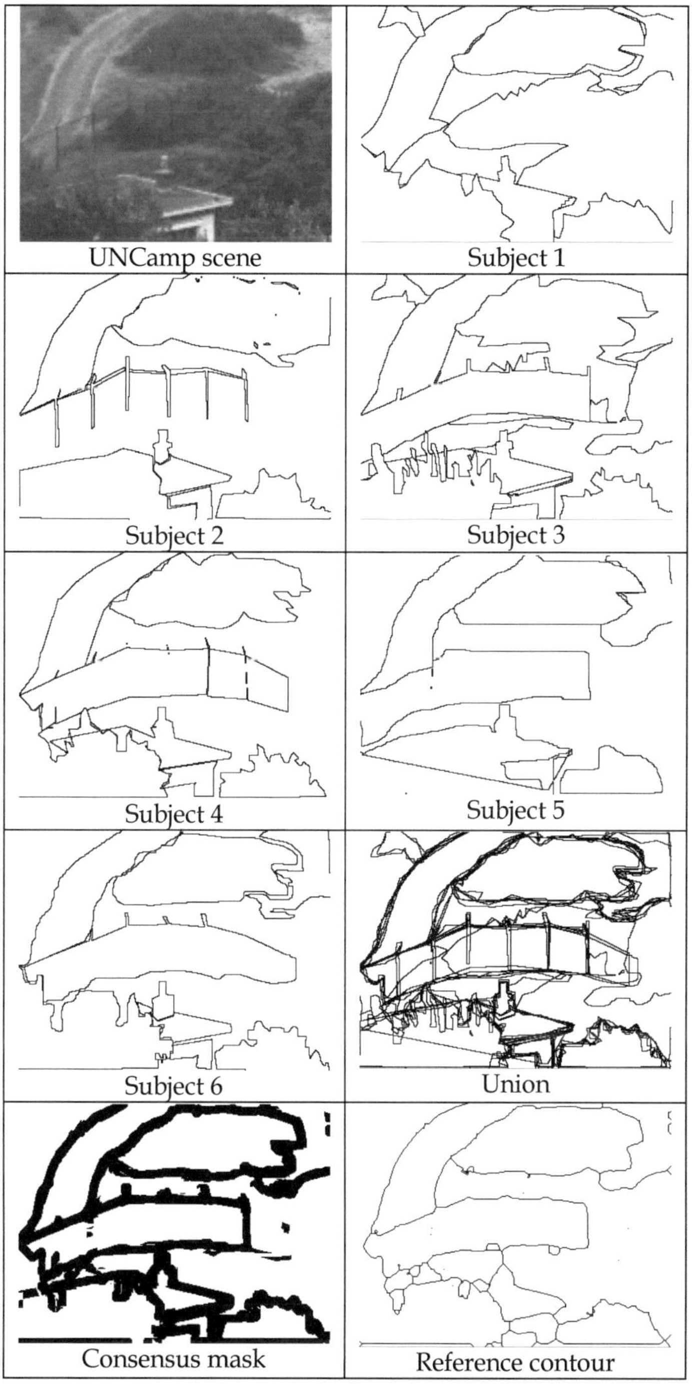

Fig. 12. Boundaries drawn by 6 human subjects for the visual image of the UNCamp scene, the union of all these boundaries, the consensus mask image (lower left) representing the thresholded sum of all boundary masks (i.e. the dilated boundary images; not shown here), and the resulting reference contour (lower right).

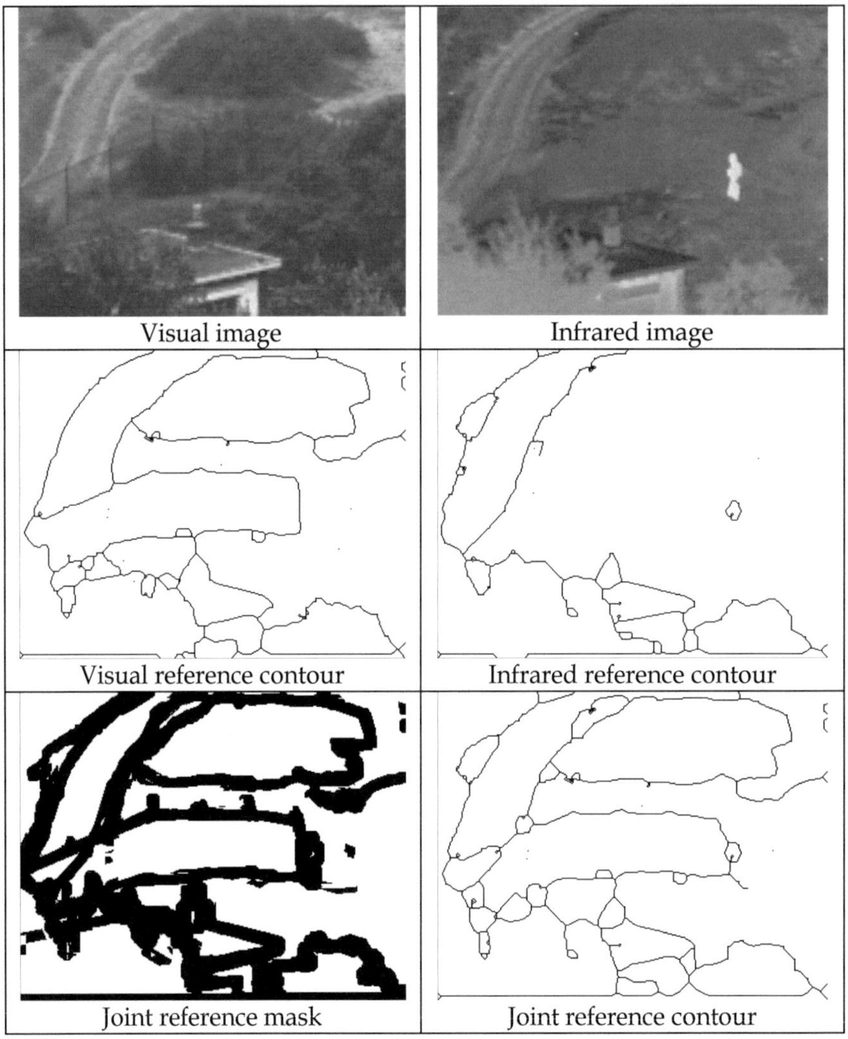

Fig. 13. The visual and infrared input images of the UNCamp scene (top row), their reference contour representations (middle row), and the joint reference contour mask and contour image (lower row).

take the intersection of the reference contour image and the subject's boundary mask image, and count the number of non-zero pixels. For each individual human subject *i* the precision (P_i) and recall (R_i) measures are then computed as the fraction of accounted pixels in both the subject's drawing and the reference contour image:

$$P_i = na_{\text{subject}} / n_{\text{subject}} \quad ; \quad R_i = na_{\text{reference}} / n_{\text{reference}} \tag{5}$$

The F-measure for each human subject *i* is then be computed from (5) as:

$$F_i = \frac{2 \cdot na_{\text{subject}} \cdot na_{\text{reference}}}{n_{\text{reference}} \cdot na_{\text{subject}} + na_{\text{reference}} \cdot n_{\text{subject}}} \tag{6}$$

The overall precision, recall and F-measures are then computed as the mean over all N subjects:

$$P = \frac{1}{N}\sum_{i=1}^{N} P_i \quad ; \quad R = \frac{1}{N}\sum_{i=1}^{N} R_i \quad ; \quad F = \frac{1}{N}\sum_{i=1}^{N} F_i \tag{7}$$

Fig. 14 shows the precision and recall measures computed for each of the individual skeletons of the visual, infrared, CWT, DWT and Pyramid fused image modalities. This figure shows that the individual manual segmentations agree to a large extent with their overall skeleton representation (median value of F=0.72). A collection of manual image segmentations can therefore be represented by a single overall skeleton.

Fig. 15 shows the precision and recall measures computed for the unified skeleton representation of the visual and infrared human boundary data, and the human boundary data for each of the (CWT, DWT and Pyramid-) fused image modalities. This result shows that the precision of the boundaries drawn by the subjects is actually quite high, meaning that the fusion schemes do not seem to introduce any spurious details. However, the fraction of recalled details is around 0.5, which is rather low. This reflects the effect that terrain details are not well perceived by the subjects in the fused images.

Summarizing, we conclude that reference contour images are a useful tool to evaluate the performance of image fusion schemes.

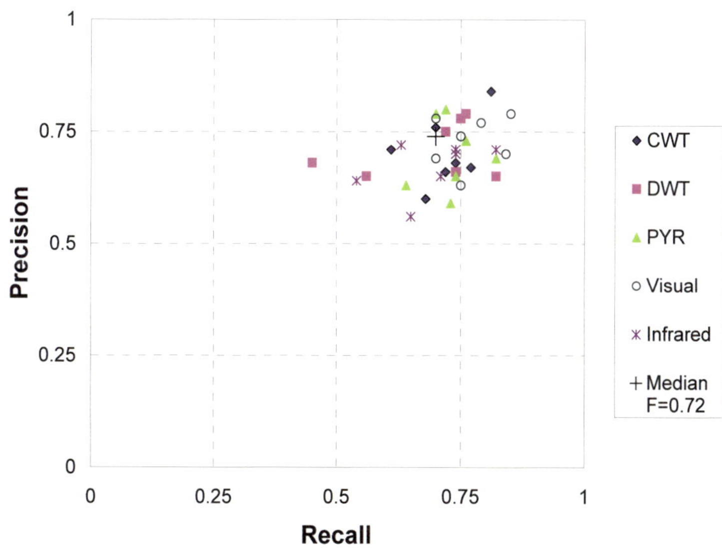

Fig. 14. Consistency between the skeleton representation of each of the individual (visual, infrared) and each of the fused (CWT, DWT, PYR) image modalities and the subject data. This figure shows that the skeleton is a reliable representation of the data.

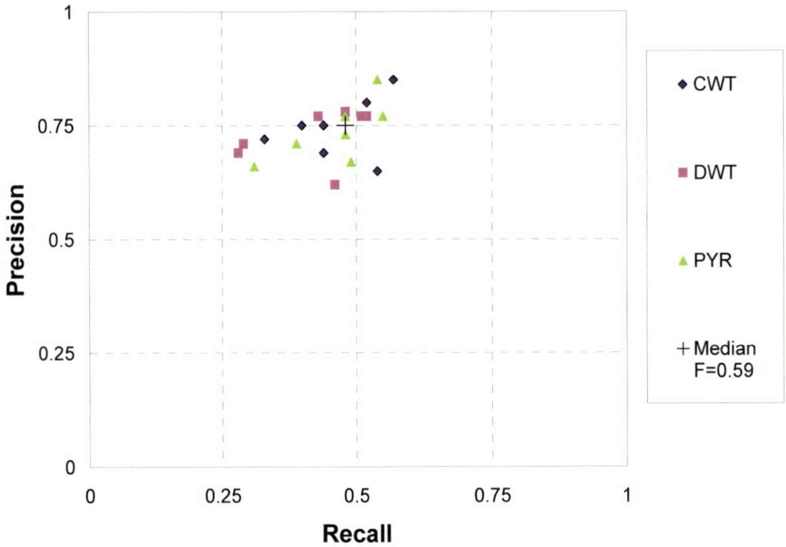

Fig. 15. Consistency between the unified skeleton representation of the visual and infrared human boundary data, and the human boundary data for each of the (CWT, DWT and Pyramid-) fused image modalities.

5. Camouflage detection

Although natural color mapping schemes provide many perceptual benefits, they are not suitable for all purposes. A typical example is the task of detecting soldiers wearing camouflage suits in a rural setting, using a two-band nightvision system sensitive to the visual and thermal part of the electromagnetic spectrum. When the false color representation of the fused nightvision image optimally agrees with the daytime appearance of the scene, the soldiers will blend in with their environment (will be camouflaged), which makes it nearly impossible to perform the task. In such cases a color mapping scheme should be used which displays the objects of interest with higher color contrast while retaining an intuitive (natural) color setting for the rest of the scene.

As an example we present the results of a color mapping which optimizes the detection of man-made camouflaged targets in a rural setting, while retaining a natural color representation of the environment.

5.1 Imagery

We registered optically aligned visual (wavelengths shorter than 700 nm) and near-infrared (NIR; wavelengths longer than 700 nm) nighttime images of a rural scene containing grass and trees, with and without targets in the scene. The targets were blue and green foam tubes (Fig. 16). For comparison we also created a standard intensified image of each scene containing both bands, since this is the type of image typically provided by standard night vision goggles. First, a red-green false color representation of the fused dual-band sensor image was obtained by mapping the visual band to the Red channel and the NIR band to the Green channel of an RGB-image (Fig. 17d). Next, for each combination of sensor outputs

Fig. 16. Images showing the two target types, the green target (a) and the blue target (b).

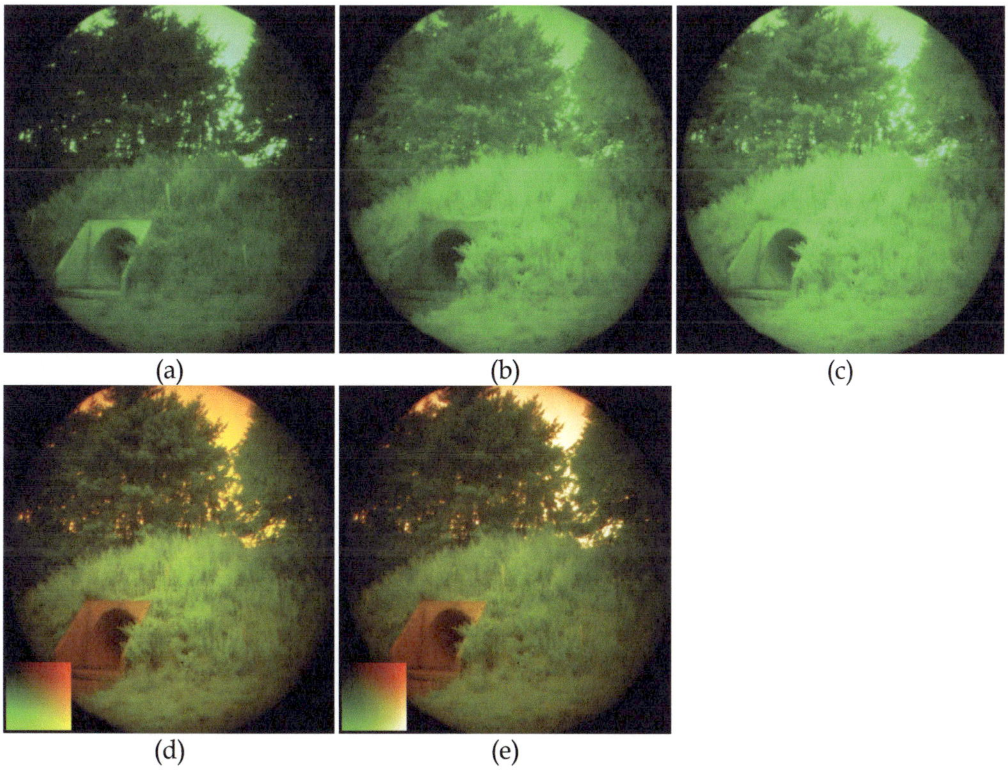

Fig. 17. Lookup table based color remapping applied to a dual-band visual (a) and NIR (b) image. (c) A regular intensified image representation for comparison (e.g. a standard night vision goggle image). (d) A red-green false color representation of the dual-band image with the visual band assigned to the Red and NIR band assigned to the Green channel of an RGB display. The inset in (d) shows all possible dual-band outputs as shades of red (large response in band 1, small in band 2), green (small response in band 1, large in band 2) and yellow (large responses in both bands). (e) The result of the color transformation. The inset shows how the colors in the inset of (d) are transformed.

(represented by a shade of red, green, yellow; see inset of Fig. 17d) a color was selected to display this sensor output. This process was implemented by transforming the red-green image (Fig. 17d) into an indexed image in which each pixel value refers to the entry of a color lookup table. When a different color lookup table is used, the colors in the indexed image are automatically transformed, such that all pixels with the same index are displayed in the same color. The method is described in detail elsewhere (Hogervorst & Toet, 2008a; Hogervorst & Toet, 2010). We found that the color transformation which maximizes the visibility of the targets while preserving the natural appearance of the scene is quite similar to the red-green representation, with a few modifications that specifically address the target colors.

The inset of Fig. 17e shows the colors assigned to all dual-band outputs (the inset of Fig. 17d) by the chosen color scheme. This color scheme emphasizes the distinction between objects containing chlorophyll (the background plants) and objects containing no chlorophyll (e.g. the foam tube targets; notable from the sharp transition between green and red at the diagonal). The dual band sensor system separates the incoming light in a part with wavelengths below 700nm and one with wavelengths above 700 nm. Since chlorophyll shows a steep rise around 700nm, this dual-band system is especially suited for discriminating materials containing chlorophyll from materials containing no chlorophyll. Elements containing chlorophyll (e.g. plants) are displayed in green (i.e. in their natural color), while objects without chlorophyll are displayed in the perceptually opposite color red. To further increase the naturalness, elements with high output in both channels are displayed in white (bottom right corner of the inset of Fig. 17e). The result of our color mapping is shown in Fig. 17e.

5.2 Experiment

We evaluated the abovementioned color mapping in a target detection paradigm. We registered both nighttime dual-band (visual and NIR) images and daytime full color digital photographs of a scene containing grass and trees, with and without targets present. Performance for detecting targets was established for imagery of the dual-band fusion system, each of the individual sensor bands (visual and NIR), standard NVG, and daytime images (taken with a regular digital photo camera). The visual angle and display area of the daytime images were matched to those of the nighttime images.

The targets were green (Fig. 18a) and blue (Fig. 18b) foam insulation tubes. The reflectance of the tubes was such the green tubes were mostly undetectable in a standard intensified

(a) (b)

Fig. 18. The green target (a) and the blue target (b) situated in a background with grass and trees.

image representation and in the NIR band (see Fig. 17), but quite distinct (as bright objects) in the visible band (see Fig. 17). In contrast, the blue tubes were mostly undetectable in the visual band, but clearly visible (as dark objects) in the NIR band and in regular intensified images (Fig. 19).

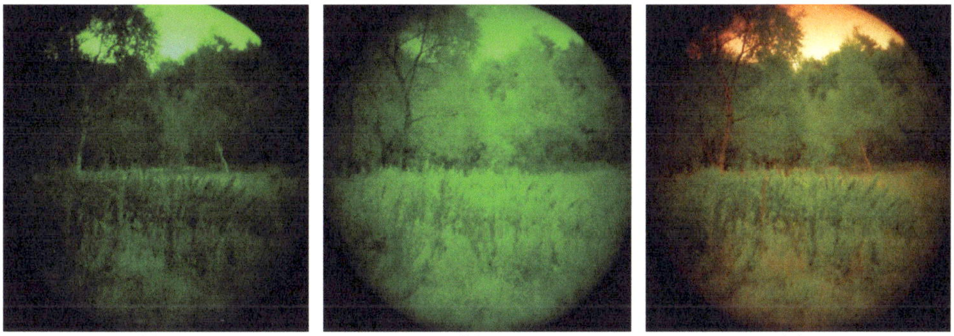

(a) (b) (c)

Fig. 19. Visual (a), NIR (b) and the color fused dual-band image (c) for a scene including a blue target. The target is visible in the NIR band as a dark tube. The dual-band image shows the target as a reddish object.

We recorded whether subjects detected the targets when present (Hits and Misses), and whether they judged there to be a target when no target was present (False Alarms and Correct Rejections). We also recorded the response times. Since no False Alarms occurred in this experiment (i.e. the False-Alarm rate was zero), observer performance is fully characterized by the Hit-rate, i.e. the fraction of targets that was detected (ph = #Hits / (#Hits + #Misses)). Observer performance was measured for 5 different image modalities:

1. Daytime: full color daylight images (taken with a standard digital daytime camera),
2. II: grayscale intensified images, combining both visual and NIR part of the spectrum,
3. VIS: grayscale intensified images representing only the visual part of the spectrum,
4. NIR: grayscale intensified images representing only the NIR part of the spectrum,
5. FC: false color images resulting from the natural color remapping method.

Seven subjects participated in the experiment. The images were shown on a CRT. The subjects indicated as quickly as possible whether a target was present or not, by clicking the appropriate mouse button. Next, the image disappeared and was replaced by a low resolution equivalent of the image, consisting of 20x15 uniformly colored squares (to prevent subjects from continuing their search after responding). We registered the time between onset of the stimulus and detection (the response time). The subject then indicated the perceived target location or clicked on an area outside the image labeled "no target found". Responses outside an ellipse with horizontal diameter of 162 and vertical diameter of 386 pixels centered on the vertically elongated target were considered as incorrect.

5.3 Results and discussion

Fig. 20 shows the fraction of hits (hit-rate) for the various sensor conditions and target colors. Shown are the average hit-rates over subjects. Not surprisingly, performance is highest in the Daytime condition. As expected (see Fig. 17 and Fig. 19), performance for detecting the green targets is high in the visual (VIS) condition and low in the image intensified (II) and NIR sensor conditions. Performance for detecting the blue targets is somewhat poorer in the single-band conditions. These targets can be detected in the NIR condition (reasonably well) and in the II condition (poorly), while they are hardly detected in the VIS condition. Detection performance for both targets is high with the false-color dual-band sensor. Optimal fusion results in performance that equals maximum performance in the individual bands. The hit-rate for the green targets is somewhat lower for the dual-band than for the visual condition. But the hit-rate for the blue targets is somewhat higher for dual-band than for NIR condition. The average hit-rate of the false color dual band sensor (0.75) is not significantly different from the average of the hit-rate for green in VIS and the hit-rate for blue in NIR (0.78). This means that this fusion scheme is near optimal. The results also show that the performance with the standard intensified imagery is clearly much worse than with the false-color dual-band NVG system.

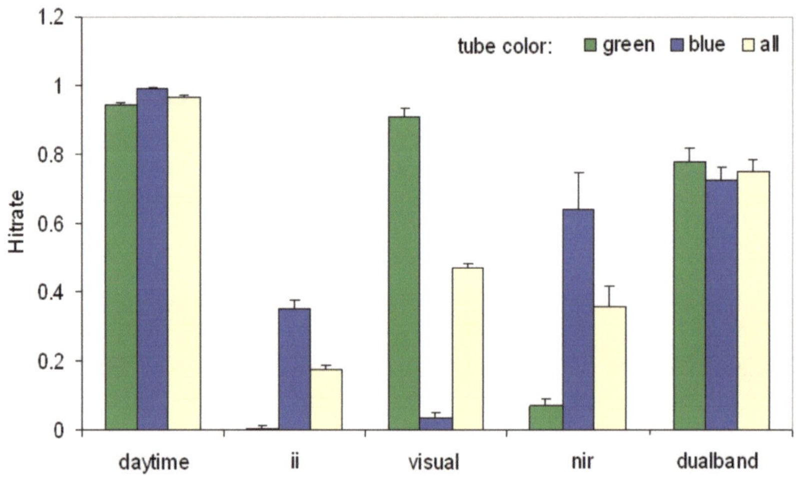

Fig. 20. Average (over all subjects) hit-rate (fraction of hits) for each of the 5 different image modalities and the 2 target colors, including the overall hit-rate ("all"). The error bars represent standard errors in the mean derived from the variance between subjects.

Fig. 21 shows the response times of the trials containing a target (shown are the geometric means over the response times, i.e. the exponent of the average log response times) for all conditions for the hits and misses. Note that the hits for the NIR and II modalities correspond primarily to the trials containing blue targets; the hits for the Visual modality correspond primarily to the trials containing green targets. The response times for the false color dual-band condition are comparable, but slightly larger than in the single-band Visual and NIR conditions. This may be due to the fact that in this condition subjects had to attend to two types of targets, while in the single band conditions only one of the target colors was apparent.

It turns out that the response times for missed targets are comparable to the response times for stimuli in which no target is present. The average response times for missed targets do not correlate with the hit-rates (see Fig. 21b). In contrast, the average response times for hits is highly correlated with the hit-rate ($r = -0.90$, $p < 0.01$, see Fig. 21b). This indicates that when targets are more easily detected, the hit-rate goes up and the response time goes down.

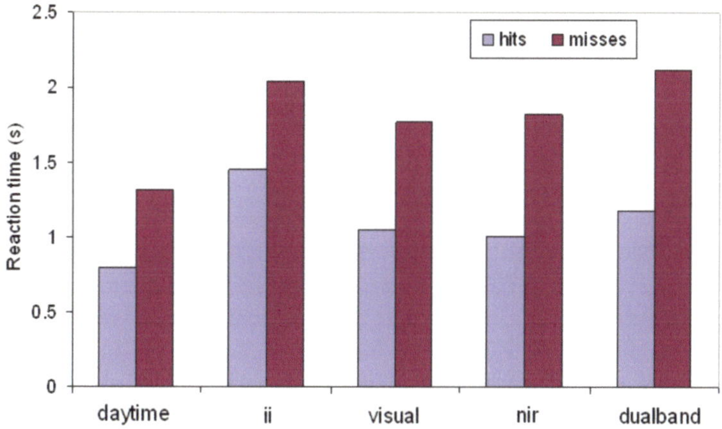

(a)

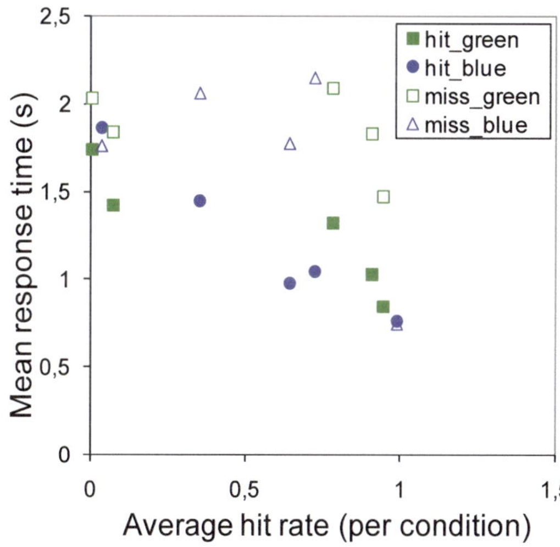

(b)

Fig. 21. (a) The geometric mean (i.e. averaged in log) response times for the various image modalities, separated for hits and misses. (b) Relationship between the hit-rate for each image modality and the (geometric) mean response times for hits and misses for the two target colors.

The results show that performance of the false color dual-band system is just as good as the maximum performance that can be attained using either of its individual bands (visual and NIR). While the green targets can be detected with the visual band of the system alone, the blue targets are mostly missed when subjects have to rely on this band alone. In contrast, the blue targets can be detected with the NIR band, but the green targets are then largely missed in this modality. With the false color dual-band image modality both targets can be detected. The total number of targets detected in the dual band image modality is the same as the total number of targets detected in the visual and modality plus the number of targets detected in the NIR image modality. This indicates that the fused color representation of the two bands is (nearly) optimal from a perceptual standpoint.

6. Conclusions

We find that observers can localize persons in a scene more accurately using fused intensified visual and thermal imagery, than with each of the individual image modalities. The addition of color does not improve this accuracy. A spatial localization task is useful tool to assess the information content of fused imagery intended for surveillance and navigation tasks.

IR and intensified visual imagery contain complementary information. IR imagery mainly contributes to the recognition of buildings and living creatures, whereas intensified visual imagery predominantly shows natural terrain features and efficiently provides the gist of the scene. Experiments testing scene recognition and situational awareness can be used to investigate the perceptual quality of images fusion and color mapping schemes.

The fusion methods used in this study degrade the perception of terrain features. Our finding that the fraction of recalled boundary contours is rather low suggests that details from the visual images are not fully transferred to the fused images. The detection of living creatures is similar in all fused images, indicating that these high-contrast details from the IR images are correctly represented in the fused images. Reference contour images obtained from human segmentations are a useful tool to systematically evaluate the quality of the representation of object boundaries in fused imagery.

The application of appropriate color mapping schemes in the image fusion process can significantly improve observer performance compared to grayscale fusion. In contrast, the use of inappropriate color schemes can severely degrade observer sensitivity. However, color mappings which are perceptually suboptimal may still have ergonomic value and lead to an overall improvement of observer performance, because they eliminate the need to switch attention between different image modalities, thereby reducing the user's cognitive workload. Color mapping schemes can also be tuned to optimize the visibility of camouflaged targets in fused imagery, thus providing larger hit rates and faster detection times. Detection and recognition experiments can be used to asses and optimize the perceptual quality of color mapping schemes.

7. References

Aguilar, M.; Fay, D.A.; Ireland, D.B.; Racamoto, J.P.; Ross, W.D. & Waxman, A.M. (1999). Field evaluations of dual-band fusion for color night vision, In: *Enhanced and Synthetic Vision 1999*, Verly, J.G. (Eds.),Vol. SPIE-3691, pp. 168-175, The International Society for Optical Engineering, Bellingham, WA.

Aguilar, M.; Fay, D.A.; Ross, W.D.; Waxman, A.M.; Ireland, D.B. & Racamoto, J.P. (1998). Real-time fusion of low-light CCD and uncooled IR imagery for color night vision, In: *Enhanced and Synthetic Vision 1998*, Verly, J.G. (Eds.),Vol. SPIE-3364, pp. 124-135, The International Society for Optical Engineering, Bellingham, WA.

Angell, C. (2005). Fusion performance using a validation approach, In: *Information Fusion 2005*.

Ansorge, U., Horstmann, G. & Carbone, E. (2005). Top-down contingent capture by color: evidence from RT distribution analyses in a manual choice reaction task. *Acta Psychologica*, Vol.120, No.3, 243-266.

Blum, R.S. (2006). On multisensor image fusion performance limits from an estimation theory perspective. *Information Fusion*, Vol.7, No.3, 250-263.

Blum, R.S. & Liu, Z. (2006). *Multi-sensor image fusion and its applications*. CRC Press, Taylor & Francis Group, ISBN , Boca Raton, Florida, USA.

Burt, P.J. & Adelson, E.H. (1985). Merging images through pattern decomposition, In: *Applications of Digital Image Processing VIII*, Tescher, A.G. (Eds.),Vol. SPIE-575, pp. 173-181, The International Society for Optical Engineering, Bellingham, WA.

Cavanillas, J.A. (1999). *The role of color and false color in object recognition with degraded and non-degraded images*. (Master's thesis) Monterey, CA: Naval Postgraduate School.

Chari, S.K.; Fanning, J.D.; Salem, S.M.; Robinson, A.L. & Haford, C.E. (2005). LWIR and MWIR fusion algorithm comparison using image metrics, In: *Infrared Imaging Systems: Design, Analysis, Modeling, and Testing XVI*, Holst, G.C. (Eds.),Vol. SPIE-5784, pp. 16-26, The International Society for Optical Engineering, Bellingham, WA.

Chen, H. & Varshney, P.K. (2005). A Perceptual Quality Metric For Image Fusion Based on Regional Information, In: Vol. SPIE-, The International Society for Optical Engineering, Bellingham, WA.

Chen, H. & Varshney, P.K. (2007). A human perception inspired quality metric for image fusion based on regional information. *Information Fusion*, Vol.8, No.2, 193-207.

Chiarella, M.; Fay, D.A.; Ivey, R.T.; Bomberger, N.A. & Waxman, A.M. (2004). Multisensor image fusion, mining and reasoning: rule sets for higher-level AFE in a COTS environment, In: *Proceedings of the Seventh International Conference on Information Fusion*, Svenson, P. & Schubert, J. (Eds.), pp. 983-990, International Society of Information Fusion, Mountain View, CA.

Correia, P. & Pereira, F. (2002). Standalone objective segmentation quality evaluation. *EURASIP Journal on Applied Signal Processing*, Vol.4, No., 389-400.

Correia, P. & Pereira, F. (2006). Video object relevance metrics for overall segmentation quality evaluation. *EURASIP Journal on Applied Signal Processing*, Vol.Article ID 82195, No., 1-11.

Correia, P.L. & Pereira, F.M. (2003). Methodologies for objective evaluation of video segmentation quality, In: *Visual Communications and Image Processing 2003*, Ebrahimi, T. & Sikora, T. (Eds.),Vol. SPIE-5150, pp. 1594-1600, The International Society for Optical Engineering, Bellingham, WA., USA.

Corsini, G.; Diani, M.; Masini, A. & Cavallini, M. (2006). Enhancement of Sight Effectiveness by Dual Infrared System: Evaluation of Image Fusion Strategies, In: *Proceedings of the 5th International Conference on Technology and Automation (ICTA'05)*, pp. 376-381.

Cvejic, N., Loza, A., Bull, D. & Canagarajah, N. (2005a). A novel metric for performance evaluation of image fusion algorithms. *Transactions on Engineering, Computing and Technology*, Vol.V7, No., 80-85.

Cvejic, N., Loza, A., Bull, D. & Canagarajah, N. (2005b). A similarity metric for assessment of image fusion algorithms. *International Journal of Signal Processing*, Vol.2, No.2, 178-182.

Davis, J.W. & Sharma, V. (2007). Background-subtraction using contour-based fusion of thermal and visible imagery. *Computer Vision and Image Understanding*, Vol.106, No.2-3, 162-182.

Dixon, T.D., Canga, E.F., Troscianko, T., Noyes, J.M., Nikolov, S.G., Bull, D.R. & Canagarajah, C.N. (2006a). Assessment of images fused using false colouring. *Journal of Vision*, Vol.6, No.6, 459-a.

Dixon, T.D.; Li, J.; Noyes, J.M.; Troscianko, T.; Nikolov, S.G.; Lewis, J.; Canga, E.F.; Bull, D.R. & Canagarajah, C.N. (2006b). Scanpath analysis of fused multi-sensor images with luminance change: a pilot study, In: *Special Session on Image Fusion Assessment. Proceedings of the 9th International Conference on Information Fusion*, Nikolov, S. & Toet, A. (Eds.), International Society of Information Fusion, Mountain View, CA.

Dixon, T.D.; Noyes, J.; Troscianko, T.; Canga, E.F.; Bull, D. & Canagarajah, N. (2005). Psychophysical and metric assessment of fused images, In: *Proceedings of the 2nd symposium on Appied perception in graphics and visualization*, Bülthoff, H.B. & Troscianko, T. (Eds.),Vol. ACM International Conference Proceeding Series; Vol. 95, pp. 43-50, ACM Press, New York, USA.

Driggers, R.G.; Krapels, K.A.; Vollmerhausen, R.H.; Warren, P.R.; Scribner, D.A.; Howard, J.G.; Tsou, B.H. & Krebs, W.K. (2001). Target detection threshold in noisy color imagery, In: *Infrared Imaging Systems: Design, Analysis, Modeling, and Testing XII*, Holst, G.C. (Eds.),Vol. SPIE-4372, pp. 162-169, The International Society for Optical Engineering, Bellingham, WA.

Essock, E.A., Sinai, M.J., DeFord, J.K., Hansen, B.C. & Srinivasan, N. (2005). Human perceptual performance with nonliteral imagery: region recognition and texture-based segmentation. *Journal of Experimental Psychology: Applied*, Vol.10, No.2, 97-110.

Essock, E.A., Sinai, M.J., McCarley, J.S., Krebs, W.K. & DeFord, J.K. (1999). Perceptual ability with real-world nighttime scenes: image-intensified, infrared, and fused-color imagery. *Human Factors*, Vol.41, No.3, 438-452.

Fay, D.A.; Waxman, A.M.; Aguilar, M.; Ireland, D.B.; Racamato, J.P.; Ross, W.D.; Streilein, W. & Braun, M.I. (2000a). Fusion of 2- /3- /4-sensor imagery for visualization, target learning, and search, In: *Enhanced and Synthetic Vision 2000*, Verly, J.G. (Eds.),Vol. SPIE-4023, pp. 106-115, SPIE -The International Society for Optical Engineering, Bellingham, WA, USA.

Fay, D.A.; Waxman, A.M.; Aguilar, M.; Ireland, D.B.; Racamato, J.P.; Ross, W.D.; Streilein, W. & Braun, M.I. (2000b). Fusion of multi-sensor imagery for night vision: color visualization, target learning and search, In: *Proceedings of the 3rd International Conference on Information Fusion*, Vol. I, pp. TuD3-3-TuD3-10, ONERA, Paris, France.

Fay, D.A.; Waxman, A.M.; Ivey, R.T.; Bomberger, N.A. & Chiarella, M. (2004). Multisensor image fusion and mining: learning targets across extended operating conditions, In: *Enhanced and Synthetic Vision 2004*, Verly, J.G. (Eds.),Vol. SPIE-5424, pp. 148-162, The International Society for Optical Engineering, Bellingham, WA., USA.

Folk, C.L. & Remington, R. (1998). Selectivity in distraction by irrelevant featural singletons: evidence for two forms of attentional capture. *Journal of Experimental Psychology: Human Perception and Performance*, Vol.24, No.3, 847-858.

Fredembach, C. & Süsstrunk, S. (2008). Colouring the near-infrared, In: *Proceedings of the IS&T/SID 16th Color Imaging Conference*, pp. 176-182.

Gegenfurtner, K.R. & Rieger, J. (2000). Sensory and cognitive contributions of color to the recognition of natural scenes. *Current Biology*, Vol.10, No.13, 805-808.

Goffaux, V., Jacques, C., Mouraux, A., Oliva, A., Schyns, P. & Rossion, B. (2005). Diagnostic colours contribute to the early stages of scene categorization: Behavioural and neurophysiological evidence. *Visual Cognition*, Vol.12, No.6, 878-892.

Green, B.F. & Anderson, L.K. (1956). Colour coding in a visual search task. *Journal of Experimental Psychology*, Vol.51, No., 19-24.

Grossberg, S. (1988). *Neural networks and natural intelligence.* MIT Press, ISBN , Cambridge, MA.

Hogervorst, M.A. & Toet, A. (2008a). Method for applying daytime colors to nighttime imagery in realtime, In: *Multisensor, Multisource Information Fusion: Architectures, Algorithms, and Applications 2008*, Dasarathy, B.V. (Eds.),Vol. SPIE-6974, pp. 697403-1-697403-9, The International Society for Optical Engineering, Bellingham, WA, USA.

Hogervorst, M.A. & Toet, A. (2008b). Presenting nighttime imagery in daytime colours, In: *Proceedings of the 11th International Conference on Information Fusion*, pp. 706-713, International Society of Information Fusion, Cologne, Germany.

Hogervorst, M.A. & Toet, A. (2010). Fast natural color mapping for night-time imagery. *Information Fusion*, Vol.11, No.2, 69-77.

Howard, J.G.; Warren, P.; Klien, R.; Schuler, J.; Satyshur, M.; Scribner, D. & Kruer, M.R. (2000). Real-time color fusion of E/O sensors with PC-based COTS hardware, In: *Targets and Backgrounds VI: Characterization, Visualization, and the Detection Process*, Watkins, W.R. et al. (Eds.),Vol. SPIE-4029, pp. 41-48, The International Society for Optical Engineering, Bellingham, WA.

Huang, G., Ni, G. & Zhang, B. (2007). Visual and infrared dual-band false color image fusion method motivated by Land's experiment. *Optical Engineering*, Vol.46, No.2, 027001-1-027001-10.

ImageFusion.Org (2007). The Online Resource for Research in Image Fusion, In: *http://www.imagefusion.org/*, Last viewed March 2007.

Jacobson, N.P. & Gupta, M.R. (2005). Design goals and solutions for display of hyperspectral images. *IEEE Transactions on Geoscience and Remote Sensing*, Vol.43, No.11, 2684-2692.

Jacobson, N.P., Gupta, M.R. & Cole, J.B. (2007). Linear fusion of image sets for display. *IEEE Transactions on Geoscience and Remote Sensing*, Vol.45, No.10, 3277-3288.

Jakobson, G.; Lewis, L. & Buford, J. (2004). An approach to integrated cognitive fusion, In: *Proceedings of the Seventh International Conference on Information Fusion*, Svenson, P. & Schubert, J. (Eds.), pp. 1210-1217, International Society of Information Fusion, Chatillon, France.

Joseph, J.E. & Proffitt, D.R. (1996). Semantic versus perceptual influences of color in object recognition. *Journal of Experimental Psychology: Learning, Memory, and Cognition*, Vol.22, No.2, 407-429.

Kong, S.G., Heo, J., Boughorbel, F., Zheng, Y., Abidi, B.R., Koschan, A., Yi, M. & Abidi, M.A. (2007). Multiscale Fusion of Visible and Thermal IR Images for Illumination-Invariant Face Recognition. *International Journal of Computer Vision*, Vol.71, No.2, 215-233.

Krebs, W.K. & Ahumada, A.J. (2002). Using an image discrimination model to predict the detectability of targets in color scenes, In: *Proceedings of the Combating Uncertainty with Fusion - An Office of Naval Research and NASA conference , April 22-24, 2002.*, Office of Naval Research and NASA, Woods Hole, MA.

Krebs, W.K.; Scribner, D.A.; Miller, G.M.; Ogawa, J.S. & Schuler, J. (1998). Beyond third generation: a sensor-fusion targeting FLIR pod for the F/A-18, In: *Sensor Fusion:*

Architectures, Algorithms, and Applications II, Dasarathy, B.V. (Eds.),Vol. SPIE-3376, pp. 129-140, International Society for Optical Engineering, Bellingham, WA, USA.

Krebs, W.K. & Sinai, M.J. (2002). Psychophysical assessments of image-sensor fused imagery. *Human Factors*, Vol.44, No.2, 257-271.

Lewis, J.J.; Nikolov, S.G.; Canagarajah, C.N.; Bull, D.R. & Toet, A. (2006). Uni-Modal versus Joint Segmentation for Region-Based Image Fusion, In: *Proceedings of the 9th International Conference on Information Fusion*, International Society of Information Fusion, Mountain View, CA.

Lewis, J.J., O'Callaghan, R.J., Nikolov, S.G., Bull, D.R. & Canagarajah, N. (2007). Pixel- and region-based image fusion with complex wavelets. *Information Fusion*, Vol.8, No.2, 119-130.

Li, G. & Wang, K. (2007). Applying daytime colors to nighttime imagery with an efficient color transfer method, In: *Enhanced and Synthetic Vision 2007*, Verly, J.G. & Guell, J.J. (Eds.),Vol. SPIE-6559, pp. 65590L-1-65590L-12, The International Society for Optical Engineering, Bellingham, MA.

Li, J.; Pan, Q.; Yang, T. & Cheng, Y. (2004). Color based grayscale-fused image enhancement algorithm for video surveillance, In: *Proceedings of the Third International Conference on Image and Graphics (ICIG'04)*, pp. 47-50, IEEE Press, Washington, USA.

Lotufo, R. & Zampirolli, F. (2001). Fast multidimensional parallel euclidean distance transform based on mathematical morphology, In: *Proceedings of the XIVth Brazilian Symposium on Computer Graphics and Image Processing (SIBGRAPI 2001)*, Wu, T. & Borges, D. (Eds.), pp. 100-105, IEEE Computer Society, Washington, USA.

Macmillan, N.A. & Creelman, C.D. (1991). *Detection theory: a user's guide.* Cambridge University Press, ISBN , Cambridge, MA.

Maragos, P. & Schafer, R. (1986). Morphological skeleton representation and coding of binary images. *IEEE Transactions on Acoustics, Speech and Signal Processing*, Vol.34, No.5, 1228-1244.

Martin, D.R., Fowlkes, C.C. & Malik, J. (2004). Learning to Detect Natural Image Boundaries Using Local Brightness, Color, and Texture Cues. *IEEE Transactions on Pattern Analysis and Machine Intelligence PAMI*, Vol.26, No.1, 1-20.

Muller, A.C. & Narayanan, S. (2009). Cognitively-engineered multisensor image fusion for military applications. *Information Fusion*, Vol.10, No.2, 137-149.

O'Brien, M.A. & Irvine, J.M. (2004). Information fusion for feature extraction and the development of geospatial information, In: *Proceedings of the 7th International Conference on Information Fusion (FUSION 2004)*, pp. 976-982, International Society of Information Fusion, Mountain View, CA.

Oliva, A. (2005). Gist of a scene, In: *Neurobiology of Attention*, Itti, L. et al. (Eds.), pp. 251-256, Academic Press.

Oliva, A. & Schyns, P.G. (2000). Diagnostic colors mediate scene recognition. *Cognitive Psychology*, Vol.41, No., 176-210.

Onyango, C.M. & Marchant, J.A. (2001). Physics-based colour image segmentation for scenes containing vegetation and soil. *Image and Vision Computing*, Vol.19, No.8, 523-538.

Piella, G. & Heijmans, H.J.A.M. (2003). A new quality metric for image fusion, In: *Proceedings of the IEEE International Conference on Image Processing*, Vol. III, pp. III-209-III-212, IEEE Press, Washington, USA.

Riley, P. & Smith, M. (2006). Image fusion technology for security and surveillance applications, In: *Optics and Photonics for Counterterrorism and Crime Fighting II*, Lewis, C. & Owen, G.P. (Eds.),Vol. SPIE-6402, pp. 640204-640204, The International Society for Optical Engineering, Bellingham, WA.

Rousselet, G.A., Joubert, O.R. & Fabre-Thorpe, M. (2005). How long to get the "gist" of real-world natural scenes? *Visual Cognition*, Vol.12, No.6, 852-877.

Sampson, M.T. (1996). *An assessment of the impact of fused monochrome and fused color night vision displays on reaction time and accuracy in target detection* (Report AD-A321226). Monterey, CA: Naval Postgraduate School.

Schuler, J.; Howard, J.G.; Warren, P.; Scribner, D.A.; Klien, R.; Satyshur, M. & Kruer, M.R. (2000). Multiband E/O color fusion with consideration of noise and registration, In: *Targets and Backgrounds VI: Characterization, Visualization, and the Detection Process*, Watkins, W.R. et al. (Eds.),Vol. SPIE-4029, pp. 32-40, The International Society for Optical Engineering, Bellingham, WA, USA.

Scribner, D.; Schuler, J.M.; Warren, P.; Klein, R. & Howard, J.G. (2003). Sensor and image fusion, In: *Encyclopedia of optical engineering*, Driggers, R.G. (Eds.), pp. 2577-2582, Marcel Dekker Inc., New York, USA.

Scribner, D.; Warren, P. & Schuler, J. (1999). Extending color vision methods to bands beyond the visible, In: *Proceedings of the IEEE Workshop on Computer Vision Beyond the Visible Spectrum: Methods and Applications*, pp. 33-40, Institute of Electrical and Electronics Engineers.

Serra, J. (1982). *Image analysis and mathematical morphology.* Academic Press, ISBN , London, UK.

Shi, J.; Jin, W.; Wang, L. & Chen, H. (2005a). Objective evaluation of color fusion of visual and IR imagery by measuring image contrast, In: *Infrared Components and Their Applications*, Gong, H. et al. (Eds.),Vol. SPIE-5640, pp. 594-601, The International Society for Optical Engineering, Bellingham, MA.

Shi, J.-S., Jin, W.-Q. & Wang, L.-X. (2005b). Study on perceptual evaluation of fused image quality for color night vision. *Journal of Infrared and Millimeter Waves*, Vol.24, No.3, 236-240.

Sinai, M.J.; McCarley, J.S. & Krebs, W.K. (1999a). Scene recognition with infra-red, low-light, and sensor fused imagery, In: *Proceedings of the IRIS Specialty Groups on Passive Sensors*, pp. 1-9, IRIS, Monterey, CA.

Sinai, M.J.; McCarley, J.S.; Krebs, W.K. & Essock, E.A. (1999b). Psychophysical comparisons of single- and dual-band fused imagery, In: *Enhanced and Synthetic Vision 1999*, Verly, J.G. (Eds.),Vol. SPIE-3691, pp. 176-183, The International Society for Optical Engineering, Bellingham, WA.

Smith, M.I.; Ball, A.N. & Hooper, D. (2002). Real-time image fusion: a vision aid for helicopter pilotage, In: *Real-Time Imaging VI*, Kehtarnavaz, N. (Eds.),Vol. SPIE-4666, pp. 83-94, The International Society for Optical Engineering, Bellingham, WA., USA.

Smith, M.I. & Heather, J.P. (2005). Review of image fusion technology in 2005, In: *Thermosense XXVII*, Peacock, G.R. et al. (Eds.),Vol. SPIE-5782, pp. 6-1-6-17, The International Society for Optical Engineering, Bellingham, WA.

Spence, I., Wong, P., Rusan, M. & Rastegar, N. (2006). How color enhances visual memory for natural scenes. *Psychological Science*, Vol.17, No.1, 1-6.

Sun, S., Jing, Z., Li, Z. & Liu, G. (2005). Color fusion of SAR and FLIR images using a natural color transfer technique. *Chinese Optics Letters*, Vol.3, No.4, 202-204.

Toet, A. (1990a). Adaptive multi-scale contrast enhancement through non-linear pyramid recombination. *Pattern Recognition Letters*, Vol.11, No.11, 735-742.

Toet, A. (1990b). Hierarchical image fusion. *Machine Vision and Applications*, Vol.3, No.1, 1-11.

Toet, A. (1992). Multi-scale contrast enhancement with applications to image fusion. *Optical Engineering*, Vol.31, No.5, 1026-1031.

Toet, A. (2003). Natural colour mapping for multiband nightvision imagery. *Information Fusion*, Vol.4, No.3, 155-166.

Toet, A. & Franken, E.M. (2003). Perceptual evaluation of different image fusion schemes. *Displays*, Vol.24, No.1, 25-37.

Toet, A. & Hogervorst, M.A. (2003). Performance comparison of different graylevel image fusion schemes through a universal image quality index, In: *Signal Processing, Sensor Fusion, and Target Recognition XII*, Kadar, I. (Eds.),Vol. SPIE-5096, pp. 552-561, The International Society for Optical Engineering, Bellingham, WA., USA.

Toet, A. & IJspeert, J.K. (2001). Perceptual evaluation of different image fusion schemes, In: *Signal Processing, Sensor Fusion, and Target Recognition X*, Kadar, I. (Eds.),Vol. SPIE-4380, pp. 436-441, The International Society for Optical Engineering, Bellingham, WA.

Toet, A., IJspeert, J.K., Waxman, A.M. & Aguilar, M. (1997b). Fusion of visible and thermal imagery improves situational awareness. *Displays*, Vol.18, No.2, 85-95.

Toet, A.; IJspeert, J.K.; Waxman, A.M. & Aguilar, M. (1997a). Fusion of visible and thermal imagery improves situational awareness, In: *Enhanced and Synthetic Vision 1997*, Verly, J.G. (Eds.),Vol. SPIE-3088, pp. 177-188, International Society for Optical Engineering, Bellingham, WA, USA.

Toet, A., van Ruyven, J.J. & Valeton, J.M. (1989). Merging thermal and visual images by a contrast pyramid. *Optical Engineering*, Vol.28, No.7, 789-792.

Tsagiris, V. & Anastassopoulos, V. (2004). Information measure for assessing pixel-level fusion methods, In: *Image and Signal Processing for Remote Sensing X*, Bruzzone, L. (Eds.),Vol. SPIE-5573, pp. 64-71, The International Society for Optical Engineering, Bellingham, WA.

Tsagiris, V. & Anastassopoulos, V. (2005). Fusion of visible and infrared imagery for night color vision. *Displays*, Vol.26, No.4-5, 191-196.

Ullman, S. (2007). Object recognition and segmentation by a fragment-based hierarchy. *Trends in Cognitive Sciences*, Vol.11, No.2, 58-64.

Ulug, M.E. & Claire, L. (2000). A quantitative metric for comparison of night vision fusion algorithms, In: *Sensor Fusion: Architectures, Algorithms, and Applications IV*, Dasarathy, B.V. (Eds.),Vol. SPIE-4051, pp. 80-88, The International Society for Optical Engineering, Bellingham, WA.

van Rijsbergen, C.J. (1979). *Information retrieval. 2nd Edition.* Butterworth-Heinemann, ISBN , Newton, MA, USA.

Vargo, J.T. (1999). *Evaluation of operator performance using true color and artificial color in natural scene perception* (Report AD-A363036). Monterey, CA: Naval Postgraduate School.

Vogel, J. & Schiele, B. (2007). Semantic modeling of natural scenes for content-based image retrieval. *International Journal of Computer Vision*, Vol.72, No.2, 133-157.

Walls, G.L. (2006). *The vertebrate eye and its adaptive radiation.* Cranbrook Institute of Science, ISBN , Bloomfield Hills, Michigan.

Wang, L.; Jin, W.; Gao, Z. & Liu, G. (2002). Color fusion schemes for low-light CCD and infrared images of different properties, In: *Electronic Imaging and Multimedia Technology III*, Zhou, L. et al. (Eds.),Vol. SPIE-4925, pp. 459-466, The International Society for Optical Engineering, Bellingham, WA.

Wang, Q. & Shen, Y. (2006). Performance assessment of image fusion, In: *Advances in Image and Video Technology*, Vol. Lecture Notes in Computer Science Volume 4319, pp. 373-382, Springer Verlag, Heidelberg/Berlin, Germany.

Warren, P., Howard, J.G., Waterman, J., Scribner, D.A. & Schuler, J. (1999). *Real-time, PC-based color fusion displays* (Report A073093). Washington, DC: Naval Research Lab.

Waxman, A.M.; Aguilar, M.; Baxter, R.A.; Fay, D.A.; Ireland, D.B.; Racamoto, J.P. & Ross, W.D. (1998). Opponent-color fusion of multi-sensor imagery: visible, IR and SAR, In: *Proceedings of the 1998 Conference of the IRIS Specialty Group on Passive Sensors*, Vol. I, pp. 43-61.

Waxman, A.M., et al. (1999). Solid-state color night vision: fusion of low-light visible and thermal infrared imagery. *MIT Lincoln Laboratory Journal*, Vol.11, No., 41-60.

Waxman, A.M.; Carrick, J.E.; Fay, D.A.; Racamato, J.P.; Augilar, M. & Savoye, E.D. (1996a). Electronic imaging aids for night driving: low-light CCD, thermal IR, and color fused visible/IR, In: *Proceedings of the SPIE Conference on Transportation Sensors and Controls*, Vol. SPIE-2902, The International Society for Optical Engineering, Bellingham, WA.

Waxman, A.M.; Fay, D.A.; Gove, A.N.; Seibert, M.C.; Racamato, J.P.; Carrick, J.E. & Savoye, E.D. (1995). Color night vision: fusion of intensified visible and thermal IR imagery, In: *Synthetic Vision for Vehicle Guidance and Control*, Verly, J.G. (Eds.),Vol. SPIE-2463, pp. 58-68, The International Society for Optical Engineering, Bellingham, WA.

Waxman, A.M.; Fay, D.A.; Hardi, P.; Savoye, D.; Biehl, R. & Grau, D. (2006). Sensor Fused Night Vision : Assessing Image Quality in the Lab and in the Field, In: *Special Session on Image Fusion Assessment. Proceedings of the 9th International Conference on Information Fusion*, Nikolov, S. & Toet, A. (Eds.), International Society of Information Fusion, Mountain View, CA.

Waxman, A.M.; Fay, D.A.; Ivey, R.T. & Bomberger, N. (2003). Multisensor image fusion & mining: from neural systems to COTS software, In: *Proceedings of the International Conference on Integration of Knowledge Intensive Multi-Agent Systems 2003*, pp. 355-362, IEEE Press, Washington, MA.

Waxman, A.M.; Gove, A.N. & Cunningham, R.K. (1996b). Opponent-color visual processing applied to multispectral infrared imagery, In: *Proceedings of 1996 Meeting of the IRIS Specialty Group on Passive Sensors*, Vol. II, pp. 247-262, Infrared Information Analysis Center, ERIM, Ann Arbor, US.

Waxman, A.M., Gove, A.N., Fay, D.A., Racamoto, J.P., Carrick, J.E., Seibert, M.C. & Savoye, E.D. (1997). Color night vision: opponent processing in the fusion of visible and IR imagery. *Neural Networks*, Vol.10, No.1, 1-6.

Waxman, A.M.; Gove, A.N.; Seibert, M.C.; Fay, D.A.; Carrick, J.E.; Racamato, J.P.; Savoye, E.D.; Burke, B.E.; Reich, R.K. et al. (1996c). Progress on color night vision: visible/IR fusion, perception and search, and low-light CCD imaging, In: *Enhanced and*

Synthetic Vision 1996, Verly, J.G. (Eds.),Vol. SPIE-2736, pp. 96-107, The International Society for Optical Engineering, Bellingham, WA.

White, B.L. (1998). *Evaluation of the impact of multispectral image fusion on human performance in global scene processing*. (M.Sc.) Monterey, CA: Naval Postgraduate School.

Wichmann, F.A., Sharpe, L.T. & Gegenfurtner, K.R. (2002). The contributions of color to recognition memory for natural scenes. *Journal of Experimental Psychology: Learning, Memory, and Cognition*, Vol.28, No.3, 509-520.

Xydeas, C.S. & Petrovic, V.S. (2000). Objective pixel-level image fusion performance measure, In: *Sensor Fusion: Architectures, Algorithms, and Applications IV*, Dasarathy, B.V. (Eds.),Vol. SPIE-4051, pp. 89-98, The International Society for Optical Engineering, Bellingham, WA.

Yang, C., Zhang, J., Wang, X. & Liu, X. (2007). A novel similarity based quality metric for image fusion. *Information Fusion*, Vol.9, No.2, 156-160.

Zheng, Y., Essock, E.A., Hansen, B.C. & Haun, A.M. (2007). A new metric based on extended spatial frequency and its application to DWT based fusion algorithms. *Information Fusion*, Vol.8, No.2, 177-192.

Zheng, Y.; Hansen, B.C.; Haun, A.M. & Essock, E.A. (2005). Coloring night-vision imagery with statistical properties of natural colors by using image segmentation and histogram matching, In: *Color imaging X: processing, hardcopy and applications*, Eschbach, R. & Marcu, G.G. (Eds.),Vol. SPIE-5667, pp. 107-117, The International Society for Optical Engineering, Bellingham, WA.

Zhu, X. & Jia, Y. (2005). A method based on IHS cylindrical transform model for quality assessment of image fusion, In: *MIPPR 2005: Image Analysis Techniques*, Li, D. & Ma, H. (Eds.),Vol. SPIE-6044, pp. 607-615, The International Society for Optical Engineering, Bellingham, MA.

Zou, X. & Bhanu, B. (2005). Tracking humans using multi-modal fusion, In: *2nd Joint IEEE International Workshop on Object Tracking and Classification in and Beyond the Visible Spectrum (OTCBVS'05)*, pp. W01-30-1-W01-30-8, IEEE Press, Washington, USA.

16

Image Fusion Methods for Confocal Scanning Laser Microscopy experimented on Images of Photonic Quantum Ring Laser Devices

Stefan G. Stanciu
Center for Microscopy – Microanalysis and Information Processing, University Politehnica Bucharest Romania

1. Introduction

Confocal Scanning Laser Microscopy (CSLM) represents one of the most important advances in optical microscopy of the last decades. It is widely accepted that the confocal microscope was invented by Marvin Minsky, who filed a patent in 1957 (Minsky, 1957). However, at that time such a system was very difficult, if not impossible, to implement, due to the unavailability of required laser sources, sensitve photomultipliers or computer image storage possibilities. A laser scanning microscope using mechanical object scanning was developed in Oxford in 1975, and a review of this work was later published (Sheppard, 1990). The Oxford microscope was the first commercial confocal microscope. Other important contributors to this era of the development of confocal microscopy were Brakenhoff (Brakenhoff et al., 1979) and Cox (Cox, 1984).

The architecture of a CSLM system provides the possibility to acquire images representing optical sections on a sample's volume. In order to achieve this, in a CSLM system an excitation source emits coherent light (laser) which is scanned across the sample surface. As it reaches the sample the light is reflected towards a detector, in reflection work mode, the same optical path being used as well in fluorescence work mode. While in conventional microscopy, the detector is subjected to light which is reflected by out of focus planes, resulting in out-of-focus blur being contained in the final image, the architecture of a CSLM system helps avoid this situation. In order to acquire images corresponding to certain optical sections, a confocal aperture (usually known as pinhole) is situated in front of the detector. More precisely, the pinhole is placed in a plane conjugate to the intermediate image plane and, thus, to the object plane of the microscope. As a result, only light reflected from the focal plane reaches the detector, out-of-focus light being blocked by the pinhole (Fig. 1). The dimension of the pinhole is variable and together with the wavelength which is being used and the numerical aperture of the objective, dictates the thickness of the volume which contributes to the collected image (Shepard et. al., 1997; Wilson, 2001).

In the case of CSLM systems, the detector is a photo multiplier tube (PMT), which presents a wide dynamic range and has high photon sensitivity suitable for detecting both strong and weak signal at a very quick refresh rates, in a time range of nano-seconds. The PMT detects light and converts photon hits into analogue electron flow as electrons leave the photocathode of the PMT, having the energy of the incoming photon. After the electrons follow a path which amplifies their number, they reach the anode of the PMT, where the accumulation of charge results in a sharp current pulse indicating the arrival of a photon at the photocathode. The continuous analogue current signal is then sampled at separate time point, digitized into discrete digital signal by analogue to digital converter (ADC), then processed by image processor resulting in digital images of the sample area contained in the system's field of view.

Besides CSLM specific advantages such as increased resolution and better contrast, the provided possibility of achieving images corresponding to optical sections represents as well a significant advantage to people working in fields such as biology, medicine, material science or microelectronics, as CSLM image stacks can be used for 3D reconstructions of the studied sample (Rigaut et al., 1991, Liu et al. 1997, Pironon, 1998, Rodriguez et al, 2003, Sugawara et al., 2005).

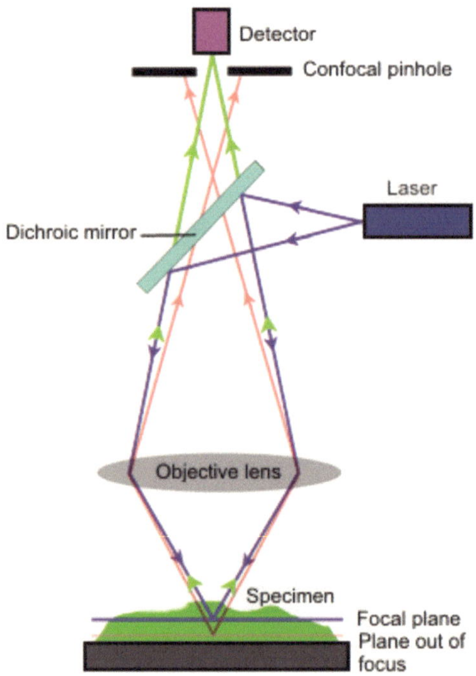

Fig. 1. Principle of Confocal Scanning Laser Microscopy

In some circumstances, a CSLM image corresponding to an optical section may contain defocused, low contrast or over-saturated areas. This problem can be present due to various reasons, such as region non-uniformity or sample regions which contribute to the image not being in the same focal plane at the same time due to non-uniform size or sample tilt (Fig. 2). For certain types of investigations conclusions can be drawn only based on images of uniform quality or uniform focus. These types of images allow better morphological observations of the sample details. One method for obtaining this type of representation is image fusion. Image fusion will provide an artificial image, which will consist of image regions belonging to different images of the CSLM stack. The purpose of this operation is to achieve an image representing a better description of the imaged scene or object than any of the individual source images. Ideally, the fusion algorithm should preserve relevant information from the fused images and suppress image regions or components which are subjected to noise or which are irrelevant in respect to a defined purpose (Nikolov, 98). Applications of image fusion have been implemented with great success in different microscopy and medical applications. For example, excellent results have been achieved in the case of three- dimensional microscopy, where certain limitations imposed by the low axial resolution of the system have been overcome by fusing images acquired at different placements of the sample (Swoger et al., 2007), while in (Forster et al., 2004) wavelet based image fusion is presented as a solution which provides good results for extending the depth of field in the case of multichannel microscopy images. In (Chen, et al 2010) an image fusion algorithm based on bidimensional empirical mode decomposition (BEMD) is applied to multi-focus color microscopic images achieving a balanced result between local feature enhancement and global tonality rendition.

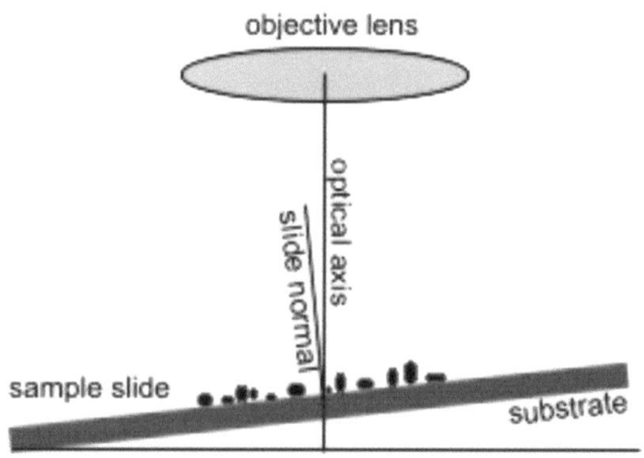

Fig. 2. Possible scenario for the acquisition of a CSLM images of non uniform focus

Image fusion can be performed in both frequency and spatial domains. Our approach, which deals with the fusion of CSLM images, was developed on a region level basis. Lately, much attention has been focused towards region-based image fusion because of its perceived advantages. With fusion rules based on combining regions instead of pixels, more useful tests for choosing the adequate regions from the source images, based on various properties of a region, can be implemented prior to fusion. Problems such as sensitivity to noise, blurring effects and misregistration in the case of pixel-fusion techniques, can be overcome by processing semantic regions rather than individual pixels (Li & Yang, 2008).
In the case of the four fusion methods that we experiment, each image in the CSLM stack is divided into the same number of square regions, same as in (Huang & Jing, 2007). Two of the proposed methods are based on a focus assesment operator, while the other two are based on a quality assesement operator. In the first two methods, which we entitled FFMAX and FFAVG, a focus assessment for the same region in all the images in the stack is calculated by Tenenabaum's algorithm (Tenengrad). In FFMAX the region of the best focus is chosen to appear in the fused image, as in (Huang & Jing, 2007), while in FFAVG, instead of building the fused image from blocks which belong to a single image, we build it by mean averaging the blocks of all images in the stack, the contribution of each source image

to the fused image being proportional to its response to the focus measure, as in (Stanciu et al., submitted 2010). The same approach is used in the 3rd and 4th presented methods, QFMAX and QFAVG, where instead of using a focus assesement operator as a decision criterion which dicates the inclusions of an image region to the fused image, a quality assesement operator is used. All four methods aim to obtain a fused image of better focus or quality uniformity, with morphological details of the structure being more visible than in any other image that contributed to the fusion.

2. Fusion methods

2.1 Focus assesment

The first two fusion methods we have experimented, FFMAX and FFAVG, are based on an image clarity measure, namely a focus measure. A well-focused image has the best average focus over an entire field of view, even though objects often reside at multiple focus planes in thick sample slides. In the case of the first two experimented methods the focus assessment dictates the inclusion or the contribution of an image region to the final fused image. Once an image of the stack is divided into blocks of a certain size, for all these blocks a focus measure is calculated. Focus measures have been deeply studied in the field of autofocusing. There are two kinds of focus measures, spatial domain focus measures and frequency domain focus measures. However, frequency domain focus measures will not be used in a real-time system because of their complexity. Detailed discussions on the topics of focus measures and auto-focusing can be found in the literature (Nayar & Nakagawa, 1994; Subbaro et al., 1992; Yeo et al., 1993; Geusebroek et al., 2000). In (Huang & Jing, 2007), several focus measures were compared according to the focus measure's capability of distinguishing clear image blocks from blurred image blocks. The results of the experiments performed on natural images showed that the Sum-Modified Laplacian (SML) can provide better performance than other focus measures when the execution time is not included in the evaluation, but other measures such as Energy of Laplacian of the image, Tenenbaum's algorithm or Energy of image gradient provided good results as well. In (Osibote et al., 2010), a comparison of automated focusing methods for brightfield microscopy was conducted. It was showed that Vollath's F4 algorithm provided best results, but in the same time Brenner and Tenenbaum's algorithm provided very good results as well. For estimating the focus of a certain region we use a spatial domain focus measure, Tenenbaum's algorithm (Tenengrad) (Krotkov, 1897; Yeo et al., 1993), which is a gradient magnitude maximization method that measures the sum of the squared responses of the horizontal and vertical Sobel masks. In its original implementation, the summation is for pixels that are above a certain threshold; however, we chose to use a variation in which all pixel locations can be included in the summation (Santos *et al.*, 1997).

$$Tenengrad = \sum_{x=2}^{M-1} \sum_{y=2}^{N-1} [\nabla S(x,y)]^2 \tag{1}$$

Where is the Sobel gradient magnitude given by :

$$\nabla S(x,y) = \sqrt{\nabla S_x(x,y)^2 + \nabla S_y(x,y)^2} \tag{2}$$

where $\nabla S(x,y)$ is

$$\nabla S_x(x,y) = \{-[f(x-1,y-1)+2f(x-1,y) \\ +f(x-1,y+1)] + [f(x+1,y-1)+2f(x+1,y)] + [f(x+1,y+1)]\}$$

$$\nabla S_y(x,y) = \{+[f(x-1,y-1)+2f(x,y-1) \\ +f(x+1,y-1)] + [f(x-1,y+1)+2f(x,y+1)] + [f(x+1,y+1)]\} \tag{3}$$

2.2 Quality assesement

For estimating the quality of image regions we have chosen to use the same quality metric as defined in (Stanciu et al, 2010) : $q_f = \mu_f \sigma_f \mu_g$, where μ_f is the average grey level of the image, σ_f is the standard deviation of the image pixels, and μ_g is the mean intensity of the gradient image. We have chosen this quality factor, as it takes into consideration three important aspects which define quality when referring to CSLM images: image brightness, image contrast and presence of edges and boundaries.

A good measure of image brightness is the average gray level of the image. Let us consider the analyzed square region as a discrete image f:[0,M-1] x [0,N-1]->[0,L-1] and let H={h(0), h(1),... h(L-1)} be its histogram. The average gray level, μ_f, immediately follows:

$$\mu_f = \frac{\sum_{i=o}^{L-1} ih(i)}{\sum_{i=o}^{L-1} h(i)} = \frac{1}{MN}\sum_{i=o}^{L-1} ih(i) \tag{4}$$

The standard deviation can be regarded as a measure of image contrast. This can be easily understood since σ is a measure of how widely spread the values in a data set are. An unbiased estimate of the standard deviation is:

$$\sigma_f = \sqrt{\frac{1}{MN-1}\sum_{i=0}^{L-1} h(i)(i-\mu_f)^2} \tag{5}$$

Another important factor that we take into consideration when choosing the reference image is related to the edges contained in the image. If an image is of good quality we can discern very clearly the objects contained in it. Edges characterize boundaries and are therefore a problem of fundamental importance in image processing. Edges represent discontinuities between image regions of rather uniform graylevel or color. In a fashion simillar to the focus assesesment method described in 2.1, we considered the Sobel edge detector (Eq. 2), where S_x estimates the gradient in the x-direction (columns), while S_y estimates the gradient in the y-direction (rows). We consider the measure of the edges contained in image f as the mean intensity of its gradient magnitude image, namely μ_g.

2.3 Fusion of square regions

In all four methods which we have experimented each of the images in the stack is divided into a set of square regions. The dimension of the square regions can be chosen according to the content of the images that are to be fused. Higher region size is equivalent to less discriminative power between image areas, while a lower region size will bring a larger number of disturbing artifacts at the boundaries of the fused regions, also known as seams.

The computational time is also directly linked to the size of the square region, larger regions being equivalent to faster processing time. Because of these aspects, a compromise should be made when choosing the size of the square region. Usually for an image of 1024 x 1024 pixels we have obtained best results for square regions of 32 and 64 pixels.

FFMAX, the first method we experimented, is simillar to the methods described in (Huang & Jing, 2007), for each square region, its inclusion in the fused image is decided by calculating its response to the Tenengrad operator in all the images in the stack (source images). The block with the maximum response to the Tenengrad operator will be included in the fused image (Fig. 3), while others will be discarded . A simillar approach is used for the QFMAX method (Stanciu et al, 2009), where instead of deciding a region's inclusion into the fused image based on a focus assesment operator, we use the quality estimate defined in section 2.2. For both FFMAX and QFMAX methods, a decision operator (F) is calculated for each square region in all images. The number of the image in the stack which contains the region of maximum response to the decision operator is introduced into the correspondence matrix. Once the correspondence matrix is completed, a fused image is constructed as presented in Fig. 3. In the case of FFMAX the decision operator is represented by the Tenengrad focus assesment operator, while in QFMAX it is represented by the quality estimate operator described in 2.2.

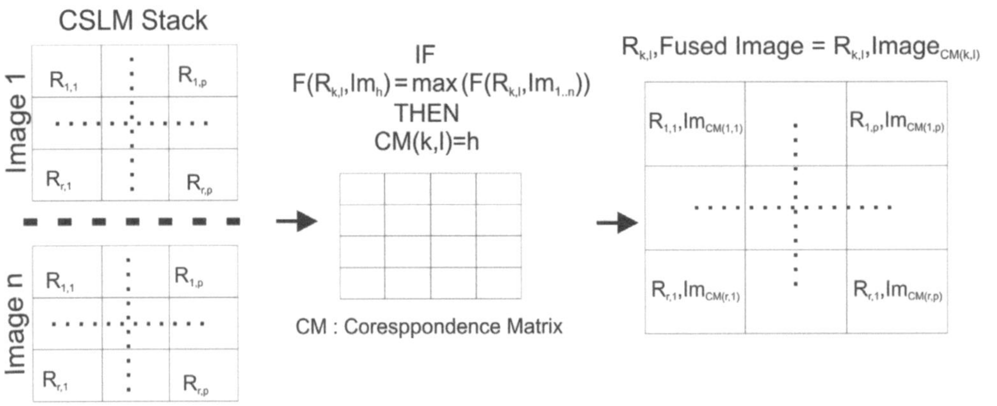

Fig. 3. Image fusion process for FFMAX and QFMAX methods

Further on, we propose two other methods FFAVG and QFAVG. In these methods each of the source images will contribute to the fused image in a certain proportion. The contribution of a square region belonging to a source image to the value of the correspondent square region in the fused image is proportional to its responses to the decision operator. Hence, the responses to the decision operator (F) represent weights in a weighted mean based image fusion process (Fig 4). In FFAVG the decision operator is represented by Tenengrad focus assessment operator, while in QFAVG it is represented by the quality estimate operator described in 2.2.

While in FFMAX and FFAVG only information regarding gradient magnitude is used in the decision regarding a region's inclusion or contribution to the fused image, in QFMAX and QFAVG along with information regarding gradient magnitude, estimates on image brightness and image contrast contribute as well to the decision criterion, which results in brighter resulted images.

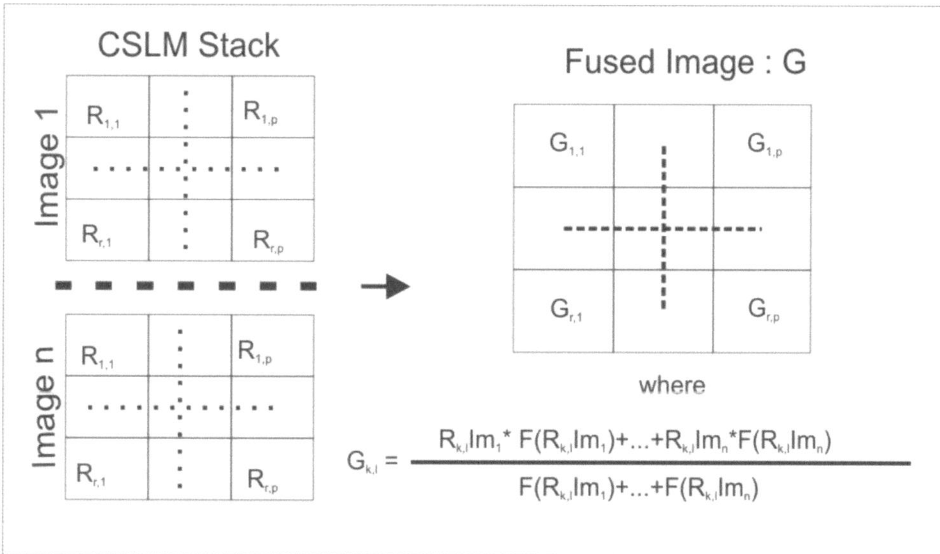

Fig. 4. Image fusion process for FFAVG and QFAVG

3. Objectives and results

3.1 Objective of the technical work carried out

The PQR 'mesa' lasers are three-dimensional (3D) whispering gallery (WG) mode lasers with doughnut type Laguerre-Gaussian (LG) beam patterns (Ahn et al., 1999). During our investigations (Stanciu et al., 2008) on this type of devices several aspects related to their geometry could not be resolved from the original images obtained by CSLM as it was not possible to have all the regions of the device structure in focus at the same time. In Figure 5 we present a stack of images obtained on PQR devices by CSLM. The number in the top left corner depicts the numerical order of optical sections in the full series. The stack consisted of 50 CSLM images acquired at different levels along the Z axis. In order to enhance the results of our investigations on PQR devices, it was needed to construct an artificial image, constructed based on the CSLM set, that would contain information from different focal planes (thus from different images corresponding to different optical sections). The four image fusion algorithms presented in 2.3 have been experimented as a solution for this problem.

The CSLM system that was used is a Leica TCS SP. The images of the PQR structures were obtained by scanning a HeNe laser beam (633nm). The power of the laser beam on the sample surface was kept at 10μW. The objective that was used was HC PL FLUOTAR 20.0 X, with a numerical aperture of 0.5.

By looking at the images in the stack (Fig. 5), we can observe that each one contains different details with their origin in different optical sections; to be more precise there are images with more details from the top of the structure (see images 25,31), and others with more details from the background (see images 37, 43).

For our investigations on the PQR devices Laser Beam Induced Current (LBIC) investigations were conducted in order to study the distribution of photocurrents density when illuminating the PQR structure with a laser beam, Fig. 6. In order to establish the relationships which occur between the sample's geometry and the photocurrent distribution comparisons over CSLM and LBIC representations of the devices were conducted.

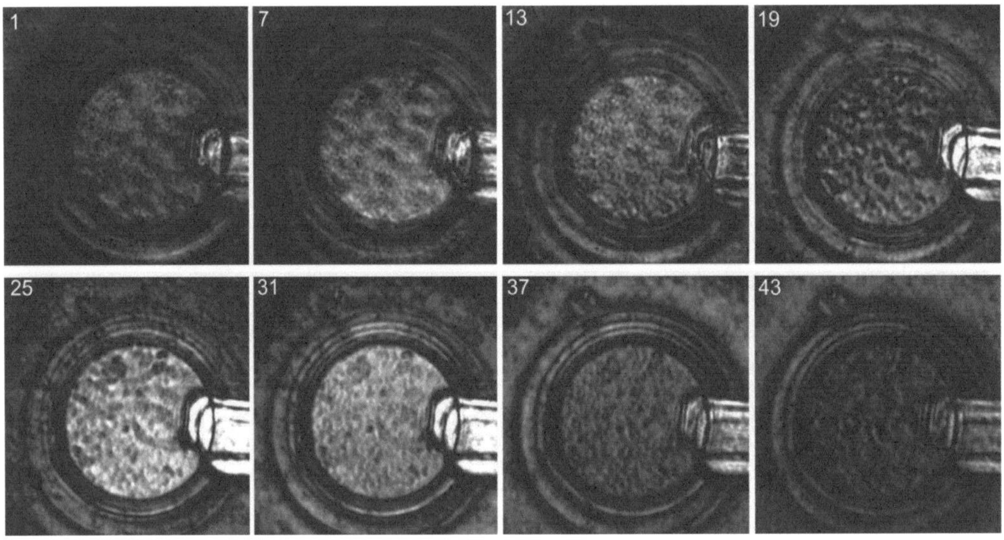

Fig. 5. Stack of PQR images obtained by CSLM

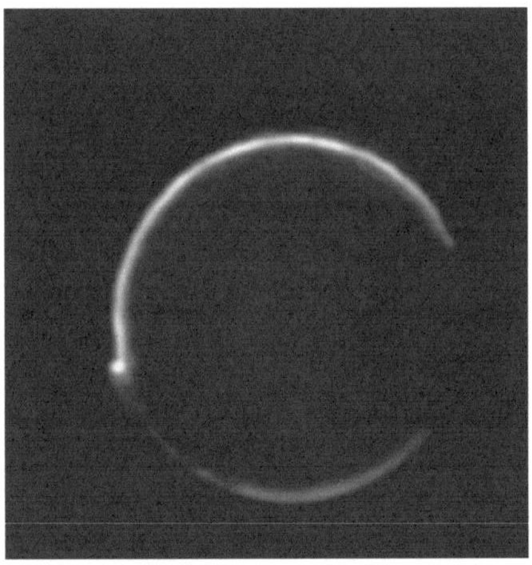

Fig. 6. Photocurrent image of the PQR laser

Our investigations on PQR devices relied on obtaining images at the same Z levels, for both induced photocurrent map obtained in Laser Beam Induced Current (LBIC) mode, and for the reflection signal of the PQR structure collected by CSLM, in order to determine the region where the current was generated. Due to the device geometry and the limitations of the investigation technique (limited depth of field and limited axial resolution), we had obtained images of generated current, by LBIC, even for Z levels for which there was no image in the reflection workmode of the CSLM, due to the structure slope. In this situations we were not able to link the physical regions of the device to the regions in which photocurrent was present. A solution to this problem was represented by the fusion of images of the CSLM stack acquired on a PQR device as described in 2.3. Comparing the photocurrent image acquired in LBIC to an artificial image containing details from different optical sections (the image resulted after image fusion) had enhanced our understanding of the phenomena which takes place in studied devices.

3.2 Results

In Fig 7 we illustrate the fused images constructed based on the CSLM stack presented in Fig. 5, by using the FFMAX method.

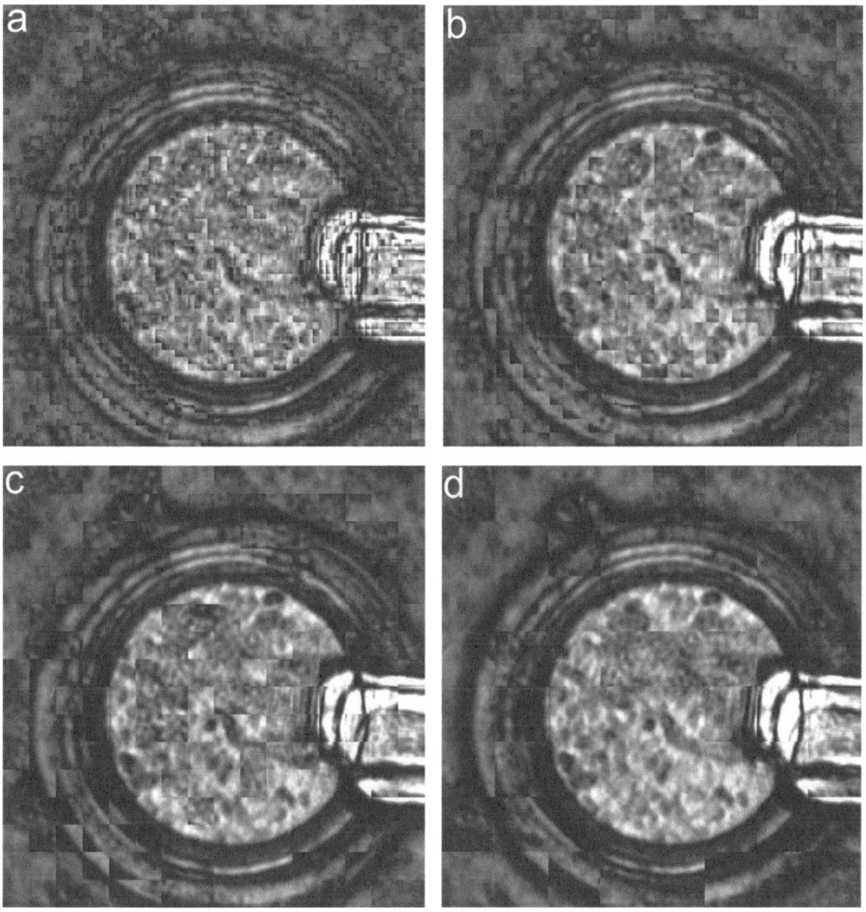

Fig. 7. Resulted images achieved by FFMAX method. The dimension of the square fused regions : a) 16 pixels, b) 32 pixels, c) 64 pixels, d) 128 pixels

The fused images consist of blocks belonging to different images in the stack according to the calculated correspondence matrix (Table 1). Each number in the correspondence matrix represents the number of the image in the stack which contributes with the respective region to the fused image.

In Fig. 8 we illustrate fused images obtained by using the QFMAX method, while in Table 2 one of the correspondences matrix resulted after a quality estimation of square regions of the initial images is presented. Both FFMAX and QFMAX methods provide fused images with better focus or quality uniformity than the intial images in the stack. However the images provided by both methods contain a large number of artefacts around the borders of the fused square regions. This problems are attenuated in the second group of methods, FFAVG and QFAVG, which are based on an averaging of the square regions having the response to a decision operator as weight.

16	16	15	42	22	22	41	40	22	40	40	40	40	40	42	41
15	44	43	40	39	35	37	18	21	18	21	21	17	34	40	41
15	40	40	22	22	31	32	35	32	16	17	17	17	21	21	40
42	42	42	18	42	33	35	33	31	31	33	24	15	12	42	42
42	42	21	36	35	33	30	27	27	26	26	27	25	11	12	16
40	22	41	37	29	30	12	13	13	27	26	28	26	24	11	37
35	20	21	35	28	26	11	25	12	11	25	11	27	11	22	14
18	36	34	17	27	12	12	11	11	25	11	11	30	26	26	21
18	37	17	31	26	12	23	26	12	11	28	33	21	24	18	24
17	36	33	30	25	11	11	24	23	24	9	30	22	17	16	18
16	35	31	16	24	23	24	22	23	10	23	10	25	22	18	18
33	33	16	21	24	24	10	24	24	10	24	24	24	27	18	8
16	16	18	23	15	26	24	9	23	23	24	25	25	29	25	25
31	16	31	16	24	20	26	24	24	24	24	27	29	16	2	30
33	33	15	31	15	14	29	26	30	29	28	18	17	33	33	30
33	31	15	15	29	28	13	12	17	15	16	16	18	29	13	12

Table 1. Correspondence matrix for FFMAX method when division into 64 pixel square regions was considered

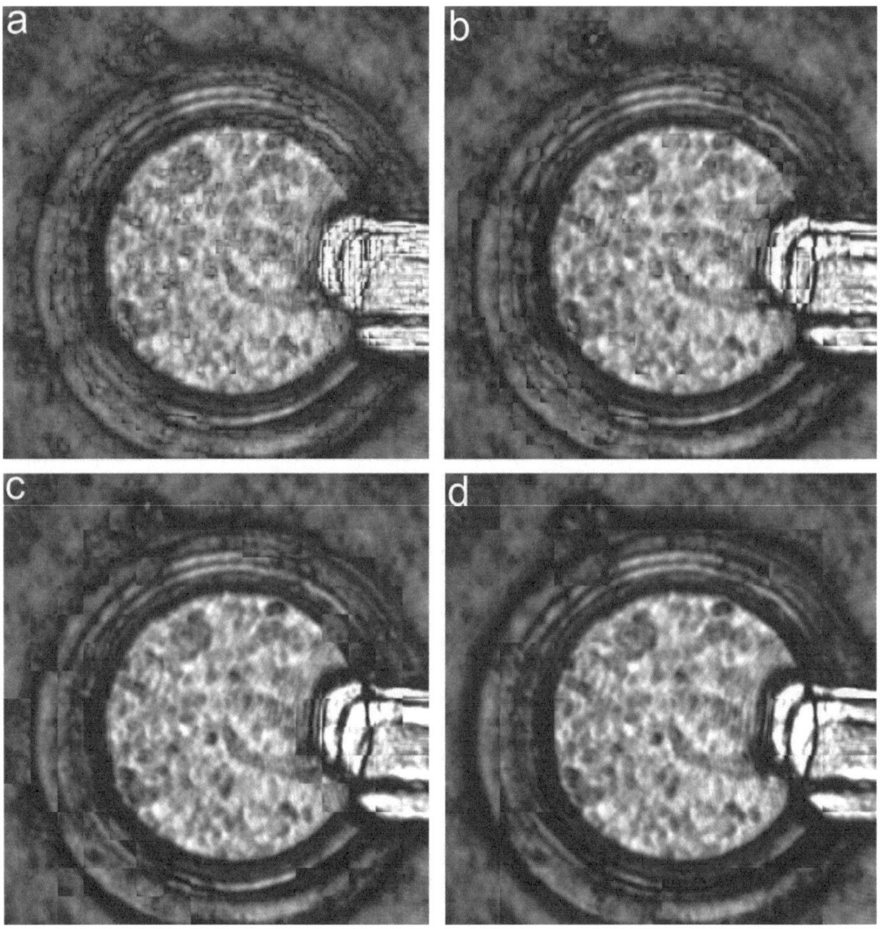

Fig. 8. Resulted images achieved by QFMAX method. The dimension of the square fused regions : a) 16 pixels, b) 32 pixels, c) 64 pixels, d) 128 pixels

16	16	44	42	41	40	40	40	40	40	40	40	40	40	42	42
15	44	42	40	22	35	37	18	21	36	36	36	40	40	40	41
44	41	39	22	18	34	32	33	32	17	17	17	35	36	39	39
40	40	39	18	36	18	35	32	31	31	27	25	15	12	37	36
41	38	20	36	36	32	30	28	28	27	27	25	24	11	12	36
39	20	40	37	29	30	28	29	27	29	28	28	11	22	11	33
35	18	38	23	29	27	29	28	28	27	27	27	27	9	22	13
34	35	20	17	28	28	27	27	27	26	27	27	31	20	24	20
18	36	18	31	28	28	27	27	26	26	27	33	22	24	17	24
18	36	21	30	26	26	26	26	26	25	25	31	24	18	18	18
17	35	16	16	26	26	26	26	25	25	25	8	26	23	20	20
34	34	17	16	29	26	25	24	24	25	24	24	8	31	20	21
34	16	31	21	16	26	26	26	24	25	24	25	26	26	31	26
34	30	31	26	22	15	26	26	26	24	24	27	29	18	2	30
34	33	16	32	29	15	23	26	29	29	28	18	17	23	29	32
35	35	31	28	28	28	26	16	17	16	16	16	23	29	31	31

Table 2. Correspondence matrix for QFMAX method when division into 64 pixel square regions was considered

In Fig. 9 and Fig 10 we illustrate the results obtained when fusing images by the FFAVG and QFAVG methods. Artefacts around square fused regions are still visible but their intensity is diminuated. However this advantage offered by averaging comes at the expense of loosing image sharpness, thus a compromise between image sharpness and intensity of border artefacts must be considered when choosing to use one of the experimented methods.

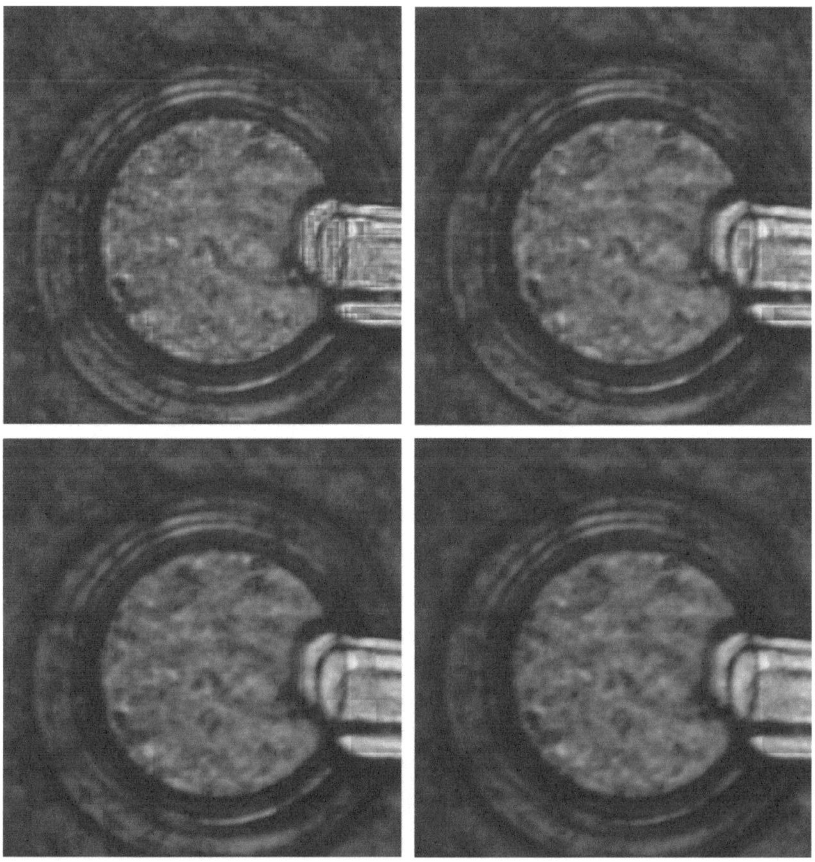

Fig. 9. Resulted images achieved by FFAVG method. The dimension of the square fused regions : a) 16 pixels, b) 32 pixels, c) 64 pixels, d) 128 pixels

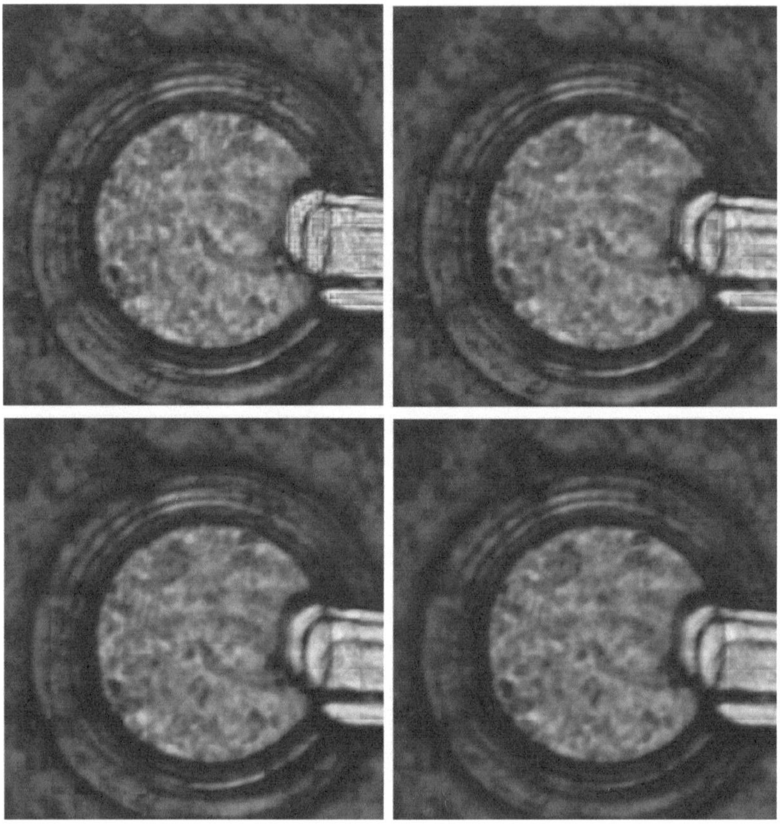

Fig. 10. Resulted images achieved by QFAVG method. The dimension of the square fused regions : a) 16 pixels, b) 32 pixels, c) 64 pixels, d) 128 pixels

4. Conclusion

In this chapter we describe the results obtained by experimenting four region based fusion methods on CSLM image stacks. The four methods have been experimented on image stacks collected on PQR devices. The presented results highlight some of the advantages and limitations of the experimented image fusion methods in connection to CSLM imaging. In the case of CSLM when different regions of the investigated area are not in focus at the same time, the collected image will contain both sharp and bright areas correspodning to the regions in focus, but also blured areas of low contrast or over saturated areas corresponding to the sample regions which contribute to the image but are not in focus. By the experimented image fusion methods we have obtained representations of the investigated sample constituted from image regions belonging to different images in the CSLM stack, corresponding to different optical sections, thus containing details from various focal planes. In two of the experimented methods, FFMAX and FFAVG, the fused image consists of image blocks of a fixed size which have been extracted or calculated from various images in the stack based on the response to the Tenengrad focus assessment operator, while in the remaining methods, QFMAX and QFAVG the contribution of an image in the stack to the fused image is decided based on a quality estimate of the sqaure regions. In two of the methods, FFMAX and QFMAX the fused imge consists of blocks which provide a maximum response to a decision operator, while in the other two, QFAVG and FFAVG all square regions from the images in the stack contribute to the fused image proportional to their response to to the decision operator. In the case of our experiments both types of methods provided artificial images which had enabled us to have a better estimate on the morphology of the studied sample in the purpose of correlating the photocurrent distribution to the device geometry than any of the source images. In the methods where the maximum response to a decision operator is considered the resulted images preserve the original sharpness but contain a large number of high intensity artefacts around the borders of the fused regions, while in the methods where averaging is performed using as weights the response to the decision operator, the intensity of the border artefacts is reduced at the cost of image sharpness.

5. Acknowledgement

The research presented in this publication has been supported by the Romanian National Program of Research, Development and Innovation PN-II-IDEI-PCE, Grant 1566/2009, UEFISCU CNCSIS.

6. References

Ahn, J. C.; Kwak, K. S.; Park, B. H.; Kang, H. Y.; Kim, J. Y. and Kwon, O'Dae, (1999), Photonic Quantum Ring, *Phys. Rev. Lett.* 82(3), 536-539

Brakenhoff, G.J.; Blom, P. & Barends, P. (1979). Confocal scanning light microscopy with high aperture immersion lenses. *Journal of Microscopy*, 117: p. 219-232, ISSN 0022-2720.

Chen, Y; Wang, L; Sun, Z; Jiang, Y and Zhai, G. Fusion of color microscopic images based on bidimensional empirical mode decomposition, *Optics Express* 18, 21757-21769 (2010), ISSN 1094-4087.

Cox, I.J. (1984) Scanning optical fluorescence microscopy. *Journal of Microscopy*, 133: p. 149-154, ISSN *0022-2720.*

Forster, B.; Van De Ville, D.; Berent, J.; Sage, D.; Unser, M. (2004) Complex Wavelets for Extended Depth-of-Field: A New Method for the Fusion of Multichannel Microscopy Images, *Microscopy Research and Technique*, vol. 65, no. 1-2, 33-42, ISSN 1097-0029.

Geusebroek, J.M.; Cornelissen, F.; Smeulders, A.W.; Geerts, H. (2000). Robust Autofocusing in Microscopy, *Cytometry*, 39, 1–9, ISSN 1552-4957.

Huang, W. & Jing, Z. (2007). Evaluation of focus measures in multi-focus image fusion. *Pattern Recognition Letters*, 28, 4, ISSN *0167-8655.*

Krotkov, E. (1987). Focusing, *International Journal of Computer Vision*, Vol. 1, 223-237, ISSN 0920-5691.

Li, S. & Yang, B. (2008). *'Region-based multi-focus image fusion' in Image Fusion: Algorithms and Applications. Ed. Tania Stathaki,* Academic Press, ISBN 0123725291.

Liu S, Weaver D, Taatjes DJ. (1997) Three-dimensional reconstruction by confocal laser scanning microscopy in routine pathologic specimens of benign and malignant lesions of the human breast. *Histochem Cell Biol.* 107:267-278. ISSN: 0948-6143

Minsky, M., Microscopy apparatus, 1961: US Patent No. 3013467, filed Nov. 7, 1957.

Nayar, S.K. & Nakagawa, Y. (1994) Shape from focus. *IEEE Transactions on Pattern Analysis and Machine Intelligence*, 16 (8), 824–831, ISSN 0162-8828.

Nikolov, S.G. (1998). *Image fusion: a survey of methods, applications, systems and interfaces, Technical Report UoB-SYNERGY-TR02,* University of Bristol, UK

Osibote, O.; Dendere, R.; Krishnan, S. & Douglas, T. (2010). Automated focusing in bright-field microscopy for tuberculosis detection, *Journal of Microscopy,* no. doi: 10.1111/j.1365-2818.2010.03389.x, ISSN *0022-2720.*

Pironon J., Canals M., Dubessy J., Walgenwitz F., Laplace-Builhe C. Volumetric reconstruction of individual oil inclusions by confocal scanning laser microscopy. *European Journal of Mineralogy* 1998; 10,p. 1143–1150, ISSN 0935-1221

Rigaut, J.P.; Vassy, J.; Herlin, P.; Duigou, F.; Masson, E.; Briane, D.; Foucrier, J.; Carvajal-Gonzalez, S.; Downs, A.M.; Mandard, A.M. (1991) Three-dimensional DNA image cytometry by confocal scanning laser microscopy in thick tissue blocks, *Cytometry,* vol. 12, pp. 511-524.

Rodriguez, A., Ehlenberger, D., Kelliher, K., Einstein, M., Henderson, S. C., Morrison, J. H., Hof, P. R., Wearne, S. L., Automated reconstruction of three-dimensional neuronal morphology from laser scanning microscopy images. *Methods* 30 (1), 2003, 94–105. , ISSN: 1046-2023

Santos, A.; De Solorzano, C.O.; Vaquero, J.J.; Pena, J.M.; Malpica, N. & Del Pozo, F. (1997) Evaluation of autofocus functions in molecular cytogenetic analysis. *Journal of Microscopy* 188, 264–272.

Sheppard, C.J.R., 15 years of scanning optical microscopy at Oxford. *Proceedings Royal Microscopical Society,* 1990. 25: p. 319-321

Sheppard, C.J.R.; Hotton, D.M.; Shotton, D. (1997). *Confocal Laser Scanning Microscopy,* ISBN 0387915141 ,Oxford

Stanciu, G.A.; Stanciu, S.G.; Hristu, R.; Kwon, O'Dae; Kim, D.K. (2008) Investigation on Photonic-Corral-Mode Quantum Qing Lasers by Laser Scanning Microscopy. *ICTON 2008 Proceedings IEEE.*

Stanciu, S. G.; Stanciu, G. A. & Coltuc, D. (2010), Automated compensation of light attenuation in confocal microscopy by exact histogram specification. *Microscopy Research and Technique,* 73: 165–175, 1097-0029.

Stanciu, S.G., Dragulinescu, M., Stanciu G.A., Sum-modified-Laplacian Fusion Methods Experimented on Image Stacks of Photonic Quantum Ring Laser Devices Collected by Confocal Scanning Laser Microscopy, submitted to *UPB Scientific Bulletin Series A*, ISSN 1223-7027.

Stanciu, S.G.; Coltuc, D.; Hristu, R.; Stoichita, C. & Stanciu, G.A. (2009) Image fusion for photonic quantum ring laser structures investigated by confocal scanning laser microscopy, *ICTON Mediterranean Winter Conference, 2009. ICTON-MW 2009 Proceedings IEEE*

Subbarao, M.; Choi, T.; Nikzad, A. (1992). Focusing Techniques. *In: Proc. SPIE. Int. Soc. Opt. Eng.*, 163–174.

Sugawara, Y., Kamioka, H., Honjo, T., Tezuka, K., Takano-Yamamoto, T., (2005) Three-dimensional reconstruction of chick calvarial osteocytes and their cell processes using confocal microscopy, *Bone,* 36, 5, Pages 877-883, ISSN 8756-3282

Swoger, J; Verveer, P; Greger, K.; Huisken, J. & Stelzer, E.H.K.(2007) Multi-view image fusion improves resolution in three-dimensional microscopy. *Opt. Express,* 15, 2007, 8029-8042, ISSN 1094-4087.

Wilson, T. (2001). Confocal microscopy: Basic principles and architectures. In: Diaspro A, editor. *Confocal and two-photon microscopy: Foundations, applications and advances,* ISBN 0471409200, New York.

Yeo, T.; Ong, S.; Jayasooriah, S.R. (1993) Autofocusing for tissue microscopy. *Image and Vision Computing,* 11, 629–639, ISSN *0262-8856.*

17

Architectures for Image Fusion

Michael Heizmann[1] and Fernando Puente León[2]
[1]*Fraunhofer Institute of Optronics, System Technologies and Image Exploitation IOSB, Fraunhoferstraße 1, D-76131 Karlsruhe*
[2]*Institute of Industrial Information Technology, Karlsruhe Institute of Technology (KIT), Hertzstraße 16, D-76187 Karlsruhe Germany*

1. Introduction

Image fusion can be defined as the combination of raw or processed images establishing the input information from different sources like cameras or other imaging sensors. Its aim is to obtain new or more precise knowledge which is the output information about the scene and which comprises, e.g., objects, events, or more complex situations. Depending on the task of the image acquisition, the output quantities can be images, features, or symbolic information such as decisions.

In automated visual inspection, the ultimate aims in most cases are to gain macroscopic geometrical information (e.g., length, width, or position of an object), to characterize the surface (e.g., reflectance properties, roughness, microstructure, occurrence of surface defects like dents, grooves or other marks), or to obtain volume properties of an object (e.g., material classification, degree of transparency, spatial distribution of components or defects). This information can then be used in various ways in industrial production engineering, e.g., for quality inspection or materials management.

In other application areas of image acquisition and processing, the tasks are similar: finally, some specific information about the observed scene is to be brought to light. Examples are autonomous vehicles, where the vision is one among the exteroceptive sensors serving to sense the surrounding of the vehicle and to recognize objects, and remote sensing, where the task is to reconstruct the properties of a remote object of interest (e.g., the Earths's surface) from acquired images.

However, many relevant scene properties cannot be determined automatically by evaluating just one image. Instead, the information of interest can often be captured in an image series by means of a properly designed imaging setup using homogeneous or inhomogeneous imaging sensors. The task of image fusion is then to collect and combine the desired information from the image series by means of an adequate extraction of the useful information.

This approach has a direct correspondence to the common visual examination performed by a human in everyday live: if a human is not able to determine the property of interest at first glance, he will alter the visual setup until this property is clearly visible with this setup or he is able to reconstruct the property in his mind.

Besides this essential justification for the use of image fusion in many situations, there are also several other task-dependent reasons:

- A higher accuracy and reliability of the inspection result can be obtained when redundant or complementary information is available. In this case, sensors which receive identical or comparable scene properties are required.
- A feature vector with a higher dimensionality than just visual intensities can be generated by evaluating distributed or orthogonal information. For this, sensors receiving different physical scene properties may be appropriate.
- The acquisition of information can be accelerated by simultaneous operation of multiple sensors of similar type.
- The costs for the acquisition of information can be reduced when several low-cost sensors are substituted for an expensive special sensor. In this case, image fusion is used for indirect measurement of the quantity of interest.

This contribution focusses mainly on theoretic considerations on the information content in image series and on systematic aspects of architectures for image fusion originating from the former considerations. The concepts presented in the contribution will be illustrated by means of several examples from automated visual inspection. They will demonstrate how these concepts can be transferred to efficient approaches for image fusion. That way, they offer a systematic approach for the conception of systems and algorithms of image acquisition and fusion, not only for automated visual inspection.

2 Acquisition of information

The basis of image fusion is established by imaging sensors delivering the data which contains the desired information of the scene. Even if there are many different types of imaging sensors with specific physical properties, they all feature some basic characteristics relevant to image fusion.

2.1 Reduction of information

The process of acquiring images can be divided into several stages: the radiance emitted from the scene is projected onto an imaging sensor by means of an optical setup, which is usually the lens, possibly equipped with optical filters. Then the imaging sensor converts this optical signal into a digitized image.

The processing chain from the scene radiance to the digitized image involves a reduction of information, which generally causes the mapping of the scene to be non-invertible. For example, the visual information emitted by the scene is reduced with respect to the following aspects when a matrix imaging sensor is used:

- Images have a finite support, i.e., they are limited spatially (by the field stop, which is usually defined by the sensor size) and temporally (even in the case that a temporal series—e.g., a video—be taken).
- The image acquisition is a projection in several respects: spatially, the three-dimensional scene is projected onto a two-dimensional imaging plane. The infinite-dimensional space of wavelengths is projected onto one spectral dimension (in the case of gray-value images), three (RGB images) or few more spectral dimensions. Finally, the exposure corresponds to a projection in the temporal dimension.
- The irradiance $E(\boldsymbol{\xi},\tau)$ on the imaging sensor with continuous support at a certain time $\tau \in \mathbb{R}$ in the image plane $I \ni \boldsymbol{\xi} := (\xi,\eta)^{\mathrm{T}} \in \mathbb{R}^2$ is spatially and temporally integrated, sampled, and quantized, thus resulting in the digital image with reduced information content.

In terms of system theory, the irradiance $E(\boldsymbol{\xi},\tau)$ is convolved with the aperture function $A(\boldsymbol{\xi})$ of a single pixel and sampled with the pixel spacings $\Delta_1,\Delta_2 \in \mathbb{R}^2$ to obtain a spatially discrete image $g(\boldsymbol{x},\tau)$, $\boldsymbol{x} := (x,y) \in \mathbb{Z}^2$:

$$g(\boldsymbol{x},\tau) := g((n\Delta_1, m\Delta_2)^{\mathrm{T}},\tau) \quad \text{with} \quad g(\boldsymbol{\xi},\tau) \propto \left(E(\boldsymbol{\xi},\tau) \underset{\boldsymbol{\xi}}{**} A(\boldsymbol{\xi}) \right) \cdot D(\boldsymbol{\xi}), \tag{1}$$

where the operator $\underset{\boldsymbol{\xi}}{**}$ denotes the two-dimensional convolution with respect to $\boldsymbol{\xi}$, $D(\boldsymbol{\xi}) := \sum_i \sum_j \delta(\boldsymbol{\xi} - i\Delta_1 - j\Delta_2)$, $i,j \in \mathbb{Z}$, describes the grid pattern of the imaging sensor, $n,m \in \mathbb{N}$ are the pixel coordinates, and $\delta(x) = 1$ for $x = 0$, $\delta(x) = 0$ else. Since the pixels do not overlap, $\mathrm{supp}\{A(\boldsymbol{\xi})\} \cap \mathrm{supp}\{A(\boldsymbol{\xi} - i\Delta_1 - j\Delta_2)\} \stackrel{!}{=} \varnothing \; \forall i,j \in \mathbb{Z}\backslash\{0\}$ holds.

Analogously, the temporal exposure can be interpreted as a convolution of the image $g(\boldsymbol{x},\tau)$, which has a continuous temporal support, with a temporal exposure function and a sampling with the refresh rate in order to get the digital image $g(\boldsymbol{x},t)$ with discrete temporal support $t \in \mathbb{Z}$.

- Further disturbances are added to the useful information, e.g., caused by thermal noise of the imaging sensor or by atmospherical disturbances in the light path.

2.2 Characteristics of imaging sensors

Sensor systems and their resulting data can be classified with respect to several properties concerning the degree of conformity of the data's information content. In the case of image fusion, the sensor systems may be characterized by the following properties:

- *Commensurability*: due to the optical projection of the three-dimensional scene onto the two-dimensional image plane, the spatial dimensions of images taken by matrix sensors always have the same physical meaning. Therefore, matrix sensors provide spatially commensurable data. Only if the imaging sensors have different numbers of dimensions (e.g., when images from matrix sensors and from line sensors are to be compared), their respective data are spatially not commensurable. In the case of color sensors (e.g., with three color values representing a color dimension) resulting in three-dimensional data, commensurability with gray-value images can be effectuated by projecting the color dimension onto one gray-value, thus resulting in two-dimensional data.
- *Homogeneity*: if the sensors capture identical or comparable physical quantities of the scene, the sensors are called homogeneous. This is an important feature for practical reasons: after the images from homogeneous sensors have been registered such that their definition areas are properly aligned, the data of the images can be combined mostly without complex preprocessing, e.g., in a data fusion. If, in contrast, the sensors are not homogeneous, a preprocessing (such as feature extraction or classification) is usually necessary to properly link the information of the images.

  The homogeneity of different images depends on the kind of processing which has been applied to the images prior to the fusion step: for example, when the images of a stereo camera pair are evaluated, a depth map is obtained, which is an inhomogeneous information compared to the original intensity images.

  The notion of homogeneity for imaging sensors may also depend on semantic aspects of the image data: if, for example, the images of a spectral series are interpreted as simple intensities which are observed from the scene, the corresponding sensor systems may be regarded as homogeneous. If, however, these images are used to characterize the scene material, they may be regarded as inhomogeneous, since they represent the spectral reflectance of the material in different bands, which can be interpreted as different physical quantities.

- *Virtuality*: in many applications, image series are recorded by a single imaging sensor which has been used several times with at least one varying illumination or acquisition parameter. Since in reality, the images are taken with the same physical sensor, the sensors referring to the images in the series are called virtual.

  The images of virtual sensors always differ in at least one imaging parameter: the acquisition time. Since this acquisition parameter is irrelevant for time-invariant scenes, virtual cameras can favorably be used to record redundant information, if no other illumination or acquisition parameter is varied during the acquisition of the image series.

- *Collocatedness*: if the positions of the imaging sensors, their orientations and pixel spacings together with the optical properties of the imaging lens are kept constant over the series, the sensors are called collocated. In consequence, the reproduction scale remains unchanged, and the images show identical areas of the scene. Collocated sensors are often realized as virtual sensors, when an illumination or acquisition parameter except the scene pose is varied for a time-invariant scene.

  A typical example of non-virtual collocated imaging sensors is a three-chip RGB-sensor, where the individual sensors for the three color values are located at the same optical position by means of a beam splitter.

  If the imaging sensors are not collocated, an image registration, e.g., by considering image features is usually required to align the images in the series by means of geometrical transforms (e.g., translation, rotation, scaling or projective transform; see, e.g., (Modersitzki, 2004)).

2.3 Image series

Once the images have been acquired, they establish the data foundation of image fusion in the form of image series $g(\boldsymbol{x}, \boldsymbol{p})$, which are functions of the discrete position vector $\boldsymbol{x}$ and a discrete parameter vector $\boldsymbol{p} := (p_1, p_2, \ldots, p_n)^{\mathrm{T}}$, $\boldsymbol{p} \in \mathbb{Z}^n$, $n \in \mathbb{N}$. The image series is obtained by taking images while the imaging parameters $p_1, p_2, \ldots$ are varied consecutively or simultaneously. Considering the acquisition of a time-invariant scene by means of a camera system, the variable parameters can refer either to the illumination or to the scene (Heizmann & Beyerer, 2005).
Useful illumination parameters comprise the position of the illumination sources relative to the scene (expressed, e.g., by the azimuth φ_{i} and the polar angle θ_{i} in a surface related coordinate system), the spatial distribution of irradiance (to describe homogeneous or structured illuminations), the illumination spectrum, its polarization state, and its coherence. Observation parameters for common camera systems are the camera position and orientation relative to the scene (in terms of the extrinsic camera parameters (Faugeras & Luong, 2001) or the scene pose), the spectral sensitivity of the sensor system including spectral filters, the polarization sensitivity of the sensor system including polarization filters, parameters of the optical system such as the focus setting, the aperture or the focal length, and the exposure time. The classical intrinsic parameters (see, e.g., (Faugeras & Luong, 2001; Shapiro & Stockman, 2001)) are not considered as relevant parameters for image fusion in most cases, since they usually cannot be varied.

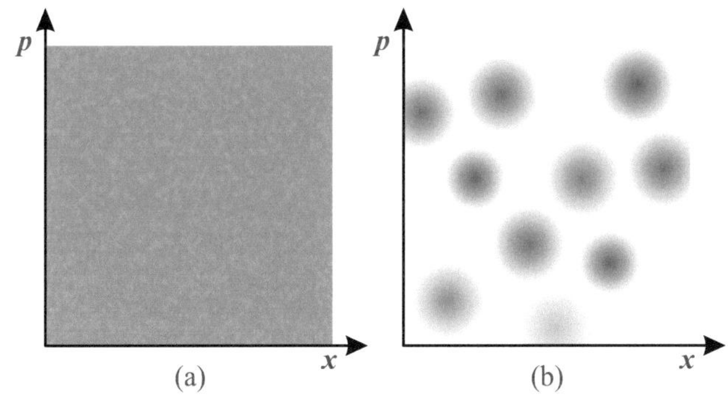

Fig. 1. Visualization of concurrent (a) and complementary (b) information: whereas in the case of concurrent information sources, the useful information (indicated as dark areas) is basically spread equally over the location-parameter domain (here simplified as one-dimensional domains each), it is concentrated in local regions for complementary information sources.

In consequence, the image series $g(\boldsymbol{x},\boldsymbol{p})$ establishes a multidimensional data object with a dimension for each varied parameter. An image $g(\boldsymbol{x},\boldsymbol{p}_i)$, $i \in \{1,\ldots,n\}$ which is sensed by the imaging sensor is a subspace of the image series for a fixed parameter vector $\boldsymbol{p}_i$.
In order to apply this definition of image series also in case that other sensor systems than cameras be used, the interpretation of the parameter vector $\boldsymbol{p}$ can be extended. If, for example, several inhomogeneous sensor systems should contribute to an image series, a nominally scaled parameter component can be used to distinguish the information sources.

3. Information content of image series

The information content in an image $g(\boldsymbol{x},\boldsymbol{p}_i)$, $i \in \{1,\ldots,n\}$, of the series $g(\boldsymbol{x},\boldsymbol{p})$ depends obviously on the imaging constellation which has been used during acquisition and, in consequence, the information content of the entire series depends on the variation of the parameter vector $\boldsymbol{p}$. Although it is often not possible to assign particular distributions of the information content in the image series to specific parameter variations, several elementary types of how information is distributed in image series can be identified. It is important to distinguish these types in order to identify suitable methods for fusing image series.

- *Redundant information*: in this case, the useful information is distributed similarly over all images of the series, i.e., it is spread equally over the location-parameter domain, see Fig. 1(a). In consequence, disturbances affect the useful information also in a similar manner. This type of relation can only be present when homogeneous sensors are used. A concurrent fusion, where all images contribute equivalently to the fusion result (e.g., by averaging over the image series), may be expedient to exploit the useful information.

  A typical example is noise reduction which can be achieved by image accumulation, i.e., averaging the intensity values for each location $\boldsymbol{x}$ over an image series acquired by homogeneous and collocated imaging sensors. If, for example, a stationary camera records n images disturbed by an additive white Gaussian noise, the observed images can be modeled as $g(\boldsymbol{x},i) = d(\boldsymbol{x}) + r(\boldsymbol{x},i)$, $i \in \{1,\ldots,n\}$, where the useful information $d(\boldsymbol{x})$ is deterministic and represents the desired scene property, and the additive noise $r(\boldsymbol{x},i)$ is the realization of a random process $R(\boldsymbol{x},i)$ with mean value $\mathrm{E}\{R(\boldsymbol{x},i)\} = 0 \; \forall \boldsymbol{x},i$ and variance $\mathrm{E}\{R(\boldsymbol{x},i)R(\boldsymbol{x},j)\} = \delta_i^j \sigma_R^2 \; \forall \boldsymbol{x},i,j$ with $\delta_i^j = 1$ for $i = j$, $\delta_i^j = 0$ else. While each original image $g(\boldsymbol{x},i)$ contains the full additive noise, i.e., $\sigma_G^2 = \sigma_R^2$, the variance of the noise in the accumulated image $f(\boldsymbol{x}) := \frac{1}{n}\sum_{i=1}^{n} g(\boldsymbol{x},i)$ is reduced to $\sigma_F^2 = \frac{1}{n}\sigma_R^2$.

- *Complementary information*: this relation applies if the useful information from homogeneous sensors is concentrated in the location-parameter domain such that, for a given location of the scene, only few images of the series are meaningful. Hence, the useful information is concentrated in local areas of the location-parameter domain, see Fig. 1(b). In order to merge the useful information, a complementary fusion is appropriate, where the contribution of an individual image to the fusion result depends on its local content of useful information. The local concentration of useful information may be caused by an inhomogeneous influence of disturbances, but it may also originate from the illumination-scene-sensor interdependence, when the susceptibility of the sensor depends on local differences in the constellation of illumination, scene, and camera (e.g., when the scene distance is varied in a focus series).

  An example is given below in Subsect. 5.1: in order to generate an image with synthetically enhanced depth of field, a focus series is taken. The useful information is identified by determining the parameter values (i.e., the scene distances) for each image location leading to a locally optimal focus indicator (Heizmann & Puente León, 2003; Puente León, 2002). Only these areas in the location-parameter domain are then used to build the fusion result.

  The same approach can be used for enhancing the image contrast by fusing illumination series (Heizmann & Puente León, 2003).

- *Distributed information*: this is the case when the useful information from homogeneous or inhomogeneous sensors is distributed over the series such that basically only the evaluation of all images allows a statement on the properties of interest. In contrast to redundant information, a single image alone does not contain enough information to conclude on the desired information. In comparison to complementary information, the useful information is not locally concentrated in the location-parameter domain. The inference from the image series to the useful information implies an image evaluation or interpretation, i.e., the image data must be transferred to a higher abstraction level (see Subsect. 4.2). Consequently, at least a feature extraction must be accomplished prior to the image fusion.

  As examples, distance maps can be generated by fusing stereo image series (Gheţa, Frese, Krüger, Saur, Heinze, Heizmann & Beyerer, 2007) or by fusing at least three images with varied directional illumination (photometric stereo) (Horn & Brooks, 1989). In the former case, the image values are interpreted as different views on the same scene which can be matched by means of epipolar geometry (Hartley & Zisserman, 2004). In the latter case, the image values are interpreted as response of the local surface shape and reflectance to the direction and intensity of the incident light. In both cases, a single image would not be enough to conclude on the desired distance map.

  A third example is given by methods of texture classification and surface inspection, when significant features are only obtainable by evaluating the entire series (Xin et al., 2004; Heizmann, 2006; Pérez Grassi & Puente León, 2007). Meaningful features for classifying topological textures can be developed especially when illumination series with varied azimuth of a directional illumination source are used, since the observed radiance of a topological texture strongly depends on the constellation of illumination. Examples in which distributed information is used are given in Subsections 5.2 and 5.3.

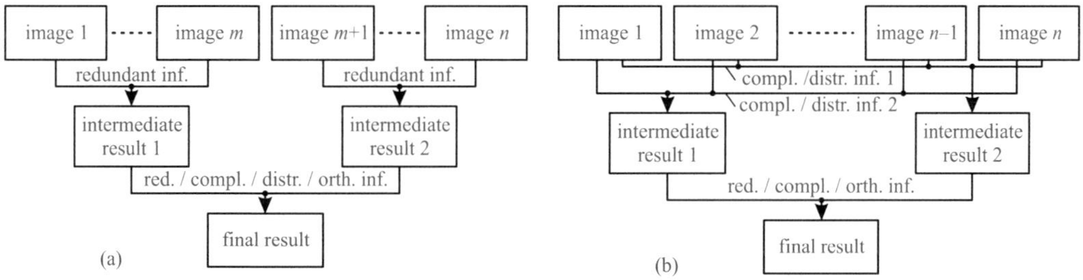

Fig. 2. Exemplary evaluation schemes for different combinations of information distributions in an image series: (a) When disjoint subsets of the image series contain redundant information, these subsets can be fused in a first stage to intermediate fusion results. The redundant, complementary, distributed or orthogonal information in these intermediate results is then fused in a second stage to the final result. (b) In the case of the image series being evaluated in more than one way, the respective information, which is usually complementary or distributed, is fused in a first stage to intermediate results, which are then fused to the final result.

– *Orthogonal information*: in this case, the images to be fused contain information on disjoint properties of the scene. Orthogonal information can be gained when inhomogeneous sensor systems, which deliver different physical properties of the scene, are deployed. It can also originate from different processing methods applied to data from basically homogeneous sensors, e.g., when reflectance information is used to generate a depth map by means of photometric stereo, the information in the resulting depth map is orthogonal to any of the original reflectance images. Since the information in the depth map and in a reflectance image is not directly linkable, a sensible fusion can only take place on the abstraction level of features or classification results.

  A typical example is the combination of 3D data of the scene and its visual appearance. Whereas the 3D data contains information on the spatial arrangement of the scene, the visual appearance is mainly governed by the reflectance of the scene. Their fusion implies the abstraction from 3D and visual data to object points featuring a position (specified in the 3D data) and a reflectance (observed in the visual image).

These basic types of distributions of the information content in the image series to be fused can also be combined in many ways. A typical combination appears when disjoint subsets of the set of all images originate from homogeneous sensors and contain redundant information, which is fused in a first stage, see Fig. 2(a). The information of the intermediate fusion results, which can be redundant, complementary, distributed or orthogonal, is then fused in a second stage to obtain the final result.

Another typical case of combination occurs when the information content of the image series can be exploited in several ways, see Fig. 2(b). Here, the usually complementary or distributed information which is extracted by the different processing methods represents intermediate fusion results, which are then fused to the final result.

The latter type of information processing usually appears when multivariate image series, in which the images differ in more than one imaging parameter, are evaluated. As an example, when images from differently positioned cameras with different focus settings are used to capture a scene, combined stereo and focus series are recorded (Gheţa et al., 2006; Gheţa, Frese, Heizmann & Beyerer, 2007). Such image series can be evaluated by exploiting the stereo and the focus information separately, e.g., by means of the approaches depth from stereo and

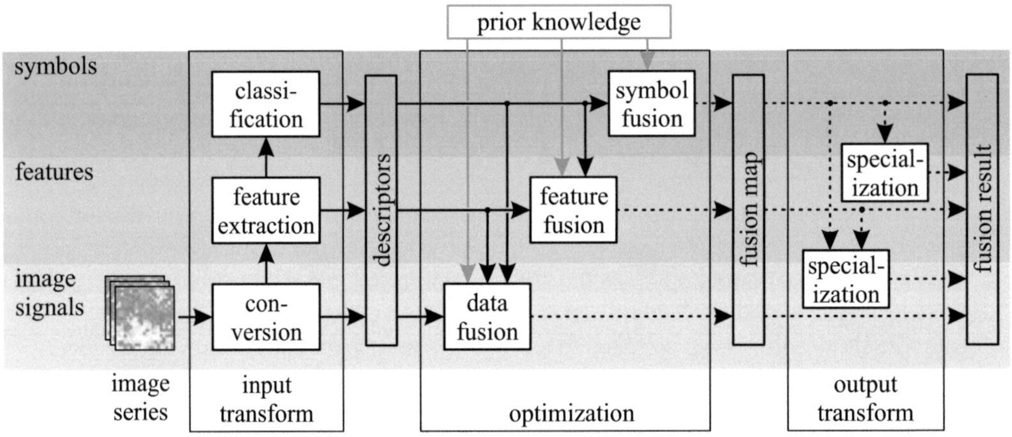

Fig. 3. General concept for image fusion (image series are indicated with continuous lines, single images are indicated with dotted lines): first, the images of the series are processed separately in the input transform in order to obtain meaningful descriptors of the useful information. During the optimization step, the useful information is selected from the descriptors. In this step, beneficial information from higher abstraction levels and prior knowledge can be included. The resulting fusion map is then converted into the desired fusion result by an output transform. During the input and the output transform, a change of the abstraction level can take place: whereas in the input transform, the image data may be lifted to a higher abstraction level in order to extract the useful information, the abstraction level of the fusion map as result of the optimization step may be lowered to obtain the desired fusion result.

depth from focus. Stereo and focus evaluations both use distributed information in the series, but each one with reference to the respective information content.

4. General concept for image fusion

Many approaches of image fusion can be traced back to a common concept with respect to an underlying processing scheme and abstraction levels involved, see Fig. 3. Although in many specific realizations, some of the processing steps or abstraction levels may be missing or cannot be strictly assigned to a step or level mentioned here, this general concept is justified since it can help to analyze existing fusion approaches and to synthesize new fusion approaches by suitably combining existing methods.

4.1 Processing scheme

In many image fusion approaches, a general processing scheme can be identified leading from the acquisition of the image series to the fusion result containing the concentrated useful information (Heizmann & Puente León, 2007), see Fig. 3.

Starting from the recorded images series, the first step is to transform the images into signals on an abstraction level where the actual combination of the useful information will take place. The aim of this input transform is to map the information in the image series onto significant descriptors such that the relevant information content becomes manifest for the following optimization step. The transform may include a conversion of the image data within the abstraction level of images or processing steps of feature extraction or classification in order to obtain information on higher abstraction levels. Since the descriptors may belong to different domains such as the spatial domain, frequency domain, parameter domain, parameter frequency domain etc., operators suitable for these domains must be used. Common operators to extract significant image features in the input transform comprise geometrical, intensity, Fourier, wavelet or morphological transforms, principal component analysis, cross-correlation, or local operators, and may not only refer to spatial dimensions, but also to any other parameter dimension.

In the second step, an optimization is performed to select the useful information from the transformed image series. By means of a suitable quality criterion, the descriptors obtained by the input transform are assessed and combined to form a fusion map which contains the desired fused information and which is afterwards used in the output transform. The optimization takes place in the descriptor domain reached by the input transform. During the optimization process, prior knowledge (e.g., known constraints, physical laws, and required or desired properties of the fusion result) which is related to the fusion task must be included in order to ensure a consistent result. Common methods for the optimization step comprise linear and nonlinear operators, energy minimization methods, Bayesian statistics, Kalman filtering, and many other methods used in pattern recognition. An example of a classification-based optimization is given in Subsect. 5.3.

To establish a comprehensive formulation of the optimization problem, energy functionals have shown to be a universal approach (Clark & Yuille, 1990; Beyerer et al., 2008). To express relevant information contained in sensor data and prior knowledge, energy terms $E_k(r(\boldsymbol{x}),.)$ are introduced. They are modeled such that the relevant information is reflected in monotonic functions, which take lower values for more desirable properties of the fusion result $r(\boldsymbol{x})$ or intermediate descriptors. The optimization task is expressed for the energy functional

$$E(r(\boldsymbol{x})) := \sum_k \lambda_k E_k(r(\boldsymbol{x}),.), \qquad k = \{1,\ldots,n\}, \qquad \lambda_k > 0. \tag{2}$$

The desired optimal fusion result is then obtained by minimizing the energy functional $E(r(\boldsymbol{x}))$ with respect to the fusion result $r(\boldsymbol{x})$. The energy formalism has several advantages: the fusion task is represented implicitly and compactly, all kinds of information and constraints can be included by introducing suitable energy terms, and the relevance of different contributions can be considered explicitly by adjusting the weights λ_k. However, the main drawback of the energy formalism is that there exists no universally applicable method for minimizing the energy functional $E(r(\boldsymbol{x}))$. Suitable minimization approaches strongly depend on the information used for the fusion, and hence, an approach found suitable for a specific task is hardly transferable to a different task.

In the last step, the fusion map representing the fused information is used as a construction plan for building the fusion result. To obtain the fusion result in the desired form, the fusion map is converted to the desired abstraction level. Depending on the domains of the descriptors and the optimization result in comparison to the abstraction level of the desired fusion result, a specialization may be used to lower the abstraction level. Examples of output transforms are the use of the fusion map as a look-up table or the trivial identity, e.g., in the case of depth maps which are obtained from fusing focus series, see Subsect. 5.1, or in the example of defect detection presented in Subsect. 5.2.

4.2 Abstraction levels

The fusion of the information in an image series can take place on different abstraction levels, see Fig. 3. In the following, three main abstraction levels are introduced: the level of the image data itself, the level of features which are extracted from the image data and which are usually used to describe scene properties, and the level of symbols which can be obtained as results of a classification step. Apparently, the assignment of a specific fusion approach to a distinct abstraction level cannot always be strict, since, e.g., the image values themselves may be interpreted as features in certain cases. The differentiation of three abstraction levels is rather intended to demonstrate how common methods of image processing and pattern recognition fit into the introduced concept for image fusion.

- *Data-level fusion* (pixel-level fusion): in this case, the combination of information takes place on the level of the image data itself, i.e., on the intensity values, without any abstraction step. The precondition of a data fusion is that the image series contains redundant or complementary information and that the images have been recorded with homogeneous sensors, such that the image intensities refer to the same physical properties of the scene.

  A typical objective is to obtain a fusion result with an image quality which is better with respect to some quality criterion, for example by means of a concurrent (e.g., to reduce the sensor noise) or a complementary fusion (e.g., to synthetically enhance the depth of field).
- *Feature-level fusion*: here, the combination of information takes place on the level of features which must have been extracted from the image series before. These features may be generated from single images (e.g., local texture features) or by a simultaneous evaluation of the entire series (e.g., the variance of intensities for an image location within a series). While the latter case applies to distributed information recorded with homogeneous sensors, possibly inhomogeneous sensors which allow the extraction of at least comparable features are sufficient in the former case.

  A first typical task of feature-level fusion is to improve the extraction of image features, e.g., with respect to their accuracy or reliability. A second typical task is to gain access to information (e.g., features) which is distributed over the series.

  An example of the latter task is the fusion of images obtained from a camera array which is equipped with different spectral filters. A possible approach for the spatial and spectral assessment of the scene is given by a region based fusion: the properties of regions in the image series are used as features and fused with respect to their disparity (to obtain the spatial reconstruction) and the spectral intensities (to obtain a spectral characterization of the scene) (Gheţa et al., 2010).
- *Symbol-level fusion* (decision-level fusion): symbolic information, which is gained by a preceding feature extraction and a classification from single images, is combined. A fusion on this abstraction level imposes the least restrictions to the relation of information in the image series and to the choice of sensors: any type of relation and inhomogeneous sensors are admissible, if the symbolic information resulting from the respective classification approaches is connectable.

  The objective of symbol-level fusion is mainly to improve the accuracy and reliability of a classification, e.g., for defect detection or object recognition. In this case, the symbolic information is given by object hypotheses established by single sensors, which are fused to a consolidated hypothesis.

During the fusion on a certain abstraction level, it may be necessary or reasonable to use information from a higher abstraction level which has been processed from single images prior to the actual fusion step.

As an example, in order to fuse complementary information, the areas in the location-parameter domain containing the desired useful information must be identified, if they are not a priori known. This identification requires a criterion which is usually at least on the abstraction level of features. In the application example of Subsect. 5.1, the criterion for identifying focussed image regions is a contrast measure on the level of features.

An important practical issue concerns the question of which abstraction level should be chosen to solve a given fusion task. There exists a tradeoff between a moderate implementation effort and an optimal exploitation of the useful information in the image series: concerning the necessary development and implementation effort, a fusion approach on a higher abstraction level is often easier to realize in comparison to lower abstraction levels. For the abstraction of single images to a higher level, standard algorithms of image processing and pattern recognition can be used in most cases. The optimization is then often performed by relatively simple operations of logical combination.

However, the quality of a fusion result obtained on an abstraction level which is as low as possible is mostly superior to the results obtained on higher abstraction levels. This can be traced back to the modification and potential reduction of the useful information during the abstraction step applied to the single images. When the information fusion is performed on a lower abstraction level, the processing which must be individually adapted to the information contained in the images and to the fusion task can ensure that the useful information is conserved for the fusion result at the best.

5. Examples

5.1 Fusion of focus series

The following example is used to demonstrate the concepts shown above, see Fig. 4: in order to evaluate a firing pin print for an automated database search, a visual image which shows the impression in detail and a depth map reflecting the spatial structure of the impression are needed (Heizmann & Puente León, 2003; Puente León, 2002). As information sources, images taken with a camera which is equipped with a macroscopic lens are to be used. Whereas a focussed image cannot be taken from the whole impression due to the limited depth of field Δ_z of the macroscope used, the depth map is a feature image which is not directly accessible from the single images.

Both tasks can be solved by applying methods of image fusion to a focus series: a series of n images $g(\boldsymbol{x},z)$, $z \in \{z_1,\ldots,z_n\}$ with varied distance z of the camera to the scene is taken such that each surface point is depicted in focus in at least one image, i.e., $z_{i+1} - z_i \leq \Delta_z \; \forall i \in \{1,\ldots,n-1\}$, and each surface point is mapped onto the same element of the imaging sensor in all images of the series. Thus, the sensors of the focus series are commensurable, homogeneous, virtual, and collocated with respect to the image plane.

In the input transform, significant descriptors for focussed imaging must be extracted from the focus series. The useful information to describe a visually sharp image is the local contrast $v(\boldsymbol{x},z)$, which can also be used to determine the in-focus plane for each image point and thus the desired depth map. A suitable descriptor for the useful information is therefore located on the abstraction level of features and determined for each image, e.g., by using the local variance.

In the optimization step, the useful information is selected from the descriptors of the images. For both tasks, the scene distance leading to the maximal local contrast represents the desired information and must be determined for each image point, i.e., $\bar{d}(\boldsymbol{x}) := \arg\max_z v(\boldsymbol{x},z)$. Although this preliminary depth map indicates the optimal scene distances based on the sensor information, it is not yet satisfactory, since high depth steps and estimation errors may occur, e.g., in surface regions with faint texture. At this point, prior knowledge stating that

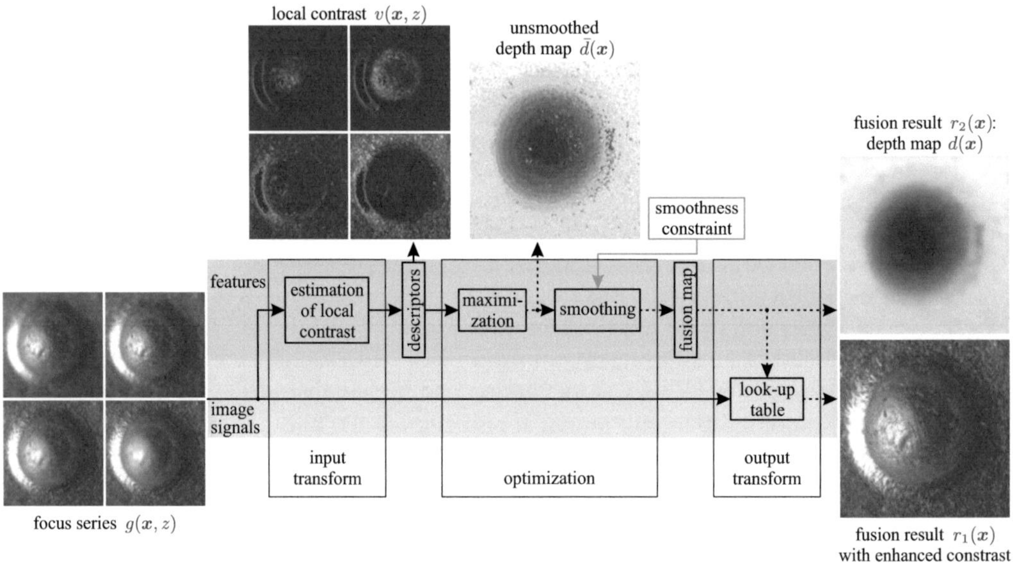

Fig. 4. Fusion of a focus series in order to obtain an image with synthetically enhanced contrast and a depth map (image series are indicated with continuous lines, single images are indicated with dotted lines): from the original image series $g(\boldsymbol{x},z)$, the local contrast $v(\boldsymbol{x},z)$ establishing a suitable descriptor of the useful information is estimated in the input transform (lighter areas have higher contrast). In the optimization step, a preliminary depth map $\bar{d}(\boldsymbol{x})$ is distilled first from the series of contrast images, which is then combined with prior information to a smoothed depth map $d(\boldsymbol{x})$ constituting the fusion map (darker areas are farther away than lighter areas). To obtain the desired image with enhanced depth of field, the fusion map is used as look-up table to compose the fusion result $r_1(\boldsymbol{x})$ from the focus series. The depth map itself represents the second desired fusion result $r_2(\boldsymbol{x})$.

the maximal inclination of the object surface is limited is incorporated in the fusion process by smoothing the preliminary depth map. The smoothed depth map $d(\boldsymbol{x})$ is then the result of the optimization step, i.e., the fusion map. It shows where the desired useful information is concentrated in the location-parameter domain.

The aim of the last step is to transform the fusion map into the desired result on the respective abstraction level. In order to construct the image with synthetically enhanced depth of field, the fusion map on the feature level must be specialized. To that aim, it is used as a lookup table: for each image point $\boldsymbol{x}$, the intensity value from the image with the respective scene distance $d(\boldsymbol{x})$ is selected from the focus series in order to form the fusion result, i.e., $r_1(\boldsymbol{x}) := g(\boldsymbol{x},d(\boldsymbol{x}))$. The second desired result, the depth map, is the fusion map, since it reflects just the vertical position of the in-focus plane, i.e., $r_2(\boldsymbol{x}) := d(\boldsymbol{x})$.

In this example, the construction of the image with enhanced depth of field can be classified as a fusion of complementary information. Although the actual combination of the input information takes place on the level of image signals, the evaluation and optimization of the useful information is performed on the abstraction level of features. The determination of the depth map, however, uses distributed information which is fused on the level of features.

5.2 Detection of defects based on illumination series

The second example is concerned with the detection of defects on membranes of pressure sensors. It is based on fusion of illumination series, and yields a feature image as the fusion result. The field of inspection is about 10 mm^2; the defects themselves are in the order of a few hundredths of a square millimeter. Figure 5(a) shows an example of a defective membrane illuminated with diffuse light. It features several local defects, whose actual position can be determined by comparing this image with the fusion result in Figure 5(c). It is obvious that images taken with a diffuse illumination hardly allow to discern intact regions from defective areas. Consequently, an inspection strategy based on an analysis of such images—i.e. without employing any fusion methods—is not likely to succeed.

Figure 5(b) shows eight of the $n = 16$ images of the original illumination series, which was obtained by rotating azimuthally a light source in steps of $\Delta\varphi = 22.5$ degrees. Due to the geometry of the machined membrane surface, images obtained with an illumination angle differing by 180 degrees one from another have a similar appearance. If now a faultless surface point $\boldsymbol{x}_0$ is observed at a certain illumination angle φ_0, its intensity $g(\boldsymbol{x}_0, \varphi_0)$ is particularly high, if the illumination direction is perpendicular to the machining grooves. Each facet of a groove acts then as a mirror that reflects the light incident from a direction perpendicular to the local direction of the groove. Consequently, the intensity signal $g(\boldsymbol{x}_0, \varphi)$ obtained for a varying illumination angle φ features a characteristic shape that allows to discern whether the point $\boldsymbol{x}_0$ belongs to a defective region or not.

By harmonic analysis of the signals $g(\boldsymbol{x}, \varphi_i)$ of the series, a suitable feature image can be defined as a measure $m(\boldsymbol{x})$ of the local defects:

$$m(\boldsymbol{x}) = \frac{|G(\boldsymbol{x}, f_\varphi = 1)|}{|G(\boldsymbol{x}, f_\varphi = 1)| + |G(\boldsymbol{x}, f_\varphi = 0)|}, \tag{3}$$

where

$$\begin{aligned} G(\boldsymbol{x}, f_\varphi) &:= \mathrm{DFT}_\varphi\{g(\boldsymbol{x}, \varphi)\} \\ &= \sum_{i=0}^{n-1} g(\boldsymbol{x}, \varphi_i) \cdot \exp\left(-\mathrm{j}2\pi \frac{i f_\varphi}{n}\right) \end{aligned} \tag{4}$$

denotes the one-dimensional discrete Fourier transform (DFT) of the series with respect to the illumination angle φ.

Equation (3) computes a feature based on the comparison of two frequency components with respect to the image intensities at the location $\boldsymbol{x}$: the fundamental oscillation, and the DC component. It is easy to recognize that the values of $m(\boldsymbol{x})$ are all within the range [0, 1], and that the ratio 0.5 is obtained when the energy of both components is the same. A value of $m(\boldsymbol{x})$ higher than 0.5 means that the fundamental oscillation—i.e. a non-defective groove texture—dominates potential defects at the location $\boldsymbol{x}$. Otherwise, $\boldsymbol{x}$ is likely to be a local defect.

Equation (3) performs the initial transform, after which an optimization and—if needed—a final transform could be performed. However, in the present case both the optimization and the output transforms are trivial, since

$$r(\boldsymbol{x}) = m(\boldsymbol{x}) \tag{5}$$

holds.

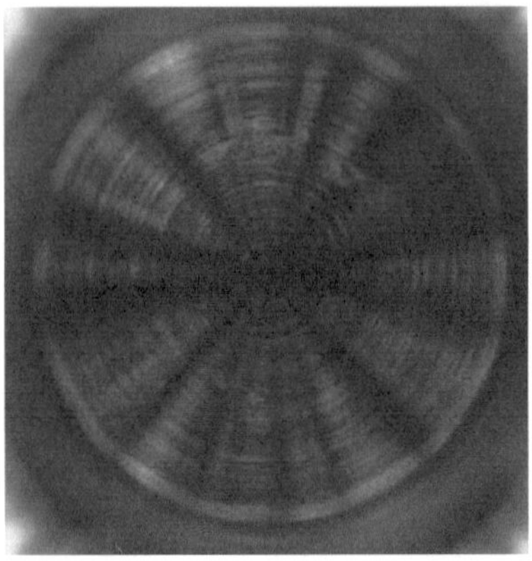

(a)

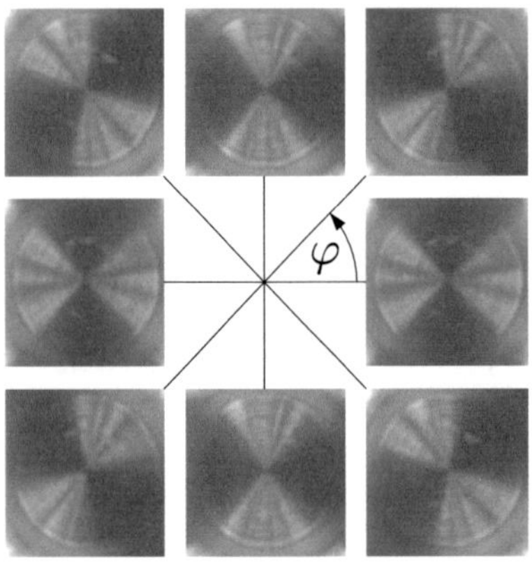

(b)

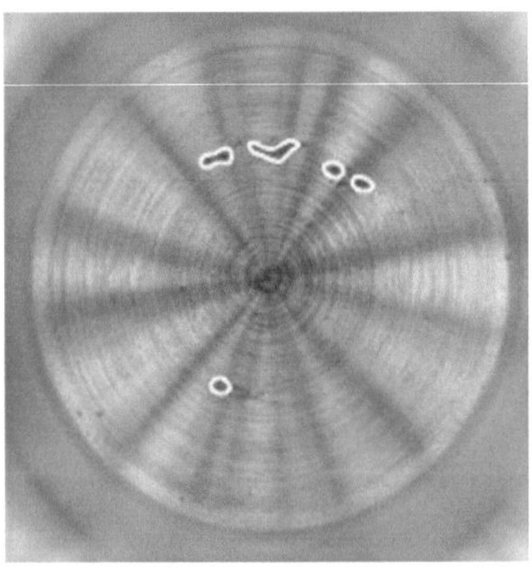

(c)

Fig. 5. Detection of defects on membranes of pressure sensors: (a) Image of a defective membrane obtained with diffuse illumination; (b) Image series of the defective membrane; (c) Fusion result with highlighted defects.

Figure 5(c) shows the feature image $r(\boldsymbol{x}) = m(\boldsymbol{x})$ obtained through fusion of the image series of Figure 5(b). The fusion result clearly highlights several defective areas, which appear darker than the faultless regions. For a better interpretation of the results, the results of a further defect detection step have been overlaid. To this end, an edge detection method based on a Laplacian-of-Gaussian (LoG) filter according to (Beyerer & Puente León, 1997) has been used.

5.3 Classification of defects based on illumination series

The method presented in the last subsection is based on a reflection model describing the intensities of a certain object or defect. Thus, both the design and computational effort will necessarily increase, if different types of defects need to be distinguished. Instead of a single feature image $m(\boldsymbol{x})$, a suitable set of features $\{m_i(\boldsymbol{x})\}$ will be necessary to discern the classes of defects in the feature space.

This example presents an alternative based on the systematic extraction of local features and a subsequent classification. A major advantage of this approach is that, after a suitable set of features has been defined, an arbitrary number of defects can be distinguished.

Additionally, if the extracted features are invariant against transforms considered to be irrelevant (e.g., translation, rotation, scaling or intensity), the computational costs remain acceptable. Moreover, thanks to the generalization capabilities of classifiers, a higher tolerance in the case of a class mismatch can be expected.

A common approach to construct a feature m out of an image $g(\boldsymbol{x})$ that is invariant against a certain transformation group T is integrating over this group:

$$m := \int_T f(t\{g(\boldsymbol{x})\})\,\mathrm{d}t = \int_P f(t(p)\{g(\boldsymbol{x})\})\,\mathrm{d}\boldsymbol{p}. \tag{6}$$

This equation is known as the Haar integral. The function $t \in T$ is a transformation parameterized by the vector $p \in P$, where P is the parameter space and f is an arbitrary, local kernel function.

In the following, we will focus on a single application scenario, in which different classes of varnish defects on wood surfaces are to be detected and classified. To achieve a maximal contrast, the pictures of the surface are taken under directional illumination, which is realized by means of a distant point light source, whose direction is described by a fixed elevation angle ϑ and a variable azimuth φ.

In this example, we aim at extracting invariant features with respect to the two-dimensional Euclidean motion, which involves rotation and translation in $\mathbb{R}^2$. The parameter vector of the transformation function is $\boldsymbol{p} = (\tau_x, \tau_y, \phi)^{\mathrm{T}}$, where τ_x and τ_y denote the translation parameters in x and y direction, and ϕ is the rotation parameter. The compactness and finiteness of this group guarantee the convergence of the integral (Schulz-Mirbach, 1995).

To process all images of the series by the Haar integral, the illumination azimuth φ needs to be added to the parameter vector $\boldsymbol{p}$, and the kernel function has to be extended accordingly to the third dimension of the input data. However, these modifications are beyond the scope of this paper. For a more comprehensive discussion of the feature extraction, we refer to (Pérez Grassi & Puente León, 2008). The resulting features do not only exhibit all invariant properties discussed above, but they also are invariant with respect to both illumination and contrast.

After extracting a set of ten features, a classification is performed by a Support Vector Machine. Since the inspected surfaces may feature areas with and without defects, the presented method is applied locally. To this end, the series of images is subdivided into local windows of 32×32

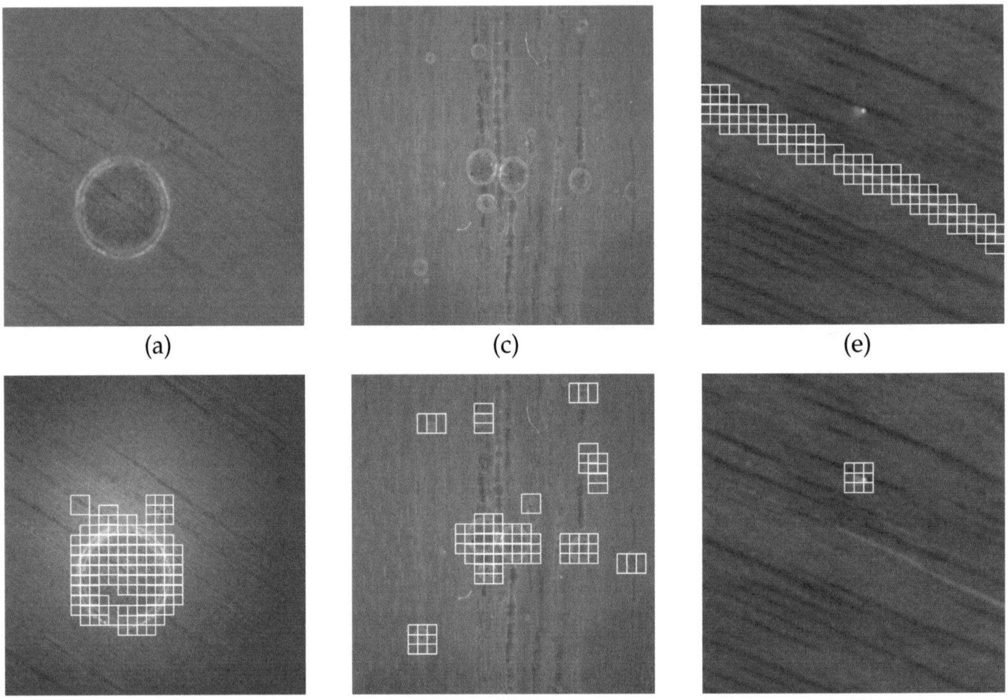

Fig. 6. Classification of different types of varnish defects on wood surfaces: (a) Surface with two craters of different radii (the smaller crater is located in the image center); (b) Classified crater regions based on image (a); (c) Varnished surface with bubbles and other varnish defects; (d) Classified bubble regions based on image (c); (e) Surface with bubble and fissure with classified fissure regions; (f) Surface with bubble and fissure with classified bubble regions.

pixels with a spatial overlap of 50 %. A 10-dimensional feature vector $\boldsymbol{m}$ is extracted from each window according to a list of kernel functions showing the same structure but with different parameters (Pérez Grassi & Puente León, 2008).

Five different classes were defined to train the system: no defect, bubble, ampulla, fissure, and crater. A group of 20 series of images of different wooden surfaces featuring different defects constituted the training list. To test the performance of the system, a disjoint list of series of images was used. Figure 6 shows a representative selection of the obtained classification results based on illumination series consisting of $n = 8$ images.

Figure 6(b) shows the inspection results for a surface showing two craters of different radii (Fig. 6(a)). Both defects were correctly classified. However, the results do not yield any information about the size of the detected defects, since craters of different sizes belong to the same class. The next example illustrates the detection of bubbles. Although the original image Figure 6(c) does not contain only bubbles, but also elongated defects, the classifier is able to distinguish between the different types of defects (Fig. 6(d)).

Finally, the Figures 6(e) and (f) show the results for a surface featuring a bubble and a fissure. The invariant approach introduced in this subsection is able to recognize both defects at one time using the same group of kernel functions.

6. Conclusion

Image fusion offers powerful tools to obtain desired information from a scene by using image series. The main precondition is to find an imaging setup with at least one varied acquisition parameter—illumination or observation parameter—such that the resulting image series contains the useful information in the form of redundant, complementary, distributed or orthogonal information. Once the image series has been acquired, a suitable procedure of image fusion can often be reduced to a standard concept for image fusion. It comprises a processing scheme consisting of an input transform, which converts the sensor information into significant descriptors, an optimization, which selects the useful information from the descriptors to generate a fusion map, and an output transform, which converts the fusion map into the desired form. The processing may take place on different abstraction levels—the levels of image signals, features, and symbols—, incorporating many common methods of image processing and pattern recognition.

7. References

Beyerer, J., Heizmann, M., Sander, J. & Gheţa, I. (2008). *Image Fusion: Theory and Applications*, Academic Press, Amsterdam, chapter Bayesian Methods for Image Fusion, pp. 157–192.

Beyerer, J. & Puente León, F. (1997). Detection of defects in groove textures of honed surfaces, *International Journal of Machine Tools and Manufacture* 37(3): 371–389.

Clark, J. J. & Yuille, A. L. (1990). *Data fusion for sensory information processing systems*, Kluwer Academic Publishers, Boston/Dordrecht/London.

Faugeras, O. D. & Luong, Q.-T. (2001). *The geometry of multiple images*, MIT Press, Cambridge (MA).

Gheţa, I., Frese, C. & Heizmann, M. (2006). Fusion of combined stereo and focus series for depth estimation, *in* C. Hochberger & R. Liskowsky (eds), *INFORMATIK 2006, Informatik für Menschen, Beiträge der 36. Jahrestagung der Gesellschaft für Informatik e.V. (GI)*, Vol. 1, Gesellschaft für Informatik (GI), Bonn, pp. 359–363.

Gheţa, I., Frese, C., Heizmann, M. & Beyerer, J. (2007). A new approach for estimating depth by fusing stereo and defocus information, *in* R. Koschke, O. Herzog, K.-H. Rödiger & M. Ronthaler (eds), *INFORMATIK 2007, Informatik trifft Logistik, Beiträge der 37. Jahrestagung der Gesellschaft für Informatik e.V. (GI)*, Vol. 1, Gesellschaft für Informatik (GI), Bonn, pp. 26–31.

Gheţa, I., Frese, C., Krüger, W., Saur, G., Heinze, N., Heizmann, M. & Beyerer, J. (2007). Depth map estimation from flight image series using multi-view along-track stereo, *in* A. Grün & H. Kahmen (eds), *Proceedings of 8th International Conference on Optical 3-D Measurement Techniques*, Vol. 2, Zürich, pp. 119–125.

Gheţa, I., Höfer, S., Heizmann, M. & Beyerer, J. (2010). A novel approach for the fusion of combined stereo and spectral series, *in* D. Fofi & K. S. Niel (eds), *Image Processing: Machine Vision Applications III*, Proceedings of SPIE Volume 7538. Paper No. 7538 0G.

Hartley, R. & Zisserman, A. (2004). *Multiple view geometry in computer vision*, 2nd edn, Cambridge Univ. Press, Cambridge.

Heizmann, M. (2006). Techniques for the segmentation of striation patterns, *IEEE Transactions on Image Processing* 15(3): 624–631.

Heizmann, M. & Beyerer, J. (2005). Sampling the parameter domains of image series, *in* E. R. Dougherty, J. T. Astola & K. O. Egiazarian (eds), *Image Processing: Algorithms and*

Systems IV, Vol. 5672 of *Proceedings of SPIE/IS&T Electronic Imaging*, pp. 23–33.

Heizmann, M. & Puente León, F. (2003). Imaging and analysis of forensic striation marks, *Optical Engineering* 42(12): 3423–3432.

Heizmann, M. & Puente León, F. (2007). Fusion von Bildsignalen, *tm – Technisches Messen* 74(3): 130–138. (in German).

Horn, B. K. P. & Brooks, M. J. (1989). *Shape from shading*, MIT Press.

Modersitzki, J. (2004). *Numerical methods for image registration*, Oxford University Press.

Puente León, F. (2002). Komplementäre Bildfusion zur Inspektion technischer Oberflächen, *tm — Technisches Messen* 69(4): 161–168. (in German).

Pérez Grassi, A. & Puente León, F. (2007). Translation and rotation invariant histogram features for series of images, *in* R. Koschke, O. Herzog, K.-H. Rödiger & M. Ronthaler (eds), *INFORMATIK 2007, Informatik trifft Logistik, Beiträge der 37. Jahrestagung der Gesellschaft für Informatik e.V. (GI)*, Vol. 1, Gesellschaft für Informatik (GI), Bonn, pp. 38–43.

Pérez Grassi, A. & Puente León, F. (2008). Invariante Merkmale zur Klassifikation von Defekten aus Beleuchtungsserien, *Technisches Messen* 75(7-8): 455–463.

Schulz-Mirbach, H. (1995). *Anwendung von Invarianzprinzipien zur Merkmalgewinnung in der Mustererkennung*, VDI Verlag, Düsseldorf.

Shapiro, L. G. & Stockman, G. C. (2001). *Computer vision*, Prentice Hall, Upper Saddle River (NJ).

Xin, B., Heizmann, M., Kammel, S. & Stiller, C. (2004). Bildfolgenauswertung zur Inspektion geschliffener Oberflächen, *tm — Technisches Messen* 71(4): 218–226. (in German).

18

Image Fusion for Computer-Assisted Tumor Surgery (CATS)

KC Wong, SM Kumta, LF Tse, EWK Ng[1] and KS Lee[1]
Orthopaedic Oncology,
[1]CAOS team, Department of Orthopaedics and Traumatology, Prince of Wales Hospital,
the Chinese University of Hong Kong,
Hong Kong
China

1. Introduction

Tumor surgeons integrate preoperative two-dimensional images and mentally formulate three-dimensional surgical plans of resection and reconstruction. The surgical procedure aims to remove tumors with clear surgical margins, while critical anatomical structures not infiltrated by tumor can be preserved. This will be particularly difficult in complex areas such as pelvis, sacrum, or when joint-saving intercalated resection is contemplated, or when custom-made prosthesis is used for reconstruction. Incorporating computer technology to aid in this surgical planning and executing the intended resection may improve precision and consequently clinical results in musculoskeletal tumor surgery.

Although primarily developed for neurosurgical applications, computer-assisted intraoperative navigation has gained acceptance and has been used effectively in orthopaedic trauma, spinal procedures and joint replacement surgery (Anderson KC et al., 20005; Gebhard F et al., 2004; Grutzner PA et al., 2004; Laine T et al., 2000; Wixson RL et al., 2005). An extended application of computer navigation assisted resection in pelvic and sacral tumors was first described in 2004 (Hüfner T et al., 2004; Krettek C et al., 2004). Computer-assisted navigation system could facilitate tumors resection and also reconstruction with custom prostheses (Cho HS et al., 2008; Cho HS et al., 2009; Kim JH et al., 2010; Reijnders K et al., 2007; Wong KC et al., 2007; Wong KC et al., 2007; Wong KC et al., 2008), joint sparing limb salvage surgery (Cho HS et al., 2009; Wong KC et al., 2007; Wong KC et al., 2008). The technique of fusing computed tomography (CT) and magnetic resonance images (MRI) was reported. The fusion image, when combined with surgical navigation, helps surgeons reproduce a preoperative plan reliably and may offer substantial clinical benefits in musculoskeletal tumor surgery (Wong KC et al., 2008). The current study represents the continuation of previous publications (Wong KC et al., 2007; Wong KC et al., 2008), which were preliminary reports of the techniques. The number of cases has increased from 13 to 22, and the average follow-up of all patients increased from 9.5 months to 32.5 months. This article is to provide more patients with longer follow-up to better assess the advantages and potential pitfalls of using the technique in musculoskeletal oncology.

Surgeons had not yet incorporated this computer technology into their routine musculoskeletal bone tumors operation. We therefore investigate the results of image fusion for Computer-Assisted Tumor Surgery (CATS) in musculoskeletal oncology with the help of a navigation system.

2. Methods

We studied 21 patients with 22 musculoskeletal tumors who underwent CATS from March 2006 to July 2009. (Table 1) A commercially available CT-based spine navigation system (Stryker Navigation, Freiburg, Germany; CT spine, version 1.6) was used. Indications for the technique included anticipated difficulties in achieving an accurate tumor resection in affected bone with complex anatomy (pelvis, sacrum) or the need for precision in making a satisfactory resection plane to accommodate a custom tumor prosthesis. Of the 21 patients, 10 were males, 11 were females, and the mean age was 32 years at the time of surgery (range, 6 - 80 years). Five tumors were located in the pelvis, seven sacrum, eight femur, and two tibia. The primary diagnosis was primary bone tumors in 16 (4 benign, 16 sarcoma) and metastatic tumors in two. The minimum follow-up was 14 months (average, 32.5 months; range, 14 – 49 months). No patient was excluded or lost follow-up in this series.

Preoperative CT and MRI examination of each patient were performed. Axial CT slices of 0.0625mm or 1.25mm thickness and various sequences of MR images in Digital Imaging and Communications in Medicine (DICOM) format were obtained. The imported image data sets were then reformatted into axial, coronal and sagittal views in the navigation system. CT and MR images for 22 cases were fused using the navigation software (Fig.1). Navigation system (Stryker Navigation, Freiberg, Germany, CT spine, version 1.6) was used for first eight patients while (Stryker Navigation; iNtellect Cranial, version 1.1) for the rest. PET images were also incorporated into the CT-MR fused images for two patients who had local recurrence following previous surgery and radiotherapy. The process of fusing multimodal image datasets had been described (Wong KC et al., 2008). A three-dimensional (3-D) bone model was created by adjusting the contrast level of the CT images. Tumor extent was defined and its volume was extracted from MR images. As different image datasets shared identical spatial coordinates after image fusion, segmented MR tumor volume was integrated into the CT reconstructed 3-D bone model. A 3-D bone tumor model was generated. All the reconstructed two-dimensional (2-D) and 3-D images were used for preoperative surgical planning. The plane of tumor resection was defined and marked using multiple virtual screws sited along the margin of the planned resection. We also integrated the computer-aided design (CAD) data of custom-made prostheses provided by the manufacturer (Stanmore Implants Worldwide Ltd, Middlesex, United Kingdom) in the final navigation resection planning for eight cases (Fig.1).

Preoperative tumor resection and prosthetic reconstruction was virtually simulated in two patients in the later part of the study by using a commercially CAD software, MIMICS® (Materialise's Interactive Medical Image Control System, Materialise, Ann Arbor, MI) that converts DICOM data into a proprietary format. The surgical plan of tumor resection and CAD prosthesis reconstruction in MIMICS format were back converted to CT data sets in DICOM format. Both original CT data sets and virtual surgical planning CT data sets were fused in the navigation software. The data sets of the fused images were then imported back into a CT-based navigation system (Stryker Navigation, Freiberg, Germany; CT spine, version 1.6) for resection planning. The navigation system was toggled to display the CT data sets with virtual surgical plans. Virtual markers (pedicle screws in CT spine navigation software) were then placed along the plane and orientation of planned tumor resection.

Case	Age (yrs)	Sex	Diagnosis	Location	Surgery	Bone reconstruction	Preoperative fusion image datasets	Navigation Planning time* (hours)	Registration error (mm)	Navigation time (minutes)	Function (MSTS score⁺)	Followup (months)	Complications and Outcome
1	46	F	Parosteal osteosarcoma	Left proximal tibia (posterior aspect)	Joint-saving resection	Vascularized fibular graft	CT angiogram and MRI	3	0.44	40	28	49	--
2	42	F	Metastatic uterine carcinoma	Left ischial tuberosity	Local resection	No	CT and MRI	1.5	0.37	13	--	49	--
3	24	F	Undifferentiated bone sarcoma	Right proximal femur	Local resection after neoadjuvant chemotherapy	Modular tumor prosthesis	CT and MRI	2.5	0.36	18	29	48	--
4	53	F	Schwannoma	Right S2 nerve root	Marginal excision via posterior approach	No	CT and MRI	1.5	0.38	15	--	44	--

5	14	M	Conventional osteosarcoma	Right femur (from subtrochanteric region to distal physis)	Joint-saving resection after neoadjuvant chemotherapy	Custom tumor prosthesis	+CT and MRI	3.8	0.50	30	30	43	--
6	80	F	Chordoma	Sacrum (below and including S2)	Resection	No	CT and MRI	2.2	0.61	35	--	42	superficial wound infection
7	6	M	Conventional osteosarcoma	Right distal femur	Joint saving resection after neoadjuvant chemotherapy	Custom extendable tumor prosthesis	CT and MRI	2.5	0.41	20	26	38	Died of distant metastases 5 months post surgery
8	54	M	Giant cell tumor	Sacrum (from S1 to S4)	Intralesional curettage	No	CT angiogram and MRI	2.2	0.45	25	--	37	Local recurrence 26 months post surgery and stabilized with bisphosphonates

9	8	M	Conventional osteosarcoma	Left distal femur	Joint saving resection after neoadjuvant chemotherapy	Custom extendable tumor prosthesis	CT and MRI	1.2	0.35	15	30	36	--
10	50	M	Recurrent chordoma	Left pelvic metastases	Resection (PII)	Custom pelvic prosthesis	CT angiogram, MRI and PET	1.8	0.46	15	23	35	Developed soft tissue local recurrence 1 year after surgery
11	18	M	Conventional osteosarcoma	Sacrum (from S1 to S5)	Total sacrectomy	No	CT and MRI	1.1	0.59	15	--	35	Postoperative wound infection Died of distant metastases 6 months after surgery

12	54	F	Recurrent chondrosarcoma	Sacrum (from S1 to S5)	Total sacrectomy	No	CT angiogram and MRI	1.2	0.68	25	--	35	Died of distant metastases 1 year after surgery
13	17	M	Recurrent malignant nerve sheath tumor	Left sciatic nerve and involving ilium and sacrum	Left hemipelvectomy (PIV resection)	No	CT angiogram, MRI and PET	1.8	0.44	30	--	33	Developed soft tissue local recurrence 5 months after surgery and died of distant metastases 11 months post surgery
14	21	F	Low grade chondrosarcoma	Left proximal femur	Joint saving resection	Custom tumor prosthesis	CT and MRI	2	0.42	50	28	32	--

15	16	F	Conventional osteosarcoma	Right ischium and acetabulum	PII + PIII resection	Custom pelvic prosthesis	CT and MRI	1.5	0.31	30	30	30	--
16	24	M	Parosteal osteosarcoma	Left distal femur	Joint saving resection	Custom tumor prosthesis	CT and MRI	3	0.34	60	28	26	--
17	41	F	Hemangioendothe-lioma	Right ilium	Resection	No	CT and MRI	1	0.59	45	--	24	--
18	55	M	Sacral chordoma	S1 and below	Total sacrectomy	Posterior instrumentation	CT and MRI	1	0.5	30	--	18	Local recurrence and distal metastases 12 months post surgery

19	42	M	Sacral chordoma	S3 and S4	Partial sacrectomy	No	CT, MRI and PET	1.5	0.49	45	--	17	--
20	6	M	Conventional osteosarcoma	Right distal femur	Joint saving resection after neoadjuvant chemotherapy	Custom extendable tumor prosthesis	CT and MRI	2	0.8	25	30	16	--
21	16	F	Low grade chondrosarcoma	Left proximal humerus	Joint saving resection	Bone graft	CT and MRI	1	0.54mm	25	30	15	--
22	18	F	Chondromyxoid fibroma	Right proximal tibia	Multi-planar resction	Bone graft	CT and MRI	1.5	0.4	45	28	14	--

Table 1. Demographic data for 22 cases in 21 patients. *Navigation planning time included time required for performing image fusion, creating 3-D bone tumor models and planning of intended resection; +MSTS = Musculoskeletal Tumor Society score. The score was obtained at the end of study period. For those patients who died during the study period, we took the maximum score that the patients could achieve following their operations

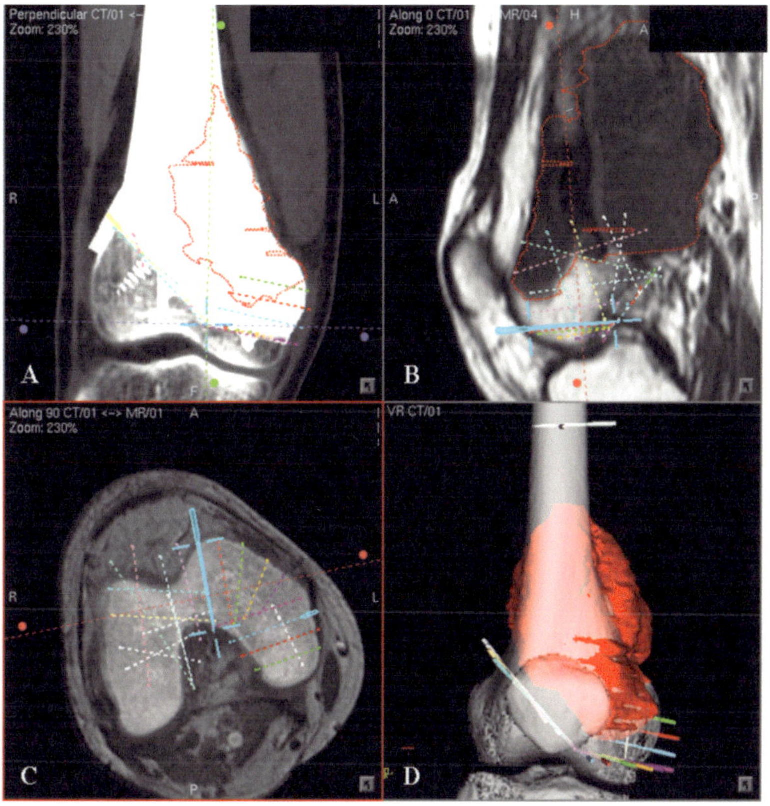

Fig. 1. (A) A coronal section of the CT images with incorporation of CAD prosthesis for Patient 16 with right distal femur parosteal osteosarcoma is shown. Conversion of CAD data of custom prosthesis to DICOM format was made possible using CAD software (MIMICS® - Materialise's Interactive Medical Image Control System). This allowed direct use of CAD data for navigation planning of tumor resection. The central cross represented the virtual marker (pedicle screw in the CT spine navigation software) that marked one of the locations of intended bone resection. (B) A sagittal section of the MR images showed the extent of the tumor. (C) A axial section of CT / MR image fusion at the intended resection of distal femur is shown. (D) A 3-D bone tumor model reconstructed from CT and MR image data sets is shown. The tumor volume was red in color. By analyzing the 2-D CT / MR fused images and 3-D model, a joint-saving resection with multiplanar osteotomies were planned at distal femur and intended bone resections were marked with virtual screws. The more precise the bone resection was, the greater number of virtual screws was needed to define the plane of resection

At the actual surgery, a dynamic reference tracker was attached to the bone in which the tumor was located. An image-to-patient registration to match precisely the operative anatomy and preoperative virtual CT images was performed by paired points and surface points matching. The navigation software calculated the registration errors which indicated any mismatch between preoperative CT images and the patient's anatomy (Fig.2). We next calibrated the navigation probe and operative instruments (drill, bone burr or diathermy) mounted with navigation trackers to the navigation system. This allowed the real-time tracking the spatial location of the tip of these instruments in relation to the patient's anatomy on the virtual preoperative images (Fig.3). The anatomic locations of virtual pedicle screws were identified and intended resection level and plane was marked using navigated tools. An oscillating saw or osteotome was used to make the osteotomy and the tumor was removed en-bloc. Skeletal defects were reconstructed using custom-made pelvic prostheses in two cases, custom-made joint-saving intercalated prostheses in six, modular proximal femur prosthesis in one, and a vascularized fibular graft in one. No reconstruction was required for twelve cases. Postoperative CT images for Patients 10, 14 and 15 were obtained and the achieved positions of custom prostheses were merged with their preoperative navigation plans. The workflow for the technique of CATS was summarized in Figure 4.

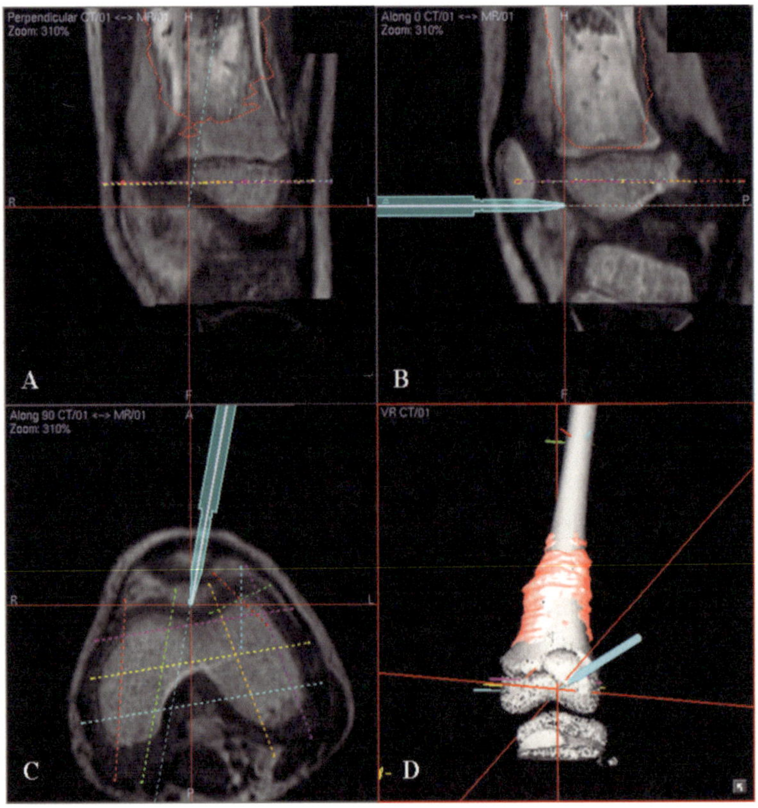

Fig. 2. (A) Coronal, (B) sagittal, (C) axial sections of CT/MR fused images and (D) 3-D bone tumor model for Patient 9 with left distal femur osteosarcoma are shown. After performing image-to-patient registration using paired points and surface matching at the surgery, we assessed the real-time matching between operative anatomy and the virtual images by running the registration probe on bone surface or by checking some anatomic landmarks. The registration was judged to be accurate and acceptable for subsequent navigation procedure as the tip of navigation probe matched well with the cartilage surface of distal femur

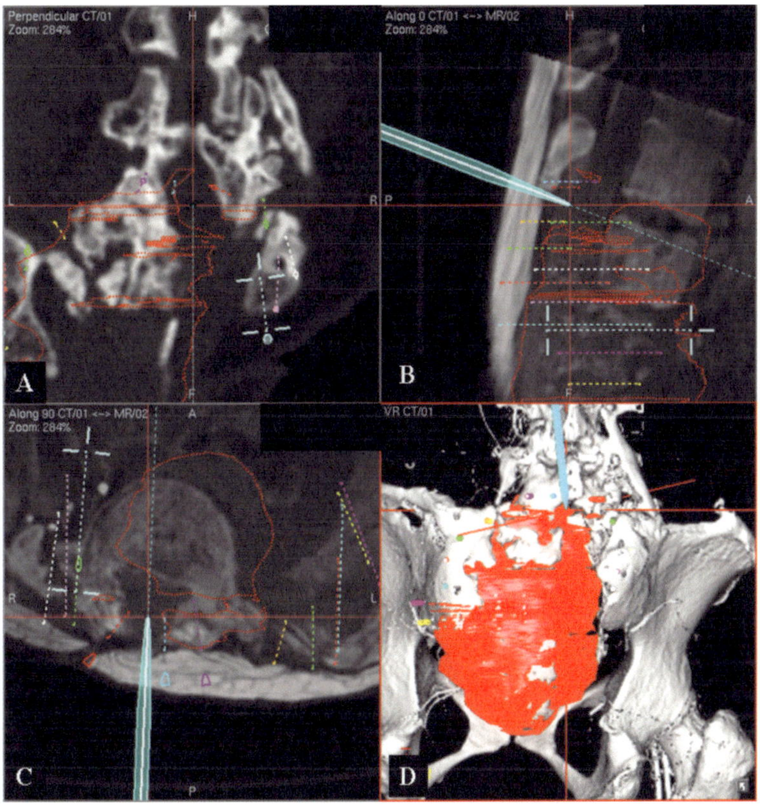

Fig. 3. (A) Coronal section of CT image, (B) sagittal and (C) axial sections of CT/MR fused images, and (D) 3-D bone tumor model for Patient 12 with recurrent mesenchymal chondrosarcoma of sacrum are shown. The patient had two previous operations and posterolateral fusion between lower lumbar spines and iliac crest. The tip of navigation probe was pointing at the location where previous laminectomy was performed at L5 level. Intraoperative navigation helped surgeons to identify with confidence the structures and intended bone resections in patients with distorted anatomy from their tumors or previous operations

We determined the results of CT-MR image fusion for CATS with the help of a navigation system by evaluating the: (1) additional information not seen on conventional images that was obtained for preoperative surgical planning; (2) the accuracy as registration error obtained intraoperatively that was defined as the average deviation between the same point in the preoperatively acquired navigation image and the actual patient's anatomy; (3) the accuracy of executing surgical plan as determined by comparing the cross sections at the resection plane and their preoperative navigation planning, assessing the fit of the custom prostheses to the remaining bone at the surgery, and assessing the histology of resection margins in all malignant tumor specimens. We did not validate the resections for Patients 4, 8 who had intralesional or marginal excision of their benign tumors and Patients 11, 12, 13,18 and 19 as their resection planes were irregular or curved; (4) time required for navigation planning; (5) time required for operative set-up and execution of the navigation procedures; (6) complications and local tumor recurrence; (7) functional outcome was assessed using the Musculoskeletal Tumor Society (MSTS) score in patients with limb salvage surgery (Enneking WF et al., 1993).

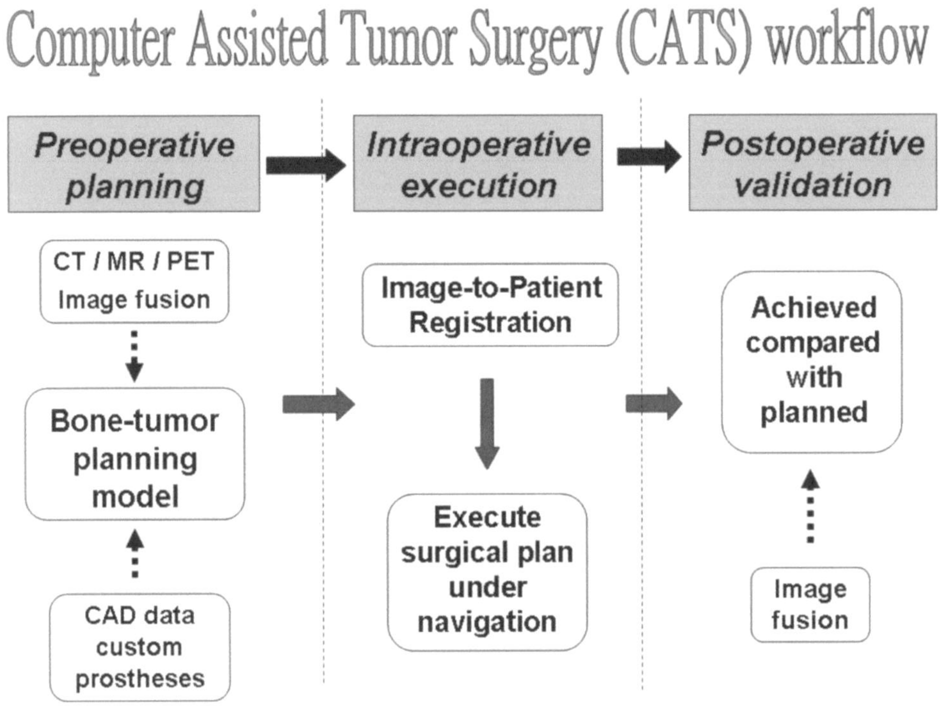

Fig. 4. The workflow of Computer-Assisted Tumor Surgery (CATS) used in the study is shown

3. Result

All tumor resections could be carried out as planned under navigation guidance. Navigation software enabled surgeons to examine all fused image datasets (CT / MRI / PET scan) together in two spatial and three spatial dimensions. It allowed easier understanding of the exact anatomical tumor location and relationship with surrounding structures. Intraoperatively, image guidance with the help of fusion images, provided precise visual orientation, easy identification of tumor extent, neural structures and intended resection planes in all cases. The bone resection could be precisely planned and executed in terms of exact level and orientation, according to the pre-defined tumor volume and data of custom prosthesis. For Patient 14 and 16, incorporation of data of CAD custom prostheses in the resection planning enabled multi-planar osteotomies and precise fit of CAD custom prostheses (Fig.5,6).

The resection achieved was as planned in 15 cases that were validated either by comparing the dimensions at the resection plane of resected specimens with that in the surgical navigation planning or merging postoperative with preoperative CT images (Fig.7). Histological examination of all resected specimens in patients with malignant tumors showed a clear tumor margin.

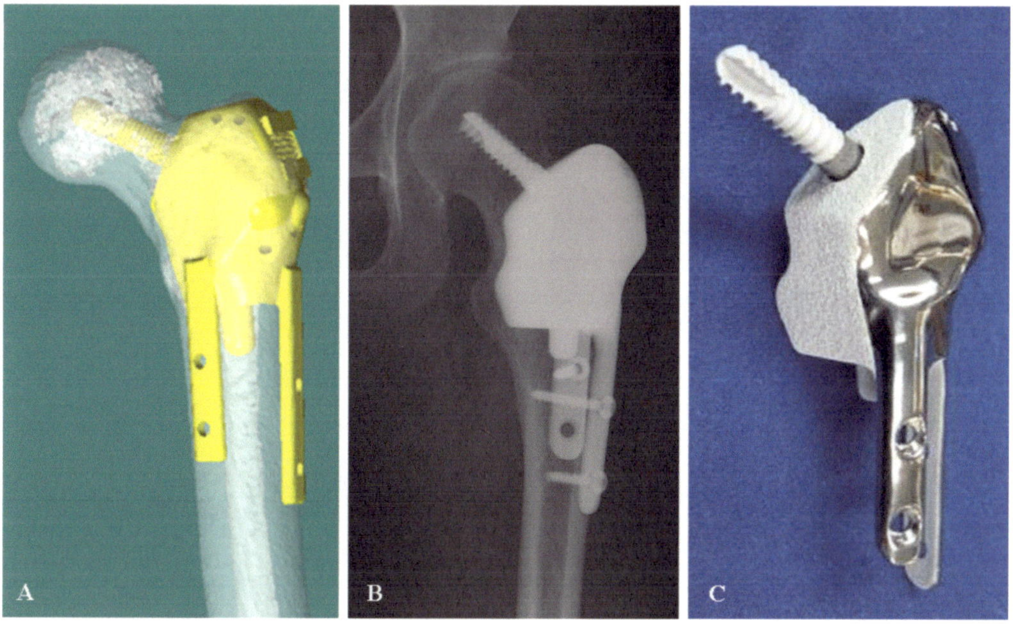

Fig. 5. (A) A joint-saving, CAD custom prosthesis in Patient 14 with low grade chondrosarcoma of left proximal femur is shown. (B) An antero-posterior view of plain radiograph of hip at postoperative one year is shown. The computer navigation technique allowed precise surgical planning, tumor resection and an accurate fit of a CAD custom prosthesis. (C) A specially designed custom prosthesis is shown. Additional extracortical plates and screw at femoral head offered excellent fixation and stability for the reconstruction. Hydroxyapatite that could facilitate osseointegration was coated at the surface of all bone-implant junctions of the prosthesis

We found the technique was particularly useful in pelvic, sacral tumors, joint-saving intercalated tumor resection and fitting of CAD custom-made prostheses.
The mean time for preoperative navigation planning was 1.85 hours (1 to 3.8). The mean time for intraoperative navigation procedures was 29.6 minutes (13 to 60). The time increased with case complexity but lessened with practice. The mean registration error was 0.47mm (0.31 to 0.8). The virtual preoperative images matched well with the patients' operative anatomy. A postoperative superficial wound infection developed in Patient 6 with sacral chordoma that resolved with antibiotic whereas a wound infection in Patient 11 with sacral osteosarcoma required surgical debridement and antibiotic. After a mean follow-up of 32.5 months (14 to 49), five patients died of distant metastases. Three out of four patients with local recurrence had tumors at sacral region. Three of them were soft tissue tumor

recurrence. The mean functional MSTS score in patients with limb salvage surgery was 28.3 (23 to 30). All patients (except one) with limb sparing surgery and prosthetic reconstruction could walk without aids.

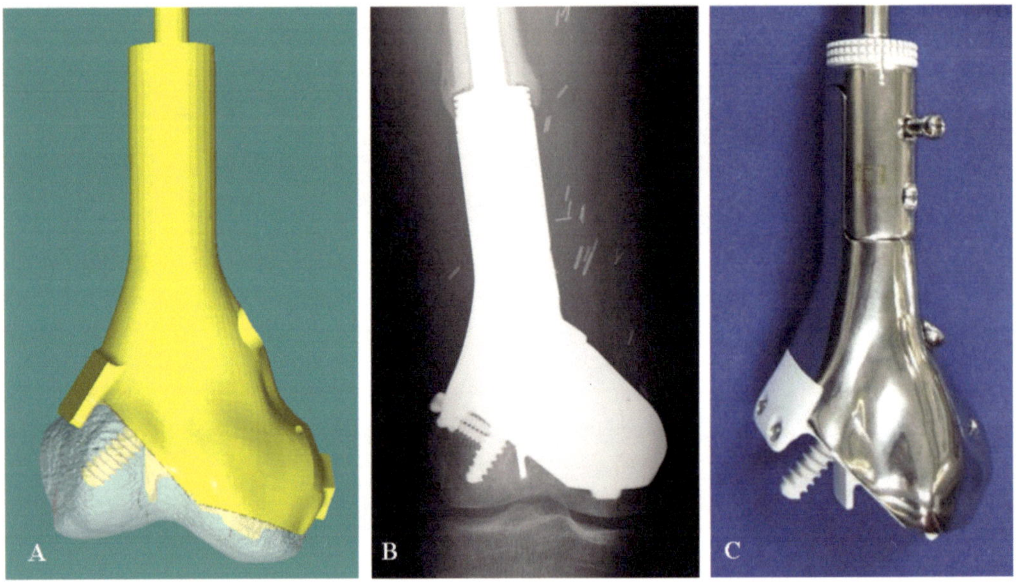

Fig. 6. (A) A joint-saving, CAD custom prosthesis in Patient 16 with right distal femur parosteal osteosarcoma is shown. With navigation planning, multiplanar osteotomies at distal femur was possible to allow joint-saving intercalated resection. The intended resection preserved soft tissue attachment (femur condylar insertion of cruciate ligaments and lateral collateral ligaments insertion) to the distal remaining bone. It allowed sufficient blood supply to the small bone segment. (B) An antero-posterior view of plain radiograph at postoperative one year is shown. Bone formation was present at the bone-implant junctions. The distal bone segment was viable without evidence of osteonecrosis. (C) A specially designed custom prosthesis is shown

4. Discussion

CT and MRI are complementary preoperative imaging investigations for planning complex musculoskeletal bone tumors resection and reconstruction. Conventionally, tumor surgeons analyze 2-D imaging information, mentally integrate and formulate a 3-D surgical plan. Difficulties are anticipated with increase in case complexity and distorted surgical anatomy. Although computer-assisted surgery has been widely used in cranial biopsies and tumor resection, only small case series with early experience are recently reported in the field of musculoskeletal tumor surgery. By including more patients with longer follow-up period in the study, we investigated the results of image fusion for CATS in musculoskeletal oncology with the help of a navigation system.

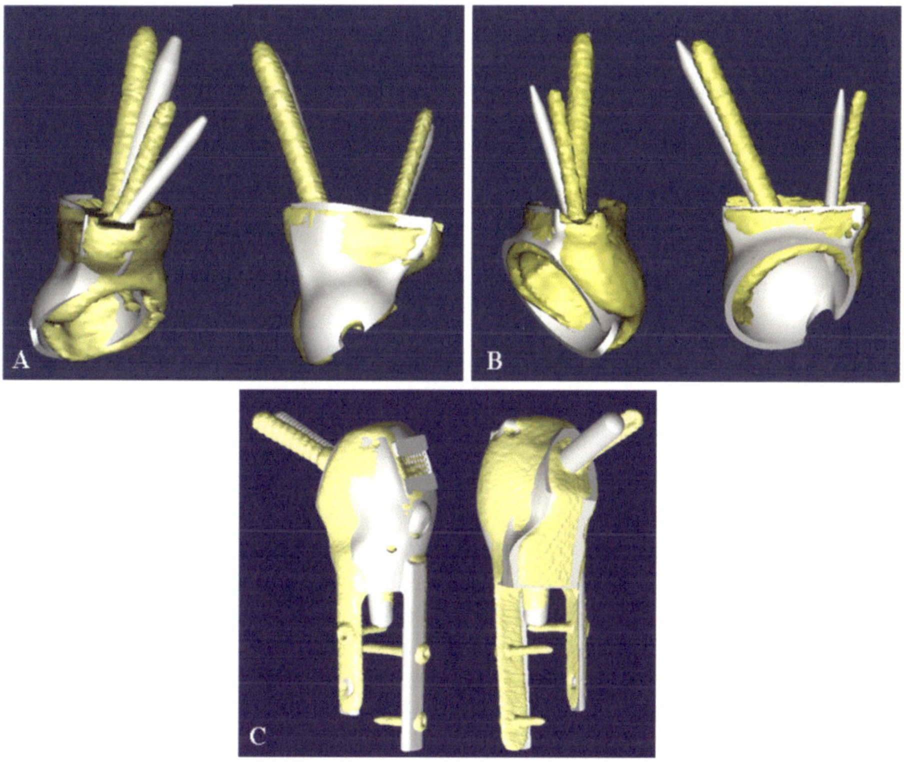

Fig. 7. Postoperative CT images were merged with preoperative planning for (A) Patient 10, (B) Patient 15 and (C) Patient 14. The achieved position (yellow colour) of a custom prosthesis could be compared to that of planned (silver color). The comparable position between the achieved and planned suggested that CATS might improve the surgical accuracy of tumor resection and reconstruction with CAD custom prosthesis

MRI based navigation has been described if fucidual markers for registration are implanted prior to MRI scanning (Kim JH et al., 2010). However, an additional operation for inserting markers is necessary. The operation is also difficult via a small wound access under local anaesthesia, in particularly if the involved bone is deep and covered by thick soft tissue. Our results showed that accurate image-to-patient registration of error < 1mm was feasible and reproducible in CT-based navigation. It was adopted for computer-assisted bone tumor surgery. Fusing multimodal images (CT / MR) could provide additional information besides bone information from CT images.

A study had investigated the surgical accuracy of an experienced surgeon in performing a pelvic tumor resection with 1-cm surgical margin (Cartiaux O et al., 2008). Authors reported that the surgeon could achieve 1-cm surgical margin (±5mm) in a probability of only 52%. The difficult pelvic anatomy and its complex geometry might contribute to the inaccuracy. Our results showed that image fusion and CATS technique allowed better surgical planning, improved intraoperative visualization and determination of intended resection. In this study, the registration error of < 1mm and the achieved resection comparable to planned resection suggested that surgeons should have a higher chance of reproducing their surgical plans and enhancing the accuracy of bone tumors surgery. This detailed and interactive image analysis is particularly helpful in difficult pelvic, sacral, or joint-saving bone tumor resections.

Currently assessing resection margins intraoperatively is possible by means of frozen section. If it is positive, they can be regarded as a guide to additional resection. When it is negative, they add no information about the distance from the tumor. Our results suggested that we could validate the clear margin and quantify the distance from the tumor boundaries by means of images navigation guidance following tumor resection at the surgery.

Reports have described the use of computer navigation in joint-saving tumor resection (Cho HS et al., 2009; Wong KC et al., 2007; Wong KC et al., 2008). We also found that the CATS technique enabled us to perform accurate joint-saving tumor resection and precise fit of CAD custom prostheses for Patient 5, 7, 9, 14, 16, 20 which would not have been possible without an accurate guide to the plane of intended resection. In Patients 14, 16, intended resection was not restricted to an osteotomy along a single plane and multiplanar osteotomies were possible around bone tumors. It could maximally preserve the adjacent normal tissue for subsequent bony reconstruction but yet achieve adequate surgical margin. The technique therefore might facilitate an accurate fit of a CAD custom prosthesis to a skeletal defect with complex geometry. We believe that the technique with similar workflow is feasible for various types of allograft reconstruction in musculoskeletal tumor surgery (Muscolo DL et al., 2006). It has great potential for allograft selection in bone bank by CT-CT image fusion; transepiphyseal resection intercalary allograft reconstruction; or hemicondylar allograft reconstruction, etc.

Although CAD/CAM software allows surgeons to perform virtual surgical simulation with the preoperative image data sets, it still relies on surgeons' experience to implement the exact surgical planning at the time of surgery. The difficulty increases with complexity of cases. Commercially available surgical navigation systems only accept medical imaging data in DICOM format and do not offer complex surgical simulation on these data. On the other hand, CAD/CAM software can import medical imaging data in DICOM format for virtual manipulation. However, the surgical simulation in its proprietary format of the software is incompatible for direct use in surgical navigation system. We find that image fusion of both the original CT data sets and virtual surgical plan data sets (CAD format is back converted to DICOM format by MIMICS software) can enhance the capacity of surgical navigation in executing virtual surgical plans. For surgical planning of musculoskeletal tumors, image fusion of virtual CT data sets with custom prosthesis and original CT data sets allow accurate planning of resection planes and thus precise fitting of custom tumor prosthesis to the residual bone segment after tumor resection. Therefore, image fusion may enable surgeons to precisely execute complex virtual surgical simulation with any CT-based surgical navigation system at the time of actual surgery.

Four patients developed local recurrence and three of them were located at sacral region in this study. The higher chance of recurrence in these patients might be explained by the fact that the nature of the tumor itself; they all had large soft tissue extraosseous tumor extension and two of them were operated as recurrent cases. Although CATS could help visualize and plan the surgery, navigation by itself could only assist and guide the final bone resection at the surgery. Surgeons still adopted conventional technique in soft tissue.

During navigation surgery, surgeons have to look at virtual preoperative images on the screen and cannot simultaneously look at the operative site and screen, which can be a source of surgical errors. Other potential sources of navigation errors may include displacement of patient's dynamic reference tracker, changes of the operative anatomy in relation to the preoperative image data, incorrect calibration of navigation tools, surgeons' perception inaccuracies or hand tremor, etc. Therefore, surgeons should have full understanding of the principles and possible errors of the computer technology, so to avoid misinterpretation of navigation information for their operations. Procedural and surgical skill training is necessary for optimal and correct use of the technique.

Limitations of this study include patients with heterogeneous diagnosis, the lack of control subjects to make a comparative assessment of clinical results. The potential benefits of the CATS technique in improving surgical accuracy may not imply good clinical results in terms of better patients' survival and reduced local recurrence. The small study size, nonrandomized and the early results may not allow us to confirm the value of using this technique, which requires additional financial investment and effort when compared to conventional technique. Without well conducted clinical trials with larger sample size, the utility of the CATS technique may not be realized.

6. Conclusion

Our study suggests Computer-Assisted Tumor Surgery (CATS) with image fusion offers advanced preoperative 3-D surgical planning and supports surgeons with precise intraoperative visualization and identification of intended resection for pelvic, sacral tumors. It enables surgeons to reliably perform joint sparing intercalated tumor resection and accurately fit CAD custom-made prostheses for the resulting skeletal defect. Long-term clinical studies and basic studies of navigation errors are necessary to confirm its value in musculoskeletal tumor surgery.

7. Reference

Anderson KC, Buehler KC, Markel DC. (2005). Computer assisted navigation in total knee arthroplasty: comparison with conventional methods. *J Arthroplasty* 2005 Oct; 20 (7 Suppl 3): 132-8.

Cartiaux O, Docquier PL, Paul L, Francq BG, Cornu OH, Delloye C, Raucent B, Dehez B, Banse X. (2008). Surgical inaccuracy of tumor resection and reconstruction within the pelvis: an experimental study. *Acta Orthop*. 2008 Oct; 79(5):695-702.

Cho HS, Kang HG, Kim HS, Han I. (2008). Computer-assisted sacral tumor resection. A case report. *J Bone Joint Surg Am*. 2008 Jul; 90(7):1561-6.

Cho HS, Oh JH, Han I, Kim HS. (2009). Joint-preserving limb salvage surgery under navigation guidance. *J Surg Oncol*. 2009 Sep 1; 100(3):227-32.

Docquier PL, Paul L, Cartiaux O, Banse X. Registration accuracy in computer-assisted pelvic surgery. (2009). *Comput Aided Surg*. 2009 Jun 9:1-8. [Epub ahead of print]

Eggers G, Mühling J, Marmulla R. (2006). Image-to-patient registration techniques in head surgery. *Int J Oral Maxillofac Surg*. 2006 Dec;35(12):1081-95.

Enneking WF, Dunham W, Gebhardt MC, Malawer M, Pritchard D. (1993). A system for functional evaluation of recontructive procedures after surgical treatment of tumors of the musculoskeletal system. *Clin Orthop* 1993; 286: 241-6.

Fehlberg S, Eulenstein S, Lange T, Andreou D, Tunn PU. (2009). Computer-assisted pelvic tumor resection: fields of application, limits, and perspectives. *Recent Results Cancer Res.* 2009; 179: 169-82. Review.

Gebhard F, Weidner A, Liener UC, Stockle U, Arand M. (2004). Navigation at the spine. *Injury.* 2004 Jun; 35 Suppl 1:S-A35-45. Review.

Grunert P, Darabi K, Espinosa J, Filippi R. (2003). Computer-aided navigation in neurosurgery. *Neurosurg Rev.* 2003 May; 26(2):73-99; discussion 100-1.

Grutzner PA, Suhm N. (2004). Computer aided long bone fracture treatment. *Injury.* 2004 Jun; 35 Suppl 1:S-A57-64.

Hüfner T, Kfuri M Jr, Galanski M, Bastian L, Loss M, Pohlemann T, Krettek C. (2004). New indications for computer-assisted surgery: tumor resection in the pelvis. *Clin Orthop Relat Res.* 2004 Sep;(426):219-25.

Kim JH, Kang HG, Kim HS. (2010). MRI-guided navigation surgery with temporary implantable bone markers in limb salvage for sarcoma. *Clin Orthop Relat Res.* 2010 Aug; 468(8):2211-7. Epub 2010 Jan 7.

Krettek C, Geerling J, Bastian L, Citak M, Rücker F, Kendoff D, Hüfner T. (2004). Computer aided tumor resection in the pelvis. *Injury.* 2004 Jun; 35 Suppl 1:S-A79-83.

Laine T, Lund T, Ylikoski M, Lohikoshi J, Schlenzja D. (2000). Accuracy of pedicle screw insertion with and without computer assistance: A randomized controlled clinical study in 100 consecutive patients. *European Spine J* 2000; 9(3): 235-40.

Muscolo DL, Ayerza MA, Aponte-Tinao LA. (2006). Massive allograft use in orthopedic oncology. *Orthop Clin North Am.* 2006 Jan; 37(1):65-74. Review.

Reijnders K, Coppes MH, van Hulzen AL, Gravendeel JP, van Ginkel RJ, Hoekstra HJ. (2007). Image guided surgery: new technology for surgery of soft tissue and bone sarcomas. *Eur J Surg Oncol.* 2007 Apr;33(3):390-8. Epub 2006 Nov 29.

Wixson RL, MacDonald MA. Total hip arthroplasty through a minimal posterior approach using imageless computer-assisted hip navigation. (2005). *J Arthroplasty* 2005 Oct; 20 (7 Supp 3): 51-6.

Wong KC, Kumta SM, Chiu KH, Cheung KW, Leung KS, Unwin P, Wong MC. (2007). Computer assisted pelvic tumor resection and reconstruction with a custom-made prosthesis using an innovative adaptation and its validation. *Comput Aided Surg.* 2007 Jul; 12(4):225-32.

Wong KC, Kumta SM, Chiu KH, Antonio GE, Unwin P, Leung KS. (2007). Precision tumour resection and reconstruction using image-guided computer navigation. J Bone Joint Surg Br. 2007 Jul; 89(7):943-7.

Wong KC, Kumta SM, Antonio GE, Tse LF. (2008). Image fusion for computer-assisted bone tumor surgery. *Clin Orthop Relat Res.* 2008 Oct; 466(10):2533-41. Epub 2008 Jul 22.

19

Multimodal Medical Image Registration and Fusion in 3D Conformal Radiotherapy Treatment Planning

Bin Li
South China University of Technology
China

1. Introduction

Medical image is the technique and process used to create images of the human body for medical science or clinical purposes, including medical medical procedures seeking to reveal, diagnose or examine disease. In the last 100 years, medical imaging technology has grown rapidly and drastically changed the medical profession. Now, physicians can use the images obtained by different medical imaging technologies to both diagnose and track the progress of illnesses and injuries. When 3D conformal radiotherapy planning (3D CRTP) is employed for tumor treatment, the relative position between the tumor and its adjacent tissues, should be obtained accurately. Generally, there are two main kinds of medical images which provide different information for diagnosis in 3D conformal radiotherapy planning (3D CRTP). They are "the anatomical images" and "the functional mages". The anatomical images, such as Computerized Tomography(CT), depict clearly primarily morphology of human body through the abundant texture, yet it is not very sensitive to the cancer. The functional mages, such as Positron Emission Tomography (PET), depict primarily information on the metabolism of the underlying anatomy. Therefore, the relative position between the tumor and its adjacent tissues could be obtained easily through analyzing the medical data sets which are fused the information of functional mages and anatomical images.

Many methods exist to perform image fusion. The very basic one is the high pass filtering technique. Later techniques are based on DWT, uniform rational filter bank, and so on. In this chapter, multimodal medical images are fused by applying wavelet transform with fusion rule of combining the local standard deviation and energy, which will be describe in detail in this chapter. Many documents presented a fusion method based on wavelet transform(Park J H et al., 2001), which is useful for image fusion. But the activity measure of the coefficients reflecting the significant information of multimodal medical images had not been considered in them. In clinic application, physicians are interested in the position signs of the tumor. The anatomical images depict clearly primarily morphology of human body through the abundant texture. So the local standard deviation is regarded as the activity measure of coefficients. Furthermore, the local energy reflects the absolute intensity of the signal change, and the large absolute intensity of the signal change reflect the obvious feature of the image. So the image feature is described in uniform by the local standard, which reflects the definition. Therefore, the local standard deviation and energy standard are selected as the activity measure of the coefficients here.

In computer vision, multi-sensor image fusion is the process of combining relevant information from two or more images into a single image. The resulting image will be more informative than any of the input images. For multimodal medical images, the important thing is the fusion of multimodal images, while the registration is the basis for image fusion. Given two image sets acquired from the same patient but at different times or with different devices, image registration is the process of finding a geometric transformation between the two respective image-based coordinate systems that maps a point in the first image set to the point in the second set that has the same patient-based coordinates, i.e. represents the same anatomic location(David M. et al., 2003). This notion presupposes that the anatomy is the same in the two image sets, an assumption that may not be precisely true if, for example, the patient has had a surgical resection between the two acquisitions. The situation becomes more complicated if two image sets that reflect different tissue characteristics [e.g. computed tomography (CT) and positron emission tomography (PET)] are to be registered. The idea can still be used that, if a candidate registration matches a set of similar features in the first image to a set of features in the second image that are also mutually similar, it is probably correct. For example, according to the principle of mutual information, homogeneous regions of the first image set should generally map into homogeneous regions in the second set(David M. et al., 2003). Usually there are several registration methods for different organs or tissues, such as rigid registration, affine registration and elastic registration(M.Betke et al., 2003) (Maintz J.B.A. et al., 1998) (T. Blaffert et al., 2004). In clinical diagnosis, the application of registration methods are just a compromise among the calculation time, accuracy and robustness. Up to now, it is still a major challenge to develop a rapid and automatic registration method whose accuracy can reach to that of manual guided registration(David M. et al., 2003) (Stefan Klein et al., 2007). For the moving organs, non-rigid registration methods are needed because the position, size and shape of internal organs and tissues are affected by the involuntary and other physiological movements of patient. Among the non-rigid registration methods, the Free-Form Deformation(FFD) method(Bardinet E et al., 1996) based on B-splines can control local deformation and change of the control points. For hierarchical B-splines is more smooth and accurate than the common B-splines, so good performance can be achieved if it is applied for floating image deformation(Lee Seungyong et al., 1997) (Ruechert D. et al., 1999) (Ino Fumihiko et al., 2005) (Zhiyong Xie et al., 2004). Thus, the presented automatic fine registration method is designed based on the hierarchical B-splines in this chapter. In 3D CRTP, the key problem for the non-rigid registration method of medical image is that it is a task of very time-consuming calculation process, which is unable to meet the clinical requirement to real-time process. In the mean time, the image data sets in 3D CRTP are so mass that it is very difficult to fuse the information of multimodal sequence images in real time. Thus some optimization measures should be taken. In this chapter, the FFD and maximum mutual information algorithm used in the presented registration method are both non-linear algorithms, so it can be taken as a multi-objective nonlinear problem. Here, the gradient descent algorithm and maximum mutual information entropy criterion are used to accelerate the searching speed for FFD coefficients. Moreover, parallel computing(Yasuhiro K. et al., 2004) (S.K.Warfield et al., 1998) can potentially further increase matching and fusion efficiency, so the parallel matching and fusion technique based on high performance computation is used in this chapter.

From the aforementioned, in order to realize effectively and efficiently the automatic registration and fusion of multimodal medical images data, an image registration and fusion method in 3D CRTP is presented in detail in this chapter. This presented automatic registration method is based on hierarchical adaptive free-form deformation(FFD) algorithm and parallel computing, and the presented parallel multimodal medical image fusion method is based on wavelet transform with fusion rule of combining the local standard deviation and energy. This study demonstrates the superiority of the presented method.

2. Algorithm description of multimodal medical image registration and fusion

The steps of the presented algorithm are illustrated in Fig. 1, which can be described as follows: First given two image sets acquired from the same patient but at different times or with different devices, e.g. CT and PET. Then the ROI is extracted by using the C-V level sets algorithm, and feature points are matched automatically which is based on parallel computing method. Then, the global rough registration and automatic fine registration of the multimodal medical images is carried out by employing principal axes algorithm and a free-form deformation(FFD) method based on hierarchical B-splines. After the registration of multimodal images, their sequence images are fused by applying an image fusion method based on parallel computing and wavelet transform with the fusion rule of combining the local standard deviation and energy.

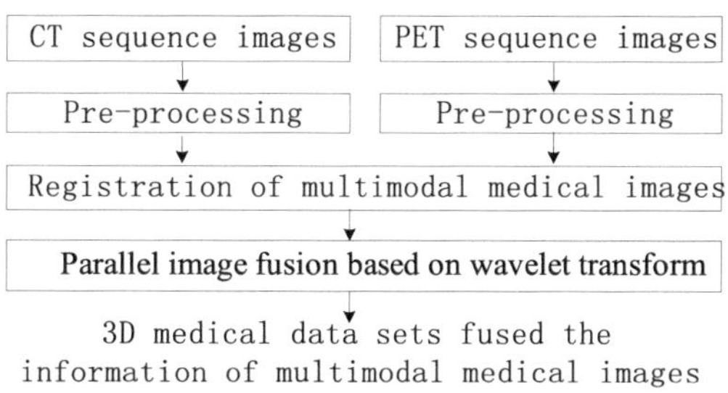

Fig. 1. Flow chart of the presented rapid registration and fusion method of multimodal medical image

3. Data preprocessing of medical images

In 3D CRTP, before the step of registration and fusion, scan data from PET and CT should be normalized or pre-processed according to the requirements of the next fusion step.

For the calculation of the fusion of PET and CT images, the standard uptake value(SUV) is frequently used for fluorodeoxyglucose(FDG) PET image to evaluate its uptake value quantitatively(S-C. Huang, 2000) (Aparna Kanakatte et al., 2007). In general, if there exists a tumor it will appear brighter than healthy cells in a PET image. This character is commonly used to identify healthy tissue from a tumor. Thus, the SUV is also named as the differential uptake ratio, or the differential absorption ratio, or the dose uptake ratio or the dose absorption ratio.

In order to obtain the tissue activity in each point, Bq/cc, units as measured by the PET/CT scanner, the pixel data is rescaled by tags "Rescale Slope" and "Rescale Intercept" available from the dicom header. The SUV is a useful quantitative way comparing tumors across different patients. For the calculation of SUV, the body weight of a patient is commonly used, sometimes, physicians prefer to use body surface or lean body mass instead. The SUV for each voxel is calculated assuming $1cc = 1g$ and applying Eq.(1).

$$SUV = \frac{YW}{D} \tag{1}$$

where W is the patient weight in kg; D is the injected dose at scan start (Bq); Y is the activity whose concentration in Bq / cc is calculated from Eq.(2).

$$Y = ax + b \tag{2}$$

where x is the original pixel intensity value, a is the rescale slope and b is the rescale intercept for each image slice of the PET scan.
According to Aparna(Aparna Kanakatte et al., 2007), the higher the SUV is, the more aggressive the tumor is. The SUV is also used to distinguish the malignant tumor and benign tumor. An SUV of 2.5 is often considered as the threshold to distinguish benign and malignancy, however, the threshold value varies for different body organs, and if taking the breathing movement in account, the SUV will increase.

4. Registration of multimodal medical images

4.1 Flow chart for image registration

The presented image registration method applying adaptive FFD which is based on hierarchical B-splines algorithm is shown as Fig.2.

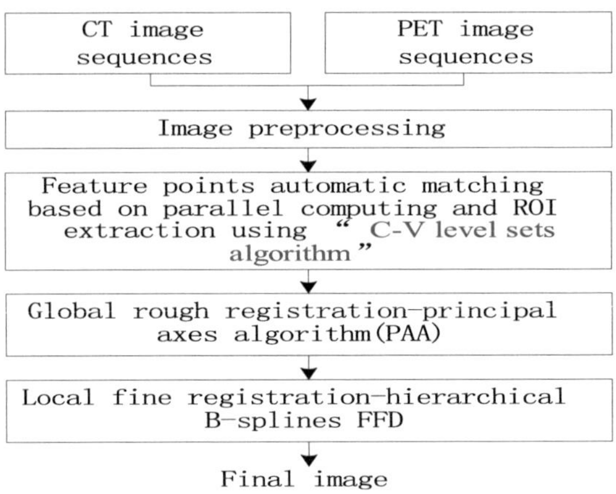

Fig. 2. Flow chart for image registration method applying adaptive FFD

The registration for medical images is a big challenge, this is because the position, size and shape of internal organs and tissues are affected by involuntary physiological movements and patient' motion when scanning, where various deformations are existent in the mean time, for example, the rigid motion of human body, the local elastic deformations of organs in motion. This will require the registration method be done about the global deformation at first, and then fine adjusting is conducted about local elastic deformation. Thus, registration process can be divided into two sub-process: one is the global rigid deformation by adopting principal axes algorithm, the other is the local elastic deformation by adopting adaptive FFD based on B-splines.

4.2 Measure of similarity for multimodal medical images

The mutual information[17,18] of multimodal medical images is taken as similarity index for registration, which is essentially the expression about the statistical characteristic of gray information between two images. An objective function can be used to define the similarity measure between the reference image and floating image.

Suppose the gray intensity of reference image is I_R, while that of the floating image is I_F, the information entropy for I_R is $H(I_R)$, it is $H(I_F)$ for I_F. Let $H(I_R,I_F)$ denote the combined information entropy of I_R and I_F, then the mutual information of two images is defined as follows:

$$MI(I_R,I_F)=H(I_R)+H(I_F)-H(I_R,I_F) \tag{3}$$

When two images are strictly matched, $MI(I_R,I_F)$ will be the maximum. For the registration of the multimodal medical images although the two images, i.e. CT and PET images, usually come from different imaging equipments, both of them are produced from the same organ of the same patient. So when the spatial positions of two images are strictly uniform, $MI(I_R,I_F)$ reaches its peak value.

Studholme(Studholme C et al., 1999) found that the value of mutual information has some relevance which is subject to the overlap degree of two images to be matched. According to Studholme(Studholme C et al., 1999), in order to eliminate the effect resulted from the relevance, the mutual information is standardized as Eq.(4). The results of experiments show that it is more robust than Eq.(3).

$$MI(I_R,I_F)=\frac{H(I_R)+H(I_F)}{H(I_R,I_F)} \tag{4}$$

4.3 Automatic matching of feature points

4.3.1 Automatic matching of feature point

The imaging principle of CT image tells that it reflects the detailed information about anatomical structure, while PET image denotes the functional information. Because the resolution of CT is higher than that of PET image, in order to realize the registration of two modals images, the PET image should be deformed to match the CT image, thus the CT image is defined as reference image, and the PET image is taken as floating image.

The main work for automatic fine registration by the FFD based on hierarchical B-splines is to find out some suitable feature points, which contain the points of ROI and the internal distribution points. For example, for the thorax, the thorax-wall is regarded as a rigid body due to its little deformation, while other organs in thorax such as heart and lung are always in the state of motion, so they are taken as non-rigid bodies. For current PET/CT scanning, the CT and PET scanning are carried out in sequence actually, not in the same time, in addition, the time for PET scanning is much longer than that of CT, thus it may lead to the difference of shapes from the PET and CT images in the same layer. For the thorax-wall is a rigid body, thus, the points on contour lines of thorax are taken as the feature points, while organs such as heart and lung, are always in motion, so internal distribution points can be randomly selected as feature points. On the other side, how to match the brighter ROI(region of interesting) of PET image with the corresponding ROI of CT image is an important task in multimodal medical image registration.

So, the operation of automatic matching of feature points is as follows, which is shown as Fig.3. ① Step 1. Shown as Fig.3(a), first the ROI with larger SUV, such as the pixel "F" of Fig.3(a), is selected from PET images by using the C-V level sets algorithm; then the corresponding feature points, such as the corresponding feature point "F′ " of "F′, are searched from CT images by using the mutual information as similarity measure. ② Step 2. Shown as Fig.3(b), the ROI, such the point "B", should be first extracted from the CT images, this can be done by using the C-V level sets algorithm. Then the corresponding feature points on the PET image, such the corresponding feature point "B′ " of "B", are searched by employing the maximum mutual information algorithm. ③ Step 3. Shown as Fig.3(c), internal distribution points are randomly selected on the internal edge. And all of the feature points are matched automatically which is based on parallel computing method. Thus automatic matching of the initial feature points are realized, and the local deformation adjustment will be done according to the follow-up gradient descent coefficients correction.

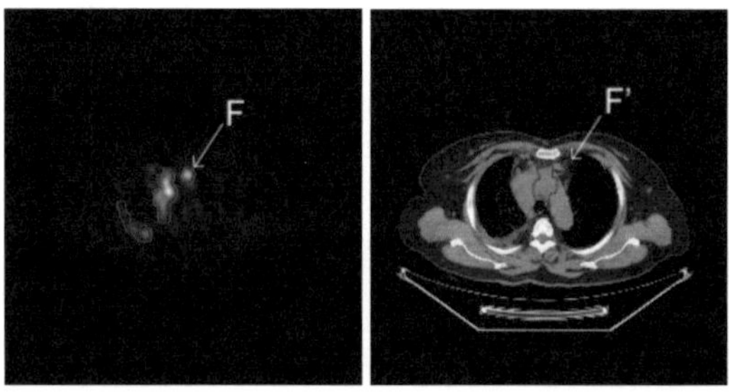

(a) step 1

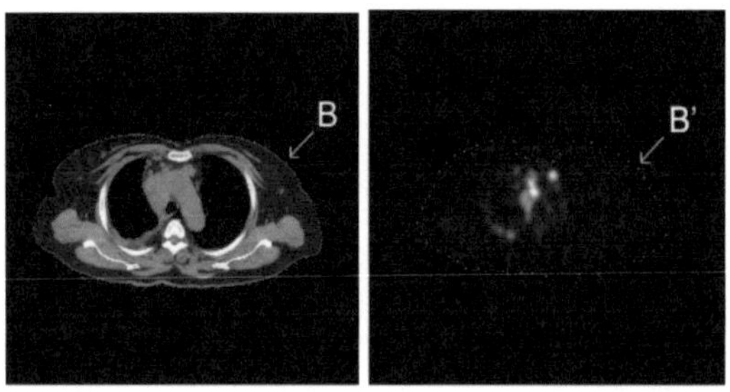

(b) step 2

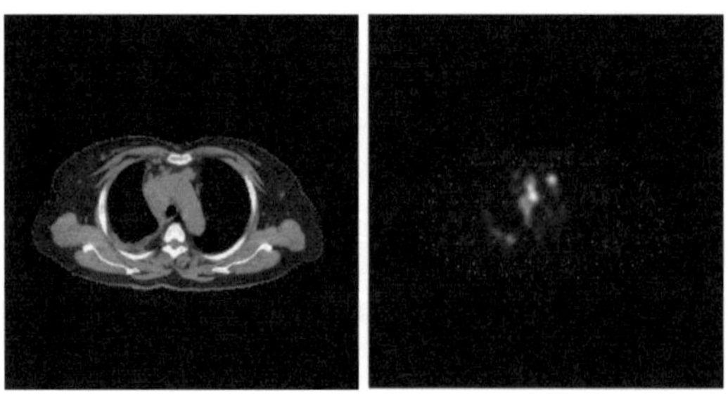

(c) step 3

Fig. 3. Illustration of automatic matching of feature points

4.3.2 ROI extraction based on improved C-V level sets method

Traditional Snake active contour modal shows some weaknesses: 1) the contour generated by initialization usually should be very near the real boundary, otherwise it will result in erroneous results; 2) the active contour is difficult to enter into concave domain.

Chan and Vese presented the C-V level set method based on optimal technique of curve evolution(Chan T F et al., 2001), simple Mumford-Shad Function, in which the image segmentation problem is connected with the optimization of Mumford-Shad Function, so that the efficiency and robustness of image segmentation are improved.

In this chapter, ROI, including the organ contour and the focus region, is extracted by the improved C-V level set method. The improved C-V level set method is based on a region-based active contour model, which avoids expensive re-initialization of the evolving level set function.

The partial differential equations(PDE) defined by level set function ϕ is:

$$\frac{\partial \phi}{\partial t} = \delta_\varepsilon(\phi)[\mu \operatorname{div}(\frac{\nabla \phi}{|\nabla \phi|}) - \nu - \lambda_1(I_0 - c_1)^2 + \lambda_2(I_0 - c_2)^2] = 0 \tag{5}$$

where, $\delta_\varepsilon(\phi)$ is slightly regularized versions of *Dirac* measure $\delta(\phi)$; $\mu,\nu,\lambda_1,\lambda_2$ represents the weight of the corresponding energy term, respectively; I_0 is the object region; c_1,c_2 is the average intensity value inside and outside contour.

The procedure for ROI extraction using the improved C-V level set method are as follows:

1. Initialize level set function ϕ_n by ϕ_0, $n=0$.
2. The initial curve is set, and the SDF(signed distance function) is also set according to the shortest distance between the point and curve, in which the value of SDF is positive inside curve, yet negative outside curve.
3. Compute $c_1 = \frac{\int_\Omega I_0 H_\varepsilon(\phi)dxdy}{\int_\Omega H_\varepsilon(\phi)dxdy}$, and $c_2 = \frac{\int_\Omega I_0(1-H_\varepsilon(\phi))dxdy}{\int_\Omega (1-H_\varepsilon(\phi))dxdy}$.
4. Solve the PDE in level set function ϕ iteratively. The iterative ϕ^{n+1} is computed by putting the global and local region value into Eq.(5).
5. Check whether the solution is stationary. If not, $n=n+1$ and repeat.

4.3.3 Auto-matching method of feature points based on parallel computing

It is well known that the process of feature-points matching accounts for the most runtime of all the registration process, that is, the feature-point-matching process is the main factor which influences the efficiency of non-rigid registration process.

Feature points are signed in CT image, then their corresponding feature points are found from PET image. The matching process of feature points, which uses local searching strategy as said in section 4.3.1, will cost much time. In the matching process of feature points, the step of searching and matching of each feature point is independent, so the matching of feature points is processed by the method of parallel computing. Parallel computing can potentially further increase matching efficiency, in order to implement efficiently the registration of multi-model medical images data, the parallel matching technique based on high performance computation is used in this chapter. The cluster computing system is very inexpensive and powerful for high-performance computing. It interconnects general-propose computers, such as workstation and PC, together to form a powerful computing platform through the rapid ethernet and the message-passing project, such as MPI(Message-Passing Interface) /PVM(Parallel Virtual Machine). In this chapter, the cluster computing system is designed to perform with MPI high performance computation-parallel image matching algorithm.

The parallel task partition strategies are a tradeoff between the communication cost and load balancing[13]. Here, the task partition could be implemented by domain decomposition. The followings are the steps of the parallel algorithm:

1. The management process broadcasts all of the data, including CT-PET image data and position of feature points in CT, to be processed to all the processes of the communication domain.
2. Each process computes the assigned start number, end number and amount of the processed feature points according to the process index.
3. The assigned feature points are matched independently in each process in turn, which is according to section 4.3.1.
4. The result is sent to the management process. And the management process receives and saves all the result.

4.4 Global rigid deformation based on principal axes algorithm

The global rough registration for rigid deformation is realized by adopting principal axes algorithm(Louis K A et al., 1995) in this chapter. First, the corresponding feature points of PET and CT images are searched by using the method presented in section 4.3, respectively. And then the centroids of two image contours are calculated, and the centroid of PET image couture is adjusted to adapt to that of CT image.

4.5 Local fine registration based B-splines adaptive FFD

When only considering local information for image registration, image deformation will be resulted, in the mean time, if elastic deformation is directly employed for image registration, it may result in mismatch. So the local elastic deformation is realized by applying the adaptive FFD based on hierarchical B-splines method. The flow chart is shown as Fig.4.

4.5.1 Registration based on B-splines FFD method

The principle of the FFD method(Huang Xiaolei et al., 2006) is that the object shape is changed and controlled through controlling the control points of control framework. The control framework and a group of basis functions constitute an entity which are some Bernstein polynomials. For B-spline only affects local deformation, so, when some of the feature points of a two-dimensional image are moved only the vicinal points are affected, not all the points in the image are deformed, so cubic B-splines tensor product of two variables is adopted as the FFD deformation function.

Let Π be a two-dimension image in $x-y$ plane. Suppose $p=(u,v)$ is a point on image Π, where $1 \le u \le m$, $1 \le v \le n$. When some deformation of image Π is generated , its shape can be represented by a vector function $\mathrm{h}(p)=(x(p),y(p))$. Let Ψ is a control point grid of $(m+3)\times(n+3)$ covering on Π. Suppose ψ_{IJ} expresses the position coordinate (I,J) in Ψ. Shape function h can be represented by ψ_{IJ} which is shown in Fig.5.

$$\mathrm{h}(u,v)=\sum_{k=0}^{3}\sum_{l=0}^{3}B_k(s)B_l(t)\psi_{(I+k)(J+l)} \tag{6}$$

Where,

$$I=\left\lfloor\frac{u}{m+2}\right\rfloor-1\,,\; J=\left\lfloor\frac{v}{n+2}\right\rfloor-1\,,\; s=\frac{u}{m+2}-\left\lfloor\frac{u}{m+2}\right\rfloor,\; t=\frac{v}{n+2}-\left\lfloor\frac{v}{n+2}\right\rfloor.$$

$B_k(s)$ and $B_l(t)$ are the uniform cubic B-spline basis function of vectors s and t, respectively. For $B_l(t)$ it can be described as follows:

$$\begin{aligned}
B_0(t)&=(-t^3+3t^2-3t+1)/6\\
B_1(t)&=(3t^3+6t^2+4)/6\\
B_2(t)&=(-3t^3+3t^2+3t+1)/6\\
B_3(t)&=t^3/6
\end{aligned} \tag{7}$$

where $0\le t\le 1$.
The expression for $B_k(s)$ is the same as for $B_l(t)$.

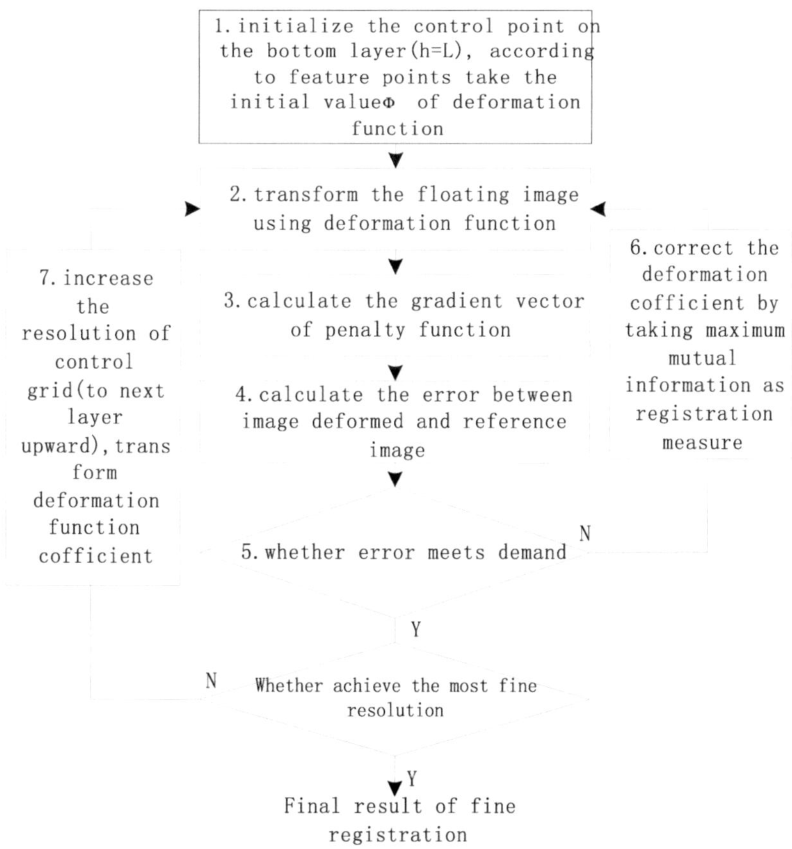

Fig. 4. Local fine registration using a free-form deformation(FFD) based on hierarchical B-splines

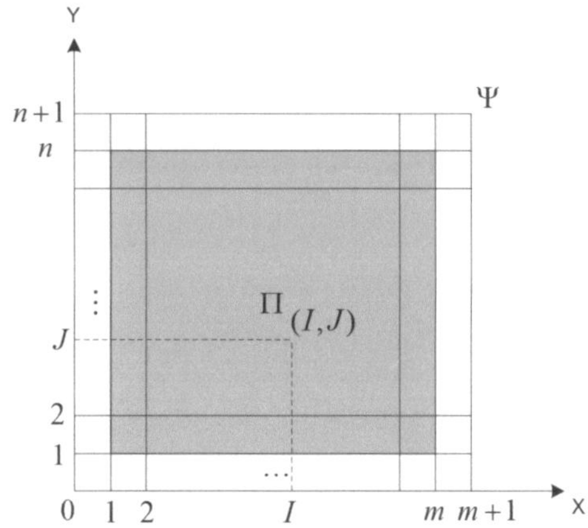

Fig. 5. Initial position of original image and control point lattice

4.5.2 Reverse mapping - elimination of the hole phenomenon

In the registration process, the image to be processed should be deformed to form a new image. In doing so, there are two kinds of methods to be selected: forward mapping and reverse mapping. For forward mapping, it is required that every pixel from input image should be mapped to output image through transformation function, which is difficult to guarantee that all the points are mapped, i.e., sometimes, some points may be omitted. When such case happens, it is called hole phenomenon. On the contrary, the reverse mapping method can enable each pixel in output image to find its corresponding point in input image, in doing so, there is no hole phenomenon to happen. In this chapter, the registration function is established based on the feature points of floating image, each pixel of the image to be matched is input to the registration transformation function, then the corresponding position of the reference image is obtained. Thus it can eliminate hole phenomenon.

4.5.3 Fine registration of multimodal medical image

For the position, size and shape of internal organs and tissues are affected by involuntary physiological movements or motions of patient, this will lead to elastic deformation in the local position of organs. However, due to the local deformation of medical image based on local information, so it is easy to result in mismatch if executing elastic deformation directly. To solve such problem, B-spline function can be selected to generates a smooth curve(or smooth plane) to approximate the control point. By comprehensively considering the accuracy of fitting function, the deformation smoothness, the calculation complexity and registration accuracy, an automatic fine registration of multimodal medical images based on hierarchical B-splines adaptive FFD is presented in this chapter. Flow chart is shown as Fig.4.

4.5.4 Implementation of fast FFD registration

In the registration process, the image to be processed should be deformed to form a new image. In doing so, there are two kinds of methods to be selected: forward mapping and reverse mapping. For forward mapping, it is required that every pixel from input image should be mapped to output image through transformation function, which is difficult to guarantee that all the points are mapped, i.e., sometimes, some points may be omitted. When such case happens, it is called hole phenomenon. On the contrary, the reverse mapping method can enable each pixel in output image to find its corresponding point in input image, in doing so, there is no hole phenomenon to happen. In this chapter, the registration function is established based on the feature points of floating image, each pixel of the image to be matched is input to the registration transformation function, then the corresponding position of the reference image is obtained. Thus it can eliminate hole phenomenon.It is well known that medical image registration is a very time-consuming task, which limits the clinical applications of such method to some degree. In order to overcome such shortcoming, some optimization measures can be taken to improve it. On this aim, a new registration method combining the FFD algorithm and maximum mutual information is presented, in which the optimization problem can be regarded as a nonlinear programming problem. This chapter adopts gradient descent method to implement fast FFD local fine registration, in which step adjusting is adapted based on maximization of mutual information.

The mutual information is taken as the cost function for the presented medical image registration method, then a global optimal solution is $\Theta^* = \arg\min_{\Theta} C(\Theta)$. In this research, the gradient descent method is used to solve the extreme value of coefficient matrix Θ. Although only the local extrema can be obtained by using the presented method, whose operation speed is much faster than the traditional ones, and due to the smoothness constraint, this method can overcome the problem of local extrema effectively in calculation process of deformation field.

The calculation process for this method is already described in Fig 3. Here some additional explanations are given as follows:

1. Gradient computation

   The gradient of cost function C is shown as follows:

$$\nabla C = \frac{\partial C(\Theta, \Phi^l)}{\partial \Phi^l} \tag{8}$$

   where Φ^l is the control grid coordinate of the l-th layer, Θ is deformation coefficient. Here, the maximum mutual information entropy is taken as the cost function C, and its gradient at the point (u,v) is a vector that can be simplified as:

$$\nabla C = | f(u,v) - f(u-1,v) | + | f(u,v) - f(u,v-1) | \tag{9}$$

2. Correction of deformation coefficient

   In the algorithm, the maximum mutual information entropy is taken as registration measure to test whether the pre-set error is achieved or not. If not achieved, the deformation coefficients should be corrected. The iterative algorithm for control points is shown as follows:

$$\Phi_i^{(t+1)} = \Phi_i^{(t)} - \mu \frac{\nabla C}{||C_i||} \tag{10}$$

   where $i \in I_C$, I_C is the grid spatial image after deformation, t is iterative number, μ is iterative step.

5. Fusion of multimodal medical image

5.1 Image fusion based on wavelet transform

After the registration of CT and PET images, their sequence images are fused by applying a image fusion method based on parallel computing and wavelet transform with the fusion rule of combining the local standard deviation and energy. The followings are the steps of the fusion algorithm:

Step 1. The CT and PET images are encoded by a 3-level wavelet decomposition with Daubechies 9/7 biorthogonal wavelet filter banks.

Step 2. Compute the average value of wavelet coefficients $D_{CT}(i,j)$ / $D_{PET}(i,j)$ of the CT and PET images.

$$\begin{cases} D_X(i,j) = \sum_{s\in S, t\in T} \omega(s,t) D_X(i+s, j+t, k, l) \\ X = CT, PET \end{cases} \quad (11)$$

Where *(i, j)* denotes the position of the center of the current window; *k* denotes the level of wavelet decomposition ($k = 1,2,3$); *l* denotes frequency band; (*s*, *t*) denotes the position in the current window; $\omega(s, t)$ denotes the weight of the coefficient in (*s*, *t*), and the further away from the center it is, the less the weight becomes; $\sum_{s\in S, t\in T} \omega(s,t) = 1$, where S and T denote the norm of the current window.

Step 3. CT and PET images are fused based on wavelet transform by employing fusion rule of combining the local standard deviation and energy.

In clinic application, physicians are interested in the position signs of the tumor. The anatomical images depict clearly primarily morphology of human body through the abundant texture. Therefore, the selected activity measure should reflect the texture pattern of the image. Each pixel value in a smooth region of a image is nearly equal, yet it changes severely in a rough region. So the local standard deviation is regarded as the activity measure of coefficients. Furthermore, the local energy reflects the absolute intensity of the signal change, and the large absolute intensity of the signal change reflect the obvious feature of the image. So the image feature is described in uniform by the local standard, which reflects the definition. Therefore, the local standard deviation and energy standard are selected as the activity measure of the coefficients.

① Let A_X denote the activity measure based on local standard deviation.

$$A_X(i,j) = \sqrt{\sum_{s\in S, t\in T} \omega(s,t) \left[D_X(i+s, j+t, k, l) - D_X(i,j) \right]^2} \quad (12)$$

Let δ_{CT} and δ_{PET} denote the weight that the activity measure based on local standard deviation assigned to CT and PET, respectively.

$$\begin{cases} \delta_{CT} = \dfrac{\left[A_{CT}(i,j)\right]^{\alpha}}{\left[A_{CT}(i,j)\right]^{\alpha} + \left[A_{PET}(i,j)\right]^{\alpha}} \\ \delta_{PET} = \dfrac{\left[A_{PET}(x,y)\right]^{\alpha}}{\left[A_{CT}(i,j)\right]^{\alpha} + \left[A_{PET}(i,j)\right]^{\alpha}} \end{cases} \tag{13}$$

Where α is a adjustable parameter. When $\alpha > 0$, the higher activity measure is, the more it weights. Here, let α equal to 1.8。
②Let B_X denote the activity measure based on local energy.

$$B_X(i,j) = \sum_{s \in S, t \in T} \omega(s,t) D_X^2(i+s, j+t, k, l) \tag{14}$$

Let δ_{CT} and δ_{PET} denote the weight that the activity measure based on local energy assigned to CT and PET, respectively.

$$\begin{cases} \varepsilon_{CT} = \dfrac{B_{CT}(i,j)}{B_{CT}(i,j) + B_{PET}(i,j)} \\ \varepsilon_{PET} = \dfrac{B_{PET}(i,j)}{B_{CT}(i,j) + B_{PET}(i,j)} \end{cases} \tag{15}$$

③After combining the local standard deviation and energy, wavelet coefficients of fused image D_F is

$$\begin{aligned} D_F(i,j) &= \left[\delta_{CT} D_{CT}(i,j) + \delta_{PET} D_{PET}(i,j)\right] \times \lambda \\ &+ \left[\varepsilon_{CT} D_{CT}(i,j) + \varepsilon_{PET} D_{PET}(i,j)\right] \times \mu \end{aligned} \tag{16}$$

Where, λ, μ are adjustable parameters, $\lambda + \mu = 1$. The image intensity gets stronger as μ increases; and the edge of intensity get sharper as λ increases, thus the blur of the edge is avoided as possible as we can if λ / μ is adjusted suitably.

Step 4. The approximate coefficients C_J^{CT} and C_J^{PET} through wavelet transform of CT and PET image are processed. $\hat{C}_J^F$ is computed by formula 21:

$$\hat{C}_J^F = (C_J^{CT} + C_J^{PET}) / 2 \tag{17}$$

Step 5. The fused image F is gotten by wavelet inverse transform using all of the wavelet coefficients D_F and the approximate coefficients.

and saves all the result.

5.2 Parallel image fusion

5.2.1 Necessity of parallel image fusion

In image fusion, it becomes more computationally expensive as the image data and its level of wavelet decomposition increase. Because parallel computing can potentially further increase fusion efficiency, the parallel image fusion technique based on high performance computation is used in this chapter. As said in section 4.3.3, the cluster computing system is very inexpensive and powerful for high-performance computing. In order to implement effectively and efficiently the fusion of mass multimodal medical images data, a parallel multimodal medical image fusion method based on wavelet transform is presented. In this chapter, the cluster computing system is designed to perform with MPI high performance computation-parallel image fusion algorithm based on wavelet transform.

5.2.2 Implement of parallel image fusion based on wavelet transform

In image fusion, it becomes more computationally expensive as the image data and its level of wavelet decomposition increase. Because parallel computing can potentially further increase fusion efficiency, the parallel image fusion technique based on high performance computation is used in this chapter. As said in section 4.3.3, the cluster computing system is very inexpensive and powerful for high-performance computing. In order to implement effectively and efficiently the fusion of mass multimodal medical images data, a parallel multimodal medical image fusion method based on wavelet transform is presented. In this chapter, the cluster computing system is designed to perform with MPI high performance computation-parallel image fusion algorithm based on wavelet transform.

Partitioning divides the problem into parts, which is the basis of all parallel programming. Partitioning can be applied to the programming data. This is called data partitioning or domain decomposition. The parallel task partition strategies are a tradeoff between the communication cost and load balancing. When an image is encoded or decoded by a M-level wavelet transform or inverse decomposition, the processed wavelet coefficients of each level are the input of the next level, so the processions between two adjacent levels are of strong correlation. But it is of high parallelism for each level to implement 1D wavelet transform/inverse decomposition row by row or column by column. Moreover, the result after implementing 1D wavelet transform/inverse decomposition is used for the next level wavelet transform. So when the sub-image is encoded by wavelet transform, the task partition could be implemented by domain decomposition. The followings are the steps of the parallel algorithm:

1. The management process broadcasts all of the data to be processed to all the processes of the communication domain.
2. The assigned rows of data are encoded/decoded by 1D wavelet transform/inverse decomposition in each of the processes, then the result is sent to the management process.
3. The management process broadcasts all of the data processed to all of the processes of communication domain.
4. The assigned columns of data are encoded/decoded by 1D wavelet transform/inverse decomposition in each of the processes, then the result is sent to the management process.
5. Repeat step 1-4, until M-level wavelet transform/inverse decomposition is finished.

From the above steps, a conclusion could be drawn that there are several times of data communication in each of M-level wavelet transform/inverse decomposition, so that the parallel efficiency is very low because the communication cost is relatively expensive, especially for the image data in miniature. Therefore, in parallel image fusion of medical sequence images, domain decomposition is applied. All the processes are processed in parallel, however in each process images are fused sequentially.

Multimodal medical sequence images are fused in 3D CRTP. The steps of the algorithm of parallel image fusion of medical sequence images are illustrated in Fig.6.

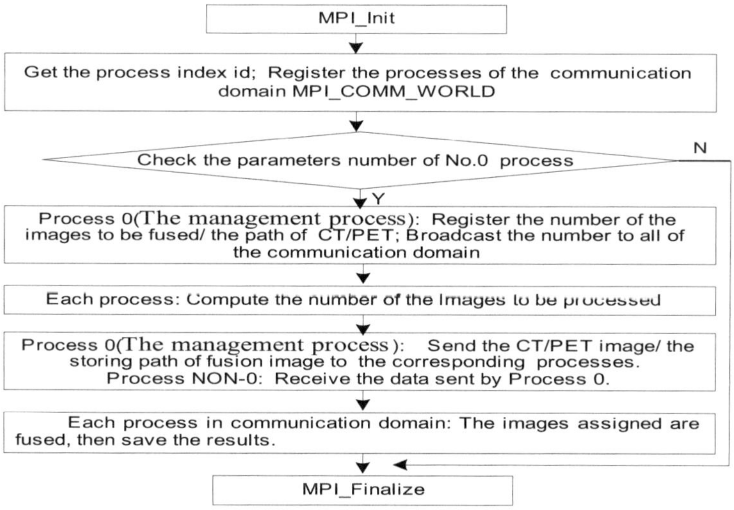

Fig. 6. The flowchart of parallel sequence images fusion

6. Experimental results in 3D conformal radiotherapy treatment planning

In this chapter, a cluster computing system is developed, whose configurations consist of: ①Operation system: Windows Server 2003; ②Network card: 100M b/s Realtek RTL8139 Family PCI Fast Ethernet NIC; ③Parallel software package: MPICH 2-1.0.5p2-win32; ④ Node configurations: processor Intel Pentium 4, CPU 3.0GHz/ 1.00GB RAM; display card, NVIDIA Quadro FX 1400. ⑤ compiler: Visual C++6.0, the programming language is C++.

6.1 Effect evaluation for medical image registration and fusion

6.1.1 Effect evaluation for registration method

The presented image registration method applying adaptive FFD which is based on hierarchical B-splines algorithm is shown as Fig.2.The original images CT(512×512) and PET(128×128), which come from the thorax image sequences, are shown as Figs 7 and 8, respectively. Fig.9 is the processing result of feature points based on parallel computing and ROI extraction by applying the C-V level sets method. The edge curve in Fig.9(a) is the result by applying the edge extraction method of C-V level sets, the regular points in the middle are the selected feature points with 8 interval pixels; the points of Fig.9(b) are the corresponding feature points of Fig.9(a). Fig.10 is the global rough registration result using the principle axes algorithm. Fig.11 is the result of local fine registration of Fig.10 by adopting the presented registration algorithm based on hierarchical B-splines adaptive FFD. Fig.12 shows the data field change pre and post registration.

The effective evaluation for registration method, especially for multimodal medical image is always very difficult. Due to multi-images to be matched are obtained at different time or under different conditions, it is difficult to find a common standardized criteria for the evaluation of the registration method. Usually the following factors are chosen to evaluate the image registration method, for example, registration speed, robustness, registration precision, etc.. For medical image registration, the registration effect should be first considered. The common evaluation methods mainly are phantom, criteria and visual method.

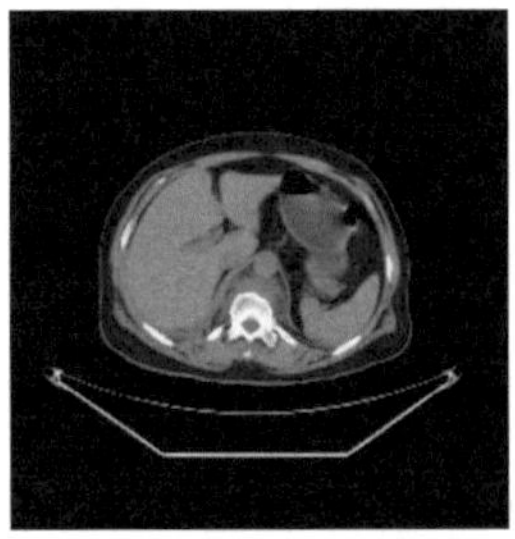

Fig. 7. CT image(reference image)

Fig. 8. PET image(floating image)

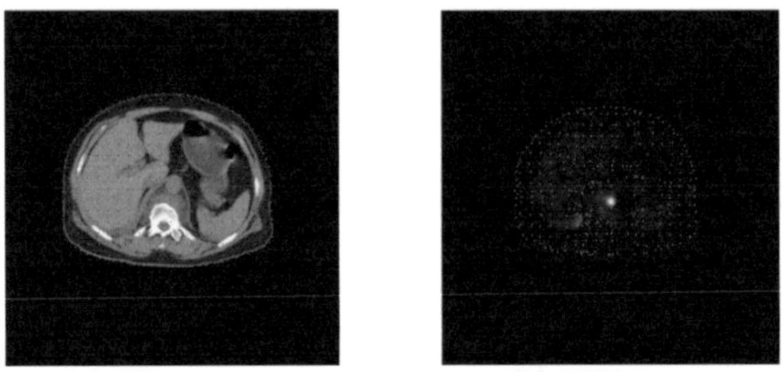

(a) CT image (b) PET image

Fig. 9. Feature points matched based on parallel computing and ROI extraction by the C-V level sets method

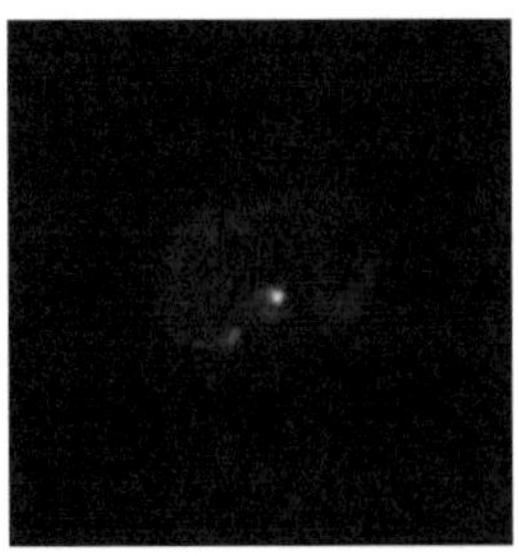

Fig. 10. Global coarse registration by PAA

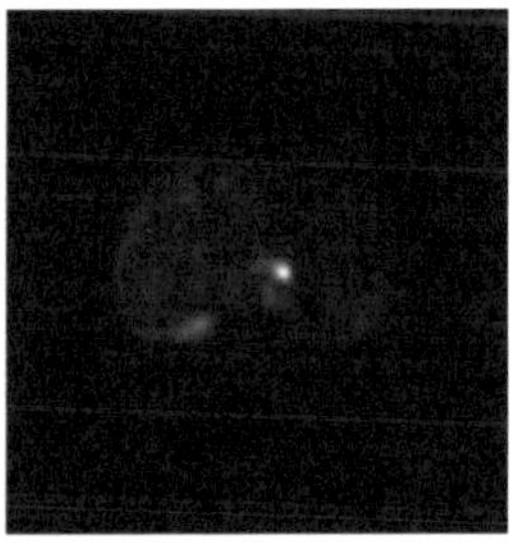

Fig. 11. Local fine registration image by FFD based on hierarchical B-splines method

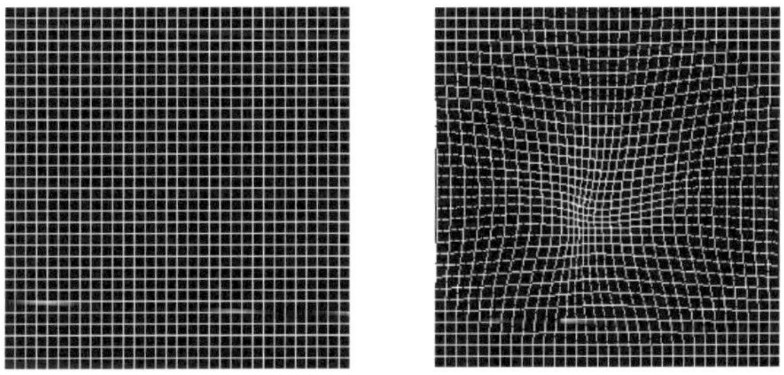

(a) Original data set (b) data set after transformation

Fig. 12. Data set change pre and post registration

The quantitative evaluation method based on image statistical characteristics is adopted in this chapter. including Maximum Information entropy(MI), Root Mean Square error(RMS error), Correlation Coefficient(CC). They can give a quantitative assessment index for registration algorithm. Generally speaking, the statistical characteristic method is currently an objective and practical evaluation method.

Suppose there are two images I_1, I_2, the size of image is $M \times N$, then the RMS is defined as follows:

$$RMS = \sqrt{\frac{\sum_{i=0}^{M-1}\sum_{j=0}^{N-1}\left(I_1(i,j) - I_2(i,j)\right)^2}{M \times N}} \tag{18}$$

If the RMS value becomes smaller, it indicates the difference between two images is small, it proves the registration effect is better. Here, the statistical characteristic CC is employed as the evaluation criteria: for registration effect

$$CC = \frac{\sum_{i=0}^{M-1}\sum_{j=0}^{N-1}\left(I_2(i,j) - \overline{I_2}\right)\left(I_1(i,j) - \overline{I_1}\right)}{\sqrt{\sum_{i=0}^{M-1}\sum_{j=0}^{N-1}\left(I_2(i,j) - \overline{I_2}\right)^2}\sqrt{\sum_{i=0}^{M-1}\sum_{j=0}^{N-1}\left(I_1(i,j) - \overline{I_1}\right)^2}} \tag{19}$$

where, $\overline{I_1}$ and $\overline{I_2}$ are the average gray values of two images: $\overline{I_1} = \frac{\sum_{i=0}^{M-1}\sum_{j=0}^{N-1} I_1(i,j)}{M \times N}$, $\overline{I_2} = \frac{\sum_{i=0}^{M-1}\sum_{j=0}^{N-1} I_2(i,j)}{M \times N}$. The CC value ranges from 0 to 1, when there is no any correlation between two images, the value is 0; vice versa, if two images are completely matched, CC tends to 1, meaning a very ideal situation. As a matter of fact,, the value of CC often is very small, especially for multimodal medical image registration.

The quantitative evaluation results for each registration method are shown in Table.1. The MI, RMS, and CC are used to evaluate each registration method, by analyzing the qualitative indexes for each method, it can be concluded that the presented registration algorithm is better than other traditional methods.

Registration method	MI	CC	RMS
Before registration	0.308430	0.648445	51.824407
Maximum mutual information	0.315437	0.671658	51.760785
Principle axes algorithm	0.280123	0.634221	52.125753
Multi-level B-splines	0.342456	0.692275	50.753875
The proposed mehtod (principle axes algorithm + H B-splines)	0.372521	0.701248	50.554238

Table 1. Comparisons among different registration methods

6.1.2 Effect evaluation for fusion method

In the experiment, CT slices(512*512*267) and PET(128*128*267) are from a male lung-cancer person. CT and PET sequence images are fused by applying the presented parallel multimodal medical image fusion method based on wavelet transform with fusion rule of combining the local standard deviation and energy. Results are shown as Fig.13, in which Fig.13(a) is No.183 CT slice of sequence images, Fig.13(b) is No.183 PET slice, Fig.13(c) is the corresponding matched result of Fig.13(a) and Fig.13(b) by using the presented registration method, and Fig.13(d) is the corresponding fusion image of them. There is some nodular shadows in basel segment of the lower lobe of left lung by viewing the CT slice. And there is a bright spot in the middle of the PET slice, which displays a high absorption region of imaging radiopharmaceuticals, yet the morphology of the cancer region is not very clear. The fusion image depict clearly the corresponding relation between the region of nodular shadows in CT slice and the region of cancer permeability in PET slice. Experimental results demonstrate that the edge and texture features of the multimodal images are reserved effectively by the presented fusion method based on wavelet transform with the fusion rule of combining the local standard deviation and energy. Therefore, the relative position between the tumor and its adjacent tissues could be obtained easily through analyzing the medical data sets which are fused the information of functional mages and anatomical images.

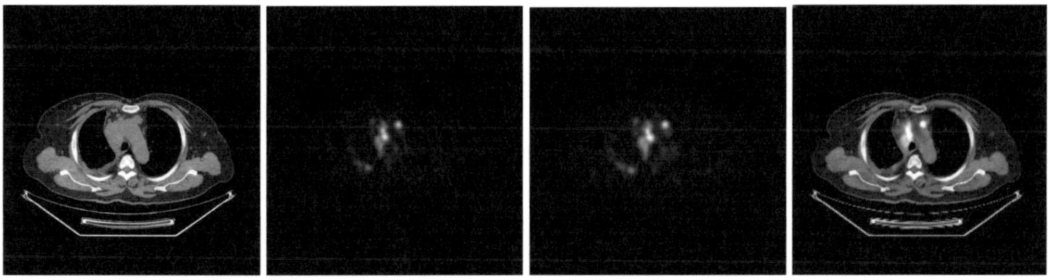

(a)Original CT image (b)Original PET image (c)Matched image (d) Fusion image

Fig. 13. Chest CT and PET image fusion

6.1.1 Effect evaluation for registration method

Generally, fusion image evaluation criteria includes the subjective evaluation and objective evaluation. The objective valuation method is used in this chapter. Various statistical characteristics of the image are used, such as mean, standard deviation, entropy and cross-entropy.

1. Standard deviation (SD) Gray variance reflects the extent of deviation from the mean of the gray value. The greater the standard deviation is, the more dispersed the distribution of gray levels is.
2. Information entropy (IE) Information entropy reflects the average amount of information that the fusion image contains. The larger the entropy is, the more information the image carries. The image's information entropy E is defined:

$$E = -\sum_{i=0}^{Z} P_i \log_2 P_i \tag{20}$$

   Where Z is the maximum gray level, P_i is the probability of i gray level.
3. Joint entropy (JE) The larger the joint entropy between fusion image and original image is, the more information the fusion image contains. The joint entropy between fusion image F and original image A is defined as follows.

$$UE_{FA} = -\sum_{i=0}^{Z_F} \sum_{j=0}^{Z_A} P_{FA}(i,j) \log_2 P_{FA}(i,j) \tag{21}$$

   Where, P_{FA} represents the joint probability density of two images.

In this experiment, the fusion results are evaluated by applying the above methods. Experiments show that the evaluation indexes of this presented method are superior to other fusion methods, the evaluation indexes of each method are shown in Table 2.

6.2 Efficiency comparison

6.2.1 Efficiency comparison for registration method

In this chapter, multimodal medical image registration is adapted based on adaptive free-form deformation and gradient descent. Moreover, the feature points are matched based on parallel computing. So, comparing to the traditional methods, the efficiency of the presented registration method has been greatly improved.

	SD	IE	JE (CT)	JE(PET)
weighted mean	328.545	4.691806	6.143996	5.620486
maximum	385.560	4.830680	8.370359	5.902740
local energy	162.497	5.052476	8.376337	6.134338
local standard deviation	415.144	5.810895	7.730113	6.800253
The presented method	383.129	5.987878	8.423761	6.997364

Table 2. Quantitative evaluation of fusion image

1. Efficiency of registration process of based on adaptive free-form deformation and gradient descent

As shown in Fig.14(a) and Fig.14(b), the average number of cycling for the presented method is about 3.12, and the registration position is searched only using about 84.24 steps. While the number of cycling for the traditional method is about 50 to 60 and more than 300 steps for searching, much larger than the presented algorithm. It demonstrates that the presented registration method is more efficient, and its searching speed is much faster than traditional algorithm.

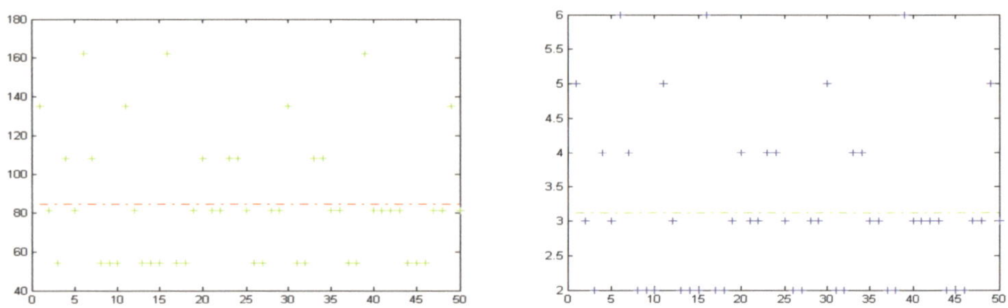

(a) Algorithm search step (b) Algorithm cycle number

Fig. 14. Efficiency of the presented algorithm based on Gradient Descent

2. Efficiency of feature-points matching based on parallel computing

In the experiment, 3 pairs CT-PET images, in which CT resolution is 512*512 and PET resolution is 128*128, are from a male lung-cancer person.

The runtime of feature-points matching based on parallel computing in the cluster computing system is shown in Fig.15.The runtime of all the registration process based serial computing is 335 seconds. The runtime of the process of feature-points matching based on serial computing is 170 seconds, and the runtime of finding the corresponding feature points of CT image from PET image is 156.5 seconds, which accounts for 92% of all the feature-points-matching process. The runtime of feature-points matching based on parallel computing using 5 processors is 32 seconds, and all the registration process costs 43 seconds. It is obvious that the runtime of registration decreases obviously. Moreover, the parallel system efficiency keeps about 0.97, thus the algorithm is of good expansibility so that the runtime will decrease more if more processors is used. It is obvious that the runtime of registration decreases obviously.

So, comparing to the traditional methods, the efficiency of the presented registration method has been greatly improved. Because, on one hand, the presented multimodal medical image registration is adapted based on adaptive FFD and gradient descent; on other hand, the feature points are matched efficiently based on parallel computing.

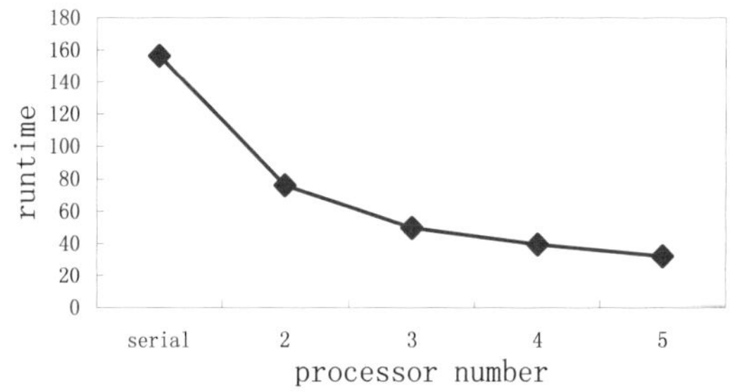

Fig. 15. Efficiency of the feature-point matching based on parallel computing

6.2.2 Efficiency comparison for fusion method

In order to evaluate the performance of parallel computing, two parameters must be introduced: the speedup factor $S(p)$ and parallel efficiency E (Yasuhiro K. et al., 2004).

$$S(p) = ts / tp \tag{22}$$

Where $S(p)$ is a measure of relative performance; p is the number of processors; tp is the execution time for solving the same problem on a multiprocessor; ts is the execution time of the best sequential algorithm running on a single processor.

It is sometimes useful to know how long processors are being used on the computation, which can be found from the system efficiency. The efficiency, E, is defined as

$$E = S(p) / p \tag{23}$$

The comparison of run time is shown in Table 3. It is obvious that the runtime of parallel sequence images fusion decreases obviously. From Table 3, the runtime of sequences image(267 images) fusion is only 43.773 seconds if using parallel computation of 6 processors, which is far less than that of sequential algorithm. Moreover, the parallel system efficiency keeps about 0.97, thus the algorithm is of good expansibility so that the runtime will decrease more if more processors is used. So it can be concluded that the calculation time is fast enough for clinical use.

	sequential algorithm	Parallel algorithm			
		processor 1	processors 2	processors 4	processors 6
runtime	251.468s	259.757s	130.103s	65.090s	43.773s
$S(p)$	--	0.97	1.93	3.86	5.74
E	--	0.97	0.97	0.97	0.96

Table 3. Time performance of parallel sequences image fusion(267 images)

6.3 Experiment results in 3D Conformal Radiotherapy Treatment Planning

The experiment results in 3D CRTPS are shown as Fig.16. Fig.16 is the interface of 3D Conformal Radiotherapy Treatment Planning System(3D CRTPS) which is developed by ourselves. Fig.16(a) and 16(b) consist of four windows respectively: No.1 is the 3D volume rendering result; No.3 and No.4 are CT image(512*512) and PET image(128*128), respectively. These slices correspond to the position showed by white line in No.1 window; No.2 is the registration and fusion result of CT and PET. The technologist can give diagnosis by using the system.

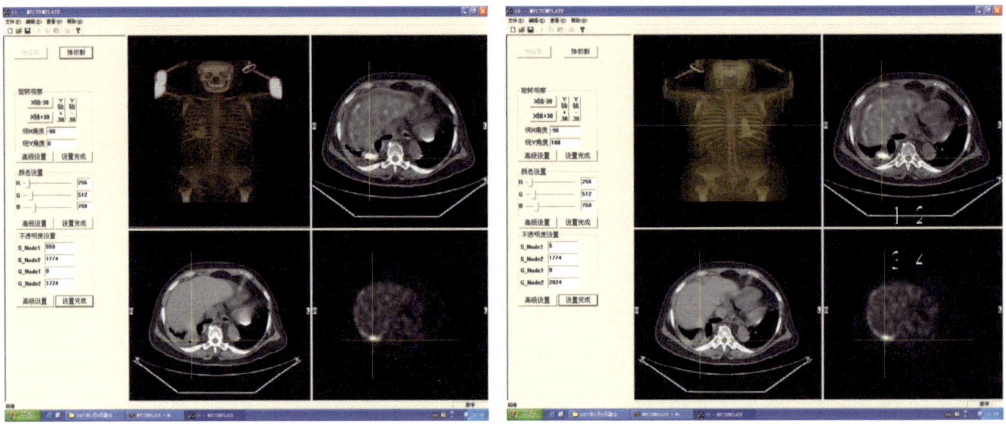

(a) Viewed from the front (b) Viewed from the back

Fig. 16. Experimental result of cases

7. Discussions and conclusions

A rapid image registration and fusion method is presented in this chapter. This presented automatic registration method is based on parallel computing and hierarchical adaptive free-form deformation(FFD) algorithm. After the registration of multimodal images, their sequence images are fused by applying a image fusion method based on wavelet transform with the fusion rule of combining the local standard deviation and energy.

The results of the validation study indicate that the presented multimodal medical image registration and fusion method can improve effect and efficiency and meet the requirement of 3D conformal radiotherapy treatment planning. And the radiologists who validated the results felt the errors were generally within clinically acceptable ranges.

By analyzing the qualitative indexes, such as MI, RMS, and CC, for each method, it can be concluded that the presented registration algorithm is better than other traditional methods. And experiments show that the evaluation indexes(SD, IE, JE) of this presented method are superior to other fusion methods, such as the weighted mean method, the maximum method, the local energy method and the local standard deviation method.

In addition, comparing to the traditional methods, the efficiency of the presented registration and fusion method has been greatly improved, because in this chapter multimodal medical image registration is realized based on gradient descent, and the feature points are matched based on parallel computing. Moreover, image fusion is also carried out by parallel computing.

8. References

Aparna Kanakatte, Jayavardhana Gubbi, Nallasamy Mani, et al.(2007). A pilot study of automatic lung tumor segmentation from positron emission tomograph images using standard uptake values, *Proceedings of the 2007 IEEE Symposium on Computational Intelligence in Image and Signal Processing (CIISP 2007)*, pp. 363-368, ISBN:1-4244-0707-9, conference location: Honolulu, HI, USA, June, 2007, IEEE, Los Alamitos

Bardinet E, Cohen LD, Ayache N. (1996). Tracking and motion analysis of the ventricle with deformable superquadrics. *Medical Image Analysis*, Vol.1, No.2, 1996, 129-149, ISSN:1361-8415

Chan T F, Vese L A. (2001). Active contours without edges. *IEEE Transaction on Image Processing*, Vol.10, No.2, 2001, 266-277, ISSN:1057-7149

David M., David R.H. , et al. (2003). PET-CT image registration in the chest using free-form deformations. *IEEE Transaction on Medical Image*, Vol.22, No.1, 2003, 120-128, ISSN: 0278-0062

Huang Xiaolei, Paragios, N.; Metaxas, D.N.(2006). Shape registration in implicit spaces using information theory and free form deformations. *IEEE Transactions on Pattern Analysis and Machine Intelligence*, Vol.28, No.8, 2006, 1303- 1318, ISSN:0162-8828

Ino Fumihiko, Ooyama Kanrou, and Hagihara Kenichi.(2005). A data distributed parallel algorithm for nonrigid image registration. *Parallel Computing*, Vol..31, No.1, 2005, 19-43, ISSN:0167-8191

Josien P. W. Pluim, J. B., Antoine Maintz, and Max A. Viergever(2003). Mutual-information-based registration of medical images: A Survey. *IEEE Transaction on Medical Image*, Vol.22, No.8, 2003, 986-1004, ISSN: 0278-0062

Lee Seungyong, Wolberg George, and Shin Sung Yong. (1997). Scattered data interpolation with multilevel B-Splines. *IEEE Transactions on Visualization and Computer Graphics*, Vol.3, No.3, 1997, 228-244, ISSN:1077-2626.

Louis K A, Atam P D, Joseph P B.(1995). Three_dimensional anatomical model_based segmentation of MR brain images through principal axes registration. *IEEE transactions on biomedical engineering*, Vol.42, No.11, 1995, 1069-1077, ISSN: 0018-9294

Maintz J.B.A., Vigergever M.A. (1998). A survey of medical image registration. *Medical Image Analysis*, Vol.2, No.1, 1998, 1-36, ISSN:1361-8415

M. Betke, H. Hong, and J. P. Ko. (2003). Landmark detection in the chest and registration of lung surfaces with an application to nodule registration. *Medical Image Analysis*, No.7, 2003, 265-281, ISSN:1361-8415

Park J H, Kim K O, Yang Y K.(2001). Image Fusion Using Multiresolution Analysis, *IEEE Int'l Conf on Geoscience and Remote Sensing (IGARSS)*, pp. 864-866, ISBN:0-7803-7031-7, conference location: Sydney, NSW, Australia, 2001, IEEE, Los Alamitos

Ruechert D., Sonoda L.I., Hayes C., et al.(1999). Nonrigid registration using free-form deformations:application to breast MR images. *IEEE Transaction on Medical Image*, Vol.18, No.8, 1999, 712-721, ISSN: 0278-0062

S-C. Huang. (2000). Anatomy of SUV. Nuclear medicine and biology, Vol.27, No.7, 2000, 643-646, ISSN:0969-8051

S.K.Warfield, F.A.Jolesz, and R.Kikinis.(1998). A high performance computing approach to the registration of medical image data. *Parallel Computing,* Vol..24, 1998, 1345-1368, ISSN:0167-8191

Stefan Klein, Marius S., josien P.W.P. (2007). Evaluation of optimization methods for nonrigid medical image registration using mutual information and B-Splines. *IEEE Transaction on Image Processing,* Vol.16, No.12, 2007, 2879-2890, ISSN:1057-7149

Studholme C, Hill DLG, Hawkes DJ (1999). An overlap invariant entropy measure of 3D medical images alignment. *Pattern Recognition,* Vol.32,No.1, 1999, 71-86, ISSN:0031-3203

T. Blaffert && R. Wiemker. (2004). Comparison of different follow-up lung registration methods with and without segmentation, *SPIE,* vol. 5370, 2004, 1701-1708, ISSN:0277-786X

Yasuhiro K., Fumihiko I., Yasuharu M., et al.(2004). High-performance computing service over the internet for intraoperative image processing. *IEEE transactions on information technology in biomedicine,* Vol.8, No.1, 2004, 36-46, ISSN:1089-7771

Zhiyong Xie, Gerald E. Farin.(2004). Image Registration Using Hierarchical B-Splines. *IEEE Transactions on Visualization and Computer Graphics,* Vol.10, No.1, 2004, 85-94, ISSN:1077-2626

20

Image-fusion for Biopsy, Intervention, and Surgical Navigation in Urology

Osamu Ukimura[1,2], M.D., Ph.D.
[1]*Institute of Urology, University of Southern California, Los Angeles,*
[2]*Department of Urology, Kyoto Prefectural University of Medicine, Kyoto*
[1]*USA,*
[2]*Japan*

1. Introduction

Due to the recent increased use of diagnostic abdominal imaging and/or serum prostate specific antigen (PSA) test, both incidental small renal tumors and low-risk prostate cancer are being detected more frequently. This leads to greater numbers of asymptomatic organ-confined early cancers in urology. Treatment strategy needs therefore to be reassessed because of the lack of comparative evidence in effectiveness and the harm of current standard radical invasive treatments especially for such early low-risk asymptomatic cancers *(Hollingsworth et al 2006, Wilt et al 2007).* The precision of the imaging for staging and localization of the diseases is an important problem so that this brings patients a benefit, avoiding the over-diagnosis of clinically insignificant cancer (which does not need to be treated) as well as under-diagnosis of advanced cancers (which definitely need to be treated.) As such, imaging technology is now evolving, and focal therapy for prostate and kidney cancer has attracted attention in urology *(Gill et al 2010, Eggener et al 2007).* Focal therapy aims to achieve targeted control or cure of the malignancy as well as preservation of organ function in order to maintain the QOL of individual patients.
Looking back on the history of urology, there was a definite step when urologists began to practise transurethral resection of bladder tumors (TUR-Bt), and this can be clearly categorised as a type of minimally invasive focal therapy. TUR-Bt can achieve the clinical control or cure of superficial bladder cancer as well as preservation of the bladder in order to maintain QOL, while allowing the patient to urinate through his or her own urethra, avoiding problematic urinary stoma on the abdominal skin. Such focal therapy can be performed generally in the out-patient day surgery, and is also repeatable at a certain interval if indicated. Should the disease become upgraded or upstaged during active surveillance after such focal therapy, the patients would reasonably accept radical treatment when indicated later.
On the other hand, historically we also find shared critical opinion against focal therapy in prostate cancer for 3 main reasons in recent years: firstly, the technological therapeutic difficulty of focal treatment; secondly, the lack of reliable imaging to localize and characterize potentially multifocal and multi-grade prostate cancers; and thirdly, the immaturity of navigation technology to achieve precise 3-dimensional targeting to the biopsy-proven cancer lesion.

However, with increased knowledge of the natural history of prostate cancer, it is now discussed that the prognostic importance of the index prostate cancer, which is a cancer with the highest grade and largest volume in an individual prostate and must determine the individual prognosis of the disease. As such, the important hypothesis has arisen that we might be able to achieve reasonable oncological control by focal therapy, targeting the index-lesion at least, while preserving the healthy parts of the prostate and peri-prostatic tissue that contribute to maintaining urinary continence and sexual function. This would be recommended for patients who are reluctant to accept active surveillance or conservative treatment (*Eggener et al, 2007*).

The current therapeutic standard for clinical localized renal cancer is surgical removal, preferably in the form of nephron-sparing surgery, supported by durable oncological outcomes and overall survival, while active surveillance and minimally invasive ablative techniques have emerged as potential alternatives in carefully selected patients (*Gill et al, 2010*).

Accordingly, for both kidney and prostate cancers, we are facing a real challenge towards endoscopic robotic-assisted surgery, focal ablative therapy, and further computer-assisted, minimally invasive ablation (such as cryosurgery, laser therapy, radiofrequency ablation), or extra-corporeal therapy (such as high-intensity focused ultrasound). A reliable image navigation system would become an essential tool, to facilitate realization of where the surgical pathological targets and vital healthy anatomies are located in the surgical field beyond the surgeon's direct vision or underneath the palpable anatomies. Image-navigation would help intra-operative appropriate decision-making before surgical exposure of the target has even been made, to minimize any iatrogenic injury to the surrounding healthy tissues, and to lead to precise surgical dissection or appropriate delivery of the ablative energy to the surgical target while preserving safe surgical margins. Real-time anatomical and pathological visualization is required for intra-operative navigation, although there may be no perfect single imaging modality to achieve this image-navigation mission. In addition, instead of free-hand control, computer-assistance and robotic control of the surgical instruments or interventional probes could increase procedural accuracy while potentially decreasing the learning curve. "Image-fusion" integrated with such computer-assistance and robotic control would become the key technology.

Active surveillance could increasingly become an important option for the management of low risk kidney and prostate cancers. The optimal biopsy protocol is still controversial in both kidney and prostate, and a new reliable biopsy protocol should be considered since the pathological evidence given by needle biopsy specimens could be one of the key components for determining the oncologic management of these organs.

To obtain reliable information from biopsy sampling, precise spatial targeting accuracy is critical. Since CT-guidance and MR-guidance require expensive facilities and significant expertise in intervention, image-fusion guidance, such as real-time US fusion with previously acquired enhanced CT for the kidney and enhanced MR for the prostate, would provide a clinically relevant opportunity for urologists. The recently emerging technology of "image-fusion" in urology includes the spatial tracking system of a 2D US probe or interventional needle with attached electromagnetic and/or optical sensors or with robotic control. Another technology involves the acquisition of real-time 3D volume data in order to track with more reality in the spatial targeted fields. This article intends to discuss the advantages and limitations in the current proposed techniques of "image fusion" in biopsy, intervention, and surgery in urology.

Among the various image-guided procedures in urology, percutaneous drainage/aspiration, percutaneous nephrostomy, percutaneous renal biopsy or renal ablative therapy (for placement of a cryo-surgery probe or radiofrequency probe), transrectal/transperineal prostate biopsy, and transperineal cryo-surgery or brachytherapy for prostate cancer could be listed as clinically frequent in diagnostic and interventional procedures. Image-guidance in urology could be performed by an urologist with expertise in imaging, but has frequently been performed with the help of an uro-radiologist. The choice of the imaging modality for kidney intervention has been based on the preference of the physicians. For prostate intervention, transrectal ultrasound (TRUS) has been the gold standard as the guidance tool for prostate biopsy delivery. However, controversial issues continue due to a current misjudgment of the true value of TRUS as well as emerging MR technology.

2. Percutaneous renal intervention

Percutaneous imaging guided biopsy and tumor ablation has an increasingly prominent role as minimally invasive management for renal tumors. Precise biopsy needle and ablative probe placement as well as safe and effective ablation are key steps for successful management. In renal intervention such as in the development of neprostomy, investigators, especially in the USA, considered fluoroscopy as an essential tool for guide-wire introduction, nephrostomy tract dilation, and nephrostomy tube placement (*Barbaric et al 1984, Ko et al 2008*). Others, especially in Europe and Japan, have preferred ultrasound guidance during puncture of the renal collecting system (*Saitoh e al 1982, Skolarikos et al, 2005*). Most often many current investigators now understand the advantages in combining the use of these 2 real-time imaging modalities for renal puncture. Since the pathologic fluid collection or renal collecting system are generally dilated to >10 mm, such a dilated collection system can be targeted so easily that image-guidance at this setting may not require very detailed anatomical signal/noise ratio or imaging expertise. On the other hand, in order to achieve precise targeting of a small renal mass, renal tumor biopsy and tumor ablative therapy are most often guided by CT fluoroscopy (*Remzi e al 2009, Leveridge et al 2010*), although it may be also precisely guided under US-guidance if performed by US experts (*Atwell et al 2007, Bassignani et al 2004*). Although US visualization of the kidney is excellent, the major disadvantages of US-guidance include the requirement of significant experience in interpretation of the peri-renal anatomy and vasculatures, difficulty of obtaining high-quality images in obese patients, and the difficulty in access of the upper-pole where the US-beam is blocked by the 11th and 12th rib-bones. The major disadvantage of CT fluoroscopy is the radiation exposure for both patients and physicians, and almost all of these CT-guided procedures were performed by radiologists because of its availability. In addition, since percutaneous CT-guided intervention generally uses un-enhanced CT images, intra-renal tumor margins are often hardly identified. Similarly, although the recent introduction of real-time MR is a promising tool, there is also the considerable issue in the availability of such expensive MR-compatible instruments and facilities. As such, pioneer experience of image-guided percutanous renal intervention required considerable expertise with such high-resolution imaging, and the limited availability of the expensive imaging modality was the significant issue for urologists. There is no doubt that enhanced CT is the most reliable, standard imaging for the diagnosis of renal mass. However, enhanced visualization of the renal tumor is dynamically transient. It does not continue long enough to be useful during entire interventional real-time procedures, and importantly, it can not be repeated often since the contrast enhancer is harmful to the renal function.

As such, to my best knowledge, the most promising solution for overcoming both the technical difficulties and the lack of availability of enhanced CT imaging is to use image-fusion of real-time imaging with pre-operatively acquired enhanced CT volume data, which can be integrated with a needle/probe tracking system by GPS(global positioning system)-like technology. Recently, various image-fusion guided techniques have been proposed, which are undergoing research to demonstrate their technical feasibility in preliminary clinical studies (*Ukimura & Gill 2008, Ukimura & Gill 2009, Haber et al 2010*). However, it may be still challenging to achieve clinically relevant accuracy in image-registration as well as in needle/probe placement, which has to be available during the limited computation time, taking into account each patient's deformable anatomies during the real-surgical procedures.

In 2002, Leroy et al reported a pioneer work on the registration of kidney contours by CT and US images, and also investigated the automated voxel based registration of CT with 3D US, achieving 3.1 mm in registration accuracy, although requiring 80 sec. in computation time (*Leroy et al 2002, Leroy et al and 2004*). In 2004, Osorio et al presented augmented reality visualization that allowed projection of pre-operative CT onto the patient's body, although this system does not achieve real-time monitoring of the procedure (*Osorio et al 2004*). In 2005, Mozer et al evaluated the accuracy of the fusion of CT with real-time US for percutaneous renal access, reporting the encouraging registration accuracy of 4.7 mm between planned and reached targets (*Mozer et al 2005*). They noted that error was mainly due to needle deflection during puncture.

For precise needle/probe placement, a GPS-like technique for navigation of the needle tract would be ideal in combination with image-fusion guidance. For this purpose, investigators have used an infrared optical tracking system, to track optical sensors which were located 3-dimensionally, and a tracking handle for guidance of the cryoprobe placement (*Haber et al 2010*). Similarly, a magnetic sensor mounted radio-frequency ablative probe can be used for real-time surgical planning to overlay 3D data of the theoretical therapeutic area onto the registered 3D volume of the CT which was pre-registered with real-time US images (*Crocetti et al 2008*).

In the fusion of two imaging modalities, image-registration has been classified as "rigid registration" or "non-rigid registration". Since the urological organs are often shifted by respiration or deformed by surgical manipulation, rigid registration may not be a sufficiently precise image-fusion for routine clinical use in urology. Recent efforts in non-rigid registration between pre-operative high-resolution imaging and real-time imaging potentially provide a new powerful opportunity to take into account the deformation of the organs in image-fusion guided intervention or surgery.

Wein et al reported a non-rigid registration for the image fusion of pre-operative contrast enhanced CT with intra-operative US images at the time of renal biopsy and radio-frequency-ablation, to achieve a fiducial registration error of 5 mm (Wein *et al* 2008). More recently, Oguro et al have proven that a non-rigid registration technique (fiducial registration error of 1.7 mm) was more accurate than a rigid registration technique (fiducial registration error of 5 mm) when fusing pre-procedural contrast-enhanced MR images to unenhanced CT images during CT-guided percutaneous cryoablation of renal tumors (*Oguro et al 2010*). The non-rigid registration technique promises to improve visualization of renal tumors using pre-procedural enhanced imaging during unenhanced CT-guided cryoablation procedures, although current limitation of the highly precise non-rigid registration does require the significantly long time of 15 minutes to perform. Further technological improvements are being investigated.

3. Augmented reality in surgical navigation

Soft tissue navigation systems in urologic surgery are evolving. The augmented reality surgical navigation technique has been most widely used in the field of neurosurgery (*Iseki et al 1997, Kawamata et al 2002*), in which there is a clear advantage of minimum organ motion in a relatively fixed surgical field within a bony frame, facilitating the registration of the 3D image data. Augmented reality for the management of intra-abdominal soft organs was challenging (*Marescaux et al 2004, Osorio et al 2004, Ukimura & Gill 2007*), because intra-abdominal organs may suffer more from respiratory motion or deformation by manipulation.

Ukimura and colleagues have demonstrated the feasibility of augmented reality in laparoscopic surgery for partial nephrectomy and prostatectomy, using optical tracking systems of the dynamic motion of the surgical instruments, with computer-assisted synchronization of the developed 3D image from the 3D volume data of enhanced CT or intra-operatively acquired 3D volume data of transrectal ultrasound images (*Ukimura & Gill 2007, Ukimura & Gill 2008, Ukimura & Gill 2009*). The approach is technically feasible, but many issues need to be resolved before its clinical wide-spread use in the fields of surgery dealing with soft tissue organs. Nevertheless, recent advancement in augmented reality in urological surgery deserves attention.

Su et al. described a stereo-endoscopic visualization system for augmented reality overlay during robot assisted laparoscopic partial nephrectomy. The stereoscopic system allows the 3D-to-3D registration system of the preoperative CT scan without external tracking devices, using image-based surface tracking technology to track gross movement, with an update rate of 10 Hz and an overlay latency of four frames to place a reconstructed 3D CT image onto the stereo video footage (*Su et al 2009*). Teber et al. reported an augmented reality assisted soft-tissue navigation system using a mobile C-Arm capable of cone-beam imaging, which required the surgeon to insert four or more needle-shaped navigation aids into the target organ (*Teber et al 2009*). Herrell et al. demonstrated an augmented reality guided laparoscopic procedure using tissue mimicking phantoms, to compare their named 'resection ratio', that was defined as the ratio of dissected tissue compared to the ideal resection, between with and without augmented reality image guidance (*Herrel et al 2009*). The resection ratio (3.26) in using image guidance was significantly smaller than that (9.01) in using no image guidance, potentially leading to a decrease of benign tissue removal while maintaining an appropriate surgical margin.

The challenge continues in the real-time tracking of organ motion and deformation, to achieve real-time dynamic navigation through an ongoing surgical procedure. In particular, conventional optical tracking systems and wired magnetic tracking systems are not suitable for tracking internal organ motion. An emerging technology, named the Calypso 4-D localization system (calypso Medical Technologies, Inc., Seattle, WA, USA), is a miniature, wireless magnetic tracking system, which was applied to tracking the prostate motion during external radiotherapy (*Kupelian et al 2007*). We have applied this new technology for an endoscopic augmented reality system to demonstrate real-time dynamic superimposition of the pre-operatively acquired CT image onto the endoscopic image of the moving organ during advancing surgical manipulation (*Nakamoto et al 2008, Ukimura & Gill 2009*). Such augmented reality image navigation with a 4D-dynamic organ tracking system, being integrated with robotic controlled surgical systems, is likely to herald higher precision surgery in the near future.

4. Image-fusion for radiotherapy, prostate biopsy, and lesion-targeted prostate intervention

Pioneer works in the image-fusion of prostate imaging were reported in the field of radiotherapy including external beam radiation therapy and brachytherapy, using fusions of CT, MR, ultrasound, and/or fluoroscopy (*Holupka et al 1996, Lau et al 1996, Kagawa et al 1997, Amdur et al 1999, Reynier et al 2004, Daanen et al 2006, Su et al 2007*). In addition, the potential value of image fusion of Doppler TRUS with MRI in the staging of prostatic cancer was discussed (*Selli et al 2007*). However, recent attention to image fusion technology for prostate cancer is more toward its value in improving the quality of prostate biopsy by precisely targeting the image-suspicious area, in mapping the 3D localization of biopsy-proven prostate cancer, as well as its value in navigating image-guided focal therapy (*Ukimura 2010*).

Real-time TRUS has been the gold standard of prostate biopsy guidance, and therapeutic intervention, because of the advantages of its real-time nature, its easy-handling, the fact that it is urologist-friendly, its relatively inexpensiveness, and its non-invasiveness. However, the current role of 2D real-time TRUS imaging to visualize the prostate anatomy as a simple delivery tool of biopsy rarely provides information on the spatial location of prostate cancer. On the other hand, diagnostic multi-function MRI for the prostate has achieved increasingly higher levels of accuracy in detection and localization of cancer in its 3D volume data (*Kirkham et al 2006, Villers et al 2006, Yakara et al 2010*). However, since real-time MR-guided targeted biopsy is still a complicated and expensive procedure, there is considerable interest in a technique of MR/ TRUS hybridized image-guided biopsy.

Reported rigid MR/TRUS fusion techniques (*Kaplan et al 2002, Xu et al 2007, Singh et al 2008, Turkbey et al 2010*) had a limitation when deformation occurred between MR and TRUS. Importantly, because the 3-D shapes of the prostate at the time of image-acquisition at preoperative MRI are likely to be different from the intra-operative TRUS images, the precise registration of each 3-D volume data is critical. In order to reduce the potential errors in rigid registration of TRUS with MRI, one solution may include preoperative MR images being obtained while a plastic outer-frame, of exactly the same shape as the real TRUS probe, is placed in the rectum, in order to simulate the deformation of the prostate caused by the absence or presence of a TRUS probe during the acquisition of MR or TRUS images (*Ukimura 2010*). For another potential solution, Hu and colleagues described a technique using a patient specific model of MR/TRUS deformation built from simulated data for image-registration (*Hu et al 2009*). A more attractive developed technique for improvement of registration in MR/TRUS image-fusion is the introduction of automatic, non-rigid (elastic) registration technology (*Baumann et al, 2009, Martin et al 2010*). This new elastic fusion technique allows making automatic segmentation of the prostate in TRUS images by deforming a patient specific 3D model built from MR image to TRUS data.

As mentioned already, unfortunately, clinical urologists generally use TRUS only as a simple delivery system for systematic sextant biopsies toward the planned segmental locations, with no detailed 3D anatomical records of the sampled localization, and by just naming the biopsy sample with a rough sextant site for review. Since urologists often need repeat biopsies, this led to the current trend of taking an increased number of initial biopsies, and also to the risk of delivering the repeat biopsy needle to spots that have previously been shown to be negative for cancer, and of failing to make the necessary deliveries for previously un-sampled locations. In order to facilitate the emerging strategy of focal therapy for prostate cancer which may require precise 3D mapping of biopsy-proven cancer, individual recording of the 3D localization of each biopsy would be the key issue. As such, transperineal template grid-based 3D mapping biopsy has been proposed (*Barzell & Melamed 2007, Onik et al 2009*). However, current ongoing transperineal template 3D mapping biopsy may require 5-mm grid based techniques to detect clinically significant cancer, resulting in a tremendous number of required biopsies, for example, over 100 samples in a large prostate. We are hoping that the improved image-fusion technique of MR and TRUS, and the elastic fusion of 3D real-time TRUS for 3D biopsy mapping techniques (*Mozer et al 2009, Ukimura 2010*) could improve the clinically relevant strategy for prostate biopsy, and also the image-guided management of prostate cancer in the near future.

5. Molecular and radionuclide imaging for urology

Targeted radionuclide therapy offers potential determination of targeted cancer specific accumulation by molecular imaging with single photon computed tomography (SPECT) or positron emission tomography (PET). In this decade, computer-assisted integration of anatomical and functional images has been demonstrated as a hybrid of PET/CT [Townsend, 2001] as well as a fusion of SPECT/CT (*Schillaci et al 2005*), providing us a new opportunity of interpretation of side-by-side or overlaid dual modalities. Cancer specific molecular imaging and radionuclide therapy is attractive for the early detection and staging of malignancies, and for the precise selection of patients who would benefit from molecular-based targeted therapy and monitoring.

18F-FDP (fluorodeoxyglucose) PET/CT has been widely used in the management of various malignancies showing an increase of glucose metabolism leading to uptake of 18F-FDP, although the urinary excretion of 18F-FDP and relatively low uptake of 18F-FDP especially in small sized foci (<5mm) of prostate cancer and some types of renal cancer were a clear limitation of its expansion in urology. At the same time, other PET tracers have recently demonstrated improved accuracy of PET/CT, which include 11C-choline, 18F-fluorocholine, 11C-acetate, and 18F- fluoride that might correlate to prognosis and localization in prostate cancer (*Wachter et al 2007, Bouchelouche& Oehr J Urol 2008, Piert et al 2009, Poulsen et al 2010*).

The fusion image of SPECT with CT might also improve the role of imaging in the diagnosis and therapy of prostate caner *(Krengli et al 2006, Sodee et al 2007)*. The usefulness of pretreatment 111-Indium capromab pendetide radio-immuno-scintigraphy plus SPECT co-registration with CT scans has been demonstrated in detection of occult metastatic disease and predicting for biochemical failure in patients who had evidence of that possibility after radiotherapy (Ellis *et al* 2008). This image-fusion capability leads to a new proposed strategy for image-guided radiation therapy to favor dose-escalation to the regions as defined by focal uptake on radio-immuno-scintigraphy fusion with anatomical image sets (CT or MRI) (*Ellis & Kaminsky 2006*).

However, there is still challenge in molecular-based diagnosis and radionuclide therapy for clinically personalized use, which requires improved detection and efficacy in large clinical trials.

6. Conclusions

Image-fusion technology would improve detection of urological malignancies and precision of intervention in minimally invasive urology, and are now increasingly under research for biopsy needle guidance and therapeutic navigation. In particular, the non-rigid image fusion of real-time US with contrast-enhanced CT/MR, 3-dimensional mapping of biopsy localization, 3-dimensional image-guided lesion-targeted ablation therapy, augmented reality, and tumor-specific diagnostic imaging have been attracting increased attention.

7. Figure legends

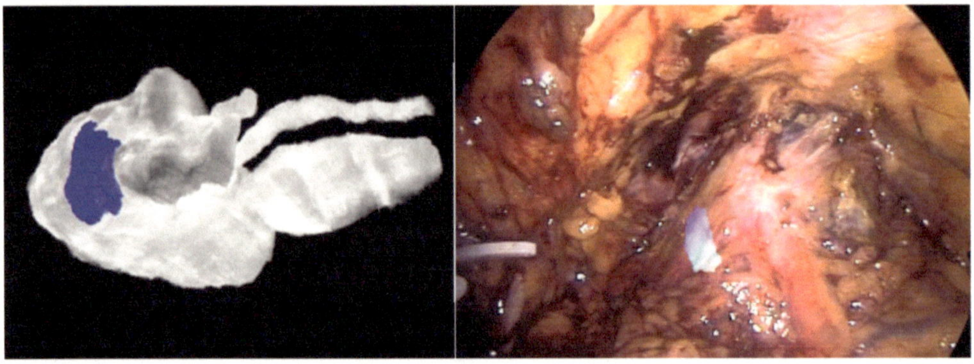

Fig. 1. Augmented reality during laparoscopic nerve-sparing radical prostatectomy
The biopsy-proven cancer area (blue), built from intra-operatively acquired 3D TRUS image, was overlaid on the real-time laparoscopic image during laparoscopic nerve-sparing radical prostatectomy

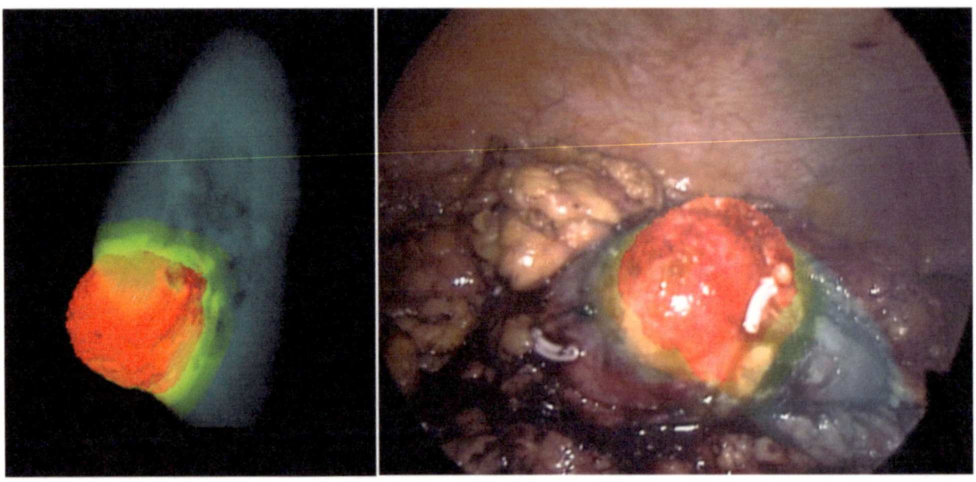

Fig. 2. Augmented reality during laparoscopic partial nephrectomy
The color-coded zonal anatomy (tumor by red, 0-5 mm margin by yeallow, 5-10 mm margin by green, beyond 10mm margin by blue), built from pre-operative contrast enhanced CT image, was overlaid on the real-time laparoscopic image during laparoscopic partial nephrectomy

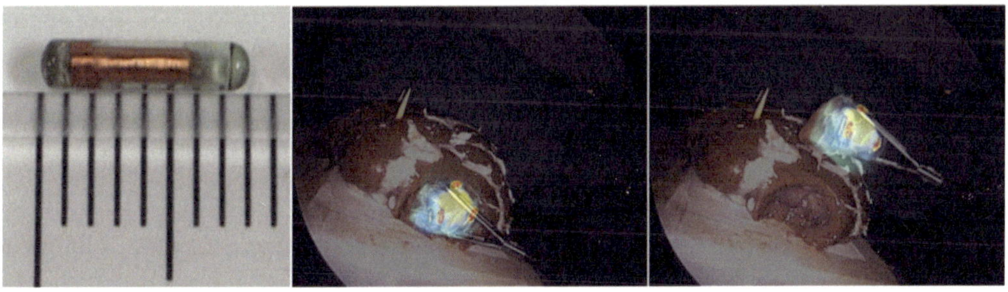

Fig. 3. 4D Augmented reality navigation
Using body-GPS (left, Calypso miniature wireless magnetic tracking system) to track real-timely the motion of the organ, 3D model of pre-operative CT was real-timely overlaid onto the laparoscopic view during ongoing surgical manipulation (middle, overlaid image at the initial position of the tumor) (right, real-timely overlaid image on the lifted-up tumor with safe surgical margin)

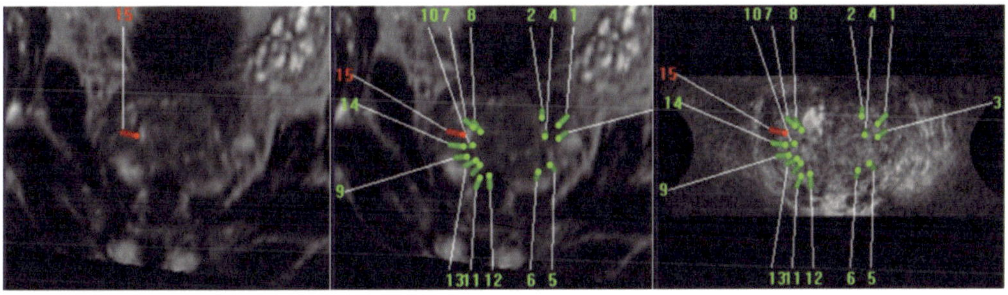

Fig. 4. MR/TRUS fusion image-guided biopsy with overlaid images of each biopsy trajectory
Left, positive cancer biopsy trajectory overlaid on the MR-visible lesion (low intensity lesion on T2 image)
Middle, overlaid images of each biopsy trajectory on the 3D MR image
Right, overlaid images of each biopsy trajectory on the 3D TRUS image

8. References

Amdur RJ, Gladstone D, Leopold KA, Harris RD. Prostate seed implant quality assessment using MR and CT image fusion. *Int J Radiat Oncol Biol Phys*. 1999;43(1):67-72.

Atwell TD, Farrell MA, Callstrom MR, Charboneau JW, Leibovich BC, Patterson DE, Chow GK, Blute ML. Percutaneous cryoablation of 40 solid renal tumors with US guidance and CT monitoring: initial experience. *Radiology*. 2007;243(1):276-83.

Barbaric ZL. Percutaneous nephrostomy for urinary tract obstruction.*AJR Am J Roentgenol*. 1984 ;143(4):803-9.

Barzell WE, Melamed MR. Appropriate patient selection in the focal treatment of prostate cancer: the role of transperineal 3-dimensional pathologic mapping of the prostate--a 4-year experience. *Urology*. 2007: 70(6 Suppl):27-35.

Bassignani MJ, Moore Y, Watson L, Theodorescu D. Pilot experience with real-time ultrasound guided percutaneous renal mass cryoablation. *J Urol.* 2004;171(4): 1620-3.

Baumann M, Mozer P, Daanen V, Troccaz J. Prostate biopsy assistance system with gland deformation estimation for enhanced precision. *Med Image Comput Comput Assist Interv.* 2009;12(Pt 1):67-74.

Bouchelouche K, Oehr O. Positron emission tomography and positron emission tomography/computerized tomography of urological malignancies: an update review. *J Urol* 179: 34-45, 2008

Crocetti L, Lencioni R, Debeni S, See TC, Pina CD, Bartolozzi C. Targeting liver lesions for radiofrequency ablation: an experimental feasibility study using a CT-US fusion imaging system. *Invest Radiol.* 2008;43(1):33-9.

Daanen V, Gastaldo J, Giraud JY, Fourneret P, Descotes JL, Bolla M, Collomb D, Troccaz J. MRI/TRUS data fusion for brachytherapy. *Int J Med Robot.* 2006;2(3):256-61.

Eggener SE, Scardino PT, Carroll PR, Zelefsky MJ, Sartor O, Hricak H, Wheeler TM, Fine SW, Trachtenberg J, Rubin MA, Ohori M, Kuroiwa K, Rossignol M, Abenhaim L; International Task Force on Prostate Cancer and the Focal Lesion Paradigm. Focal therapy for localized prostate cancer: a critical appraisal of rationale and modalities.*J Urol.* 2007;178: 2260-7.

Ellis RJ, Kaminsky DA. Fused radioimmunoscintigraphy for treatment planning. *Rev Urol.* 2006;8 Suppl 1:S11-9.

Ellis RJ, Zhou EH, Fu P, Kaminsky DA, Sodee DB, Faulhaber PF, Bodner D, Resnick MI. Single photon emission computerized tomography with capromab pendetide plus computerized tomography image set co-registration independently predicts biochemical failure. *J Urol.* 2008 ;179(5):1768-73;

Gill IS, Aron M, Gervais DA, Jewett MA. Clinical practice. Small renal mass. N Engl J Med. 2010; 362:624-34.

Haber GP, Crouzet S, Remer EM, O'Malley C, Kamoi K, Goel R, White WM, Kaouk JH. Stereotactic percutaneous cryoablation for renal tumors: initial clinical experience. *J Urol.* 2010;183:884-8.

Haber GP, Colombo JR, Remer E, O'Malley C, Ukimura O, Magi-Galluzzi C, Spaliviero M, Kaouk J. Synchronized real-time ultrasonography and three-dimensional computed tomography scan navigation during percutaneous renal cryoablation in a porcine model. *J Endourol.* 2010 Mar;24(3):333-7.

Herrell SD, Kwartowitz DM, Milhoua PM, Galloway RL. Toward image guided robotic surgery: system validation. *J Urol* 2009; 181:783–789.

Hollingsworth JM, Miller DC, Daignault S, Hollenbeck BK. Rising incidence of small renal masses: a need to reassess treatment effect. *J Natl Cancer Inst.* 2006; 98 :1331-4.

Holupka EJ, Kaplan ID, Burdette EC, Svensson GK. Ultrasound image fusion for external beam radiotherapy for prostate cancer. *Int J Radiat Oncol Biol Phys.* 1996;35:975-84.

Hu Y, Ahmed H, Allen C, Pends´e D, Sahu M, Emberton M, Hawkes D, Barratt D. MR to Ultrasound Image Registration for Guiding Prostate Biopsy and Interventions. *MICCAI*, vol. 1, pp. 787–794, 2009.

Iseki H, Masutani Y, Iwahara M, et al. Volumegraph (overlaid three-dimensional image-guided navigation): Clinical application of augmented reality in neurosurgery. *Stereotact Funct Neurosurg*1997; 68:18.

Kagawa K, Lee WR, Schultheiss TE, Hunt MA, Shaer AH, Hanks GE. Initial clinical assessment of CT-MRI image fusion software in localization of the prostate for 3D conformal radiation therapy. *Int J Radiat Oncol Biol Phys*. 1997;38:319-25.

Kaplan I, Oldenburg NE, Meskell P, Blake M, Church P, Holupka EJ. Real time MRI-ultrasound image guided stereotactic prostate biopsy. *Magn. Reson. Imaging* 2002; 20: 295–9.

Kawamata T, Iseki H, Shibasaki T, et al. Endoscopic augmented reality navigation system for endonasal transsphenoidal surgery to treat pituitary tumors: Technical note. *Neurosurgery* 2002;50:1393.

Kirkham AP, Emberton M, Allen C. How good is MRI at detecting and characterising cancer within the prostate? *Eur. Urol.* 2006; 50: 1163–74.

Ko R, Soucy F, Denstedt JD, Razvi H. Percutaneous nephrolithotomy made easier: a practical guide, tips and tricks. *BJU Int*. 2008;101(5):535-9.

Krengli M, Ballarè A, Cannillo B, Rudoni M, Kocjancic E, Loi G, Brambilla M, Inglese E, Frea B. Potential advantage of studying the lymphatic drainage by sentinel node technique and SPECT-CT image fusion for pelvic irradiation of prostate cancer. *Int J Radiat Oncol Biol Phys*. 2006 Nov 15;66(4):1100-4.

Kupelian P, Willoughby T, Levine, et al. Multi-institutional clinical experience with the Calypso system in localization and continuous, real-time monitoring of the prostate gland during external radiotherapy. *Int J Radiat Oncol Biol Phys* 2007;67:1088–98.

Lau HY, Kagawa K, Lee WR, Hunt MA, Shaer AH, Hanks GE. Short communication: CT-MRI image fusion for 3D conformal prostate radiotherapy: use in patients with altered pelvic anatomy. *Br J Radiol*. 1996;69:1165-70.

Leroy, Mozer P, Payan Y, Richard F, Chartier-Kastler R, and Troccaz J: Percutaneous renal puncture: requirements and preliminary results, *Surgetica* 02, 303-309, 2002.

Leroy A, Mozer P, Payan Y, Troccaz J. Rigid registration of freehand 3D ultrasound and CT-scan kidney images. In: Barillot C (ed): *Proc MICCAI 2004*, New York: Springer, pp 837-844, 2004

Leveridge MJ, Mattar K, Kachura J, Jewett MA. Assessing outcomes in probe ablative therapies for small renal masses. *J Endourol*. 2010;24(5):759-64.

Marescaux J, Rubino F, Arenas M, et al. Augmented-reality-assisted laparoscopic adrenalectomy. *JAMA* 2004;10;292:2214.

Martin S, Troccaz J, Daanenc V. Automated segmentation of the prostate in 3D MR images using a probabilistic atlas and a spatially constrained deformable model. *Med Phys*. 2010 ;37(4):1579-90.

Mozer P, Leroy A, Payan Y, Troccaz J, Chartier-Kastler E, Richard F. Computer-assisted access to the kidney. *Int J Med Robot*. 2005 ;1(4):58-66.

Mozer P, Baumann M, Chevreau G, Moreau-Gaudry A, Bart S, Renard-Penna R, Comperat E, Conort P, Bitker MO, Chartier-Kastler E, Richard F, Troccaz J. Mapping of transrectal ultrasonographic prostate biopsies: quality control and learning curve assessment by image processing. *J Ultrasound Med*. 2009 ;28(4):455-60.

Nakamoto M, Ukimura O, Gill IS, Mahadevan A, Miki T, Hashizume M, Sato Y: Realtime organ tracking for endoscopic augmented reality visualization using miniature wireless magnetic tracker. In: Dohi T, Sakura I, Liao H (Eds): MIAR 2008, pp 359-366, 2008

Oguro S, Tuncali K, Elhawary H, Morrison PR, Hata N, Silverman SG. Image registration of pre-procedural MRI and intra-procedural CT images to aid CT-guided percutaneous cryoablation of renal tumors. *Int J Comput Assist Radiol Surg*. 2010 in press

Onik G, Miessau M, Bostwick DG. Three-dimensional prostate mapping biopsy has a potentially significant impact on prostate cancer management. *J. Clin. Oncol.* 2009: 27, 4321–4326.

Osorio A, Traxter O, Merran S, Dargent F, Ripoche X, Atif J. Real-time fusion of 2D fluoroscopic and 3D segmented CT images integrated into an augmented reality system for percutanous nephrolithotomies (PCNL). RSNA INORAD 2004, ref 9101 DS-i.

Piert M, Park H, Khan A, Siddiqui J, Hussain H, Chenevert T, Wood D, Johnson T, Shah RB, Meyer C. Detection of aggressive primary prostate cancer with 11C-choline PET/CT using multimodality fusion techniques. *J Nucl Med*. 2009;50(10):1585-93.

Poulsen MH, Bouchelouche K, Gerke O, Petersen H, Svolgaard B, Marcussen N, Svolgaard N, Ogren M, Vach W, Høilund-Carlsen PF, Geertsen U, Walter S. [(18)F]-fluorocholine positron-emission/computed tomography for lymph node staging of patients with prostate cancer: preliminary results of a prospective study. *BJU Int.* 2010 PMID: 20089104

Remzi M, Marberger M. Renal tumor biopsies for evaluation of small renal tumors: why, in whom, and how? *Eur Urol*. 2009;55(2):359-67.

Reynier C, Troccaz J, Fourneret P, Dusserre A, Gay-Jeune C, Descotes JL, Bolla M, Giraud JY. MRI/TRUS data fusion for prostate brachytherapy. Preliminary results. *Med Phys*. 2004;31(6):1568-75.

Saitoh M, Watanabe H, Ohe H. Single stage percutaneous nephroureterolithotomy using a special ultrasonically guided pyeloscope. *J Urol*. 1982;128(3):591-2.

Schillaci O. Hybrid SPECT/CT: a new era for SPECT imaging? *Eur J Nucl Med Mol Imaging* 2005;32(5):521–4.

Selli C, Caramella D, Giusti S, Conti A, Tognetti A, Mogorovich A, De Maria M, Bartolozzi C.Value of image fusion in the staging of prostatic carcinoma. *Radiol Med*. 2007;112:74-81.

Singh AK, Kruecker J, Xu S et al. Initial clinical experience with real-time transrectal ultrasonography-magnetic resonance imaging fusion-guided prostate biopsy. *BJU Int*. 2008; 101: 841–5.

Skolarikos A, Alivizatos G, de la Rosette JJ. Percutaneous nephrolithotomy and its legacy. *Eur Urol*. 2005;47(1):22-8.

Sodee DB, Sodee AE, Bakale G. Synergistic value of single-photon emission computed tomography/computed tomography fusion to radioimmunoscintigraphic imaging of prostate cancer. *Semin Nucl Med*. 2007;37:17-28.

Su LM, Vagvolgyi BP, Agarwal R, Reiley CE, Taylor RH, Hager GD. Augmented reality during robot-assisted laparoscopic partial nephrectomy: toward real-time 3D-CT to stereoscopic video registration. *Urology*. 2009;73 :896-900.

Su Y, Davis BJ, Furutani KM, Herman MG, Robb RA. Seed localization and TRUS-fluoroscopy fusion for intraoperative prostate brachytherapy dosimetry. *Comput Aided Surg*. 2007;12:25-34.

Teber D, Guven S, Simpfendörfer T, Baumhauer M, Güven EO, Yencilek F, Gözen AS, Rassweiler J. Augmented reality: a new tool to improve surgical accuracy during laparoscopic partial nephrectomy? Preliminary in vitro and in vivo results. *Eur Urol*. 2009;56(2):332-8.

Townsend DW. A combined PET/CT scanner: the choices. J Nucl Med 2001;42(3):533–4.

Turkbey B, Xu S, Kruecker J, Locklin J, Pang Y, Bernardo M, Merino MJ, Wood BJ, Choyke PL, Pinto PA. Documenting the location of prostate biopsies with image fusion. *BJU Int*. 2010 in press

Ukimura O, Nakamoto M, Desai M, HErts B, Aron M, Haber GP, Kaouk, J, Miki T, Sato, Y, Hashizume, M, Gill IS. Augmented reality visualization during laparoscopic urologic surgery: The initial clinical experience. *J Urol* 2007; 177(suppl) 348, 102nd AUA2007 Abstract V1052.

Ukimura O, Mitterberger M, Okihara K, Miki T, Pinggera GM, Neururer R, Peschel R, Aigner F, Gradl J, Bartsch G, Colleselli D, Strasser H, Pallwein L, Frauscher F. Real-time virtual ultrasonographic radiofrequency ablation of renal cell carcinoma. *BJU Int*. 2008;101:707-11.

Ukimura O, and Gill IS. Image-assisted endoscopic surgery: Cleveland Clinic Experience. *J Endourology* 22:803-810, 2008

Ukimura O, Gill IS. Augmented reality for computer-assisted image-guided minimally invasive urology. Chapter 17. In: Ukimura O, Gill IS, (Eds). *Contemporary interventional ultrasonography in urology*. Springer; 2009. p. 179–84.

Ukimura O, and Gill IS: Image-fusion, augmented reality, and predictive navigation. *Urol Clin North Am* 36; 115-123, 2009

Ukimura O. Evolution of precise and multimodal MRI and TRUS in detection and management of early prostate cancer. *Expert Rev Med Devices*. 2010;7(4):541-54.

Ukimura O, Hirahara N, Fujihara A, Yamada T, Iwata T, Kamoi K, Okihara K, Ito H, Nishimura T, Miki T. Technique for a hybrid system of real-time transrectal ultrasound with preoperative magnetic resonance imaging in the guidance of targeted prostate biopsy. *Int J Urol*. 2010; 17:890-3

Villers A, Puech P, Mouton D, Leroy X, Ballereau C, Lemaitre L. Dynamic contrast enhanced, pelvic phased array magnetic resonance imaging of localized prostate cancer for predicting tumor volume: correlation with radical prostatectomy findings. *J. Urol*. 2006; 176: 2432–7.

Wachter S, Tomek S, Kurtaran A, Wachter-Gerstner N, Djavan B, Becherer A, Mitterhauser M, Dobrozemsky G, Li S, Pötter R, Dudczak R, Kletter K. 11C-acetate positron emission tomography imaging and image fusion with computed tomography and magnetic resonance imaging in patients with recurrent prostate cancer. *J Clin Oncol*. 2006; 24:2513-9.

Wein W, Brunke S, Khamene A, Callstrom MR, Navab N. Automatic CT-ultrasound registration for diagnostic imaging and image-guided intervention. *Med Image Anal*. 2008;12(5):577-85.

Wilt TJ, MacDonald R, Rutks I, Shamliyan TA, Taylor BC, Kane RL. Systematic review: comparative effectiveness and harms of treatments for clinically localized prostate cancer. *Ann Intern Med*. 2008;148 :435-48

Yakar D, Hambrock T, Huisman H et al. Feasibility of 3T dynamic contrast-enhanced magnetic resonance-guided biopsy in localizing local recurrence of prostate cancer after external beam radiation therapy. *Invest. Radiol.* 2010; 45: 121–5.

Xu S, Kruecker J, Guion P et al. Closed-loop control in fused MR-TRUS image-guided prostate biopsy. *Med. Image Comput. Comput. Assist. Interv.* 2007; 10: 128–35.